ISBN 978-0-266-02297-8
PIBN 10959896

1 MONTH OF
FREE
READING

at

www.ForgottenBooks.com

By purchasing this book you are eligible for one month membership to ForgottenBooks.com, giving you unlimited access to our entire collection of over 1,000,000 titles via our web site and mobile apps.

To claim your free month visit:

www.forgottenbooks.com/free959896

DIGEST ANNOTATIONS

By special request of the Judges, an effort has been made to give, in each syllabus and index paragraph, a reference by number to the analogous topic and section of the new 1919 Washington State Digest.

REPORTER

WASHINGTON REPORTS

VOL. 116

CASES DETERMINED

IN THE

SUPREME COURT

OF

WASHINGTON

———

MAY 26, 1921 – SEPTEMBER 2, 1921

———

ARTHUR REMINGTON
REPORTER

SEATTLE AND SAN FRANCISCO
BANCROFT-WHITNEY COMPANY
1922

OFFICIAL REPORT

Published Pursuant to Laws of Washington, 1905, page 330

Under the personal supervision of the Reporter

JUN 28 1922

PRINTED, ELECTROTYPED AND BOUND
BY
FRANK M. LAMBORN, PUBLIC PRINTER

JUDGES

OF THE

SUPREME COURT OF WASHINGTON

DURING THE PERIOD COVERED BY THIS VOLUME

Hon. EMMETT N. PARKER, Chief Justice

DEPARTMENT ONE

Hon. MARK A. FULLERTON

Hon. O. R. HOLCOMB

Hon. KENNETH MACKINTOSH

Hon. J. B. BRIDGES

DEPARTMENT TWO

Hon. WALLACE MOUNT

Hon. JOHN F. MAIN

Hon. JOHN R. MITCHELL

Hon. WARREN W. TOLMAN

Hon. L. L. THOMPSON, Attorney General
C. S. REINHART, Clerk

JUDGES OF THE SUPERIOR COURTS

Hon. John Truax..........Ritzville..Adams, Benton and Franklin
Hon. Chester F. Miller......Dayton..Asotin, Columbia and Garfield
Hon. Wm. Grimshaw.........Wenatchee ....Chelan
Hon. John M. Ralston......Port Angeles....Clallam and Jefferson
Hon. Geo. B. Simpson.......Vancouver ....Clarke
Hon. Homer Kirby.......Kalama..Cowlitz, Klickitat and Skamania
Hon. Sam B. Hill...........Waterville........Douglas and Grant
Hon. C. H. Neal.............Okanogan........Ferry and Okanogan
Hon. Geo. D. Abel
Hon. Ben Sheeks } ....Montesano..............Grays Harbor
Hon. Ralph C. Bell
Hon. Guy C. Alston } ....Everett.........Island and Snohomish
Hon. Boyd J. Tallman
Hon. A. W. Frater
Hon. Mitchell Gilliam
Hon. Everett Smith
Hon. J. T. Ronald } ...Seattle ....King
Hon. King Dykeman
Hon. Otis W. Brinker
Hon. Calvin S. Hall
Hon. Austin E. Griffiths
Hon. Walter M. French......Port Orchard.................Kitsap
Hon. John B. Davidson......Ellensburg ....Kittitas
Hon. W. A. Reynolds.........Chehalis ....Lewis
Hon. Joseph Sessions.......Davenport ....Lincoln
Hon. John M. Wilson
Hon. D. F. Wright } ......Olympia..........Mason and Thurston
Hon. H. W. B. Hewen........South Bend....Pacific and Wahkiakum
Hon. Daniel H. Carey........Colville......Pend Oreille and Stevens
Hon. W. O. Chapman
Hon. M. L. Clifford
Hon. E. M. Card } ....Tacoma ....Pierce
Hon. W. D. Askren
Hon. W. P. Brown
Hon. Ed. E. Hardin } .....Bellingham....San Juan and Whatcom
Hon. Augustus Brawley.....Mt. Vernon....................Skagit
Hon. Wm. A. Huneke
Hon. Bruce Blake
Hon. Joseph B. Lindsley } ..Spokane ....Spokane
Hon. Hugo E. Oswald
Hon. R. M. Webster
Hon. Edward C. Mills........Walla Walla.............Walla Walla
Hon. R. L. McCroskey........Colfax ....Whitman
Hon. Geo. B. Holden
Hon. V. O. Nichoson } .....Yakima ....Yakima

TABLE

OF

CASES REPORTED

TABLE

OF

CASES CITED BY THE COURT

STATUTES
CITED AND CONSTRUED

ERRATA

Page 157, line 1, for *240* read *340*
Page 269, line 8 from bottom, for *McNeely* read *McNeeley & Co.*

ERRORS NOTED IN PREVIOUS VOLUMES

Vol. 110 Wash.

Page 134, for line 18 from top read *of the superior court for Thurston county affirming*

CASES

DETERMINED IN THE

SUPREME COURT

OF

WASHINGTON

[No. 16353. *En Banc.* May 26, 1921.]

THE STATE OF WASHINGTON, *on the Relation of William M. Short et al., Plaintiff*, v. J. GRANT HINKLE, *as Secretary of State, Respondent.*[1]

CONSTITUTIONAL LAW (39)—STATUTES (2-3)—LEGISLATIVE POWERS—ACTS—TIME OF TAKING EFFECT—DETERMINATION OF EMERGENCY. The Administrative Code (Laws 1921, p. 9, ch. 7) is not subject to referendum under Art. 2, § 1, of the state constitution as amended; in view of the emergency clause which recites that the revenues of the state are insufficient to support the state government and its existing public institutions and that it is necessary that the existing administrative agencies of the state government be consolidated and coordinated in order to bring the cost of supporting the state government and its existing institutions within the possible revenue of the state; which is a statement of fact, which the court cannot, from its judicial knowledge, say does not exist.

SAME. In a mandamus proceeding to compel the secretary of state to submit to referendum a legislative act reciting an emergency for its taking effect immediately, the court is without power to grant the writ, in view of the presumption of verity attaching to the legislative declaration of emergency, unless it can say from judicial knowledge that a patent contradiction exists upon the face of the enactment sufficient in law or in reason to justify the court's denial of the declaration of emergency.

SAME. A legislative act is properly one for the support of the government, if its purpose is to give the government and its existing public institutions the greatest benefit from the revenues which are actually received, and also to protect the resources of the state from which such revenues are derived.

[1] Reported in 198 Pac. 535.

SAME. Where a legislative enactment is composed of many separate sections, some of which the court in the exercise of its judicial knowledge must know to be emergent, a mandamus proceeding to compel the secretary of state to submit the entire act to popular vote under the referendum provisions of the state constitution must fail.

HOLCOMB, TOLMAN, MAIN, and MITCHELL, JJ., dissent.

Application filed in the supreme court February 14, 1921, for a writ of mandamus to compel the secretary of state to receive and file a proposal for the referendum of the administrative code. Denied.

Geo. H. Rummens, Tracy E. Griffin, and *P. M. Troy,* for relators.

The Attorney General, for respondent.

MACKINTOSH, J.—This is an original proceeding in mandamus to compel the secretary of state to receive and file the proposal and affidavits of the relators for the referendum of Laws of 1921, ch. 7, p. 12, being an act entitled "An Act relating to, and to promote efficiency, order and economy in, the administration of the government of the state, prescribing the powers and duties of certain officers and departments, defining offenses and fixing penalties, abolishing certain offices, and repealing conflicting acts and parts of acts," and commonly known as the administrative code.

Chapter 7 consists of 138 sections, the final section being:

"Whereas the revenues of the state are insufficient to support the state government and its existing public institutions as at present organized, and whereas it is necessary that the existing administrative agencies of the state government be consolidated and coordinated in order to bring the cost of supporting the state government and its existing institutions within the possible revenues of the state, therefore this act is necessary for the support of the state government and its existing public institutions, and shall take effect immediately.'' Laws of 1921, p. 69, § 138.

Article 2, § 1, of the state constitution is as follows:

''The legislative authority of the State of Washington shall be vested in the legislature, consisting of a senate and house of representatives, which shall be called the legislature of the State of Washington, but the people reserve to themselves the power to propose bills, laws and to enact or reject the same at the polls, independent of the legislature, and also reserve power, at their own option, to approve or reject at the polls any act, item, section, or part of any bill, act or law passed by the legislature. . . .

''The second power reserved by the people is the referendum, and it may be ordered on any act, bill, law or any part thereof passed by the legislature, except such laws as may be necessary for the immediate preservation of the public peace, health or safety, support of the state government and its existing public institutions, either by petition signed by the required percentage of the legal voters, or by the legislature as other bills are enacted. Six per centum, but in no other case more than thirty thousand, of the legal voters shall be required to sign and make a valid referendum petition.

''No act, law, or bill, subject to referendum, shall take effect until ninety days after the adjournment of the session at which it was enacted. No act, law or bill approved by a majority of the electors voting thereon shall be amended or repealed by the legislature within a period of two years following such enactment. But such enactment may be amended or repealed at any general, regular or special election by direct vote of the people thereon.''

The respondent declined to accept and file the proposal and affidavits for the reason that § 138 does not permit of the act being referred. The relators' position is that § 138 is of no effect for the reason that the act is not emergent.

The relators take their stand flatfootedly upon our decision in the case of *State ex rel. Brislawn v. Meath*, 84 Wash. 302, 147 Pac. 11, that being a case which involved an act of the legislature passed in 1915 (Laws of 1915, ch. 6, p. 19) in relation to the board of state land commissioners, the act being an amendment of the prior law (Laws of 1909, p. 757, ch. 223). Under the law of 1909 the board was made up of the commissioner of public lands, the state fire warden, and the members of the state board of tax commissioners. The act of 1915 merely substituted for the state fire warden and the board of tax commissioners the secretary of state and the state treasurer, and to this amending act was added a section which stated that the act was necessary "for the immediate preservation of the public peace and safety and the support of the state government and shall take effect immediately." This court, in passing upon this emergency clause, held that an emergency clause attached to an act was subject to review by the courts, and that the clause would be held unconstitutional where the act, on its face, shows that the declaration is false, but that if, from an examination of the act, it be doubtful as to whether an emergency exists in fact, that the question of emergency would be treated as a legislative question, and the act would be upheld. The court there further decided that, by reason of the fact that there were being merely substituted two officers on a board in the place of other state officers, that the court could determine, from its judicial knowledge, that there was no emergency, and that the final clause of the act was inoperative.

The alpha and omega of the relators' argument is that ch. 7, of the Laws of 1921, p. 12, makes no more change in the theretofore existing plan of state government than did the act of 1915 in relation to the composition of the board of state land commissioners. It is unnecessary to review the reasons assigned by the majority and minority opinions in the *Brislawn* case, and it is unnecessary to determine whether the *Brislawn* case was properly or improperly decided. It is sufficient to take that decision as it appears in the books and apply to it the facts in the instant case, facts obtained by an examination of Laws of 1921, p. 12, ch. 7, and not assertions based upon only a casual reading thereof. The fallacy of relators' position lies in the unfounded premise, i. e., that ch. 7 is "nothing more than a broad, comprehensive scheme for transferring the duties now performed by various state officers and subordinates under the present form and plan of state government to other officers and departments created by the act." Grant the premise, and under the *Brislawn* case relators' position may be correct, but the premise is found to be unwarranted upon a careful and exact analysis and understanding of the act. The act says that the revenues are insufficient to support the state government in its then existing form, and that in order for the state, as an institution, to continue to function its expenditures must be so reduced as to fall within the possible revenue, and to effect this purpose the act abolishes many offices, boards and commissioners, provides against the duplication of duties and responsibilities in administration, coordinates the operation of the business of the state, classifies employees, provides for expenditures in cases of emergency, authorizes the exchange between state institutions of supplies, provides a cost accounting system, sustains building programs, and authorizes the preparation of estimates for appropriations. Without going into the act section by section it, in general, provides a more efficient method of carrying on the state government. The court is not concerned with whether—for the reason that it cannot know—the results anticipated by the new plan will be achieved. Under the *Brislawn* decision, the court can only hold § 138 invalid, if from its knowledge, which it possesses as a court, it can say that no necessity exists for such a change in the method of conducting the state government in the face of the legislative declaration that public funds were not sufficient to uphold the state government under the prior existing plan.

The legislature possessed the opportunity (and is conclusively presumed to have availed itself of that opportunity) to know the facts and has declared that a precarious financial condition prevails. We are asked to say that the solemn statement of the legislature is false, and to say so, not because we are possessed of any knowledge upon the subject, but because we are ignorant upon it. We can take no testimony; we have no machinery with which to gather the facts, which the legislature is presumed to be possessed of, but, totally in the dark, we are asked to substitute our personal prejudices, predilections and preconceptions for the presumably enlightened judgment of those deputed by the constitution of the state to inquire into and determine these factual problems. It is only when the court, following the *Brislawn* case, can say, from its judicial knowledge, that a patent contradiction exists upon the face of a legislative enactment, that, in law or in reason, it can deny the legislative declaration of emergency. As Judge Parker says in the case of *State ex rel. Reclamation Board v. Clausen*, 110 Wash. 525, 188 Pac. 538:

"It may well be doubted that there has ever come to the American courts any more vexatious question than that of determining whether or not a particular purpose for which public funds were sought to be raised by taxation and expended is a public purpose, when the particular purpose in question lay within that twilight

zone wherein the minds may reasonably differ as to
such purpose being a public one; the bounds of which
zone are ever changing with the passing of time, and
within which new problems of public welfare always
first appear. That such a question, when arising in the
courts, has proven so vexatious is, we apprehend, because of its inherent nature, in that, in its last analysis,
it is not one of exclusive legal logic, but is one more or
less of policy and wisdom, properly determinable in the
light of public welfare, present and future, in a broad
sense; and hence is not a pure judicial law question, except in those cases clearly outside of the twilight zone
we have alluded to. . . .

"Plainly, since a correct solution of our present
problem, because of its inherent nature, calls for the
consideration of something more than pure legal principles, suggests that we exercise a great degree of caution to the end that we shall not usurp powers which do
not constitutionally belong to us. This court has adhered steadfastly to the general rule, in common with
other courts of our country, that a statute cannot be
declared unconstitutional unless it clearly so appears.
Is not this rule of peculiar force in its application to
the question of whether or not a legislative act authorizing the levy of a tax and the expenditure of public
moneys so raised is for a public purpose? We are decidedly of the opinion that it is."

When the court speaks of the determination of the validity of a section such as 138 being a judicial question,
it is meant that courts will inquire into the fact as to
whether a necessity exists, an inquiry necessarily based
upon proof, but proof, limited by law, to so-called judicial knowledge. But to resolve the immediate problem,
obviously its intricate and complicated nature requires
the exertion and application of an amount of expert
knowledge, experience and judgment, necessarily without the scope of the restricted doctrine of judicial
knowledge, and, as we have intimated, properly commanded only by the legislature. In its nature, the at-

tenuated theory of judicial knowledge, in the presence
of so considerable a mass of fact as the administrative
code, cannot afford proof sufficient to overcome the
declaration of the legislature, even though that declaration were naked and unsupported by the presumption
of verity. To apply judicial knowledge to the resolution of peculiarly factual problems would "amount to
turning the supreme court into an irresponsible House
of Lords," as Theodore Roosevelt said, in referring to
the *Bakeshop* cases, "a position which the people of
the United States would never stand."

Relators speciously argue that the declaration of the
legislature that some change in the method of administration is necessary in order to bring the cost of operating the state government within its revenues is, *ipso
facto*, false, for the reason that the state always possesses the power of taxing in any amount that is necessary to perpetuate any form of administration which
may be in existence. This is an enamelled argument
which might be brightly attractive to those fortunate
citizens who contribute nothing by way of taxes to the
support of the state. Although the state possesses unlimited power of taxation such unlimited power does
not produce unlimited revenue and a point is attain-
able—and the legislature declares it is already reached
—where additional taxation produces nothing but defaulted realty and personalty in the hands of the col-
lector, and when the levy of additional taxes creates
burdens which parch the source of revenue, the levies
tend to destroy rather than support the state government. It is certain, as was said in the case of *State v.
Pitney*, 79 Wash. 608, 140 Pac. 918, Ann. Cas. 1916 A
209:

"If a state of facts can reasonably be presumed to
exist which would justify the legislation, the court must
presume that it did exist and that the law was passed

for that reason. If no state of circumstances could exist to justify the statute, then it may be declared void because in excess of the legislative power.''

In *State ex rel. Blakeslee v. Clausen,* 85 Wash. 260, 148 Pac. 28, Ann. Cas. 1916 B 810, the court said, in reference to ''support'':

''The intent and purpose of the people, as gathered from the words of the constitution and the circumstances attending the adoption of the seventh amendment, impels the holding that the people intended to use the word 'support' in its fullest sense. When so considered 'support' includes appropriations for current expenses, maintenance, upkeep, continuation of existing functions, as well as appropriations for such new buildings and conveniences as may be necessary to meet the needs and requirements of the state in relation to its existing institutions.

''In Webster's New International Dictionary, the word 'support' is given the following definitions: 'To furnish with funds or means for maintenance; to maintain; to provide for, to enable to continue; to carry on.'

''In the absence of an express reservation, it would be a usurpation on the part of any court to say that an appropriation directed to the maintenance of the existing activities of the state is subject to the referendum. The first right of government is the right of self-preservation, and to say that the people intended, in the absence of an express reservation, to allow the government or its institutions to be crippled or embarrassed in any way would be to say that the people intended that the government could not sustain itself through the mediumship of the ordinary and recognized methods of legislation.''

See, also, *State ex rel. Anderson v. Howell,* 106 Wash. 541, 181 Pac. 37; *State ex rel. Case v. Howell,* 85 Wash. 281, 147 Pac. 1162.

If the purpose of the act is to give the government and its existing public institutions the greatest benefit from the revenues which were actually received, and also to protect the resources of the state from which those revenues derive, then the act is properly one for the support of the government.

There is another reason why the relators must fail in their attempt to refer this act, and that is that they are seeking reference of the entire act, and if there is any section or portion of it of which the court can say there is an emergency their proceedings must fall. If it should be conceded that as to certain sections or portions of the act the court could say, from its judicial knowledge, that the changes made were not necessary for the support of the state government and its existing institutions, yet the relators are making a general attack and are not seeking to refer those sections only which the court might judicially declare not to be emergent. There are, however, many separate sections which the court in the exercise of its judicial knowledge must know are emergent, and, as we have already indicated, from our judicial knowledge we cannot say that the act as a whole is not emergent. Those sections referring to the protection of agriculture, game and fish are, from their very nature, concerned with things necessary for the support of the state and its existing institutions. Those sections dealing with labor and industry show a necessity exists to overcome the conflict of jurisdiction and inefficiency of the existing form of administration of which the court has judicial knowledge from the many cases coming before it involving these questions. One instance of this conflict is the difference existing between the commissioner of labor and the state safety board, to which this court has devoted its attention. *State ex rel. Younger v. Clausen,* 111 Wash. 241, 190 Pac. 324. Instances might be multiplied of where the act in itself contains evidence of the necessity which the judicial knowledge of this court confirms.

To summarize then our conclusions: Taking the *Brislawn* case as the law, we find that in that case the court had before it a scheme which merely changed the personnel of one of the state commissions and between that change of membership of a minor board and the support of the state government there was no natural connection. In the act before us there are certain facts which, if they were considered by themselves, are similar to the facts in the *Brislawn* case, but these facts are only a part of an entire plan proposed to reorganize the administration of the state's business, upon what, the legislature deems, are businesslike principles. This court is not called on to consider the act section by section, disregarding the act as a whole, especially since the relators are not making specific attack upon any special sections but are attacking the act as a whole. Moreover this case differs from the *Brislawn* case in that in the *Brislawn* case the legislature merely stated that a necessity existed, and this was but a conclusion by the legislature that it was engaged in a constitutional proceeding. This court refused that legislative dictum in the light of the facts of which the court had judicial knowledge. In the act before us, however, the legislature makes a specific statement of fact that the revenues of the state are not sufficient to support the state government or its existing institutions as they were then organized, and that it was necessary to coordinate the affairs of the state, "in order to bring the cost of supporting the state government and its existing institutions within the possible revenues of the state." This is a declaration of fact and unless the court from its judicial knowledge can say this fact does not exist it must be taken as true. *State ex rel. Govan v. Clausen*, 108 Wash. 133, 183 Pac. 115; *State ex rel. Lister v. Clausen*, 108 Wash. 146, 183 Pac. 120. For the reasons stated, the writ is denied.

PARKER, C. J., FULLERTON, BRIDGES, and MOUNT, JJ., concur.

HOLCOMB, J. (dissenting)—"All political power is inherent in the people, and governments derive their just powers from the consent of the governed, and are established to protect and maintain individual rights." Constitution of Washington, art. 1, § 1.

Section 32 of the same article declares:

"A frequent recurrence to fundamental principles is essential to the security of individual rights and the perpetuity of free government."

It seems that the majority have forgotten those positive declarations of our fundamental law. It seems, also, that they are imbued with the idea that there are some instances in which the courts may not inquire into the validity of a legislative act under the restrictions of the constitution. Our primary obligation is to the constitution.

"In monarchical governments, the independence of the judiciary is essential to guard the rights of the subject from the injustice of the crown; but in republics it is equally salutary, in protecting the constitution and laws from the encroachments and tyranny of faction. . . . Nor is an independent judiciary less useful as a check upon the legislative power, which is sometimes disposed, from the force of party, or the temptations of interest, to make a sacrifice of constitutional rights; and it is a wise and necessary principle of our government, . . . that legislative acts are subject to the severe scrutiny and impartial interpretation of the courts of justice, who are bound to regard the constitution as the paramount law, and the highest evidence of the will of the people." 1 Kent, Commentaries, 294, 295.

"This, then, is the office of a written (free) constitution: to delegate to various public functionaries such of the powers of government as the people do not intend to exercise for themselves; to classify these powers according to their nature, and to commit them to separate agents; to provide for the choice of these agents by the people; to ascertain, limit and define the extent of the authority thus delegated; and to reserve to the people their sovereignty over all things not expressly committed to their representatives." Hurlbut on Human Rights and their Political Guaranties.

"It is idle to say the authority of each branch is defined and limited in the constitution, if there be not an independent power able and willing to enforce the limitations. Experience proves that it is thoughtlessly but habitually violated; and the sacrifice of individual rights is too remotely connected with the objects and contests of the masses to attract their attention.

"From its every position, it is apparent that the conservative power is lodged with the judiciary, which, in the exercise of its undoubted right, is bound to meet every emergency; else causes would be decided not only by the legislature, but, sometimes, without hearing or evidence." Gibson, Chief Justice, in *De Chastellux v. Fairchild*, 15 Pa. St. 18.

"Without the limitations and restraints usually found in written constitutions the government could have no elements of permanence and durability; and the distribution of its powers and the vesting their exercise in separate departments would be an idle ceremony." *People v. Draper*, 15 N. Y. 532, Brown, J.

"It cannot be denied that the one great object of written constitutions is to keep the departments of government as distinct as possible; and for this purpose to impose restraints designed to have that effect. And it is equally true that there is no department on which it is more necessary to impose restraints than upon the legislature. The tendency of things is almost always to augment the power of that department . . ."

"The constitution being the supreme law it follows of course that every act of the legislature contrary to that law must be void. But who shall decide this ques-

tion? Shall the legislature itself decide it? If so, then
the constitution ceases to be a legal and becomes only
a moral restraint upon the legislature. If they and they
only are to judge whether their acts be conformable
to the constitution, then the constitution is admonitory
or advisory only; not legally binding; because, if the
construction of it rest wholly with them, their discretion in particular cases may be in favor of very erroneous and dangerous constructions. Hence the courts of
law, necessarily, when the occasion arises, must decide
upon the validity of particular acts. . . .

"Without this check, no certain limitations could
exist on the exercise of legislative power." 3 Daniel
Webster, Independence of the Judiciary, Works, p. 29.

During the last forty years of the nineteenth century
and the first decade of the twentieth, popular unrest
and distrust of legislatures resulted, in numerous
states, in a return to the primitive system of direct
legislation, modified by modern systems of election.
The result in this state was the adoption in 1912 of the
seventh amendment to the constitution, which is, in substance, set forth in the majority opinion. By plain and
simple, apt and certain words, it withdrew from the
legislature the power to finally enact legislation, with
certain clear exceptions, and reserved them to the
people.

The emergency declared in the act under consideration is that, it is "necessary for the support of the state
government and its existing institutions."

That it may be a better system of administration and
operation of the state's activities, may, for the purpose
of this argument, be readily conceded. With the de-
sirability or results of such a system, or the policy or
the expediency of it, courts have no concern. We are
here to declare the law, not to defend, or assail policies.
That this system is immediately necessary for the support of the state and its existing institutions is plainly,

utterly and emphatically fallacious. This is proven by
the fact that for thirty-two years the state existed and
the successive and cumulative wisdom of sixteen legislatures evolved the system of administration heretofore existing. It remained for the seventeenth legislature to suddenly enact, almost without debate, or deliberation, a revolutionary act, completely changing
the existing system of administration, transferring the
duties of a number of bureaus, commissions and officials to ten new, highly paid officials, with numerous
highly paid assistants; and it is declared that this new
and extremely revolutionary system is so immediately
necessary that an emergency exists, and that the act
cannot wait the lapse of ninety days from the adjournment of the session at which it was enacted.

The proposition is preposterous. There is no declaration that unless put into effect before June 8, 1921,
the state would become insolvent, or that its several
agencies transformed and transferred to the new would
cease to function under the old system. It may be noted
that the same legislature that declared this system to
be necessary, "in order to bring the cost of supporting
the state government and its existing institutions within the possible revenues of the state," appropriated the
total sum of $10,637,289.88 from the general fund for
the support and maintenance of the state and its existing institutions for the biennium ending in 1923, as
against a total appropriation by the legislature of 1919,
for the support of the state and its then existing institutions from the general fund of $10,561,000.42. There
has never been a more supreme example of an act of
the legislature intended to be reserved by the seventh
amendment for the right of referendum to the people.
It is an act of the utmost importance to the people of
the state. It is a much more obvious legislative evasion

of the seventh amendment that that under consideration in the case of *State ex rel. Brislawn v. Meath*, 84
Wash. 302, 147 Pac. 11, in which our present learned
chief justice concurred with the majority in deciding
that there could not be any immediate emergency as
declared by the legislature. And that case was right,
and the attempt to distinguish this case from it by the
majority is a vain attempt at a distinction without a
difference. That case was thoroughly considered, un-
answerably reasoned, and its determination was the
only logical result under the seventh amendment.
Otherwise that amendment, as to the reserve power of
the people to have measures referred for their acceptance or rejection, is merely solemn and empty phrase-
making, and the legislature is at liberty to evade it, by
a mere *ipse dixit* whenever it is so inclined.

The legislature is very powerful, but not all powerful. It is not like the British parliament, or other parliamentary bodies, which exercise sovereign authority,
and may even change the constitution at any time by
declaring the parliamentary will to that effect. Our
constitutions consist entirely of commands to, and limitations and restraints upon, the several governmental
agencies. They were created for the protection of the
minority against the tyranny of the majority.

"In America after a constitutional question has been
passed upon by the legislature, there is generally a
right of appeal to the courts when it is attempted to
put the will of the legislature in force. For the will of
the people, as declared in the constitution, is the final
law; and the will of the legislature is law only when it
is in harmony with, or at least is not opposed to, that
controlling instrument which governs the legislative
body equally with the private citizen." Cooley, Con_
stitutional Limitations (7th ed.), p. 6.

"While every possible presumption is to be indulged
in favor of the validity of the statute, . . . the

courts must obey the constitution rather than the law-making department of government, and must, upon their own responsibility, determine whether, in any particular case, these limits have been passed." *Mugler v. Kansas*, 123 U. S. 623.

Courts are both cautious and reluctant to override a law duly enacted by the legislature; and that caution and that reluctance are to be applauded. We have gone as far as the courts of any state and as far as judicial ingenuity and judicial oaths could possibly go in upholding legislation of doubtful constitutional validity, upon the theory that every possible presumption is to be indulged in favor of the validity of the statute. The rule of reason should be applied to every case.

"To what purpose," said the great Chief Justice, John Marshall, in *Marbury v. Madison*, 1 Cranch (U. S.) 49, "are powers limited, and to what purpose is that limitation committed to writing; if these limits may, at any time, be passed by those intended to be restrained? The distinction between a government with limited and unlimited powers is abolished, if those limits do not confine the person on whom they are imposed, and if acts prohibited and acts allowed are of equal obligation. It is a proposition too plain to be contested, that the constitution controls any legislative act repugnant to it; or, that the legislature may alter the constitution by an ordinary act.

"Between these alternatives there is no middle ground. The constitution is either a superior, paramount law, unchangeable by ordinary means, or it is on a level with ordinary legislative acts, and like other acts, is alterable when the legislature shall please to alter it. . . .

"Certainly all those who have framed written constitutions contemplate them as forming the fundamental and paramount law of the nation and consequently the theory of every such government must be, that an act of the legislature repugnant to the constitution is void."

As if in answer to the oral argument made here by the *Attorney General*, and the idea that seems to prevail in the minds of the majority, that the constitution does not specify who shall declare the conditions to support which the constitutionality of the act must be determined, exist, and that the seventh amendment does not so specify, that the legislature is therefore the exclusive judge of the existence of these conditions, the great chief justice in the case above quoted, further said:

"If any act of the legislature, repugnant to the constitution, is void, does it, notwithstanding its invalidity, bind the courts and oblige them to give it effect?

"It is emphatically the province and duty of the judicial department to say what the law is. . . .

"If then, the courts are to regard the constitution; and the constitution is superior to any ordinary act of the legislature; the constitution, and not such ordinary act, must govern the case to which they both apply."

In this case we have a legislative declaration which is manifestly made for the purpose of preventing any referendum to the people upon the act, otherwise it would not be in the act. It was enacted for that sole purpose, and the majority of this court say that the courts are bound by that declaration and cannot inquire beyond its enactment.

The act before us states as its purpose the consolidation of numerous departments, commissions, bureaus and officials into fewer departments for the purpose of co-ordinating their activities, and securing greater efficiency and greater economy, and transfers the duties of the boards, bureaus, commissions and officers that are abolished, to the new departments.

In 1915 the legislature consolidated the duties of several commissions and bureaus and transferred certain duties to one board, called the board of state land com-

missioners, and declared that the act was "necessary
for the immediate preservation of the public peace,
and safety, and the support of the state government,
and shall take effect immediately." The act was by no
means as comprehensive as the present act, but it was
brought before this court to contest the validity of the
emergency clause. In that case Judge Chadwick,
speaking for the court, said:

"Where there is a declaration in the constitution
that no law shall take effect unless in a case of emergency to be declared by the legislature, it may be truth-
fully said that the general rule is that a court will not
review the declaration of the legislature; but where the
people have put upon the legislature a limitation in the
way of a specific definition of its power, and an elimi-
nation of acts of a certain character, the rule is that
the declaration of an emergency must conform to the
constitutional requirement. . . .

"At the general election held in November, 1912, the
people of the state adopted the initiative and referendum amendment to the constitution. By this amendment, it was provided that no law or bill subject to the
referendum shall take effect until ninety days after
the adjournment of the legislature at which it was enacted, and that all laws shall be subject to referendum
except such as may be necessary for the immediate
preservation of the public peace, health or safety, support of the state government and its existing public institutions. . . .

"It is the contention of the respondents that the provision for an emergency in the amendment is in no
respect different from that contained in the constitution, art. 2, § 31, and that the courts are powerless to
inquire into the act or discretion of the legislature; that
we are governed by the same rules and by the same considerations which have moved the courts since the establishment of our government to put no judicial restraints upon legislative discretion. . . .

"The judicial aversion to a review of legislative discretion, in so far as it relates to emergency clauses, is

no more thoroughly established than the equivalent
declaration that courts have power to declare laws unconstitutional. Now there is no more reason for saying that a bill is an emergency measure, when upon its
face it is not, and from the very nature of its subject-
matter cannot be, just because the legislature has said
it is so, than there is for declaring a law to be unconstitutional when it has been passed by the legislature
with the constitution and its limitations lying open
before it. The sense and discretion of the legislature,
as well as its power to discriminate between an act
falling clearly without and one falling clearly within
the constitution, should, if we are consistent, be given
the same weight as a declaration that an act is emergent, but few courts have so held since *Marbury v. Madi-*
son, 1 Cranch, (U. S.) 49, although their inconsistencies
have long been apparent to the lay mind. In the one
case we have said that we will inquire, in the other we
have said that we will not inquire, saying meanwhile
that we will indulge every presumption in favor of a
law and will not declare it unconstitutional unless it is
clearly violative of the constitution.

"The object of the amendment, in so far as it
touches the taking effect of bills or laws, was to secure
the right of review. In paragraph 'b' of the same
section it is provided:

" 'The second power reserved by the people is the
referendum and it may be ordered on *any* act, bill, law,
or *any part* thereof passed by the legislature, except
such laws as may be necessary for the immediate preservation of the public peace, health or safety, support
of the state government and its existing public institutions.'

"If specific reservation in words of the right to subject *all* laws to the referendum were not enough, the
preamble of the amendment makes it clear that the
people intended to assert that the revised and amended
clause of the constitution permitting emergent legislation should not be a dead letter, as was § 31, which was
expressly repealed. They said:

" 'The legislative authority of the State of Washington shall be vested in the legislature, consisting of the

senate and house of representatives, which shall be called the legislature of the state of Washington, but the people reserve to themselves the power to propose bills, laws, and to enact or reject the same at the polls, independent of the legislature, and also reserve power, *at their own option,* to approve or reject at the polls any act, item, section or part of any bill, act or law passed by the legislature.' Laws of 1911, p. 36.

"The people said to the legislature, make such laws as you will, but you may not legislate so as to take away our rights to pass upon the law you have just enacted, 'except such laws as may be necessary for the immediate preservation of the peace, health or safety, support of the state government and its existing institutions.'" *(State ex rel. Brislawn v. Meath, supra).*

After discussing the fact that under the original constitution and § 31, art. 2 thereof, the legislature had unlimited power to declare emergencies without the right of review by the people, the writer of the foregoing opinion continues:

"But here no such declaration is final, and should be given no immediate effect unless it can be fairly said that the act is necessary to preserve the health, peace or safety of the state or to support the government or its institutions."

and quotes from *Mugler v. Kansas,* 123 U. S. 623, to the effect that courts are not bound by mere forms, nor are they to be misled by mere pretenses. The opinion continues:

"The reservation in the amendment is a declaration of 'Thou shalt not', except it be for the safety or support of the state. . . . .
 . . . "power has been withheld, in so far as a withholding can be made by apt and certain words."

The opinion further says:

"The true rule is: The referendum cannot be withheld by the legislature in any case except it be where the act touches the immediate preservation of the pub-

lic peace, health, or safety, or the act is for the financial
support of the government and the public institutions
of the state, that is, appropriation bills. If the act be
doubtful, the question of emergency will be treated as
a legislative question, and the doubt resolved in favor
of emergency made by the legislative body.

"Emergency, in the sense of the present constitution, does not mean expediency, convenience or best
interest. There is no room for construction or specu-
lation. The declaration is equivalent to saying that
the referendum shall not be cut off in any case except
in certain enumerated instances, none of which now
occur. . . .

"The essence of our reasoning is not that the legislature has abused its discretion; that is really immaterial; but that the people shall have a right, if they see
fit, to review its acts and place the stamp of approval
or disapproval upon it."

It was there concluded:

"The real question is, Can the people, as distinguished from a representative legislative body, indulge in constructive legislation and reserve that right
without interference by the legislature or the courts,
except where, in certain enumerated instances, they
have waived the right in order that the immediate necessities of health, peace and safety and the support of
the government and our public institutions may be met
by their representatives duly convened in legislative
session? Section 2 of the act amending § 6605, violates
the Seventh Amendment to our constitution, and is
void. The act will take effect ninety days after the
legislature has adjourned."

In *State ex rel. Mullen v. Howell,* 107 Wash. 167, 181
Pac. 920, involving the method of ratifying or rejecting
the eighteenth amendment to the constitution of the
United States, Chadwick, C. J., again writing the opinion for the court, again reviewed the reasons for the
adoption of the seventh amendment to our state consti-

tution, known as the direct legislative amendment, among other things said:

"No cases have been cited, and we may confidently say that there are none holding to the rule of strict construction where the power of the whole people is in question. . . . .

"It is well known that the power of the referendum was asserted, not because the people had a willful or perverse desire to exercise the legislative function directly, but because they had become impressed with a profound conviction that the legislature had ceased to be responsive to the popular will. They endeavored to, and did—unless we attach ourselves to words and words alone, reject the idea upon which the referendum is founded, and blind ourselves to the great political movement that culminated in the seventh amendment —make reservation of the power to refer every act of the legislature with only certain enumerated exceptions. . . .

" 'The theory of our political system is that the ultimate sovereignty is in the people, from whom springs all legitimate authority'." Citing Cooley, Constitutional Limitations (6th ed.), p. 39.

And in that case one of our learned associates, Judge Mackintosh, concurred with the majority and wrote a special concurring opinion in which he said:

"By the adoption of the initiative and referendum amendments the people of this state became a part of the legislative branch of the state government, and all legislative actions, except those especially exempted, are subject to their participation. The reasons which have led up to this modern form of legislation are as set forth in Judge Chadwick's opinion and, upon both authority and reason, no curtailment of this power should now be judicially sanctioned. If the people have declared their intention to assert their authority over the legislature in acts many of which are of temporary or small importance, it was surely their intention to preserve to themselves the right of reviewing legislative action of lasting and great importance, . . .

It would be idle to say that the right of referendum
could be exercised in the unimportant matters and not
in the important.

"The dissenting opinion of Judge Parker indulges
in altogether too narrow and restricted an interpretation of the right of referendum, and seems to be entirely out of harmony with the course of the decisions
of this court upon this and kindred matters arising
under laws affecting modern legislative and governmental functions. By strict adherence to dictionary
definitions, this dissenting opinion crushes the spirit
of the constitutional provisions under consideration,
and if it were the prevailing view in this case, would
mark a step backward by a court which has come to
be recognized as rather liberal in its interpretation of
legislation aimed at the correction of social and public
evils.''

And yet, we have here not merely *a step* backward,
but a long march backward in the interpretation of the
force and effect of the referendum clause of the
seventh amendment.

The emergency declared is that the act "is necessary
for the state government and its existing institutions."
Apply the simplest rules of construction to this declaration of emergency and it must fall. It is not, and
does not pretend to be, an act carrying an appropriation for either *existing* or *future* public institutions. It
abolishes *existing* institutions and substitutes new
ones.

In *State ex rel. Blakeslee v. Clausen*, 85 Wash. 260,
148 Pac. 28, we held, Judge Parker concurring, that
the seventh amendment to the constitution, art. 2, § 1,
subd. (b) giving the right of referendum upon all laws
except such as may be necessary for the "immediate
preservation of the public peace, health and safety,
(and the) support of the state government and its existing public institutions" contemplates "support" as

including appropriations for current expenses, maintenance, upkeep, continuation of existing functions, as well as appropriations for such new buildings and conveniences as may be necessary for the needs and requirements of the state in relation to its *existing* institutions, but did not contemplate exemption from the referendum where the law brought the state into a new activity, or provided for a new function, so that it might be fairly said that it did not pertain to the *support* of the government *as then organized,* or to any (then) *existing institution.*

That precisely covers the situation here.

The present act *abolishes seventy existing* institutions and substitutes new ones to go into existence April 1, 1921.

Nor can it be said that it is necessary for the future support of the state government as it must be organized for the future, for the language of the constitution is that an emergent matter must be for the "support of the state government *and* its *existing* public institutions"; and by no possible straining of language can it be said that anything is *emergent unless* it is *immediate,* or approximately so, and nothing can be in immediately necessitous circumstances unless it is in existence.

Here we have the constitution with its seventh amendment before us, and an act of the legislature with a declaration of an immediate emergency, which is manifestly, as everyone knows, a mere pretense. It constitutes a positive legislative usurpation of power reserved by the people to themselves, and the majority say that the declaration is final and conclusive by the mere negation that it is non-justiciable. We have weakly vacillated from the rule adopted in the *Brislawn* case, *supra.* We have placidly closed our judicial eyes to a legislative usurpation of rights withdrawn and reserved "by apt and certain words", to the people by the seventh amendment. We have abrogated judicial power to inquire into the validity of a legislative assertion of power; we have judicially countenanced the nullification of the seventh amendment as to the referendum—a result devoutly desired by some, but not by any considerable number of the people. It is an impotent outcome to labors in framing and adopting the amendment, withdrawing and reserving from the legislative power to fully and finally legislate in all matters except a few instances, that seemed to promise vastly more. At any rate, the law has become unsettled and its continuity broken.

The courts are the conservators of the rights guaranteed by the constitution to the people and to the individuals composing the people.

"It is requisite that the courts of justice should be able, at all times, to present a determined countenance against all licentious acts; and to deal impartially and truly, according to law, between suitors of every description, whether the cause, the question, or the party be popular or unpopular. . . . .

"Courts should be more constant and determined else the law becomes unsettled and may even become an object of scorn and derision." Kent Commentaries, p. 294.

The referendum right and power of the people may be a slow and clumsy system and may be objectionable to many. But this is a government eminently "of the people, by the people, and for the people," and they adopted this system and made it a part of the fundamental and paramount law. It is not for us to destroy it by judicial construction.

For the foregoing reasons I dissent.

The emergency clause attached to this act should be stricken under the seventh amendment of the constitution, so as to permit the act to be subject to the referendum.

TOLMAN, J., concurs with HOLCOMB, J.

MAIN and MITCHELL, JJ. (dissenting)—We concur in the conclusion arrived at in the dissenting opinion written by Judge Holcomb, for the reason that the *Brislawn* case was correctly decided and is controlling. It would serve no useful purpose to further discuss that case. The only way for an inquiring mind to determine whether the majority or the minority view of it is correct is to read that opinion and consider its application to the law here under consideration. If there is any difference between the two cases the present case is more clearly subject to the referendum than was the *Brislawn* case.

[No. 16310. *En Banc.* May 28, 1921.]

HENRY CONGER, *as Receiver etc., Appellant,* v. PIERCE COUNTY *et al., Respondents.*[1]

NAVIGABLE WATERS (30-3)—RIPARIAN RIGHTS—INJURIES CAUSED BY STRUCTURES—EROSION. Laws 1913, p. 156, authorizing contiguous counties to cooperate in the improvement, confinement and protection of rivers and their banks, tributaries and outlets, the waters of which work damage by inundation or otherwise, has for its object the protection of adjoining lands from overflow, and does not contemplate the improvement of the stream for navigable purposes.

WATERS AND WATER COURSES (35, 72)—DIVERSION—FLOWAGE—ACTION FOR INJURIES. Where adjoining counties, under express legislative authority, improve a navigable stream for the purpose of preventing it from overflowing its banks and doing damage to public property, they are liable to a landowner, under Const., art. 1, § 16, prohibiting the damaging of private property for public use without compensation, if, because of such improvements and the manner in which they are made, his property is eroded and washed away.

[1]Reported in 198 Pac. 377.

Constitutional Law (43, 51)—Police Power—Nature and Scope —Deprivation of Property. The police power of the state, while permitting the regulation of private property even to its destruction, under the necessity of the public health, peace or welfare, does not extend to the taking of private property for public use without compensation to the owner.

Waters and Water Courses (44)—Damages (9)—Direct or Consequential—In General. The erosion and washing away of a property owner's land on the banks of a stream, due to deflecting the current of the stream by improvements in the channel made by defendants, cannot be said to be an indirect or consequential damage, where it appears that defendants through their engineer had knowledge that such an injury would probably result from the improvement.

Holcomb, J., dissents.

Appeal from a judgment of the superior court for Pierce county, Clifford, J., entered April 28, 1920, granting a nonsuit and dismissing an action for damages caused by erosions due to certain river improvements. Reversed.

Davis & Neal, for appellant.

J. W. Selden, John A. Sorley, F. D. Nash, Malcolm Douglas, Howard A. Hanson, and *Bert C. Ross,* for respondents.

Bridges, J.—This is an action to recover damages caused by certain erosions, the result, it is alleged, of changes in and improvements of the Puyallup river, made by the defendants, which river, in part, forms the boundary line between the defendant counties and empties into Commencement Bay, at or near Tacoma. The complaint alleged, and the plaintiff's testimony tended to show, the following facts: On December 17, 1917, and for a number of years prior thereto, the Tacoma Meat Company, a corporation, owned a small tract of land bordering on the Puyallup river, near its mouth, on which land it had erected various buildings in which it had carried on a general slaughtering and packing establishment. Within these buildings were considerable quantities of valuable machinery and other personal property. Prior to the making of the improvements hereinafter mentioned, the Puyallup river was a tortuous, navigable stream, which had been in the habit of overflowing its banks during the rainy seasons, and thus doing much damage to the bridges, roads and other public property of the defendants. In 1913, the legislature enacted a law which authorized any two counties, under certain circumstances, to jointly improve streams which flowed through both of such counties, or formed the boundary line between them, so as to correct, as far as might be, their habit of overflowing their banks and thereby causing damage. By virtue of this enactment, the defendants entered into a contract, under date of January 19, 1914, for the purpose of straightening and deepening the channel of the Puyallup river and abating the flood tendencies. This contract formed a district within which such improvements should be made, and the plaintiff's property is located in the extreme northwesterly portion of such district.

After entering into the contract, the counties proceeded to make the improvements and in many places they straightened the stream and widened and deepened it, and placed various improvements along and upon the banks with a view of keeping the waters from eroding them. A few hundred feet immediately above the plaintiff's property, the river, previous to its improvement, took a wide bend to the southwest, and as the waters so ran they were in the habit of hitting the northeasterly bank at a point slightly up stream from the plaintiff's property, which act caused the waters to be deflected in such a way that very little, if any, erosion had occurred on the plaintiff's property in many years. In improving the stream, the defendants eliminated the bend just mentioned by causing the channel of the stream to be straightened, and, as a result of such straightening and the placing of concrete blocks on the banks for their protection, the waters of the stream were caused to come forcibly in contact with the bank on which plaintiff's property was situated, and during a high freshet in the winter of 1917, and after the defendants had completed their work of improving the river, there was such erosion of the plaintiff's lands as to cause its buildings to lose their foundations and to be floated, together with their contents, out into Commencement Bay, or Puget Sound. The particular causes of the erosions are alleged to be, the straightening of the channel in such manner as to throw the current of the stream against the river bank at the point of plaintiff's location; the placing of concrete protection on the bank opposite and a little above plaintiff's property in such way as to deflect the waters against the bank of the river where plaintiff's improvements were located, and the failure of the defendants to protect the banks along that part of the stream where plaintiff's property was situated.

When the plaintiff had rested its case, the trial court granted the defendants' motion to take the case from the jury and enter judgment dismissing the action. Later such judgment was made and entered and the plaintiff has appealed. Since there was sufficient testimony to carry the case to the jury on the theory that respondents' acts had caused the damages suffered by appellant, we will henceforth speak of the damage as being caused by respondents, realizing, of course, that, at best, it was a question for the jury.

The arguments before this court have taken such a wide and varied range that it seems necessary for us

at this time to show what the exact question before us
is. In the first place, the appellant is not seeking any
damage because its land and property were flooded.
As a matter of fact, the waters, at the time in question,
were so high as that all of plaintiff's property was
flooded, but plaintiff seeks recovery only for damage
done by erosion of his lands. In this way the direct
question of damage by flooding is not involved. The
testimony tends to show that the erosion was caused by
such of the waters as were in the channel of the stream
and that the overflow waters did not cause any erosion.
Again, although this stream is navigable within the improved district, we have concluded that the law applicable to improving navigable steams in aid of navigation is not directly involved. While the improvements
made by the respondents may or may not have improved the stream for navigation, the purpose of the
improvement was not in aid of navigation, but to correct the tendency of the stream to overflow its banks.
The legislative enactment authorizing the counties to
do this work (Laws of 1913, p. 156) does not contemplate the improvement of the stream for the purpose
of making it more navigable. Its title, which is as follows, quite correctly shows the purpose of the act:

"An act authorizing counties to contract together
for administrative and financial cooperation in the
improvement, confinement and protection of rivers and
the banks, tributaries and outlets thereof, whose
waters flowing into or through such counties work
damage by inundation or otherwise, authorizing the
levy of taxes and the creation and disbursement of special funds for such purposes, delegating the power of
eminent domain in aid of, and providing generally
ways and means for the accomplishment of such purposes and the performance of such contracts."

The direct question before us is, whether a county
which straightens and otherwise improves a navigable

stream for the purpose of preventing it from overflowing its banks and thereby doing damage to the public
property, where such improvements are made by virtue of express authority of the legislature, is liable to
a landowner if, because of such improvements, and the
manner in which they are made, his property is eroded
and washed away. The trial court stated its position,
and as we understand it, that of the respondents, in
the following language:

"The Puyallup river, at the point in controversy, is
a navigable and tidal stream. The state in its sovereign right is owner of the bed and banks and body of
the stream, and as such owner may make such changes
in the course of the river, and may improve the same
by widening or deepening or straightening a channel,
or in any other manner it may see fit, and it is not liable
to the owner of the shore land for any damage that
may result from so doing, either directly or indirectly.
It owes no duty to the shore land owner to protect him
from resulting damage on account of any improvement
the state may make upon its own property in the banks
or bed of the stream, and the shore land owner has no
right to any protection from the result of the state's
acts in dealing with the river channel and the waters
flowing therein. . . ."

The parties to the action have elaborately discussed
the law of outlaw, or surface, waters. In our opinion,
those questions are not in this case, and to undertake
to discuss them would be to create confusion in a question already sufficiently difficult. The appellant is
complaining only of the action of those portions of the
waters which were within the bed of the stream. It is
not complaining of any overflowed, outlaw or surface
waters. Certainly, so long as the waters are confined
to the bed and banks of the stream they cannot be outlaw waters.

It seems certain that had a private individual or private corporation caused the damage which the appellant alleges, there would be a liability. While a private individual has a right, under certain circumstances, to protect himself against overflow, surface and outlaw waters, he cannot so change the stream in an effort to protect his own property, as that he will thereby flood or erode the property of someone else. It seems to us that the authorities are quite unanimous in this regard. A few of them are as follows: *Judson v. Tidewater Lumber Co.*, 51 Wash. 164, 98 Pac. 377; *Johnson v. Irvine Lumber Co.*, 75 Wash. 539, 135 Pac. 217; *Valley Ry. Co. v. Franz*, 43 Ohio St. 623, 4 N. E. 88; *Crawford v. Rambo*, 44 Ohio 279, 7 N. E. 429; *Freeland v. Pennsylvania R. Co.*, 197 Pa. 529, 47 Atl. 745, 80 Am. St. 850, 58 L. R. A. 206; *Gerrish v. Clough*, 36 N. H. 519; *Bowers v. Mississippi & R. R. Boom Co.*, 78 Minn. 398, 81 N. W. 208, 79 Am. St. 395; *Morton v. Oregon Short Line Ry. Co.*, 48 Ore. 444, 87 Pac. 151, 120 Am. St. 827, 7 L. R. A. (N. S.) 344, and note; *Town of Jefferson v. Hicks*, 23 Okl. 684, 102 Pac. 79, 24 L. R. A. (N.S.) 214, and note.

But respondents contend that when they improved this river they were acting under direct legislative authority, and that what they did was for the state, and that when the state, either directly or through its appointed agents, acts for the good of the public, it cannot be made to respond for damages which may result to the private individual. They advocate the doctrine that the private individual, under such circumstances, must suffer for the public good. A wilderness of authorities are cited both in support of and against this proposition. It seems to us that a recurrence to certain fundamental principles may assist us in reaching a correct conclusion. One of the greatest contributions of the English speak-

ing people to civilization is the protection by law of the
private individual in the enjoyment of his property and
his personal liberties against the demands and aggres-
sions of the public. No better illustration of the progres-
sive growth of this principle can be found than that contained in our various state constitutions with reference
to the taking of private property for a public use. It
has been said that this power is a necessary incident to
government and was before and did not grow out of
constitutions. If so, the Federal constitutional provision, that private property should not be taken for a
public use without compensation being made, was but
a written expression of a right which already existed,
being placed in the constitution for the purpose of em-
phasizing the desire to protect the rights of the individual. The national constitution and the constitutions
of the earlier states went no farther than to provide
that private property should not be taken for a public
use without compensation being made. Later constitutions added to these provisions the idea that the compensation must be made before the taking is accomplished. Still later constitutions, including that of the
state of Washington, added an additional element, to-
wit, that private property may not be taken or damaged for the public use without compensation being
first made. Const., art. 1, § 16. It is true that this is
not an eminent domain proceeding but the principles of
law involved in the power to take private property for
a public use are involved here, because respondents
are seeking to justify the damage alleged to have been
done by them on the theory that they were acting by
virtue of law and as an arm of the state, and for the
use of the state, and for the public good.

Since, therefore, our constitution expressly forbids
the taking or damaging of private property for a pub-

lic use except upon just compensation first made, on
what theory can respondents be relieved from any
damage to appellant's property as a direct result of
the improvements which were made in the Puyallup
river? Certainly not simply because they were acting
as an arm of the state, or alone because they were acting for the good of the public, or simply on the theory
that the individual must suffer for the public good. To
hold that they would be relieved on any of these
grounds would be entirely to disregard the express provisions of our constitution. The state itself cannot
take or damage private property for a public use, without compensating the owner; nor can it authorize a taking or damaging which is prohibited to it. The only
other principle of law under which respondents might
be relieved would be the police power of the sovereign,
because the only ways known to the law whereby private property may be taken or damaged by the public
are by the principles of eminent domain or those of the
police power. (If there may be a taking by taxation
that principle does not interest us here). Indeed, it is
the police power theory upon which respondents seem
most strongly to rely. It is probable that this power
is the most exalted attribute of government, and, like
the power of eminent domain, it existed before and in-
dependently of constitutions. It is easy to understand
the principles upon which the police power doctrine is
based, but difficult to define in language its limitations.
It is not inconsistent with nor antagonistic to the rules
of law concerning the taking of private property for a
public use. Because of its elasticity and the inability
to define or fix its exact limitations, there is sometimes
a natural tendency on the part of the courts to stretch
this power in order to bridge over otherwise difficult
situations, and for like reasons it is a power most

likely to be abused. It has been defined as an inherent
power in the state which permits it to prevent all
things harmful to the comfort, welfare and safety of
society. It is based on necessity. It is exercised for
the benefit of the public health, peace and welfare.
Regulating and restricting the use of private property
in the interest of the public is its chief business. It is
the basis of the idea that the private individual must
suffer without other compensation than the benefit to
be received by the general public. It does not authorize the taking or damaging of private property in the
sense used in the constitution with reference to taking
such property for a public use. Eminent domain takes
private property for a public use, while the police
power regulates its use and enjoyment, or if it takes
or damages it, it is not a taking or damaging for the
public use, but to conserve the safety, morals, health
and general welfare of the public. Lewis, Eminent Domain, § 6, writes of this subject:

"Everyone is bound so to use his own property as
not to interfere with the reasonable use and enjoyment
by others of their property. For a violation of this
duty the law provides a civil remedy. Besides this
obligation, which every property owner is under to the
owners of neighboring property, he is also bound so
to use and enjoy his own as not to interfere with the
general welfare of the community in which he lives. It
is the enforcement of this last duty which pertains to
the police power of the state so far as the exercise of
that power affects private property. Whatever restraints the legislature imposes upon the use and enjoyment of property within the reason and principle of
this duty, the owner must submit to, and for any inconvenience or loss which he sustains thereby, he is
without remedy. It is a regulation, and not a taking,
an exercise of police power, and not of eminent domain.
But the moment the legislature passes beyond mere
regulation, and attempts to deprive the individual of

his property, or of some substantial interest therein, under pretense of regulation, then the act becomes one of eminent domain, and is subject to the obligations and limitations which attend an exercise of that power."

In the case of *Askam v. King County*, 9 Wash. 1, 36 Pac. 1097, speaking of police power, this court said:

". . . while it is undoubtedly true that in extreme emergencies the rights of private parties as to property must yield to the requirements of the public, yet to authorize such interference the emergency must be such as to make the action necessary."

The specific question, then, is: were the respondents in the exercise of the police power in making the improvements they made in the river in question? Our answer must be in the negative. The legislative act under which they made the improvement is entirely bare of any expression which would indicate that the legislature considered that public necessity demanded or required the making of the improvement. Section 1 of the Laws of 1913, ch. 54, p. 156, being the act by virtue of which these improvements were made, provides that whenever any river shall flow in part through two counties, or shall form the boundary line between them:

". . . and the waters thereof have in the past been the cause of damage, by inundation or otherwise, to the roads, bridges or other public property situate in or to other public interests of both such counties, or the flow of such waters shall have alternated between the said counties so at one time or times such waters shall have caused damage to one county, and at another time or times to the other county, and it shall be deemed by the boards of county commissioners of both counties to be for the public interests of their respective counties that the flow of such waters be definitely confined to a particular channel, situate in whole or in part in either county. . . ."

then the counties interested may jointly make the desired improvement.

The act provides that the expense of making such improvement shall be raised by an annual tax on all the property in the county, which tax is to be levied and collected as any other county tax. The act nowhere intimates that the counties would be relieved from any damages that may be done to private property; on the contrary, they are authorized to exercise the power of eminent domain for the purpose of acquiring lands on which the river may be straightened. The contract between the respondents, under which the work was done, directly recognizes that the river in the past has overflown its banks and thereby damaged the roads, bridges and other private property of the two counties, and that because thereof litigation between them had arisen, and that the purpose of the contemplated improvement is to settle such pending litigation and make improbable future suits, and to avoid future damage to the roads and bridges of the two counties. It will thus be seen that this improvement was not made to preserve public health, peace, morals or welfare; it was not done to reclaim large tracts of land which otherwise might have been a waste; the idea of impelling necessity, which seems to be the chief ingredient of the police power, is entirely absent. Respondents cite many cases which they contend support them in their argument of non-liability. While we have carefully read all of them, we cannot here take the space to digest them, nor even cite all of them. The leading ones are: *Lamb v. Reclamation Dist.*, 73 Cal. 125, 14 Pac. 625, 2 Am. St. 775; *Cubbins v. Mississippi River Comm.*, 241 U. S. 351, 60 L. Ed. 1040; *Bass v. State*, 34 La. Ann. 494; *Hughes v. United States*, 230 U. S. 24; *McCoy v. Board of Directors*, 95 Ark. 345, 129 S. W. 1097, 29 L. R. A. (N. S.)

396; *Bedford v. United States*, 192 U. S. 217; *Gray v. Reclamation Dist.*, 174 Cal. 622, 163 Pac. 1024.

The decisions in some of these cases are based upon constitutional provisions which only prohibit the taking of private property without compensation, and are, therefore, at least to that extent, not in point in view of our constitutional provision. Others of the cases cited involve improvements made in aid of navigation and are not in point or material here. Others of the cited cases arise in instances where the state, or some subdivision of it, has made improvements in streams solely for the purpose of preventing them from overflowing their banks, and by such improvements reclaiming or saving to the state and its people large tracts of land, which are essential to the welfare of the public. Of this class, the case of *McCoy v. Board of Directors*, concerning the Arkansas river, and *Gray v. Reclamation District, supra,* concerning the Sacramento river, may be considered leading cases. The last cited case is particularly elaborately considered by the California supreme court. The reclamation district in that case built dikes, levees and other works purely for the purpose of confining the waters of the Sacramento river within its banks, in order to reclaim very extensive tracts of otherwise valueless lands. Because of such improvements, the plaintiff's lands were overflown and damaged. The court applied the police power to these facts and held the district was not liable. Without approving or disapproving the conclusion of the court in that case and in others along the same line, they are easily distinguishable from the case at bar. In those cases there are elements on which the police power is rightly based, but which facts are entirely absent from the case at bar. There the controlling purpose of the improvement was to reclaim and save to the people large tracts of rich lands which, because of inundation, were worthless. To that extent the public welfare was involved. Here the controlling purpose was the protection of the roads and bridges of the respondent counties. Neither the state nor the people of the state or counties were interested in the improvement except in a very indirect way, and as taxpayers.

We are confident that any damage that may have been done by the respondents cannot be excused under any reasonable interpretation of the law of police power. While no cases exactly in point have been cited or found by us, the following are a few of a great number which, in principle, support our views: *Burrows v. Grays Harbor Boom Co.*, 44 Wash. 630, 87 Pac. 937; *Askam v. King County, supra; Ordway v. Village of Canisteo*, 21 N. Y. Supp. 835; *Noonan v. City of Albany*, 79 N. Y. 470, 35 Am. Rep. 540; *Bradbury v. Vandalia Levee and Drainage Dist.*, 236 Ill. 36, 86 N.E. 163, 19 L. R. A. (N. S.) 991; *Barden v. Portage*, 79 Wis. 126, 48 N. W. 210; *Jefferson v. Hicks*, 23 Okl. 684, 102 Pac. 79, 24 L. R. A. (N. S.) 214; Lewis, Eminent Domain, §§ 115, 285, 306.

In the case of *Burrows v. Grays Harbor Boom Co., supra*, the facts were: that the driving company had built several splash dams for the purpose of creating artificial freshets in order to assist in the driving of saw logs down the river towards market. The testimony showed that these artificial freshets caused Burrows' lands to be eroded. The latter by his action sought, among other things, to enjoin the creation of artificial freshets because of the damage they did to his lands. Substantially the same argument was made by the driving company in that case as is made by the respondents here. It was there contended that the driving company was a quasi-public corporation, directly authorized by legislative act, to create artificial freshets for the public good, and that it could not be held liable for damages caused by them. This court refused to adopt that view and held that if the driving company caused Burrows' lands to be eroded by its artificial freshets it would be liable therefor in damages. Answering this argument, Judge Dunbar, speaking for the court, said:

"This provision in the fundamental law (our constitutional provision with reference to taking of private property for public use) was construed by this court in *Brown v. Seattle*, 5 Wash. 35, 31 Pac. 313, 32 Pac. 214, 18 L. R. A. 161, and in many subsequent cases, to mean just what it said: and it can make no possible difference whether the property abuts on a street or river or whether the invader of that right is a municipality, an individual, or a boom company; the constitutional guaranty applies equally in both cases."

Why, indeed, on general principles, should not the counties be liable if the damage to appellant is the direct result of the changing of the river channel and the currents of the stream? The counties were protecting themselves and their roads and bridges. May they do this in such a way as to injure private property without becoming liable therefor? Certainly not. They are in no better position than would be an individual who should do exactly the same thing. By the legislative authority they had a right to straighten the stream and change the currents thereof, but that legislative authority did not absolve them from liability for such damages as might directly result from such improvements.

But respondents contend that, in any event, they are not liable here because the damage to appellant was not the direct result of improvements made by them, but was only what is sometimes termed indirect, or consequential, damages, for which there can be no liability. It is difficult to give any definition showing the difference between a direct and an indirect or consequential damage. This, however, may be easily shown by certain illustrations. Private property may be damaged and its value lessened because it is located close to some public building, such as a jail or hospital or public hall, yet such damage is purely incidental and not recoverable. The noise consequent on the operation of railroad trains upon private right-of-way, may depreciate the value of adjoining private property and be an annoyance to those living in the immediate neighborhood, but such damage is purely consequential and is not recoverable. But the injury to appellant's property, if caused as contended for by it, cannot be considered of this nature. The alleged erosion of its land and thereby the destruction of its property would be the direct result of the act of the respondents in straightening the channels of the river, and thereby changing the currents of the stream. There was testimony tending to show that respondents' engineers must of necessity have known that the improvements which they were making would cause the appellant's property to be eroded and probably washed away. Under these conditions it cannot be said that the damages are so remote and disconnected with the improvement of the river as to be purely incidental or consequential.

Briefly, we hold that if the damage in question was caused by the action of respondents in straightening the Puyallup river and thereby changing its currents, then the appellant is entitled to have its case submitted to a jury. It follows from what we have said that the trial court erred in taking the case from the jury. The judgment dismissing the action is reversed and the cause remanded for trial.

PARKER, C. J., MACKINTOSH, FULLERTON, MAIN, TOL-MAN, and MITCHELL, JJ., concur.

HOLCOMB, J. (dissenting)—The foregoing opinion is an exceedingly able and admirable one, but I am unable to bring myself to concur in it.

I agree with the conclusions of the trial judge quoted in the majority opinion. I am firmly of the opinion that the act under which the work was done by the counties was an act under the police power. The improvements were certainly for the public welfare. It is assuredly in the interests of public welfare to improve the stream so as to prevent flooding and destruction of county roads and bridges. If the safety of travel by the public is not the public welfare, it is difficult to conceive what would be.

It is determined that the Puyallup river is a navigable river. As such its sovereignty is in the state, the state having asserted absolute title and control of the beds, shores and banks of navigable rivers. It is determined that the work by the counties was lawfully performed, and the counties had previously obtained the necessary rights-of-way and made compensation for any damage by reason of such taking and change of the channel of the stream.

Therefore, the damage to appellant, if attributable to respondents, is consequent upon a lawful act of respondents, and is *damnum absque injuria*. Wiel (3d ed.), Water Rights, § 248; Dillon, Municipal Corporations (4th ed.), § 995; Cooley, Constitutional Limitations, p. 300; *Hill v. Newell*, 86 Wash. 227, 149 Pac. 951; *Morton v. Hines*, 112 Wash. 612, 192 Pac. 1016. Other authorities could be cited from our own and other courts, but the above citations are sufficient to sustain my view. I therefore dissent.

[No. 16217. Department One. May 28, 1921.]

C. August Wunsch, *Respondent*, v. Consolidated Laundry Company, *Appellant*, George Sillman et al., *Defendants*.[1]

PLEADING (112)—AMENDMENT OF COMPLAINT—NEW OR DIFFERENT CAUSE OF ACTION. A trial amendment of a complaint, even if it changes the cause of action from one sounding in tort to one sounding in contract, is permissible under the code.

SAME (109)—CONDITION OF CAUSE — ASKING CONTINUANCE. The amendment of a complaint in the course of a trial cannot be claimed as prejudicial on appeal, where defendant did not demand time to prepare to meet the new allegations.

EVIDENCE (48)—COMPETENCY—VALUE OF CORPORATE STOCK. In an action to recover the value of stock in an old corporation all the property of which had been transferred to a new corporation, under an agreement for an issue of new stock "dollar for dollar," evidence of the value of the stock in the new corporation was admissible as tending to show the value of the stock of the old corporation.

STIPULATIONS (3)—CONCLUSIVENESS AND EFFECT—PERSONS CONCLUDED. Under a stipulation between parties to an appeal in an action to recover the value of corporate stock that, in case the supreme court should hold plaintiff entitled to a money judgment, then no question shall be raised as to the amount of the money judgment rendered by the trial court, the appellant is concluded from urging on appeal that the stock had no value.

CORPORATIONS (172)—PROPERTY AND CONVEYANCES—DISPOSAL OF CORPORATE ASSETS. A transfer of all the property of a corporation by its officers and some of its stockholders to a trustee to be by him transferred to a new corporation on its organization would not defeat the right of dissenting or omitted stockholders to sue the purchasing company for the value of the stock.

Appeal from a judgment of the superior court for Spokane county, Webster, J., entered May 24, 1920,

[1]Reported in 198 Pac. 383.

upon findings in favor of the plaintiff, in an action to recover the value of certain corporate stock. Affirmed.

Charles E. Swan, for appellant.

F. A. McMaster, for respondent.

FULLERTON, J.—The respondent, Wunsch, instituted this action on behalf of himself and his assignors, O. C. Nelson, F. A. Nelson, Minnie Fletcher and W. R. White, against the appellant, Consolidated Laundry Company, and others, to recover the value of certain shares of stock held by them in a corporation whose property, it was alleged, appellants had taken and converted to their own use. The trial court, on the hearing, dismissed the action as to the codefendants of the appellant corporation and entered a judgment against it in the sum of eight hundred and seventy-four dollars. This appeal followed.

The Hotel Laundry Company, the corporation whose property is alleged to have been converted, was organized, in the early part of the year 1918, to do a general laundry business in the city of Spokane. Its chief promoter was one Charles Roberts, who seems to have been the active manager of the corporation during the months it engaged in business. To assist in the promotion of the corporation, Roberts engaged the services of the respondent and his assignors (with the exception of F. A. Nelson), agreeing to give them severally as compensation, in addition to a weekly wage, a certain number of shares of the corporation. On the organization of the corporation, pursuant to the agreement, shares of stock were issued, to the persons named, in the following amounts: to Wunsch fifty shares, to O. C. Nelson twenty shares, to Fletcher ten shares, and to White fifty shares, each of such shares having a face value of ten dollars. F. A. Nelson, to whom was

issued one hundred and fifty shares, paid for his stock
by turning over to the corporation certain laundry
equipment, which he had theretofore used in the operation of a laundry owned by himself individually. The
number of shareholders, on the organization of the corporation, totaled about ninety.

The corporation continued in business until the
month of October of 1918. Whether it had been a
profitable or a losing venture the evidence is in dispute. It had, however, during this time accumulated
property of a considerable value and had incurred a
considerable debt. In the month named, a number of
the stockholders of the corporation, some of whom
were trustees, met to consider its affairs. This meeting was not held pursuant to a call of the trustees or
pursuant to any notice given, and it does not appear
that a majority of the stock of the corporation was
represented thereat. At the meeting the stockholders
present agreed to abandon the corporation and the business as conducted by it, organize a new corporation
with an increased capital stock, turn over to the new
corporation all of the property assets and good will
of the existing corporation, and require the new corporation to assume the debts of the old. It was agreed
also that stock of the new corporation should be issued
to the stockholders of the old "dollar for dollar." Pursuant to this agreement, the appellant corporation was
organized. To it was transferred all of the property
of the old corporation, and it assumed and agreed to
pay all of the debts of the old corporation. Shares of
stock of the new corporation were issued and delivered
to all the shareholders of the old corporation in proportion to their holdings therein, save and except to
the respondent and his assignors. No stock was delivered or tendered to them for the reason that the

organizers of the new corporation, after investigation, concluded that the stock issued to them by the old corporation was issued without consideration.

From the evidence introduced at the trial, the court found that the respondent and his assignors were holders for value of the stock issued to them by the first of the corporations, that it had a value at the time of the transfer in the sum of $874, that the transfer of the property of the first corporation to the second was not in conformity with the rules of law, and was made without the knowledge or consent of the respondent or his assignors, and concluded, as matter of law, that the respondent was entitled to recover.

In the course of the proceedings, the court allowed the respondent to amend his complaint. It is urged that this was error, the reason given being that the amendment changed the cause of action from one sounding in tort to one sounding in contract. But we cannot conceive that the amendment had this effect. If the form of the action was tort prior to the amendment, it was so afterward. The amendment but added some additional facts, brought out in the evidence at the trial, which were not contained in the original complaint. If, however, we were to concede that the amendment had the effect contended for, we could not concede that it would be fatal to the right of recovery. In this state it is provided by statute that there shall be but one form of action for the enforcement and protection of private rights, and it is especially enjoined by statute what the complaint shall contain. One of the requirements is that it contain a plain and concise statement of the facts constituting the cause of action without unnecessary repetition. Manifestly, under the liberal provisions of our statute relating to amendments, which even permits amendments in this court, if the complaint alleges what was formerly denominated a tort and the evidence tends to show a breach of duty or a breach of contract, the complaint may be amended to conform therewith. The defendant has, of course, in such a case, as he has in the case of all amendments to complaints, the right to time sufficient to prepare to meet the new allegations, but he cannot, if he does not demand the right but tries the cause on the new issues, afterwards claim that he was prejudiced thereby.

In addition to showing the exchange of the stock in the old corporation for stock in the new on a basis of par value, the trial court permitted the respondent to show the par value of the stock in the new corporation and that none of it had ever been sold for less than its par value. It is contended that, because the question at issue was the value of the stock in the old corporation, this evidence was inadmissible. But the evidence clearly had some tendency to show the value of the stock in the old corporation, and the trial court had the right, and this court would have the right were the question before us, to consider it for that purpose.

It is next contended that the evidence overwhelmingly shows that the first of the corporations was insolvent and that its stock at the time of the transfers had no value whatsoever. But the appellants are concluded by the record from urging the question in this court. Prior to the preparation and settlement of the statement of facts, in order that the testimony introduced at the trial, relating to the character and value of the property of the first corporation transferred to the later one might be omitted therefrom, the parties stipulated:

"Now therefore it is hereby stipulated and agreed by and between the appellant and respondent, through their respective attorneys, that if the supreme court shall hold that the plaintiff, or either or any of his

assignors, is entitled to recover a money judgment
against the appellant herein, then and in that event no
question shall be raised by either party as to the
amount of such money judgment as rendered by the
trial court."

Since the amount and value of the property the corporation had on hand at the time of the transfer was
a material element in determining the value of its
stock at that time, the stipulation concludes an inquiry
in this court as to its value.

The final contention is that the respondent has no
cause of action against the appellant in any event. The
argument is this: (We quote from the brief.)

"If the respondents have a cause of action at all,
whether for conversion or in contract, their right of
action is against the individuals whose actions it is
claimed were wrongful and illegal, and they are not
entitled to a judgment of any kind against the appellant. The alleged conversion occurred before the appellant corporation was organized, and neither the
corporation nor its stockholders were liable for wrongful acts committed by persons in their individual
capacity. The same situation exists with respect to
the alleged contract, as set forth in plaintiff's second
amended complaint. If such an agreement was made,
it was the act of the individual defendants, and not the
act of the appellant corporation, which was not then
in existence."

In explanation of some of the facts here asserted,
which might be otherwise obscure, it may be stated
that the stockholders and trustees of the first of the
corporations, at the time they concluded to make the
reorganization, transferred all of the property of the
corporation to trustees to hold the property pending
the organization of the new corporation, and that the
property was conveyed to the new corporation through
the medium of these trustees. But the second corpora-

tion can claim no immunity based on these facts. The trustees acquired no interest by the transfer other than the bare legal title to the property, and the transaction, in so far as the rights of the respondent and his assignors are concerned, was equivalent to a direct transfer from the one corporation to the other. On the principal question, it is said by Fletcher in his Cyclopedia, Corporations (vol. 7, § 4798) that . . . .

"where a sale of all corporate property is illegally made by corporate officers without consent of the stockholders, a dissenting stockholder may sue the purchasing company for the value of his stock."

In *Ervin v. Oregon R. & Nav. Co.*, 20 Fed. 577, 27 Fed. 625, one Villard organized a new corporation, purchased and caused to be transferred to it a majority of the stock of the Oregon Steam Navigation Company. Thereupon Villard and the new corporation elected, as directors of the Oregon Steam Navigation Company, the directors of the new corporation and caused the directors to make a sale of the property of the old corporation to the new corporation at an inadequate price, and to dissolve the old corporation. At the suit of a minority stockholder in the old corporation, it was held that the directors, by their ownership of the majority of the stock, and the exercise of the powers of the corporation, were trustees of the property and that their sale of the property to the new corporation at an inadequate price was a breach of the trust, rendering them and the new corporation liable for the actual value of the interests of the plaintiff in the old corporation; and this notwithstanding the defendants had the right under the existing statutes to dissolve the corporation and distribute its assets, and notwithstanding they proceeded in so doing in compliance with the statutes. See, also, *Jones v. Missouri-Edison Elec.*

Co., 144 Fed. 765; *Tanner v. Lindell R. Co.*, 180 Mo. 1, 79 S. W. 155, 103 Am. Rep. 534.

The sale in this instance was made without even the forms of law, and the corporation is liable because it was the beneficiary of the transaction, receiving property thereby to which it was not justly entitled.

The judgment is affirmed.

PARKER, C. J., HOLCOMB, BRIDGES, and MACKINTOSH, JJ., concur.

[No. 16475. Department One. May 28, 1921.]

JAMES H. DOWNEY, *Appellant*, v. R. A. WILBUR *et al., Respondents.*[1]

APPEAL (23)—DECISIONS REVIEWABLE—SUITS IN EQUITY. The provision of the constitution, Art. 4, § 4, denying appellate jurisdiction to the supreme court where the original amount in controversy is less than $200, does not preclude appeal from an injunctive order made in a proceeding to have property declared a homestead and exempt from execution upon a judgment for $55.82.

Motion to dismiss an appeal from a judgment of the superior court for Pierce county, Askren, J., entered February 6, 1921. Denied.

Fayette J. Partridge, for appellant.

Kelly & MacMahon, for respondents.

MITCHELL, J.—James Downey sued and recovered judgment against R. A. Wilbur and wife, in a justice of the peace court, in the sum of $55.82. He then filed a duly certified transcript from the docket of the justice of the peace in the county clerk's office, upon which the clerk issued a writ of execution. The sheriff made a levy upon the property in which Wilbur and wife resided, and advertised it for sale. Prior to the date

[1]Reported in 198 Pac. 268.

fixed for the sale, R. A. Wilbur filed in the office of the
county auditor his duly acknowledged statutory declaration of homestead of the property advertised to be
sold, and at once commenced proceedings in the superior court for an order setting the property aside as exempt from levy and sale. He alleged its value to be not
exceeding $1,000. This proceeding was contested by
the judgment creditor and, upon a trial, the court entered an order setting the property aside as a homestead, declaring it free from the execution and enjoining the sheriff from selling it. James Downey has taken
an appeal from that order.

Wilbur and wife have moved to dismiss the appeal
upon the ground that this court is without jurisdiction
to hear it. The argument is that the original amount
in controversy, $55.82, is insufficient to give this court
jurisdiction under art. 4, § 4, of the constitution. In
our opinion, the position is untenable. The thing in
controversy in this appeal is real property, according
to the order and judgment of the superior court, and
which respondents allege to be of the value of $1,000.
It is an appeal not by Wilbur and wife, directly or indirectly, from the money judgment against them, but by
Downey from a final judgment made in favor of Wilbur
and wife at the conclusion of a separate proceeding instituted by them by which they have had removed from
their real property the lien of a levy and had it declared free under the exemption laws. It was a proceeding on the equity side of the court that resulted
in an injunctive order from which the appeal has been
prosecuted.

Respondents rely upon the cases of *Leites v. Peterson*, 68 Wash. 474, 123 Pac. 773; *Wade v. Weber*, 82
Wash. 591, 144 Pac. 901; and *State ex rel. Swan v. Superior Court*, 105 Wash. 167, 177 Pac. 679. Those

cases considered situations decidedly different from this one. In their order they were: (1) an appeal from an adverse judgment of the superior court in an action by a judgment debtor to restrain the enforcement of a judgment of a justice of the peace, which had been affirmed by the superior court, for less than $200; (2) an appeal from an adverse judgment of the superior court affirming on a writ of certiorari a judgment of a justice of the peace for less than $200; and (3) an original mandamus application in this court to compel the superior court to dismiss an action at law for the recovery of money in the sum of only $125. In the two first cases just referred to, the appeals to this court were taken by those who were debtors in the judgments of the justices of the peace to indirectly secure a review of those judgments—indirect methods of appeal in cases where direct appeals were denied by the law. Neither of the three cases just mentioned is applicable here, where the appeal is at the instance of the creditor in the original judgment because of an order procured after that judgment upon a proceeding by the debtors affecting their homestead exemption. The appeal in no way seeks a review of the judgment of the justice of the peace, which is favorable to the appellant and from which no appeal to this court is attempted in any manner by the respondents.

The motion to dismiss the appeal is denied.

PARKER, C. J., TOLMAN, FULLERTON, and HOLCOMB, JJ., concur.

[No. 16441. Department One. May 31, 1921.]

HERBERT E. WILLSON *et al.*, *Respondents*, v. ANTON
BETSCHART *et al.*, *Appellants.*[1]

APPEAL (24)—DECISIONS REVIEWABLE—AMOUNT IN CONTROVERSY.
Under Art. 4, § 4, of the state constitution prohibiting the appellate
jurisdiction of the supreme court in "actions at law for the recovery
of money or personal property when the original amount in controversy or the value of the property does not exceed the sum of
two hundred dollars," a judgment for $142 for damages to real
property, the title to which was in no way involved, is not appealable.

Appeal from a judgment of the superior court for
Pierce county, Card, J., entered October 30, 1920, upon
findings in favor of the plaintiff, in an action in tort.
Appeal dismissed.

H. W. Lueders, for appellants.

Jesse Thomas, for respondents.

MITCHELL, J.—Suit was brought in the superior
court to recover the sum of $142 to reimburse the plain-
tiffs for the cost of replacing a glass front in a building owned by them which they alleged had been broken
through the negligence of the defendants. They recovered judgment in the amount sued for. The defendants have taken an appeal.

The respondents have moved to dismiss the appeal
for the reason that the original amount in controversy
is not sufficient to give this court jurisdiction.

Article 4, § 4, of the constitution, defining the appellate jurisdiction of this court, provides that . . .
"its appellate jurisdiction shall not extend to civil actions at law for the recovery of money or personal
property when the original amount in controversy or

[1] Reported in 198 Pac. 269.

the value of the property does not exceed the sum of two hundred dollars, unless the action involves the legality of a tax, impost, assessment, toll, municipal fine, or the validity of a statute.'' The provision is plain and emphatic, and without doubt covers this case. Such has been our uniform holding in similar cases. *Henry v. Thurston County,* 31 Wash. 638, 72 Pac. 488; *State ex rel. Lack v. Meads,* 49 Wash. 468, 95 Pac. 1022; *Hall v. Cowen,* 51 Wash. 295, 98 Pac. 670.

Appellants' argument that the rule is not applicable because the claim originally grew out of damage to real property is without merit. The title to real property is in no way involved. The test is not to be found in the origin of the obligation, but in the character of the suit and the recovery sought. The language of the constitution forbids appellate jurisdiction in civil actions at law for the recovery of money when the original amount in controversy does not exceed $200. This is that kind of action.

Nor is it sound to argue that the rule is avoided because the action was one in tort rather than one in contract. The words of the constitution authorize no such distinction. ''When a recovery of money only is sought, no matter whether the action is in tort or in contract, the pecuniary restriction applies.'' Cyc., Appeal and Error, vol. 2, p. 545.

Appeal dismissed for want of jurisdiction.

PARKER, C. J., TOLMAN, FULLERTON, and HOLCOMB, JJ., concur.

[No. 16103. *En Banc.* June 1, 1921.]

J. H. PRICE *et al., Appellants,* v. HUMPTULIPS DRIVING COMPANY *et al., Respondents.*[1]

WATERS AND WATER COURSES (58)—PRESCRIPTION—ADVERSE CHARACTER OF APPROPRIATION. The filing by a public service corporation with the secretary of state of the plat and notice required by law showing that it was organized for the purpose of driving logs in a certain river was not sufficient to initiate an adverse claim or assertion of a legal right necessary to the support of prescriptive title.

INJUNCTION (10, 11, 43)—DEFENSES—LACHES—INCONVENIENCE TO PUBLIC. Where plaintiffs acquiesced for a long series of years in the use by a public service corporation of splash dams to produce artificial freshets, the plaintiffs themselves making use of the freshets for the same purpose, and having knowledge that such use of the stream caused erosion of their lands, their application to enjoin further use of the stream by defendant should be denied, since injunctive relief would cause serious public inconvenience and loss without corresponding advantage to plaintiffs.

Appeal from a judgment of the superior court for Grays Harbor county, Hewen, J., entered July 24, 1920, upon findings in favor of the defendants, in an action to enjoin the creation of artificial freshets in a river. Affirmed.

W. H. Abel, E. E. Boner, and *M. J. Gordon,* for appellants.

Theodore B. Bruener and *John T. Welsh,* for respondents.

MACKINTOSH, J.—This is an action in equity wherein the plaintiffs seek to enjoin the defendants from creating artificial freshets in the Humptulips river, and to prevent the change of the channel of that river and to restrain the defendants from trespassing upon plain-

[1]Reported in 198 Pac. 374.

tiffs' lands which abut upon that river. The defendants claim the right to create the artificial freshets and
to do the acts complained of, based upon prescription.

The Humptulips river rises in the Olympic mountains and, by a tortuous channel through heavily tim-
bered country, reaches Grays Harbor. The Humptulips is a meandered stream and, in its natural state,
was floatable for logs. In 1900, the defendant incorporated as a public service corporation for the purpose of
driving logs down the Humptulips river, past and
through the lands involved in this proceeding. Within the statutory time, it filed in the office of the secretary of state the required plat and notice. In 1903, it
had finished a splash dam on one of the branches of the
river several miles above the plaintiffs' land. This
dam has been continuously used since that time. In
1907, another splash dam was completed upon the other
branch of the river also several miles above the plaintiffs' property, and likewise this dam has been in continuous operation since its completion. By means of
these two dams, the waters of the river were impounded and artificial freshets were created to assist in driving logs down the river. These artificial freshets have
added to the natural erosion created by the current and
have caused the river to encroach upon the plaintiffs'
adjacent land. The defendant, since 1900, has been upon the river, improving the channel, straightening its
course, removing rocks and obstructions, and doing
other things necessary to facilitate the driving of logs,
and in doing this has gone upon the banks of the river
and has used donkey engines thereon for the purpose
of sacking logs. All these things were necessary to the
successful driving of the stream, and have been done
for more than ten years prior to the commencement of
this suit.

The property in question here, prior to 1912, has been owned for many years by the Lytle Logging and Mercantile Company. In 1904, 1905 and 1906, this company logged into the river and consented to the defendant entering upon its lands, sacking logs and creating artificial freshets and changing the channel. In 1912, the Lytle Logging and Mercantile Company sold the property to the intervener, Walker Timber Company, which was also engaged in logging, and which continued to consent to the use made of the land by the driving company, and the creation of artificial freshets, and this permission was never withdrawn until shortly before this action was instituted. In October, 1919, the intervener contracted to sell the property to the plaintiffs, who, in November, 1919, started this suit.

The trial court denied the injunction on the ground that the defendant is a public service corporation, performing a public function, and that it had taken the lands of the plaintiffs for its corporate purposes, and that the taking had been complete for many years, and therefore the plaintiffs were not entitled to equitable relief. The court also found against the defendant's claim of prescriptive easement.

Without a minute or detailed review of the testimony upon which the lower court came to the conclusion concerning the use of the plaintiffs' land by the defendant's employees and machinery, and the encroachment upon the banks by the additional erosion caused by the artificial freshets, it is enough to say that a consideration of the testimony satisfies us that the trial court arrived at a proper conclusion and was correct in holding that the defendant's claim of prescriptive right could not be sustained. The testimony satisfies us that the acts done by the defendant were done with the permission and the active acquiescence of the plaintiffs

and their predecessors in interest; several written
documents appear in the testimony which fortify this
conclusion, and, with the trial court, we also agree in
holding that the filing of the plat and notice with the
secretary of state, as required by law, did not initiate
an adverse claim, nor was it the assertion of a legal
right which is necessary to support a prescriptive title.
Article 1, § 16, of the state constitution, prevents such
filing from having the effect claimed for it by the defendant. As was said by this court in *Peterson v.
Smith*, 6 Wash. 163, 32 Pac. 1050:

"The land owner need do nothing before his property has been condemned by a municipal or public
service corporation."

See, also, *State ex rel. Smith v. Superior Court*, 26
Wash. 278, 66 Pac. 385; *Nicomen Boom Company v.
North Shore etc. Co.*, 40 Wash. 315, 82 Pac. 412.

The filing of the notice and plat gave the defendant
only the prior right of location on this stream for driving and booming purposes, and did not start the statute of limitations running against the plaintiffs or their
predecessors or initiate any right in hostility to their
title.

We do not agree, however, with the trial court in
holding that this case falls within the operation of the
rule announced where public service corporations, having taken possession of private property and constructed thereon improvements to be used in carrying on of
public service, have been allowed to continue in the use
of the property, and the property owner has been denied injunctive relief and the corporation has been compelled to proceed to condemn. *Kakeldy v. Columbia &
Puget Sound R. Co.*, 37 Wash. 675, 80 Pac. 205; *Domrese
v. Roslyn*, 89 Wash. 106, 154 Pac. 140; *Habermann v.
Ellensburg etc. Co.*, 100 Wash. 229, 170 Pac. 571; *Irwin*

v. J. K. Lumber Company, 102 Wash. 99, 172 Pac. 911.
The acts sought to be enjoined by this suit are not acts
of taking which have already occurred, but acts which
are likely to occur by the continued operation of the
defendant. In other words, the plaintiffs are not seeking to enjoin the defendant from the use of the property which it has already taken without condemnation,
but is seeking to enjoin the future infliction of damages. The plaintiffs are not in the position of the plaintiffs in the cases just above cited, but are in the position of those who, seeing a public service corporation
about to enter upon their property, seek to enjoin the
corporation before it has taken possession. Although,
upon the legal principles which we have thus discussed,
we are in agreement with the plaintiffs' contention, we
cannot agree that they are entitled to the relief which
they seek. The granting of equitable relief is not a matter of right but of grace, and before plaintiffs are entitled to the favorable decree of equity there must be
justice in their claim. After the plaintiffs and their
predecessors have acquiesced in the conduct of the defendant and public interest will be jeopardized by
granting the relief prayed for, and such a grant would
cause serious public inconvenience or loss without a
corresponding advantage of the plaintiffs, the chancery court will not enjoin. Where, under mutual agreement, the plaintiffs, knowing all the facts, having long
delayed in entering the portals of the equitable tribunal, and that delay has been without good excuse, the
doors are closed against them, for to allow them at this
time to enter would result in greater damage to the
defendants than that which the plaintiffs would suffer.

Here we have a situation where for twenty years the
plaintiffs and their predecessors had notice that the
defendant was using the stream in the exercise of its

public service functions, where for more than sixteen years they have observed the use of their lands by the defendant, and the erosion thereof by the artificial freshets, and not only have they stood by in silence, but they have actively participated in the enterprise. It was to their advantage that the streams and the contiguous banks be so used. They have taken the benefit of the operations of the defendant for the purposes of getting their timber to market, they have been, in effect, joint adventurers with the defendant in the opening up of this timber area. Not until they had reaped the benefits of this association do we find them objecting to the operation. Their conduct does not appeal to the conscience of the chancellor. By their own pleadings and proof, they established that all the acts heretofore done have been with their permission, and by these pleadings and proof they defeat the defendant's claim of a prescriptive right, and by these same pleadings and proof they establish the inequity of their own position. In 1903, the defendant built the first dam, and the second in 1907. Both of these entailed the expenditure of large sums of money, both have been operated continuously since their construction; large sums of money have also been expended in straightening the river, in removing obstructions and similar work. The plaintiffs' predecessors have consigned their logs to the defendant, conscious that their own lands were being eroded by the artificial freshets and that the Humptulips river was being devoted to a public purpose. During that time the plaintiffs' predecessors often requested additional artificial freshets, so that their logs might be more quickly brought to market. The logs of many other landowners on the river were and are being consigned to the defendant. To now enjoin the defendant would result in shutting down of many logging camps, the discontinuance of the employment of many men, thousands of logs in the river would be kept from market, milling companies would be hampered by lack of logs, and public interest demands that no such untoward results be allowed for the benefit of one who, after all these years of acquiescence and knowledge and benefits received, now seeks the termination of this condition.

In 1909, the Lytle Logging & Mercantile Company, in an action against the defendant, reported in 60 Wash. 559, 111 Pac. 774, sought damages for changing the course of the river across a portion of the land involved in this suit. That action, by its complaint, sought damages for future as well as past erosions to the portion of the land, but the judgment does not disclose whether future erosions were compensated for. If they were, the plaintiffs, of course, cannot again recover for them, and all the lands affected should have been included in that action. *Kline v. Stein*, 46 Wash. 546, 90 Pac. 1041, 123 Am. St. 940; *Collins v. Gleason*, 47 Wash. 62, 91 Pac. 566, 125 Am. St. 891; *Brechlin v. Night Hawk Mining Co.*, 49 Wash. 198, 94 Pac. 928, 126 Am. St. 863. In any event, having then elected to proceed at law, and the use of the river being the same now as it was at the time the suit was begun in 1909, it would be inequitable to now compel the defendant to stop its continued use.

As the trial court said: ''the large cost of defendant's dams, large quantities of logs in the river requiring immediate transmission, are elements which the court should consider in granting or refusing an injunction. While the holding is that the action of the defendant had been by sufferance, nevertheless, the plaintiffs have endured the same for a long period and should not now be allowed to peremptorily interrupt the business of the defendant driving company at this time by injunction." *Mahoney Land Co. v. Cayuga Investment Co.,* 88 Wash. 529, 153 Pac. 308; *Robertson v. Seattle,* 37 Wash. 137, 79 Pac. 610.

"The equitable doctrine of acquiescence is freely applied to cases involving eminent domain rights. The underlying principle of the constitutional provisions allowing the taking of private property is that it is to be devoted to public use. Hence, when a landowner stands by until the public has acquired an interest in the use, there is strong reason for applying the doctrine, in addition to the familiar grounds covering its application to other cases. The United States supreme court in a recent case has laid down the rule in no uncertain language: 'If one, aware of the situation, believes he has certain legal rights, and desires to insist upon them, he should do so promptly. If by his declarations or conduct he leads the other party to believe that he does not propose to rest upon such rights, but is willing to waive them for a just compensation, and the other party proceeds at great expense in the expectation that payment of a fair compensation will be accepted and the right waived—especially if it is in respect to a matter which will largely affect the public convenience and welfare—a court of equity may properly refuse to enforce those rights, and, in the absence of an agreement for compensation, compel him to submit the determination of the amount thereof to an impartial tribunal.' Accordingly, when a landowner stands by and makes no attempt to enjoin a railroad company from building over his land until large expenditures have been made, or the road has been completed, injunctive relief will be denied, and the party will be left to his remedy at law for damages. The same principle applies to the laying of pipes or to a taking for any other public use. And although permission is granted to take upon the distinct understanding that compensation is to be made, an injunction will not issue, after the work has been done, for the purpose of enforcing payment. The doctrine also applies to cases involving the rights of railroads in streets." Vol. V, Pomeroy's Equity Jurisprudence, § 1886.

See, also, *McCarthy v. Bunker Hill etc. Co.*, 164 Fed. 927; 22 Cyc. 778, 784; *Hardin v. Olympic Portland Cement Co.*, 89 Wash. 320, 154 Pac. 450; *Woodard v. West Side Mill Co.*, 43 Wash. 308, 86 Pac. 579.

"An injunction is an extraordinary remedy, and does not follow as of right even when a case of wrongful act is made out on one side and consequent injury on the other. In equity a decree is of grace rather than of right, and the court will always consider whether it will not do a greater injury by enjoining an act than would result from permitting the act to continue and leaving the party injured to his remedy in damages." *Ferry-Leary Land Co. v. Holt & Jeffery*, 53 Wash. 584, 102 Pac. 445.

For the reason that we find no equity in the plaintiffs' action, it is dismissed. The judgment of the lower court is affirmed.

PARKER, C. J., FULLERTON, TOLMAN, MITCHELL, and MAIN, JJ., concur.

BRIDGES, J., took no part.

[No. 16563. Department Two. June 2, 1921.]

THE CITY OF BELLINGHAM, *Appellant*, v. BELLINGHAM
PUBLISHING COMPANY, *Respondent.*[1]

NEWSPAPERS (2)—LEGAL PUBLICATIONS—DAILY PAPERS. A newspaper published every day except Monday is a daily newspaper,
within the requirement of Laws 1921, p. 293, §§ 1, 6, providing that
no newspaper shall be considered a legal newspaper for the publication of legal notices unless it shall have been published continually,
legal holidays and Sundays excepted, as a daily newspaper.

SAME (2)—CHANGE OF NAME—EFFECT. The change of name of
a newspaper from "The American Reveille" to "The Bellingham
Reveille", not being a change in the identity of the paper, would
not affect the legality of the publication of legal notices under a contract made prior to the change of name.

Appeal from a judgment of the superior court for
Whatcom county, Brown, J., entered May 9, 1921, in
favor of the defendant upon an agreed statement of
facts, in an action to determine the validity of a contract. Affirmed.

T. D. J. Healy, for appellant.

C. W. Howard, for respondent.

PARKER, C. J.—This cause was presented to the
superior court for Whatcom county for final disposition upon the merits, upon an agreed statement of
facts under §§ 378-380, Rem. Code, relating to agreed
cases. The purpose of the action is to have judicially
determined whether or not the city may lawfully avoid,
and treat as no longer binding upon it, a contract
entered into by it with the defendant publishing company for the publication in its newspaper of the city's
legal notices during the year 1921.

The controversy has arisen because of a change in
the name of the defendant's newspaper, and also be-

[1] Reported in 198 Pac. 369.

cause of the passage of the act of the legislature of
1921, entitled: "An Act relating to and regulating the
publication of legal and other official notices and fixing
the fees therefor;" (Laws of 1921, Ch. 99, p. 293)
furnishing, as it is claimed, grounds for the contention
that the defendant's newspaper is not, and especially
will not be after the going into effect of the act of
1921, which will soon occur, "a legal newspaper" for
the publication of the city's legal notices. Upon submission of the cause to the superior court, judgment
was rendered against the city, holding, in substance,
that the defendant's newspaper was, and will continue
to be during the whole of the year 1921, if its publication be continued as when this case was commenced,
a legal newspaper for the publication of the city's
legal notices during the whole of the year 1921.
From this disposition of the cause in the superior
court, the city has appealed to this court.

The controlling facts may be summarized as
follows: Respondent publishing company is, and for
several years past has been, a domestic corporation of
this state, and the publisher of a daily newspaper,
printed and published in the English language, in the
city of Bellingham, of general circulation in that city,
being published on every day of the week except Monday. Prior to May 1, 1921, respondent's newspaper
was named and known as "The American Reveille,"
the Sunday issue being designated as "The Sunday
American Reveille." On May 1, 1921, the name of
the paper was changed by respondent to "The Bellingham Reveille," the Sunday edition being designated
as "The Bellingham Sunday Reveille." Otherwise,
the paper has in all respects been, and will continue to
be, printed, published and circulated as now being
printed, published and circulated. During the late

session of the legislature, there was passed an act
entitled as above quoted, which was approved by the
Governor on March 16 and will soon become effective.
The following are the only provisions of that act which
we need here notice:

"Section 1. No newspaper shall be considered a
legal newspaper for the publication of any advertisement, notice, summons, report, proceeding or other
official document now or hereafter required by law
to be published unless such newspaper shall have been
published in the English language continually (legal
holidays and Sundays excepted) as a daily or weekly
newspaper, as the case may be, in the city or town
where the same is published at the time of the publication of such official document, for at least six months
prior to the date of such publication, and shall be
printed either in whole or in part in an office maintained
at the place of publication: . . ." [Laws of 1921,
p. 293, § 1.]

"Sec. 6. Where any law or ordinance of any incorporated city or town in this state provides for the
publication of any form of notice or advertisement
for consecutive days in a daily newspaper, the publication of such notice on legal holidays and Sundays may
be omitted without in any manner affecting the legality of such notice or advertisement: *Provided*, That
the publication of the required number of notices is
complied with." Laws of 1921, p. 295, § 6.

Our principal inquiry seems to be, will respondent's
newspaper be "a legal [daily] newspaper" for the
publication of the city's legal notices after the going
into effect of the act of 1921? The language of § 1
above quoted may seem to lend support to the view
that respondent's newspaper will not be a daily legal
newspaper after the going into effect of the act, having in view the fact that respondent's newspaper has
not been, and will not thereafter be, published on Mon-
days; from which fact there seems room for arguing

that the paper has not been, and will not be, "published . . . continually (legal holidays and Sundays excepted) as a daily . . . newspaper . . . for at least six months . . . ." We are of the opinion, however, that this language is not intended as a definition of what constitutes a weekly or daily newspaper, speaking generally; but that the only purpose of this language is to define and prescribe the period during which a daily or weekly newspaper shall have been maintained and published regularly as such before it shall be "considered a legal newspaper for the publication of" legal notices. We do not overlook the words, "legal holidays and Sundays excepted," parenthetically embodied in § 1; but those words, we think, mean only that the publication, or failure of publication, of holiday and Sunday issues, shall be ignored in determining whether or not the paper has been regularly and continuously published for six months. If the publication of a paper on every week day, save Monday, makes it a daily paper, such continued publication for a period of six months manifestly makes it a "legal [daily] newspaper for the publication of" legal notices. In *Fairhaven Pub. Co. v. Bellingham,* 51 Wash. 108, 98 Pac. 97, 16 Ann. Cas. 420, the status of the predecessor of this same paper was drawn in question, and in holding that it was in law a daily paper this court said:

"The only question we are required to notice is whether The Morning Reveille is a daily paper, within the meaning of that term as it is used in the city charter. We think it is. The term daily, as applied to the publication of newspapers, is relative. It has never been given the exclusive meaning of every day of the week, month or year, but papers published every day except Sunday, or every day except Monday, or every day except both Sunday and Monday, are regarded by the general public as daily papers. This court in *Puget Sound Publishing Co. v. Times Printing Co.*, 33 Wash. 551, 74 Pac. 802, held that a paper published every day except Sunday and legal holidays was a daily paper, and cited approvingly a case from California which held that a paper published every day except Monday was such a paper. A paper omitting both days may be less a daily publication than either of these cited instances, but it is not so widely different from them as to require it to be put into a distinct class. It is a daily paper in the popular sense, and it was in this sense that the term was used in the city charter.''

Nor do we think that § 6 of the act argues to the contrary of our conclusion. That section manifestly was embodied in the act merely for the purpose of enabling the publication of legal notices to be omitted from holiday and Sunday issues of newspapers, *"Provided, That the publication of the required number of notices is complied with;"* that is, that the publication of a notice daily for the required number of consecutive days, omitting holiday and Sunday issues, will be regarded as a consecutive daily publication of such notice.

Does the change of the name of respondent's newspaper render it a different newspaper from its predecessor in name, during the six months next following such change in name? We are quite convinced that the mere change of the name from ''The American Reveille'' to ''The Bellingham Reveille,'' in view of the other conceded facts shown by this record, is not a change in the identity of the paper; and that being our conclusion, it follows that such change of name has not affected, and will not affect, the legality of the publication of the city's legal notices therein during any portion of the year 1921; assuming, of course, that the paper will be continued to be printed and published as printed and published at the time of the commencement of this action.

The judgment is affirmed.

MITCHELL, MACKINTOSH, MAIN, and TOLMAN, JJ., concur.

[No. 15992. *En Banc.* June 7, 1921.]

MARY E. JARRARD, *Respondent*, v. G. T. JARRARD, *Appellant.*[1]

DIVORCE (47-1)—DECREE—VACATION—COLLUSION—EVIDENCE—SUFFICIENCY. Collusion of parties to a divorce action is not established by a showing that, after a wife had knowledge of the pendency of the action, she demanded a property settlement, intimating that otherwise she would defend and defeat the action, and the negotiations between them finally resulting in an agreement that the wife should receive title to the home property in full of her property rights.

SAME (49)—VACATION—PUBLIC INTEREST—DISCRETION. The action of a trial court in setting aside a default decree of divorce and permitting the defendant to defend the action, where application was made promptly after default and no change in conditions had occurred, was a proper exercise of discretionary power vested in courts because of the public interest or policy attaching to divorce actions.

Appeal from a judgment of the superior court for Spokane county, Blake, J., entered May 17, 1920, upon findings in favor of the plaintiff, in an action to set aside a divorce decree. Affirmed.

D. R. Glasgow, for appellant.

W. C. Donovan, for respondent.

TOLMAN, J.—The respondent, on January 3, 1920, signed and verified a petition, which was duly filed two days later (whether served in the interim does not appear), in and by which she sought to have set aside

[1]Reported in 198 Pac. 741.

a decree of divorce entered by default on December 30, 1919, in favor of her husband, the appellant here. The petition charges that the decree was obtained by reason of fraud practiced by the prevailing party, (a) in obtaining service by publication by mailing a copy of the summons and complaint to her, general delivery, Portland, Oregon, when he knew her street address in that city, alleging that she never received the papers which were so mailed, and (b) charging in effect that the husband testified falsely upon the trial of the divorce action that a property settlement had theretofore been made, and that he knew of no reason for his wife having left him, when in fact he induced and persuaded her to leave and gave her money with which to do so, and making further allegations, which, if true, would defeat the husband's action and probably entitle the wife to a divorce. Appellant, by answer, took issue upon these allegations. The case came on for trial before a judge other than the one who had heard the divorce case, and from a judgment vacating the decree of divorce and permitting respondent to appear in, answer and defend the divorce action, the case is brought here on appeal.

The trial court found that there was no fraud in the matter of the service of the summons, and no irregularity therein, with which finding we are in entire accord. He also found that there was collusion between the parties prior to the entry of the decree, that respondent has a meritorious defense to the divorce action, and that public policy demands that the decree be vacated and the wife be permitted to defend.

We are not satisfied that collusion is here shown, as collusion is usually defined. The wife, after she had knowledge of the pendency of the action, demanded a property settlement, and intimated that, unless a set-

tlement satisfactory to her was made, she would defend and defeat the action. All her demands were
made by letters written to her husband's attorney, and
we see nothing collusive in his answers thereto, his
submission of the demands to his client, or in the
agreement which was reached that the wife should receive title to the home property in full of her property
rights.

We are satisfied that there was a sufficient showing
of a meritorious defense to warrant the court, under
Rem. Code, § 235, were this other than a divorce action, in permitting the defendant, served by publication, to appear and defend the action. The legislature
seems to have excepted divorce actions from the operation of this statute upon no other theory, so far as we
can judge, than that, within the year, the situation
might so change as to make it unwise to disturb a decree; but where the application is made, as here,
promptly and within a very few days of the rendition
of the judgment, and no change in conditions has occurred, the reason for the rule does not exist.

But, in any event, speaking of this section of the
statute in *Chaney v. Chaney,* 56 Wash. 145, 105 Pac.
229, Mr. Justice Parker said:

"It did not take away any rights possessed by the
parties having judgments rendered against them, but
gave additional rights to parties having judgments
rendered against them upon service by publication. In the absence of this provision, a judgment rendered upon service by publication could not
be set aside for any different reason than could other
judgments. This section is not the whole law upon the
subject of setting aside divorce decrees, simply because such decrees are excluded from its operation."

And in *Graham v. Graham,* 54 Wash. 70, 102 Pac.
891, after reviewing the previous decisions of this
court upon this subject, it was said:

"It would seem, therefore that, notwithstanding the doctrine frequently announced that a decree of divorce will never be vacated because of the probable evil consequences following the severance of a new relation, bearing as it might after-begotten children, the better rule is that, notwithstanding the decree, a court will reopen and try the case if the decree is the result of fraud practiced upon the other party or upon the court."

And in the same case, in discussing the grounds upon which a decree of divorce may be vacated, it was further said:

"It is contended, however, that, the lower court having had complete jurisdiction, a mere offer to prove that the decree was obtained as the result of perjured testimony and was fraudulently obtained is insufficient. Whatever the rule may be when the divorce proceeding is collaterally inquired into, it must be remembered that this is a direct application, timely, and diligently prosecuted, and no harm can result to any innocent person by a further inquiry as to the justice of respondent's cause.

"Aside from these considerations, the interest of the public in all actions for divorce is such that a policy has grown up in accord with enlightened sentiment to discourage and deny divorces unless claimed upon proper grounds and sustained by an honest disclosure of the facts. There is much in the record that prompts further inquiry."

It is apparent from the record before us that the respondent knew of the pendency of the action in ample time to have made her defense before the default was taken against her, and that no sufficient excuse is now offered for her failure to do so. She, therefore, having had opportunity to defend and defeat her husband's charges before judgment, and having failed without sufficient reason or excuse to do so, should not now be heard to complain; and, if her interest were the only

interest at stake, no doubt the trial court would have
denied the prayer of her petition and held her bound
by the decree; but, in part at least, the judgment of the
trial court is based upon public policy, and the interest
of the public is the only interest which here demands
consideration. Public policy as to divorce actions has
been defined:

"Marriage is a relation in which the public is deeply
interested and is subject to proper regulation and control by the state or sovereignty in which it is assumed
or exists. The public policy relating to marriage is
to foster and protect it, to make it a permanent and
public institution, to encourage the parties to live together and to prevent separation. This policy finds
expression in probably every state in this country in
legislative enactments designed to prevent the sunder-
ing of the marriage ties for slight or trivial causes, or
by the agreement of the husband and wife, or in any
case except on full and satisfactory proof of such facts
as by the legislature have been declared to be cause
for divorce. Such provisions find their justification
only in this well-recognized interest of the state in the
permanency of the marriage relation." 9 R. C. L.,
p. 252.

And in *Faulkner v. Faulkner*, 90 Wash. 74, 155 Pac.
404, it was said:

"The real question then is, should the court have set
the decree aside when the fact appeared because of
the public interest. That it has such power may be conceded, and perhaps, if the fact timely appeared, it
might be its duty to do so. But when the fact is made
to appear after the right of appeal has expired, the
court may be confronted with conflicting public interests, and a duty to determine the course which will
best promote such interests. In other words, the matter becomes one of discretion with the court to be reviewed on appeal only when such discretion is abused."

In furtherance of this public policy, as it is thus defined, much discretion must be vested in the trial

courts, and when, as here, the application is made almost instantly and the condition of the parties has not changed, and the trial court, after hearing and seeing the parties and their witnesses, is of the opinion that public policy requires that the decree be set aside and the party complaining be allowed to defend, we are not inclined to interfere. Indeed, in view of the state's interest, the *nisi prius* judges should be encouraged to exercise sound discretion in all such cases, to the end that divorces be not granted "except on full and satisfactory proof of such facts as by the legislature have been declared to be cause for divorce." 9 R. C. L., *supra.*

The judgment appealed from is affirmed.

HOLCOMB, MOUNT, MITCHELL, BRIDGES, and FULLERTON, JJ., concur.

[No. 16372. Department One. June 9, 1921.]

SACAJAWEA LUMBER & SHINGLE COMPANY, *Appellant,* v. SKOOKUM LUMBER COMPANY *et al., Respondents.*[1]

ATTORNEY AND CLIENT (21)—DISMISSAL AND NONSUIT (6)—CONTROL OF LITIGATION—PARTIES ENTITLED TO DISMISS. Parties to an action have the right to compose their disputes and dismiss the action without first paying or consulting their attorneys.

CORPORATIONS (128)—OFFICERS AND AGENTS—DEALINGS WITH CORPORATION. The president of a corporation had no authority to dismiss an action by the corporation upon the vote of its board of directors, where the majority therefor depended on the vote of one of the defendants who was a director in the plaintiff corporation; since a director in a private corporation has no power to vote upon a proposition wherein his individual interest is opposed to that of the corporation which he represents.

Appeal from an order of the superior court for Thurston county, Wilson, J., entered October 18, 1920,

[1] Reported in 198 Pac. 1112.

overruling plaintiff's motion to set aside an order of dismissal. Reversed.

F. Campbell and *H. H. Johnston,* for appellant.

Bridges, J.—By this action the plaintiff sought to recover damages of the defendants because of a breach of contract. At the time of the institution of the suit and for sometime thereafter, the defendant Tucker was the owner of one-third of the capital stock of the plaintiff and was also one of its directors. One Richard W. Jamieson was also a director and the owner of one-third of the capital stock, and Julius LaVergne and his mother were the owners of the remainder of the stock, and the former was a director and the president of the company. While the suit was pending, there was a directors' meeting at which the president of the plaintiff company was authorized to settle the litigation with the defendants and to cause the suit to be dismissed. By virtue of this authority, the president later made a settlement, and a stipulation was entered into between the parties to the action, upon which the court entered an order dismissing the action. Thereafter the plaintiff moved to set aside the order of dismissal and to reinstate the case, for the alleged reasons that plaintiff's attorneys had not been consulted concerning the settlement of the litigation or the dismissal of the case, and that their compensation had not been paid, and because the board of directors was without power to authorize the president to settle the litigation and cause the case to be dismissed, and because there was fraud in the whole transaction leading up to the dismissal of the case. This motion was supported and opposed by certain affidavits. After a hearing upon these affidavits, the court denied the motion to set aside the order dismissing the action, and the plaintiff has appealed. Respondents have not appeared in this court.

The only question before us is whether or not the court was justified in refusing to set aside the order dismissing the action.

In a proceeding such as this, we cannot say that the affidavits show active fraud or overreaching in arriving at the settlement or dismissal of the action. Nor can we hold that the parties could not settle their differences and dismiss the action without first paying or consulting with their attorneys. The parties to an action always have the right to compose their disputes and are not under any legal obligations to first pay their attorneys or to consult with them concerning the settlement. The only substantial question before us is whether there was a valid authorization by the board of directors to the president of the appellant corporation to settle the litigation and dismiss the action.

It appears from the record that when the meeting of the board of directors opened, all of the directors, to wit: Mr. LaVergne, Mr. Tucker and Mr. Jamieson were present. At once thereafter it was announced to the meeting that Mr. Tucker had sold his capital stock in the appellant to Mr. Buchanan, who is one of the defendants in this case. Thereupon Mr. Tucker resigned as a director and Mr. Buchanan was elected in his stead. The meeting then proceeded to authorize the president of the appellant to settle the litigation and to cause the dismissal of the action. Mr. LaVergne and Mr. Buchanan voted in favor of this proposition, and Mr. Jamieson refused to vote and probably objected to the proceedings. The appellant takes the position that since Mr. Buchanan was one of the defendants in the case, it was against public policy for him to exercise his vote as a director on the question of settling the litigation, and that his vote was a nullity and consequently there was but one valid vote in favor of the proposed settlement, which, of course, was less than a majority of the three directors. Since the dismissal of the case rested entirely upon a settlement of the litigation, and since the president in making the settlement and dismissing the suit acted by virtue of the supposed authorization of the board of directors, if, as a matter of law, Mr. Buchanan was not authorized to vote, then it must follow that the president was without authority to do the things complained of.

A director of a corporation occupies a strictly fiduciary capacity and it is always his duty to fully represent the interests of the corporation of which he is a director. While there is some authority to the contrary, the majority of the courts and text writers hold that a director in a private corporation has no power to vote upon a proposition wherein his individual interest is opposed to that of the corporation which he represents. At page 92, 14a C. J., the rule is stated as follows:

"A director who is disqualified by personal interest from voting on a particular matter before the meeting, cannot be counted for the purpose of making a quorum or a majority of the quorum. The act done is invalid where his presence is necessary to constitute a quorum, or where his vote is necessary to the passage of the resolution, regardless of the fairness or good faith of the transaction. . . ."

In the case of *Burns v. National Mining, Tunnel & Land Co.*, 23 Colo. App. 545, 130 Pac. 1037, the court said:

"A board of directors of a solvent corporation may borrow money from one or more individual members of the board, and give the corporation's note for it, and even mortgage the corporate property to secure it, where the transaction is in good faith. . . . If the presence and vote of the director loaning the money is necessary to constitute a quorum, and to make a majority upon such vote, however, the act is voidable at the instance of the corporation or its stockholders. The trust relation existing between the directors and the stockholders of a corporation ought not to permit such an act, and a court of equity will scrutinize all contracts made in this way and set them aside, regardless of the good faith of the transaction."

At 10 Cyc. 790, the rule is stated as follows:

"A director cannot with propriety vote in the board of directors upon a matter affecting his own private interest any more than a judge can sit in his own case; and any resolution passed at a meeting of the directors at which a director having a personal interest in the matter voted will be voidable at the instance of the corporation or the shareholders, without regard to its fairness, provided the vote of such director was necessary to the result."

See, also, the following cases to the same effect: *Heublien v. Wight*, 227 Fed. 667; *Curtin v. Salmon River etc. Co.*, 130 Cal. 345, 62 Pac. 552, 80 Am. St. 132; *O'Rourke v. Grand Opera House Co.*, 46 Mont. 609, 133 Pac. 965; *United States Rolling Stock Co. v. Atlantic & Great Western R. Co.*, 34 Ohio St. 450, 32 Am. Rep. 380. Other cases involving this question may be found in the cases above cited.

But the question under discussion is not a new one to this court. In the case of *Parsons v. Tacoma Smelting & Refining Co.*, 25 Wash. 492, 65 Pac. 765, we said:

"The policy of the law forbids a trustee to assume a double function where there are adverse interests considered. . . . While there are observations by some of the text writers and expressions in some judi-

cial opinions refining upon acts which may be merely
voidable, and not *per se* void, where an interested trustee's vote is necessary to adopt, we think on principle,
and in the better-considered cases, such acts, when consummated by the necessary vote of the interested trustee, are voidable upon complaint of a stockholder."

We there quoted from the case of *Munson v. Syra-
cuse etc. R. Co.*, 103 N. Y. 58, 8 N. E. 355, 57 Am. Rep.
701, as follows:

" 'The contract bound the corporation to purchase,
and Munson, as one of the directors, participated in the
action of the corporation in assuming the obligation,
and in binding itself to pay the price primarily agreed
upon between the plaintiffs and Magee. He stood in
the attitude of selling as owner and purchasing as trustee. The law permits no one to act in such inconsistent relations. It does not stop to inquire whether the
contract or transaction was fair or unfair.' "

We also there quoted from *Bassett v. Fairchild*, 132
Cal. 637, 64 Pac. 1082, 52 L. R. A. 611, to the following
effect:

" ' .   .   .   there is no legal quorum of directors
present when action is attempted to be taken on a matter as to which one of the directors necessary to make
the quorum is interested.' "

In the recent case of *Wonderful Group Mining Co. v.
Rand*, 111 Wash. 557, 191 Pac. 631, discussing a somewhat similar question, we said:

"The record in this case shows clearly that the rule
of law which provides that a trustee may not vote
upon his own compensation was violated by the resolution of June 3, and that the act of the trustees in passing a series of resolutions awarding money to four out
of five members of the board was void. . . . Granting that the board of trustees might compensate officers
but not trustees for past services, it is the rule that,
where concerted action of this kind is taken, the pass-

ing of a resolution awarding such pay must be had without the vote of any one pecuniarily interested in the resolution.''

It must, however, be conceded that this court has not at all times been entirely consistent on this question. In the case of *Pitcher v. Lone Pine-Surprise etc. Min. Co.*, 39 Wash. 608, 81 Pac. 1047, Judge Root, speaking for the court, took a position apparently opposed to that announced in the previous case of *Parsons v. Tacoma Smelting & Refining Co., supra*. But in the *Pitcher* case no reference was made to the *Parsons* case. Manifestly, that case was not called to the attention of the court. A careful review of the whole question and the authorities convinces us that the rule of the *Parsons* and *Wonderful Group Mining Co.*, cases, *supra*, is supported by the better reason and is in accord with the great weight of authority.

Applying the law to the facts of this case, we conclude that Mr. Buchanan had no right to vote as a trustee for the appellant for the settlement of disputes between that company and himself, and that, consequently, the president of the appellant was without authority to dismiss the action.

The judgment is reversed, and cause remanded with directions to set aside the judgment dismissing the action.

PARKER, C. J., MACKINTOSH, FULLERTON, and HOLCOMB, JJ., concur.

[No. 16166. Department One. June 10, 1921.]

HAZEL DANIEL, *Respondent*, v. J. I. DANIEL, *Appellant*.[1]

REFERENCE (2)—COMPULSORY REFERENCE — STATUTES — VALIDITY.
Rem. Code, § 369 *et seq.*, expressly providing that a compulsory reference may be ordered by the trial court where the issues involve a long account on either side, does not contravene Const., Art. 4, §§ 1, 6, 23, creating courts, defining their jurisdiction, and providing for the appointment of court commissioners.

COURTS (2)—JURISDICTION—NATURE AND SOURCE. Const., Art. 4, § 6, defining the jurisdiction of the superior courts, does not purport to control the manner in which such courts shall exercise jurisdiction, but this is left as a prerogative of the courts and of the lawmaking power, which can be lawfully exercised in any manner which the constitution does not directly prohibit.

ACCOUNT (7)—DEFENSES—PROFITS FROM ILLEGAL TRANSACTIONS.
The fact that profits arising from the use of premises were derived largely from their lease for immoral purposes would not deprive a part owner of the premises of a right to an accounting after the transaction had been completed and closed, where such part owner had not been a party or privy to the illegal transaction.

SAME (14)—EVIDENCE (75-77)—SECONDARY EVIDENCE—GROUNDS FOR ADMISSION—FAILURE TO KEEP BOOKS. In an action for an accounting for moneys collected for plaintiff's benefit and wrongfully withheld, defendant cannot complain of the indirect and circumstantial character of the evidence of moneys received, where he kept no books of account showing either the gross earnings of the property or the cost of its upkeep during the period of the accounting.

INTEREST (5, 7)—ACCOUNTS—UNLIQUIDATED DEMANDS. The rule that interest is not allowed upon unliquidated demands is inapplicable where a definite sum was collected by defendant during a term of years, of which sum plaintiff was entitled to a certain share; and it was proper for a referee, in stating the account by yearly periods, to allow interest on the balances from the end of each yearly period down to the time of the accounting.

SAME (5)—ACCOUNTS. Under Rem. Code, § 6250, providing that every forbearance of money shall bear interest at a fixed rate, recovery of interest is authorized where one fails to account to another for moneys collected in the latter's behalf.

[1] Reported in 198 Pac. 728.

COSTS (48)—REFEREE'S FEES. An allowance of a referee's fees as costs under a statute therefor does not deprive a litigant of any constitutional right, inasmuch as costs are a part of the burden of litigation.

Appeal from a judgment of the superior court for Spokane county, Blake, J., entered July 16, 1920, upon findings in favor of the plaintiff, in an action upon an accounting taken by a referee appointed by the court. Affirmed.

Cyrus Happy and *O. C. Moore*, for appellant.

George W. Belt and *Fred M. Williams*, for respondent.

FULLERTON, J.—This is an appeal from a judgment entered upon an accounting. The case prior hereto was before us on another aspect, and will be found reported in *Daniel v. Daniel*, 106 Wash. 659, 181 Pac. 215. In the cited case, we affirmed the trial court, which adjudged that the respondent was the owner of an undivided one-twelfth interest in certain real property situated in the city of Spokane, and was entitled to an accounting for a one-twelfth interest in the rents, issues and profits thereof during the time her interests were withheld from her by the appellant. The amount found to be due was the sum of twenty-four thousand five hundred and thirty dollars, and for this sum the judgment appealed from was entered.

After the cause had been remanded on the first appeal, the trial court appointed a referee to take the accounting. It is contended that this was beyond the power of the trial court, and that, in consequence, all proceedings had thereunder are null and void. In the language of the appellant's learned counsel:

"Our constitution does not provide for the appointment of a referee, but clearly contemplates that all judicial proceedings shall be either in one of the courts provided by the constitution or before a court commissioner, for the appointment of which provision is made by the constitution. We·therefore contend that the order of reference, made without consent of appellant, and all proceedings thereunder are illegal and without judicial force or effect."

The provisions of the constitution cited as the foundation for the contention are §§ 1, 6, and 23, of article 4, of that instrument. The first of these sections vests the judicial power of the state in a supreme court, superior courts, justices of the peace and such inferior courts as the legislature may provide. The second of the sections defines the jurisdiction of the superior courts, and the third empowers the superior court to appoint court commissioners, and defines their powers and duties when so appointed. We cannot think these sections have a bearing upon the question suggested. They but create the courts and define their jurisdiction; in no way do they purport to regulate or control the manner in which the courts shall exercise jurisdiction. The latter is left as a prerogative of the courts themselves and of the law-making power, and can be lawfully exercised in any manner which the constitution does not directly prohibit. The legislature has acted on the matter. By the code (Rem. Code, § 369 et seq.), it is expressly provided that a compulsory reference may be had where the issues involve a long account on either side. It is true the statute was actually enacted prior to the formation and adoption of the constitution, but that instrument itself provided (§ 2, art. 27), that "All laws now in force in the territory of Washington which are not repugnant to this constitution shall remain in force until they expire by their own limitation, or are altered or repealed by the legislature. . "

The law has not expired by any limitation nor has it been altered or repealed by the state legislature.

We are clear also that the statute is not repugnant to the constitution. To refer a cause, involving the taking of an account, to a master has, from the earliest times, been the recognized practice of the courts of chancery, and in all of the American states to which our attention has been directed, where the legal and chancery powers are exercised by the same tribunal, statutes have been enacted authorizing such a reference. These statutes, with substantial uniformity, have been upheld by the courts. In this state the practice has been repeatedly exercised since the adoption of the constitution, and in at least two instances we have held a compulsory exercise of the power within the province of the court. *Lindley v. McGlauflin*, 57 Wash. 581, 107 Pac. 355; *Poultry Producers Union v. Williams*, 58 Wash. 64, 107 Pac. 1040, 137 Am. St. 1041. In neither of these cases, it may be conceded, was the precise question suggested, but we cannot think that this fact destroys the cases as authority. We cannot conclude therefore that the court acted without its powers in directing a compulsory reference.

In the early part of the period over which the appellant was compelled to account for the profits of the premises, and the period during which the greater gains therefrom were derived, the premises were leased to women engaged in the practice of prostitution to be used for such practices. It is urged that this use of the premises was contrary to public morals, and in consequence the court should not compel an accounting for profits so derived, as to do so would be in effect to recognize and enforce an illegal transaction. There are courts which maintain the principle that a division of

profits arising from an illegal or immoral transaction
will not be enforced between participants therein, even
though the transaction has been completed and closed,
and nothing is asserted but the title to money which
has arisen from the transaction. But this conclusion
is opposed by some courts, if not a majority, and we
have heretofore aligned ourselves with the opposing
courts. *McDonald v. Lund*, 13 Wash. 412, 42 Pac. 348,
52 Am. St. 57; *Standard Furniture Co. v. Van Alstine*,
31 Wash. 499, 72 Pac. 119; *Stirtan v. Blethen*, 79 Wash.
10, 139 Pac. 618, 51 L. R. A. (N. S.) 623.

We cannot, however, concede that the present case
falls within the rule sought to be invoked. The respondent was, in this instance, in no sense a party or privy
to the illegal transaction through which the profits she
seeks to recover were gained. At the time they were
gained the appellant was holding and managing the
property as his own, without recognition of any right
therein in the respondent, and it was wholly because of
his individual act that the property was put to an immoral use. To require him to account for the profits
gained is not, therefore, to enforce an illegal transaction to which the respondent was at one time a party;
it is but to require him to account for money acquired
by the wrongful use of her property. To refuse to
require the accounting would be to punish the innocent
rather than the guilty party, and this is not the purpose
of the rule relied upon. Its purpose is to discourage
illegal transactions, and when this purpose is better
subserved by recognizing and enforcing the transaction
than it is by ignoring it, courts have never hesitated so
to do.

The appellant next questions the amount of the recovery recommended by the referee and confirmed by the

court, contending that the recovery is too large. He
also objects to much of the evidence introduced by the
respondent to establish the amount of the recovery,
contending that it is remote and of a hearsay nature.
But neither of these contentions requires extended discussion. The evidence as we read it tends reasonably
to support the amount of the recovery, and the evidence,
by which the amount of the recovery was sought to be
established, was the best evidence of which the case
from its nature was susceptible. The appellant kept no
books of account showing either the gross earnings of
the property or the cost of its upkeep during the period
of the accounting, and he is not in a position to complain because the evidence of the respondent was more
or less indirect and circumstantial. Since it was his
duty to account, and since his withholding of the respondent's share of the earnings was wrongful, courts of
equity do not in such cases (in the language of Mr. Justice Story) "proceed upon the notion that strict justice is done between the parties, but upon the ground
that it is the only justice that can be done, and that it
would be inequitable to suffer the fraud or negligence
of the agent to prejudice the rights of the principal."

The report of the referee states the account by yearly
periods, and allows interest to the respondent on the
balances found, at the legal rate, from the end of each
yearly period down to the time of the accounting. It
is contended that the allowance of interest is unauthorized; the argument being that the demand was unliquidated and that interest is not recoverable on unliquidated demands. But the case falls within the principle
of the case of *Modern Irr. & Land Co. v. Neely*, 81
Wash. 38, 142 Pac. 458, in which we held the rule contended for inapplicable. There the plaintiff had made
the defendant its exclusive sales agent for the sale

of certain of its land. During the continuance of the
contract sales were made aggregating large sums which
were received by the defendant. No regular account-
ings were had, the defendant, at first frequently, but
latterly at long intervals, turning over to the plaintiff
sums which he claimed balanced the account. The
action was begun at the close of the relationship, the
plaintiff contending that the defendant had retained
moneys which properly belonged to it. The trial court
found there was a large sum due the plaintiff, and in
casting the account struck quarterly balances, and allowed interest on such balances from each quarterly
period down to the time of the entry of the judgment.
On the appeal it was contended, as it is contended here,
that the demand was unliquidated and that interest is
not allowable on unliquidated demands. Answering
the objection we said:

"It is true, of course, as a general rule, interest is
not allowed upon unliquidated demands. This rule,
however, like nearly all general rules, has its exceptions. Courts will not hesitate to make it yield to the
equities of a given case. . . . The evidence was
conflicting upon these points, but a consideration of the
entire record convinces us that the whole difficulty arose
from the remissness of the defendants in the matter
of accounting at reasonable intervals. In such a case,
it would be most inequitable to deny interest on balances cast at reasonable intervals, the means for determining such balances being always at hand." *Modern Irr. & Land Co. v. Neely, supra.*

So in this case, there was a definite sum actually collected by the appellant, of which the respondent was
entitled on its collection to a certain share. It was the
appellant's duty to account to her for this share. He
failed to so account, and failed even to keep a definite
record of the amounts collected. Manifestly it would

be inequitable to say that he has, by his breach of duty, relieved himself from paying interest on such sums as can now be ascertained he has wrongfully withheld.

It is also argued that interest is not a creation of the common law but is purely of statutory origin, and that we have no statute authorizing the recovery of interest in cases of this sort. But if it be true that the asserted principle is the now applicable rule, we think there is such statutory authority. By the code (Rem. Code, § 6250) it is provided that every loan or forbearance of money shall bear interest at a fixed rate, and there was here, clearly, a forbearance of money.

The court allowed the referee fees based on the rate fixed by statute. Objection is made to this on the ground that the statute is unconstitutional. The argument made in support of the contention is ingenious, but we cannot regard it as tenable. The case of *State ex rel. Rochford v. Superior Court,* 4 Wash. 30, 29 Pac. 764, on which the principal reliance is placed is not in point. There the trial court sought to charge to the county the fees of a stenographer appointed to take the testimony on a trial held before it, and the right was denied because of want of statutory authority. It was not denied that the legislature could provide for a stenographer and make his fees payable from county funds. Costs are a part of the burden of litigation, and no litigant is deprived of a constitutional right by statutes which impose such costs upon him.

Other questions are raised and discussed in the briefs, but these, as we view them, were foreclosed by the judgment in the principal case, and cannot again be considered.

The judgment is affirmed.

PARKER, C. J., BRIDGES, MACKINTOSH, and HOLCOMB, JJ., concur.

[No. 16316. Department One. June 10, 1921.]

W. F. HAYS, *Appellant*, v. SUMPTER LUMBER COMPANY
et al., *Respondents.*[1]

CONTINUANCE (4)—PENDENCY OF OTHER ACTION—ISSUE NOT DE-
PENDENT ON OUTCOME. In an action for damages for failure to prosecute and pay the costs of an appeal from the Federal district court
to the circuit court of appeals, it is proper to deny a continuance
pending the outcome of litigation in the Federal court to quiet title
to certain lands.

Appeal from an order of the superior court for
Pierce county, Fletcher, J., entered March 1, 1920, dismissing an action on contract, after plaintiff's refusal
to proceed when denied a continuance. Affirmed.

W. F. Hays, in propria persona.

E. R. York and *Peters & Powell,* for respondents.

FULLERTON, J.—The appellant Hays instituted this
action against the respondents, Sumpter Lumber Company, a corporation, and J. J. Hewitt, and Henry
Hewitt as administrators of the estate of Henry
Hewitt, Jr., deceased, to recover in the sum of $2,602,-
500. The claim was based upon a contract entered into
between the appellant and Henry Hewitt, Jr., whereby
the appellant contracted to sell to Hewitt his interests
in certain timber lands. At the time of the execution
of the contract, the interests of the appellant in the
lands were represented by sheriff's certificates of sales
issued on the sales of the lands under execution. In
the contract it was provided that Hewitt should pay to
the appellant a certain fixed sum in the case the lands
were redeemed from the sales by the judgment debtors,
and should pay another fixed sum and deed to the appellant an undivided one-half interest in the land in

[1]Reported in 198 Pac. 723.

the case the sales should pass to deeds. The lands were not redeemed from the sales, and sheriff's deeds were subsequently executed to Hewitt. Hewitt thereafter, with the written consent of the appellant, conveyed the lands to the respondent Sumpter Lumber Company, although neither the payment nor the deed agreed to be made to Hays was made. The lands were at all times adversely claimed by a corporation known as the Sound Timber Company. This corporation held the legal title to the property at the time of the execution sales, and was neither a judgment debtor in, nor a party to, the action in which the judgment was entered on which the sales were had. With the matters in this condition, the respondent Sumpter Lumber Company began a suit in equity in the United States district court against the Sound Timber Company to quiet its title to the lands. The Sound Timber Company answered in the suit, in which it denied title in the plaintiff, averred title in itself, and prayed that its title be quieted as against the plaintiff. On a trial had on the merits, the Sound Timber Company prevailed, and the present appellant, who is an attorney at law and who represented the Sumpter Lumber Company in the suit, gave notice of appeal to the United States circuit court of appeals. Before the appeal was perfected, Henry Hewitt, Jr., died, and the Sumpter Lumber Company as well as the representatives of Henry Hewitt, Jr., refused to proceed further with the appeal. The present appellant thereupon had himself substituted as party appellant, and prosecuted the appeal on his own behalf and at his own cost. The appeal resulted in an affirmance of the decree of the district court. *Hays v. Sound Timber Co.*, 261 Fed. 571.

To charge the respondents in the present action, the appellant alleged that Henry Hewitt, Jr., was the presi-

dent of the Sumpter Lumber Company, and as such
caused the suit to quiet title to be instituted, and
promised on behalf of himself and on behalf of that
company to advance the costs necessary for the prosecution of the appeal; and further alleged:

"That plaintiff as attorney for the said Sumpter
Lumber Company, about the time of said appointment
of said defendants as such administrators, duly applied
to them to take and prosecute the required appeal to
the Circuit Court of Appeals aforesaid from the said
decree of April 29th, 1918, both in their capacity as
administrators of said estate, and as the successors in
interest of the said Henry Hewitt, Jr., to the said
Sumpter Lumber Company, but said defendants
neglected and did not take any step toward the prosecution of said appeal, but thereafter and without the
knowledge or consent of this plaintiff and for the purpose of defrauding, cheating and swindling this plaintiff out of all his rights and interests in and to said
lands, fraudulently conspired and confederated with
the defendants the said Sound Timber Company, its
officers, agents and attorneys, for the purpose of preventing an appeal to be taken from said decree of
April 29th, 1918, and as a part of said conspiracy and
fraud wrongfully equipped the defendant, the Sound
Timber Company, its officers, agents, attorneys and
servants with affidavits and papers in substance declaring it to be the purpose of said Sumpter Lumber
Company and its said officers and successors in interest, not to appeal from said order of April 29th, 1918,
and to enable the said Sound Timber Company and
themselves to wrongfully and fraudulently defeat this
plaintiff both in his capacity as the attorney for the
said Sumpter Lumber Company in making and per-
fecting said appeal, and in his own individual capacity
as the beneficial owner in and to all the interest of said
lands in pursuance of said contract of sale of November
19th, 1908, by which the said defendants in pursuance
of said conspiracy have so interfered with this plaintiff in the prosecution of said appeal, both as said
attorney and in his individual capacity aforesaid, in-

volving an unnecessary and additional cost and expense
to him in and about the premises of at least ten
thousand ($10,000) dollars and by which the said
Hays has been required to advance out of his own
means all of the expenses in the preparation of records,
transcripts and expenses necessary in the premises
in the sum of at least five thousand ($5,000) dollars, all
of which the said Henry Hewitt, Jr., by the terms of
his agreement with this plaintiff was to have paid and
advanced out of his own funds.

"That by the terms of said contract of November
19th, 1908, the said Henry Hewitt, Jr., was to pay
plaintiff for an undivided one-half interest in the lands
covered by said sheriff's certificates to the said Hays,
at the time of the 'vesting' of title under said certificates in the said Henry Hewitt, Jr., in the sum of
ninety thousand ($90,000) dollars less two thousand
five hundred ($2,500) dollars which was paid down at
the time of making said purchase and obtaining the
assignment of said certificates to him.

"That said title thereafter duly vested in the said
Henry Hewitt, according to the terms of said writing,
by virtue of the sheriff's deeds thereunder, and the
failure and refusal of said Henry Hewitt, Jr., as the
president of said corporation and his successors in
interest and the said corporation itself, and the said
heirs of the said Henry Hewitt, Jr., and each of them,
to duly prosecute an appeal from the decree aforesaid, all in violation of the terms of said agreement of
November 19, 1908, by which plaintiff has been made
to lose the undivided one-half interest in and to all of
said lands and may yet be forced to lose it, also the
title thereto so to be given, to this plaintiff, to said
lands, of the reasonable value of two million five hundred thousand ($2,500,000) dollars, also the further
sum of eighty-seven thousand five hundred ($87,500)
dollars, aforesaid, all of which the defendants and
each of them well knew would flow as a consequence
of their said acts."

The respondents put in issue the allegations of the
complaint, and thereafter noted the cause for trial.

At the time the cause was called for trial, the appellant
moved for a continuance. On this motion the statement
of facts shows the following:

"Be it remembered that on the 25th day of
February, 1920, the case of W. F. Hays, plaintiff,
versus the Sumpter Lumber Co., and the Henry Hewitt
estate was duly called for trial before the Honorable
John D. Fletcher, one of the judges of said court,
presiding in department No. 3, plaintiff appearing in
person and the defendants being represented by their
counsel, Messrs. Peters & Powell, and E. R. York,
Esq., and the oral application of the plaintiff for a
continuance of the case being made upon the ground:
first, that the subject matter of this action out of
which this action has grown is now pending in the
United States circuit court of appeals with notice to
said court of the purpose and intention of suing out
a writ of certiorari from a judgment entered in that
court, to the Supreme Court of the United States directing the circuit court of appeals to transmit the
record in said case for a final hearing of said case upon
merits.

"That upon further representation to the court that
a final determination in the United States supreme
court in favor of the appellant would determine the
rights of the plaintiff in this case in so far as his claim
goes to the money judgment sought herein and would
give to the defendant in this suit an interest of one-
half the entire lands involved in that suit if judgment
is favorable under the decision of the supreme court,—
the purpose of said suit being to quiet title to some
25,000 acres of timber lands, which was the subject
matter of the contract sued upon in this action.

"That suit being undetermined by the United States
supreme court, it is impossible for this court to proceed with the trial of this case upon the merits, and
grant full and complete relief to the plaintiff and to
the defendant, and that a trial at this time would be
premature and ineffectual for any purpose.

"The subject matter of the litigation being the title
to said timber lands, if determined in said court fav-

orably to the petitioner and appellant, then his rights
now sought in this action will have been satisfied and
adjudicated and this action would be at an end in
so far as such incidental expenses or costs as might
be incurred by a natural appellant or litigant in the
case were concerned.   This is in view of the necessary
substitution in said Sumpter Lumber Co. case of this
plaintiff in the present action.

"The said case in the United States circuit court
of appeals being entitled: United States circuit court
of appeals, for the ninth circuit. W. F. Hays substituted as appellant for Sumpter Lumber Co., a
corporation, pursuant to order entered April 8, 1919,
appellant, versus Sound Timber Co., a corporation,
appellee.   Upon appeal from the United States district court for Washington.

"That upon these facts being stated, the court found
that the application for continuance of this present
action is without merit, and is denied.

"To which denial the plaintiff then and there excepted, and exception was allowed by the court.   The
Court: Let the record show that the above statement
is taken in lieu of an affidavit, such proceedings being
consented to by the attorneys for the defendant. You
may proceed with the trial on the merits.   Mr. Hays:
The plaintiff refuses to proceed or submit further to
the jurisdiction of this court, upon the ground that it
is without jurisdiction of the subject matter and therefore any judgment it might render in this case would
be void.   The Court: On that statement let an order
be entered dismissing the action.   Mr. Hays: Your
honor will allow exception.   The Court: Exception
allowed."

The appellant argues in support of his claim of error,
that, while an emergency existed for instituting the
action (the emergency being to avoid the short statute
of limitations) no emergency existed for the immediate
trial of the action; and, since a favorable decision by
the supreme court of the United States on the writ
of error will vest title to the lands mentioned in him

and render it unnecessary to litigate further many of
the questions he here seeks to litigate, justice required
that the cause be continued to await the outcome of
the proceedings in that court, as to do so might save
him from the burden and cost of litigating matters
which a favorable decision would render it unnecessary
to litigate. The reference is here to that part of the
complaint which seeks to charge the respondents with
the value of the lands in case it should finally be determined that they have been lost to the parties. But
we are clear that no cause of action is stated in this
regard. As we held in *Vanasse Land Co. v. Hewitt*, 95
Wash. 643, 164 Pac. 196, construing the very contract
here relied upon, the subject-matter of the contract
was the sale and purchase of land and no action would
lie to recover the purchase price if the title to the land
did not pass by the execution sale. It must follow that
this action in no way hinges on the result of the proceedings in the United States supreme court. Whether
the proceedings result favorably or unfavorably to the
appellant, he is equally prohibited from recovering the
value of the lands from the respondents. If the complaint states a cause of action at all, it states a cause of
action because of the breach of the contract to prosecute and pay the costs of the appeal from the judgment
of the district court to the court of appeals. But as
this issue was in no way dependent on the outcome of
the pending proceedings, it could have been tried at
the time the defendant sought to try it as well as at
any other time. There was therefore no showing
authorizing a continuance, and it follows as of course
that no error was committed by denying the application.

The judgment will be affirmed.

PARKER, C. J., HOLCOMB, BRIDGES, and MACKINTOSH,
JJ., concur.

[No. 16377.   Department One.   June 10, 1921.]

THE STATE OF WASHINGTON, *Respondent*, v. J. G. WASHBURN, *Appellant*. [1]

WITNESSES (78)—CROSS-EXAMINATION—LIMITATION TO SUBJECTS OF DIRECT EXAMINATION. Where the testimony of a witness as to certain facts had been stricken by the court, the refusal of the court to allow the cross-examination of the witness for the purpose of laying a foundation for his impeachment with reference to the stricken testimony was proper.

EVIDENCE (186)—BODILY CONDITION—NON-EXPERT EVIDENCE—ADMISSIBILITY—IN GENERAL. In a prosecution for rape, it is admissible for a woman, present at the time of the examination of the prosecutrix by a physician, to state what she observed, as the same was not expert testimony.

CRIMINAL LAW (25)—EVIDENCE—WEIGHT AND EFFECT. The state is not bound in a criminal prosecution to produce witnesses who agree entirely in their statements concerning a transaction, the question of their credibility being for the jury to determine.

APPEAL (121, 405)—PRESERVATION OF GROUNDS—REVIEW—BURDEN OF SHOWING ABUSE OF DISCRETION. Where the record on appeal does not set forth the showing made by the defendant to secure a continuance, it must be presumed that the trial court properly exercised its discretion in refusing to grant a continuance.

CRIMINAL LAW (299)—TRIAL—RECEPTION OF EVIDENCE—REBUTTAL. Error cannot be predicated on the fact that a witness for the state, called in rebuttal of defendant's testimony upon matters not covered by her testimony in chief, had been permitted to restate the whole case, where her examination was confined to four questions addressed to proper rebuttal testimony.

Appeal from a judgment of the superior court for Lewis county, Abel, J., entered April 6, 1920, upon a trial and conviction of rape. Affirmed.

Gus L. Thacker, for appellant.

Herman Allen, J. H. Jahnke (*John I. O'Phelan*, of counsel), for respondent.

[1] Reported in 198 Pac. 980.

HOLCOMB, J.—The appellant appeals from a verdict and judgment convicting him on an information charging him with having wilfully, unlawfully and feloniously carnally known and abused Bula Morgus, a female child over the age of ten years and under the age of fifteen years, and not the wife of appellant, in Lewis county, Washington, on December 2, 1918.

The evidence in the case shows that, on December 2, 1918, Bula Morgus was almost twelve years of age. Her parents reside in South Bend, Washington. For about two weeks prior to December 2, 1918, she had been on a visit to her uncle in St. Helens, Oregon. Leaving St. Helens to return home, she was accompanied by the wife of her uncle to Kalama, Washington, she continuing the journey from Kalama, Washington, by herself, to Chehalis, Lewis county, where it was necessary for her to make a change of trains to proceed to South Bend. While at the depot in Chehalis, she became acquainted with appellant. He took her to a restaurant and gave her her dinner, and when she had finished and returned to the depot the train had departed for South Bend, so that she could not go on that night. Appellant then suggested that they go to Centralia and secure rooms there, to which the girl consented, and they went by street car to Centralia. Appellant took the girl to the Landers Hotel, and registering for both as "Mr. and Mrs. Brown," they were assigned a room. The girl was not in the presence of the landlady of the hotel when appellant registered. Appellant and the girl went to a show, and returned afterwards to the hotel and went up to the room. The landlady of the hotel shortly afterwards went to the room and asked appellant if the girl was his wife. He stated that she was. The landlady asked him why the girl wore her hair down in braids, and wore such short dresses.

Appellant explained that that was because they were traveling on the road so much. He stated to the landlady that the girl was seventeen years of age and that they had been married for about a year and a half. The landlady then left them and did not molest them further. Appellant and the girl occupied the room that night, both occupying the same bed, and the offense, according to the girl's testimony, was committed that night.

The first assignment of error by appellant is that the court erred in refusing him the right to lay the foundation for impeaching witness John Morgus, the father of the prosecuting witness.

Morgus testified as witness for the state and, among other things, testified as to the visit of the girl to St. Helens, her return journey, stopping at Chehalis, and going on to Centralia with appellant. All of this testimony was over the objection of counsel for appellant and, on motion, was stricken by the court and the jury instructed to disregard it. Counsel for appellant then questioned Morgus as to his acquaintance with a Mrs. Leber of South Bend, and upon objection being sustained thereto upon the ground that it was not proper cross-examination, appellant offered to lay the foundation by the witness that he had made statements to Mrs. Leber to the effect that he did not know anything about the journey of the girl to Chehalis and Centralia from St. Helens, and that the girl did not always tell the truth in any event.

The testimony of Morgus having been stricken respecting the journey of the girl from St. Helens to Chehalis and Centralia, the offer of proof made by counsel for appellant was certainly improper. The proposed questioning of the witness Morgus was not within the scope of his direct examination, was not proper cross-examination, and was certainly not a proper method of attempting to impeach the prosecuting witness.

The next error claimed is that the court allowed the witness Amanda Williams to testify as an expert and give impeaching testimony of Dr. Kennicott, who was another of the state's witnesses.

No testimony was asked of Mrs. Williams as an expert. She was merely asked to state what she saw at the examination of the girl by Dr. Kennicott. This was perfectly proper and competent. The whole of her testimony was confined to what she observed during the examination. Her testimony disagreed somewhat with that of Dr. Kennicott, but the state is not bound to produce witnesses who agree entirely in their statements concerning a transaction. The question of credibility of witnesses is for the jury to weigh and determine.

The next error assigned is that the court refused to grant a continuance to enable appellant to secure the testimony of one S. M. Ragan. Ragan was a person mentioned by appellant as having occupied a room in another hotel in Centralia than the one shown by the state, in company with appellant on the night of December 2-3, 1918. He had been subpoenaed as a witness at the previous trial of the same case in September, 1919, and appeared two days late for the trial. Upon this trial counsel for appellant made an attempt to show why Ragan was late at the previous trial, and also some kind of a written showing to the court to explain the necessity of the attendance of Ragan as a witness, the materiality of his testimony, and why counsel believed he was not present when the case was tried in March, 1920. Whatever showing appellant made to the trial court as to the materiality of the testimony of Ragan and the circumstances excusing his nonattendance in March, 1920, is not before us, not having been brought up in the record. We are therefore obliged to presume that the trial court correctly exercised its discretion upon whatever the showing was in refusing a continuance.

The next error assigned is that the court allowed Mrs. Landers, a witness for the state, to restate the whole case in rebuttal. There is no merit whatever in this contention. Mrs. Landers was the landlady of the hotel at which it was shown appellant and the girl stayed all night. She was asked and answered four questions to rebut evidence given by appellant. Her testimony in rebuttal was proper rebuttal testimony of the testimony of appellant, which had not been covered by her testimony in the case in chief. In any event, it cannot be presumed that appellant was prejudiced thereby.

The judgment is affirmed.

PARKER, C. J., BRIDGES, MACKINTOSH, and FULLERTON, JJ., concur.

[No. 16248. Department One. June 10, 1921.]

TIMEWELL INVESTMENT COMPANY, *Appellant*, v.
ERNESTINE S. BECKWITH *et al.*,
Respondents.[1]

EVIDENCE (52)—COMPETENCY—RES GESTAE—ACTS ACCOMPANYING
TRANSACTION—BOOK ENTRIES. Where the issue in an action was as to
whether a person who purchased certain judgments against real
property was acting as the agent of the plaintiff or of the defendant,
book entries made at the time of purchasing the judgments were admissible as a part of the res gestae in favor of the one making
them to show the capacity in which he acted, to corroborate testimony as to the transaction, and to rebut inferences that might be
drawn or attempted to be drawn if the books were not produced.

PRINCIPAL AND AGENT (9)—EVIDENCE—WEIGHT AND SUFFICIENCY.
In an action to establish a trust arising from the procurement of
the assignment of a judgment by a person alleged to be acting as
agent for plaintiff, held that the burden of proof resting upon plaintiff to prove the agency was not sustained by a preponderance of
the evidence.

Appeal from a judgment of the superior court for
Pierce county, Card, J., entered July 31, 1920, dismissing an action to vacate certain execution sales of
real property. Affirmed.

Jesse Thomas, for appellant.

F. H. Murray and *Burkey, O'Brien & Burkey,* for
respondents.

HOLCOMB, J.—By this appeal the appellant endeavors
to reverse a judgment of dismissal by the trial court
upon conflicting evidence. The pleadings are voluminous and not necessary to set forth here. The object of
the action, as stated in the appellant's notice of *lis
pendens,* was to ''establish a trust, or to vacate certain
execution sales of real property, or to compel the

[1]Reported in 198 Pac. 735.

assignment of the sheriff's certificate of sale of real
property, and for general relief." The real property
to be affected by the action is described as follows: lots
1 and 2, block 821; lots 11 and 12, block 1016; lots 11 and
12, block 1420, map of New Tacoma, Washington Territory.

Appellant admits that, although the decision of the
lower court was, as it believes, based upon untenable
ground, yet, the case being of equitable cognizance, its
trial here is *de novo,* and the burden rests upon the
appellant to show that it proved the agency by a preponderance of the evidence.

The burden also rested upon the appellant in the
lower court to prove the agency by a preponderance of
the evidence. The lower court saw and heard the witnesses and was much better able to judge of the credibility than are we.

The evidence on behalf of appellant was to the effect
that, about the latter part of April, 1919, J. C. Heitman, president, general manager, and principal stockholder of the Fidelity Rent & Collection Company, went
to W. R. Sturley, assistant treasurer and general manager of appellant, at his place of employment in the
Bank of California, in Tacoma, and interviewed him in
regard to lots 11 and 12, block 1016, map of New Tacoma, situated at South Eleventh street and Yakima avenue; that Heitman represented to him that appellant
had lost certain other property in Tacoma by foreclosure, when Heitman could have sold its equity and
saved something for it, had it been placed in Heitman's
hands for sale, and that the 11th street and Yakima avenue property would go the same way unless steps were
taken to realize on the equity before it was too late;
that Sturley stated to him that there were two judgments which were liens against the property—one

held by Blanche B. Parker of Seattle for about ten
thousand dollars, and one by the National Bank of
Tacoma for a deficiency of more than fifteen hundred
dollars. Sturley told Heitman that Mrs. Parker's attorney had intimated to him that Mrs. Parker would
give him a release of her judgment for $200 cash; that
it was then agreed between them that Heitman would
see Mrs. Parker and ascertain what he could get a release or assignment of the Parker judgment for, and
report back to Sturley, and Sturley would arrange with
the National Bank of Tacoma for a release from the
judgment held by that bank, and as soon as the lots
were relieved from the judgment liens, Heitman would
find a purchaser for them. Sturley testifies that Heitman first said he thought he could sell them for $12,000,
and that he (Sturley) told him to "go to it"; that Heitman never reported back, and he supposed he had not
been able to make any deal with Mrs. Parker, and that
the matter had fallen through. On September 13, 1919,
he learned that the 11th street and Yakima avenue
property had been levied upon under an execution, and
he approached Mr. Murray, the attorney for Mrs. Parker, and was told by Murray that he did not know anything about it, that he was not then handling the affairs
of Mrs. Parker, and that he had better see Heitman.
He then saw his own attorney and he and a Mr. Young
went and called upon Heitman, and offered to reimburse him for the amount he had paid for the judgment,
and his expenses, which Heitman refused. The assignment of the judgment from Mrs. Parker to Mrs. Beckwith is dated May 1, 1919, and was acknowledged before
a notary public on that day. The property was sold on
execution on the judgment assigned to Mrs. Beckwith
on October 25, 1919, who purchased all three properties
subject to the other existing prior encumbrances. On

November 24, 1919, this suit was commenced and the
lis pendens filed in the auditor's office.

On the other hand, Heitman testifies that he was for
some time authorized by Mrs. Beckwith, a woman of
some means, residing in Rochester, New York, to invest
some money for her in Tacoma property such as Heitman would recommend; that, prior to his calling upon
Sturley, he had discovered the condition of the three
parcels of property involved herein, and had an attorney investigate the judgment liens against them, who
investigated and reported the same prior to April 17,
1919; that he then went to Sturley and offered one
thousand to fifteen hundred dollars for a quitclaim deed
"on behalf of a client of his", which Sturley refused.
Heitman had also, prior to going to Sturley, inquired
of Mr. Hellar, a representative of the National Bank of
Tacoma, to learn for what price the bank would release
or assign its deficiency judgment, but had not yet received the information from the bank, and after Heitman's interview with Sturley, Sturley was notified by
Mr. Hellar the next day that Heitman had tried to buy
the judgment and that the bank had declined. At about
the same time—just prior to, or just after, his visit to
Sturley—Heitman went to Seattle and interviewed
Mrs. Parker relative to the purchase of her judgment.
She asked $250, but within three or four days she went
to Tacoma and visited Heitman, when he offered her
$225 for an assignment of the judgment, which she
accepted. This assignment was drawn up but the name
of the purchaser left blank. Mrs. Parker, before executing the assignment, asked the name of the purchaser and was thereupon told that it was Ernestine S.
Beckwith, and that name was written into the instrument. The money was paid to Mrs. Parker by check of

the Fidelity Rent & Collection Company, and the amount was immediately charged on the books of the Fidelity Rent & Collection Company to the respondent Beckwith, the entry being made in the books by the bookkeeper of the Fidelity Rent & Collection Company on the same day and in the regular course of business. All subsequent disbursements in connection with the levy and sale were likewise charged to the respondent Beckwith on the company's books as soon as the disbursements were made.

Respondent Beckwith's brother had expected to be in Tacoma in time for the sale, but did not arrive until early in December following, when he repaid the Fidelity Rent & Collection Company the money advanced in the purchase of the judgment and making the sale, amounting to $520.80. The notice of the levy and sale, showing respondent Beckwith as owner of the judgment, was published in the Tacoma Daily Index, a paper of very general circulation among banks and business houses in Tacoma. Heitman was the active manager of the Fidelity Rent & Collection Company, and had been for about sixteen years, and had never operated individually as a real estate broker.

Appellant first complains that the court erred in permitting the respondents to show that an account was opened upon the books of the Fidelity Rent & Collection Company between it and Ernestine S. Beckwith on May 1, 1919, charging the latter with the $225 paid for the assignment of the Parker judgment.

The closing of the negotiations with Mrs. Parker, the execution of the assignment, the payment of the purchase price, and the entry of that payment in the company's cash book and ledger, were all parts of the same transaction, and were all parts of the *res gestae*. The claim of Sturley that Heitman was his agent in buying the judgment was denied by Heitman, who testified that he was not acting in his individual capacity, but only as manager of the Fidelity Rent & Collection Company, and that it was acting solely as the buying agent of respondent Beckwith. Book entries made by one party at the time of the transaction are competent evidence as a part of the *res gestae.* 11 Ency. Evidence 416. They are admissible in favor of the party making them as well as against such party. 10 R. C. L. 182. They are admissible also to rebut inferences that might be drawn or attempted to be drawn if the books were not produced, and to corroborate the testimony of the persons testifying to the transaction. 22 C. J. 892; and to show the capacity, whether as owner, trustee, agent, etc., in which the party acted. 10 R. C. L. 166.

The book entries were, therefore, properly admitted and were clearly competent, and tended to corroborate the testimony of Heitman that he individually did not attempt to act as agent; that the agent in the transaction was the Fidelity Rent & Collection Company, and that it was the agent of Ernestine S. Beckwith, at the time appellant alleged Heitman to be its agent. Heitman was also corroborated by the attorney employed to investigate the deficiency judgment and liens against the property, as being in April, 1919, prior to the 17th. Such evidence all tends to controvert the testimony of appellant to show that Heitman was the agent of appellant. The burden of proof being upon appellant to establish the agency by a fair preponderance of the evidence, we agree with the lower court that it failed to do so. We should be inclined to so hold had the trial court found otherwise. This being our view of the evidence, the other errors assigned by appellant are immaterial.

The judgment is affirmed.

PARKER, C. J., BRIDGES, MACKINTOSH, and FULLERTON, JJ., concur.

[No. 16434. Department One. June 10, 1921.]

MARTHA SMITH, *Respondent*, v. LOUIS FRATES, *Appellant*.[1]

APPEAL (386)—REVIEW—PARTIES ESTOPPED—ACQUIESCENCE. Error cannot be assigned on modification of a decree for divorce so as to permit the mother to visit children awarded to the father, where the attorney for the father conceded in open court the right of the mother to visit her children.

COSTS (24)—SECURITY—CHARACTER OF PARTIES—ANCILLARY PROCEEDINGS. A petition for the modification of a divorce decree being an ancillary proceeding and not an original action, would not subject petitioner to the operation of Rem. Code, § 495, requiring non-resident litigants to furnish security for costs.

SAME (88)—REMEDIES FOR COLLECTION—STAY OF SUBSEQUENT PROCEEDINGS. A motion for a stay of proceedings upon a petition for the modification of a divorce decree until petitioner should satisfy the costs in the divorce action was properly denied where it was shown that she was wholly unable to satisfy them.

Appeal from a judgment of the superior court for King county, Frater, J., entered October 28, 1920, modifying a decree in a divorce action. Affirmed.

Howard O. Durk, for appellant.

Elias A. Wright and *Sam A. Wright,* for respondent.

HOLCOMB, J.—Upon a former appeal in this case, an adjudication as to the custody of the children was made by this court, and a history of the case given. *Smith v. Frates,* 107 Wash. 13, 180 Pac. 880.

[1]Reported in 198 Pac. 732.

Respondent filed her petition for a modification of the decree so as to permit her to visit her minor children. Appellant thereupon moved the court for a stay of proceedings, upon two grounds: first, until respondent should furnish security for costs; and second, until such time as she should pay the judgment against her in this action, for costs on the former appeal, amounting to $103.55.

When the petition came on for hearing upon the merits, the attorney for appellant, in open court, made the following concession:

"As to the right of this woman to see her own children, I suppose there is no doubt that the court will grant that right, but the contention that Mr. Frates has ever denied that right, according to his own testimony, is absolutely false."

There was no testimony taken in the case after counsel for appellant conceded the right of respondent to have the decree modified to the extent prayed, and there was only one proposition of law upon which the trial court was called to pass by the appellant, and that was the question of the stay of proceedings. The court entered an order modifying the previous decree as to the custody of the children, so as to give respondent the right to visit the children at certain stated times after notice to appellant, and at certain places, and under certain restrictions imposed by the court.

Appellant, in this state of the record, is in no position to urge as error the modification by the court of the original decree of divorce, as well as the judgment of this court in the case of *Smith v. Frates, supra.* A litigant cannot be allowed to adopt one position in the trial court and the opposite position in this court.

As to the first ground for the motion for stay of proceedings, namely, that respondent was a nonresident of

King county, which, under the statute and decisions of
this court, entitle appellant to the bond demanded
(Rem. Code, § 495), it cannot be sustained. Respondent's petition was not an original proceeding, but merely an ancillary proceeding to the original action which
had been brought in King county, where the parties at
that time resided. Although respondent has since removed to Yakima county, the original action, being for
divorce, brought in the county where plaintiff resided,
her subsequent removal does not give grounds for requiring security for costs under § 495, *supra*.

Nor is the second ground for the motion for stay of
proceedings tenable. The costs arose out of the same
case and not out of an independent former action. Affidavits were presented to the trial court by both
parties as to the ability or inability of the respondent
to first satisfy the costs before she could be heard upon
her petition, and it was reasonably shown that respondent was wholly unable to satisfy the costs. In *Archi-
bald v. Lincoln County*, 50 Wash. 55, 96 Pac. 831, 126
Am. St. 886, 18 L. R. A. (N. S.) 902, a stay of proceedings was ordered by the lower court until the plaintiff
therein paid the costs of a former case, which had been
dismissed. This court held that the lower court abused
its discretion under the showing made by the party
that she was absolutely without means, and reversed
the order.

The trial court properly exercised its discretion in
this case in refusing to stay the proceedings.

The order is affirmed.

PARKER, C. J., BRIDGES, and MACKINTOSH, JJ., concur.

FULLERTON, J., concurs in the result.

[No. 16386. Department One. June 10, 1921.]

NORTH END WORKERS SUPPLY COOPERATIVE ASSOCIATION,
Appellant, v. RUDOLPH SABLICH *et al.,*
Respondents.[1]

WILLS (11)—DISTINGUISHED FROM OTHER DISPOSITIONS OF PROP-
ERTY. A written instrument reciting that it is "Last writing or testament. Leaving all my estate, Rudolph Sablich, these two lots located . . . . to J. Zatkovich, and he out of that must pay,"
(certain named beneficiaries), shows an intent to make a will, and
not an authorization to sell as agent of the owner.

PRINCIPAL AND AGENT (29, 34)—EXPRESS AUTHORITY—POWER TO
SELL—KNOWLEDGE. An agreement to sell certain real estate by an
alleged agent, reciting that the owner of the lots had gone abroad
and left a signed statement to sell, "but said signed statement is not
a full power of attorney", was sufficient to indicate to the purchaser
the limit of such agent's authority.

SAME (8)—EVIDENCE OF AGENCY—DECLARATION OF AGENT. Under
the rule that neither agency nor the scope of agency can be established by the declarations of the alleged agent, a recital of one's
self "as agent" of the owner in a notice relating to certain real
estate would not constitute proof of agency.

IMPROVEMENTS (2)—STATUTORY PROVISIONS. In an action for
specific performance of a contract for sale of land, which was un-
enforceable by reason of the lack of authority of an alleged agent
to sell, the plaintiff would not be entitled to recover the value of
improvements placed on the land, since Rem. Code, §§ 797-799,
allow such recovery only in possessory actions for the recovery of
real property upon which permanent improvements have been made.

Appeal from a judgment of the superior court for
Pierce county, Chapman, J., entered November 17,
1920, upon findings in favor of the defendants, in an
action for specific performance. Affirmed.

P. L. Pendleton, for appellant.
Remann & Gordon, for respondents.

[1]Reported in 198 Pac. 738.

HOLCOMB, J.—Rudolph Sablich, respondent, came to America about the year 1906. He in time acquired title to two lots in Tacoma.

In November, 1913, being about to depart for his old home on a visit, he made provision for the disposal of his estate, should anything happen or befall him. This instrument was dated November 26, 1913, and being in a foreign tongue, was translated by an interpreter, as follows:

"Tacoma, Washington 26th November, 1913. Last writing or testament. Leaving all my estate, Rudolph Sablich, these two lots located on 49th street, leaving to J. Zatkovich, and he out of that must pay Brother Matt Sablich $100, his two children $50 each and to the sisters each $50, and he also to sister's girl Tortzi $50, and when John Satkovich pays all of these, which amount to $350, and then these two lots remain his, and the same must be paid within one year; and now there, these two lots is all done, three witnesses, Witness M. Lucic, Winko Lucic, also Winko Zardas, owner Sablich, Rudolph."

Respondent left very shortly for Europe, leaving the above instrument and his deed and abstract with his friend John Zatkovich, to whom his affairs had been entrusted in that instrument.

While he was abroad, the European war came on and he could not return to America. He returned to America at the first opportunity with his wife, whom he married while abroad, and came direct to Tacoma about August or September, 1920.

In May, 1919, appellant company, desiring the property in question, lots 3 and 4, block 24, Seaview addition, entered into negotiations with John Zatkovich for their purchase. Appellants and Zatkovich executed a writing as follows:

"Received of North End Workers Supply Co-Operative Association, a corporation, the sum of $250 as earnest money and part payment of lots 3 and 4, block 24, Seaview addition to Tacoma, Washington, the agreed purchase price is $500, there being a balance owing of $250. It is agreed that the owner of the lots, Rudolph Sablich, has gone abroad and left a signed statement to John Zatkovich to sell the lots, but said signed statement is not a full power of attorney, and the deed of conveyance will be sent to the owner abroad for signature, and in the meantime the buyers may have peaceable possession of said lots, and work on the same. On return of the deed, if the title is good, the North End Workers Supply Association shall pay the remaining $250. If the title is not good and cannot be made good, the $250 shall be returned to the company as soon as ascertained that the title is not good. If after five months the owner does not be found and sign a deed, the seller or agent agrees to give the company a bond for a deed, to protect the company from loss in case the owner after the company improves the property refuses to sign.

"Dated May 23, 1919.

"Rudolph Sablich,
"Accepted: By John Zatkovich.
"North End Workers Supply Association,
"By Albert Luisch, President.
"Attest: Frank Cvitanovich, Secretary."

Zatkovich had not heard from Rudolph Sablich, the owner, for about five years. He testified: "I offered a price to sell the property because I did not know really if Rudolph Sablich lived or not; I figured it would be a good idea to sell the property and give the money to his folks back in the old country."

A deed was mailed to respondent which was never returned, but in June, about a month after the execution of the alleged contract, Zatkovich received his first knowledge of respondent for five years, in the form of

a letter written before the deed could reach respondent. Within two days after gaining knowledge that his
friend was alive, he caused notice to be served on appellants not to proceed with the building on the lots.
The notice was as follows:

"Tacoma, Washington, June 11, 1919.
"North End Workers Co-Operative Association, City.
"Gentlemen: On May 23, 1919, as agent for Rudolph
Sablich, the owner of lots 3 and 4, block 24, Seaview addition to Tacoma, I entered into a certain agreement
with you, signed upon your behalf by Albert Luisch,
president, and Frank Cvitanovich, secretary, a copy of
which you undoubtedly have, and to which reference is
hereby made for contents thereof.

"I desire to notify you that I have just received a
letter from Rudolph Sablich which shows that he was
alive on February 24, 1919. As you are aware, I did
not have full power of attorney to sell these lots for the
owner, and the signed statement which I have, signed
by the owner, I have been informed is in the nature of
a last will, giving me authority to sell the lots in the
event of the death of Rudolph Sablich, and not under
other conditions. In this letter, which I recently received from him, he tells me that he is married. This,
I am informed, revokes the will given to me, so that my
authority is entirely gone to, in any manner, represent
the owner. I am therefore tendering back to you herewith the two hundred fifty dollars ($250) paid as earn-
est money and part payment on the lots, and ask that
the agreement be cancelled. If you do not desire to accept it, I am willing to send the deed to Rudolph to be
executed by himself and his wife. If they, or either of
them refuse to sign, however, I notify you that I will
not be responsible to your company in any manner for
any loss that you may sustain by reason of improvements placed by you upon the property, or in any other
manner. You are notified that, so far as I am concerned, if you proceed to improve the property, you do
so at your own peril, with knowledge that the property

does not belong to you, and that the owner has not agreed to sell and convey it to you.

"If you do not accept the two hundred fifty dollars ($250) herewith tendered to you, please be advised that I am holding the same for you and subject to your order, and I notify you that I will personally not give to you a bond for a deed, reference to which is made in the contract referred to, entered into on May 23, 1919.

(Signed) "John Zatkovich."

At that time some grading had been done and a small quantity of lumber had been delivered on the ground, but no construction had been commenced, and no evidence of value of either grading or lumber was offered. Appellants ignored the notice, erected their building, and have continuously occupied it since its completion in the fall of 1919.

When respondent arrived in Tacoma in the early fall of 1920, he learned for the first time of the possession of appellant and the erection of the building. They tendered him $250 and demanded a deed. He refused and appellants commenced this action for specific performance, based on the instrument executed by Zatkovich to it.

All the authority Zatkovich had was the writing given by Sablich prior to his departure for Europe. Although appellant made repeated attempts to get Zatkovich to admit that he had some other authority than that written instrument, Zatkovich continually asserted that he had no other authority, and the existence of the written instrument would tend to establish the authority of Zatkovich as that contained in the written instrument, and none other. That instrument, while it was very imperfectly executed, was undoubtedly intended as a will. It attempted to give the property to Zatkovich with certain testamentary dispositions to others. There was nothing in the instrument authorizing Zat-

kovich to sell and account to Sablich for the proceeds.
It said: "these two lots located on 49th street, leaving
to J. Zatkovich, and he out of that must pay," etc.; and
that when the amounts specified to be paid, aggregating
$350, were paid as therein provided, then the two lots
remained his (Zatkovich's). Appellant concedes that
the instrument of 1913 was not a power of attorney
authorizing Zatkovich to make a deed, but claims that,
under our decision in *Littlefield v. Dawson*, 47 Wash.
644, 92 Pac. 428, an agent may be even orally authorized
by his principal to make a contract binding upon the
principal for the sale of lands. The case cited does not
so decide, but decided that the agent, having made an
oral contract under a written contract of agency for the
sale of specific lands, and the contract having been
acted upon and ratified by the agent's principal, that
the vendee could enforce performance. This case is
not like that in any particular. In that case the agent's
contract creating his authority contained this provision:

"We agree to convey the same or cause the same to
be conveyed by good and sufficient warranty deed to the
person or persons designated by you (the agent)".

And the court asked:

"If the authority to make a binding contract was not
included in the terms of the agency of what force are
the above words."

There was no such authority in the instrument given
by Sablich to Zatkovich in 1913.

The instrument received by appellant in negotiating
for the lots contained the clear statement that the owner
of the lots, Sablich, had gone abroad and left a signed
statement with Zatkovich to sell the lots, "but that said
signed statement is not a full power of attorney." This

indicated to appellant the limit of Zatkovich's authority; and furthermore, Luisch, one of the witnesses to the
instrument of 1913, was also one of the officers of appellant, and a witness for appellant at the trial of this
case, and testified that he knew the contents of the instrument of 1913, and endeavored to establish that Sablich made Zatkovich his agent to sell the real estate.
That being the situation, appellant must be held to have
had exact knowledge of the limitations of the authority
of Zatkovich, and that Zatkovich could not convey title
to the lots unless Sablich was dead, and then convey
them as executor. Conceding, for argument's sake,
that the instrument would have been effective as a will
had Sablich died, he did not die, and the instrument
never became effective.

When Zatkovich gave his notice to appellant that the
contract theretofore executed and delivered by him for
the sale of the lots to appellant was at an end, he designated himself as agent for Rudolph Sablich. Upon
this appellant seems to contend that, Zatkovich having
declared himself agent, it is proof of his agency. It is
fundamental law that one cannot establish agency, nor
the scope of agency, by declarations of the alleged
agent.

Zatkovich gave prompt notice to appellant of the
fact of Sablich's being alive, and of his (Zatkovich's)
incapacity to convey the real estate; tendered the two
hundred fifty dollars he had received as earnest money
back, and demanded that the agreement be cancelled.
At that time appellant had done but very little work
towards improving the premises by construction of the
building, and had only a small amount of material upon
the premises. Appellant chose to ignore the notice, and
proceed at its own risk to erect the building upon the
premises.

Upon this situation, appellant seems to contend that it is entitled to recover the value of the improvements under the betterment statutes, Laws of 1903, p. 262, Rem. Code, §§ 797-8-9. Those statutes were enacted in connection with the statutes providing for possessory actions for the recovery of real property upon which permanent improvements have been made, etc. This is not a possessory action under the statutes, but an action for specific performance of a contract, and the betterment statutes can in no way apply.

The judgment of the trial court is right, and is affirmed.

PARKER, C. J., FULLERTON, BRIDGES, and MACKINTOSH, JJ., concur.

[No. 16246. Department One. June 14, 1921.]

F. B. WILCOX, *Respondent*, v. V. B. MOBLEY *et al.*, *Appellants*.[1]

LIENS (2)—RIGHT TO LIEN—CONSENT OF OWNER. Where the owner of a truck under a conditional sale contract had not authorized and had no notice of repairs placed thereon, his interest in the truck could not be subjected to a lien for labor and material thereon, since Laws 1917, p. 229, authorizes such chattel liens only in case of labor performed or material furnished "at the request of the owner."

Appeal from a judgment of the superior court for Lewis county, Reynolds, J., entered September 23, 1920, in favor of the plaintiff, in an action to foreclose a mechanics' lien. Reversed.

George L. Spirk, for appellant.

MACKINTOSH, J.—The appellant, on October 31, 1919, sold a truck and delivered possession thereof to the

[1]Reported in 198 Pac. 728.

defendant Mobley under a conditional sale contract, which was filed, on November 4, in the office of the auditor of Lewis county. The respondent, in December, began this action to foreclose a chattel lien, alleging that he had performed labor and furnished material on the truck on November 3. The lien notice made no mention of the appellant. By answer, the appellant denied its liability for the claim and alleged that it was the owner of the truck and that at no time had it ordered, sanctioned or authorized any repairs, and had no notice that they were being made, and alleged that no authority existed on the part of any one to order any repairs on appellant's behalf. Judgment was entered against the appellant for the amount of the lien, and foreclosure and sale were ordered. From this judgment, the appellant has prosecuted an appeal.

Chapter 68, Laws of 1917, p. 229, limits the right of a lien of one who has performed labor or furnished material to one who has performed the labor or furnished the material "at the request of the owner." It being indisputable from the evidence that the appellant was the owner of the truck at the time the labor was performed and the material furnished, and there being no evidence that these things were done at the appellant's request, or at the request of any one acting for or on its behalf, and it appearing that the appellant had not ordered, sanctioned or authorized, or had notice of or ratified the performance of the labor and the furnishing of the material, the judgment was erroneous in so far as it affects the appellant, and is reversed.

PARKER, C. J., BRIDGES, HOLCOMB, and FULLERTON, JJ., concur.

[No. 16402. Department One. June 14, 1921.]

P. A. POLLEY et al., Respondents, v. F. W. PEABODY et al., Appellants.[1]

PRINCIPAL AND AGENT (6)—EVIDENCE (154)—PAROL EVIDENCE OF AGENCY—ADMISSIBILITY. In an action against an agent for fraud in misrepresenting the true price of land purchased by him for the plaintiffs under a verbal agreement, parol evidence is admissible to establish the agency, notwithstanding the existence of written instruments in the transaction, where such instruments do not state the employment and the parol evidence does not seek to alter or vary their terms.

Appeal from a judgment of the superior court for Snohomish county, Bell, J., entered April 20, 1920, upon the verdict of a jury in favor of the plaintiff, in an action to recover certain money advanced to an agent. Affirmed.

Earl W. Husted, for appellants.

D. W. Locke and *C. T. Roscoe*, for respondents.

MACKINTOSH, J.—The Polleys prosecuted this action to recover from the Peabodys certain sums of money alleged to have been given to F. W. Peabody in pursuance of a verbal agreement whereby he was employed as the Polleys' agent to purchase for them certain property in Snohomish county, and to advance for them a portion of the purchase price by way of a loan. They allege they paid to Peabody the sum of $1,013.75, but that he used only the sum of $771.50 in making payment for the premises, and that he had retained the balance, less reasonable compensation for his services, and this action is for the sum of such balance, to wit, $204.75. By affirmative defense, the appellants allege that the property was purchased by the respondents under a written memorandum. In their reply, respond-

[1] Reported in 198 Pac. 731.

ents admit the memorandum, but deny that the memorandum amounted to a contract.

The essential question in the case is whether the appellant was the agent of the respondents. Although the appellants allege many errors, the only one they have seen fit to argue is whether the trial court was in error in admitting parol evidence to establish the agency. The evidence is amply sufficient to sustain the respondents' position, if it was properly admitted. The written evidence consists of four instruments; first, a receipt signed by Peabody for $50, as earnest money to be returned if the property was not secured; second, a receipt signed by Peabody for $50, to be applied on the purchase price of $950; third, a receipt signed by one Otto for $50, upon the purchase price of $850; and fourth, an escrow memorandum between respondents and appellants, showing the price to be $750. The parol evidence was not introduced for the purpose of varying or altering the escrow agreement, but merely to establish the fact that Peabody had been employed as the respondents' agent, and while acting as such agent had purchased the premises in question with their money, concealing from them the true price at which he had made the purchase, and falsely and fraudulently representing to them that the price paid was in excess of the price for which he had actually secured the property. The escrow agreement does not state the contract whereby the respondents employed the appellant, and, moreover, there was sufficient evidence to show that the signature of the respondents to it had been secured by fraud and misrepresentation.

Examination of the case discloses no error, and the judgment is affirmed.

PARKER, C. J., BRIDGES, HOLCOMB, and FULLERTON, JJ., concur.

[No. 16411. *En Banc.* June 14, 1921.]

THE STATE OF WASHINGTON, *on the Relation of*
American Savings Bank & Trust Company,
Plaintiff, v. THE SUPERIOR COURT FOR
OKANOGAN COUNTY, *C. H. Neal,*
Judge, Respondent.[1]

CORPORATIONS (195)—ACTIONS—VENUE—TRANSACTION OF BUSINESS.
Where a trust company in the course of its business acquired by
foreclosure fruit land in another county which it was compelled to
cultivate until able to dispose of it, such cultivation would not constitute the transaction of its ordinary or customary business in such
county, and hence it would not be liable to suit therein under Rem.
Code, § 206, providing that "an action against a corporation may be
brought in any county where the corporation transacts business."

VENUE (9-1)—DOMICILE—CODEFENDANTS. Under Rem. Code, § 207,
providing that actions must be tried in the county in which the
defendants, or some of them, reside, a joint action against a corporation resident in another county and an individual who is a resident
of another state was improperly brought in a county where neither
resided, though real property belonging to both defendants had been
attached on the ground of the non-residence of one of the defendants.

PARKER, C. J., and HOLCOMB, J., dissent.

Application filed in the supreme court March 31,
1921, for a writ of prohibition to the superior court for
Okanogan county, Neal, J., to restrain the trial of a
case and compel the granting of a change of venue.
Granted.

Farrell, Kane & Stratton, for relator.

J. Henry Smith, P. D. Smith, and *W. C. Brown,* for
respondent.

TOLMAN, J.—The relator, the American Savings
Bank & Trust Company, a corporation, was incorporated under the laws of this state in the year 1901; its

[1]Reported in 198 Pac. 744.

articles of incorporation naming its principal place of business as being in King county, and authorizing it to carry on the business of banking, with the usual powers pertaining to banks and trust companies. The relator has never had an office for the transaction of business in Okanogan county, and at no time has it maintained an officer, agent, or other person upon whom process against it could be served, resident in said county. Nor has the relator ever transacted any business in Okanogan county except as hereinafter referred to.

In September, 1916, the relator and one Murray, in the usual course of business in King county acquired a promissory note made by one Peterson for $25,000, and interest, together with a mortgage, given to secure the same, upon certain real estate consisting of orchard land situated in Okanogan county.

In August, 1918, the relator and Murray, as owners of the note and mortgage referred to, employed J. Henry Smith, an attorney at law practicing in Okanogan county, to foreclose the $25,000 mortgage, and thereafter, apparently with the knowledge and consent of the relator, P. D. Smith and W. C. Brown, also attorneys practicing in Okanogan county, were associated with J. Henry Smith as attorneys for plaintiff in such foreclosure action. The action to foreclose the mortgage was commenced in Okanogan county and prosecuted to a judgment of foreclosure, from which an appeal was taken, and the judgment of foreclosure was thereafter affirmed by this court in *American Sav. Bank & Trust Co. v. Peterson*, 112 Wash. 101, 191 Pac. 837. In the meantime, the real estate covered by the $25,000 mortgage, which was so foreclosed, being in part subject to the lien of a prior mortgage for $10,000, the relator and Murray, to protect themselves, acquired this first mortgage, procured it to be fore-

closed by the same attorneys, and thereafter upon foreclosure sale purchased all of the property subject to
the mortgages for the amount due thereon. In the
month of March, 1919, for the purpose of protecting
and preserving the property so acquired, the relator,
and Murray took possession of the orchard lands covered by the mortgages and proceeded to cultivate,
prune, spray and care for the same, extended the irrigation system for the better irrigation and care of the
orchards, harvested the crop therefrom in the years
1919 and 1920, and are continuing in such possession
and care of the property, through their employees, for
the sole purpose, as relator alleges, of preserving the
value of the orchards and preventing the deterioration
of the property until such time as the lands may be
sold at prices and upon terms satisfactory to them,
relator alleging that they are making every effort to
so sell and have not had the intention at any time to
engage in farming or fruit raising, save only as an
incident to preserving the value of these lands until
they can realize thereon.

In February, 1921, P. D. Smith, J. Henry Smith and
W. C. Brown began an action in the superior court for
Okanogan county against the relator and Murray to
recover a balance of $2,000 claimed to be due them as
attorney's fees earned in the foreclosure proceedings
hereinbefore referred to. Summons and complaint
were personally served upon the relator in King
county, Washington, on February 7, 1921, and an affidavit in due form was filed setting forth that Murray
was a non-resident of the state of Washington, and a
writ of attachment was sought and issued against him
under which the sheriff of Okanogan county levied
upon the interest of Murray in the real estate which
had been the subject of the foreclosure suits hereinbefore mentioned; and since that time the plaintiffs in

that action have proceeded regularly to serve the summons and complaint upon Murray by publication, he being a resident of the state of Montana, which publication was proceeding in due course but had not been completed at the time of the issuance of the alternative writ herein. In due course, and within twenty days after service upon it, relator appeared specially in said action and objected to the jurisdiction of the court on the ground that the relator had no office nor agent in, and was not transacting business in, Okanogan county, within the contemplation of § 206, Rem. Code. These objections to the jurisdiction being overruled, the relator, still preserving its special appearance, made demand for a change of venue to King county, accompanied by an affidavit of merits, and a demurrer to the complaint, which demand was by the trial court denied. Thereupon the relator sought and obtained an alternative writ of prohibition to be issued out of this court directed to the respondent, as judge of the superior court for Okanogan county, restraining the superior court from proceeding further as against relator until the further order of this court, and requiring it to show cause why it should not be permanently restrained from further proceeding in said cause as against the relator.

The statute reads:

"An action against a corporation may be brought in any county where the corporation transacts business or transacted business at the time the cause of action arose; or in any county where the corporation has an office for the transaction of business or any person resides upon whom process may be served against such corporation, unless otherwise provided in this code." Rem. Code, § 206.

It is not contended that the relator maintained an office or transacted any of its banking or trust business

in Okanogan county, or that any person there resided
upon whom process against the relator could be served.
We have heretofore held that the mere bringing and
prosecution of an action does not constitute the doing
of business within the meaning of similar statutes.
Marble Sav. Bank v. Williams, 23 Wash. 766, 63 Pac.
511; *Lilly-Brackett Co. v. Sonnemann,* 50 Wash. 487,
97 Pac. 505. This being the settled law, it would seem
to follow that the incidental care and preservation of
the fruits of such an action would come within the same
rule. By the terms of our statute, Laws of 1917, ch. 80,
p. 291, § 37, a bank or trust company may acquire real
estate only for certain purposes or in the collection of
debts and foreclosure of its liens and securities; and
therefore it must be assumed here that relator was, in
its relation to this property, pursuing only its statutory rights to collect its debt. To care for the property, preserve by cultivation and the adding of the
necessary means of irrigation was as much a part of
the collection of its debt as was the acquiring of the
title by means of the foreclosure. The natural result
of the care and preservation of orchard lands is the
production of a crop, and that this should be marketed
and the proceeds as realized applied in satisfaction of
the cost of cultivation, treated as income on the debt
which is in process of collection or as payment *pro
tanto,* does not appear to affect the principle involved.

What is meant by the statutory term "transaction of
business" is very well defined by the following:

"It is frequently stated that the words 'doing business' and 'transacting business,' as used in statutes
imposing conditions on foreign corporations, refer
only to the transaction of the ordinary or customary
business in which a corporation is engaged, and do not
include acts not constituting any part of its ordinary
business. In other words, the test applied is, Is the

corporation engaged in the transaction of that kind of business, or any part thereof, for which it was created and organized? If so, it 'does business,' within the meaning of the constitutions and statutes. If not,—if the act it is doing or has done is not within the purpose of the grant of its general powers and franchises, —it is not the business to which the constitutional or statutory requirement is directed." 12 R. C. L., § 49, p. 71.

And we have already approved and followed this rule. *Rich v. Chicago, Burlington & Quincy R. Co.*, 34 Wash. 14, 74 Pac. 1008; *State ex rel. Wells Lumber Co. v. Superior Court*, 113 Wash. 77, 193 Pac. 229.

We conclude that relator does not, and did not at the time the cause of action arose, transact business in Okanogan county within the statutory meaning of that term.

It is contended, however, that the superior court of Okanogan county had jurisdiction under the terms of Rem. Code, § 207, which provides:

"In all other cases the action must be tried in the county in which the defendants, or some of them, reside at the time of the commencement of the action, or may be served with process, subject, however, to the power of the court to change the place of trial, as provided in the next two succeeding sections."

Of course, had Murray resided in Okanogan county, or had he there been personally served with process, there would be no question as to the right to there proceed. But since Murray was a nonresident of the state, the mere fact that he owned property in that county, which it was sought to attach, cannot be permitted to overweigh relator's rights. While it may be more orderly to proceed against a nonresident defendant in a county in which he has property which is to be attached, the law does not require it, but expressly directs that writs of attachment may issue to other

counties. Rem. Code, §§ 655, 656. And since § 206 of
the code is intended for the benefit of corporation
defendants residents of the state, the statute may not
be set aside, or its force avoided by electing to sue a
nonresident codefendant in a particular county when
equal relief may be obtained against the nonresident
defendant by suing both in the county where the resident corporation transacts business.

Nor was the nonresident defendant Murray served
with process in Okanogan county within the meaning
of the statute. True, the summons was there being
published, but with the intent in law that notice of the
pending action should by that means reach Murray at
his foreign domicile, where also the statute requires a
copy of the summons and complaint to be addressed
and mailed to him. The service referred to in § 207
of the code is undoubtedly personal service; but, in any
event, when relator raised this issue, the service by
publication had not proceeded to a point where Murray
could be said to have been served anywhere or at all,
in fact had not then been commenced.

Section 207 is applicable in so far as it provides that
actions must be tried in the county in which the defendants, or some of them, reside; and since Murray
resides in none of the counties of this state and relator
resides in King county, we conclude that the action
should have been brought in, or transferred to, King
county for trial.

The permanent writ will issue.

FULLERTON, MAIN, MITCHELL, BRIDGES, and MACKIN-
TOSH, JJ., concur.

HOLCOMB, J. (dissenting)—It seems to me that this
decision is utterly unsound.

Prior to 1909, the statute provided:

"An action against a corporation may be brought in any county where the corporation has an office for the transaction of business, or any person resides upon whom process may be served against such corporation. . . ." Bal. Code, § 4854.

In 1909, this statute was amended so as to read: (Rem. Code, § 206), as follows:

"An action against a corporation may be brought in any county *where the corporation transacts business or transacted business at the time the cause of action arose;* or in any county where the corporation has an office for the transaction of business, or any person resides upon whom process may be served against such corporation, unless otherwise provided in this code." (Italics mine.)

As pointed out by Mr. Justice Mount in *Strandall v. Alaska Lumber Co.*, 73 Wash. 67, 131 Pac. 211, the words "where the corporation transacts business or transacted business at the time the cause of action arose" were inserted into the previous statute evidently for the purpose of authorizing suits to be brought in the county where the corporation transacts business, whether it has an office for that purpose in such county or not.

The present decision would practically eliminate the amendatory provisions of the act of 1909, found in § 206, and prevent such corporation as the relator, which is doing a banking and trust business, from being sued in any county other than the county where it has its office or any person resides upon whom process may be served against such corporation.

It is said in the majority opinion that the business of operating its land as a farm or orchard in Okanogan county is not a part of relator's corporate business, and therefore is not transacting business in Okanogan county within the statutory meaning of the term. This reasoning is fallacious because the relator, although a bank and trust company, has power incidental to its principal powers of acquiring land through foreclosure and otherwise; of doing business in any county of the state, and incidentally, of managing its lands, actively for the purpose of profit, as it has done in this case for two years. These are certainly incidental powers, and therefore transactions under them constitute "transacting business" within the meaning of the statute.

It is to be presumed the corporation acts only in conformity with its charter powers, and that all its transactions are authorized.

If this reasoning is not correct, then all those who have dealt with the relator as a farmer or orchardist, such as those who furnished supplies and materials for the operation of its farm or orchard, having any controversy with the relator as to the amount due for such supplies and materials, would be obliged to go to King county, the county of relator's residence, in order to maintain an action against it, because it has not been doing business in Okanogan county with these persons with whom it dealt directly and made express or implied contracts.

In my opinion, the statute, Rem. Code, § 206, should receive a liberal construction as to what is the "transaction of business" by a corporation in a county, rather than a strained one. It is evident that the legislature had that in view when enacting § 206. It is no more unjust, or a matter of hardship, upon a corporation transacting any kind of business, either primary or incidental to its corporate powers, to be sued and jurisdiction maintained in a county other than the county of its residence, than it was to require it to go to Okanogan county to maintain its action to foreclose its mortgage upon lands in Okanogan county.

It seems to me that the suggestion of respondents that § 206 should be construed so that a corporation may be sued in the county where it transacts business "upon all matters growing out of the business so transacted in such county," is correct, and that that rule would prevent injustice or hardship and would be calculated to best meet the needs of all concerned.

For these reasons I dissent,

PARKER, C. J., concurs with HOLCOMB, J.

[No. 16494. Department Two. June 15, 1921.]

GEORGE E. SNYDER et al., Respondents, v. JOHN STRINGER, as Sheriff of King.County, et al., Appellants.[1]

HUSBAND AND WIFE (45)—COMMUNITY PROPERTY—WHAT LAW GOVERNS—PROPERTY ACQUIRED IN ANOTHER STATE. Personal property acquired in another state by one of the spouses of a community composed of husband and wife domiciled in this state is presumptively community property, and hence not liable for the separate debt of one of the spouses; the fact that the law where the property was acquired would make it separate property not affecting its status in this jurisdiction.

Appeal from a judgment of the superior court for King county, Marion Edwards, judge.pro tempore, entered December 18, 1920, upon findings in favor of the plaintiff, in an action to determine the ownership of an automobile and its liability to seizure on execution. Affirmed.

F. W. Girand and Fred M. Williams (Attwood A. Kirby, of counsel), for appellants.

Gates & Helsell, Harry L. Cohn, and Robert Weinstein, for respondents.

[1]Reported in 198 Pac. 733.

PARKER, C. J.—This was a proceeding in the superior court for King county under Rem. Code, §§ 573-577, relating to adverse claims to property levied upon. The plaintiffs, Snyder and wife, as a community, sought recovery of an automobile, claimed by them as their community property, which had been levied upon by the defendant sheriff under a writ of execution issued upon a judgment rendered against the plaintiff Snyder in favor of the defendant Merkel. Proper affidavit and bond having been furnished to the defendant sheriff, he delivered the automobile to the plaintiffs, and thereafter the cause came regularly on for trial upon the merits as to the ownership of the automobile and its liability to seizure and sale in satisfaction of the judgment rendered against Snyder in favor of the defendant Merkel. Findings and judgment were made and rendered by the superior court, adjudging the automobile to be community property of the plaintiffs and not subject to seizure and sale in satisfaction of the judgment rendered against Snyder. From this disposition of the cause, the defendants have appealed to this court.

We think there is no room for serious controversy as to what the controlling facts of the case are. They may be summarized as follows: Respondents Snyder and wife were married in July, 1917, and ever since then have been residents of the state of Washington. In February, 1919, there was duly rendered in the superior court for Spokane county a money judgment, against respondent Snyder and in favor of appellant Merkel, for the sum of $2,500, upon an obligation incurred by Snyder long before his marriage, which obligation and judgment were not, and never became, a debt or obligation of the community composed of respondents. The business of respondent Snyder, consisting wholly of the business of the community, called him frequently, and for periods of considerable duration, out of this state, and particularly into the states of Montana and Iowa. While in Iowa in May, 1920, he purchased there the automobile here in question, with funds which for present purposes we may regard as having been earned by him in his business in that state and in Montana. He brought the automobile to this state, and thereafter it was seized by appellant as sheriff under an execution issued upon the judgment rendered against Snyder in favor of appellant Merkel. This proceeding was thereupon commenced by respondents, seeking recovery of the automobile, and resulted as above noticed. It was proven upon the trial that, by the laws of both Montana and Iowa, the earnings of a husband during coverture become his separate property and become liable to levy and sale in satisfaction of his individual debts.

Counsel for appellant, while conceding that community property cannot, in this state, during coverture be seized and sold to satisfy the separate debts of the husband, invoke the general rule that the ownership of property brought into this state from another state remains unchanged; so that, if such property be separate property of the husband when brought here, it so remains, and becomes subject to seizure and sale to satisfy his separate debts, notwithstanding it may have been earned during coverture; citing *Freeburger v. Gazzam*, 5 Wash. 772, 32 Pac. 732; *Brookman v. Durkee*, 46 Wash. 578, 90 Pac. 914, 123 Am. St. 944, 13 Ann. Cas. 839, 12 L. R. A. (N. S.) 921; and *Meyers v. Albert*, 76 Wash. 218, 135 Pac. 1003. The *Freeburger* decision seems to assume, rather than decide, that the property acquired in Kansas was there the separate property of the wife. The real point decided seems to be that the property did not change its character as to ownership by being brought into this state; that is, that it did not thereby become community property, though acquired during coverture. The place of the actual domicile of the husband and wife seems not to have been noticed in that decision. The *Brookman* and *Meyers* decisions render it plain that the properties there involved were acquired in states other than Washington, while the husband and wife were actually domiciled· in those states, and became under the laws of those states the separate property of one or the other, and so remained when brought into this state.

Our decision in *Colpe v. Lindblom*, 57 Wash. 106, 106 Pac. 634, we think, is in principle decisive here in favor of the respondents. The property there involved was in this state, having been purchased by the husband with moneys earned by him in Alaska during coverture. Holding that the property was community property, Judge Gose, speaking for the court, said:

"The appellants urge that the interest of the appellant Dawson in the premises was his separate property. The evidence which forms the basis for the contention is that the money which Dawson put into the property was earned by him at Nome, Alaska, and that, under the laws of that place, his earnings were his separate estate. The record discloses that both the husband and wife were at Nome, he working at different things, as she expressed it, and she keeping house. The wife further testified that the marriage occurred at Phoenix, Arizona, about seventeen years before the trial. We have not been able ·to discover from the record whether Nome was their domicile or merely their temporary abode. As we have stated, in this state the presumption is that all property acquired by either spouse after marriage is community property. This rule is so well established that the citation of authority is not neces. sary. The law of the domicile controls as to personal property acquired during coverture. *Thayer v. Clarke* (Tex. Civ. App.), 77 S. W. 1050. In the absence of evi_

dence as to the domicile of the parties at the time the
money was earned, the presumption will be indulged
that the domiciliary law is the same as our own. *Clark
v. Eltinge,* 29 Wash. 215, 69 Pac. 736.''

It seems to be argued by counsel for the appellants
that, by this language, the court had in mind the presumption that the laws of Alaska were the same as our
own in the absence of proof; but, clearly, we think, this
is not what the court meant; for near the beginning of
the quoted language it is said, ''under the laws of that
place (Alaska), his earnings were his separate estate.''
We think it clear that, since the court was unable from
the record to determine where the domicile of the husband and wife was at the time of earning the money
which purchased the property, it would be presumed
that, in whatever state or territory that domicile was,
the laws of such state or territory were the same as
our own; manifestly proceeding upon the theory that
the husband and wife were not domiciled in Alaska, but
were only there temporarily.

We are of the opinion that, for the purpose of determining by the courts of this state the ownership of this
automobile, that is, as to whether it is community or
separate property, both spouses being domiciled in this
state when the automobile was acquired in the manner
we have noticed, the *situs* of the property, to-wit, the
automobile, must be deemed to be that of the domicile
of respondents; whatever may be said as to its *situs* for
the purpose of determining its liability to seizure and
sale to satisfy the individual debts of respondent Snyder while it was in Montana, or Iowa, by the courts of
those states.

The judgment is affirmed.

MITCHELL, MAIN, MACKINTOSH, and TOLMAN, JJ., concur.

[No. 16159. Department Two. June 17, 1921.]

W. T. Pettijohn, *Appellant*, v. A. L. Ray, *Respondent*.[1]

Contribution (4)—Persons Entitled. Where a joint purchase
of harvesting machinery on deferred payments was made by two
farmers, and thereafter, under an alleged agreement between them,
one was released from liability by the seller, the payment by the
other of the balance due to the seller would not entitle the payor
to contribution against his copurchaser.

Appeal (413)—Review—Verdicts—When Not Set Aside. Where
there was sufficient evidence to go to the jury, the appellate court
will not interfere on the ground of its inability to determine which
items were found in favor of one party and which in favor of the
other.

Same (343, 347)—Briefs—Specification of Errors—References.
Error assigned on the refusal of the trial court to give a requested
instruction cannot be considered on appeal, where neither the
instruction nor its substance is set forth in the brief or any argument made upon it or the record of it disclosed.

Appeal from a judgment of the superior court for
Walla Walla county, Mills, J., entered December 12,
1919, upon the verdict of a jury rendered in favor of
the plaintiff, in an action on contract. Affirmed.

John C. Hurspool, for appellant.

E. L. Casey, for respondent.

Tolman, J.—Appellant, as plaintiff below, brought
this action to recover on five causes of action, praying
for judgment in the aggregate of $2,078.48. The action
was tried to a jury, which returned a general verdict
in plaintiff's favor in the sum of $721.66, upon which a
judgment was entered. Plaintiff has appealed from
the judgment, contending that, under the evidence in
the case, he should have recovered a much larger
amount.

The parties were neighboring farmers and had transactions back and forth running over a number of

[1]Reported in 198 Pac. 981.

years. The evidence was vague and unsatisfactory in
many respects, conflicting on all vital points of any
importance, and no useful purpose will be served by
setting forth the issues or the testimony, except as
may be necessary to understand what we consider to
be the only debatable point of law raised by the appeal.

It appears that, before the harvest in the year 1915,
appellant and respondent jointly purchased a harvesting outfit from one Rogers, for the sum of $1,200, on
credit; but whether the obligation was oral or reduced
to writing and signed by one or both does not appear.
There was evidence from which the jury might have
found that, in the year 1915, respondent's lands were
summer-fallowed; that he had no crop to harvest that
year, and that it was agreed between them that appellant should use the harvesting machinery so purchased and owned jointly, during that year, becoming
an insurer thereof while so using it, and would return
it to respondent before the harvest in 1916 in good
order and operating condition, for respondent's use in
that year. All agree that, while appellant was in the
sole possession of and threshing with the outfit in 1915,
it was destroyed or very seriously damaged by fire,
and that he did not return it in good condition to respondent before the 1916 harvest.

It is also admitted that, shortly before the harvest of
1916, respondent purchased for $425 what remained of
the machinery, though respondent contends, and testified, that he, relying on the previous agreement to return in good order, which was then impossible of fulfillment, purchased the full title from appellant for the
sum mentioned; while appellant contends, and testified, that there was no such agreement to return in
good order; that the fire loss was a joint loss, and that
respondent purchased only the outstanding half interest in the machinery, his liability to pay Rogers

one-half of the original purchase price still remaining unaffected by the subsequent transaction between them. That this would be true as against Rogers, if nothing else appeared, may be conceded, but there was testimony from which the jury might have found that Rogers was advised of what respondent claims was the agreement between the parties, acquiesced therein, never made any demand upon respondent for any portion of the purchase price, settled other matters with respondent in the year 1918, and then gave him a written receipt in full of all accounts against him, understanding that this account no longer existed, and thereafter looked only to appellant for his money. At any rate, appellant paid Rogers various sums on account from time to time, and just before bringing this action paid to Rogers, by giving his note, the remainder due on the original purchase of $750, which he now contends represented the $600 originally to have been paid by respondent, and interest accrued thereon, which amount he here seeks to recover as one of his causes of action.

The respondent's defense is based upon the theory that, by agreement, each should be an insurer while in possession of and using the joint property. Appellant, by his reply, pleaded the statute of limitations, and contends that the fire, having occurred in 1915, respondent's right to recover his loss was barred by the three-year statute of limitations before he (appellant) paid Rogers in full and became entitled to contribution from respondent.

Whether respondent's set-off was no part of the mutual accounts between the parties, but was for damages arising out of the breach of an independent contract such as would not be kept alive by the existence of the mutual accounts, as appellant contends, or whether, seeking no affirmative relief, respondent's defensive rights would still remain unaffected by the statute, need not be here determined, because, if Rogers acquiesced in the asserted agreement of the parties that, after the fire, appellant became and was his sole debtor, and thereafter, looking only to him for payment, he released respondent, then clearly appellant acquired no rights by paying Rogers, and that payment cast no duty on respondent to contribute. Hence we cannot interfere with the verdict upon this ground.

We find that there was evidence sufficient to go to the jury upon all of the other issues. Merely because we cannot determine from the verdict which items the jury found in favor of one party and which in favor of the other is not ground for our interference. .

Error is assigned upon the refusal of the trial court to give appellant's requested instruction number one. Neither this requested instruction nor its substance is set forth in the brief. No argument is offered thereon, nor reason given, why it is thought the court erred in refusing it, and if the requested instruction is preserved in the record we have, in a somewhat intensive study of the case, not happened to find it. Under these conditions, we cannot consider it.

Finding no error, the judgment appealed from is affirmed.

PARKER, C. J., MAIN, and MITCHELL, JJ., concur.

[No. 16227. Department One. June 21, 1921.]

THE STATE OF WASHINGTON, *Respondent*, v. FRED E. WOODS *et al., Appellants.*[1]

CRIMINAL LAW (55)—FORMER JEOPARDY—INTOXICATING LIQUORS—DIFFERENT OFFENSES IN SAME ACT. An acquittal of the offense of opening up, conducting and maintaining a place for the sale of intoxicating liquors would not be a bar to a subsequent prosecution for unlawfully having in possession intoxicating liquors, though the two prosecutions were based upon substantially the same evidence, since the one offense is not included within the other under the provisions of the statute relating to intoxicating liquors.

INTOXICATING LIQUORS (30)—OFFENSES—ILLEGAL POSSESSION. Under a statute making the possession of intoxicating liquor unlawful, it is no defense to a prosecution therefor that defendants came into possession thereof during the time when, under the laws of the state, such possession was lawful.

SAME (6)—PROHIBITION—POSSESSION OF INTOXICATING LIQUOR—EIGHTEENTH AMENDMENT. The Volstead Act, passed pursuant to the 18th amendment to the constitution of the United States, does not supersede the state statute relating to the unlawful possession of intoxicating liquors.

Appeal from a judgment of the superior court for Snohomish county, Bell, J., entered July 26, 1920, upon a trial and conviction of the crime of unlawful possession of intoxicating liquor. Affirmed.

O. T. Webb and *Coleman & Fogarty*, for appellants.

Thos. A. Stiger and *Q. A. Kaune*, for respondent.

FULLERTON, J.—The defendants, Wood and wife, were convicted in the superior court of Snohomish county upon an information charging them with the offense of unlawfully having in their possession intoxicating liquor other than alcohol, and appeal from the judgment and sentence pronounced against them.

At the time of their arraignment upon the information, the defendants, in addition to a plea of not

[1]Reported in 198 Pac. 737.

guilty, interposed a plea of former acquittal of the offense charged. At the trial, in substantiation of the latter plea, they offered in evidence the record of a cause in the superior court of Snohomish county, in which they had been tried for and acquitted of the crime of being jointists; that is, of the crime of opening up, conducting and maintaining a place for the unlawful sale of intoxicating liquor; offering in the same connection to show that the evidence introduced on behalf of the state to secure a conviction in that case was substantially the same evidence as the evidence on which the state relied for conviction in the instant case. The trial court excluded the proffered evidence, and its action in so doing forms the basis of the first error assigned. But we find no error in the ruling. The acquittal in the one case could operate as a bar to a conviction in the other only on the principle of included offenses, and we think it manifest that the offense of opening up, conducting and maintaining a place for the sale of intoxicating liquor does not necessarily include the offense of unlawfully having intoxicating liquor in possession. There is no necessary connection between the two offenses. A person may open up, conduct or maintain a place for the sale of intoxicating liquor, without himself engaging in such sale; he may do so for the purpose of furnishing a place for the sale of such liquor by others. An information for the one offense therefore would not inform a defendant that he must meet the other, and it must follow that on a charge of the one he could not be legally convicted of the other. The converse of the proposition must also follow, namely, that an acquittal of the one offense will not bar a conviction of the other.

The case of *State v. Burgess*, 111 Wash. 537, 191 Pac. 635, cited and relied upon by the defendants, rather supports than militates against the conclusion

here reached. The precise question was not there presented, but it was recognized that a person might be
guilty of a violation of this particular section of the
statute without himself having unlawful possession of
intoxicating liquor.

Nor does the case of *State v. Spillman*, 110 Wash.
662, 188 Pac. 915, support a contrary view. We were
there considering the clause of the statute relating to
bootleggers—persons who carry about with them intoxicating liquor for the purpose of unlawful sale—
and held that the offense of unlawful possession of intoxicating liquor was necessarily included in the
offense of bootlegging, as a person could not well carry
about with him intoxicating liquor for the purpose of
unlawful sale without having unlawful possession of
such liquor. But the holding does not require the further holding that the offense of unlawful possession is
necessarily included in the offense of being a jointist.

The appellants requested the court to give to the
jury the following instruction:

"You are further instructed that even though you
should be convinced beyond a reasonable doubt, that
the defendants did, at the time and place set forth in
the information, have in their possession intoxicating
liquor. yet I instruct you that if you believe that said
defendants came into lawful possession of said liquor
during the time when, under the laws of this state, it
was lawful to have possession of intoxicating liquor,
or should you have a reasonable doubt as to such fact,
then you must acquit the defendants."

This instruction the court refused and the second
error assigned is predicated thereon. But the question
suggested does not require extended discussion. It
was before us in the case of the *State v. Giaudrone*, 109
Wash. 397, 186 Pac. 870, where we determined, in harmony with the view here taken by the trial court, that

the manner of the acquisition of intoxicating liquor did not affect the question of rightfulness of possession.

Finally, it is contended that the statute under which the appellants were convicted is superseded by the Federal statute, commonly known as the Volstead act, enacted pursuant to the Eighteenth amendment to the Federal constitution (see 41 U. S. Statutes at Large, p. 305). But this question was likewise before us in *State v. Turner,* 115 Wash. 170, 196 Pac. 638, where a conclusion contrary to the contention was reached. The question there involved, it is true, related to the other provisions of our act—the provisions relating to "jointists" and "bootleggers"—but the principle announced is determinative here.

The judgment is affirmed.

PARKER, C. J., HOLCOMB, MACKINTOSH, and BRIDGES, JJ., concur.

[No. 327. Department One. June 21, 1921.]

In the Matter of the Proceedings for the Disbarment of RUFUS L. SHERRILL.[1]

ATTORNEY AND CLIENT (8)—DISBARMENT PROCEEDINGS—ADDITIONAL CHARGES—POWERS OF BOARD. In disbarment proceedings before the state board of law examiners, it is within the powers of the board to allow the filing of additional charges after a hearing has been entered upon, a continuance being granted to give the accused full opportunity to meet the new charges.

SAME (9)—DISBARMENT PROCEEDINGS—PUNISHMENT. The verification of a complaint in disbarment proceedings by a member of the board of law examiners charged with the duty of trying the accused raises no presumption of unfairness in the proceedings, since such power is expressly conferred on the board by statute.

Proceedings filed in the supreme court January 31, 1921, for the disbarment of an attorney, upon the find-

'Reported in 198 Pac. 725.

ings of the state board of law examiners against the accused. Judgment of disbarment.

Leo & Flaskett, for accused.

The Attorney General and *John H. Dunbar, Assistant,* for the state.

FULLERTON, J.—This is a proceeding for the disbarment of Rufus L. Sherrill, an attorney at law, duly licensed to practice in the courts of this state.

The complaint against Mr. Sherrill, as originally filed with the state board of law examiners, contained two charges; the substance of the first being, that he had wrongfully appropriated to his own use money sent him in his capacity as an attorney by a judgment debtor for the purpose of satisfying a judgment; and the second, that he was of immoral and dissolute habits, a habitual drunkard, and had been guilty of violating the liquor laws of the state, and had paid fines and served jail sentences upon convictions for such offenses. On the filing of the complaint, the board appointed a time and place for hearing the same, and caused notice thereof to be served on Mr. Sherrill. At the time and place appointed, Mr. Sherrill appeared and filed a written answer to the charges; the answer being in substance a general denial of the charges, save that he expressly admitted that he had been found guilty and had paid fines and had served jail sentences for unlawfully having in his possession intoxicating liquors. The hearing then proceeded upon the charges on which issue was taken, in which hearing evidence was introduced both in support and in disproof of the charges. On the conclusion of the testimony, the attorney representing the prosecution announced to the board that since the filing of the complaint on the pending charges, additional charges against the accused had been brought to his attention which he desired to investigate, and moved the board for a continuance of the hearing to some future day certain with leave to file a supplemental complaint in case he found sufficient substantiation of the charges. To this Mr. Sherrill, who was then appearing on his own behalf, made no objection, and on the suggestion of a date by the chairman of the board, answered that it was satisfactory. The hearing was then adjourned until Wednesday, November 10, 1920, the chairman directing that any complaint containing additional charges be served upon the accused at least ten days prior to the time to which the hearing was adjourned.

On October 22, 1920, an amended and supplemental complaint was filed with the secretary of the board. This complaint contained the charges set forth in the original complaint in substantially the language there pursued, and contained in addition two further charges; the first of which is that he aided and abetted one Julia B. Smith in the practice of criminal abortion, and the second, that after the conviction of Mrs. Smith for the crime of criminal abortion, and after her sentence to a term in the penitentiary, he sought to persuade certain witnesses, who testified for the state at her trial, to make false affidavits for use in an application which he contemplated making to the governor of the state for her pardon.

The amended and supplemental complaint was served on Mr. Sherrill more than ten days prior to the adjourned hearing. At that time Mr. Sherrill appeared in person and by counsel, and filed certain written objections to any further proceedings. These objections were overruled by the board, whereupon evidence was introduced on behalf of the prosecution in support of the additional charges. An adjournment was then taken to a later day, at which time counsel alone appeared; Mr. Sherrill personally making no further appearance. At this hearing the proceedings were conducted to a close, and later on the board returned into this court a transcript of the proceedings together with their report, finding the charges sustained and recommending that the accused be disbarred.

In this court it is contended, on behalf of the accused, that the board exceeded its powers in permitting the amended and supplemental complaint to be filed and in retrying the cause upon the additional charges set forth therein. It is argued that amendments to complaints in proceedings of this sort are governed by the statute permitting amendments to complaints in ordinary civil actions, and that there was no sufficient cause shown for allowing the amendment in this instance. But we think this a special proceeding to which the statutes referred to are inapplicable. The hearing before the board is not in its nature strictly judicial. By the statute creating the board, they are empowered only to entertain the complaint, hear and take evidence thereon, and report the evidence with their recommendations to this court, where the final judgment is entered. It is essential, of course, that the complaint against the accused state definitely and clearly the grounds of the charges against him, and that he be given full and ample opportunity to make his defense thereto, but it is not a requirement that the proceedings take any particular course, or that they comply with the practice governing the proceedings in the superior or other courts. Here the complaint was definite and certain in its charges, the accused was given ample time and a full opportunity to present his defense, and we cannot think that because the board allowed additional charges to be filed after the hearing had been entered upon, it in any way acted irregularly or without authority, much less that it so far exceeded its powers as to render the proceedings void.

The complaint was verified by a member of the board to the effect that he believed it to be true. It is argued that this is to make the board both the accuser and the judge, and that the proceedings are void for this reason. But this is a power expressly conferred on the board by the statute, and no presumption of unfairness or partiality arises from the fact. A similar objection was made to the act establishing a railroad commission (Laws 1905, p. 145), which permitted the commission created thereby to institute proceedings "on its own motion" against public carriers. But we held this not fatal to the act, or as rendering void proceedings instituted on a complaint verified by one of the commissioners. *State ex rel. Oregon R. & Nav. Co. v. Railroad Comm.*, 52 Wash. 17, 100 Pac. 179.

The merits of the controversy we shall not discuss. Recognizing the serious consequences of the proceedings to the accused, and the rule of law that the accusations should be proven by a clear preponderance of the evidence, we have no hesitancy in saying that the evidence justifies the conclusion that the accused has been guilty of conduct demonstrating his unfitness to practice as an attorney at law.

It will therefore be the judgment of the court that the license heretofore granted the accused to practice law in this state be revoked, that he be disbarred, and that his name be stricken from the roll of attorneys.

Parker, C. J., Holcomb, Mackintosh, and Bridges, JJ., concur.

[No. 16094. *En Banc*. June 21, 1921.]

H. HEINO *et al., Respondents*, v. LIBBY, McNEILL & LIBBY, *Appellant*.[1]

SEAMEN (2)—SHIPPING ARTICLES—CONTRACTS—"MERCHANT SHIPS"
—WHAT LAW GOVERNS. A vessel engaged in domestic commerce between ports of one state and noncontiguous territory is a merchantman subject to the operation of maritime law, and the shipping regulations promulgated by the United States statutes.

SAME (2)—ARTICLES—PERFORMANCE OF CONTRACT—SURVEY—ABANDONMENT OF SHIP—SEAWORTHINESS—EVIDENCE—SUFFICIENCY. Where shipping articles are signed by men employed as seamen, fishermen, beachmen and trapmen, under a contract to sail a vessel from Seattle to a port in Alaska, work during the fishing season as fishermen, beachmen or trapmen, and at the close of such season sail the vessel back to Seattle, the contract as a whole is of a maritime character, notwithstanding the extra provisions covering fishery services.

SAME—WAGES—FORFEITURE. Seamen employed under shipping articles to sail a vessel on the return voyage from an Alaskan port to Seattle, have no justification for abandoning their contract on the ground of the unseaworthiness of the vessel, where a survey of the vessel was made by three disinterested master mariners, and also by a board of survey consisting of the commander of a U. S. coast guard cutter and three other officers of his ship, the surveyors in both instances finding the vessel seaworthy and fit to make the voyage from Alaska to Seattle; and their refusal to serve as seamen, without making any demand for a survey, constituted them deserters under the statutes of the United States.

SAME—WAGES—FORFEITURE—DESERTION. A deserting seaman not only forfeits his wages or emoluments which he has earned, but also forfeits the right to recover upon a quantum meruit for services rendered in part performance of his contract.

SAME—WAGES—ISSUANCE OF CERTIFICATES—EFFECT. Labor certificates issued to a crew of seamen and fishermen, stating the amounts that would become due them on fulfillment of their contract would not estop the employer to deny the right of recovery, where the certificates were secured by coercion after the crew had become deserters under their shipping contract.

FULLERTON, J., dissents.

[1] Not yet reported in Pacific Reporter.

Appeal from a judment of the superior court for King county, Smith, J., entered April 27, 1920, upon the verdict of a jury rendered in favor of the plaintiffs, in consolidated actions to recover seamen's wages, after a trial on the merits. Reversed.

Kerr & McCord and *Stephen V. Carey*, for appellant.
H. E. Foster, for respondents.

HOLCOMB, J.—These actions, ten in number, were brought by ten of a crew of seamen and fishermen, suing for themselves and as assignee for collection of eighty-four others, to recover wages claimed to have been earned by them under a contract of employment. The ten cases were consolidated for trial under the title of *Heino v. Libby, McNeill & Libby*. From six to twelve cases are included in each suit. In each suit the plaintiff alleges his employment and that of his assignors and that he was given certificates showing stated amounts which appellant refused to pay.

Appellant answered in each case, the answer in the *Heino* case being typical of all, denying that the several amounts claimed by the plaintiffs were earned, alleging that certain lesser sums were earned, which would be owing by appellant were it not for matters affirmatively alleged. Appellant then affirmatively alleged that, on April 8, 1919, respondents and their assignors entered into a contract with appellant in the form of shipping articles, and a certain supplementary agreement, whereby respondents and their assignors engaged themselves as seamen and fishermen for the season of 1919, and, as such, agreed to sail the ship "Abner Coburn" from Seattle to Libbyville, Alaska, and to work as fishermen during the fishing season, and on the conclusion thereof to sail the "Abner Coburn" back to Seattle. It is further alleged that, upon the arrival

of the ship at Libbyville, the crew conspired together
to violate their contract by refusing to navigate the
ship back to Seattle; that, in furtherance of the conspiracy, the crew pretended that the vessel was in a
leaky condition and unseaworthy, and thereupon the
appellant had the vessel surveyed by three master
mariners, and by the officers of the United States coast
guard cutter "Unalga"; but that, notwithstanding
such surveys and the demand of the master that the
crew fulfill their contract, they refused to do so, and
deserted the ship. Appellant then alleged that, on
account of the refusal of the crew to perform their
contract, appellant was subjected to expenses aggregating something over $36,000, and by reason of the pro-
visions of the contract, appellant became entitled to
recover from each member of the crew $5 for each day
they severally refused to work.

Respondents replied, putting in issue the matters alleged in appellant's affirmative answer.

The total amount claimed by the several respondents
upon their own and the assigned claims was $26,029.22.
Upon a trial to the court and a jury, the jury returned
a verdict for $25,613.76.

Appellant operates a number of salmon canneries in
Alaska on Bristol Bay, and one of the canneries is located at Libbyville, Alaska. The usual method of operating these canneries is to fit out an expedition, which
leaves Seattle in the spring in time to reach the cannery by the time the fish begin to run. The canneries
are operated during the run of the fish, and when that
is over the expedition returns to Seattle. During the
season of 1919, the sailing ship "Abner Coburn",
owned by appellant, was assigned to the expedition to
Libbyville. She left Seattle on April 10, 1919, having
on board a cargo of cannery and fishery supplies and
about 325 or 330 men. The men on board were under

contract to perform the labor and were divided into three groups, namely: (1) seamen, fishermen, beachmen and trapmen; (2) monthly men; (3) China crew.

The first group (seamen, fishermen, beachmen and trapmen) was composed of about one hundred men who, before leaving Seattle, signed shipping articles in the office of the United States shipping commissioner, by which they engaged themselves to sail the "Abner Coburn" to Alaska, work during the fishing season as fishermen, beachmen or trapmen, and at the close of the fishing season to sail the vessel back to Seattle. These men were all members of the Alaska fishermen's union. Their contract of employment consisted of the usual form of shipping articles prescribed by title LIII, Revised Statutes of the United States, to be executed with respect to vessels or merchant ships, together with a supplemental agreement known as a "fisherman's contract", which provides in detail as to the duties and compensation of these men. The two documents, namely, the shipping articles and the fishermen's agreement, were executed together and constituted one contract. The form of the fishermen's agreement is agreed to each year by representatives of the salmon packers operating in Alaska, and the officials of the Alaska fishermen's union, and the form so agreed to becomes the uniform contract applicable to all canneries in Alaska.

Under the agreement, the seamen and fishermen were entitled to certain fixed sums known as "run money", as compensation for sailing the ship to and from Alaska, together with further allowances depending upon the number and kind of fish caught during the season.

These cases concern only wages claimed to be due seamen and fishermen, the monthly men and China crew not being involved.

When the vessel left Seattle with its cargo of cannery supplies, it was loaded down to the 24 foot draught. When about seven hundred miles outside of Cape Flattery, nearly one-half of the distance to Unimak Pass, the ship encountered a squall which lasted about twenty-four hours, on about April 18, 1919, and began to take water, and took water to the extent of nine or ten inches per hour. Some of the crew then became alarmed and demanded of the master that he return to Seattle. A petition was circulated aboard ship and signed by many members of the crew, and monthly men, and presented to the master, making this demand, but he declined to turn back, being of the opinion that he could as safely go forward to Unimak Pass as to put back an equal distance to ·Seattle; for, on reaching Unimak Pass he could, if necessary, put into Dutch Harbor. After this squall, the vessel proceeded to Bristol Bay, not finding it necessary to stop at Dutch Harbor. Upon the master's refusal to put back, the crew became insubordinate, and for a time refused to set sail as ordered. The ship arrived at Bristol Bay about May 8, 1919, and proceeded to discharge her cargo. Although the vessel had leaked considerably on the voyage, the cargo was not damaged by water. From the time she started to leak, about April 18, until she arrived in Bristol Bay, she continued to take in more or less water, but the power pumps were always adequate to take care of the water and it was never necessary to operate the hand pumps.

When the vessel was partly unloaded, the leak was discovered at about the 19-foot draught line, and it was found that several butts had opened up, probably caused by the storm, and thus caused the vessel to leak. A "butt" is a joint between the ends of two planks on the side of the ship. The planks are about eight inches wide, and the space between the ends of the two planks, about a quarter of an inch wide, is called a "butt" and is filled with oakum to make it water tight. The oakum had worked out of several of the butts. The unloading of the vessel had caused her to come up out of the water so that the leaking butts were exposed. When the vessel had been completely unloaded, appellant caused her to be overhauled and fitted for the return voyage, and, among other things, caused the leaking butts to be repaired.

When the crew arrived at Libbyville, they held a meeting and agreed among themselves that under no circumstances would they sail the ship on the return voyage, and so notified the superintendent of appellant's cannery. This determination was made by the crew before the vessel was unloaded and before it was known why she had leaked on the trip to Alaska.

After the vessel was repaired, appellant, on about July 8, caused her to be surveyed by three disinterested master mariners from other ships then in Bristol Bay, and as a result of their examination they pronounced the ship seaworthy and in all respects fit to make the return trip to Seattle.

On August 12, the ship was loaded and ready to make the return trip. The vessel did not have a full cargo for the return voyage, and as loaded for the return trip the butts which had leaked on the up trip were above water. The master then ordered the crew aboard for the return voyage, but because of the previous agreement among themselves, they refused to go aboard. The men were then assembled on shore, the master read to them the certificate made by the three master mariners, the roll of the crew was called, and each man individually asked to go aboard, and each individually refused to do so. In the meantime the general superintendent, Svenssen, of appellant, had arrived at Libbyville, and took charge of the situation. He had various consultations with the members of the crew endeavoring to get them to fulfill their contract, but without success. As a last resort he took steps to have the United States coast guard cutter "Unalga" sent to the scene of the trouble. Captain Dodge, commander of the "Unalga" was ordered by his superiors at Washington to go to Libbyville where he arrived with his vessel September 6. He immediately appointed a board of survey consisting of himself and three other officers of the ship. This board proceeded to survey the Coburn and, after a complete examination, pronounced her seaworthy and fit to make the voyage to Seattle. He then assembled the crew in a bunk house and informed them of the conclusions reached by himself and his officers, and endeavored to persuade them to make the return voyage, without success, the crew still persisting in their refusal to go aboard the vessel. On August 26, the fishermen's union headquarters at Seattle telegraphed to Selenius, "delegate" or representative of the crew, advising that the crew sail the vessel home because it had been certified to be seaworthy.

To induce them to go aboard Captain Dodge made various proposals to them. He offered to tow the Coburn to Unimak Pass and then convoy her the remainder of the way to Seattle, but the men refused to go aboard under these conditions. He offered to tow the Coburn all the way to Seattle if a sufficient number of her crew would go aboard to steer her on the trip down, which proposal was also refused. The men were at no time violent but simply stubbornly determined. That condition of affairs continued from September 6 to September 16, and by that time bad weather was approaching and it was necessary to do something to get the men out of the country. Finally Captain Dodge made an arrangement whereby he took the crew

aboard his own vessel, the "Unalga," and towed the
Coburn with the monthly men to Dutch Harbor, where
he arrived on September 17. The Coburn made the
voyage from Libbyville where she left on September
15, to Unalaska, Dutch Harbor, without any difficulty
whatever.

The seamen and fishermen were quartered on shore
at Dutch Harbor until October 12, when they were put
aboard a steamer, together with the China crew, and
sent to Seattle, appellant advancing the transportation
charges.

Shortly after the departure of the steamer with these
men aboard, the "Unalga" sailed from Dutch Harbor
leaving the Coburn there. Appellant failing in its efforts to procure a crew to sail the Coburn, was compelled to have her towed by steamer "Cordova" to
Seattle, where she arrived on November 12. The
master and monthly men made the trip on the Coburn
from Libbyville to Dutch Harbor, and thence to Seattle
and the vessel leaked but an inconsequential amount
on the trip down, and discharged her cargo at Seattle
without any damage. The proof shows that a wooden
vessel will leak more when being towed than when
being sailed.

During the trip from Libbyville to Dutch Harbor,
when the Coburn was towed by the "Unalga," a
distance of four hundred fifty miles, Lieutenant Anderson, a subordinate of Captain Dodge of the "Unalga"
was put aboard the Coburn to keep Captain Dodge informed of the conditions aboard the Coburn, and no
leaking or other trouble was reported to Captain
Dodge.

While at Libbyville and on September 12, Captain
Dodge made an agreement with the representatives of
the fishermen and beachmen whereby it was agreed that
safe transportation should be furnished the fishermen

and beachmen from Libbyville to Unalaska, and from
Unalaska to Seattle on a seaworthy vessel, excluding
the "Abner Coburn", and that all expenses were to be
paid by Libby, McNeill & Libby from the time the men
left Libbyville until they arrived at Seattle. This
agreement the men who represented the fishermen,
beachmen and others, testified was authorized by Captain Svenssen, the general superintendent of appellant,
and also declared by him to have been by and with
his authority, representing appellant. Captain Dodge
and Captain Svenssen, however, both testified that the
agreement was not authorized nor ratified by Captain
Svenssen, or the appellant. Captain Dodge testified
that it was made under the stress of the circumstances
existing at the time, because it was absolutely necessary that the men be gotten out of Libbyville and that
region at once or they could not be gotten out at all
during the winter, and would suffer great hardships
and privations. On the arrival of the Coburn in Seattle, this agreement was repudiated by appellant
whose officers insisted that the crew had violated their
agreement and that appellant would stand strictly
upon the contract between it and the men.

Prior to the sailing of the ship from Seattle, she was
surveyed by a representative of the San Francisco
board of marine underwriters, who was a master
mariner of over thirty years experience, and who
found her fit for the voyage, and issued a certificate
to that effect. After her return to Seattle from this
voyage she was again surveyed by the same representative of the underwriters, and found practically tight
and seaworthy and the cargo came out in good condition.

It is not necessary to set forth the contract between
appellant and the men in full, for it is exactly such a
contract as was held by this court in *Danielson v. Libby,*

McNeill & Libby, 114 Wash. 240, 195 Pac. 37, to come within the designation of "Seaman's Contract" and governed by maritime law.

Respondents assert that the "Abner Coburn" was not a merchant ship and therefore not governed by the laws applicable to merchant ships. They argue that "appellant has not advised the court whether it is claiming under the 'Harter Act' (Federal Statutes) or claiming simply for reasons that are historic. This expedition was not launched under any provisions of the laws of the United States. It was simply a private enterprise for private pursuits."

The "Harter Act" alluded to by respondents in no way applies to this matter. That act was an act of Congress of February 13, 1893; 27 Stat. L. 445. It provides that agreements added to bills of lading relieving the owner, etc., of a vessel sailing between the United States and foreign ports from liability for negligence in proper loading, stowage, custody, care or proper delivery of merchandise, are void. That no bill of lading shall contain any agreement whereby the obligations of the owner to exercise proper diligence, properly equip, man, provision, and outfit such vessel and to make such vessel seaworthy and capable of making the intended voyage, or to relieve the master, etc., of the vessel from carefully handling and stowing her cargo, and properly to care for and deliver the same; nor shall the vessel, her owner or owners, charterers or master be held liable for losses arising from dangers of the sea or other navigable waters, acts of God or public enemies, or the inherent defect, quality, or vice of the thing carried, or for insufficiency of package or seizure under legal process, or for any loss resulting from any act or omission of the shipper or owner of the goods.

It will thus be seen that the act applies only to liabilities and immunities of carriers to shippers of merchandise.

The "Abner Coburn" was not a ship of war, nor a police patrol vessel, nor a private pleasure yacht, but was engaged in domestic commerce between ports of the state of Washington, and noncontiguous territory and was therefore a merchantman.   .

"A ship or vessel employed in foreign or domestic commerce and in the merchant service is a merchantman." Black's Law Dictionary, 773.

The owner and master of the ship would have been subjected to penalties had they not complied with the shipping regulations provided by the United States statutes, title LIII, and the men were protected in their rights by those same statutes.

Moreover, it has become indisputably established that such a contract as the one before us is of a maritime character. In *Domenico v. Alaska Packers' Assn.*, 112 Fed. 554, a similar contract by men "to act as seamen on a voyage to and from the salmon fishing grounds in Alaska, to work as fishermen during the season, assist in canning the fish on shore, and loading them on board for transportation," is one maritime in its nature. The court there observed:

"It will be noticed that the principal subject of the contract upon the part of the libelants was for the rendition of services as fishermen at Pyramid Harbor, and included work in the cannery on shore, in preserving the fish caught by them, and also the labor of placing the fish on board the Two Brothers for transportation to San Francisco. The contract is, however, maritime in its nature. The fact that, while engaged in fishing at Pyramid Harbor, the libelants slept on shore and mended their nets and cared for the fish on shore, and that this was contemplated by the contract, does not make it any the less a maritime contract which a court of admiralty has jurisdiction to enforce."

This case was affirmed by the circuit court of appeals for the ninth circuit, in 117 Fed. 99. And the same kind of a contract in *North Alaska Salmon Company v. Larson*, 220 Fed. 93, 135 C. C. A. 661, was held to be a maritime contract. Benedict's Admiralty (4th ed.), § 143 was quoted to the effect that, "if a contract is maritime in itself it carries all its incidentals with it, and the latter, though nonmaritime in themselves will be heard and decided." The same rule was declared in *Union Fish Co. v. Erickson*, by the circuit court of appeals, ninth circuit, 235 Fed. 385, which was affirmed by the United States supreme court in the same case on certiorari, 248 U. S. 308, in which the principle was declared that, "those who pursue commerce and put to sea are subject to the maritime law."

The contract being maritime, these respondents and their assignors had a right, if they desired, to bring their suits in admiralty in a United States district court. But they had the alternative right to sue at common law in a common law court by virtue of the third subd. of § 24, of the United States judicial code, which provides that district courts of the United States shall have jurisdiction of admiralty or maritime actions, "saving to suitors in all cases the right of a common law remedy where the common law is competent to give it." But it is well established that although the respondents had the right to sue in admiralty, and had an alternative right to sue in common law actions in the state courts, their reciprocal rights, duties and obligations are governed by the rules and principles of admiralty law. *The Osceola*, 189 U. S. 158; *Chelentis v. Luckenbach S. S. Co.*, 243 Fed. 536. In the last case, in the opinion of the circuit court of appeals, it was declared:

"The contract of a seaman is maritime and has written into it those peculiar features of the maritime law that were considered in the case of *The Osceola,* supra; and although because of these peculiarities such contracts are almost invariably litigated in admiralty courts, still the contract must be the same in every court, maritime or common law."

In reviewing the decision of the circuit court of appeals in the above case, the opinion of the supreme court of the United States, 247 U. S. at p. 384, stated:

"The distinction between the rights and remedies is fundamental. A right is a well founded or acknowledged claim; a remedy is the means employed to enforce a right or redress an injury. Bouvier's Law Dictionary. Plainly, we think, under the saving clause a right sanctioned by the maritime law may be enforced through any appropriate remedy recognized at common law; but we find nothing therein which reveals an intention to give the complaining party an election to determine whether the defendant's liability shall be measured by common law standards rather than those of the maritime law. Under the circumstances here presented, without regard to the court where he might ask relief, petitioner's rights were those recognized by the law of the sea."

In *Knickerbocker Ice Co. v. Stewart,* 253 U. S. 149, the supreme court of the United States cites and quotes the above cited cases, and others, quoting the *Erickson* case in 248 U. S. 308, to the effect that,

"In entering into this contract the parties contemplated no service in California. They were making an engagement for the services of the master of the vessel, the duties to be performed in the waters of Alaska, mainly upon the sea. The maritime law controlled in this respect, and was not subject to limitation because the particular engagement happened to be made in California. The parties must be presumed to have had in contemplation the system of maritime law under which it was made."

And in the case last cited, the supreme court further said:

"As the plain result of these recent opinions and the earlier cases upon which they are based, we accept the following doctrine: The Constitution itself adopted and established, as part of the laws of the United States, approved rules of the general maritime law, and empowered Congress to legislate in respect of them and other matters within the admiralty and maritime jurisdiction. Moreover, it took from the states all power, by legislation or judicial decision, to contravene the essential purposes of, or to work material injury to, characteristic features of such law or to interfere with its proper harmony and uniformity in its international and interstate relations. To preserve adequate harmony and appropriate uniform rules relating to maritime matters and bring them within control of the federal government was the fundamental purpose; and to such definite end Congress was empowered to legislate within that sphere."

Appellant, upon those terms, contends that, as a matter of law, the crew had no right to set up their judgment as against the judgment of the master confirmed as it was by disinterested independent surveys. That the contentions of the crew were purely obstinate, unreasonable and not in good faith, to the effect that the ship was not seaworthy for the return voyage, and that, agitated by their constituted agent or agents, they entered into the ill-advised agreement, not, under any circumstances, to return on the "Abner Coburn" regardless of its real condition, regardless of any surveys and certificates as to the seaworthiness of the vessel, and stubbornly adhered to it as a body, and therefore became deserters.

On the other hand, respondents contend that the seaworthiness of the vessel was a fact to be determined by the jury as any other fact, and that the evidence justifies the verdict of the jury that the vessel was

not seaworthy, and therefore justified the men in discharging themselves at Libbyville, Alaska, and refusing
to return on her, and that furthermore, under their
contract the men had a perfect right to quit the employ
of the company at any time, referring to subdivision
"f" of § 12 of the supplemental contract between the
men and appellant.

Subdivision "f" of § 12 of the supplemental contract
is as follows:

"(f) A fisherman refusing to go fishing or work
otherwise shall be considered as having quit the employment of the company, and shall be paid in accordance with § 18, and the company released from all
further obligations to him."

Section 18 is as follows, so far as here material:

"(b) Any man who is discharged, or who quits
shall be paid only half run money and all his other
earnings, including for the day of discharge or quitting.
If no substitutes are hired to take the place of a quitting or discharged man, the run money so deducted
shall be equally divided among all the men of the cannery signing this contract.

"(c) Men discharged shall be given free transportation to home port, including maintenance, but
this obligation shall not apply to men quitting."

We cannot perceive how the above quoted portions
of the contract in any way justify the men. They had,
under this contract, no right to quit as a body by col-
luding and combining together in order to bring about
the abandonment of the ship or the enterprise on which
the ship was engaged, and if they quit singly, and
without cause, they had no right to more than one-half
the "run-money" or remaining compensation, nor to
transportation back to Seattle, under the provisions of
the contract.

Being governed by maritime law, as before seen, the
men have no right to conspire together to abandon the

ship and its enterprise before the voyage is completed. They signed up for the voyage from Seattle to Libbyville, and any other ports in Alaska which the master might see fit to touch, and for the salmon fishing season of 1919, and to return by the same ship, and man the ship from Libbyville to Seattle, at the end of the season. Thus, the duration of the voyage was fixed by the contract. When the ship landed at Libbyville, the voyage was not complete. Shore duties were then required of some of the crew, and when the fishing season was completed, sea duties were again required of them to return the ship to Seattle. Although the ship may have appeared to them to be in a dangerous condition on the first half of the voyage, that from Seattle to Libbyville, its safe arrival at Libbyville proved that the fears of the crew were unfounded. It is almost indisputably established that the ship was put in a seaworthy condition for the return trip, if it had ever been in an unseaworthy condition, and the master and the monthly men risked their lives upon the ship for the return trip to Seattle, although under tow because of not having a crew to handle it (which method of handling would have made it leak more than if sailed by the crew), and arrived in Seattle, with the cargo, safely.

In the *C. F. Sargent,* 95 Fed. 179, the crew had shipped as seamen for a voyage from Tacoma to Honolulu and thence to San Francisco, before their final discharge, either direct or by way of one or more ports on the Pacific Coast. Proceeding from Tacoma to Honolulu, where the cargo was discharged, the vessel returned in ballast from Honolulu to Seattle where a cargo was taken on for San Francisco. After the cargo was loaded at Seattle the crew left the vessel, claiming that she leaked and was unseaworthy. They then libeled the ship for their wages. The evidence showed that the vessel was in a leaky condition on the trip from Tacoma to Honolulu, and that it was necessary for the crew to perform considerable labor in manning the pumps, but she reached Honolulu in safety, and on the return voyage to Seattle, when light, she took in but little water. At Seattle the leak was located and repaired and a certificate of seaworthiness was given by the agent of the underwriters. The United States district court, sitting in admiralty, said:

"Under the circumstances shown by the uncontradicted evidence, the seamen were not authorized to determine the question as to the seaworthiness of the ship, and they cannot be relieved from their obligations to perform their contract under the shipping articles which they have signed, on the ground of unseaworthiness. If they in good faith believed that it was unsafe for the ship to go to sea, they might have demanded a survey, which, if fairly made by competent persons, would be treated by the court as conclusive for the purpose of determining whether the men should or should not be discharged before completion of the voyage."

It will be observed that the above case holds that, on the question of the seaworthiness of the ship, the men should not be relieved from their obligations to perform their contract on the ground of unseaworthiness unless they demanded a survey, and that if the survey was fairly made, by competent persons, it would be treated by the court as *conclusive* for the purpose of determining whether the men should or should not be discharged before the completion of the voyage. In this case the men did not demand a survey; but two surveys, which appear to be fair, and made by entirely disinterested and competent persons, were made, as to the seaworthiness of the Coburn, and the results thereof made known to the men, who refused to be bound by them.

In *The Condor*, 196 Fed. 71, the district court said:

"A judge should, of course, be careful not so to construe the law as to force the crew to risk their lives on an unseaworthy ship; but, on the other hand, if they may finally choose, without subsequent question, to regard any injury to the ship as absolving them from further service, the condition of their master will be quite helpless. Here they probably knew the actual fact that no crew could be got nearer than Valparaiso. The situation was not, so far as I can see, that of a crew harshly held to a bargain now become dangerous, but of one, not sincerely afraid, but attempting to exploit the necessities of their master. If so, it is surely a very dangerous practice to encourage, and one which directly promotes insubordination and mutiny. Discipline on the sea is not like that on the land in ordinary industrial employments. The relations between master and man requires an authority which is not necessary when both parties have immediate recourse to constituted authority. No doubt countless misery and brutality has arisen from the exercise of master's authority; but the substance of that authority still remains in civilized countries, and must remain if men are to put to sea for weeks, out of reach of the usual methods of keeping order.

"So long as a master does what he can to obtain impartial outside opinion, acts within reasonable bounds of a fair judgment, and trusts his life upon the venture equally with his men's, his decision must control as to whether the voyage shall break up, and the whole ship's company is bound by it. To hold otherwise is to imperil his authority and the whole safety of ships and those upon them."

Under § 8345 (title LIII) United States Compiled Statutes, 1918, it is provided that first and second officers under the master, or a majority of the crew of any vessel bound on any voyage shall, before the vessel shall have left the harbor, if it is discovered that the vessel has a leak or is otherwise unfit in her crew, body, tackle, apparel, furnishings, provisions or stores, to

proceed on the intended voyage, require such unfitness
to be inquired into, the master, upon request of the first
and second officer under the master, or such majority of
the crew, forthwith apply to the judge of the district
court of that judicial district, if he shall there reside,
or, if not, of some justice of the peace of the city, town
or place, for the appointment of surveyors, taking
with him two or more of the crew who shall have made
such request, and providing a penalty for failure to
comply with such demand; and § 8346 *supra,* provides
that the judge or justice in the domestic port shall
upon such application of the master or commander,
issue a precept directed to three persons in the neighborhood, the most experienced and skillful in maritime
affairs that can be procured, to make a survey of the
matters complained of. Section 8347, *supra,* provides
that if, "after judgment that such vessel is fit to proceed on her intended voyage, . . . the seamen,
or either of them, shall refuse to proceed on the voyage
he shall forfeit all wages that may be due him."

It is not in the record whether or not there was any
judge of the United States district court or any justice
of the peace of a city, town or place, residing at Libbyville where the ship was in harbor. At any rate, a
majority of the crew, as provided by statute, never demanded any survey by competent and disinterested
persons in that harbor. The surveys procured by appellant were undoubtedly disinterested and competent,
fairly made, and procured in good faith by appellant,
from humanitarian as well as legal motives. Such
being the case, when the men in a body refused to return to the ship and actually abandoned and deserted
her, they must either be held to a strict performance
of the contract, or they are amenable to the statute applying in such cases which makes them deserters, reading as follows:

"Whenever any seaman who has been lawfully engaged or any apprentice to the sea service commits any of the following offenses he shall be punished as follows:

"First: for desertion by forfeiture of all or any part of his earnings, board and clothes, and of all or any part of the wages, or emoluments which he has then earned."

Desertion by a seaman in law consists in quitting the ship and her service without leave and without justifiable cause, and with intent not to return to his duty. *The Mary C. Conery*, 9 Fed. 222; *The William H. Clifford*, 165 Fed. 59. And by general martime law as well as by statutes desertion is followed by forfeiture of all wages earned. *The Mary C. Conery, supra;* the *C. F. Sargent*, 95 Fed. 179.

"And a deserting seaman is not even entitled to recover upon a *quantum meruit* for services rendered in part performance of his contract." *The Liederhorn*, 99 Fed. 1001 (syllabus).

Upon the above stated facts and the foregoing principles of maritime law, appellant requested that the verdict of the jury be directed in favor of appellant, which was refused.

Upon the submission of the case to the jury, the trial court instructed the jury as follows:

"If seamen find that the vessel is unseaworthy and they have reason to believe that she is so unseaworthy as to endanger their lives at sea, and they in good faith do so believe, they may lawfully refuse to go to sea on her. Both law and reason require that a vessel shall be seaworthy before seamen are bound to go aboard her, and navigate her at sea. If you believe from a preponderance of the evidence that when the Coburn was prepared for the return trip to Seattle she was in such condition that ordinarily prudent seamen had reason to apprehend imminent danger; that she could not be navigated upon the sea without danger to the lives of the men, and that the seamen did so believe in good faith, and had reasonable grounds for their belief, then they would be justified in refusing to sail the vessel to Seattle, and they would be entitled to receive the compensation to which they were entitled upon their certificates when adjusted and settled."

The above instruction entirely disregards the uncontradicted evidence, that while the vessel had leaked on the voyage up she had been repaired, and had been surveyed by disinterested and competent master mariners, and found to be seaworthy for the return trip, and was obviously not in the same condition as she was in on the trip up after the storm of April 18, and that the seamen had not complied with the law of the sea that they should demand a competent survey of the vessel as to seaworthiness, and that they had obdurately, in the face of all the facts as to the seaworthiness of the ship for her return trip, refused to return in her, thereby evidencing not good faith, but bad faith and unreasonableness. On the contrary, under the laws of the sea, or maritime law, the jury should have been instructed, if the case was submitted to the jury at all, as requested by appellant:

"Seamen are not authorized to determine for themselves the question of the seaworthiness of their ship. If they in good faith believe the ship is unfit to go to sea, they may, before leaving the harbor, demand a survey and if that survey is fairly made, by competent persons, such survey must be treated as conclusive for the purpose of determining whether the seamen should or should not proceed on the voyage."

And the jury should further have been instructed, if the case were submitted to it, that,

"If the crew, notwithstanding the opinion of the master that the ship was in fact seaworthy, had reasonable grounds to believe the contrary, the master was not compelled to do more than to do what he could under the circumstances to obtain an impartial survey by other competent persons, and if, when the dispute arose between the master of the 'Abner Coburn' and her crew as to the seaworthiness of the vessel, the master did do what he could to obtain an impartial survey by other competent masters, and that such other competent masters pronounced the ship seaworthy, such survey became binding and conclusive upon the crew, and if the crew then persisted in refusing to go aboard the ship in obedience to the master's orders, they became deserters and subjected themselves to the forfeitures provided by law for cases of desertion.''

But we are convinced, under the law and the facts governing this case, that the crew of the Coburn wilfully and unreasonably acted upon their own opinion as to the seaworthiness of the vessel to make the return trip to Seattle; refused to be governed by the disinterested and ·independent surveys made by competent master mariners;.refused to go aboard the ship in response to the master's order; demanded no survey by impartial persons competent to make such survey, and wilfully refused to make the return voyage to Seattle without just cause or reason; and under such circumstances they became deserters. Such being the case they forfeited their wages and all emoluments then earned.

Respondents contend, however, that appellants are bound by the fact that they issued to the men labor certificates in Alaska, before the men returned, for the amount of the wages which would become due them for the voyage, and having sued on these certificates, the company is estopped to deny their right of recovery. These labor certificates were issued by the company's officers and agents in Alaska, stating the amounts which would become due the men if the contract were fulfilled, and that they were issued under protest as having been coerced from the company's officers and agents by the conduct of the men in Alaska. This contention is undoubtedly borne out by the testimony of the company's officers and agents, and Captain Dodge of the United States coast guard cutter "Unalga," and all the circumstances surrounding the transaction. A somewhat similar situation existed in *Domenico v. Alaska Packers Ass'n.*, 112 Fed. 554, cited in this opinion, upon other matters, wherein the libelants undertook to show that certain apparatus provided by the respondent were defective, and on that account they demanded increased wages. Sustaining the contention of the libelants the court held that:

"Where a person who has bound himself by contract to render services refuses to do so unless paid more than the contract price, the parties may enter into a new contract by which an increase in compensation is to be paid for the same service, and in such case the subsequent performance of the contract by the promisee is sufficient consideration for the new agreement, and where persons who have contracted to render services refuse without lawful excuse to perform the same unless paid a greater compensation, the employer has his election to sue for damages for breach of the contract, or to enter into a new and substituted contract for the payment of the compensation demanded; and the fact that the former remedy is worthless because the employees are not able to respond in damages, and the employer is induced thereby, and to save himself from greater loss, to yield to the demands of the employees and agree to pay a higher compensation for the same service does not constitute duress which will render the new contract invalid."

But on appeal to the circuit court of appeals for the ninth circuit, that court, in 117 Fed. 99, disagreed with the district court, saying:

"After having entered upon the discharge of their contract and at a time when it was impossible to secure other men in their places, the libelants, without any

valid cause, absolutely refused to continue the services
they were under contract to perform, unless the appellant would consent to pay them more money. Consent
to such demand under such circumstances, if given,
was, in our opinion, without consideration, for the
reason that it was based solely upon the libelants'
agreement to render the exact services and none other,
that they were already under contract to render
(italics ours). The case shows that they willfully and
arbitrarily broke that obligation. As a matter of
course they are liable to the appellant in damages, and
it is quite probable, as suggested by the court below in
its opinion, that they may have been unable to respond
in damages. . . . . Certainly it cannot be justly
held upon the record in this case that there was any
voluntary waiver on the part of the appellant of the
breach of the original contract.''

King v. Railway Co., 61 Minn. 482, 63 N.W. 1105, is
cited and quoted as follows:

''No astute reasoning can change the plain fact that
the party who refuses to perform, and thereby coerces
a promise from the other party to the contract to pay
him an increased compensation for doing that which
he is legally bound to do, takes an unjustifiable advantage of the necessities of the other party. Surely
it would be a travesty on justice to hold that the party
so making the promise for extra pay was estopped from
asserting that the promise was without consideration. A
party cannot lay the foundation of an estoppel by his
own wrong, where the promise is simply a repetition
of a subsisting legal promise. There can be no consideration for the promise of the other party, and there
is no warrant for inferring that the parties have voluntarily rescinded or modified their contract. The
promise cannot be legally enforced, although the other
party has completed his contract in reliance upon it.''

The opinion also cites and quotes from *Lingenfelder
v. Wainwright Brewing Co.*, 103 Mo. 578, 23 Am. St.
900, to the same effect, and distinguishes and rejects a
number of cases cited counter thereto and cites a num-

ber of cases to sustain the holding of the circuit court
of appeals in the case quoted.

We are of the opinion that the reasoning and decision in the above case by the circuit court of appeals
are controlling in this analogous situation.

Here, the men deserted and abandoned the ship and
its enterprise in a body, at a remote point where other
men could not be obtained to continue the enterprise
and voyage, and where, from humanitarian motives
alone, it was absolutely impossible to evade the duty
of returning the men from that region to the initial
port; and because they unanimously abandoned and
deserted the ship and refused all efforts to persuade
them to perform their duty and fulfill their contract,
they compelled the appellant to give them certificates
of labor performed while in Alaska or on the voyage
thereto, and to furnish them maintenance and transportation out of that region; all of which constituted
duress of the most forceable kind, and gives no validity
to the labor certificates issued in Alaska, or to recovery
upon the original contract wilfully forfeited and
abandoned by the men themselves.

Therefore, although mindful that we "should be
careful not to so construe the law as to force a crew to
risk their lives on an unseaworthy ship," we are convinced by the record in this case, and the law applying,
that appellant did everything in its power to humanely
care for these men, and paid out a great deal of money
in excess of their contract pay, on account of their unreasonable, obstinate and arbitrary conduct, and that
the men forfeited and are not entitled to recover their
wages. The jury should have been instructed to render
a verdict for appellant.

The judgments are reversed and the cases dismissed.

Parker, C. J., Tolman, Main, Mackintosh, Bridges,
and Mitchell, JJ., concur.

FULLERTON, J. (dissenting)—This is an action brought by the respondents, who were plaintiffs below, to recover upon a written contract for services performed. The cause was tried in the court of its origin by a jury, who found that the plaintiffs and their assignors had earned under the contract sums aggregating $25,613.76, and judgment was entered in their favor for these sums. This court, in the foregoing opinion, does not question the finding of the jury as to the amount earned by the plaintiffs under the contract, but finds, contrary to the finding of the jury, that there was a breach of the contract, and as matter of law concludes that because of the breach there has been a forfeiture of the sums earned, and directs that there be no recovery. The sum stated represents practically a year's earnings of nearly one hundred men, and the effect of the holding is to take from them this considerable sum and vest it in the defendant, their employer. I can but believe the result is due to the application of erroneous principles of law, and I feel justified, because of the importance of the case to the plaintiffs, in stating, although somewhat at length, the grounds for my belief.

In the first place, I think the majority have placed a construction upon the contract that it cannot legally bear. It is held that the contract is one and entire, that it is in its effect the same contract that a seaman enters into when he binds himself to a vessel to serve as a seaman thereon for a stated period, or for a given voyage, and that the same rigorous rules are applicable thereto that are applicable to the ordinary seaman's contract. With this I cannot agree. As shown by the opinion, the contract consisted of two parts, the one entirely separable and distinct from the other. The first part consisted of ordinary shipping articles by

which the plaintiffs agreed to act as seamen in sailing
the vessel, "Abner Coburn," from the port of Seattle in
the state of Washington to the defendant's cannery, on
Behring Sea, in the territory of Alaska, and to act as
seamen in sailing the vessel on its return voyage at a
later period. In the second part of the contract, they
agreed to catch salmon for the defendant in the waters
adjacent to the cannery during the period of the salmon
run. For the performance of the first part of the contract, they were each to receive certain stated and
definite sums, measured by the capacity in which they
acted; and for the performance of the second part,
they were to be paid a price for the number of fish
caught and delivered, the price varying according to
the variety of the fish.

The first part of the agreement may be essentially
maritime in its nature, and it may be that the ordinary
shipping articles were necessary to be entered into
before its performance was entered upon. But it is
clear to my mind that the second part of the agreement
was in no sense maritime as that term is understood in
admiralty. No shipping articles were necessary to be
entered into by any one as a condition precedent to its
performance. In fact, the present record shows that a
number of persons engaged in fishing along with the
plaintiffs who did not and who were not asked to sign
the shipping articles. But more than this, the business from its nature cannot be maritime. In a maritime contract the person agrees to serve as a seaman
on a vessel engaged in commerce as a common carrier
for a given period of time or for a given voyage. In the
other, the work is not performed on a common carrier.
The fishing is done in small boats operated by the fishermen themselves; the boat engages in no form of
trade, and the work involves no element of public interest, but is purely of a private nature. It seems to

me to follow conclusively from these differences that
the breach of one part of the contract cannot be a
breach of the other, and if the majority are correct in
holding that there was a breach of the contract to navigate the vessel, and that because of the breach the
plaintiffs have forfeited their right to the compensation agreed to be paid for that service, they are in
error in holding that the breach operates as a forfeiture of their earnings under the second part of the
contract.

The cases cited by the majority, as I read them, do
not sustain the contrary conclusion. In none of them
was the particular question raised or discussed. The
cases are, for the most part, all instances where the
plaintiffs, suing on the contracts, brought their suits in
the admiralty courts, and where objection was made to
the jurisdiction of the court because the contracts were
not maritime in character. The jurisdiction was sustained on the theory that a contract, maritime in part,
carries its incidentals with it, and the latter though
non-maritime will be heard and decided. It was not,
however, decided in any of the cases that the rules
applicable to the maritime part of the contract will be
applied in determining the issues not maritime, much
less was it decided that a breach of the maritime part
of the contract, although sufficient to work a forfeiture
of wages earned thereunder, would work a forfeiture
of the earnings under that part of the contract essentially non-maritime.

In the next place, I think the majority have given an
unwarranted effect to the so-called surveys made of the
vessel while it was at anchor at the cannery in Behring
Sea. It is true that the Federal statute provides for a
survey of a vessel when a majority of the crew may
deem it unseaworthy for any cause, and further provides that if upon such a survey the vessel is pro-

nounced seaworthy any seaman who refuses to proceed
on the voyage shall forfeit all wages that may be due
him. But the statute also provides the manner of
selecting the surveyors, and enough appears in the
majority opinion to show that the statute was not in
· this respect even substantially pursued. The survey
therefore had no official sanction. Legally, the findings
of the surveyors were nothing more than the expressed
opinions of private individuals. I am aware that the
majority say that these surveys "were undoubtedly
disinterested and competent, fairly made and procured
in good faith by the" defendant; but, conceding that
the evidence justified the statement, I am unable to
understand just what it signifies. The defendant is
claiming the right in virtue of a statute to forfeit to
itself a large sum of money which belongs to the plaintiffs, and certainly it is no hardship to say that, before
it is permitted to do so, it show a strict compliance with
the statute. Forfeitures are never favored. It is only
where the inflexible rules of law will permit of no other
course that they will be granted. Here, I may repeat,
there was no compliance nor attempted compliance
with the statute. Since the right of forfeiture, in so
far as this branch of the case is involved, depends upon
the statute, I can but think the majority in error in
holding that the surveys justify an adjudication of forfeiture.

And here I may properly notice the further holding
that seamen are not authorized to determine for themselves the question of the seaworthiness of their ship.
This is not an absolute rule. Its application depends
upon circumstances. If the vessel is in a port where
the ordinary processes of government are functioning,
seamen who believe the vessel in which they are required to sail is unseaworthy, are by statute required
to demand a survey, and if the survey is made in ac-

cordance with the terms of the statute, the seamen are
concluded by it. But the rule has no application to
conditions such as were here shown. The vessel was
on a bleak, uninhabited coast, hundreds of miles from
any place where organized form of government existed.
Contrary to the statement in the majority opinion, the
record does show that there was no judge of the United
States district court, or justice of the peace residing at
Libbyville to whom application for a survey could be
made. One of the defendant's own witnesses expressly
testifies that there were no others at the cannery except
the cannery people. By the terms of the statute, the
officers named are the only persons authorized to appoint surveyors. To apply for a survey would have
been a useless procedure on the part of the seamen, and
seamen, no more than any other class of persons, are
required to do useless things in order to preserve their
rights. Their rights, therefore, to determine the seaworthiness of the vessel stood as they did stand prior
to the enactment of the statute, and what these rights
were is stated by Judge Curtis in *United States v. Nye*,
Fed. Cas. No. 15,906, in the following language:

"I think the correct rule is, that after the men have
rendered themselves on board, pursuant to their contract, and before the voyage is begun, they may lawfully refuse to go to sea in the vessel, if they have
reasonable cause to believe and do believe the vessel to
be unseaworthy. But the presumption is that the
vessel was seaworthy; and the seamen must prove that
they acted in good faith and upon reasonable grounds
of belief that the ship was not in a fit condition to go
to sea by reason of unseaworthiness. If they prove
this, they are justified in their refusal."

Again, I am unable to agree with the majority in the
assumption that the facts of the case are before us for
decision. These facts are important. For example, it
is found on conflicting testimony that the agreement

made at the cannery after the close of the work to transport the crew from the cannery to Unalaska, and from Unalaska to Seattle on a seaworthy vessel at the expense of the defendant, was not authorized by the defendant or any of its authorized agents; it is found on conflicting testimony that the seamen wrongfully conspired together for the purpose of bringing about an abandonment of the ship, or the enterprise on which the ship was engaged; it is found on conflicting testimony that the ship, by the repairs made upon it by the carpenter while at the cannery placed the vessel in a seaworthy condition; it is found on conflicting testimony that the labor certificates, showing the amount of the earnings, were issued under coercion; and finally it is found that the plaintiffs deserted and abandoned the ship at a remote point where other men could not be obtained, and that because of these and other facts, the men became deserters.

In my opinion these were facts which this court is without power to determine on conflicting testimony; that they were questions for the jury in the court below, and that their findings on them are conclusive upon this court. As stated in the majority opinion, the United States judicial code does not give exclusive jurisdiction to the admiralty courts in maritime causes. The act saves "to suitors in all cases the right of a common law remedy where the common law is competent to give it." There is no question here that the common law can give the remedy. If this were not true this court should dismiss the action for want of jurisdiction, not reverse it and direct a judgment for the defendant. Since the act saves to suitors the common law remedy, it saves to them the remedy as it is usually administered at common law. One of the oldest of these remedies is to have the facts of the controversy determined by a jury, and I can conceive of no reason,

certainly none is stated by the majority, why the plaintiffs did not have the same right in this cause as they
would have in any other cause triable in a common law
court, to have the facts of the cause determined by a
jury. The conclusion reached by the majority on the
question is, moreover, contrary to our holdings in the
cases of *Larson v. Alaska Steamship Co.*, 96 Wash.
665, 165 Pac. 880, L. R. A. 1917F 671, and *Sandanger v.
Carlisle Packing Co.*, 112 Wash. 480, 192 Pac. 1005.
These were actions for personal injuries suffered by
seamen, due to defects in the equipment of the vessels
on which they were sailing. One of the questions submitted in each of the cases was whether the remedy of
admiralty or the remedy of the common law should be
applied. The court held in each case, "that the common law courts of a state have jurisdiction concurrent
with the Federal courts when proceeding *in personam,*
and that the state court will grant the relief that a
common law court would have granted had the case
been originally triable in such court," and applied the
remedy of the common law, although the remedy dif-
fered from that afforded in admiralty. The majority
do not notice these cases, but I can see no way in
which they can be reconciled with the rule now announced, namely, that the saving clause in the statute
confers only "an alternative right to sue in common
law actions in the state courts," and "that the reciprocal rights, duties and obligations of the parties are
governed by the rules and principles of admiralty
law."

As I have before indicated, the ultimate question for
the determination of the jury was whether or not the
plaintiffs had reasonable cause to believe that the vessel was unseaworthy at the time they refused to return
upon her. This issue they found in favor of the plain-

tiffs, and in my opinion, there was abundant evidence
in the record to justify the finding. The vessel was
old, having been built in the year 1882. She was acquired by the defendant in 1913. Prior to that time
she was commissioned as a merchant vessel, although
for a year previous she had lain inactive in the harbor
of San Francisco. After the defendant acquired her,
she was not used in the merchant service, but was used
solely for carrying supplies and fishermen to the different canneries operated by the defendant, making but a
single trip each year. In 1917, while being sailed to a
cannery, she sprang a leak in the first gale encountered,
and was brought back, temporarily repaired, and taken
to the cannery in tow. In 1918, she encountered ice on
her trip, and the evidence of the carpenter is that on
this occasion she received severe strains. On the trip
here concerned she also sprang a leak at the first gale
encountered. This leak was, to my mind, much more
serious than the majority seem to consider it. Water
poured into the hold of the vessel in sufficient quantities to cause it to rise therein at the rate of ten inches
an hour. The vessel was over three hundred feet in
length, with a beam of thirty-eight feet, and it requires
no very intricate mathematical calculation to show that
the quantity was considerable. It was sufficient at any
rate to thoroughly frighten the crew. Many of these
were men who, in their earlier years, had followed the
sea, and men who would know a dangerous leak in a
vessel as well as would any other person. No ordinary
leak would cause them concern, and the fact that they
were alarmed is in itself evidence that the leak was
unusual and dangerous.

I think, too, that the evidence fairly shows that the
leak was sufficiently alarming to cause the master of
the vessel concern, despite his subsequent contrary
assertions. In his radiograms sent to the owners at

the time, he mentioned not only the fact that the vessel
was leaking, but the rate per hour of the leak, and
asked for instructions. Manifestly, if he had regarded
it as nothing but the usual and expected, it would not
have occurred to him to mention the fact. It is true
that the pumps took care of the water during the remainder of the voyage, but to do this they were kept
in operation continuously. Moreover, the journey was
made in fair weather. What would have happened had
another gale been encountered can only be conjectured.
I am aware that it is said in the majority opinion, as
an argument that the leak was not dangerous, that "the
power pumps were always adequate to take care of the
water and it was never necessary to use the hand
pumps." But I can find nothing in the evidence that
indicates that the vessel had hand pumps, except as
these pumps might be so called. The captain's testimony concerning the pumps was that the vessel had
no pumps other than the power pumps, but that these
were so arranged that they could be used as hand
pumps, if the power failed.

I cannot but feel, also, that the majority have mini-
mized the condition the vessel was found to be in after
she had reached her destination and was unloaded.
The carpenter testifies that he found two open butts on
the port side of the vessel, and an open seam and an
open butt on the starboard side. These he remedied
by recaulking. But he testifies that the most trouble-
some condition of the vessel arose from an injury to
the parts surrounding the rudder post. His description of the affected parts is given in terms too nautical
to convey to my mind any very definite idea as to what
the parts were, but it can be gathered from his testimony that on some such part the fastenings had given
way leaving the rudder post loose; that the loosened
parts would open as strain was put upon the rudder,

letting water enter into the hold of the vessel. These defects he could remedy only partially. The loosed parts of the vessel he could not refasten; the best he could do was to fill the openings with oakum and hold it in place by tacking over it sheet lead, which would only partially stop the leak.

When the vessel returned to Seattle, even Lloyds surveyor became alarmed at her condition and insisted that she be overhauled. In this work it was found that some of the heavy timbers forming the keelson had become so far decayed that an ordinary chisel could be driven by hand through pieces 14 by 14 inches in size. In making the repairs it was found necessary to remove these decayed pieces and install new timbers in their place and to further strengthen the keelson by fastening thereto additional heavy timbers running for the full length of the vessel. The vessel was further strengthened by the insertion of two new deck beams with knees, and by the insertion of "two big iron rods", with turn buckles, running from stem to stern directly beneath the main deck.

What was learned as to the condition of the vessel when she was overhauled could not, of course, be known to the men at the time they refused to return on the vessel. The boat's behavior, however, was such as to indicate with unerring certainty its real defect. It was shown that the rigging of the vessel stood staunch and tight before loading and immediately thereafter became slack. This was explained to mean that the load had caused the keel to bend downward at the middle of the vessel which resulted in the cupping of the top of the vessel, and thus a shortening of the distance between the fastenings of the stay lines of the rigging. The converse of the proposition would also be true. A bending in the other direction, which could well happen when the vessel was riding a storm, would cause the vessel to spread at the top, which would account for the parting of the butts and the opening of the seams on the planking of the vessel's sides. Clearly, these conditions rendered the boat unsafe for these turbulent northern seas, where gales and storms are the rule rather than the exception at the season of the year the boat was required to return. But it is said the boat returned in safety. So it did. But it was loaded with cargo only to its sixteen foot draft line. Had it carried these three hundred and more men in addition to its cargo it would have been subjected to different tests. It came down in tow, and it is noticeable that the course of the tow followed the coast line on its journey, although a direct course would have been several hundred miles shorter. The vessel also gave evidence of its inherent weakness on its return journey, even with its light load. At one point it encountered the "tail end" of a storm, and immediately began to leak, taking some eight inches of water in twenty-four hours' time.

I can but feel, also, that the majority have unduly censured the conduct of the men. In spite of the seeming inference to the contrary in the majority opinion, there was no unseemly behavior among them at any time. The captain of the boat is witness to this, and both the agent of the defendant and the chief officer of the revenue cutter testify that there was no disorder while the men were on shore at the cannery. Stress is laid on the fact that the men held a meeting immediately after landing at the cannery and announced that they would not return on the vessel before the cause of the leak was discovered. But the men then knew the history of the vessel, knew that it developed a weakness whenever it encountered a storm, and the fact that they gave the notice thus early is to my mind evidence of good conduct and good faith on their part rather

than an indication of concert and design to injure the
defendant wilfully; it gave the defendant notice in
ample time to meet the emergency. The defendant, it
is true, gave no heed to the notice, possibly under the
belief that the exigency of the situation at the close of
the fishing season would cause the men to return in the
vessel despite their belief of its unseaworthiness. And
it was because it gave no heed to the notice that it was
later obliged to call to its aid the revenue cutter. But
even the officer of that vessel, as I have said, testifies to
the good behavior of the men, and testifies, though perhaps unwittingly, to facts which show their good faith.
After he had completed his so-called survey and had
determined to his own satisfaction that the vessel was
seaworthy, he called on the men to sail her home in accordance with their agreement. They refused.   He
then caused certain sections of the United States Revised Statutes to be read to them, and informed them
that they were in danger of losing their earnings if
they did not obey. They answered that danger of loss
of earnings was nothing when compared to danger of
loss of life. He then informed them that it was within
his power to arrest them as vagrants and to cause their
conviction as such in the Alaska courts. They answered that breaking rocks on Alaska roads was pre-
ferable to a watery grave. It is in evidence also that
certain of the men, believing that there was no other
alternative than a return on the vessel, traveled on foot
for many miles on that barren coast to a point where
they could take passage home on another vessel.

It seems to me that there was here sufficient evidence
to warrant even the court in finding that the vessel
was in fact unseaworthy, that the men acted in good
faith and within their just rights in refusing to return
on the vessel, and that they were in no sense deserters.
But if I am wrong in this conclusion, I think the judg-

ment directed by the majority erroneous for another reason. If it be a fact that the vessel was seaworthy, and the men were wrong in their belief that it was not, they should be held to be constructive rather than wilful deserters, and under such a holding no principle of law or justice requires that their entire earnings be forfeited. At most they should be held to make good only the actual and necessary loss their mistake caused the defendant.

The defendant's actual outlay in towing the vessel on its return voyage and transporting the men home, as set forth in its answer, is less than $17,500. It alleged in its answer that its total damage was $66,204.41. This was made up in part by charging the men for the extra wages paid and the extra supplies furnished to the China crew and the shore men for the time of the delay caused in completing the arrangements for their transportation after the close of the fishing season. But the defendant was given notice that the men would not return on the vessel immediately on its arrival at the cannery before the commencement of the fishing season, and in ample time to enable the defendant to make other arrangements for their return transportation at the close of that season. It did not heed the notice, and made the arrangements only after it failed to coerce the men to return on the vessel after such close. The delay was thus the result of the defendant's own fault and neglect, and I know of no principle of law which will permit a person to enhance his damages by his own fault and neglect. The balance of the item is made up by charging the men five dollars for each day the crew was detained while arrangements were being made for returning them home. As I read the contract the clause therein supposed to authorize this charge applies only to a refusal to work on the fishing grounds at the work of fishing, not for any refusal to sail the vessel. But if it can be said that the refusal to sail the vessel was a refusal to work within the meaning of the contract, the delay for which the charge is made was not, as I have shown, the fault of the men. Not being so, they should not be charged with it, and the utmost sum that should be deducted from the wages earned is the actual and necessary expenditure caused by the men, namely, the actual cost paid in towing the vessel, plus the actual cost paid as transportation for the crew.

There are trial errors urged by the appellant which I have not noticed and which might possibly require a new trial, but upon the grounds discussed in the majority opinion, I can find no sufficient reason for a reversal.

[No. 340. *En Banc.* June 21, 1921.]

In the Matter of the Proceedings for the Disbarment of GEORGE OLSON.[1]

ATTORNEY AND CLIENT (9-1)—DISBARMENT PROCEEDING—APPEAL. A finding of the state board of law examiners exonerating an attorney from the charge made against him in disbarment proceedings is not appealable, the only right of appeal granted by statute (Laws 1917, ch. 115, as amended by Laws 1919, ch. 100) being reserved to the person whose license has been annulled or revoked.

SAME (9-1). Under the inherent power of the supreme court to suspend or disbar attorneys, the court may, at its option, examine charges against an attorney, notwithstanding the procedure outlined by statute to be followed in case of inquiry by the board of law examiners.

Proceedings filed in the supreme court February 14, 1921, for the disbarment of an attorney. Dismissed.

Carroll Hendron, for the state.

Tucker & Hyland, Jay C. Allen, and *W. R. Bell,* for accused.

[1] Reported in 198 Pac. 742.

HOLCOMB, J.—Proceedings were instituted before the state board of law examiners upon a complaint against George Olson for his disbarment from the practice of law in the state of Washington, the original complaint being upon two charges or counts. The first charge was that he perpetrated a fraud upon Henry J. Gorin, in that he induced Henry J. Gorin to execute his promissory note for $4,000 upon the representation that he would receive as consideration therefor twenty-five shares of the capital stock of the Broadway State Bank of Seattle, of the value of $160 per share, and would be employed by the bank as its attorney at a salary of $1,000 per annum. It was further alleged that confidential relations existed between Gorin and Olson in that they had associated together in various capacities, and that by reason thereof Gorin believed the statements of Olson, and relied thereon, and delivered his note for the above amount to Olson, but never received the stock or the employment, and that the bank was then insolvent and the stock worthless, all of which was known to Olson.

The second charge in the original complaint was to the effect that Olson, as attorney in a certain cause, prepared findings of fact, conclusions of law and decree in the superior court of Washington, for King county, which conformed with the decision of the court as orally announced, and upon which opposing counsel endorsed his approval, but that Olson did not present the decree, served by copy upon opposing counsel, to the court, but presented one of a different purport which was signed and filed.

A hearing was had upon the charges of the original complaint, and the matter was taken under advisement by the board of law examiners. Thereafter, another complaint was filed against Olson, charging him with mismanagement and breach of trust with reference to the handling of the estate of Hans Bergman, deceased, whereby he acquired and appropriated property belonging thereto to his own use, the charges in which complaint were heard by the board of law examiners at subsequent dates. After hearings on the complaints, the state being represented by counsel, the Seattle bar association by counsel, and Olson by counsel, the board of law examiners reported to this court that it "had carefully considered and weighed all oral and documentary evidence submitted relative to all the charges set forth in said complaints and is of the opinion that the evidence submitted does not sustain any of said charges, and therefore recommends that said charges should be dismissed."

Upon its findings and recommendations being filed, the Seattle bar association, by its attorney, filed objections and exceptions to the report and findings, and the matter was heard before this court *En Banc*.

Counsel for respondent Olson urge that no objections or exceptions can be presented to this court from the findings and recommendations of the board of law examiners by the state or on its behalf, on the ground that the statute, Laws of 1917, ch. 115, p. 421, as amended by the Laws of 1919, ch. 100, p. 243, (Pierce's 1919 Code, §§ 167, 168 and 169), makes no provision for such procedure.

Section 169, Pierce's Code, reads in part as follows:

"Any person whose license has been annulled or revoked may petition the supreme court of the state to review the findings of the board, and to reverse or modify the same, in which event the board shall file with the supreme court a complete transcript of the evidence and proceedings of the case together with its findings, which findings shall constitute a *prima facie* case, and the burden shall be on the appellant to show wherein such order of the board was unlawful. The supreme court shall fix rules for the procedure in such appeals and shall, after hearing, render judgment therein. If it shall find that the order of the board was not in accordance with law, the court shall reverse or modify the same; or may remand the same to the board for further investigation and consideration. But if the board did not exceed its authority and appellant had a fair trial, the court shall affirm the order of the board."

It will be seen that, under the statutes now in force, no one but the person whose license has been annulled or revoked may proceed as of right in this court against the findings of the board of law examiners to reverse or modify the same.

But under the inherent power of this court to admit, suspend or disbar attorneys at law, notwithstanding the statute gives the right as a matter of course only to the person whose license has been annulled or revoked to object to and have a review of the same, we have felt obliged, in a matter of such importance to the bar and the public, to consider that we may, at our own option, examine into the charges against an attorney proceeded against before the state board of bar examiners, even though his license has not been recommended to be revoked or annulled by the board. We may not feel in duty bound to do so in all such cases, but the importance of this case was such that we have felt disposed to do so.

The voluminous record has been examined with considerable care. The charges against the attorney appeared to be very serious, and we especially thought that the first and third charges were particularly grave; but after examining the record we are unable to arrive at any conclusion differing from that of the state board of law examiners.

The most that can be said against the attorney as to the present charges is that he seems to have had an unnecessary propensity for voluminous and circuitous proceedings in transacting business where simplicity and direct methods would have been much more commendable. Some of the things complained of against him seemed at first to have been well founded, but after straightening out the great complexity and circumlocution of his transactions, they appear not to have harmed those involved.

We are of the opinion that the findings and recommendations of the board of law examiners must be and are approved and affirmed.

PARKER, C. J., TOLMAN, BRIDGES, and MITCHELL, JJ., concur.

MAIN, J., concurs in the result.

[No. 15844. Department One. June 22, 1921.]

In the Matter of the Estate of WILLIAM H. WATKINS.[1]

WILLS (20)—VALIDITY—INTENT—UNDUE INFLUENCE—EVIDENCE—SUFFICIENCY. A will which was sufficient as to substance and execution would not be invalidated by reason of having been made as part of the ritualistic ceremony of a secret order, where it sufficiently appears from the testimony of the surviving witness that it was executed by the maker at the time with testamentary intent, notwithstanding a disagreement among members of the order as to whether the making of a will was required of candidates (BRIDGES and MACKINTOSH, JJ., dissenting).

Appeal from a judgment of the superior court for Adams county, Hill, J., entered September 25, 1919, dismissing a will contest. Affirmed.

Lee & Kimball and *W. O. Lewis,* for appellants.

Adams & Miller and *Miles F. Egbers,* for respondents.

[1]Reported in 198 Pac. 721.

FULLERTON, J.—William Henry Watkins died in Adams county in this state on December 10, 1916, leaving estate therein consisting of real and personal property. He left as his heirs at law four children, two sons and two daughters, each of whom had reached the age of majority. At the time of his death no will was found, and one John C. Allen was appointed administrator of the estate. The administrator proceeded with the administration and in due time reported the estate as ready for distribution. At this time one of the daughters appeared by petition, producing what she alleged to be a will of the decedent, and asked that the instrument be admitted to probate as his last will and testament and that the property of the estate be distributed according to the terms thereof. A time was fixed by the court for hearing the petition, at which time proofs were submitted of its due execution and an order entered admitting it to probate. This was done over the protest of certain of the other heirs of the estate and proceedings were immediately instituted by them in contest of the will. The contest was subsequently heard, resulting in an order sustaining the will and a dismissal of the contest proceedings.

The purported will was found in the archives of a secret society known generally as the Masonic order. As presented here, it is a sheet of paper folded so as to form four pages. Heading the first page were printed instructions in these words:

"Write, now, in good faith, your last will and testament precisely as if you were about immediately to be engaged in battle and expected to fall in the action."

Following this were the printed words:

"In the name of God, Amen! I, ..., being of sound mind and memory, but knowing the uncertainty of human life, do now make and publish this, my last will and testament, that is to say;"

The instrument was completed so as to take the form of a will by Mr. Watkins himself. He wrote his name in the blank space left in the printed form, and wrote underneath it the following:

"I wish my property, whatever it may be, divided into five parts and my youngest daughter to receive two parts, and the other to the other three children.
"W. H. Watkins."

The instrument bears the names of two persons, signing in the place usually accorded witnesses. The second page was blank. On the third page there was printed certain admonitory directions, followed by a series of questions to which answers were required. These were followed by an obligation, signed by Watkins, in which he promised, among other things that he would "never improperly make known the mode of my admission into this degree." The fourth page was blank. The matter on the third page does not purport to have relation to the part comprising the will. In form the instrument was sufficient to constitute a duly executed will, provable as such under the laws of this state.

It developed in the testimony that the instrument was executed on November 16, 1903, some thirteen years prior to the death of Mr. Watkins, at a time when there was being conferred on him a degree of the secret order mentioned. It was testified by members of the order that the making of a will was a part of the ceremony of the particular degree, required of all candidates who had not theretofore made a will. The members of the order testifying did not however, altogether agree as to the purpose of the requirement. One testified that it was a ceremonial only, a part of the ritualistic work, and not intended as a testamentary disposition of property. Two others testified to a contrary view; the substance of their testimony being that all members of the order who had taken this degree were expected to die testate, and that while the will executed on the particular occasion, like all other wills, was subject to modification by subsequent codicils or revocation by subsequently executed wills, it is intended and regarded as testamentary.

There would seem to be no legal objection to regarding a will so executed as a valid will. The time, place or circumstance of the execution of an instrument in form testamentary are material only as they bear upon the question of intent. It is well settled, of course, that an instrument offered for probate as a will, however formal may have been its execution, will not be admitted to probate as such unless it was executed by the testator with testamentary intent. If it is executed under compulsion, undue influence, as a part of a ceremonial, for the purpose of deception, or for the purpose of perpetrating a jest, it is not a will, but the fact that it was executed at a time when the testator was taking a degree in a secret order is not alone sufficient to reject it as a valid testamentary disposition of property. A valid will may be made under these circumstances as well as under any other. The question being one of intent, if it fairly appears that the testator intended it as his will, there is no valid legal reason because of the place of its execution why the courts should not give it effect as such.

It remains to inquire whether the testator intended the instrument to be his will and testament. The evidence on the question is somewhat meager, but we think the decided weight of the evidence is that he so regarded it. The surviving witness to the will testified that it was executed with testamentary intent, and that the testator at the time of its execution declared it to be his last will and testament. His evidence was taken by deposition to which were attached cross-interrogatories. To one of these, inquiring whether the testator talked with him about it or to any one else in his presence concerning it, the witness answered: "All he said was that if he never made another will that one would do. I can't remember that he said anything else."

It appeared, however, from the testimony of another witness that at the close of the ceremony Mr. Watkins remarked, "that is quite a josh." It is argued that this shows that Mr. Watkins himself did not regard the making of the will to be anything more than a ceremonial. But we think the witness' testimony as a whole shows that the remark was made with reference to the requirement that a will be executed rather than to the instrument executed as a will; a part of the witness' further testimony being the following:

"Q. Was there anything said by Mr. Watkins as to whether or not he was executing a will? A. Yes, sir; it was expressly understood that he was executing a will. Q. What, if anything, did he say with relation to having made a will? A. Well, he said that that was his will; that he signed that as his will, his last will and testament. . . . . As I say, it is the custom that the request be made and complied with by every candidate. He is asked if he has made a will, and, if he has not he is requested to do so, and he has to do so before he can proceed any further."

The disagreement among the members of the order as to the purport of the requirement is not of moment. The question in each case must necessarily be, what was the intent of the particular individual, and here, we think, the trial judge correctly determined that the deceased executed this instrument intending it to be his last will and testament.

The judgment is affirmed.

PARKER, C. J., and HOLCOMB, J., concur.

BRIDGES, J. (dissenting)—I am unable to concur in the foregoing opinion. I readily agree with the correctness of the statement therein that no instrument should be held to be a last will and testament unless the proof shows the intent of the maker that it should be such. But mere preponderance of evidence should not be sufficient; the evidence should be such as to clearly, convincingly and satisfactorily establish the intention. I do not think the testimony in this case is of the class indicated. It fails to convince me that the maker of the purported will intended it to be a final disposition of property. The making of a will is an important and solemn business; the testator usually deliberates the subject, and when the will is made he keeps it in his possession or under his control. He generally chooses his own time to make it and his witnesses to it. It seems to me that all of the conditions and circumstances surrounding the making of this instrument argue with great force against the idea that it was made with that seriousness and solemnity with which wills are customarily made. As pointed out by the court's opinion, it was made as a part of the ritualistic work of a secret society into which the deceased was being initiated. One witness testified that the deceased, at the time of making the instrument, said he thought it was "quite a josh." The testimony also conclusively shows that at least some of the members of the society who had previously been initiated into it, and who probably had been required to make similar purported wills, believed that it was not intended that the instrument so made was to be considered a final will and testament. The deceased here may have been of like mind. This purported will was made some thirteen years prior to decedent's death, during all of which time it was lodged in the secret archives of the society.

I greatly fear that the holding of the court in this
case will lead to the presentation and probation of
many instruments in the form of wills which were
never intended to be such. I frankly concede that a
valid will might be made under the circumstances this
instrument was made, but certainly the testimony of
the intention of the testator should be much stronger
than is shown in this case, to authorize the probation
of it as a final disposition of property. I think the
judgment ought to be reversed.

MACKINTOSH, J., concurs with BRIDGES, J.

[No. 16387. Department One. June 22, 1921.]

GEORGE A. CORUM *et al., Respondents,* v. GUST
BLOMQUIST *et al., Appellants.*[1]

NEGLIGENCE (38)—ACTIONS—EVIDENCE—SUFFICIENCY. In an action for damages for the death by drowning of an minor son in a
swimming pool, operated by defendants, a motion for nonsuit was
properly denied, where, upon an issue as to whether defendant furnished a reasonably attentive and competent attendant, the evidence
showed that the boy while using the pool was missing from ten to
fifteen minutes without his absence being noted, and when brought
out of the water breathed a few times under manual manipulation.

APPEAL (373)—REVIEW—SCOPE—THEORY OR GROUNDS—GRANT OF
NEW TRIAL. An order granting a new trial will not be reversed on
appeal, when the grounds upon which the trial court ruled do not
appear in the record.

NEGLIGENCE (35)—ACTIONS—EVIDENCE—PREVIOUS ACCIDENTS—AD-
MISSIBILITY. In an action for damages for the death of a young child
in a swimming pool, alleged as due to the negligence of the attendant
to reasonably observe the movements of those using the pool, evidence of previous accidents therein is inadmissible.

Appeal from an order of the superior court for
Grays Harbor county, Reynolds, J., entered October
13, 1920, granting plaintiffs' motion for a new trial,

[1]Reported in 198 Pac. 727.

after a verdict rendered by a jury in favor of plaintiffs, in an action for damages. Affirmed.

William E. Campbell and *Martin F. Smith*, for appellants.

W. H. Abel and *John D. Ehrhart*, for respondents.

MACKINTOSH, J.—The appellants operate a swimming pool in a building owned by them at Hoquiam, and on July 10, 1919, the respondents' eleven year old boy was there drowned. The complaint charges that the bed of the pool sloped from a few inches to eight feet in depth, and was a dangerous, yet attractive, place for small children, and that such children were likely to be injured or drowned, and that, with knowledge of these conditions, the appellants operated the pool without placing a responsible person in charge, and negligently committed the care of the pool to their daughter, a girl lacking in judgment, experience, skill or ability to safeguard the children who frequented the pool. The case was tried to a jury and resulted in a verdict for the respondents, who moved for a new trial, which was granted, and from that order the appellants bring the case here.

Appellants allege that the court committed error in granting the new trial and committed error in refusing to grant appellants' motion for a nonsuit. Upon the respondents' suggestion in their brief that the abstract of the testimony furnished by the appellants is inadequate, we have read the statement of facts, which discloses that the respondents produced no testimony of any negligence in the construction or operation of the swimming pool other than that relating to the failure of the employee in charge to be reasonably attentive. The testimony upon this point, which would entitle the respondents' case to be considered by a jury, was that the respondents' son was missing for from ten to fifteen minutes without his absence being noted. This presented a question of fact for the jury to determine whether, if that statement is true (and it is open to some doubt for the boy, after being brought out of the water, breathed a few times under manual manipulation), a competent attendant, exercising reasonable care, should have discovered the boy's disappearance earlier than was actually done. There is no other element of negligence in the case, for there is no question that, after the discovery of the boy, everything that could be done by anyone was done and as speedily and efficiently as was humanly possible. Upon this attenuated string, the respondents rely to hold the liability of the appellants, which the jury tied with as attenuated a knot, having returned a verdict in the sum of one dollar. There being the evidence to which we have referred in the case, the court was not in error in refusing to grant the appellants' motion for nonsuit.

The grounds upon which the court granted respondents' motion for a new trial do not appear in the record, and under our rule which provides that the granting of a new trial will not be reversed under such conditions, we cannot do other than affirm the lower court.

Although it is not necessary for the decision of this case, in order to obviate the necessity for a further appeal in the event of a new trial, it may be said the evidence which was admitted relative to previous accidents in this swimming pool was improper for the reason that the only question of negligence, as we have seen in this case, is the failure of appellants' daughter to reasonably observe the movements and whereabouts of those using the pool. The judgment is affirmed.

Parker, C. J., Bridges, Fullerton, and Holcomb, JJ., concur.

[No 16519. Department One. June 22, 1921.]

W. L. BEYER, *Appellant*, v. M. P. ZINDORF *et al.*,
Respondents.[1]

HIGHWAYS (33)—CONSTRUCTION — CONTRACTS — RESERVE FUND.
Under a contract between the state and a contractor for the construction of a highway pursuant to Rem. Code, §§ 5867-5878, which
does not authorize the retention of a percentage of the contract
price for the protection of those supplying labor and material, no
trust fund is created in favor of the latter by the provisions of the
contract to the effect that part of the price earned might be retained
to be applied by the state at its discretion upon any claims due and
unpaid, the contract further providing that, on failure of the contractor to complete the contract according to its terms, the state
was authorized upon notice to take over the work and complete it,
and the contractor should not be entitled to any balance of the
amount payable under his contract unless such unpaid balance
should exceed the expense incurred by the state in finishing the
work.

Appeal from a judgment of the superior court for
Thurston county, Wright, J., entered March 31, 1921,
upon findings in favor of the plaintiff as against the
contractor and dismissed as to the state, in an action
to recover for labor and materials furnished on a state
highway. Affirmed.

Fred M. Bond, for appellant.

The Attorney General and *O. R. Schumann, Assistant,* for respondents.

MACKINTOSH, J.—Plaintiff desires to recover for
labor and material performed and furnished on a state
highway under a contract entered into August 5, 1916,
between the state highway board and the defendant,
M. P. Zindorf. The contract contemplated the grading
of part of the National Park highway, located in
Pacific county. Under the contract, the price to be

[1]Reported in 198 Pac. 977.

paid for the work amounted to $25,550.21. The work was to be completed by August 20, 1917. On account of the failure of Zindorf to complete his work according to his contract, the state highway department took charge of the job on August 31, 1917, and completed it fifteen months thereafter, at a cost of $18,834.57. Zindorf had been paid under the contract the sum of $12,285.22, and he had also earned, but not been paid, a retained percentage of 20 per cent, amounting to $3,397.01, and upon his last monthly statement an estimated amount of $1,302.82. In other words, there was retained the sum of $4,699.83 at the time the state highway department took over the contract. The state highway department used up in completing the contract all this and several thousand dollars in addition.

The plaintiff performed labor and furnished materials to the job while it was being carried on by Zindorf, and not being paid therefor he filed his claim with the state highway department, claiming an interest in the retained percentage as a trust fund. His claim, together with other claims assigned to him, amounts to $3,581.11.

Plaintiff is seeking judgment against the state upon the theory that the retained percentage was a trust fund, which had been used by the state, which was therefore rendered liable. Plaintiff secured judgment below against Zindorf, but his action was dismissed as against the state and its officers, and from this latter portion of the judgment he has appealed.

As much of the contract as it is necessary for us to set forth is as follows:

IV.

"Should the contractor at any time refuse or neglect to supply a sufficiency of properly skilled workmen, or of material of the proper quality, or fail in any respect to prosecute the work with promptness and diligence, or fail in the performance of any of the agreements herein contained, the state highway commissioner shall be at liberty, after three (3) days' written notice to the contractor, to provide any such labor and materials and deduct the cost thereof from any moneys then due or thereafter to become due to the contractor under this contract; and if the state highway commissioner shall consider that such refusal, neglect or failure is sufficient ground for such action, he may, by written notice, terminate the employment of the contractor for said work and enter upon the premises and take possession of all materials, tools, and appliances thereon, for the purpose of completing the work included under this contract, and employ, by contract or otherwise, any person or persons to finish the work, and provide the materials therefor; and in case of such discontinuance of the employment of the contractor, he shall not be entitled to receive any further balance of the amount to be paid under this contract until the work shall be fully finished, at which time, if the unpaid balance of the amount to be paid under this contract, shall exceed the expense incurred by the state highway commissioner in finishing the work, such excess shall be paid by the state to the contractor, but if such expense shall exceed such unpaid balance, the contractor shall pay the difference to the state treasurer."

VII.

"Partial payments under this contract, not to exceed eighty per cent (80%) of the work done, shall be made at the request of the contractor once each month, said payments to be made upon estimates of the state highway commissioner. In case of lump sum price, a schedule of prices to be used as basis of partial payments, shall be based upon the prices in the preliminary estimate, which prices shall be increased or reduced in the same ratio that the lump sum price bears to the preliminary estimate. Final payments for said work shall be made within thirty (30) days of the final completion and acceptance of the entire work by the state highway commissioner, Provided, That the state highway commissioner may require the contractor to show to the satisfaction of said commissioner before

the making of such final payment, that all just debts
due all laborers, mechanics, material men, and persons,
who have supplied such contractor, or sub-contractor,
with materials or goods of any kind for this work,
have been paid, and, Provided, further, That if prior
to any payment being made the state highway commissioner receives notice from any person or persons that
any laborers, mechanics or materialmen, or other persons who have furnished or supplied said contractor,
or any sub-contractor, with any labor, service,
material, goods or provisions of any kind, in connection with the construction of said portion of the National Park Highway that may be ordered for said portion of the National Park Highway have claims against
said contractor, or any sub-contractor, for any such
service or things, and for which any such laborers,
mechanics, materialmen, or other persons, would be
entitled to a lien under the laws of this state were said
highway not a public highway, or proper claim against
the bond in such cases required by law, the state highway commissioner may, in his discretion, retain out of
the payments then due or to become due said contractor, an amount, in addition to the twenty per cent
(20%) above provided to be retained until the final
completion of said work, sufficient to cover all such
claim or claims of which notice shall have been so given,
until such claim or claims shall have been fully satisfied and paid and receipts in full for the same shall
have been furnished by said contractor or to the state
highway commissioner, and the said contractor hereby
expressly agrees to pay all such claims.''

We have already stated the theory upon which the
appellant seeks recovery, and it thus becomes necessary to examine the contract to determine whether by
its terms it creates such a trust fund as claimed.

This court has held that where the contract reserves
a balance for the protection of materialmen and
laborers, that such reserve balance is a trust fund, and
the municipality making the contract is under obligation to hold it as such for their benefit. But this rule,

as we take it, has been applied only in those cases where the contract unmistakably provides for such a fund.

The case of *State ex rel. Bartelt v. Liebes,* 19 Wash. 589, 54 Pac. 26, had to do with a contract which provided that no payment was to be made to the contractor until the work was completed and "all labor paid thereon." The assignee of the contractor brought suit against the city to compel the delivery of bonds to the contractor under the contract. Certain unpaid laborers and materialmen intervened, and the court held that the contract was valid, and that by its terms a trust fund was created in favor of such unpaid laborers and materialmen.

The court, in *First National Bank v. Seattle,* 71 Wash. 122, 127 Pac. 837, followed the *Liebes* case, *supra,* and held that a contract which expressly provided for the retention by the city of thirty per cent of the contract price to secure the payment of laborers and materialmen created a trust in their behalf; the contract, in that case, expressly binding the city to withhold the designated percentage.

In *Maryland Casualty Co. v. Washington Nat. Bank,* 92 Wash. 497, 159 Pac. 689, the court had before it a contract providing that the contractor might receive current payments of eighty per cent, but that twenty per cent should not be paid until after the work had been accepted and the municipality satisfied that the laborers and materialmen had been paid. The court held that such a contract was for the protection of the laborers and materialmen, following the *Liebes* and *First National Bank* cases, *supra.*

The contract in the case of *Denham v. Pioneer Sand & Gravel Co.,* 104 Wash. 357, 176 Pac. 333, provided "for the withholding by the county of twenty per cent of the contract price for the satisfaction of unpaid

labor and material claims." We there re-announced
the doctrine that the reserved percentage was a trust
fund for the benefit of laborers and materialmen.

In all of these cases the contracts expressly or necessarily impliedly bound the municipalities to hold out
a certain percentage for the benefit of laborers and
materialmen.

In *Northwestern Nat. Bank v. Guardian Casualty
& Guaranty Co.*, 93 Wash. 635, 161 Pac. 473, the contract provided that, "The said contractor agrees to pay
the wages of all persons . . . and for all materials
purchased therefor, and the said city of Bellingham
may withhold any and all payments under this contract until satisfied that such wages, assistance and
materials have been fully paid for." The court said
in regard to that contract:

"It did not contain the usual provision for the
payment of a certain percentage of the estimated value
of work as it progressed, and for a retention of a certain percentage by the city until the work was completed to meet any unpaid labor and material claims,
nor did it contain any provision for the holding up of
any sum by the city, except that above quoted."

The decision of the court was that in those contracts which provided for the retention of a certain
balance for the benefit of laborers and materialmen,
such retained percentage was a trust fund, but:

"It is only where there is a clear and express
reservation in the contract of a fund to be held up
for the benefit of laborers and materialmen that there
is any fund the contractor may not effectually assign
by an assignment made prior to his default and notice
of such default to the board or, as in this case, to the
city, and that it is only as to such reserve fund that
the labor and material claims have any priority over
such assignments, hence only as to such reserve fund
that there is any right of subrogation in favor of the
bondsmen . . .

"In the case before us . . . The contract itself contained no provision for an absolute reserve of any percentage as security for labor and material claims. It contained nothing but a provision permitting the city to withhold payment until satisfied that all labor and material claims had been paid."

Both appellant and respondents agree that the contract alone covers this case and it is not to be considered in regard to any statute, for the reason that Rem. Code, §§ 5867-5878, under which the state highway board was contracting for the construction of this road, contains no provision in regard to the retention of any trust fund.

An examination of the contract shows that there is no express provision for the creation of a trust fund, nor is there any provision which has that necessarily implied result. Under paragraph seven the contractor, as a matter of right, received each month payments not in excess of eighty per cent of the work done, the unpaid balance to be paid thirty days after final completion and acceptance of the entire work. It is provided that before final payment all debts shall have been paid, and that the state highway commissioner may retain, in addition to the twenty per cent, enough to cover claims that may be filed until such time as the contractor should show receipts for all such payments. Although the contract provides that the contractor shall receive only eighty per cent per month and the balance 30 days after the completion of the work, with a provision allowing the state to require the contractor to show that he had paid all his bills, the measure of the appellant's rights is whether this twenty per cent has been placed beyond the control of the contractor, and it seems to us, upon an examination of the contract, that it was no more placed beyond his control than was the reserve in the *Northwestern*

National Bank case, *supra.* In that case the contract
provided that the municipality might withhold "any
and all payments under this contract until satisfied
that such wages, assistance and materials have been
fully paid for." If that was not an absolute reserve,
the provision in this case that the state highway commissioner "may require the contractor to show to the
satisfaction of said commissioner before making such
final payments that all just debts . . . have been
paid," does not create an absolute reserve. Although
the contract provides the state highway commissioner
"may" withhold twenty per cent of the contract price,
and, as a matter of fact, he did so withhold such
amount, the fact that the withholding may have been
optional only made it impossible for the contractor
to collect the entire price before final acceptance, and
required him to satisfy the commissioner that he had
paid all the debts, if the commissioner so chose, yet
the contractor was entitled to the 20 per cent within
30 days after final completion, if the commissioner
did not require him to show that he had paid all claims,
the contract being that the commissioner "may" so
require such payment to be shown.

In *Dowling v. Seattle,* 22 Wash. 592, 61 Pac. 709,
where the contract provided that "the city of Seattle
may withhold any and all payments under this contract until satisfied that such wages, assistance and
materials have been fully paid for," it was held:

"It is true that the city, by virtue of a provision
of the agreement which we have hereinbefore noted,
might have withheld all payments from the contractor
until it was satisfied that all just claims for labor and
materials had been fully paid; but it does not follow
from that fact, as contended by the learned counsel
for appellants, that it was obliged to do so, and that,
having done otherwise, it should now be held to be a
trustee of the laborers and material men, and, as such,

liable to them directly for the amount of the fund assigned and of the bonds delivered to the contractor."

In the *Northwestern National Bank* case, *supra*, this court, in referring to the *Dowling* case, *supra*, held it to be still good law, and that the provision just quoted meant nothing but permission granted to the city to withhold payments.

Taking the contract as a whole, and giving it the interpretation which would best effect the intention of the parties (*Dyer v. Middle Kittitas Irr. Dist.*, 25 Wash. 80, 64 Pac. 1009, and *Norton v. State*, 104 Wash. 248, 176 Pac. 347), it will be seen that the contract contemplated the use by the state highway commissioner of all amounts earned by the contractor and not yet paid to him in carrying out the contract, in the event the state highway commissioner was forced to complete the work. This was what was done in this case. To say that this was unauthorized would be to read out of the contract that section which provides for this very contingency. Section seven was inserted for the purpose of aiding the commissioner in securing the performance of the contract, but does not take the title of the twenty per cent from the contractor. *Columbia Brick Co. v. District of Columbia*, 1 App. D. C. 351; *Jones v. Savage*, 24 Misc. Rep. 158, 53 N. Y. Supp. 308; *Epeneter v. Montgomery County*, 98 Iowa 159, 67 N. W. 93. See, also, *State ex rel. Fairhaven v. Cheetham*, 17 Wash. 131, 49 Pac. 227.

We find no merit in the other contentions made by the appellant, and the judgment is therefore affirmed.

PARKER, C. J., BRIDGES, FULLERTON, and HOLCOMB, JJ., concur.

[No. 16142. Department Two. June 25, 1921.]

J. R. McKEAND, *Appellant*, v. CARL BIRD *et al.*, *Respondents.*[1]

TAXATION (152)—FORECLOSURE OF LIEN—AFFIDAVIT—NONRESID-ENCE—SUFFICIENCY. The superior court acquired no jurisdiction of tax foreclosure proceedings by a private party against a nonresident defendant, where the affidavit for publication of the summons was contradictory, reciting that affiant believes that the defendant is not a resident of the state, and that he has deposited a copy of the summons and notice in the post office at Pasco, . . . directed to the defendant at his place of residence, to wit, at Pasco; since Rem. Code, § 228, requires the affidavit to show a mailing of the copy directed to the defendant at his place of residence, unless the affidavit state that such residence is not known to affiant.

Appeal from a judgment of the superior court for Franklin county, Truax, J., entered June 15, 1920, in favor of the defendants, in an action to quiet title, tried to the court. Affirmed.

Chas. W. Johnson, for appellant.

B. B. Horrigan, for respondents.

MITCHELL, J.—The decision in this case depends upon the validity of two tax foreclosure cases had in the superior court of Franklin county, wherein the real property is located.

The plaintiff is the grantee of the purchaser at the tax foreclosure sales, while the defendants are the grantees of Fred P. Yandeau, who owned the property at the time of the assessment of the property, delinquency in payment of the taxes, issuance of the C. D.'s and the foreclosure proceedings including the tax sales. Upon the trial of the case, the superior court entered judgment finding that the defendants are the owners in fee simple of the lands free and clear of

[1]Reported in 199 Pac. 293.

any claim on the part of the plaintiff, for whose benefit
the judgment declares the defendants have paid to the
clerk of the court for the plaintiff the sum of $615.13
in full satisfaction of plaintiff's prior lien for taxes,
penalty, interests and costs. The plaintiff has appealed.

There was no personal service of process in the tax
suits nor appearance by Fred P. Yandeau, the defendant named therein; nor did he have any notice or
knowledge of the pendency of the tax cases. The validity
of the judgments in those cases depends upon the proceedings for substituted service by the publication of
summons.

Fred P. Yandeau resided at Pasco, the county seat
of Franklin county, from the time of acquiring the
property in August, 1908, until March 1, 1909, at which
time he went to California, where he has since resided.
After going to California, he regularly paid taxes on
the property until the spring of 1914—the last payment being the taxes levied in the year 1913—by correspondence from La Jolla, California. The evidence
shows that a part at least of his correspondence from
that place was kept on file in an orderly manner in the
office of the county treasurer and that the official dupli-
cate tax receipts in the treasurer's office show Yandeau's residence to be La Jolla, California. The evidence further shows that the certificates of delinquency
foreclosed were for the taxes levied in the years 1914
and 1915, and that the preparation and making of the
affidavits, for the publication of summons in the tax
foreclosure cases, were by persons who were residents
of Pasco. In each of the affidavits, it was stated,

"That he (affiant) believes that the defendant above
named is not a resident of the state of Washington, and
cannot be found therein. That he has deposited a copy
of the summons and notice of foreclosure in this action
in the post office at Pasco in said county, state of

Washington, directed to the said defendant at his place of residence, to-wit: at Pasco, in the state of Washington, with the postage thereon duly paid.'"

The statements in the affidavits as to the defendant's residence were positively contradictory, and it was not even stated that Pasco was the last known place of residence of Yandeau, nor was it stated that his residence was unknown. The slightest diligence by way of inquiry at the treasurer's office, which ordinarily is supposed to be advised of the address of a non-resident taxpayer, would have readily shown that Yandeau's address was La Jolla, California. That inquiry would have qualified the maker of the affidavits, upon which the publications of summons were based, to have complied with the essentials mentioned in the statute, and at the same time to have carried out the purpose and policy of the statute that the owner of the property shall have his day in court. In cases wherein the defendant is not a resident of the state or cannot be found therein, Rem. Code, § 228, as to the service of summons by publication, provides for the filing of an affidavit of the plaintiff, his agent or attorney, with the clerk of the court, stating, among other things, that the affiant has deposited a copy of the summons and complaint in the post office, directed to the defendant at his place of residence, unless it is stated in the affidavit that such residence is not known to the affiant. That section of the code is applicable to tax foreclosure proceedings commenced by a private party. *Felsinger v. Quinn*, 62 Wash. 183, 113 Pac. 275. And as late as the case of *Moller v. Graham*, 101 Wash. 283, 172 Pac. 226, occasion was found to repeat the rule announced in the case of *Wick v. Rea*, 54 Wash. 424, 103 Pac. 462, as follows:

"While the argument is forceful and is supported by respectable authority, this court is committed to the doctrine that a summons in tax foreclosure proceedings must comply with the statutes. Otherwise the court acts without jurisdiction. The rule, as stated in 17 Ency. Plead. & Prac., 45, 'The right to serve process by publication being of purely statutory creation and in derogation of the common law, the statutes authorizing such service must be strictly pursued in order to confer jurisdiction upon the court,' was adopted in *Thompson v. Robbins,* 32 Wash. 149, 72 Pac. 1043, and has been followed in the following cases: *Smith v. White,* 32 Wash. 414, 73 Pac. 480; *Dolan v. Jones,* 37 Wash. 176, 79 Pac. 640; *Woodham v. Anderson,* 32 Wash. 500, 73 Pac. 536; *Williams v. Pittock,* 35 Wash. 271, 77 Pac. 385; *Young v. Droz,* 38 Wash. 648, 80 Pac. 810; *Owen v. Owen,* 41 Wash. 642, 84 Pac. 606; *Bartels v. Christenson,* 46 Wash. 478, 90 Pac. 658; *Bauer v. Windholm,* 49 Wash. 310, 95 Pac. 277; *Gould v. Knox,* 53 Wash. 248, 101 Pac. 886; *Hays v. Peavy, ante* p. 78, 102 Pac. 889; *Gould v. Stanton, ante* p. 363, 103 Pac. 459; *Gould v. White, ante* p. 394, 103 Pac. 460.''

Because of the conclusion that the court was without jurisdiction to render the judgments in the tax cases, we find it unnecessary to discuss other contentions made by the respondents, disputed by the appellant, that the tax sales and deeds were void.

Judgment affirmed.

PARKER, C. J., MAIN, and TOLMAN, JJ., concur.

[No. 16564. Department Two. June 25, 1921.]

CARL S. WEATHERWAX *et al., Appellants,* v. GRAYS
HARBOR COUNTY *et al., Respondents.*[1]

DRAINS (4-1)—ESTABLISHMENT BY CITIES—AREA LYING WITHIN
CORPORATE LIMITS. The power to establish diking and drainage districts within the corporate limits of cities and towns being conferred by Rem. Code, §§ 4120 and 4162, the county commissioners
have no authority, under the powers granted by Id., § 4226-1 *et seq.*
as amended and supplemented by Ch. 130, Laws 1917, p. 517, to
create such a district where the territory to be included lies wholly
within the corporate limits of a city.

Appeal from a judgment of the superior court for
Grays Harbor county, Abel, J., entered May 10, 1921,
denying the relief sought by plaintiff, in an action to
enjoin the establishment of a proposed diking and
drainage district. Reversed.

W. E. Campbell, for appellants.

George Acret (E. E. Boner, of counsel), for respondents.

MITCHELL, J.—Proceeding under the provisions of
ch. 176, p. 611, Laws of 1913 (Rem. Code, § 4226-1),
and of ch. 130, p. 517, Laws of 1917 (the latter act
being largely amendatory of the former) the owners
of certain property situated within the city of Aberdeen, a city of the second class, presented to the board
of county commissioners of Grays Harbor county their
petition for the establishment of a diking and drainage
improvement district embracing their lands together
with those of other owners, all of which lands are situate within the corporate limits of the city. Thereupon,
this action was commenced by taxpayers on behalf of
themselves and all others similarly situated, owners

[1] Reported in 199 Pac. 303.

of property within the proposed improvement district, to enjoin and restrain the board of county commis-sioners from establishing the proposed diking and drainage district. Upon the hearing of the cause, the trial court denied the relief sought and the plaintiffs have appealed.

It is stated by the appellants, and agreed to by the respondents, that the case involves the single question: Is the board of county commissioners authorized to establish a diking and drainage improvement district lying wholly within the corporate limits of an incorporated city or town.

An examination of the statutes shows there are different methods of procedure for the establishment and maintenance of diking and drainage improvement districts, in each of which methods the costs of construction and of maintenance shall be a charge upon the property within the district. By the acts of 1913 and 1917, already referred to, and under which these proceedings were instituted, it is provided that the establishment and maintenance of such improvement district shall be under the management and control of the county authorities. In § 39, ch. 130, p. 552, of the act of 1917, it is provided:

"Nothing in this act contained shall be construed as in anywise modifying or repealing any of the provisions of chapter 115 or of chapter 117 of the Laws of 1895, or the acts amendatory thereof or supplemental thereto, or affecting any proceedings heretofore or that may hereafter be had under the provisions of said acts."

Chapters 115 and 117 of the Laws of 1895, referred to in the law of 1917, together with the acts amendatory or supplemental thereto, provide the other plan for the establishment and maintenance of diking and drainage improvement districts. They provide for proceedings

initiated before the board of county commissioners of
the county wherein the property is situated that finally
results in the creation and establishment of a legal
entity as a public corporation known and designated as
diking or drainage district No.——— of the county of
——— of the state of Washington, with the right of
eminent domain and the right to sue and be sued by and
in the name of its own board of commissioners, having
perpetual succession and required to adopt and use a
seal.

In ch. 115, p. 291, Laws of 1895 (Rem. Code, § 4162),
it is provided as follows:

"Sec. 23. Any town or city already incorporated,
or which may hereafter be incorporated, may exercise
the functions of a drainage district under the provisions of this act, or the whole or any portion of any
such town or city may be included with other territory in a common district under the provisions for the
establishment thereof as provided for herein."

A similar provision is found in § 26, ch. 117, p. 323,
Laws of 1895 (Rem. Code, § 4120), for the establishment of diking districts.

It thus clearly appears to be the intention of the legislature to confer upon cities and towns the power to
exercise the functions of such improvement districts
in those cases where all of the property within the improvement district is situated entirely within the
limits of an incorporated city or town, but that in the
event all of the property included within the proposed
improvement district embraces property other than a
portion or all of the area of a city or town that then
the improvement district for diking and drainage purposes may be established and maintained by a district
organized as a separate municipal corporation.

The acts of 1895 still being in effect, and the legislature in 1917 having construed its act of that session

as in nowise repealing or modifying the earlier acts of 1895, it follows, we think, that the jurisdiction is with the city of Aberdeen and not the county authorities for the establishment and maintenance of the proposed diking and drainage improvement district, and that the relief prayed for by the appellants should have been granted by the trial court.

This construction of the statute responds to the manifest intention of the legislature and harmonizes with the general rule that two municipal corporations cannot have jurisdiction and control, at one time, of the same territory, for the same purpose.

Reversed with directions to enter judgment accordingly.

PARKER, C. J., MACKINTOSH, MAIN, and TOLMAN, JJ., concur.

[No. 16234. Department One. June 28, 1921.]

JOHN R. NEVINS, *Respondent*, v. LEE A. SCACE *et al.,* *Appellants.*[1]

DAMAGES (3, 106)—CERTAINTY AS TO AMOUNT—EVIDENCE—ADMISSIBILITY. Upon an issue as to damages through an architect's breach of contract in the preparation of plans and specifications for a hospital building, which could not be constructed within the estimate, an item of damages in the sum of $1,000 for costs of excavating the basement for the building, prior to discovery of inability to bring the expense of construction within the estimate, was properly withdrawn from the jury, where the excavation also included a cesspool and a long drain leading thereto, which were not included in the plans, and the defendants were unable to segregate the cost of the cesspool and drain items from the excavation.

NEW TRIAL (19)—VERDICT CONTRARY TO EVIDENCE—POWER OF COURT. The inability of the court to follow the minds of the jury in arriving at a verdict upon conflicting claims of the parties is not a ground for the granting of a new trial.

[1]Reported in 199 Pac. 305.

Appeal from a judgment of the superior court for
Lewis county, Hewen, J., entered August 6, 1920, upon
the verdict of a jury rendered in favor of the plaintiff,
in an action to recover for services rendered. Affirmed.

C. D. Cunningham, for appellants.

Aust & Terhune and *Forney & Ponder*, for respondent.

BRIDGES, J.—The plaintiff sought to recover of defendants $1,739.86, less certain payments, for drawing
plans and specifications for a hospital which defendants contemplated building on Seminary Hill, in Centralia, Washington, and also, $1,260 for like services for
a hospital to be constructed in the down-town district
of the same city. He claims to have performed these
services at the request of the defendants, for which
he was to be paid for each set of plans an amount equal
to 3% of the cost of construction of the building, and
that the cost of constructing under the first plans
would have been $57,900, and under the second plans,
$42,000. He admits the payment by defendants to him
of $950, which he applied on account of the first plans,
thus leaving due him $789.86 for them, and $1,260 for
the second plans.

Defendants admitted that both sets of plans had
been drawn by the plaintiff for them, and that they had
agreed to pay him for his services an amount equal to
3% of the construction cost, but they claim that the
plaintiff guaranteed that the hospital to be erected
under the first plans would not cost in excess of
$40,000, and that the lowest bid for constructing under
them was an amount in excess of $57,000, and that be-
cause of such excessive cost they were unable to, and
did not use the first plans, and ought not to be required
to pay for them. They admit, however, that they con-

structed the down-town hospital under the second plans
drawn by the plaintiff, and that they thereby became
indebted to him in the sum of $1,260, of which amount
they claim to have paid $1,050, leaving a balance of
$210; but they claimed damages against the plaintiff in
the sum of $1,000, such damages growing out of the
inability to construct the hospital under the first plans
for the price guaranteed by the plaintiff. They assert
that after those plans were drawn and before they
knew that the building could not be constructed within
the amount guaranteed by the plaintiff, they spent
$1,000 in digging a basement or cellar for the hospital,
as provided by the first plans and that such $1,000 was
a complete loss to them because of plaintiff's fault.
This $1,000 item was, during the trial, by the court
taken from the jury for reasons which we will more
fully explain hereafter. The case was tried to a jury,
which brought in a verdict in favor of the plaintiff for
$860. The defendant's motion for new trial having
been denied, judgment was entered on the verdict, and
the defendants have appealed therefrom.

It is first contended that the court erred in taking
from the jury the consideration of the item of $1,000
damages on account of the excavation made under the
first, or Seminary Hill, plans. The testimony showed
that these plans provided for an excavation under the
kitchen and part of the dining room of the hospital.
The appellants not only made this excavation but also
excavated for a large cesspool, and a long drain leading
thereto, which latter were not covered by the plans.
The testimony showed that the appellants had paid
$1,300 for all of this excavation, but no evidence was
introduced showing the cost of the excavation provided
for by the plans and specifications. The appellants
introduced but one witness on this feature of the case,
and he was wholly unable to segregate the cost of the

excavation for the building from the cost of the excavation for the drain and cesspool. On this account the trial court held that the question of damages for excavating could not be submitted to the jury. We have no doubt of the correctness of the court's ruling in this regard. In no event could appellants recover for the cost of excavating for the cesspool and drain; they could recover only for the excavations for the building. The witness was able to tell the cost of all the excavations but did not and could not make any segregation. Consequently, there was a complete absence of testimony as to the cost of excavations for the building. It is true that, after the court made its ruling, the appellants made a specific offer to show by the witness then on the stand a segregation of the costs in the items of excavation, but such offer was useless because the witness had time and again stated that he could not make such segregation.

It is next claimed that the appellant was entitled to a new trial because the verdict was inconsistent with any theory of the case as presented to the jury, either by the testimony or the instructions of the court. Their argument is that if the jury found for the respondent only on account of the second plans, liability for which was admitted, then the verdict could only have been for $210; but if the jury found for respondent on account of both the first and second plans, then the verdict must have been for an amount twice as large as that returned by the jury. While it is difficult for us to tell how the jury arrived at the amount of its verdict, it is perfectly plain that they allowed recovery, at least in part, on both sets of plans. But courts cannot grant new trials simply because they are unable to follow the minds of the jury in arriving at its verdict. In the case of *Haefele v. Brackett*, 95 Wash. 625, 164 Pac. 244, we said:

"But we do not understand that a verdict will be set aside as within the rule of mistake or compromise or that it is impossible under the theory of either party, unless it shows upon its face that the jury has given way to passion or prejudice or has acted in willful disregard of its duty to consider the testimony, and a true verdict rendered."

There is nothing on the face of this verdict which shows that the jury refused to follow the evidence. The most that can be said is that if the jury meant to find for the respondent for both plans drawn by him, then their verdict could have been for a larger sum. But, in this respect only, the respondent could complain. Appellants will not be heard to complain because the verdict against them was not large enough. A careful reading of the record convinces us that the judgment should be affirmed.

PARKER, C. J., MACKINTOSH, FULLERTON, and HOLCOMB, JJ., concur.

[No. 16368. Department One. June 28, 1921.]

WALTER DeLong, *Respondent*, v. NORTHWEST MOTOR
COMPANY, *Appellant*.[1]

PRINCIPAL AND AGENT (42, 57, 58-1)—EVIDENCE—SUFFICIENCY. In
an action against a principal for the conversion of an automobile
by its agent, a verdict against defendant was warranted by evidence showing its sales agent in attempting to make a sale of one
of defendant's cars to plaintiff offered to take a car owned by plaintiff and credit it on the purchase price; that, though the bill of
sale for plaintiff's car was made direct to the sales agent, the car
was placed among defendant's second-hand cars, and kept there until
its disappearance; that a mechanic employed by defendant to examine cars was required to procure an order from the main office
for the delivery of the car from the second-hand department for
that purpose, which was given him by the sales agent, at the time
the only one in charge of the main office; and that there was
nothing in the evidence putting plaintiff upon inquiry or notice
that the sales agent was exceeding his authority.

Appeal from a judgment of the superior court for
King county, Allen, J., entered October 8, 1920, upon
the verdict of a jury in favor of the plaintiff, in an
action for damages for the conversion of an automobile.
Affirmed.

Kerr, McCord & Ivey, for appellant.
Ogden & Clarke, for respondent.

HOLCOMB, J.—The only errors alleged on this appeal
are that the court erred, first, in denying appellant's
motion for judgment *non obstante veredicto;* and, second, in denying appellant's motion for a new trial. At
the conclusion of the evidence, appellant asked for a
directed verdict, which was denied.

The suit was for $1,150 damages for the conversion
of a Mitchell automobile which had been delivered to
one Doty, a sales agent of appellant, who had been in

[1]Reported in 199 Pac. 233.

the employ of the appellant from 1917 until about September, 1919, when, after one or more defalcations, he absconded.

Appellant contends that there was not sufficient evidence of the authority of Doty, as agent of the company, to enter into any such transaction as respondent made, and that the transaction was not ratified by appellant.

The facts were submitted to the jury upon instructions as to the question of agency, not excepted to by appellant, and no instructions requested by appellant other than as given by the court.

Having examined and analyzed the evidence, we conclude that the evidence was sufficient to prove the agency and authority of Doty. Doty was appellant's authorized sales agent and respondent knew him in no other capacity. He had come to the office, where respondent was employed, a great many times for the purpose of attempting to sell automobiles to persons connected with the concern. He solicited respondent to purchase an Essex car, and on being informed that respondent had a Mitchell car, agreed to take it in exchange for an Essex car and attempt to secure a credit of $1,400 for the Mitchell car. The Mitchell car was delivered to him, and, although the bill of sale was made direct to Doty, the car was taken to the place where appellant kept its used or second-hand cars about the first of July, and remained there for some time. Doty finally asserted that he could not get approval of a credit exceeding $1,150, to which respondent assented. A mechanic, who was employed by respondent to examine as to the condition of the car in a certain respect, of which information had been given respondent by Doty, was obliged to go to the main office of appellant, not to the place where it kept its second-hand cars, and procure an order to the agent in charge of the used car department, for the delivery of the car from the place where the second-hand cars were kept, to him. He got the order, although no one was in the office at the time except Doty, who gave him the order. He took the car out to test it, and returned it to the place where appellant kept its second-hand cars. From there it disappeared some time later, probably having been sold by Doty.

The officers of appellant contend that the manner in which Doty placed the car where appellant kept its second-hand cars was irregular, not according to its usual course of business, and without any record of the transaction; but of that the respondent had no knowledge, and is not at fault. The company should have kept better check upon its agents, and upon the cars in its place of business.

Other circumstances and inferences to be derived from the evidence justified the jury in finding that Doty, although defrauding appellant, was acting as agent of appellant in this particular transaction. There was nothing in the evidence or circumstances to put respondent upon notice or inquiry that Doty was exceeding his authority in this transaction.

The judgment is affirmed.

PARKER, C. J., MACKINTOSH, BRIDGES, and FULLERTON, JJ., concur.

[No. 16460. Department One. June 28, 1921.]

CORA TURNER et al., Appellants, v. TJOSEVIG-KENNECOTT COPPER COMPANY et al., Respondents.[1]

PLEADING (14)—ALLEGATIONS INCONSISTENT WITH WRITTEN INSTRUMENTS. Where a cause of action is pleaded as being founded upon certain contracts which are set out, the pleadings must give way to the contrary provisions of the contract.

CORPORATIONS (55, 60) — STOCK — SALES — PLEDGES — TITLE OF PLEDGEE. A contract for stock in a corporation in consideration of mining claims sold to the corporation is valid and legal where it provided that the money payment was to be derived from sales of the balance of the stock; that the entire capital stock should be held in pledge by a bank, to be released and sold in certain blocks, from the proceeds of which sales certain sums were to be paid on the purchase price due the claim owners; and that, in the event of failure of the corporation to meet the purchase price, it should forfeit all rights to have the unsold shares returned to it, but that such unsold stock should become the property of the claim owners.

SAME (28)—CAPITAL STOCK—REDUCTION. Under a contract providing for the sale of mining claims to a corporation, all of the stock of which except a certain number of shares given the claim owners was to be sold and the proceeds turned over to them, the stock, pending sales, being deposited in bank as a pledge for the purchase price, there was no diminution of the capital stock or assets, within the prohibition of Rem. Code, § 3697, where no stock had been issued which was not paid for, and nothing was taken out of the assets to pay for the stock.

SAME (83)—CAPITAL STOCK—RIGHT TO VOTE—PLEDGES. A pledge of the entire capital stock of a corporation to secure performance of a contract to pay for the property acquired by the corporation would not constitute the pledgee a stockholder.

Appeal from an order of the superior court for King county, Hall, J., entered September 21, 1920, sustaining a demurrer to the complaint, in an action to secure the return of money paid for corporate stock. Affirmed.

[1]Reported in 199 Pac. 312.

James F. Ailshie and *Walter B. Allen,* for appellants.

Chadwick, McMicken, Ramsey & Rupp, for respondents Hay, Gazzam, McDougall and Roberts.

Ballinger, Battle, Hulbert & Shorts, for respondents Christian Tjosevig *et al.*

MACKINTOSH, J.—The appellants presented to the court a complaint containing two causes of action; they alleged that they were stockholders in the defendant corporation, and that they brought the suit for the benefit of themselves, as stockholders, and all other stockholders of the company. The first cause of action seeks the appointment of a receiver; the second cause of action alleges that the defendant corporation has a capitalization of 2,500,000 shares of stock, of the par value of one dollar per share; that the corporation entered into certain dealings with the defendants, Tjosevig, which resulted in the corporation purchasing from them a number of quartz mining claims in Alaska, and paying for the property by issuing to the Tjosevigs 2,499,995 shares of the capital stock, and that the Tjosevigs accepted the stock and in exchange therefor deeded to the corporation the mining claims, and that ever since such date the corporation has been, and now is, the owner thereof; that thereafter, the Tjosevigs entered into a contract with the corporation by which the corporation was given the right to sell any portion of the stock held by the Tjosevigs, except 135,000 shares, at different prices, with the agreement that all receipts by the corporation above such prices should belong to the corporation.

It further alleged that the agreement between the Tjosevigs and the corporation was that in case of the sale of a part of the stock of the former, and a failure to make the balance of the payments to the Tjosevigs, the corporation would forfeit its right to sell the bal-

ance of the stock, and that the Tjosevigs would then
remain the owners of whatever number of shares of
stock might remain unsold. It is then alleged that the
corporation sold 500,000 shares of stock, and that the
defendant trustees of the corporation wrongfully purchased from the Tjosevigs all the remaining shares of
stock and paid Tjosevigs $141,000 in cash therefor
from funds in the treasury of the corporation. Further, that these acts were contrary to § 3697, Rem.
Code, which provides that it shall be unlawful for trustees to in any way pay to stockholders of a corporation
any part of the capital stock of the company, or reduce
the capital except in the manner provided; also, that
the acts were in violation of § 3704, Rem. Code, which
provides that the capital stock of a corporation may
be lawfully increased or diminished only in certain
specified ways. The complaint then alleges that the
appellants have demanded that the defendant trustees
take steps to secure the return of the money paid to the
Tjosevigs for the purchase of their stock to the treasury of the company, but that this request has been denied, and that appellants are therefore prosecuting this
action for the benefit of themselves and all other stockholders of the company. The prayer of the complaint
is that the trustees of the company be held personally
liable for the sum paid to the Tjosevigs.

The defendant corporation demurred to each cause
of action on the ground that it did not state facts
sufficient to constitute a cause of action; likewise the
defendant trustees and the Tjosevigs demurred. The
court sustained the demurrer of the corporation and
the trustees to the second cause of action, and sustained
the Tjosevigs' demurrer to the entire complaint. From
this disposition of the demurrers the appellants bring
the record here.

Attached to and made a part of the complaint are various exhibits, comprising the agreements between the Tjosevigs and the defendant corporation in relation to the purchase of the mining claims and the organization of the company. An examination of these exhibits refutes the legal effect of them plead by the appellants. The rule is that where a cause of action is plead as being founded upon certain contracts which are set out, the pleadings must give way to contrary provisions of the contract. *Lawson v. Sprague,* 51 Wash. 286, 98 Pac. 737; *Clark v. Cross,* 51 Wash. 231, 98 Pac. 607; *Jordan v. Coulter,* 30 Wash. 116, 70 Pac. 257. From the contracts it appears that the Tjosevigs were the owners of mining claims in Alaska and that a mining promoter, who had an option for the purchase of the mines, interested the defendants named as trustees in the subsequently organized corporation in their purchase. It also appears that these men organized a corporation and followed the procedure allowed by Rem. Code, § 2347, and that they purchased the Tjosevigs' claims by agreeing to pay for them $175,000 in money and 135,000 shares of the capital stock. In order that the company might be allowed to sell the stock to raise the money necessary to pay the cash portion of the purchase price, and at the same time protect the Tjosevigs, it was agreed that the Tjosevigs would make a deed to the property under a contract providing that the entire capital stock of the company, less the five shares necessary to qualify the trustees, should be held in pledge by a bank, and that this stock should be released in certain blocks and sold, and that out of the proceeds of such sale certain fixed sums should be paid to the Tjosevigs to be applied on the purchase price. The contracts then provide that, in the event of failure of the corporation to meet the purchase price, the company should forfeit all of its rights to have the shares of stock in the hands of the trustees yet unsold returned to it, but that the unsold stock should become the property of the Tjosevigs.

Although this is not the ordinary method of acquiring mining claims by a corporation organized for the purpose of purchasing claims owned by someone else, it was a perfectly lawful and businesslike arrangement. It offered protection to the purchaser and seller alike. What the appellants complain of is the performance of this contract by the corporation. The claims were sold in consideration of the money and stock to be delivered. All that has been done is that the company has procured the money from the sale of the stock, which it had a perfect right to do, and has paid all of the purchase price to the Tjosevigs and has delivered the stock to them and taken title to the property. We cannot see how this is in any way a diminution of the capital stock or of assets of the company. Nothing was taken out of the assets by the trustees to pay for the stock; no stock has been issued which has not been paid for, and the case does not fall within the decision in *Kom v. Cody Detective Agency*, 76 Wash. 540, 136 Pac. 1155, which was a case involving the right of a corporation to purchase and retire its own stock with capital funds. Here each share of stock, sold or unsold, is represented by money or assets of the company; if unsold, by the stock itself; if sold, by money or other assets. All that has been done is to pledge the capital stock to pay the purchase price of these claims.

Nor can the appellants find solace in the argument that the Tjosevigs became the owners of the entire capital stock when it was pledged with them to secure the performance of the contract. They were mere pledgees and not stockholders. *Burgess v. Seligman*, 107 U. S. 20.

We find nothing in the complaint as read in the light of the contracts themselves which was sufficient to withstand the demurrers, and the judgment is therefore affirmed.

PARKER, C. J., BRIDGES, FULLERTON, and HOLCOMB, JJ., concur.

[No. 16334. Department One. July 1, 1921.]

LEO G. GOSTINA *et al., Respondents,* v. A. L. RYLAND *et al., Appellants.*[1]

ADJOINING LANDOWNERS (3)—ENCROACHMENTS. An adjoining property owner having an absolute legal right, under Rem. Code, § 943, to an action to abate a nuisance caused by overhanging branches of trees, the defendants cannot defend on the ground that the action is inspired by spite.

NUISANCE (5)—PRIVATE NUISANCE—GROUNDS FOR INJUNCTION. Acquiescence for several months in a nuisance occasioned by overhanging branches and the spreading vines of a creeping plant would not constitute an estoppel against a right of action by an adjoining owner to abate the nuisance occasioned thereby.

ESTOPPEL (48)—EQUITABLE ESTOPPEL—ACQUIESCENCE—LACHES. In an action to abate a nuisance under Rem. Code, § 943, granting the right where there is an obstruction to the free use of property essentially interfering with the enjoyment of life and property, proof of some actual and sensible damages, although insignificant, will sustain plaintiff's right to have the nuisance abated.

MACKINTOSH and BRIDGES, JJ., dissent.

Appeal from a judgment of the superior court for King county, Gilliam, J., entered January 14, 1920, upon findings in favor of the plaintiffs, in an action to abate a nuisance, tried to the court. Affirmed.

Walter B. Allen, for appellants.

Warren Hardy, for respondents.

[1]Reported in 199 Pac. 298.

HOLCOMB, J.—These adversaries own and reside upon adjoining lots in the city of Seattle. Appellants have owned and resided upon their lot for many years. Respondents bought their lot in August, 1918. There are growing upon appellants' lot a Lombardy poplar tree, situated about two feet from the division line fence separating the properties; also a fir tree in the rear of appellants' premises, situated within two feet of the division fence. It is alleged that some branches of the trees overhang the premises of respondents. Appellants also maintain a creeping vine, growing in a rustic box on top of a large stump, a few feet from the division fence, which is trained downward from the stump and it is alleged that parts of the creeping plant go through and under the division fence, and onto the lawn on respondents' premises. There are also some raspberry bushes and a rose bush at the rear of appellants' premises growing near the line which the respondents allege are permitted to hang over the division fence.

On July 28, 1919, respondents caused their attorney to give notice in writing to the appellants that the branches of the fir tree (then mentioned as a pine tree) standing upon appellants' premises, extended over the lot of respondents, and that the needles therefrom fell upon the lawn of respondents, injuring the same; and that the ivy planted in the yard of appellants ran under the fence and onto the lawn of respondents. Demand was made that appellants, within ten days, cut off the branches of the fir tree at the point where they crossed the boundary line, and remove the ivy from respondents' property, and to keep the tree and ivy from further encroaching upon their property.

This demand not having been complied with, about
fifteen days thereafter respondents began their action
under the statute, Rem. Code, §§ 943, 944 and 945, for
the abatement of a nuisance, and for such other and
further relief as might seem equitable and just.

Issue was joined as to the overhanging branches and
encroaching ivy constituting a nuisance. Findings of
fact and conclusions of law and judgment ordering
abatement of the nuisances by appellants within sixty
days, and in case of failure by them, ordering the
sheriff to do so, were entered in favor of the respondents by the trial court, and this appeal resulted.

Appellants desired to defend on the theory that the
action by respondents was merely for spite and vexa-
tion, and first complain because the court excluded evidence offered by them to the effect that, when respondents purchased their property adjoining that of appellants, they knew of the existence and condition of
the trees and shrubs, and expressed their admiration
therefor, and had no objection to their maintenance as
they were upon the property of appellants, until after
they had had some sort of personal disagreement,
which caused their action in regard to the trees and
shrubs. The court rejected all such evidence and
offered proof, on the ground that it was immaterial,
because where branches of trees overlap adjoining
property, the owner of the adjoining property has an
absolute legal right to have the overhanging branches
removed by a suit of this character.

Section 943, Rem. Code, provides:

" . . . whatever is injurious to health, or indecent, or offensive to the senses, or an obstruction to
the free use of property, so as to essentially interfere
with the comfortable enjoyment of the life and property, is a nuisance, and the subject of an action for
damages and other and further relief."

Section 944, *supra,* provides:

"Such action may be brought by any person whose property is injuriously affected, or whose personal enjoyment is lessened by the nuisance. . . ."

It cannot be said that acquiescence in the existence of the alleged nuisance for the period of a few months is such as to constitute estoppel or equitable laches. Whatever may have been respondents' sentiments regarding the situation and character of the trees and shrubs at one time, when they entered upon the enjoyment of their own possessions, after occupancy for a few months they gave notice on July 28, 1919, that their permissive acquiescence in the existence of the alleged nuisances, at least as to the fir tree and the ivy, had ceased, and that they required the encroachment to be stopped.

In *Lonsdale v. Nelson,* 2 B. & C. 311, it is held by the English court that:

"Nuisances by an act of commission are committed in defiance of those whom such nuisances injure, and the injured party may abate them, without notice to the person who committed them; but there is no decided case which sanctions the abatement, by an individual, of nuisances from omission, except that of cutting the branches of trees which overhang a public road, or the private property of the person who cuts them. The permitting these branches to extend so far beyond the soil of the owner of the trees, is a most unequivocal act of negligence, which distinguishes this case from most of the other cases that have occurred. The security of lives and property may sometimes require so speedy a remedy as not to allow time to call on the person on whose property the mischief has arisen, to remedy it. In such cases an individual would be justified in abating a nuisance from omission without notice. In all other cases of such nuisances, persons should not take the law into their own hands, but follow the advice of Lord Hale, and appeal to a court of justice."

"Trees whose branches extend over the land of another are not nuisances, except to the extent to which the branches overhang the adjoining land. To that extent they *are* technical nuisances, and the person over whose land they extend may cut them off, or have his action for damages, if any have been sustained therefrom, and an abatement of the nuisance against the owner or occupant of the land on which they grow, but he may not cut down the tree, neither can he cut the branches thereof beyond the extent to which they overhang his soil." Wood, Nuisances (3d ed.), § 108.

"It may be understood that any erection upon one man's land, that projects over the land of another, as well as any tree whose branches thus project, *doing actual damage,* or anything that interferes with the rights of an adjoining owner, is an actionable nuisance." Wood, Nuisances, § 106.

From ancient times it has been a principle of law that the landowner has the exclusive right to the space above the surface of his property. To whomsoever the soil belongs, he also owns to the sky and to the depths. The owner of a piece of land owns everything above it and below it to an indefinite extent. Coke, Litt. § 4.

"On the same principle it is held that the branches of trees extending over adjoining land constitute a nuisance—at least in the sense that the owner of the land encroached on may himself cut off the offending growth." 20 R. C. L. 433, 434, 435, § 49, the cases cited.

"But whether a suit for an injunction and damages may be maintained without proof of actual damage is a point upon which the authorities are not very clear or satisfactory. According to some of the decisions, sensible appreciable damage must be shown in order to give the overhanging branches the character of nuisance; in other words, the fact that the branches extend over another's land does not constitute them a nuisance *per se.*" 20 R. C. L. p. 433, 434, 435, § 49.

Thus in *Countryman v. Lighthill,* 24 Hun (N. Y.) 405, 82 Hun (N. Y.) 152 (not an ancient case as respondents state, but decided in 1881) it was held that:

"The overhanging branches of a tree, not poisonous or noxious in its nature, are not a nuisance *per se,* in such a sense as to sustain an action for damages. Some real, sensible damage must be shown to result therefrom."

The complaint which does not describe the damages caused will not state a cause of action.

That is our view.

It is generally the rule that "One adjoining owner cannot maintain an action against another for the intrusion of roots or branches of a tree which is not poisonous or noxious in its nature, his remedy in such case is to clip or lop off the branches or cut the roots at the line." 1 C. J. 1233, § 94.

See, also, *Countryman v. Lighthill, supra; Crowhurst v. Amersham Burial Board,* 4 Exchequer Div. 5; *Hoffman v. Armstrong,* 48 N. Y. 201, Sickles, Vol. 3; *Lyman v. Hale,* 11 Conn. 177, 27 Am. Dec. 728; *Skinner v. Wilder,* 38 Vt. 115, 38 Am. Dec. 645; *Harndon v. Stutz,* 124 Iowa 440, 100 N. W. 329; *Tanner v. Wallbrumm,* 77 Mo. App. 262.

It is therefore well settled that the powerful aid of a court of equity by injunction can be successfully invoked only in a strong and mischievous case of pressing necessity and there must be satisfactory proof of real substantial damage. *Tanner v. Wallbrumm, supra.*

Hence, were it not for our statute of nuisances, the respondents herein would not be accorded any judicial relief. But our statutes accord a remedy for a very slight nuisance: "Whatever is . . . . an obstruction to the free use of property, so as to essentially interfere with the comfortable enjoyment of the life and property." Rem. Code, § 943.

But in this case the respondent did describe some annoyance and damage—insignificant, it is true, so insignificant that respondents did not even claim them or prove any amount in damages—but simply proved that the leaves falling from the overhanging branches of the poplar tree caused them some additional work in caring for their lawn; and that the needles from the overhanging branches of the fir tree caused them some additional work in keeping their premises neat and clean, and fell upon their roof and caused some stoppage of gutters; and that sometimes, when the wind blew in the right direction, the needles blew into the house and annoyed the occupants. We cannot avoid holding, therefore, that these are actual, sensible damages, and not merely nominal, and although insignificant, "the insignificance of the injury goes to the extent of recovery and not to the right of action." *Henry v. Shepherd*, 52 Miss. 125.

The respondents in this case certainly had one remedy in their own hands, and under all the authorities could, without notice, if they had not encouraged the maintenance thereof, after notice if they had (which they gave), have clipped the branches that overhung their premises at the line.

"And although the right so to trim must be conceded, this does not dispose of the case, as the watching to see when trimming would be necessary, and the operation of trimming, are burdens which ought not to be cast upon a neighbor by the acts of an adjoining owner. . . . . . if the trees were innocuous, it might well be held . . . . that the occupier of the land projected over would have no right of action . . . . from similar grounds of general convenience." *Crowhurst v. Amersham Burial Board, supra.*

Since they had the statutory right to bring an action for abatement, and have shown some actual and

sensible damages, although insignificant, we consider
that we have no option but to sustain it. The remainder of the trees will doubtless shed their leaves
and needles upon the respondents' premises; but this
they must endure positively without remedy.

The appellants' contention that "One who has slept
upon his rights for a considerable time by acquiescing
in the alleged nuisance will be denied equitable relief
and left to his remedy at law", 29 Cyc. 1231, cannot
apply here. The cases cited by appellants under this
head show delays not of months, but of years. That
principle is applied where one has encouraged the nuisance and allowed the party to go on and make a heavy
expenditure under the reasonable belief that no objection would be made; or where the damages were small
and the injury not of a continuous and permanent nature. 2 Wood, Nuisances (3d ed.), § 785.

The courts look beyond the injury to the consequence
of their action and if fair redress can be had at law
they will not tie up important industries or operations
by injunction unless the equities of the case demand.
Varney v. Pope, 60 Me. 192; *Sparhawk v. Union Pass
R. Co.*, 54 Pa. St. 401.

Here respondents did not encourage an active nuisance or nuisance by commission, but for a short time
permitted an omission when they gave notice of the
cessation of their permission. No expenditure had
been encouraged, and incurred on the part of appellants. It cannot be considered that respondents slept
upon their rights for such a considerable time, by
acquiescing in the alleged nuisance, so that they would
be denied equitable relief; nor is this equitable relief,
but legal and statutory relief. *Carl v. West Aberdeen
Land & Imp. Co.*, 13 Wash. 618, 43 Pac. 890. While it
has some appearance of being merely a vexatious suit,

appellants admit that the tree-boughs do overhang respondents' lot to some extent. There is sufficient foundation in fact to sustain a case, and the authorities are clearly with respondents.

The judgment of the lower court is affirmed.

PARKER, C. J., and FULLERTON, J., concur.

MACKINTOSH, J. (dissenting)—To have the acts complained of in this case constitute a nuisance, under § 943, Rem. Code, they must be acts (1) injurious to health; or (2) indecent; or (3) offensive to the senses, or (4) an obstruction to the free use of the property so as to essentially interfere with the comfortable enjoyment of the life and property. It is conceded that the acts do not come within classifications 1, 2 or 3, but it is held that such acts amount to an obstruction of the free use of the property so as to essentially interfere with its comfortable enjoyment. I cannot agree with such a result. For the trivial encroachment of the branches of a tree, and the growth of a few vines under a fence do not appear to me to amount to *such an obstruction* as to *essentially interfere* with the respondents' comfortable enjoyment of their property, and are not such circumstances as will entitle respondents, under § 944, Rem. Code, to institute an action, it being provided in that section that the action may be brought by a person whose property is *injuriously* affected or whose *personal enjoyment* is lessened.

I agree with the writer of the opinion in his characterization of this action as vexatious, and I think that the statutes on nuisances are hardly susceptible of the interpretation given them, which has rendered the action not only vexatious but successful.

I therefore dissent.

BRIDGES, J., concurs with MACKINTOSH, J.

[No. 16471. Department Two. July 1, 1921.]

In the Matter of the Estate of JOHN F. CURTIS.[1]

APPEAL (81)—RIGHT TO APPEAL—PARTIES—DISMISSAL—IN GENERAL. An appeal of parties of record will not be dismissed on the ground that they did not appear below, where attorneys filed an affidavit showing their authority and appearance in their behalf.

EXECUTORS AND ADMINISTRATORS (1, 29½)—NECESSITY OF ADMINISTRATION—ADMINISTRATORS DE BONIS NON. Where an executor for an estate died after eighteen years of incumbency without having closed and procured distribution of the estate, nor given the notice to creditors ordered by the court at the time of his appointment, the court had jurisdiction to appoint an administrator *de bonis non* with the will annexed; since creditors of the estate had not been conclusively barred; and Rem. Code, § 1368, providing nonliability of an estate for debts unless letters of administration be granted within six years after death of the decedent is inapplicable in view of the actual appointment of an executor.

SAME (165)—COMPENSATION—RATE AND COMPUTATION — ALLOWANCE. Where the services of an administrator *de bonis non* consisted wholly in giving notice to creditors, procuring appraisement of the property of the estate, rendering a final account and procuring an order of final settlement, discharge from creditors, and decree of distribution, an allowance of $600 should be reduced to $250.

HUSBAND AND WIFE (58, 60)—COMMUNITY PROPERTY—PRESUMPTION—EVIDENCE—SUFFICIENCY. The presumption of the community character of property acquired during coverture is not overcome by a showing that the separate property and community earnings of the spouses were commingled in the acquisition of what is claimed as community property.

WILLS (86)—RIGHTS OF DEVISEES—ELECTION. The duty of a widow to elect whether she will take under her husband's will devising to her a life use in specific realty or under her own right as a community owner need not be exercised until the time of distribution, where her right has not been disputed.

ESTOPPEL (61)—PERSONS TO WHOM AVAILABLE. Estoppel of a widow to claim a community interest in real estate which her husband's will treated as separate property from which she was to have a net income for life cannot be asserted by heirs who never complied with the provisions of the will for her net income.

[1] Reported in 199 Pac. 309.

Appeal by legatees from a judgment of the superior court for King county, Jurey, J., entered December 18, 1920, decreeing a settlement and distribution of an estate, after a hearing upon exceptions to the final account of the administrator. Modified.

Geo. McKay, Winter S. Martin, and *Roy D. Robinson,* for appellants.

Shorett, McLaren & Shorett, for respondents.

HOLCOMB, J.—John F. Curtis died in King county, Washington, in 1893. He left a will which was thereafter duly probated in, and by, the superior court of King county, disposing of his estate. After certain usual and customary provisions, the provisions of the will in controversy and most material in this matter, were these:

"Third: I give and bequeath to my beloved wife Ellenor the rents and use of all my personal estate of every description whatever, money I may have on hand at the time of my death and all securi*etes* for money, indebtedness, chances (choses) in action, subject only to the payment of my debts and funeral expenses.

"Fourth: I give the use of the building and rents to receive on lot number three, block twenty-six in the town of Sprague, now recorded in Lincoln county, state of Washington—

"Fifth: I give the use of lots one and two, block nin-ty-eight, David D. T. Denny-s fifth addition to Seattle, King county, state of Washington—also the use and collection of rents on 3 houses on John street and two on lots No. 2 running on said lot to alley.

"Sixth: I give the use of lots No. 1 and 2, block sixteen, and the use and collection of rent on the house built on lot 1, corner Adams and 12th street extension to Fairhaven, situated in Fairhaven, Whatcom county, state of Washington.

"Seventh: All my money received from rents or lease of lots to be received by my wife Ellenor or her

agents and to take out fifty dollars from said rentals
for her maintenance and support and the ball/ance left
in the bank drawing interest and not to be drawn out
except for repairs of houses and taxes and street
grades and in case one of the houses burn down, and to
make out a yearly report to my son Leonard Harvey
John Curtis, giving detail and receipts of all work done
yearly. I make these provisions and stipulations so as
to give a correct account so it will enable my son Leonard as to the wants of all buildings and taxes and repairs and all other items.— should there be not money
enough coming in from rents my son Leonard must
make up the amount for the support of my wife Ellenor maintenance and the f-ur heirs will have to pay
equal share—no lots nor any of the houses to be sold
if possible.

"Eighth: At the death of my wife Ellenor all the
property of every description and all moneys in banks
coming from the receiving of the rents to be given over
to the rightful heirs begotten by me and the lawful
heirs are Mary Eliza Ellen Facer, now in Colorado,
Matilda Sarah Winterburn Fairweather, of Spokane,
Leonard Harvey John Curtis of this state of Wash.,
Anson Erastus Jeptha Curtis, of Albina, Oregon, at
the death of my wife Ellenor this property herein described must be divided equally as the four heirs m-y
decide on—this to be done as soon as my wife Ellenor
*h*is bur*r*ied, all funeral expenses to come out of the
estate.

"Eighteenth: To my wife Ellenor until her death
to live in the house on corner of John and Bissmar-k
street if she wishes or she can live in any of the house-
she chooses until/ her death and *if* is apparent to the
executor that she becomes demented or sickness over-
takes her and her reason leaves her for the executor to
take hold of it and do the business for her. All the
furniture I die possessed with, and bedding and clothes
for her own and to be given to whom she likes. I would
prefer Lizzie Cox to have them."

By other paragraphs of his will, he left small bequests of personal articles to certain of his own child-

ren, and also children of the surviving wife. He nominated his son Leonard Harvey John Curtis as executor and provided that he should not be obliged to give security before obtaining letters testamentary. Leonard Harvey John Curtis, upon the admission of the will to probate, was granted letters testamentary, without bond. The executor died in 1911, without having closed and procured distribution of the estate and without, in fact, having given notice to creditors, although an order so to do had been made by the superior court for King county upon the admission of the will to probate, and his appointment as executor.

The widow, Ellenor Curtis, was a second wife of the testator, and had no children by him, but had three children by a previous marriage. Elizabeth Curtis, the first wife of decedent, died in The Dalles, Oregon, in February, 1881, leaving four children, who were the four children and representatives of deceased children involved in this proceeding. The testator and his first wife had lived in the state of Washington from about the year 1870 to about the year 1879, and had acquired property in what was then Fairhaven (now Bellingham), Whatcom county, Washington, and a tract of land near Silver Lake and Castle Rock, Cowlitz county, Washington, and real estate in The Dalles, Oregon, after their removal there, which they used for a home, and a small house which was rented to their son, Anson. After the death of the first wife in 1881, the surviving husband visited his old home in England, and on his return trip in December, 1881, he married Ellenor Curtis at La Porte, Indiana. He immediately came west after his marriage and took a position with the Northern Pacific Railway Company as master mechanic, at Pasco, Washington, removing in about three months to Sprague, Washington, where his duties had been transferred. His wife came west to join him at Sprague in the summer of 1882. In his capacity as railroad master mechanic, Curtis earned between $200 and $250 per month, and retained the position until the spring of 1883, or a little over one year. He then went to Seattle. While living at Sprague he built a residence, probably costing, according to the testimony, in the neighborhood of $3,000. On April 6, 1883, he sold and conveyed the property at The Dalles, Oregon, for $2,500. On June 11, 1883, or a little over two months thereafter, he acquired the Seattle property, which is now in dispute, for a consideration of $1,000, which was paid in cash, and the conveyance immediately made by deed. This property was later improved with five small frame houses, the first one of which to be built was occupied as a home by Curtis and wife, and the other four were rented.

Leonard Curtis, as executor of the last will of John F. Curtis, filed two meager reports after his appointment, but did nothing further up to his death in 1911.

In the year 1919, the present administrator was appointed administrator with the will annexed *de bonis non* on the application of Ellenor Curtis, the surviving widow. No notice of the application for the appointment of the present administrator was given, the court making an order that no notice was necessary. The present administrator, with the will annexed *de bonis non,* caused an inventory to be prepared, had appraisers appointed, and had the property appraised. The property was appraised as community property of the value of $15,000. He published notice to creditors as directed by the order entered in 1893, and after the expiration of the time for serving and filing claims against the estate he prepared and filed his final account and petition for distribution, and gave the customary notice of hearing thereon. Prior to the hearing, objections were filed to the necessity for an administrator with the will annexed, and also objections to the manner of distribution proposed by the administrator.

The attorneys for appellants originally appeared for Anson Curtis and also all the other legatees who would join with him. Thereafter, during the proceedings, the attorneys named as objectors all of the surviving heirs and descendants of John F. Curtis, save and except the widow, as those for whom they appeared. A motion was made by respondents to dismiss the attempted appeal of John Facer, Frederick Facer, Cora A. Facer Pauley, and Eunice Facer Struthers, for the reason that they neither served nor filed nor made any objections to the final account and petition for distribution before the entry of the decree of settlement and distribution.

We will deny the motion to dismiss the appeal as to the foregoing named persons, presuming that the attorneys were authorized to, and did, appear for all the aforenamed persons, which authority is supported by affidavits filed by attorneys Martin and McKay.

The first complaint of appellant is that the court below should have sustained their objections to the probate proceedings appointing Edward R. Taylor as administrator *de bonis non* with the will annexed. They urge that all of the property belonging to the estate was delivered over to the parties entitled thereto, according to the terms of the will; that during the administration of Leonard Curtis all the debts of the estate were paid, and that the estate was practically closed; that there was no property not administered, and property not administered only gives the court jurisdiction to appoint an administrator *de bonis non*.

It is argued that the policy of our statute (Rem. Code, § 1368) reading:

"No real estate of a deceased person shall be liable for his debts unless letters testamentary or of administration be granted within six years from the date of the death of such decedent."

is against allowing the probate proceedings to be revived as this was.

We are of the opinion, contrary to the contention of the respondent, that appellants made their objections at the first opportunity to the appointment of this administrator, but that their objection is untenable for the reason that: (1) the statute (§ 1368, Rem. Code), does not apply, because letters testamentary had been applied for and granted within six years after the death of decedent, and the probate was open and continuous, and in the hands of the executor named in the will from that time to the date of the death of that executor; and (2) that the executor had not conclusively barred creditors against the estate, for the reason that he had not published notice to creditors as required by law and by the order of the court, and we have held that in order to determine whether there was any creditor or creditors it was necessary to publish notice, and until the order of the court is complied with any claims which may exist would not be barred. *Donnerberg v. Oppenheimer,* 15 Wash. 290, 46 Pac. 254; *McFarland v. Fairlamb,* 18 Wash. 601, 52 Pac. 239; *In re Collins' Estate,* 102 Wash. 697, 173 Pac. 1016; *State ex rel. Mann v. Superior Court,* 52 Wash. 149, 100 Pac. 198.

The completion of the probate and conclusive barring of creditors being justified, the administrator *de bonis non* was entitled to some allowance for his services. The trial court allowed and credited him, as against the appraised value of the estate remaining, the sum of $600, and for commissions earned, and of this appellants complain. His services consisted wholly in giving notice to creditors, causing appraisers to be appointed and appraisement of the property of the estate made, and rendering a final account and settlement, and procuring an order of final settlement, discharge from creditors, and decree of distribution, and for such services, not requiring the passing on claims of creditors, no handling of funds or personal property and disposing of the same, we think $600 allowed by the trial court greatly excessive. That allowance is hereby modified and reduced to the sum of $250, which we consider very ample.

Appellants next complain of the findings of the court that the real estate involved in this appeal is community property of John F. Curtis deceased, and Ellenor Curtis, his surviving wife, and in decreeing distribution to the appellants of the remainder of one-half of the property in controversy instead of the entire property after the termination of the life estate of respondent widow.

After diligently reading the entire record, including a full statement of facts, we are unable to say that the evidence is sufficiently strong and convincing to overthrow the presumption of the community status of the property arising from the fact that the property was acquired during coverture of the testator and his surviving widow. There is no strong and convincing evidence controverting the fact that at the time of the acquisition of the property in question, the testator had considerable earning capacity, at a time when the purchasing power of a dollar was considerably greater than now; that Ellenor Curtis also had some little property, and that at most separate property of each, and community earnings were commingled in the acquisition of this property. *In re Slocum's Estate,* 83 Wash. 158, 145 Pac. 204.

Appellants then contend that if we find that the property involved was community property, then, under the terms of the will, the widow was required to elect and take either under the will or against it; and they contend that she has conclusively elected to take under the will, and therefore confined to her life estate in the property, and the distribution made by the court is incorrect.

Conceding that the testator by his will made provision for his widow which he was under no legal obligation to make, and that he dealt with the entire estate as if it were his separate property, devising to her a life use of specifically described real estate, and that she was therefore required, under our decisions in *Herrick v. Miller,* 69 Wash. 456, 134 Pac. 189, and *Prince v. Prince,* 64 Wash. 552, 117 Pac. 255, to elect whether she would take under the will or under her own right as community owner, we are of the opinion nevertheless that she was not required to make such election, where her right had not been disputed, until distribution. This she has done. She petitioned for distribution and declared that the property was community property. *In re Smith's Estate,* 108 Cal. 115, 40 Pac. 1037.

Nor are appellants in any position to assert estoppel and laches on the part of the widow when they themselves did not comply with the provisions of the will during the eight years of the executorship of Leonard Curtis, and ten years since the death of the executor, Leonard Curtis, to contribute sufficient to assure the widow a net income of fifty dollars per month, and maintain the status of the real estate as separate

estate, the remainder of which would be distributed to
the residuary devisees upon the termination of the life
tenure.

The distribution made by the court will be affirmed.

The decree will be modified as hereinbefore specified
fixing the administrator's commissions at $250, and
the appellants will recover costs of appeal.

PARKER, C. J., TOLMAN, MAIN, and MITCHELL, JJ.,
concur.

[No. 16484. Department One. July 7, 1921.]

THE STATE OF WASHINGTON, *on the Relation of C. L.
Morris, Plaintiff*, v. JOHN TRUAX, *Judge etc.,
Respondent.*[1]

APPEAL (237)—SUPERSEDEAS — RIGHT TO — JUDGMENTS AFFECTING
RIGHTS. Where a receiver, appointed in a suit by mortgagees, was
required by stipulation of the parties to make reports only to the
mortgagees, but was subsequently ordered, at suit of minority stockholders, to make report to the court, and was adjudged in contempt
for failure to so report after dismissal of the action in which he had
been appointed receiver, he is entitled, on appeal from the order
requiring him to report and adjudging him in contempt, to have
the order requiring a receivership report superseded pending the
appeal, where it appears he is acting in good faith, that the question to be presented to the appellate court is debatable, that no injury
will result to the stockholders that cannot be compensated in damages, and that his appeal might be rendered nugatory by repeated
citations for contempt.

Application filed in the supreme court April 21, 1921,
for a writ of mandamus to compel the superior court
for Benton county, Truax, J., to supersede, pending an
appeal, an order requiring a receiver to file a report.
Granted.

[1]Reported in 199 Pac. 306.

Lee C. Delle, for relator.

Parker, LaBerge & Parker and *Robinson, Murphy & Murphine,* for respondent.

FULLERTON, J.—On March 16, 1916, and for some time prior thereto, the Kiona-Benton Land & Water Company, a corporation, owned a large tract of irrigated land, situated in Benton county, a considerable portion of which it had planted to a commercial orchard. Prior thereto it had encumbered the property by two mortgages covering separate tracts; the one running to the North American Mortgage Company and the other to the International Mortgage Bank. In the early part of the year named, separate foreclosure proceedings were instituted to foreclose the mortgages, and in each of the suits, apparently by consent and stipulation between the parties, the relator C. L. Morris was appointed receiver of the mortgaged property. While the showing in this court is more by way of recital than by direct averment, it can be gathered from the record as a whole that there were no creditors of the land company other than the mortgage holders and that the interested parties agreed that the receiver should take the control and active management of the mortgaged property and determine whether the mortgages could be ultimately paid from the earnings of the property, or whether it would be necessary to prosecute the foreclosure proceedings to judgment and sale; it being stipulated and agreed that the receiver should make annual reports of his doings as such to each of the mortgage companies and to the land company, but that he need not make any report to the court. These annual reports were made pursuant to the arrangement, and the foreclosure proceedings were allowed to rest.

On December 8, 1920, one Henry C. Ewing, a minority stockholder of the defendant corporation, petitioned the superior court in which the foreclosure proceedings were pending, praying that the receiver be required to make a report to the court of his doings as such receiver. The application was resisted, but the court nevertheless required the report to be made and filed on or before April 6, 1921. Prior to the day fixed for filing the report, the plaintiffs and the defendant in the mortgage foreclosure suits settled the matters of difference between them, and entered into a stipulation the material parts of which follow:

"1. That the defendant has fully settled and discharged all of the indebtedness due and owing from the said defendant to the said plaintiff in the above entitled cause;

"2. That the plaintiff has heretofore executed and delivered a full and complete release and satisfaction of the mortgage, and the notes thereby secured, the subject matter of this suit;

"3. That all of the plaintiff's costs and disbursements, including attorney's fees, have been fully paid and discharged by the defendant; all other or further costs and charges, including that of the receivership herein, together with the receiver's compensation and attorney's fees to be paid by the defendant as of course;

"4. That the plaintiff has no further claims against the defendant in this cause or interest in the subject matter of this litigation; and this cause shall be dismissed against the defendant with prejudice, and the *lis pendens* of record cancelled and discharged;

"5. That upon the presentation and filing of this stipulation the court shall forthwith and without notice whatsoever to either party hereto, make and enter an order dismissing the above entitled cause with prejudice, no costs to be taxed to either party, cancelling and discharging of record the *lis pendens* heretofore filed of record in the office of the County Auditor of said

Benton county, and discharging the receiver and exonerating his bondsmen;

"6. It is further stipulated and agreed that the
plaintiff is fully satisfied with all and singular the acts
and doings of the receiver, C. L. Morris, herein; that
he has faithfully, efficiently and honestly administered
his said trust, which has been and is now in all things
satisfactory to the plaintiff, and by reason of said Morris' personal attention to his said trust he greatly increased the value of plaintiff's mortgage security and
prevented it from sustaining a loss, which it was threatened with at the time this cause was begun; that each
year said receiver rendered a full itemized and detailed
report showing his transactions during that year, which
said statements were found to be correct and accurate;
that this plaintiff hereby expressly waives the rendering and filing of any account or report whatsoever in
this cause, and hereby respectfully asks the court to
discharge said receiver, and exonerate his bond, without the necessity of, and so as to relieve the said defendant and the said receiver of the costs and expense and
labor involved in the preparing and filing of reports,
and for the further reason that the encumbering of the
records and files in this cause after the plaintiff's
claims have been fully settled and its mortgage released, with the immense amount of detail matter necessary in order to make up a proper and complete report will now only cause the defendant herein added
and unwarranted expense and greatly increase the cost
in the furnishing of many separate abstracts of title
to the many separate tracts of real estate involved in
this matter, the said receiver having also each year
during his said receivership rendered and filed with the
said defendant company like full and complete itemized
and detailed reports of his acts and doings as such receiver, all of which are now on file with the records
and files of said defendant company and open to inspection of all of its officers and stockholders and all
other persons properly interested therein, and all of
which reports have been fully examined and found to
be correct by the proper officers of this defendant and

duly approved by them; and the said plaintiff and defendant do hereby stipulate and agree that the said receiver be discharged forthwith without the filing of any report whatsoever, and that his bondsmen be and it is hereby fully discharged and exonerated of all liability whatsoever in the premises.

"That at a meeting of the stockholders of said defendant duly and regularly called and held on this 2nd day of April, 1921, the said stockholders of said corporation by several resolutions duly and regularly adopted fully approved, ratified and confirmed the settlement made with the plaintiff herein."

The stipulation was presented to the court on April 6, 1921, whereupon the court entered the following order:

"Upon the reading and filing of the stipulation entered into between the plaintiff and defendant in the above entitled cause, and as based thereon, it is now hereby ordered, adjudged and decreed by the court, as follows:

"1. That the above entitled cause be, and the same is hereby dismissed, with prejudice;

"2. That the notice of *lis pendens* heretofore recorded in the county auditor's office of this county be, and the same is hereby cancelled and discharged; and the county auditor is hereby directed to make the proper entry on the margin of the record;

"3. That no costs shall be taxed to either party, the same having been adjusted between the parties hereto.

"The receivership proceedings, however, are not discharged and the receiver is required to file a report as heretofore ordered."

On the same day the defendant land company moved the court to vacate that part of each of the orders of the court requiring the receiver to file a report, basing the motion on the ground of the changed conditions, in which motion the receiver afterwards joined. On April 8, 1921, and before this motion was heard, the stock-

holder before mentioned applied to the court for a
citation directed to the receiver, requiring him to appear before the court on a day certain and show cause
why he should not be punished for contempt for failing
to comply with the court's order requiring him to file
a report with the court showing his doings as such receiver. The citation was issued as requested, fixing
the return day on April 13, 1921. The receiver appeared on the day appointed, and, after disclaiming
that any willful or defiant contempt of the court or its
orders was meant by his failure to comply with the
order, challenged the jurisdiction of the court to continue the proceedings against him after a dismissal of
the suits in which he was appointed. The court overruled his objections and entered the following order:

"This cause coming on to be heard upon an order
duly made and entered in this court on the 8th day of
April, 1921, requiring said C. L. Morris to appear before this court at the hour of ten o'clock a. m. on the
13th day of April, 1921, at the court room in the court
house at Prosser, Benton county, Washington, and
show cause, if any he had, why he should not be punished for contempt for failing to file a report as receiver, coming on to be heard on this 13th day of April,
1921, the state of Washington and the relator, Henry
C. Ewing, appearing by Fred Parker, their attorney,
and the said C. L. Morris appearing in person and with
his attorney, Lee C. Delle, and the said defendant having heretofore filed and served his demurrer herein,
and the matter having been submitted to the court on
said demurrer, and duly argued, and after listening to
the arguments of counsel and being fully advised, the
demurrer is overruled and exception allowed, defendant refusing to plead further and electing to stand upon his demurrer, and the court having heard and considered testimony oral and documentary, whereupon
defendant Morris was then asked by the court if he
had any cause to show why judgment of the court

should not now be pronounced and defendant saying nothing except as he before has said, and electing to stand on his demurrer and challenging the jurisdiction of the court, and it appearing to the court that the said C. L. Morris was on the 16th day of March, 1916, by an order of this court duly made and entered appointed as receiver in a cause pending in this court, being cause No. 2140, wherein North American Mortgage Company was plaintiff and the Kiona-Benton Land & Water Company was defendant, and that the said Morris thereafter duly qualified as such receiver, entered upon the discharge of his duties as such, took charge of the property of defendant and ever since has been and now is the duly appointed, qualified and acting receiver in said cause, and has never been discharged; that on the 17th day of March, 1921, by an order of this court duly made and entered in said cause upon the petition of the relator, Henry C. Ewing, the said C. L. Morris as such receiver was ordered and directed to file in this court on or before the 6th day of April, 1921, his report as such receiver, which order is in words and figures following: [Here follows copy of the said order of March 17th, 1921, heretofore set forth] and it appearing to the court that the said C. L. Morris has failed to file his report as such receiver or any report in pursuance of said order, and has failed to comply with the same as in said order directed by the court, that the said Morris is in contempt of court because of his failure to comply with said order.

"It is now here ordered and adjudged by the court that the said C. L. Morris is in contempt of this court for the reasons aforesaid, and

"It is further ordered, adjudged and decreed that the said Morris be punished for such contempt by the payment of a fine of $100.00, and

"It is further ordered that unless the said Morris shall file in the office of the clerk of this court his report as such receiver as in said order required on or before five o'clock p. m. on the 23rd day of April, 1921, that he be taken into custody by the sheriff of Benton county, and confined in the county jail of Benton county at Prosser, Washington, until he complies with said order, and files said report, and that he pay the costs and disbursements of this proceeding to be taxed according to law; to all of which defendant excepts and exceptions are allowed."

The receiver thereupon, through his attorney, stated to the court that it was his intention to appeal from the judgment and order of the court, and requested the court to fix the amount of a supersedeas bond necessary to be given by him to stay execution on the judgment entered against him until he could have his appeal from the judgment heard and determined in this court; further requesting that the supersedeas include a stay of any further proceedings against him, pending the appeal, on the orders requiring him to account. The court took the application under advisement, and later on in the same day entered the following order:

"The court having entered judgment herein against defendant C. L. Morris, receiver, adjudging him to be guilty of a contempt as alleged and having fixed the penalty or punishment on account thereof, counsel for defendant now requests that a *supersedeas* bond on appeal be fixed by the court and considerable argument by the respective attorneys follows as to the extent and scope of such a bond under the statute.

"It is accordingly ordered by the court that the supersedeas bond pending an appeal to the supreme court be and the same is hereby fixed at the sum of $500; that such a bond if properly conditioned under the statute will stay the following portions of the judgment or order in the contempt proceeding:

"It will supersede the portion requiring $100 and costs to be paid, and it will stay the portion of said judgment requiring defendant to be confined in jail.

"It will not stay any judgment, decree or order entered heretofore in the case of *North American Mortgage Company v. Kiona-Benton Land & Water*

Company, Case No. 2140 of this court concerning which and wherein said contempt was committed.

"Exceptions are allowed to all parties."

On the filing of this order the receiver instituted the proceedings now before us. He seeks a writ of mandamus compelling the lower court to supersede, pending his appeal, that part of its order requiring him to file a report. In his application he again disaffirms any willful contumelious disobedience of the court's order, but avers that the order was invalid when made, or if not then invalid, has been superseded by the second order wherein the suits in which he was appointed receiver were settled and dismissed. He avers also that he is prosecuting his appeal in good faith, and that he desires to do so unhampered by repeated citations compelling him to show cause why he should not be punished for contempt for disobedience of the orders; further averring, in this connection, that one of the counsel for the relator in the contempt proceedings has stated that a further application for his punishment will be made if he does not file a report prior to the time fixed by the court in the contempt judgment.

It seems to us that the record presents a proper case for granting the relief applied for. It may be that to grant a writ of this sort is rather within the discretionary power of the court than within the strict legal right of the applicant, but where the court is convinced, as it is here, that the applicant is acting in good faith, that the question he seeks to present to the court on the appeal is debatable, that no injury will result to the stockholders which cannot be compensated in damages, and that the appeal may be rendered nugatory, or, at least, so hampered as to compel its abandonment by the appellant, by repeated citations for contempt, justice requires that the relief be granted.

We think it unnecessary to pursue the inquiry. The writ will issue commanding the judge of the superior court to fix the amount of a proper supersedeas bond which will, in addition to staying execution on the judgment for contempt, stay, pending the appeal, the orders of the court requiring the receiver to file a report.

PARKER, C. J., HOLCOMB, MACKINTOSH, and BRIDGES, JJ., concur.

[No. 16415. Department One. July 7, 1921.]

LOUISE SPOTTS *and* LOIS SPOTTS *by her Guardian,* LOUISE SPOTTS, *Appellants,* v. WESTLAKE GARAGE COMPANY, *Respondent.*[1]

WITNESSES (35)—COMPETENCY—TRANSACTIONS WITH PERSONS SINCE DECEASED—INTEREST IN EVENT. Rem. Code, § 1211, disqualifying a person from testifying as to transactions with a decedent respecting the renewal of a lease, is inapplicable in the case of a lessee who had parted with all interest under the lease, and was not a party to the record.

CONTRACTS (66)—LANDLORD AND TENANT (15)—LEASE—CONSTRUING INSTRUMENTS TOGETHER. An agreement for renewal of a lease, bearing same date as the lease and making reference to that instrument, must be considered as a part of the leasing agreement and supported by the same consideration; the fact that the renewal agreement was not acknowledged until five days after the date of the lease being immaterial.

LANDLORD AND TENANT (30)—EXTENSIONS AND RENEWALS—COVENANT FOR RENEWAL. Under a lease providing for renewal at the expiration of the term at the same rentals paid during the last year of the term, the lessee is entitled to a renewal at the reduced rental paid during the last year of his tenancy, under a modification of the rental terms of the original lease.

[1]Reported in 199 Pac. 294.

LANDLORD AND TENANT (15)—LEASE—CONSTRUCTION AND OPERA-
TION—CONDITIONS. A condition in a lease requiring the lessees to
deliver a bond in the sum of $5,000 as security for the performance
of its terms was waived by the acceptance of $1,000 in lieu thereof,
which sum was to be returned on the substitution of $2,400 in stock
of the corporation to be formed by the lessees, and on tender of the
stock the lessor said he did not care for it, that he had used the
$1,000, and asked that the sum be applied on the rent, and at no
time thereafter during the term of the lease ever demanded the delivery of the $5,000 bond.

SAME (15). The failure of a lessee to pay the rent due for certain months under a lease must be deemed waived by a subsequent
agreement modifying rentals for the future, which made no reference to the prior delinquent rent, and hence such failure would not
defeat the lessee's right to renewal of the lease under the agreement
between the parties.

SAME (15). Slight damages resulting from alterations or failure
to repair would not defeat the right of a lessee to a renewal of his
lease under an agreement providing therefor at the expiration of
the original term.

Appeal from a judgment of the superior court for
King county, Jurey, J., entered January 6, 1921, upon
findings in favor of the defendants, in an action for
unlawful detainer, tried to the court. Modified.

G. Ward Kemp, for appellants.
McClure & McClure, for respondent.

HOLCOMB, J.—In this action for unlawful detainer,
appellants set up a lease made and entered into between appellants Louise Spotts and her now deceased
husband, A. L. Spotts, on April 26, 1915, for a term of
five years from the first day of July, 1915, to L. G.
Horr and August R. Klaiber, as lessees. The premises
demised were described as lots 9 and 10, in block 14,
of an addition to the city of Seattle as laid off by the
heirs of Sarah A. Bell, in King county. It was alleged
that the term of the lease had terminated, and that
respondent was holding over without right.

The rental stipulated in the lease was $24,500 for

the term of five years, payable in monthly installments of $408, on the first day of each and every month during the term, save that the last installment specified was $428. By agreement between the parties to the lease, the lessees assigned the leasehold to a corporation agreed to be organized and which was organized, called the Westlake Garage Company, this respondent.

Respondent for answer admitted the execution of the lease, and pleaded a renewal agreement made between the parties as of the same date as the date of the lease, April 26, 1915, and which respondent alleged was intended to be, and was, a part of the same contract of lease; and also alleged that under the terms of the renewal agreement respondent had, on May 11, 1920, or before the expiration of the original lease term, notified appellants that it elected to renew the lease of the premises for an additional year, *at the rate paid during the previous year,* under and by virtue of certain written instruments recited in the notice, as follows:

"Lease executed and acknowledged April 26, 1915, between A. L. Spotts and Louise Spotts, his wife, as lessors, and August Klaiber and L. G. Horr, as lessees.

"Written consent by A. L. Spotts and Louise Spotts, his wife, to the assignment by August L. Klaiber and L. G. Horr of said lease to a corporation, said consent having been executed April 26, 1915.

"Receipt for $1000 executed April 26, 1915, by A. L. Spotts and Louise Spotts, his wife, to L. G. Horr.

"Agreement for modification of time of payment of rent executed March 16, 1917, by A. L. Spotts and Louise Spotts, his wife, and Westlake Garage Co., a corporation.

"Agreement executed and acknowledged April 26, 1915, by A. L. Spotts and Louise Spotts."

Appellants replied to the affirmative answer setting up affirmatively that the agreement (for renewal) was

void for uncertainty, lack of equity and of consideration; that, if valid, the rights had been waived by the
defendants failing to pay rents, make repairs and keep
up securities, and failure to give proper notice of intent to hold over.

The questions presented by appellants upon this appeal are: (1) Whether there ever was any valid agreement for renewal; (2) if there was any agreement,
whether it was waived by failure of the tenant to perform its obligations under the lease, and (3) if the
tenant is entitled to a renewal, then on what terms and
for what period.

Appellants first contend that the court erred in receiving testimony from Horr, one of the original
lessees, to the effect that the agreement for renewal
was made as a part of the agreement of lease, and that
the lease would not have been accepted by the lessees
without an agreement for renewal on the terms provided therein. Appellants argue that Horr, having
been a party to the original lease, covenanting to pay
for the entire period the sum of $24,500, is an inter-
ested party, notwithstanding the fact that Horr sold
his stock in the respondent corporation organized to
take over the lease, two and one-half years before the
trial, and had no connection whatever with the respondent company. The objection was made that since
Spotts was dead, and this action prosecuted by Mrs.
Spotts individually and as guardian of the infant
daughter of herself and deceased husband, the statute,
Pierce's 1919 Code, § 7722 (Rem. 1915 Code, § 1211),
precludes Horr from testifying because of his supposed interest. The contention is untenable. Horr
was neither a party to the record, nor a party in interest. He was merely a witness in the case. He could not
cross-examine witnesses, nor introduce any evidence

in his own behalf. He was not bound by the admissions or acts of any party or attorney on either side of the case. He was therefore a competent witness. *Sackman v. Thomas,* 24 Wash. 660, 64 Pac. 819; *Denny v. Schwabacher,* 54 Wash. 689, 104 Pac. 137, 132 Am. St. 1140; *Showalter v. Spangle,* 93 Wash. 326, 160 Pac. 1042.

Regardless of the competency of Horr as a witness, in regard to the above transaction (the renewal agreement), it was executed by Mr. and Mrs. Spotts; recites that they were lessors, and Klaiber and Horr were lessees "in that certain indenture of lease bearing even date herewith," and the instrument recites the date of April 26, 1915. It is evident, therefore, that it was intended by the parties to the renewal agreement that it should be considered as a part of the agreement of lease and the terms of the instrument itself, and had the same consideration. Nor does the fact that the renewal agreement was not acknowledged by the lessors until May 1, 1915, militate against that conclusion.

The renewal agreement provided among other things as follows:

"II. It is distinctly understood and agreed between the parties hereto, that the lessees in said lease, their successors or assigns, shall be entitled, subject to all the conditions hereinbefore stated, to a renewal of said lease annually after the present term thereof expires until the tenth year from the date hereof, at any rate offered by any third person to the lessors herein, their heirs or assigns, but in the event the lessors, their heirs or assigns, are unable to obtain a better offer for the leasing of the said premises than the lessees are paying at such time, then, and in that event, the lessees herein, their successors or assigns, shall be entitled, at their option, to such renewal for the ensuing year at the rate paid during the previous year."

A preceding provision of the renewal agreement stipulated that the lessees should pay as rental during the renewal period a rent equal to any *bona fide* offer by any third person to the lessors which they should be able to obtain.

On March 27, 1920, appellants served notice upon respondent that they had a *bona fide* offer for the rental of the demised property for a period of three years, beginning July 1, 1920, and ending July 30, 1923, for a total rental of $27,000, payable at $750 each month in advance, the first $750 for July, 1920, to be deposited by April 3, 1920, and a cash deposit of an additional sum of $3,000 to be delivered to lessors on or before July 1, 1920, to insure the performance of the lease by the lessees, and so much thereof as may not be used for damages to apply on the rental for the last four months of the three-year term; the lessees further agreeing to keep up all repairs to the building and garage, except ordinary repairs to the roof and walls of the building; the lessees to have six per cent per annum interest on the $3,000; all further terms of the lease to be the same as the terms of certain paragraphs of the lease of respondent.

The trial judge found, upon ample proofs, notwithstanding the evidence was somewhat conflicting, that appellants did not have a *bona fide* offer as stated in the above notice; that the proposed lessee above referred to was one Wagner; that Wagner did not have $3,000; that his father-in-law, who was interested in the matter with him, refused to take the lease of the property at a rental of $750 per month, and refused to finance Wagner in taking the lease upon the property, and that the notice above mentioned was not given nor served upon respondent by appellants in good faith;

and that respondent was not required either to accept or reject the same.

During the term of the lease respondent had become delinquent in the payment of the rent in the aggregate amount of $972 for nine months prior to February, 1916, and appellants then served notice on respondent to pay the delinquent rent or vacate the premises. In March, 1917, a modification agreement was sought and obtained by respondent, in the form of a written memorandum, whereby the rents for the remainder of the term of the lease were materially changed both as to time and amounts of monthly installments. Nothing was said in this agreement about the payment of the aforesaid delinquent rents. By this modification agreement, the rents for the remainder of the term from the first day of March, 1917, to and ending on the 30th day of June, 1920, were fixed as follows: On the 12th day of April, May, June, July and August, 1917, $350 for each month; on the 12th day of each succeeding month for six months, $354.05; for the next ensuing twelve months, beginning with March, 1918, on the 12th day of each month, the sum of $404.35; for the next ensuing twelve months, beginning March, 1919, on the 12th day of each month, the sum of $476.15; and for the four months commencing March, 1920, the sum of $408 on the first day of each month, except the last month, for which the rent was fixed at $428. The evidence uncontrovertibly showed and the trial court found that the rents as above fixed were promptly paid and that respondent had not violated any of the terms relating thereto in any substantial particular.

The modification as to rentals must be considered in no other way than a change of the amounts of rental to be paid from and after the time fixed by the agreement, March 1, 1917, to July 1, 1920, and the rents, therefore, for the last year, were fixed as follows:

For the last month $428; for the three preceding months, $408; for the eight preceding months, $476.15, and those were the rentals respondent notified appellants it desired for the renewal term. Notwithstanding this finding, the court concluded that the respondent was entitled to a renewal for the ensuing year, after the termination of the original lease on July 1, 1920, at the rents fixed in the original lease. With this conclusion we cannot agree. As said above, the rentals were undoubtedly modified by that agreement so that the rentals for the last year were changed, doubtless in consideration of the fact that nine months' rent prior to March 1, 1917, had been delinquent. We are also of the opinion that the nine months' delinquent rent was waived by appellants when the modification agreement was made, and that the nonpayment thereof does not in any way interfere with the renewal of the lease. We conclude, however, that the rentals to be paid after the renewal of the lease, in the absence of a *bona fide* offer for an increased rental, must be fixed at $476.15 for the first eight months; $408 for the next three months, and $428 for the last month each year of the renewal term.

Appellants vehemently argued, however, that the lessee is not entitled to a renewal on any terms, because of several reasons. Passing the first contention that the renewal agreement was void and without consideration, and the second, that the nonpayment of rent during the original term precluded a renewal of the lease for the additional time, both of which contentions we have heretofore discussed, it is next contended that the original lease provided that the respondents should give security for the performance of the terms of the lease, which was violated. The original lease provided as follows:

"Lessees agree that they will execute and deliver to lessors, a bond with good and sufficient sureties, to be acceptable to lessors in the full penal sum of $5,000, or other satisfactory security, conditioned that lessees will, in all respects, carry out the terms and conditions of this lease, and pay the rental for said premises for said term according to the terms and conditions thereof."

At the time the lease was executed, Mr. and Mrs. Spotts executed an agreement by which they acknowledged receipt from Horr of the sum of $1,000 to be held as collateral security for the faithful performance of the terms and conditions of the lease, with a proviso that Horr could, at any time during the term of the lease, substitute for the $1,000 in cash, stock of the value of $2,400 in the corporation to be organized. This agreement further provided that Horr was to receive six per cent interest on the $1,000 from the date of the agreement, April 26, 1915, to a date thirty days prior to the substitution of the stock for the $1,000. This $1,000 in cash was accepted by the lessors as satisfactory security at the time of the execution and delivery of the lease, instead of a bond for $5,000. After the organization of the respondent corporation, as agreed, and the delivery of the assignment to it, Horr went to Mr. Spotts and told him that the lessee was ready to put up the $2,400 in stock, and draw down the $1,000. Spotts told Horr that he had used the $1,000 and asked if he could take it out on the rent. Thereupon the $1,000 was applied upon the rent due, and when Horr wanted to put up the stock of the corporation as security, Spotts told Horr that he did not care anything

about the stock. At no time thereafter during the term
of the original lease was the $5,000 bond demanded of
respondent.

We are of the opinion that when the $1,000 was re-
duced to payment of rent, and the $2,400 in corporate
stock was declined (and that during the early period of
the lease), and no $5,000 bond thereafter required, the
matter of security to be furnished by the lessee must
be deemed to have been waived. Any any rate, appellants should have demanded the security under the
terms of the original lease after respondent notified
appellants of its intention to exercise its option for
renewal, instead of which, on June 1, 1920, appellants
served notice upon respondent to vacate the premises.

It is also contended that respondent is not entitled
to a renewal of the lease for the reason that it has
violated the provision of the lease providing for repairs
by the lessees.

The lease provides, in § 6, that the lessee shall not
have the right to make any additions or alterations in
the building without the written consent of the lessors,
and that at the expiration of the term, or other termination of this lease they will quit and surrender the
premises, leaving the same in as good condition as they
were in when lessees took possession thereof, damage
by fire and the elements excepted.

The evidence shows that some damages have been
caused to the garage building by the use thereof by
lessees, as a garage, and that the same could be repaired at an expense of not to exceed $90 to $100. The
trial court, however, believed that even some of these
items were structural in their nature, rather than repairs, and that the remainder were insignificant.
Under the terms of the lease above stated, there would
be no breach of the covenant to repair until the end of

the term. 24 Cyc. 1112; Tiffany, Landlord and Tenant, p. 781.

On the whole, upon the essential questions in this controversy, the findings of the trial court are amply supported by competent evidence. We cannot, however, agree with the conclusion of the trial court as to the agreed rental that was to be paid for the last year of the original lease, and which should be paid for the renewal term.

In accordance with our own conclusion upon that phase of the matter, the judgment of the trial court is modified so that the respondent may renew the lease for the ensuing twelve months upon the payment each year of $476.15 for the first eight months thereof; $408 for the next three months thereof, and $428 for the last month thereof. Annually until the expiration of ten years from June 26, 1915, unless evicted for cause, respondent will be entitled to renewal upon the same terms, unless a *bona fide* offer to appellants from any third person of better rent shall have been obtained by appellants, at the rate paid during the previous year, in conformity with paragraph 2 of the renewal agreement. In all other respects the judgment is affirmed.

Appellants having recovered substantial benefits in this appeal, will recover costs of appeal.

PARKER, C. J., MACKINTOSH, BRIDGES, and FULLERTON, JJ., concur.

[No. 16296. Department One. July 7, 1921.]

JONES-SCOTT COMPANY, *Appellant*, v. ELLENSBURG
MILLING COMPANY, *Respondent*.[1]

CONTRACTS (40)—VALIDITY—STATUTES—LEVER ACT. The Lever
Food Control Act fixing a minimum price for wheat is not a prohibition against sales at a price in excess thereof.

SALES (68)—DELIVERY—TENDER OR OFFER—NECESSITY. Where a
purchaser of wheat directed the seller not to make the first shipment at the time provided in the contract of sale, a delivery or tender of delivery of the wheat was not a condition precedent to a right
of action for damages for repudiation of the contract by the purchaser.

SAME (143)—REMEDY OF SELLER—ACTIONS—MEASURE OF DAM-
AGES. The measure of damages for breach of contract to deliver a
quantity of wheat, where no definite time was fixed for delivery, is
the difference between the contract price and the market price at
the date of the demand and refusal of performance.

Appeal from a judgment of the superior court for
Kittitas county, Davidson, J., entered July 26, 1920,
upon findings in favor of the defendant, in an action
for breach of contract, tried to the court. Reversed.

C. R. Hovey and *Gose & Crowe*, for appellant.

Austin Mires, Carroll B. Graves, and *Arnold L.
Graves*, for respondent.

MACKINTOSH, J.—The contract which is the basis of
this law suit was before this court for consideration in
the case of *Jones-Scott Co. v. Ellensburg Milling Co.*,
108 Wash. 73, 183 Pac. 113, where the correspondence
in regard to the sale of the 10,000 bushels of wheat is
set forth in full, and therefore need not be repeated
here. Although it is probably true that the contract
was an oral one, and the writing merely took it with.
out the statute of frauds, still, there is some language

[1]Reported in 199 Pac. 238.

in the former opinion which gives support to the contention of the respondent that the court held the contract to be a written one, and, therefore, entered into on October 13, 1917, and although the appellant claims that the contract was one as of the date of August 11, 1917, yet, in view of the former opinion of this court, and the theory upon which the lower court tried the case we will dispose of this contention of the appellant adversely to it, and, for the purpose of this case, proceed upon the theory that the contract was a written one, entered into on October 13, 1917.

Under the contract, the respondent was to pay for the 10,000 bushels of blue stem wheat at $2.44 per bushel, f. o. b., cars Eureka Flat points, the first shipment to consist of one car, about November 1, the balance of the wheat to be taken "as fast as I can". None of the wheat was ever delivered, and this action is for damages for failure to receive and pay for it.

It is the respondent's claim that the contract is invalid because in violation of the United States food control act, dated August 10, 1917, and commonly known as the Lever act. Respondent argues that by the terms of that Federal legislation, it was unlawful for the parties here to have fixed a price for wheat in excess of the fair price fixed by the government. The act, upon being read, however, does not lend itself to any such interpretation. It merely provides, as far as wheat is concerned, for the fixing of a *minimum* price. The purpose of the act is very apparent; to encourage the production of wheat by the farmers of the country to meet the stress of war demands. Respondent, however, recognizing that the act fixes only a minimum price resorts to § 4 of the act, which provides against discrimination and unfair practices and unjust and unreasonable charges for necessaries, and provides against any agreements for excessive prices, and claims that the contract before us violates all those provisions of § 4, and cites us to our decision in *Henrikson v. Pacific Coast Packing Co.*, 109 Wash. 644, 187 Pac. 377, as authority for the position that any contract in violation of the Federal food control act is void. There is little comfort, however, for the respondent in its resort to § 4 of the act, for the United States supreme court, in the case of *United States v. Cohen Grocery Co.*, 255 U. S. 81, holds § 4 to be unconstitutional, being vague, indefinite and uncertain. Thus we may dispose of the respondent's contentions in this regard by saying that the Lever act has no application to the contract.

It is next urged by the respondent that the appellant has never performed its contract and cannot therefore recover, for the reason that the appellant failed to perform its contract to deliver one car about November 1, and that the claimed repudiation of the contract by the respondent was not a breach of the contract. A resort to the evidence in the case, however, convinces us that on or about November 1, the appellant was directed by the respondent not to make the shipment on that date, and this fact is testified to positively by the appellant's manager, and the respondent's denial consists of his statement that "I don't think so; I don't remember." A careful reading of the testimony of the two witnesses, the managers of each of the companies, which, in effect, is all the testimony in the case, is conclusive that the failure to deliver on November 1 was due to the respondent's act and not to that of the appellant.

The other argument in regard to the failure to perform the contract is that the appellant is not entitled to demand performance by the respondent until it had itself performed, or tendered performance, and that in the present case respondent was not obligated to pay for the wheat until it had been delivered, and no delivery having taken place, consequently no payment was due. Bound up in this argument is the claim that the respondent, by the contract, was not obliged to pay more than the fair minimum price fixed by the government, and was not obligated to comply with the price specified in its contract with the appellant. The evidence is clear and satisfactory that in December or January the respondent refused to accept the wheat, (it may be said here that a great deal of the testimony relating to the conduct of the appellant's business, which was that of buying wheat from the growers and selling it to the millers, is of very little consequence in the case, and does not refute the positive statements of appellant's witnesses that it had on hand, or available, wheat with which to fill the contract,) and repudiated all obligation to pay the contract price; such refusal, of course, obviated the necessity of making a delivery.

There then only remains the question as to the measure of damages. That measure is the difference between the contract price and the market price, at the date of the demand and refusal, there being no definite time fixed for the delivery, *Menz Lumber Co. v. McNeely*, 58 Wash. 223, 108 Pac. 621, 28 L. R. A. (N. S.) 1007; *Oriental Trading Co. v. Houser*, 87 Wash. 184, 151 Pac. 242; *Hughes v. Eastern R. & Lumber Co.*, 93 Wash. 558, 161 Pac. 343. The contract price was fixed at $2.44 per bushel. The appellant's demand for performance was on January 7, 1918, and the price of wheat at Eureka Flat points at that date was testified to as being $2.00½ per bushel. A computation based on these figures must result in a judgment for the appellant in the sum of $4,350. The judgment of the lower court will be reversed, and the judgment entered for the appellant for $4,350, with interest.

PARKER, C. J., and BRIDGES, J., concur.

[No. 16439. Department Two. July 7, 1921.]

JOHN J. SNYDER et al., Respondents, v. E. O. MARKEN et al., Appellants.[1]

JUDGMENT (195-1)—CONCLUSIVENESS—COPARTIES—EFFECT. Where two persons wholly unrelated in business, each driving his own car, become involved in a collision between the two cars which caused injury to a third person, suing both of them for damages, a judgment against such third person is not conclusive in a subsequent suit by one car owner against the other to recover damages for the latter's alleged negligence; the rule being that parties to a judgment are not bound by it in subsequent controversies between each other unless they were adversaries in the action wherein the judgment was entered.

Appeal from a judgment of the superior court for King county, Tallman, J., entered November 13, 1920, upon the verdict of a jury rendered in favor of the plaintiffs, upon sustaining a demurrer to defendants' affirmative defense, in an action for personal injuries sustained in an automobile collision. Affirmed.

Hartman & Hartman, for appellants.
Flick & Paul, for respondents.

MITCHELL, J.—This action grows out of a collision of two automobiles, one belonged to the plaintiffs and the other to the defendants. At the time of the accident, Mr. and Mrs. Snyder had as fellow passengers in their

car Mr. and Mrs. James M. Woods. As a result of
the accident, Mr. and Mrs. Woods were injured and so
were Mr. Snyder and his car. Mr. and Mrs. Woods
sued both the Snyders and E. O. Marken to recover
damages for their injuries alleged to have been caused
by the negligence of those defendants. In that action,
there was a verdict and judgment in favor of all the
defendants therein. Thereafter, the present action was
commenced by Mr. and Mrs. Snyder to recover damages for Mr. Snyder's injuries in the same accident,
which, they alleged, were caused by the negligence of
the defendants Marken and wife.

The defendants, in their answer, in addition to general denials, interposed an affirmative. defense showing the former suit of Mr. and Mrs. Woods and the
result of it. They further alleged that in that suit the
defendants therein appeared separately, and that
Snyder and wife by their answer admitted that E. O.
Marken was negligent and admitted that Woods and
wife were injured in the accident. It is further alleged
that, at the trial of that case, the undisputed evidence
showed that Woods and wife were injured; and that
the judgment in that case was a final determination
that E. O. Marken was not negligent in connection with
the accident, and that the plaintiffs herein are thereby
estopped from now claiming that the defendants
E. O. Marken and wife or either of them was guilty
of any negligence whatever in the accident. A general
demurrer to the affirmative defense was sustained.
From a verdict and judgment for the plaintiffs, the
defendants have appealed.

The question in the case is: Where two persons,
wholly unrelated in business, each driving his own car,
become involved in a collision between the two cars

which causes an injury to a third person, who unsuc-
cessfully sues both car owners to recover damages for
their alleged negligence, may one of the co-defendants
in the former suit thereafter sue the other to recover
damages alleged to have been caused by the latter's
negligence on that same occasion?

Whatever may be the rule in equitable actions, where
the constant practice is to decree between all the parties
including co-defendants upon proper proofs and under
pleadings which among other things bring the respective claims and rights of the co-defendants between
themselves under judicial cognizance, or in actions at
law involving constructive negligence and liability
over, or actions at law upon contracts of indemnity or
suretyship, we think the present case is controlled by
the general rule that parties to a judgment are not
bound by it in subsequent controversies between each
other unless they were adversaries in the action wherein the judgment was entered. 15 R. C. L. p. 1013, § 487;
23 Cyc. 1279, § 11; Freeman, Judgments (4th ed.), § 158.

The object of the action by Mr. and Mrs. Woods
was not to determine the rights of all the parties thereto, each as against all others, whether plaintiffs or
defendants. It was to determine only their rights
against those defendants. Neither of the defendants
in that case was called upon in defending his position
to do anything other than to meet the charge that he
was guilty of negligence so far as Mr. and Mrs. Woods
were concerned, unless perchance there was the defense of contributory negligence charged against Mr.
and Mrs. Woods, or some other affirmative defense of
which there is no advice in the affirmative defense interposed in the present case. It was unnecessary for
either defendant in that case to show that the other

defendant was negligent—that was the burden the plaintiffs therein assumed. The defendants therein made no issue between themselves by their separate answers, nor did they attempt to do so. That these plaintiffs, in their separate answer in that case, admitted that Mr. and Mrs. Woods were injured in the accident was binding upon no one other than Mr. and Mrs. Snyder, and the admission, by these plaintiffs in that same answer, that E. O. Marken was negligent in connection with the accident was unimportant. It does not appear whether therein they specifically admitted the negligence of Mr. Marken or whether they did so by not denying that charge contained in the complaint of Mr. and Mrs. Woods. The legal effect would be the same, it was binding on no one. By that admission, Mr. and Mrs. Snyder presented no issue to Mr. Marken. They were not answering any pleadings of his nor were they interposing any pleadings under our code of practice which he could move against, demur or reply to, or join issue in any manner upon. They were not crossing swords with each other, they were each only defending himself against the charge of negligence made upon him by Mr. and Mrs. Woods. In such a case, the finding and judgment of the court that neither of the parties defendant was guilty of negligence as to those plaintiffs do not conclude and determine any of the mere relative rights of the defendants therein as between themselves. *Harvey v. Osborn*, 55 Ind. 535; *Keagy v. Wellington Nat. Bank*, 12 Okl. 33, 69 Pac. 811.

The case of *Boston & M. R. Co. v. Sargent*, reported first in 70 N. H. 299, 47 Atl. 605, and on the second appeal in 72 N. H. 455, 57 Atl. 688, is relied on by the appellant. It was a case wherein a constructive tort-

feasor sued to recover contribution, or indemnity under
an implied contract, from a co-defendant who was primarily liable for the damages. The suit followed one
wherein the injured party had recovered judgment
against a railroad company and a shipper for the destruction of a store house near the railroad tracks by
fire communicated from a stove in the car on which the
shipper's goods were stored, the car being in the shipper's control. The shipper had had his day in court
upon the charge of his negligence and suffered a judgment therefor that he was directly obligated to pay, and
in the subsequent suit by the railroad company (upon
its paying the judgment) against the shipper upon his
implied contract of indemnity, it was held by the New
Hampshire court that he was estopped by the former
judgment from showing that he exercised due care
in heating the car and that the railroad company was
guilty of actual (not constructive) negligence which
was the sole cause of the burning of the store house,
for those issues were found against him in that suit.
Even in the case between the railroad company and the
shipper it was held that the railroad company could
not have indemnity unless it showed that, by the exercise of proper care, it could not have prevented the injury, and that since such fact was not litigated in the
suit for the loss of the store house, it was incumbent
upon the railroad company in its suit against the shipper to establish that it could not have prevented the
injury by the exercise of such care. But that case is
not authority in the consideration of the present one
wherein, when co-defendants, these parties in the suit
of Mr. and Mrs. Woods were charged as separate and
distinct tort-feasors, each being accused of actual negligence. They were in no way related to each other
by contract, direct or implied, and have not until the

present suit had any opportunity to litigate their relative rights and liabilities growing out of the accident.

Judgment affirmed.

Parker, C. J., Main, Tolman, and Bridges, JJ., concur.

[No. 16423. Department One. July 7, 1921.]

Joseph Sussman, as *Tacoma Junk Company*, *Respondent*, v. Sam Gustav, as *Pacific Junk Company, Appellant*.[1]

Sales (55)—Rescission by Buyer—Failure to Deliver. After formal unconditional demand for delivery, accompanied by tender of the balance of the agreed purchase price, the buyer is not bound to accept the seller's offer of performance after suit brought, but was entitled to stand upon his claim for damages.

Sales (154)—Remedies of Buyer—Action for Breach—Measure of Damages. Where a seller of scrap iron repeatedly promised for almost a year to make delivery, and the purchaser was willing at all times to receive the iron, the damages for breach of contract to deliver were properly measured by the difference between the contract price and the market value at the time of the final demand shortly before suit brought; the claim of the seller that the breach was prior in time being untenable.

Appeal from a judgment of the superior court for King county, Grover E. Desmond, judge *pro tempore*, entered September 18, 1920, upon findings in favor of the plaintiff, in an action on contract, tried to the court. Affirmed.

Jay C. Allen and *E. W. Howell*, for appellant.

Blackburn & Gielens and *Jones, Riddell & Brackett*, for respondent.

Parker, C. J.—The plaintiff Sussman commenced this action in the superior court, seeking recovery of damages which he claims to have suffered from the failure of the defendant Gustav to deliver to him one hun-

[1] Reported in 199 Pac. 232.

dred tons of scrap iron in compliance with a contract
for the purchase of the iron from the defendant. The
cause came regularly on for trial upon the merits and
resulted in the court awarding judgment of nonsuit in
favor of the defendant at the close of the evidence
introduced in behalf of the plaintiff. An appeal to
this court from that judgment resulted in its reversal
and the remanding of the cause to the superior court
for a new trial. 109 Wash. 459, 186 Pac. 882. A new
trial was accordingly had before the court without a
jury, resulting in findings and judgment awarding to
the plaintiff recovery as prayed for; from which the
defendant has appealed to this court.

On November 8, 1916, appellant gave to respondent
in writing a two-day option for the purchase from him
of one hundred tons of scrap iron at $11.50 per ton f.
o. b. Seattle. On November 10 this option was accepted,
and on November 14 respondent paid, and appellant
accepted, upon the agreed price of the iron, the sum of
$500. The trial court found, among other things, as
follows:

"That at the time of the entry into the contract described in the complaint herein, it was orally agreed
between the plaintiff and the defendant that defendant
should begin making delivery of the iron immediately
after the 1st day of January, 1917.

"That from the first of the year 1917 up to the 19th
day of November, 1917, the plaintiff many times demanded of the defendant delivery of the said iron;
that the defendant kept continually promising to the
plaintiff that he would make delivery of the same, but
failed to do so.

"That defendant had ample opportunity to procure
cars upon which to deliver said iron, but failed to do
so; that during all of the said period of time defendant was buying and selling similar iron and making
deliveries thereof to other parties.

"That at the time of the commencement of this

action on the 19th day of November, 1917, and for
approximately six weeks prior thereto, the fair and reasonable market value of scrap wrought iron f. o. b.
Seattle, Washington, was $25 per ton.

"That defendant has never paid the plaintiff the sum
of $500 deposit on the purchase price of said iron."

Judgment was awarded in favor of respondent for
an amount equal to the difference between the contract price of $11.50 per ton and the found market
value of the iron on November 19, 1917, of $25 per ton;
and also the sum of $500, the amount which respondent
had paid upon the agreed purchase price; the court
proceeding on the theory that the contract was
breached on November 19, 1917, the date of the commencement of this action.

In their last analysis, the contentions here made by
counsel for appellant present little else than questions
of fact. It is argued that the evidence shows that appellant was at all times prior to the commencement of this
action willing to deliver the iron as agreed. We are
quite convinced that the evidence does not so show,
but that, while he so repeatedly expressed himself by
promises made to respondent, he continually put respondent off and neglected to do anything looking
towards the actual delivery of the iron up to the time of
the commencement of the action. Looking to the final
consummation of the purchase contract, or of putting
appellant in the attitude of finally refusing to deliver
the iron and thus breaching the contract, respondent
caused the formal unconditional demand to be made
upon appellant for the delivery of the iron as agreed,
at the same time tendering to him the whole of the
balance of the agreed purchase price. Such demand
not being complied with, this action was commenced a
few days thereafter. It is true that, after the commencement of this action, appellant again offered to

deliver the iron, but manifestly respondent was not under any legal obligation to pay any further attention to such offer or promise, but was entitled to stand upon his claim for damages for breach of the contract, if the contract was in fact breached, as we think the evidence clearly shows it was at or shortly before the time of the commencement of this action.

Some contention is made in behalf of appellant that if the contract was breached at all it was breached several months before the commencement of this action when the market value of the iron was considerably less than $25 per ton, and that in any event respondent's recovery should have been measured accordingly. We are quite convinced, however, that in view of appellant's repeated promises to deliver the iron up to near the commencement of this action, and respondent being willing to receive the iron up until near the commencement of this action, appellant is in no position to successfully claim that the breach of the contract occurred prior to the time found by the court, to wit, just prior to the commencement of this action. That being true, the court was fully warranted in measuring respondent's damage for the breach by the difference between the contract price and the market value of the iron at the time of the final demand therefor shortly before the commencement of this action. The following, among numerous authorities which might be cited, lend support to this conclusion: *Menz Lumber Co. v. McNeeley & Co.*, 58 Wash. 223, 108 Pac. 621; *M'Dermid v. Redpath*, 39 Mich. 372; *Brown v. Sharkey*, 93 Iowa 157, 61 N. W. 364; *Trask v. Hamburger*, 70 N. H. 453, 48 Atl. 1087; *Roberts v. Benjamin*, 124 U. S. 64.

The judgment is affirmed.

FULLERTON, HOLCOMB, MACKINTOSH, and BRIDGES, JJ., concur.

[No. 16271.   Department One.   July 8, 1921.]

THE STATE OF WASHINGTON, *Respondent*, v. JOHN PICO,
Appellant.[1]

CRIMINAL LAW (191)—TIME OF TRIAL—CONTINUANCE—DISCRETION
OF COURT. The refusal of the court to grant a continuance in a criminal case, because of the inability of counsel for accused to attend
owing to professional duties in another court, was not an abuse of
discretion, where the court gave the defendant reasonable opportunity to select other counsel, and, on his failure so to do, appointed
counsel to defend him.

Appeal from a judgment of the superior court for
Clallam county, Ralston, J., entered February 28, 1920,
upon a trial and conviction of criminal syndicalism.
Affirmed.

George F. Vanderveer and *Ralph S. Pierce*, for
appellant.

William B. Ritchie, T. F. Trumbull, and *Frank L.
Plummer*, for respondent.

HOLCOMB, J.—Although sixty-eight errors were
claimed, appellant in his brief states that "with the
exception of the refusal of the court to grant a continuance as requested by defendant, this appeal presents
no distinctive question of either fact or law," not presented in other briefs by the same counsel in other
cases before the court, involving convictions under the
criminal syndicalism statute.

The questions raised have heretofore been decided in
State v. Hennessy, 114 Wash. 351, 195 Pac. 211.

As to the continuance, the granting or refusing thereof is ordinarily a matter of discretion to be exercised
by the trial court. *Thompson v. Territory*, 1 Wash.
Terr. 547; *Blanton v. State*, 1 Wash. 265, 24 Pac. 439;

[1]Reported in 199 Pac. 289.

State v. Underwood, 35 Wash. 558, 77 Pac. 863; *State v. Carpenter*, 56 Wash. 670, 106 Pac. 206; 16 C. J. 451.

The demand herein was based upon the inability of Messrs. Vanderveer and Pierce, retained to defend appellant, to conclude their labors in an important trial then in progress at Montesano, Grays Harbor county, and appear in court at Port Angeles, Clallam county, on February 16, 1920, when this case was set for trial.

The termination of the trial at Montesano was for some days uncertain. It might have ended in ample time for counsel to reach Port Angeles and proceed with the trial. The trial court in Clallam county doubtless had sufficient reasons for not disarranging its calendar, unless it became imperatively necessary to secure a fair trial to appellant. Meantime the trial judge gave appellant every reasonable opportunity to select other counsel for himself, without avail, and finally the court appointed counsel to defend appellant and ordered the case to proceed. The accused had the constitutional right to be represented by counsel, but not by any particular counsel when such individual attorneys were so engaged that their services were unavailable.

"A request for continuance on the ground of the absence of a certain counsel is not looked upon by the courts with favor, especially where such counsel is attending to professional duties in another court, or in some other manner would retard the operation of the court by his personal convenience or business." 16 C. J. 455.

See, also, *Territory v. Lobato*, 17 N. M. 666, 134 Pac. 222, L. R. A. 1917A 1226.

We are of the view that the trial court did not manifestly abuse its discretion, in this instance, in denying the continuance.

The judgment of conviction is affirmed.

PARKER, C. J., FULLERTON, and BRIDGES, JJ., concur.

[No. 16463. Department One. July 8, 1921.]

E. A. COFFIN, *Appellant*, v. JAMES E. BLACKWELL *et al.*, *Respondents*.[1]

MUNICIPAL CORPORATIONS (315)—POLICE POWER—RETROACTIVE ORDINANCES—PROTECTION AGAINST FIRE. A city, in the exercise of the police power, has a right to enact an ordinance, retroactive in effect, to compel a building owner to make necessary changes to reduce the fire hazard of a structure erected prior to the passage of the ordinance.

SAME (50)—ORDINANCES—CONSTRUCTION AND OPERATION. The building code of Seattle, providing, in § 1035 of the part relating wholly to "alterations and repairs" of existing buildings, that "nothing in this part shall be construed to prevent the superintendent of buildings from requiring unsafe or dangerous structures to be made safe under the powers granted elsewhere in this code," has a special and limited effect to the control only of alterations and repairs.

SAME (50). The building code of Seattle, § 103, providing that "nothing in the building code shall be construed as requiring that buildings heretofore constructed and equipped must be reconstructed, rearranged or otherwise equipped unless it be by ordinance specially provided," took from the administrative officers of the city all power to require reconstruction or equipment, unless specifically provided by ordinance to that effect.

SAME (50). Section 110 of the Seattle building code empowering the superintendent of buildings to require a building to be demolished or vacated when he finds "(c) That such building is unsafe to human life or property from any cause whatever or in imminent danger of so becoming," authorizes physical abatement by the officer when the danger is unmistakable and emergent.

SAME (50). Under § 9 of the "fire hazard" ordinance of the city of Seattle, providing that nothing therein shall be construed to require the alteration of elevators in any building constructed in full accordance with a permit issued by the superintendent of buildings, "unless such alterations or installation is manifestly necessary for the safeguarding of life and property or is specifically required by ordinance subsequently passed by the city council," the administrative officers of the city had no power, in the absence of a showing of immediate and unmistakable necessity, to require the reconstruction of an elevator shaft except under the sanction of a special ordinance passed for the express purpose of ordering the change.

[1]Reported in 199 Pac. 239.

Appeal from a judgment of the superior court for
King county, Gilliam, J., entered December 2, 1920, dismissing the action and dissolving a temporary restraining order prohibiting the enforcement of certain
changes in a building to conform to the building code.
Reversed.

Carroll B. Graves, for appellant.

Walter F. Meier and *Nelson T. Hartson,* for
respondents.

HOLCOMB, J.—It is conceived that the subjoined
statement (except as otherwise specifically noted) presents undisputed record facts.

This suit was waged to enjoin the superintendent of
buildings. the fire marshal, and the chief of the fire department, officers of the city of Seattle, from closing a
building, referred to in the complaint, in an effort to
enforce compliance with a notice and directions that
certain alterations and changes be made in that building. One Angie B. Collins, sometimes referred to as
the John Collins Estate, was originally made a party
defendant, but, prior to the trial, was dismissed from
the action, and an amended complaint was filed. The
cause was heard and determined upon the issues tendered by the amended complaint and the answer thereto.

The building under consideration is the Hotel Knickerbocker, in Seattle. This building was designed, constructed, and leased for hotel purposes, and, at all the
times mentioned, was being occupied and operated as
a hotel. It is seven stories in height, with six guest
rooms on the ground floor, and fourteen rooms on each
of the other floors, or ninety rooms in all. All floors
are served by one elevator.

On June 22, 1920, this building was let and demised
to appellant for a term of two years and five months,

commencing July 1, 1920. The appellant went into possession under this lease immediately, and ever since has remained in possession.

On about June 25, 1920, respondent officers served notice upon the owner of the building that certain changes and alterations must be made therein. The chief and radical alteration had relation to the enclosing of the elevator shaft and the notice required that alteration to be as follows:

"(4) The elevator must be enclosed in the basement with fire-proof construction and on the upper floors with partitions of four (4) inch solid wood, plastered both sides. All doors leading to the elevator shaft, must, of course, be fire-proof doors, in accordance with Section 663 of the building code."

The items 1, 5, 7, and 8 of the notice are not material, resistance thereto having been waived at the trial, and those changes either have been made or will be made in compliance with the instructions, but items 2, 3, 4, and 6, are within the objections urged by appellant.

On August 4, 1920, an additional notice was served by the respondent officers upon the Collins estate, and a copy thereof was transmitted to the plaintiff at the Knickerbocker hotel, wherein it was declared that if the alterations required by the notice of June 25, 1920, were not complied with, the building, or a portion thereof, would be closed. The effect of these two notices was to declare the intention of the officers, upon their own determination, unless such alterations were made, to prohibit the operation of the hotel, and thus interfere with and prohibit the carrying on of appellant's hotel business.

The Knickerbocker hotel was constructed in the year 1907, under a permit granted by the superintendent of buildings, dated January 8, 1907. The present ordinance, and the ordinances under which the city officers were claiming the right to act, were enacted in the year 1913, and in subsequent years. There was no contention that the building was not constructed in compliance with the terms of the permit for its construction.

The hotel building, structurally, does not comply with the present ordinances, nor is it a fireproof or mill building within the meaning of the ordinances. The building is situated inside of the second building district of the city. In order to comply with the ordinance relating to buildings in the second building district, this structure must either be a fireproof building or a mill building. Building Code, § 210. Sections 217-226 define fireproof building construction, and §§ 236-247 define mill building construction. It is not claimed by the respondent officers that the construction, arrangement or equipment of the building is contrary to the provisions of the building code for the purpose for which the building was used or occupied, namely, for hotel purposes, but only that changes were required under the general provisions of the code relating to all classes of buildings in that building district.

The building code was adopted in 1913 and the codification in evidence contains all amendments to May 1, 1920. Section 103 of this code reads as follows:

"Nothing in the building code shall be construed as requiring that buildings heretofore constructed and equipped must be reconstructed, rearranged, altered or otherwise equipped unless it be by ordinance specifically so provided."

An ordinance approved September 28, 1920, amended § 103 to read as follows:

"Section 103. Nothing in the building code shall be construed as requiring that buildings heretofore constructed and equipped, must be reconstructed, rearranged, altered or otherwise equipped except as may be required under authority of Section 110 of this code and other provisions of law relating thereto.''

Section 110 empowers the superintendent of buildings to direct and require a building to be vacated, removed or demolished by notifying, in writing, the owner, lessee, or person in charge, whenever he finds the following conditions to exist:

''(a)   That such building has been erected, altered or repaired subsequent to the passage of this ordinance in a manner contrary to the provisions thereof or the permit issued hereunder.

''(b)   That the construction, arrangement or equipment of such building or portion thereof, is contrary to the provisions of this Code for the purpose for which such building is used or occupied.

''(c)   That such building is unsafe to human life or to property *from any cause whatever* or in imminent danger of so becoming. (Italics ours.)

''(d)   That such building is not provided to the extent and in the manner required by ordinance with proper and sufficient means of egress in case of fire or of fire protective and fire extinguishing apparatus or of light and ventilation.''

Defendants introduced a third (called the ''fire hazard'') ordinance, numbered 36,299. The pertinent sections in that ordinance are §§ 8 and 9, which read as follows:

''Section 8.   The fire marshal is authorized and empowered, acting in conjunction with the superintendent of buildings, to direct and require that any building, or portion thereof, be reconstructed, rearranged, altered, repaired or provided with fire preventive or extinguishing equipment whenever he shall find that the means of egress from the same, or of preventing the origin or spread of fire, or of extinguishing fire, are insufficient, inadequate or do not comply with the provisions of the ordinances of the city relating thereto, and to direct and require that any building, or portion thereof, be vacated, removed, or demolished by posting a notice on such building or structure, and notifying in writing the owner, lessee or person in charge whenever it be found by him that such building or portion thereof constitutes a fire hazard, which should be abated or is unlawfully or dangerously occupied or is not provided to the extent or in the manner required by ordinance, with proper and sufficient means of egress in case of fire or panic, or with fire protective and fire extinguishing construction, apparatus or equipment.

"Section 9. Nothing in this ordinance contained shall be construed to require the alteration, of the number, location or construction of exits, aisles, halls, passageways, stairways, elevators, or the installation of fire preventive or extinguishing equipment in or on any building constructed in full accordance with a permit issued by the superintendent of buildings, unless such alterations or installation is manifestly necessary for the safeguarding of life and property or is specifically required by ordinance, subsequently passed by the city council; or unless the use and occupancy of such building has been changed subsequent to the issuance of said permit in such a manner as to necessitate such alterations or installation."

This ordinance took effect August 30, 1916. Section 113 and § 1096 of the building code and § 45 of ordinance No. 36,299 provide penalties for violation of these ordinances upon conviction thereof.

A further enactment of the building code, which respondents cite as bearing upon this matter, is § 1035 of the building code contained in the chapter or "part" of that code relating wholly to "alterations and repairs" of existing buildings, which section reads:

"Nothing in this part shall be construed to prevent the superintendent of buildings from requiring unsafe or dangerous structures to be made safe under the powers granted elsewhere in this code."

Judgment was rendered dismissing the action, and dissolving the temporary injunction, from which plaintiff appeals, and assigns as errors:

(1) The court erred in holding that the defendant officers had the authority to require the alterations determined upon by them; (2) the court erred in holding that the defendant officers could execute their determination by threat and force instead of resorting to the procedure authorized by law and by ordinance; and (3) the court erred in dismissing the action, dissolving the injunction, and rendering judgment for the defendants.

In our view, § 1035, being contained in the chapter or "part" of the ordinance regulating and controlling alterations and repairs to existing buildings by the owners, of their own volition, manifestly has but a special and limited effect, having relation only to the control and regulation of alterations and repairs by the officers charged therewith, either during the progress of the alterations and repairs, or thereafter, and that the section has no general effect otherwise.

We are fully in accord with the proposition advanced by respondents, that the city, in the exercise of the police power, has a right to enact an ordinance retroactive in effect, to compel a building owner to make necessary changes to reduce the fire hazard of a structure erected prior to the passage of the ordinance. This proposition was fully sustained in *Seattle v. Hinckley,* 40 Wash. 468, 82 Pac. 747. It is clear also that the city asserted this power and right in the enactment of the several ordinances involved herein. Nor are the penalty provisions exclusive, for they are not adequate to enforce all needful regulations in such matters. The general building code, however, in itself, § 103, wherein it is provided that "nothing in the building code shall be construed to require that buildings heretofore constructed and equipped must be reconstructed, rearranged, altered or otherwise equipped, unless it be by ordinance specifically so provided," while in force, assuredly took from any of the administrative officers of the city the power to require such reconstruction, rearrangement, alterations or equipment, unless specifically provided by ordinance to that effect, and there is no such ordinance enacted in regard to this property.

Nor is there any doubt that, under the provisions of § 110 of the building code heretofore quoted, the executive officers charged therewith would have a right to require that a building that is manifestly unsafe to human life or property, from any cause whatever, or in imminent danger of so becoming, be removed or destroyed. That condition occurs when the peril is imminent and manifest—that is, unmistakable—and such as to constitute at the time an emergent danger. In all such cases, a physical abatement by the executive officers would be sustained.

In this case it was shown that the building in question was built under a permit, and under regulations in force at the time of its erection. The changes required by the officers of the city would require the expenditure of approximately $3,000, and suspend the operation of the elevator for a considerable period, and put plaintiff's hotel business at a standstill, and drive much of its business away; and if the threat of the officers to close the building, or a part of it, should be effectuated, that would drive its business away.

The trial judge, in deciding the case, made the following observations:

"It is quite evident from the facts in the case that the alterations required by the city officers are reasonably necessary for that purpose. The present condition of the building is such as to be extremely hazardous for the guests in case of fire, to escape. The alterations as required greatly reduce the hazard and may be the means of preventing the loss of life in case of fire.

"If the rights of the city were limited to the building code, ordinance No. 31578, there would be no question but that the alteration required by the superintendent of buildings and the fire marshal, could not be enforced, unless a separate ordinance be passed specifically providing for it. However, the later ordinance, No. 36299, and particularly paragraphs 8 and 9 of said ordinance, seems to me to furnish ample authority to the fire marshal and the superintendent of buildings to require reasonable alterations for the purpose of preventing the origin and spread of fire. It is quite evident from the facts in the case that the repairs required by the city officers are reasonably necessary for that purpose. The present condition of the building is such as to be extremely hazardous for the guests in case of fire, to escape. The alterations as required greatly reduce this hazard, and may be the means of preventing the loss of life in case of fire. . . . . .

"In reaching my conclusions I am not overlooking the fact that the city at the trial conceded that the building in question when constructed, complied with all of the building ordinances of the city of Seattle, and that the plaintiff conceded at the trial that the building, as constructed, does not comply with the present building ordinances which have been enacted in the meantime."

The "fire hazard" ordinance, No. 36,299, as heretofore noted, took effect August 30, 1916. Section 103 of the building code ordinance, after the amendment on September 28, 1920, reads:

"Nothing in the building code shall be construed as requiring that buildings heretofore constructed and equipped, must be reconstructed, rearranged, altered or otherwise equipped except as may be required under authority of Section 110 of this code, and other provisions of the law relating thereto."

Section 110 only empowers the superintendent of buildings to direct and require a building to be vacated, removed or demolished by notifying in writing the owner, lessee, or person in charge, whenever he finds the conditions existing heretofore noted in subdivisions a, b, c, and d. And the other provisions of the law referred to in § 103, as amended, other than that of § 110, specifically referred to, and the penalty provisions, cannot refer in any way, by inference, intendment, or otherwise to any general city legislation other than §§ 8 and 9 of the "fire hazard" ordinance, No. 36,299. But § 9 of the "fire hazard" ordinance limits and restricts the application of that ordinance in the same way that § 103 of the building code before amendment did, unless "specifically required by ordinance," except where "manifestly necessary for the safeguarding of life and property."

The building code or other ordinances do not authorize the respondent officers, except in case of manifest necessity, to close or vacate a building or remove or demolish it, because of the failure or refusal of any person to comply with any notice or requirement by them, but provides only for a criminal prosecution in case of the violation of any ordinance provision. This, of course, is qualified by previous observations to the effect that in case of imminent peril, or emergent danger existing in a building erected under the former ordinances, or under any ordinance, it could be abated as a nuisance at any time without notice.

We are of the opinion, therefore, that the city could not proceed in regard to the building of appellant and require the building to be reconstructed, rearranged, repaired or equipped except by proceeding under the provisions of § 103 in the original building code, or § 9 of the fire hazard ordinance, by first enacting an ordinance specifically requiring such alterations and installations. There is no testimony in this case showing that any immediate public necessity requires the physical

abatement of this building or any part of it. The most
the evidence shows is that the rearrangement of the
building as indicated by the fire marshal, and the superintendent of buildings, would tend to lessen the danger
from fire to inmates of the building, but in no sense is
it shown to be imminently hazardous. Buildings in
such condition are to be regarded as protected from
mere executive interference by the building code, under
§ 103, and § 103 as amended, and § 9 of the fire hazard
ordinance, "unless such alterations or installation are
manifestly necessary for the safeguarding of life and
property, or are specifically required by ordinance
subsequently passed by the city council." As heretofore remarked, "manifestly necessary" means an immediate and unmistakable necessity.

For these reasons we conclude that the judgment of
the trial court is erroneous, and it is reversed.

PARKER, C. J., BRIDGES, and MACKINTOSH, JJ., concur.

[No. 16470. Department One. July 8, 1921.]

PENNINGTON & COMPANY, *Respondent*, v. HEDLUND BOX
& SHINGLE COMPANY, *Appellant*.[1]

SALES (25)—CONSTRUCTION OF CONTRACT—PROVISIONS IN GENERAL.
A printed letter head containing a provision stating "No offers binding on us until returned and accepted in writing" would have no
effect in governing clear and specific language evidencing specified
terms accepted and agreed to by both of the parties, or acted upon.

SALES (8)—REQUISITES—CONTRACTS BY CORRESPONDENCE. A consummated contract is not shown by correspondence arriving at the
terms of an agreement for the sale of a commodity, but which was
not entered into by reason of the failure of the buyer to execute and
deliver a formal written order as required by the seller.

Appeal from a judgment of the superior court for
Yakima county, Taylor, J., entered April 28, 1920, upon
findings in favor of the plaintiff, in an action on contract, tried to the court. Reversed.

Hamblen & Gilbert and *Richards & Fontaine*, for
appellant.

Preble, McAuley & Meigs, for respondent.

HOLCOMB, J.—The lower court gave judgment for
respondent for damages for the breach of an alleged
contract for the sale and delivery to it of 100,000 apple
box shooks. The measure of recovery as fixed by the
court was the sum of the difference between the cash
market value f. o. b. Yakima, Washington, of ten
thousand of such box shooks, on each of the ten different dates upon which such boxes should have been
shipped, and the stipulated price of such ten thousand
boxes on each of the ten dates so determined. In March,
1919, the Yakima Valley Traffic & Credit Association, a

[1]Reported in 199 Pac. 235.

corporation, in which the principal fruit buyers of the Yakima region were interested, and which had for one of its members the respondent, Pennington & Company, addressed a letter to the appellant at Spokane, Washington, who was engaged in the manufacture of box shooks, stating that the membership of the association had decided to form a pool for the purchase of box shooks, and asking appellant to quote prices upon from one to three million boxes of the specifications enclosed. All of the correspondence which followed, covering a period of a month, was carried on by the Yakima Valley Traffic & Credit Association, with appellant.

On March 29, 1919, appellant wrote the following letter to the association:

"Yakima Traffic & Credit Association,
     c/o Mr. I. L. Plette,
        "Yakima, Washington.

"Gentlemen: All agreements and contracts are contingent upon strikes, accidents, fires, delays to carriers and other delays unavoidable or beyond our control. Quotations are based upon terms herein stated; are made subject to change without notice and to prior sale of stock. Delivered prices are based on freight rates in effect at time prices are made. Advances in freight rates will increase prices proportionately. No offer is binding upon us until returned and accepted in writing. We do not guarantee safe delivery, nor against loss in transit. Claims will not be allowed unless made within five days of receipt of goods and entire shipment is held intact.

"We enclose confirmation of our telegram to you on this date.

"Now we can take care of your orders to the extent of 15 car loads of apple boxes at the present time and we suggest that Mr. Pennington take say 10 cars and the Washington Fruit & Produce Company take 5 cars. Then later on, we have no doubt, but what we can furnish Mr. Pennington with the balance of his requirements.

"The boxes will, of course, all be made of Western White Pine, well manufactured with ends ¾" thick and sides 5/16". The ends will contain possibly 20% of two pieces each fastened with corrugated staples put in by machinery to a smooth fit. Sides will be of one piece. T. & B. of four pieces, that is, two tops and two bottoms. Four cleats. All K. D.

"The price is $14.00 per 100 net f. o. b. at 15c frt. rate from Spokane, Wash.

"The deliveries are to start in April and continue at the rate of one car per week. We have some other orders to deliver also, so do not anticipate that any one of your members buying from us will receive a big bunch of boxes from us all at once. This is merely representative of our schedule and it will naturally vary somewhat.

"ThersM: The price is net. Buyer to pay frt. bill as goods are received for which we will give him credit, except for the Federal Taxes on the freight expenses themselves. We also wish to use Trade Acceptances on each car covering sixty days time from date of shipment. We may decide to let each car be invoiced on open account, but either way should not matter.

"Thanking you very kindly for calling us, we remain,
      "Yours very truly,
          "HEDLUND BOX & SHINGLE COMPANY,
                          "By D. A. Hedlund."

The first paragraph above set forth was a printed paragraph just below the address and on all the letters from appellant. To this letter the association made reply under date of March 31, as follows:

"Hedlund Box & Shingle Co.,
      "Spokane, Washington.

"Gentlemen: Referring to your letter of March 29th. Please confirm orders for 100,000 apple box shooks, specifications as shown for Pennington & Company, and 50,000 for Washington Fruit & Produce Company at terms mentioned.

"If in the market for any further orders at the price of 14c please advise and I will endeavor to place for you.

"Yours very truly,

"Y. V. TRAFFIC & CREDIT ASS'N,
"I. L. Plette, Manager."

On April 2, appellant wrote the association, as follows:

"Yakima Traffic & Credit Association,

"Yakima, Wash.

"Gentlemen: We have your letter of the 31st ultimo for which we thank you.

"Today we are sending contracts to Pennington & Co., and the Washington F. & P. Co., and as soon as these are returned to us signed by them we will be ready to go ahead on deliveries.

"Just at present we do not want to accept any more orders as we always wish to deliver what we agree to and there are many elements, labor, etc., which may prevent us from doing more than are already agreeing to do.

"Later on we shall be pleased to take the matter up with you again and trust you will have the orders and that we will be able to make deliveries.

"Yours very truly,

"HEDLUND BOX & SHINGLE COMPANY,
"By D. A. Hedlund."

The contract referred to in this letter was never sent to Pennington & Company, no form of contract was ever executed, no orders for shooks were ever sent by Pennington & Company to appellant, and on April 15, appellant again wrote the association saying: "as yet we have not received the order from Pennington & Company for any apple boxes. Therefore we have decided to withdraw our offer which we have no doubt will be satisfactory to you."

The questions of law discussed by appellant upon this appeal are these: (1) Did the negotiations between the parties as exhibited by the correspondence in question constitute a contract? and (2) did the court apply the proper rule of damages and fix the proper amount of damages in its judgment?

In support of its first proposition, appellant contends, first, that the minds of the parties did not meet as to the quantity of box shooks to be furnished; and second, no written contract or order was ever signed by the respondent Pennington & Company.

Attention is first called to the letter of appellant dated March 29, in which appellant made a proposition to take care of the association's orders to the extent of fifteen carloads of apple boxes at the present time, and suggested that Mr. Pennington take ten cars, and the Washington Fruit & Produce Company take five cars. Then it was suggested that later on appellant could furnish Mr. Pennington the balance of his requirements. Instead of accepting the proposal for fifteen carloads of apple boxes, the association mentioned 100,-000 apple box shooks for Pennington & Company in its reply. This, it is insisted, is a marked variation from the terms of the offer. The evidence shows that a carload of apple box shooks contains from eight to ten thousand shooks. We consider this variation immaterial since the letter of April 2, sent by appellant to the association stating, that contracts were being sent to Pennington & Company, and the Washington Fruit & Produce Company, and as soon as the contracts were returned to the appellant, signed, the appellant would be ready to go ahead on deliveries, either accepted the order of the association for 100,000 apple box shooks, or intended that contracts be signed stating the shooks by carload lots instead of box shook quantities, as ordered by the association.

A more serious question is the question of whether or not a contract was consummated at all.

Appellant attaches importance to the fact that each letter head of appellant contained in the heading this stipulation; "No offers binding on us until returned and accepted in writing." We attach no importance to that stipulation in the printed portion of the letter head, because, clear and specific language agreeing to specified terms accepted and agreed to by both of the parties, or acted upon, of course constitutes a contract, and the printed letter head would have little or no influence in changing the clear and specific language of the agreement as otherwise evidenced. *Sturm v. Boker*, 150 U. S. 312; *Summers v. Hibbard, Spencer, Bartlett & Co.*, 153 Ill. 102, 38 N. E. 899; *Sturtevant Co. v. Dugan*, 106 Md. 587, 14 A. & E. Ann. Cas. 675.

However, there was more evidence in this case explicitly pointing to the intention of the appellant not to consider the agreement consummated until a written formal contract had been prepared and signed. In another letter from appellant to the association, dated March 14, appellant stated that "the writer expects to be in Yakima next week, when he will call on you in hopes that you will then be ready to sign up a contract for your requirements." The writer of this letter was D. A. Hedlund. In the letter of April 2, replying to the letter of the association of March 31, it was stated that the contracts for Pennington & Company and for the Washington Fruit & Produce Company would be sent, and plainly intimated that appellant would *not* be ready to go ahead on deliveries until the contracts were returned to appellant signed by the parties to whom the deliveries were to be made.

Undoubtedly appellant had in mind that the principal rather than the agent with whom it had theretofore been dealing in the negotiations, should be bound by formal contract, and this it had a right to insist upon, and until the contract should be reduced to writing as the evidence of the terms of the agreement, there is nothing binding upon either of the parties, unless it had been acted upon by one or the other. In this case neither of the parties had acted upon the contract except that respondent insists that it had resold the box shooks which it had ordered. But it did not order any. It had merely arrived at the terms of an agreement to be entered into, which was not entered into. This feature of the case, we consider, is controlled by our decision in *Empson Packing Co. v. Lamb-Davis Lumber Co.*, 112 Wash. 75, 191 Pac. 833, and by *Schulze v. General Elec. Co.*, 108 Wash. 401, 184 Pac. 342; *Sparks v. Mauk*, 170 Cal. 122, 148 Pac. 926; *Aftergut Co. v. Mulvihill*, 25 Cal. App. 784, 145 Pac. 728; *Barber v. Burrows*, 51 Cal. 404; *Morrill v. Tehama Consolidated Mill & Mining Co.*, 10 Nev. 125; *McDonnell v. Coeur d'Alene Lumber Co.*, 56 Wash. 495, 106 Pac. 135; *Donnelly v. Currie Hdw. Co.*, 66 N. J. 388, 49 Atl. 428; *Ocala Cooperage Co. v. Florida Cooperage Co.*, 59 Fla. 394, 52 South. 13.

The respondent therefore had no right of recovery. The judgment below is erroneous, and is reversed.

PARKER, C. J., FULLERTON, BRIDGES, and MACKINTOSH, JJ., concur.

[No. 16341. Department One. July 8, 1921.]

E. S. THAYER, *Respondent*, v. YAKIMA TIRE SERVICE COMPANY, *Appellant*. [1]

SALES (179-1)—CONDITIONAL SALES—EFFECT OF ASSIGNMENT. Where a judgment creditor attached an automobile held by his debtor under a conditional sale contract providing for forfeiture in case of default in deferred payments, the seller of the car, in proving ownership on his motion to dissolve the attachment, was entitled to show that his assignment of the conditional sale contract, absolute on its face, was given merely as collateral.

Appeal from a judgment of the superior court for Yakima county, Holden, J., entered October 25, 1920, upon findings in favor of the plaintiff, dismissing a writ of attachment. Affirmed.

Wm. G. Smith, for appellant.

Williamson & Luhman, for respondent.

MACKINTOSH, J.—The Yakima Tire Service Company, on August 10, 1920, began an action against O. H. Ames, on a promissory note, and recovered judgment, and thereafter sued out a writ of attachment. On the writ, the sheriff took into his possession an automobile, which, on November 24, 1919, had been sold to Ames by E. S. Thayer, doing business as the Elgin Motor Company. On August 20, 1920, the Elgin Motor Company filed its affidavit of ownership, under § 573, Rem. & Bal. Code, and upon a hearing on the issues thus tendered, the superior court found the Elgin Motor Company was the owner of the car, and dismissed the writ of attachment of the Yakima Tire Service Company, from which order that company has appealed.

The sale on November 24, by the Elgin Motor Company to Ames, was made under an ordinary conditional

[1] Reported in 199 Pac. 224.

sale contract, which called for an initial down payment
(which was made) and for specified monthly payments
thereafter. The contract provided that on default by
Ames of any of these installments, the Elgin Motor
Company might retake the car, in which event all of
Ames' interest therein should be forfeited. On the
same day on which the contract was entered into, the
Elgin Motor Company assigned the contract to the
First National Bank, of Yakima, and, as a part of the
assignment, guaranteed to the bank the deferred payments to be made by Ames. Ames defaulted in his
first payment, and the Elgin Motor Company made the
payment to the bank. Ames, with regularity, defaulted in the three subsequent payments, and the
amount of those payments was charged by the bank
against the Elgin Motor Company's account. In
March, 1920, when it became apparent that Ames had
no ability nor intention of making the payments which
were to extend throughout the year 1920, the testimony is undisputed that Ames and Thayer agreed
that the contract might be cancelled, with redelivery to
Thayer. The contract still remained in possession of
the bank, and as the installments became due the
amounts thereof were charged against the Elgin Motor
Company's account. The Yakima Tire Service Company's claim that Ames had an interest in this machine
which was subject to their attachment as judgment
creditor, is based upon the fact that the Elgin Motor
Company, having placed of record an assignment of
the contract to the First National Bank, which was
absolute on its face, must be conclusively presumed to
have parted with its title to the bank, and the bank,
never having declared a forfeiture of the conditional
sale contract, it was still in force, and that Ames' inter_
est in the machine, whatever it might be, was subject
to attachment.

Without determining what the rights of judgment creditors may be by way of attachment of property for which the debtor is paying under a conditional sale contract, the question presented by the Yakima Tire Service Company may be answered by a reference to the evidence, which uncontradictedly shows the assignment to the bank was, as a matter of fact, purely as collateral to a loan. The judgment creditor, not being a *bona fide* purchaser for value, of course, has no right, to prevent the proof that an assignment, absolute on its face, is, as a matter of fact, given as collateral.

What we have already said in regard to the transaction between the Elgin Motor Company and Ames disposes of other contentions of the Tire Company, for it is apparent that after March, 1920, Ames had no interest in this car which could be reached in the manner pursued here. The judgment of the trial court was correct and is affirmed.

PARKER, C. J., BRIDGES, FULLERTON, and HOLCOMB, JJ., concur.

[No. 16413. Department One. July 8, 1921.]

JAMES O'BRIEN, *Respondent*, v. GRIFFITHS & SPRAGUE
STEVEDORING COMPANY, *Appellant*.[1]

APPEAL (370)—REVIEW—THEORY OF CASE IN LOWER COURT.
Where, in a personal injury action by a stevedore injured in the
hold of a vessel as the result of improper signals given by a hatch
tender, the defendant tried the case throughout on the theory that
the hatch tender was a vice-principal, it cannot on appeal assume
the position that, under the rules of the admiralty courts, a stevedore
working in a vessel's hold and the hatch tender are fellow servants
in loading the vessel.

DAMAGES (88)—EXCESSIVE—INJURY TO LEG. A verdict for $10,000,
for injuries to plaintiff's leg, about five inches above the ankle, for
which he was in the hospital sixty-eight days and the leg was rendered about one-half inch short, with a slight backward bow, was
excessive, and should be reduced to $5,000.

Appeal from a judgment of the superior court for
King county, Allen, J., entered September 22, 1920,
upon the verdict of a jury, in an action for personal
injuries. Modified.

Trefethen & Findley, for appellant.

James R. Gates and *Henry W. Pennock*, for respondent.

MACKINTOSH, J.—The appellant was loading a vessel in the Seattle harbor and employed the respondent,
who was stationed in the hold, stowing away railroad
rails, which were being handled under the direction of
a hatch tender stationed on the upper deck, one of
whose duties was to signal the winch drivers. The
negligence alleged against the appellant is that the
hatch tender gave the winch drivers improper signals
which resulted in a load of rails striking the respondent's legs, causing a fracture of the right leg about five
inches above the ankle, from the effect of which injury

[1]Reported in 199 Pac. 291.

the respondent lay in the hospital for sixty-eight days, and the limb has been left 2/5ths to 1/2 inch short, with a slight backward bow.

The appellant complains of the verdict of $10,000 on two grounds; first, that there was not sufficient evidence to justify it, and, second, that it is excessive.

The argument of the appellant upon the first point is that the rules of the admiralty courts should have been applied to this action, although it admits that the state court had concurrent jurisdiction over it with the admiralty court. Its argument is based upon the fact that, under the rules of admiralty, the hatch tender and the respondent were fellow servants. This objection cannot now be urged for the following reason: the appellant from its first appearance in this case until the filing of its briefs, tried the case upon the theory that the common law rules of fellow servant, as they have been established by the decisions of this court, were governing. No mention was made in the pleadings or at the trial of the applicability of any rule of admiralty. The appellant's answer was a common law answer and plead the common law defenses. No attack was made upon the respondent's pleadings wherein it was alleged that the hatch tender was a vice-principal. No evidence was introduced or contention made throughout the trial that this was not the relationship between the hatch tender and the respondent. The appellant's defense was that the negligence which proximately caused the injury was that of the yardarm winchman, and that he was a fellow servant. No instructions were proposed by the appellant advancing the fellow-servant rule nor its applicability to the hatch tender; no exceptions were taken to instructions which were given upon the theory that the hatch tender was a vice-principal, and in this court, for the first time, it

is suggested that the admiralty rules govern the case.
This court has held in *Jacobsen v. Rothschild*, 62 Wash.
127, 113 Pac. 261, that a hatch tender, as to an employee in the respondent's position, occupies the relationship of vice-principal to him. The case cannot be
presented by the pleadings and proof and instructions
in the lower court upon one theory, and then presented
for the first time in this court upon a different one. As
we said in *Driver v. Galland*, 59 Wash. 201, 109 Pac.
593:

"But there is another reason why the appellants
cannot prevail in this case. It has been the uniform
holding of this court that we will determine a case here
upon the theory upon which it was tried below, and
that alleged errors which are not called to the attention
of the lower court could not be reviewed here. . . .
In order to determine exactly what was tried below
and what it was the intention of the parties litigant to
try, we must resort to the pleadings and the testimony
offered, the instructions of the court, instructions objected to and instructions asked, and to the character
of the trial generally."

The supreme court of Wisconsin, considering this
same question, has this to say; in the case of *Leora v.
Minneapolis, St. P. etc. R. Co.*, 156 Wis. 386, 146 N. W.
520:

"At the threshold of this case we are met with the
objection that the plaintiff was employed in interstate
commerce when injured, and hence that the case is
governed by the federal statute regulating actions for
injuries suffered by employes of interstate carriers.

"This objection was not made in the trial court, nor
was it made in the briefs filed in this court upon the
appeal, but was first raised upon the oral argument.
The question is important and far reaching. It is not
in the strict sense, a jurisdictional question, because
the court has power to try the case whichever law be
applicable. If a defendant can carry its case through

the trial court without raising the question of the application of the federal law, and, when defeated, come to this court and for the first time raise the question successfully, it possesses a very valuable advantage. It can experiment through both courts with one law and, if defeated, commence over again under the other law, thus securing two trials, even though the first trial be without objection or exception. Such a conclusion should not be reached unless it is inevitable. Every instinct of fairness and justice cries out against it. It is a question which seems likely to occur with more or less frequency so long as the two laws exist side by side with varying and contradictory provisions on essential matters. The line which divides employment in interstate commerce from employment in intrastate commerce is at times very shadowy and difficult to draw. If the question may lie dormant in the trial court and be raised for the first time in the court of last resort, it is very certain that many a case fairly tried under the terms of one law, and in which every right secured to the parties by that law has been carefully safeguarded, will have to be reversed and a new trial awarded because of an objection never brought to the attention of the trial court.

"There is a well established legal principle which forbids this result, and that is the principle of consent or waiver. This principle has been frequently applied in cases where it is claimed in the appellate court for the first time that a law, under which a recovery has been had in the trial court, is unconstitutional."

See, also, on this same point: *Rice v. Stevens*, 9 Wash. 298, 37 Pac. 440; *Yarwood v. Billings*, 31 Wash. 542, 72 Pac. 104; *Sanders v. Stimson Mill Co.*, 34 Wash. 357, 73 Pac. 688; *Normile v. Thompson*, 37 Wash. 465, 79 Pac. 1095; *Standard Furniture Co. v. Anderson*, 38 Wash. 582, 80 Pac. 813; *Nielsen v. Northeastern Siberian Co.*, 40 Wash. 194, 82 Pac. 292; *Lesser Cotton Co. v. St. Louis etc. R. Co.*, 114 Fed. 133; *Union Pacific R. Co. v. Whitney*, 198 Fed. 784; *Pine Belt Lumber Co. v. Riggs*, 80 Okl. 28, 193 Pac. 990; *Wickern v. United*

States Express Co., 83 N. J. 241, 83 Atl. 776; *Madden
v. Hughes,* 185 N. Y. App. 466, 78 N. E. 167; *Hanson
v. Chicago, M. & St. P. R. Co.,* 157 Wis. 455, 146 N. W.
524; *Chicago etc. R. Co. v. Rogers,* 150 S. W. (Texas)
281.

Upon the second point, we are constrained to agree
with the appellant's position. So far as our examination has led us, we cannot find any verdict in this
amount which has been allowed to stand for any injury
similar to that suffered by the respondent. Under all
the circumstances of the case, and taking into consideration the earning power of the dollar, the verdict is
grossly excessive and should be reduced to the sum of
$5,000, and the order of the court, therefore, will be
that if the respondent will within 30 days after the
receipt of the remittitur by the superior court, consent
in writing to take a judgment in the amount of $5,000
then a new judgment shall be entered in his favor for
that sum, otherwise the trial court is instructed to
grant appellant a new trial.

PARKER, C. J., BRIDGES, FULLERTON, and HOLCOMB,
JJ., concur.

[No. 16416. Department Two. July 8, 1921.]

Robert Lindstrom, *Respondent*, v. Seattle Taxicab Company et al., *Appellants.*[1]

Municipal Corporations (383, 391)—Use of Streets—Contributory Negligence of Pedestrian. Where a pedestrian is placed in imminent danger through the wrongful and negligent act of an automobile driver, the question whether he acted with due prudence in avoiding the danger is one for the jury, in an action for personal injuries inflicted by being run down by the automobile.

Trial (120)—Deliberations of Jury—Coercing Agreement. Coercion of a jury is not shown by the fact that the jury, after a day and night of deliberation, were brought into court and admonished by the judge not to be stubborn; not to be afraid to change their minds; that they should reason with one another; that the case had been well tried; that a disagreement would necessitate a new trial; and that the present jury should agree, if possible, though the judge took it upon himself to advance the admonition without any request from the jury for further instructions.

Appeal from a judgment of the superior court for King county, Tallman, J., entered December 11, 1920, upon the verdict of a jury in favor of the plaintiff, in an action for personal injuries. Affirmed.

W. A. Gilmore and *Van Dyke & Thomas*, for appellants.

Carl J. Smith and *H. E. Foster*, for respondent.

Tolman, J.—Respondent as plaintiff brought this action to recover for personal injuries. From a verdict against them in the sum of $2,000, and a judgment entered thereon, the defendants have appealed.

The only eyewitnesses to the accident who testified upon the trial, were the respondent and the appellant Erickson, the driver of the taxicab. Respondent testified in substance that, at the time in question, he walked

[1] Reported in 199 Pac. 289.

down Fourth avenue, in the city of Seattle, to James
street, where he stopped for an instant because there
was an automobile passing in one direction, and a
street car coming from the other; that he heard the
brakes applied to the street car and knew it would
stop before crossing the cable line on James street.
He therefore proceeded to cross Fourth avenue on
the crossing at the intersection with James street,
keeping a lookout for approaching traffic. As he
passed over the first street car track so that he could
see to the east of the approaching car, he saw appellant's taxicab coming south on the left side of the
street car, and on the east street car track, and distant from him some seven or eight feet. He had heard
no sounding of a horn or other signal, and did not know
of the approach of the taxicab until it was in close
proximity to him. As to what then occurred he testified as follows:

"Q. And you say you took one long step? A. Yes,
as soon as I saw that cab I took that big step. I
thought I would make it anyway; but instead of going
right straight ahead then he swing over to his left
the same way I was going, and the car knocked me
down. Q. How is that? A. As soon as I see, he swing
that way, I stepped as far as I could, but the car
grabbed me at the side and threw me down . . .
Q. Are you able to tell the jury just what portion of the
taxicab it was that actually hit your body, whether it
was the door— A. Just about the door of the cab."

And again:

"Q. Did you hear the approach of the automobile
until you got to the point 'H' when you first saw it
at 'I'? A. No, sir, I did not hear it. Q. Are you able
to tell the jury how far it was after you saw the automobile, that he commenced to turn further to the left?
A. He was just about ten feet away from me. He was
just close to me, and he thought I would back up, but

instead I ran ahead to get to the sidewalk. Q. What, if any, attempt did he make to slow up? A. He did not slow up. I did not see him slow up, or I would have made it. Q. What? A. He did not slow up. If he had slowed up I would have made it."

Appellant Erickson fixes the place of the accident at a different point, between street intersections, where the taxicab would have had the right of way, and under circumstances tending to show that respondent was guilty of contributory negligence, but his testimony in the main, agrees with that of respondent to the effect that respondent was struck by, or ran into, the taxicab so that he came into contact with the body at or near the door of the taxicab.

While admitting that there was testimony from which the jury could have found that the accident happened at a street intersection, where respondent had the right of way, appellants contend that the evidence justifies only the conclusion that respondent ran into the taxicab, and that therefore their request for an instructed verdict, or their motion for a new trial should have been granted. We think, however, that this was a question for the jury. It must be borne in mind that, according to respondent's testimony he was placed in imminent danger through the wrongful and negligent act of the driver of the taxicab in passing to the left of the street car, and proceeding upon the wrong side of the street. As was said in *Sheffield v. Union Oil Co.*, 82 Wash. 386, 144 Pac. 529:

"Being in imminent danger, an emergency was presented, and whether, under this emergency, the respondent acted with due prudence is, under all the authorities, a question of fact for the jury. The law does not scrutinize too carefully an act done by one who has been put in a position of danger by the one who inflicts injury upon him, leaving it for the jury to say under such circumstances whether the act in seeking to avoid the danger was the act of an ordinarily prudent man.''

The case was submitted to the jury during the forenoon of Friday, and, not having agreed upon a verdict on Saturday morning at 9:30 o'clock, the jury was brought into court, and the following took place:

''The court: Members of the jury: I have been informed that thus far you have been unable to agree. Am I right about that? Foreman: You are. The court: May I inquire how you stand? Don't tell which side you are for, but the number. How do you stand? Foreman: Eight to four. The court: It occurred to me, members of the jury, that a word from the court at this time might assist you. Jury duty is very difficult, of course. It is sometimes difficult for one man to make up his mind on a question. Therefore, I realize how difficult it is for twelve people to make up their minds on a certain subject sometimes. However, in my opinion it is not impossible and should not be impossible for you people to agree. There are a few things that you should keep in mind. In the first place, a juror should not be obstinate. A juror should not be stubborn. There is another way of putting it that is more forcible than elegant, a juror should not be bull headed. You must realize that there is nothing wrong or criminal about one changing one's mind after listening to the argument of other jurors, or a juror should not feel that because she or he voted one way once that he or she must never change her or his mind. If the other jurors convince you that you are wrong, don't be afraid to change your mind. The old saying that has gotten to be a proverb is that a wise man sometimes changes his mind, but a fool never does. Don't feel because you voted a certain way that you must not change your mind. Disagreements are very undesirable. This case will have to be decided by some twelve people, and some twelve people will agree, and they won't know in all probability any more about the case than you know about it. This case was well tried to you, and ably presented by the lawyers on both sides.

Everything was brought out in all probability that
could be brought out; so some twelve people will have
to decide this case, and I see no reason why you twelve
people should not decide it. You should agree, if possible, and I think it is possible for you to agree. Reason one with the other. Don't go away and obstinate-
ly sit down and say I voted and I will vote that way
until the stars fall. That isn't the position to take.
Talk the matter over and continue to talk it over.
Don't all talk at one time, but reason together and see
if someone isn't wrong, and agree, if possible, and I
think it is possible for you to agree. I want to repeat,
some twelve people will decide this case, and why can't
you twelve people? You look to me to be reasonable
men and women, and I see no reason why you should
not decide this case. Now, members of the jury, go
back and see if you can't agree upon a verdict."

Shortly after again retiring the jury returned the
verdict upon which judgment was entered. It is contended that in this the court seriously erred, and that
not having asked for further instructions, the court's
interference was an assault upon the minds and con-
sciences of the jurors, which amounted to coercion. We
had occasion to pass upon a somewhat similar case in
Mott Iron Works v. Metropolitan Bank, 90 Wash. 655,
156 Pac. 864, where it was said:

"Before returning to the jury room, the court admonished its members at considerable length to the
effect that they should listen to each other, consult
with each other, and make an effort to agree; that they
should not be stubborn; that they need not be convinced beyond a reasonable doubt, but should bring in
a verdict upon what might seem to them a fair preponderance of the evidence; this and much more to the
same effect. It is urged that this tended to minimize
the essential duty of a juror to return a verdict according to his own judgment and conscience. We find nothing in it calculated to coerce the judgment or lay the
conscience of any reasonable juror."

It is true that there additional instructions were asked for and the court's admonition was limited by the statement that the jurors should base their verdict upon what might seem to them to be a fair preponderance of the evidence. In a proper case, whether or not additional instructions were requested, a reasonable admonition to agree, if possible, is permissible, though care should always be exercised not to cause any juror to disregard or abandon his honest convictions as to what is established by the evidence, and agree to a verdict which he honestly believes to be unsupported by a preponderance of the evidence. The inquiry as to how the jury stood, followed by the language used by the court in this case, is not to be commended, and while it is possible that the judgment of some juror might have been overborne thereby, yet, in view of the court's previous instructions, still before the jury giving the correct rule for its guidance, we cannot assume that any juror was improperly influenced or coerced by what was said.

We have examined with care the errors assigned upon the giving and refusal to give instructions, but cannot discuss these matters in detail without unduly extending this opinion. It is sufficient to say that we find no reversible error therein and that, taken as a whole, the instructions given fairly advised the jury as to the law applicable.

Judgment affirmed.

PARKER, C. J., HOLCOMB, MAIN, and MITCHELL, JJ., concur.

[No. 16485. Department Two. July 8, 1921.]

GERMAN-AMERICAN MERCANTILE BANK *et al.*,
Respondents, v. H. E. FOSTER,
Appellant.[1]

CORPORATIONS (46)—STOCK SUBSCRIPTIONS—ACTIONS ON—AMEND-
MENTS. A subscriber to the capital stock of a banking corporation
would not be released by the amendment of its articles of incorporation so as to change its name and increase its capital stock for the
purpose of absorbing the assets and assuming the liabilities of another bank, since such amendment did not end the corporate existence of the original bank.

SAME (46). An error in judgment on the part of the bank examiner in permitting one bank to absorb another, resulting in loss
to the former, would not constitute a defense against the liability of
a nonassenting stockholder in an action to recover on his subscription to the capital stock of the original bank.

Appeal from a judgment of the superior court for
King county, Ronald, J., entered June 19, 1920, upon
findings in favor of the plaintiff, in an action to recover
on stock liability, tried to the court. Affirmed.

Carl J. Smith, for appellant.

D. E. Twitchell, for respondents.

TOLMAN, J.—This action was instituted to recover
from appellant $500 and interest as superadded liability
accruing by reason of his ownership of five shares of
the capital stock of the respondent bank, of the par
value of $100 each. From a judgment as prayed for,
this appeal is taken.

Appellant subscribed for, and became the owner of,
the stock in question at the time of the incorporation of
the bank in April, 1911. The bank was incorporated as

[1]Reported in 199 Pac. 814.

the German-American Bank, the amount of its capital stock not being shown in the record. In 1915, the bank filed amended articles of incorporation, changing its name to that of German-American Mercantile Bank, and increasing its capital stock to $200,000. Appellant opposed the making of these changes, but thereafter accepted the new stock certificate in lieu of the one first issued to him, which, on its face, shows the change of name, etc. In large part appellant's defenses in the trial court, and assignments of error here are based upon the assumption that the German-American Bank ceased to exist in 1915, and that the German-American Mercantile Bank was a separate and distinct corporate entity; and that the bank examiner, by permitting the latter to succeed the former and absorb the assets and assume the liabilities of the Mercantile National Bank, had caused the appellant to lose the value of his stock in the German-American Bank. Appellant's affirmative answer and his cross-complaint based upon this theory, were, on motion, stricken by the trial court. We see no error in such ruling. There was but one corporation. The amending of its articles did not end its existence, or change appellant's status as a stockholder; and if the amendment was effected as the statute requires (and it is not alleged otherwise) appellant was bound thereby whether he assented or not.

Nor would an honest error in judgment on the part of the bank examiner, if there was such, and the permitting of the absorbing of another banking institution, though loss followed, be a defense to this action.

All of the other points raised by appellant are decided against him in *Hanson v. Soderberg*, 105 Wash. 255, 177 Pac. 827. Still adhering, as we do, to the views therein expressed, a rediscussion of the subject seems unnecessary.

Finding no error the judgment appealed from is affirmed.

PARKER, C. J., HOLCOMB, MAIN, and MITCHELL, JJ., concur.

[No. 16209.   Department Two.   July 12, 1921.]

HOWARD PARKER et al., Appellants, v. ANNIE C. PARKER, Respondent.[1]

TRIAL (149-1)—TRIAL BY COURT—DECISION. An order of the court, granting a new trial in an action tried without a jury after delivering an oral opinion in favor of one of the parties, was in legal effect simply the reopening of the case for further proof for the benefit of both parties; since under Rem. Code, § 367, in the trial of an issue of fact by the court, its findings, conclusions and judgments must be in writing, and under Id., § 402, the party moving for new trial must, within two days after notice in writing of the decision of the court, file and serve his motion for a new trial.

Appeal from an order of the superior court for King county, Hall, J., entered August 16, 1920, upon granting defendant's motion for a new trial, in an action on promissory notes. Remanded.

Million & Houser and *J. L. Corrigan,* for appellants.

Shank, Belt & Fairbrook (*G. P. Haight,* of counsel), for respondent.

MITCHELL, J.—This is an action at law to recover on two promissory notes. The answer denied generally the allegations of the complaint and pleaded several affirmative defenses. Trial was had by the court without a jury. At the conclusion of the introduction of the testimony, the court delivered an oral opinion in favor of the plaintiffs. Defendant moved for a new trial for the reasons: (1) insufficiency of the evidence

[1]Reported in 199 Pac. 723.

to justify the decision, and that the same is contrary to law; and (2) error in law occurring at the trial and excepted to at the time by the defendant. The clerk's docket entry shows "defendant's motion for a new trial is granted." There were no findings of fact or conclusions of law given in writing by the trial court and filed with the clerk; nor was there any formal order granting the motion for a new trial signed by the judge and filed with the clerk.

The plaintiffs have appealed and have assigned as error the granting of defendant's motion for a new trial. Section 367, Rem. Code, provides:

"Upon the trial of an issue of fact by the court, its decisions shall be given in writing and filed with the clerk. In giving the decision, the facts found and the conclusions of law shall be separately stated. Judgment upon the decision shall be entered accordingly."

Section 368, Rem. Code, provides:

"The order of proceedings on a trial by the court shall be the same as provided in trials by jury. The finding of the court upon the facts shall be deemed a verdict, and may be set aside in the same manner and for the same reason, as far as applicable, and a new trial granted."

Section 402, Rem. Code, in part, provides:

"The party moving for a new trial must, within two days after the verdict of a jury, if the action was tried by a jury, or two days after notice in writing of the decision of the court or referee, if the action was tried without a jury, file with the clerk, and serve upon the adverse party, his motion for a new trial, designating the grounds upon which it will be made . . ."

In the case of *Russell v. Schade Brewing Co.*, 49 Wash. 362, 95 Pac. 327, it was pointed out: " . . . particularly in view of our statute, a distinction must be made between a mere opinion of a trial court and its decision." A trial court is at liberty, after an oral opinion, upon further reflection to change its views upon the facts or law or both, for the purpose of a decision which the statute requires to be given in writing and filed with the clerk.

In the case just cited, it was held that written findings are necessary under the statute in actions at law tried by the court without a jury, manifestly, as stated in the opinion, because there is no verdict, so-called, until the findings have been given in writing and filed with the clerk. It is plain therefore, since a motion for a new trial follows a verdict of a jury or a decision by a court in an action at law tried without a jury and that there were no findings of fact or decision given in writing and filed with the clerk in this case, that the legal effect of the court's action, as shown by the docket entry that the motion for a new trial was granted, was simply to reopen the case for further proof for the benefit of both parties. It was but the exercise of power inherently and necessarily lodged in the court, at that stage of the trial.

Remanded with instructions to proceed accordingly.

Parker, C. J., Main, and Tolman, JJ., concur.

[No. 14917. Department Two. July 14, 1921.]

W. S. DOUGLASS, *Respondent*, v. TILLICUM DEVELOPMENT COMPANY, *Appellant*.[1]

PUBLIC LANDS (20)—POSSESSORY RIGHTS—TOWNSITES—ADVERSE CLAIMS—AFFIDAVIT—SUFFICIENCY. The object of the Townsite Act of Congress, March 2, 1867, and of Rem. Code, § 9469, for the purpose of carrying the Federal act into effect, being for the benefit of the occupant of the land at the time of entry, the failure of a claimant to state in his affidavit of possessory rights who was the occupant of the lots at the time of entry of such townsite, would not be sufficient to defeat his title upon a contest by another, where the evidence showed the former claimed directly under a conveyance from one who was the occupant at the time of the townsite entry.

SAME (21)—TOWNSITES—RIGHTS ACQUIRED BY ENTRY. In a contest over lots under the Federal Townsite Act, where the court found plaintiff and his predecessor in interest had been in exclusive possession of all the lots, his failure to enclose some of the lots would not affect his title thereto, where the court further found they had been left unfenced for road and pasturage purposes.

Appeal from a judgment of the superior court for Okanogan county, Neal, J., entered May 27, 1918, upon findings in favor of the plaintiff, in an action to obtain title to certain land, tried to the court. Affirmed.

W. C. Gresham, for appellant.

J. W. Graham, for respondent.

MAIN, J.—The parties to this action are rival claimants to certain lots or tracts of land in the government townsite in Loomis, in Okanogan county. The trial resulted in findings of fact and conclusions of law and judgment sustaining the plaintiff's claim of title. From this judgment the defendant appeals.

No bill of exceptions or statement of facts has been brought to this court and the case must therefore be

[1]Reported in 199 Pac. 451.

determined upon the findings. The essential facts as there stated may be summarized as follows: The government townsite of Loomis was entered in the manner and form provided by law on the 19th day of January, 1912. On the 17th day of February, 1912, the respondent entered into possession of the lands in controversy and ever since that date has been in actual and exclusive possession thereof. The respondent's predecessor in interest in the property had claimed, improved and resided upon the same for a period of sixteen years prior to the transfer to the respondent and at that time the improvements upon the property were of the value of about $3,000. On August 30, 1913, for the purpose of acquiring a certificate covering the lands in controversy the respondent filed an affidavit with the proper officer, which affidavit is made a part of the findings. Subsequently and on September 4, 1913, the appellant made a similar claim supported by affidavit, which is also made a part of the findings. The respondent's affidavit, among other things, states that he went

"into possession of said lots on February 17, 1912, and has ever since said time, been, and now is in the exclusive possession of said lots; that affiant and claimant is entitled to the possession of all of said lots and to a deed therefor, as against all other persons or claimants to the best of his knowledge and belief; that he is the occupant of all of said lot and was at the time of the entry of such townsite at the United States land office."

The appellant claims that this affidavit is defective in two respects: First, that it does not concisely state the facts constituting the possession or right to possession or occupancy of the land; and, second, that the findings of fact as made by the trial court show that the respondent was not in possession and had no

right to the possession of the lands at the time of the
entry of the government townsite of Loomis.

On March 2, 1867, an act of Congress was approved
which provided for the relief of inhabitants of cities
and towns upon public lands. The legislature of this
state in 1909, for the purpose of carrying out the objects of the Federal act, passed an act prescribing
certain rules and regulations which claimants should
conform to. Laws of 1909, p. 836, ch. 231, § 31 (Rem.
Code, § 9469), of this act provides that every person
claiming under it and the Federal act must within the
time there specified present an affidavit to the officer
named.

"in which must be concisely stated the facts constituting the possession or right of possession of the
claimant and that the claimant is entitled to the possession thereof and to a deed therefor as against all
other persons or claimants, to the best of his knowledge
and belief, and in which must be stated who was an
occupant of such lot or parcel of land at the time of
the entry of such townsite at the United States land
office . . ."

It will be observed that by this statute the affidavit
should set out the facts constituting possession or the
right to possession and also who was the occupant of
the land at the time of the entry of such townsite.

It will be admitted that the act of Congress, as well
as the state act, is for the benefit of the occupant of
the land at the time of the entry. *Lockwitz v. Larson*,
16 Utah 275, 52 Pac. 279. The affidavit in question
fails to state that the respondent claimed through another who was the occupant at the time of the entry
of the townsite. To this extent at least the affidavit
is defective. The trial court, however, found the fact
to be that the respondent did claim directly under a
conveyance from the one who was the occupant at

the time of the entry. There was here within the time prescribed an effort made in good faith to comply with the law with only a technical defect. It would be a harsh rule that would deprive the respondent of his property, including the improvements thereon, for failure to embody in his affidavit every detail required by the law when the findings of the court show a full compliance with the law.

This is not a case where there was no attempt within the required time to make a claim. Cases holding, therefore, that where there is no such attempt that the claimant's rights are gone are not here in point.

The appellant makes a claim that, according to the findings, three or four lots or parts thereof had never been fenced or enclosed by the respondent or his predecessor in interest. There is a further finding to the effect that the respondent and his predecessors never used the land for any purpose other than that of a roadway passing through the same and used a small portion as pasturage. In another place, as already pointed out, it is expressly found that the respondent since the date of entry into possession had continued in actual and exclusive possession of all of said lots and tracts of land and that he had made his home upon and constantly resided thereon and that the respondent's predecessor in interest had claimed, improved and resided upon the property for a period of sixteen years prior to the transfer to the respondent. Under these findings the appellant would not be entitled to that portion of the lots which had not actually been fenced or enclosed by the respondent or his predecessor.

The judgment will be affirmed.

PARKER, C. J., MITCHELL, and TOLMAN, JJ., concur.

[No. 16293. Department Two. July 14, 1921.]

LOUISE JOHNSTON, *Respondent*, v. CHARLES J. JOHNSTON, *Appellant*.[1]

APPEAL (45)—DECISIONS APPEALABLE—ORDER AWARDING CUSTODY OF CHILD. An order modifying the order made in a divorce proceeding awarding the custody of a minor child is appealable.

SAME (102)—RIGHT TO APPEAL—CESSATION OF CONTROVERSY—LAPSE OF TIME. An order awarding the custody of a child to one parent for a prescribed period, "and until the further order of this court," being a continuing order unaffected by the expiration of the prescribed period, is appealable.

SAME (175)—REQUISITES FOR TRANSFER—MOTION TO VACATE JUDGMENT. The rule requiring an application to the superior court to correct an irregular order before appealing therefrom does not apply where judgment was entered without power or authority in the court to render the judgment.

DIVORCE (96, 97)—CUSTODY OF CHILD—POWER TO AWARD—JURISDICTION OF JUVENILE COURT. A judge of the superior court sitting as a judge of the juvenile court, and who had not tried the divorce action in which custody of the child was awarded to a parent, would have no power to modify the order for its custody upon the report of the juvenile officer, there being no showing that the child was dependent or delinquent under the provisions of Rem. Code, § 1987 *et seq.*, known as the juvenile act.

Appeal from a judgment of the superior court for Kitsap county, Dykeman, J., entered June 22, 1920, modifying an order in divorce for the custody of a minor child. Reversed.

Tucker & Hyland (Ford Q. Elvidge, of counsel), for appellant.

H. E. Gorman, for respondent.

MAIN, J.—This is an appeal from an order taking the custody of a child from its father and awarding it to the mother. On July 5, 1916, the plaintiff was

[1]Reported in 199 Pac. 737.

awarded a decree of divorce from her then husband, the defendant. The trial court found both parties suitable persons to have the custody and control of their only child, a daughter, who was then six years old, but awarded its custody to the father, reserving to the mother the right to see it at all reasonable times and places. In March, 1919, the plaintiff filed a petition asking that the decree relative to the custody of the child be modified and that the custody be awarded to her. The allegations of this petition, after being amended, were denied by the defendant, and upon the issues thus framed, the cause, on May 17, 1920, came on for trial before the Honorable Walter M. French, judge of the superior court for Kitsap county. A hearing was had on that date in which both parties introduced testimony, and at the conclusion thereof the trial judge indicated a desire to have a report on the matter from the juvenile officer of his court. The proceedings were thereupon adjourned until such time as the report could be received.

Before the report of the juvenile officer was received, Judge French departed from the state to be gone some little time, and directed that all juvenile matters in his court should be heard by Honorable King Dykeman, one of the judges of the superior court of King county, or another judge of the latter county. On June 22, 1920, Judge Dykeman, while sitting as a visiting judge in Kitsap county, made an order awarding the custody of the child to the plaintiff, its mother. This order was based upon the report of the juvenile officer which was then on file. From the order awarding the custody of the child to the mother, the defendant appeals.

The respondent moves to dismiss the appeal for three reasons, which will be briefly considered. First, it is claimed that the order is not a final order and

therefore is not appealable. In *Irving v. Irving,* 26
Wash. 122, 66 Pac. 123, where there was an appeal
from a similar order, it was held that "the statute
permits an appeal from orders and judgments of this
character." Since the decision of that case, it has
been the uniform practice of this court to entertain
such appeals. Anything that may have been said to
the contrary in *Tierney v. Tierney,* 1 Wash. Terr. 569,
cannot now be regarded as the law.

Second, it is claimed that the appeal should be dismissed because the period named in the order during
which the custody should be changed has expired and
that there is nothing now to appeal from. The order
recites that the custody of the child should be given
to the mother "during the period of school vacation
during the months of June, July, and August and until
the further order of this court." Under this order,
the period during which the mother would hold the
custody of the child would not expire with the end
of the month of August named in the order, but would
continue until the further order of the court. Orders
containing this latter provision as above indicated were
held to be appealable in *Irving v. Irving, supra.*

The third position on the motion is that the judgment entered by Judge Dykeman was irregular and
that, before an appeal would lie, it was necessary to
make an application to the superior court to have a
proper judgment entered. The judge entering the
order did not hear the testimony upon the trial, and
as above stated, based the order upon the report of
the juvenile officer. This was not an irregular judgment, but one entered without power or authority to
do so. It does not come with the rule of the case of
State ex rel. Hennessy v. Huston, 32 Wash. 154, 72
Pac. 1015, where it was held that it was necessary,

under the facts of that case, to make an application to the superior court to correct an irregular order before appealing therefrom.

The motion to dismiss the appeal will be denied. Upon the merits, there can be little ground for controversy. The case came on before Judge French and the issue as to the custody of the child was regularly tried and referred to the juvenile officer for a report. It is not claimed that the child was dependent or delinquent under the terms of the juvenile act (Rem. Code, § 1987 *et seq.*). The child not coming within the provisions of this act, Judge Dykeman, while sitting as a judge of the juvenile court for Kitsap county, would have no right to interfere with its custody based solely upon the report of the juvenile officer, and, since he did not hear the testimony upon the trial, had no power or authority to enter the judgment. Rem. Code, § 54, subd. 2.

The judgment will be reversed and the cause remanded.

PARKER, C. J., MITCHELL, and TOLMAN, JJ., concur.

[No. 16303. Department Two. July 14, 1921.]

THE STATE OF WASHINGTON, *on the Relation of E. M. Martin, Appellant,* v. THE CITY OF SEATTLE and HARRY W. CARROLL, *as City Comptroller, Respondents.*[1]

MUNICIPAL CORPORATIONS (68) — EMPLOYEES — COMPENSATION. Where a civil service employee of the city of Seattle was laid off because of lack of work in the department in which he was employed, his subsequent reinstatement, on the discharge of another employee of the department who was found ineligible because of nonresidence in the city, would not entitle him to compensation during the time he was separated from the service.

Appeal from a judgment of the superior court for King county, Jurey, J., entered September 30, 1920, upon sustaining a challenge to the evidence, dismissing a mandamus proceeding to compel the issuance of a city warrant. Affirmed.

Jas. A. Dougan, for appellant.

Walter F. Meier and *Nelson T. Hartson,* for respondents.

MAIN, J.—The relator, E. M. Martin, a civil service employee of the city of Seattle, brought this action in mandamus for the purpose of compelling the city to issue to him a warrant for salary which he claimed he was entitled to.

On the 26th day of July, 1919, and for some time prior thereto, there was employed, under the engineering department of the city, eleven drawbridge tenders of which the relator was one. On the date mentioned, the relator and one G. M. Brinkerhoff were laid off for lack of work by the head of the department under

[1] Reported in 199 Pac. 449.

which they were employed. Of the nine bridge tenders retained, Thomas O. Hornbeck was one. After the relator was laid off, he complained informally to the civil service commission of the city that Hornbeck was ineligible because he was at the time residing outside the corporate limits of the city, and on October 30, made a formal complaint to the commission relative to Hornbeck's continued employment. On November 4, the commission held a hearing and determined that Hornbeck was not a resident of the city, and was therefore not entitled to further employment, and he was discharged from the service. Up to the time of his discharge, Hornbeck received the salary of the position in which he was serving. The civil service rules provided that all employees in that service, with certain exceptions which are not here material, should be "actual residents of the city of Seattle during such service". After Hornbeck was discharged, the relator was certified by the commission as a preferred eligible, and on the 18th of November, 1919, re-entered the service as a bridge tender. Thereafter he brought this action, claiming that, since the city had retained in its employ Hornbeck, who was ineligible under the civil service rules for employment, the relator's discharge from the service was wrongful, and that he was entitled to the salary during the time that he was laid off.

It is not claimed that there was work in the department at the time for more than nine bridge tenders. It is recognized that discharge from the service for lack of work was a good and sufficient reason. Reliance is placed upon the case of *State ex rel. Roe v. Seattle*, 88 Wash. 589, 153 Pac. 336, where it was held that a civil service employee, discharged by the department in which he was employed for "lack of veracity and integrity'', which charge upon appeal to the civil service commission was held to be unfounded, was entitled to compensation during the time that he was separated from the service. But the rule of that case does not cover the facts in this case. There is no question here but what there was not sufficient work for the entire eleven bridge tenders, and that it was necessary to lay off two of them. The fact that there was retained a bridge tender who, under the rules, was not entitled to employment, would not justify directing that the city pay to the relator the salary during the time that he was not in the service.

The charter of the city provides, "that every officer or employe in the classified civil service shall hold office until removed or retired." Hornbeck was in the classified civil service, and under this provision of the charter, held the employment until he was removed. To hold that, under the facts in this case, the relator was entitled to prevail, it would be necessary to go further than the court has gone in any case heretofore decided relative to a civil service employee's right to compensation during the time that he was separated from the service.

The judgment will be affirmed.

PARKER, C. J., MITCHELL, and TOLMAN, JJ., concur.

[No. 16367. Department Two. July 18, 1921.]

In the Matter of the Condemnation of Property for
BOTHELL WAY.

THE CITY OF SEATTLE, *Respondent,* v. JAMES R. WOOD
et al., Appellants.[1]

EMINENT DOMAIN (125)—DAMAGES — EVIDENCE — ADMISSIBILITY.
In condemnation proceedings for the establishment of a street improvement, the fact that the established grade of the street will
place it in some instances several feet above, and in other cases
several feet below, the adjoining property constitutes an element of
damages to the owners for the taking of their property.

Appeal by defendants from a judgment of the superior court for King county, Jurey, J., entered May
17, 1920, awarding damages in eminent domain proceedings, after a trial on the merits. Reversed.

Carkeek, McDonald, Harris & Coryell, for appellants.

Walter F. Meier and *Edwin C. Ewing,* for respondent.

PER CURIAM.—This is an eminent domain proceeding, commenced in the superior court for King county
by the city of Seattle, looking to the acquiring and
damaging of property by the city to such extent as will
enable it to open and extend a street, to be known as
Bothell Way, at a specified grade along its entire
course. The cause came regularly on for trial before
the court sitting with a jury, upon the question of
awarding compensation for the property taken and
damaged; and resulted in verdicts and judgments
awarding to the several owners compensation for their
property so taken and damaged. Among the owners

[1] Reported in 199 Pac. 450.

to whom such awards were made, were James R. Wood and wife and Stone-Easter, Inc.; who, deeming themselves aggrieved, as they claim, because of the inadequacy of their awards, have appealed therefrom to this court.

The sole question to be here decided is as to whether the trial court erred in refusing to allow counsel for appellants to introduce evidence tending to show that their lands, abutting upon the street, would suffer damages by the proposed physical improvement of the street at the grade specified and established by the terms of the city ordinance providing for the commencement and prosecution of the eminent domain proceeding.

The theory of counsel for appellants is that they will suffer damages because of such established grade and improvement of the street, because the grade is at some points several feet above, and at other points several feet below, their adjoining lands. The theory of the trial court's ruling, apparently, is that the grade established by the ordinance, being an original established grade, the damage to appellants' adjoining lands by reason of such establishing of the grade and improvement of the street will be only consequential, and that appellants are, therefore, not entitled to prove, or have awarded in this proceeding, any damages which may result to their adjoining lands. This question was recently reviewed at length by us sitting *En Banc* in, *In re Petition of the City of Seattle*, 115 Wash. 535, 197 Pac. 784, where we reached a conclusion determinative of the question in appellants' favor in this case. We are satisfied with our conclusion there reached. The judgments in this case awarding damages to appellants are reversed, and the cause is remanded to the superior court with directions to award them a new trial.

[No. 16390. Department Two. July 20, 1921.]

H. P. McGlothern, *Appellant*, v. The City of Seattle et al., *Respondents.*[1]

Municipal Corporations (354)—Use of Streets—Regulation of Jitneys—Ordinances—Powers of Council. An ordinance imposing on the city council the duty of passing on applications for jitney bus permits is not objectionable as authorizing legislative action independent of the mayor.

Constitutional Law (113)—Equal Protection of Laws—Regulation of Business. The issuance of permits for auto stage lines running to outlying towns and the refusal of jitney bus permits within the city limits does not constitute a violation of the equal protection clause of the state constitution, art. 1, § 12.

Municipal Corporations (354)—Use of Streets—Regulation of Jitneys—Powers of Council. Where a committee of the city council, after investigating applications for jitney bus permits, reported a resolution to the effect "that all applications now pending be denied" for the reason their object was to serve districts already supplied with adequate street car service, but that it be understood that applications for permits to serve districts now without street car facilities would be considered when received, the adoption of the resolution by the council was in effect no more than the rejection of existing applications and not an attempt by resolution to modify the ordinance under which the council was acting.

Constitutional Law (113)—Equal Protection of Laws—Class Legislation—Jitney Busses—Regulations. The guaranty of equality of rights under the Federal Constitution (Amend. 14) is not contravened by a municipal ordinance regulating the use of the city streets by jitney busses.

Municipal Corporations (354)—Use of Streets—Regulation of Jitneys—Powers of Council and Method of Proceeding. Under the recognized rule that a city has the power to control the use of its streets in the interest of public peace, safety, and welfare, it possesses authority to refuse to permit jitney bus routes to be established in the congested business section of the city.

Appeal from a judgment of the superior court for King county, French, J., entered November 17, 1920, dismissing an action for an injunction to restrain en-

[1]Reported in 199 Pac. 457.

forcement of a city ordinance regulating jitney busses, after a trial on the merits to the court. Affirmed.

W. R. Crawford and *Morris B. Sachs,* for appellant.
Walter F. Meier, George A. Meagher, and *Charles T. Donworth,* for respondents.

MITCHELL, J.—Plaintiff, in his own behalf and in behalf of others similarly situated, together with a large number of other persons who intervened in the action as plaintiffs, seek to enjoin the city of Seattle from enforcing the provisions of ordinance number 40886, entitled,

"An ordinance relating to and regulating the operation of certain kinds of 'for hire' motor vehicles, prescribing penalties for the violation thereof and declaring an emergency,"

and to enjoin obedience by the city of its own resolution or action by which the plaintiffs were refused permits to operate jitney busses on certain portions of the streets of the city. A temporary injunction was granted during the pendency of the action. Upon issues joined, a trial was had that resulted in a judgment denying relief and dismissing the action. Plaintiff has appealed, and upon giving a supersedeas bond in the amount fixed by order of the court, has continued the temporary injunction during the appeal.

The portions of the ordinance pertinent to this case are as follows:

"Sec. 2. Any person desiring to operate a jitney bus shall apply to the city council by filing with the city comptroller on a form to be provided by said comptroller, an application for a jitney bus permit which application shall describe the route over which it is desired to operate, including the specification of certain fixed termini, the schedule of time upon which the same will be operated, the rate of fare (which shall not exceed the rates hereinafter specified) to be charged, and the capacity of the jitney bus to be used.

"Sec. 3. Immediately upon the filing of an application for a jitney bus permit, as herein provided, the city comptroller shall furnish a copy thereof to the superintendent of public utilities, who shall, without delay, investigate the same and make a report thereon, in writing, to the city council, recommending either the granting of the permit applied for, with or without modification of the route, termini, schedule, rate of fare or capacity specified in said application, or the refusal of the same. Said report shall set forth fully the reasons for the recommendations therein made. Upon receipt of said report the city council may direct the city comptroller to issue a permit in accordance with the recommendations of the superintendent of public utilities, or with such modifications thereof as the city council shall specify."

Section 4 provides that every jitney bus permit shall specify the route, with fixed termini, over which the permittee is authorized to operate a jitney bus, the schedule of time upon which it shall run, etc. By section 6 there is reserved to the city council the power and authority to modify the route, termini, schedule, or rate of fare specified in any permit. Section 8 provides, among other things, against the operating of any jitney bus on the streets without having secured a permit to do so. Section 10 provides that any person violating or failing to comply with any of the provisions of the ordinance shall be deemed guilty of a misdemeanor, and, upon a conviction, punished in the manner therein specified. It is further declared in the ordinance that the then existing conditions in transportation by the "for hire motor vehicles," affected by the ordinance, were unsafe and that the public peace, health, safety and welfare were injuriously affected and would be, by the continuation thereof, without regulation, and that an emergency existed making

it necessary that the ordinance become effective from
and after its passage and approval by the mayor. The
ordinance was passed by the council on May 10, 1920,
and approved by the mayor on the following day.

Upon the passage and approval of the ordinance,
the city notified the jitney bus operators of its purpose
to enforce the ordinance, whereupon these plaintiffs
and others filed, between May 20, 1920, and June 1,
1920, some two hundred and nineteen applications for
permits and thereafter twelve other applications were
filed. At the time of commencing this suit no action
had been taken on eleven of the applications, thirty-
three had been granted and one hundred and eighty-
seven (including those made by plaintiffs herein) had
been rejected.

It is contended that the ordinance is invalid: (1) because, by § 3 thereof, attempt is made to give the council alone, not acting with the mayor, the power to
regulate the use and control of the streets; while the
charter of the city provides that such power is legislative in character and must be exercised by the legislative power consisting of the council and mayor; and
(2) because it vests in the council alone the power to
issue licenses; or, more exactly, it is contended that,
under the charter, the power to issue licenses must be
exercised in each and all applications for permits by
ordinance to which the office of mayor pertains, rather
than by resolution or order of the council alone as
provided in § 3.

The views mistake the character of the act of the
city council in passing upon such applications. The
ordinance is the legislative expression for carrying
out the charter provision, while the duty imposed upon the council to pass on applications made under the
terms of the ordinance is not of a legislative nature

and may be properly exercised under the terms of the ordinance, by its order or resolution, independent of the mayor.

It is claimed that, because of possible inequalities in the enforcement of the ordinance, it violates § 12, art. 1, of the state constitution. This subject is fully discussed, and answered against appellant's contention, in the case of *State ex rel. Schafer v. Spokane*, 109 Wash. 360, 186 Pac. 864, and in *Allen v. Bellingham*, 95 Wash. 12, 163 Pac. 18, wherein ordinances not essentially unlike the one in the present case were considered. The argument of appellant, by way of illustration, that certain permits had been granted to others under this ordinance loses its value, for the reason that they were granted to auto stage lines connecting Seattle with outlying towns and sections—a class of service entirely distinct from the jitney bus business, such as these applicants desired permits for, as was well pointed out in the *Allen v. Bellingham* case; and the record shows that, in the recommendation of the committee on city utilities that was adopted by the city council (next to be discussed herein), it was determined to take all proper action to prohibit, if necessary, the auto stage licensees from operating as ordinary jitney busses within the city limits.

The applications here involved were placed in the hands of the superintendent of public utilities who, upon investigation, made a report thereon to the city council, which in turn referred the report to its committee on city utilities. The committee made an investigation and reported to the city council its recommendations (spoken of in the record here as a resolution), "that all applications now pending be denied and that the reports of the superintendent of public utilities thereon be placed on file." It was further stated in the report that, in making its recommendations that pending applications for jitney permits be rejected, "which applications were to serve sections of the city already supplied with adequate street car service," the committee wished it understood that *bona fide* applications for permits to serve districts now without street car facilities would be considered by the committee when received. The report of the committee was adopted by the council. It is argued that the adoption of the resolution was an attempt to change and modify the ordinance which the council, in that manner, had no power to do. It is evident, however, that the purpose and legal effect of its action with reference to the applications was to reject them, which it had the right to do under its general powers and the terms of the ordinance. Its manner of doing so by adopting the report of its committee making that recommendation was a matter wholly within the choice of the city council.

Lastly, it is contended that the ordinance is unconstitutional and void, being in contravention of that portion of the fourteenth amendment to the Federal constitution guaranteeing equality of rights. An adverse answer to the argument is found in the case of *State ex rel. Schafer v. Spokane, supra,* and the cases therein cited. We can see no Federal question in this case. Indeed, the argument that the ordinance undertakes to give arbitrary power to discriminate between persons of the same class is clearly met by the case of *Schoenfeld v. Seattle,* 265 Fed. 726, wherein one of the present intervening complainants attacked this same ordinance and, in addition to adopting our decisions with reference to the plenary powers of cities as to such users of the streets, it was held that the ordinance here in question violated no vested right to the use of the streets for the carrying on of a private business as a common carrier, and that the ordinance is not unreasonable, discriminating or arbitrary.

It may be further stated that, while these applications were pending, there were a number of conferences, formal and informal, between the representatives of the appellants and the committee on city utilities, concerning the routes applied for. The record before us is indefinite as to the exact location of those routes. It does appear, however, by abundant proof, that the main controversy was over the establishment of the termini of the routes with reference to traffic in the congested business section of the city. The testimony shows there was consideration or mention by the committee of the plan of operating the jitney busses from points removed several blocks from the most densely traveled sections of the streets. To this the appellants objected. One of the members of the committee testified:

"As I recall, all these applications involved one principle, that they wanted to come down town and we wanted to keep them off those streets. There was no chance for a compromise at that time and we could not get together and this was decided on."

Other members of the committee testified similarly. That is, it appears the city authorities were undertaking to remedy a situation which the city had legislatively found and declared to be unsafe to the public peace, health, safety and welfare, by the enforcement of an ordinance necessitated by that condition. The controversy is one which calls in question the very power of the city to control its streets, a question upon which under the well-established rule in this state and generally there can be no doubt. The city has that authority and was engaged in the proper exercise of it at the time this suit was brought. Such was manifestly the opinion of the trial court in entering the judgment which has been appealed from, and its judgment is hereby affirmed.

PARKER, C. J., MAIN, FULLERTON, and TOLMAN, JJ., concur.

[No. 16406. Department One. July 21, 1921.]

JENS PEDERSEN, *Respondent*, v. OTHO F. NORRIS *et al.*, *Appellants*.[1]

PHYSICIANS AND SURGEONS (11)—ACTIONS FOR MALPRACTICE—QUESTION FOR JURY. The negligence of a dentist in the extraction of a tooth, upon removing a gold crown, is a question for the jury, where the plaintiff testified the tooth was sound, though a majority of the witnesses testified the tooth was diseased, and there was testimony that the tooth was loose, and that the bridge could not be removed without extracting the tooth to which it was attached.

SAME (12)—INSTRUCTIONS. In an action for damages for negligently extracting a tooth where there was conflicting evidence as to its soundness, a requested instruction, that "if said tooth was diseased, then I charge you . . . . the extraction was a benefit to the plaintiff and not a damage," was properly refused, since it would not follow as a matter of fact or of law that a tooth which was diseased or not sound should be extracted.

Appeal from a judgment of the superior court for Pierce county, Chapman, J., entered November 12, 1920, upon the verdict of a jury rendered in favor of the plaintiff, in an action for malpractice. Affirmed.

Emil N. Stenberg, for appellants.

P. L. Pendleton, for respondent.

BRIDGES, J.—The defendant, E. E. Keith, was an assistant of, and working for, his codefendant, Otho F. Norris, in the dental offices of the latter, in

[1] Reported in 199 Pac. 732.

the city of Tacoma. In June of 1920, the plaintiff
visited the offices of the defendants and requested the
defendant Keith to remove a gold crown, or bridge,
from certain of his teeth. In the act of removing it,
one of the teeth to which it was attached was extracted, and plaintiff brought suit against the defendants for damages because of the alleged negligent extraction of the tooth, which he contended was sound.
There was a verdict for the plaintiff in the sum of $650.
The court denied defendants' motions for nonsuit, instructed verdict, judgment notwithstanding the verdict and for new trial. Judgment was entered upon
the verdict, and the defendants have appealed.

One of appellants' contentions is, that the respondent's testimony failed to make a case to be submitted
to the jury. While a majority of the witnesses testified that the tooth was diseased, and there was testimony that it was loose and that the bridge could not
be removed without extracting the tooth with it, and
that there was neither negligence on the part of appellants nor damage to respondent, yet there was also
competent evidence to the effect that the tooth was
sound and was not loose, and the defendant Keith
was negligent in extracting it. Nothing could be
gained by repeating, in detail, the testimony on this
question; suffice it to say that a reading of the record
convinces us that there was sufficient testimony on the
part of the respondent to require the court to submit
the case to the jury upon the merits.

The appellants requested the court to give the following instruction: "The plaintiff in his complaint
alleges that the tooth that came out was a sound tooth.
This is denied by the defendants, so if you find that said
tooth was diseased, and such diseased condition, in
any degree, loosened said tooth, then you will find for
the defendants, and if said tooth was diseased and

said plaintiff at said time was seeking relief, then I charge you the extraction was a benefit to the plaintiff and not a damage, and you must hold for the defendants." Complaint is made that the court refused to give this instruction. We think the request was too broad. It would not follow, as a matter of fact or as a matter of law, that a tooth which was diseased or not sound, should be extracted. The court stated the law when it told the jury, in connection with other instructions, that the question is: "Did the defendants, through the defendant E. E. Keith, exercise ordinary care and skill in removing the gold crown from plaintiff's teeth and in their treatment of the plaintiff. Unless you find from a preponderance of the evidence that said defendants did not exercise ordinary care and skill, then you should return a verdict for the defendants." But other instructions given by the court were nearly as broad as that requested by the appellants, for he told the jury that if the appellants "wrongfully and carelessly extracted a sound tooth from plaintiff's jaw, then your verdict should be for the plaintiff . . . ", and that the plaintiff must prove, by preponderance of the evidence, that at the time of the extraction of the tooth the same "was a sound tooth." We have no doubt that the instructions, taken as a whole were fully as favorable to the appellants as they were entitled to have them. We do not find any reversible error; the judgment is affirmed.

PARKER, C. J., MACKINTOSH, FULLERTON, and HOLCOMB, JJ., concur.

[No. 16428. Department One. July 21, 1921.]

A. L. WHIPPLE, *Appellant,* v. INDUSTRIAL INSURANCE
COMMISSION, *Respondent.*[1]

MASTER AND SERVANT (121-2)—WORKMEN'S COMPENSATION—REME-
DIES—APPEAL—REVIEW. Under Rem. Code, §§ 6604-5, 6604-20, an
award by the industrial insurance commission for an injury, properly classified as "permanent partial disability" not being subject to
review by the courts, except for arbitrary or capricious action on its
part, an award of $400 will not be disturbed where it appears the
commission acted upon the testimony of competent physicians, some
of them considering plaintiff's injury to be very severe and probably
lasting, while others concluded that his injury was not so severe.

Appeal from a judgment of the superior court for
Pierce county, Clifford, J., entered January 6, 1921,
upon findings in favor of the defendant, upon appeal
from an order of the industrial insurance commission,
after a trial on the merits to the court. Affirmed.

Govnor Teats, Leo Teats, and *Ralph Teats,* for appellant.

The Attorney General and *John H. Dunbar, Assistant,* for respondent.

BRIDGES, J.—On April 1, 1919, the appellant was injured while engaged in his duties as an employee of
a shingle mill located in Lewis county, Washington.
He made application to the industrial insurance commission for compensation under the workmen's compensation act of this state. Ultimately the commission
classified his injury as a permanent partial disability,
and he was awarded the sum of $400, in addition to
time lost. Being dissatisfied with the award, he appealed to the superior court of Pierce county, where,
after a hearing, the order of the commission was

[1]Reported in 199 Pac. 455.

affirmed. He has appealed to this court from that judgment.

In his complaint in the superior court he alleged that the commission "made an award or final settlement in the sum of $400, allowing only for the permanent partial disability of the plaintiff, which said award is insufficient according to law for the injury received by the plaintiff, and which said award was in fraud of all the rights of the plaintiff and done without consideration of the plaintiff's injury, and done by said commission arbitrarily and illegally. . . . That said award should have been for permanent partial disability and in the sum of $2,000."

The appellant seems not to dispute the correctness of the classification of his injury, to-wit, permanent partial disability, but contends that the sum awarded him was insufficient, considering the severity of his injury. Section 6604-5 (f) Rem. Code, defines a permanent partial disability, and fixes specific amounts to be paid for certain common injuries, and provides that "compensation for any other permanent partial disability shall be in the proportion which the extent of such disability shall bear to that permanent partial disability above specified which most closely resembles and approximates the degree of such other disability, but not in any case to exceed the sum of $2,000."

Section 6604-20 Rem. Code, provides as follows:

"Any employer, workman, beneficiary or person feeling aggrieved at any decision of the department affecting his interests under this act may have the same reviewed by a proceeding for that purpose, in the nature of an appeal, initiated in the superior court of the county of his residence (except as otherwise provided in subdivision (1) of section numbered 6604-5) in so far as such decision rests upon questions of fact, or of the proper application of the provisions of this act, it being the intent that matters resting in the discretion of the department shall not be subject to review. . ."

It has become the settled doctrine of this court that where an injured person has been properly classified under the workmen's compensation act, the amount to be paid is entirely discretionary with the commission, and its award will not be reviewed by the courts, except for arbitrary or capricious action on its part in making the award. In the case of *Parker v. Industrial Insurance Dept.*, 102 Wash. 54, 172 Pac. 830, Judge Chadwick, speaking for the court, said:

"The meaning of the act is that all questions going to the classification of an injured workman and his right to participate in the insurance fund are questions of fact and subject to review, upon appeal, by court or jury; but the amount of the award upon a proper classification is a matter resting in the broad discretion of the department and will not be interfered with:

" 'Unless possibly, their decision might be reviewed by the courts upon such a question were they charged with capricious or arbitrary action in fixing the amount of their award.' *Sinnes v. Daggett, supra*, 80 Wash. 673, 142 Pac. 5.

"Whether an injured employee comes within one class or another is a fact, and an injured workman may not be made subject to an erroneous classification without a right of review. . . .

" 'Questions of fact' within the meaning of the act, means all questions resting in fact, and all facts necessary to be ascertained before a workman is classed as a beneficiary, and upon which his classification is made. Discretion means the conduct of the department with reference to all matters pertaining to the administration of the claim after the workman is properly classified."

The same doctrine was announced in *Chalmers v. Industrial Insurance Comm.*, 94 Wash. 490, 162 Pac. 576; *Sinnes v. Daggett*, 80 Wash. 673, 142 Pac. 5; *Foster v. Industrial Insurance Comm.*, 107 Wash. 400, 181 Pac. 912.

Under the statute as construed by this court, we are prohibited from considering the question as to whether appellant has been properly and sufficiently compensated for his injury in cases where the injury has been properly classified, unless we can find from the testimony that the commission, in making the award, acted fraudulently or arbitrarily and without reference to the facts. We have read the testimony and are convinced therefrom that the commission in making its award acted honestly and with the intention of complying with the letter and spirit of the statute. The testimony shows that at the instance of the commission the appellant was examined by several well known physicians. As is very often the case, the physicians disagreed. Some of them considered appellant's injury to be very severe and probably lasting, whereas other equally competent physicians concluded that his injury was not so severe. Under these circumstances, we cannot hold that the commission acted capriciously or arbitrarily, or without a due and honest consideration of appellant's rights. The lower court, who heard the witnesses, refused to believe that the commission had acted arbitrarily, and we think its judgment in that regard was correct and should be upheld. The judgment is affirmed.

PARKER, C. J., MACKINTOSH, FULLERTON, and HOLCOMB, JJ., concur.

[No. 16356. Department One. July 21, 1921.]

THE STATE OF WASHINGTON, *Respondent*, v. CHARLES
ANDERSON, *Appellant*.[1]

INTOXICATING LIQUORS (6) — PROHIBITION — BOOTLEGGING — 18TH
AMENDMENT. Prosecution under state laws for bootlegging and conducting illegal liquor joints is lawful as in aid of the enforcement
of the 18th amendment to the constitution of the United States and
the Volstead act passed pursuant thereto.

CRIMINAL LAW (407) — APPEAL — RECORD — AFFIDAVITS AS TO SEPA-
RATION OF JURY. On appeal from an order denying a motion for new
trial in a criminal case, on the ground the jury had been allowed
to separate without the consent of the defendant, it will be presumed that the defendant knew of the separation and waived the
error, where the affidavits upon which his motion was based are not
attached to the statement of facts.

Appeal from a judgment of the superior court for
Spokane county, Hurn, J., entered July 24, 1920, upon
a trial and conviction of being a jointist. Affirmed.

Crandell & Crandell and *McCarthy, Edge & Lantz,*
for appellant.

William C. Meyer and *James Emmet Royce,* for respondent.

MACKINTOSH, J.—Appellant was convicted under an
information charging him with being a jointist, and he
has appealed.

He complains that the information was drawn under
an act which is unconstitutional, and that it fails to
allege facts sufficient to charge a crime. This court
has already considered the question of the constitutionality of the jointist and bootlegging act, and decided
the question presented by the appellant adversely to
his position: *State v. Rousseau,* 111 Wash. 533, 191

[1]Reported in 199 Pac. 449.

Pac. 634; *State v. Burgess,* 111 Wash. 537, 191 Pac. 635; *State v. Hessel,* 112 Wash. 53, 191 Pac. 637.

It is suggested that the jointist act is unconstitutional for the reason that it conflicts with the eighteenth amendment to the Federal constitution. This contention has already been considered by this court in *State v. Turner,* 115 Wash. 170, 196 Pac. 638, and *State v. Woods, ante* p. 140, 198 Pac. 737. The question is therefore no longer an open one.

It is finally claimed that there was misconduct of the court and jury, in that the jury were allowed to separate during a short recess taken in the trial, without the consent of the defendant. The affidavits upon which this matter was urged, on the motion for a new trial, are not attached to the statement of facts, and, indulging in the presumption which makes for the regularity of trials, the record is barren of any showing that the appellant at the time did not know of the separation, he must be held to have known of it, and to have made no objection thereto, and to have proceeded with the trial of the case. Under such circumstances he must be held to have waived the error. *State v. Shuck,* 38 Wash. 270, 80 Pac. 444.

PARKER, C. J., BRIDGES, FULLERTON, and HOLCOMB, JJ., concur.

[No. 16357. Department One. July 21, 1921.]

F. J. CUMMINGS, *Appellant*, v. ARTHUR ERICKSON *et al.,* *Respondents.*[1]

PARTNERSHIP (1)—THE RELATION—COMMUNITY OF INTEREST. A partnership between farmers is not established by the fact that they farmed certain tracts on shares, where it appears they kept separate trading accounts, and also maintained a debtor and creditor account between themselves.

FRAUDULENT CONVEYANCES (16)—PROPERTY TRANSFERRED—EXEMPT PROPERTY. Grain needed for stock and seed by a farmer and householder, being exempt from attachment or levy and sale on execution, under Rem. Code, § 563, could be transferred to a creditor to apply on indebtedness to him, free from the lien of attachment or execution levy.

PAYMENT (11) — APPLICATION — RIGHTS OF PARTIES — SECURED DEBT—PRESUMPTIONS. Where a creditor, holding both secured and unsecured claims against a debtor, allows part of the property on which he has a mortgage to be sold and the proceeds are placed in his hands to apply on the debtor's account, the creditor must apply the proceeds to the secured debt, in the absence of an understanding to the contrary.

Appeal from a judgment of the superior court for Okanogan county, Neal, J., entered June 7, 1920, upon findings in favor of the defendants, in an action for an accounting, tried to the court. Affirmed.

W. H. Patterson, for appellant.

W. C. Brown and *P. D. Smith,* for respondents.

MACKINTOSH, J.—What, from the pleadings, seems to be a Hyrcanian wood, becomes, after an investigation of the record, a three-cornered controversy involving an accounting. The appellant was a creditor of the respondents Erickson; part of his claim being secured by a mortgage, and part of it consisting of an open account. The respondent Urban also claimed to be a

[1]Reported in 199 Pac. 736.

creditor of the Ericksons, while the appellant contends
that Urban and the Ericksons were partners in the
conduct of a couple of farms in Okanogan county. The
facts as found by the trial court (and which our review
of the testimony does not warrant us in disturbing),
may be summarized as follows: In January, 1917, the
Ericksons had rented two tracts of land, one of them
being rented on shares, the owner to receive one-third
of the crop and the Ericksons two-thirds. The respondent Urban came to Okanogan county early in the
winter of 1917, bringing with him several head of
cattle. His purpose was to find a suitable farm, but
being unable to do so, he "joined forces with the
Erickson Brothers in farming the Huntley place and
Indian allotment", and sold to the Ericksons several
head of cattle and some horses for $1,575, the Erick-
sons becoming indebted for the entire amount. The
arrangement between the Ericksons and Urban was
that Urban was to receive an equal share with the
Ericksons of the crops.

The Ericksons dealt at the merchandise store of the
appellant, where they carried an open account, the
unpaid balance of which, in 1916, amounted to $451.96.
This indebtedness, in 1917, had increased to $1,315.25,
and represented purchases for the benefit of the Ericksons. Urban traded at another town and had no connection with the account of the appellant. On November
27, 1917, the Ericksons gave a promissory note for the
amount due the appellant, and secured by two chattel
mortgages covering cattle, horses, machinery and automobile, and the future crops, and mortgages were also
given to secure further advances in the sum of $500.
During 1918, the Ericksons continued to trade with
the appellant on open account, which, in December,
1918, amounted to $1,017.28. In November, 1918, the
Ericksons informed the appellant that they would have

to dispose of some of the property covered by the mortgages in order to pay the note, and consent was given to this arrangement, and the receipts of this sale, amounting to $975, were credited by the appellant on the open account. In December, 1918, the Ericksons delivered to the appellant wheat of the value of $685.75; they then demanded from the appellant their note and mortgages, insisting they had been paid, and at this time the Ericksons were given a statement of their account by appellant, showing he had credited all the receipts from the sale of the mortgaged property and wheat on the open account, and claimed a balance of $343.47 due on the note and mortgage. The Ericksons objected to this, and in the spring of 1919, their objections not having been met, further negotiations were carried on between Ericksons and the appellant, the Ericksons all the time insisting that the mortgages had been paid. About May 1, 1919, cattle and horses owned by the Ericksons were turned over to Urban to apply on their debt to him, and in October, 1919, Urban advertised these cattle and horses and some machinery for sale.

The appellant started this action for his unpaid balance, claiming that there was a balance still owing him on the note, and that the property offered by Urban for sale was property upon which he held a mortgage. The 1919 wheat crop was threshed by Urban, and after paying the share due the landowners, the balance was taken by Urban to apply on the Ericksons' indebtedness to him.

It is the contention of the appellant (1) that Urban and the Ericksons were partners, (2) that the grain which was taken over by Urban was partnership property, and was not exempt from attachment and execution in an action upon the partnership debt, and (3) that the Ericksons, not having directed the application of the proceeds from the sale of the mortgaged property to the satisfaction of the mortgage indebtedness, that it was in the power of the appellant to make that application upon the open account. The trial court concluded from the facts as they have been detailed, that no partnership existed between Urban and the Ericksons, and for that conclusion the evidence preponderates. That conclusion, of course, answers the first contention of the appellant. (2) It appearing from the evidence that the Ericksons were farmers and householders and needed the grain for themselves and their stock and for seed, they had a right to claim it as exempt from attachment and levy and sale on execution, under § 563 Rem. & Bal. Code, and being thus exempt in the hands of the Ericksons, they could transfer it to Urban to apply on their indebtedness to him. (3) The authorities are to the effect that where a creditor holds claims, some secured and some on open account, when funds of the debtor come into the creditor's hands, in the absence of any direction from the debtor, or any agreement as to how they shall be applied, that the creditor may apply them on either account at his option, but this rule is subject to certain exceptions, one of them (recognized by many authorities), is that where a creditor has allowed part of the property on which he has a mortgage to be sold and the proceeds are placed in his hands in extinguishment of his debt, or to apply on the debtor's account, in the absence of an understanding to the contrary, the presumption must be that the proceeds will be applied to the secured debt. This court has recognized this distinction in the case of *Sturtevant Co. v. Fidelity & Deposit Co.*, 92 Wash. 52, 158 Pac. 740, where it is said:

"It is elementary law that a 'creditor may apply a payment voluntarily made by a debtor without any specific appropriation where there are two or more

debts, to whichever debt he pleases'. . . . The rule
is not without its exceptions, one of which is stated in
the text of 30 Cyc. 1237 as follows:

" 'Another exception to the rule that the creditor has
the right to apply the payment obtains when the money
with which the payment is made is known to the creditor to have been derived from a particular source or
fund, in which case he cannot, without the consent of
the debtor, apply it otherwise than to the exoneration
of the source or fund from which it was derived.' "

Cases which hold to this rule that where money is
derived from a particular source or fund, must be ap-
plied to the relief of the source or fund from which
derived are as follows: *Boyd v. Jones,* 96 Ala. 305, 11
South. 405, 38 Am. St. 100; *Strickland v. Hardie,* 82
Ala. 412, 3 South. 40; *Lyon v. Bass,* 76 Ark. 534,
89 S. W. 849; *Massengale v. Pounds,* 108 Ga. 762, 33
S. E. 72; *Ellis v. Mason,* 32 S. C. 277, 10 S. E. 1069;
Brighton v. Doyle, 64 Vt. 616, 25 Atl. 694; *Chaney v.
Remey,* 19 Ky. Law 1258, 43 S. W. 235.

For the foregoing reasons we affirm the judgment of
the superior court.

PARKER, C. J., BRIDGES, FULLERTON, and HOLCOMB,
JJ., concur.

[No. 16162. Department Two. July 21, 1921.]

EDMUND C. BARNEY, *Respondent*, v. J. A. ANDERSON,
Appellant.[1]

MASTER AND SERVANT (2)—RELATION—EVIDENCE OF EMPLOYMENT.
In an action for personal injuries, the relation of master and
servant between defendant and plaintiff was established by evidence
showing that defendant, who was the owner of several farms, employed plaintiff to work on a hay-baling machine for a period of six
weeks and possibly longer, if he could find hay to bale on the outside; that, after finishing work on one of defendant's farms, the
machine was moved to a neighbor's farm to bale his hay, the defendant feeling obliged to do his neighbor's baling because the latter had gone out of his way to do the defendant's threshing; and
that there had never been any intimation to the plaintiff of any
change in his employment substituting a new master in place of his
employer.

SAME (77)—MASTER'S LIABILITY—VICE-PRINCIPALS—FOREMAN—
AUTHORITY OF SUPERINTENDENCE—DELEGATION OF DUTY. The fact that
the foreman of the baling machine, in his absence, was accustomed
to delegate the duty of operating it to his brother, constituted the
latter a vice-principal of defendant, charged with the duty of furnishing plaintiff a reasonably safe place in which to work.

SAME (77). In determining whether an employee occupies the
position of vice-principal, the power of superintendence and control
is the test, and not the question whether he had authority to employ
or discharge workmen.

SAME (113)—CONTRIBUTORY NEGLIGENCE—METHODS OF WORK. The
fact that a safer method of oiling a baling machine existed does not
establish contributory negligence on the part of plaintiff, where it
appears there was no danger in the method pursued until the machine was started without any notice to him by the person under
whose order he was working and who negligently took no notice of
the situation of plaintiff.

SAME (20-1)—MASTER'S LIABILITY—WORKMEN'S COMPENSATION
ACT. Accidental injury while engaged in work connected with the
operation of a hay-baling machine on a farm does not come within
the purview of the industrial insurance act.

SAME (130-1)—ACTIONS—ADMISSIBILITY OF EVIDENCE—EXISTENCE
OF RELATION. A letter written by defendant to the foreman in

[1] Reported in 199 Pac. 452.

charge of a hay-baler concerning the delivery of the machine to the foreman's brother for the latter's own use was properly excluded in an action by a servant against defendant for personal injuries due to negligence in the operation of the baler, where the writing of the letter or its subject-matter was in no way, either directly or indirectly, called to the attention of plaintiff.

DAMAGES (86)—INADEQUATE DAMAGES—INJURY TO ARM. Damages to plaintiff in the sum of $4,000 for the loss of his right arm about six inches below the shoulder should be increased to $7,500, where the evidence showed he was twenty-three years of age, an experienced woodsman who during six years had earned from $4.40 to $9.00 per day, and in recent farm work had earned from $5.00 to $8.00 per day.

Cross-appeals from a judgment of the superior court for Spokane county, Hurn, J., entered May 14, 1920, upon findings in favor of the plaintiff, in an action for damages, tried to the court. Reversed on plaintiff's appeal.

Zent & Jesseph, for appellant.
Lee & Kimball, for respondent.

MITCHELL, J.—This is an action for damages for personal injuries alleged to have been sustained by the plaintiff while employed by the defendant. The case was tried without a jury and resulted in a judgment in favor of the plaintiff. The defendant has appealed. Also the plaintiff has cross-appealed, claiming the award was too small. The parties will be spoken of as plaintiff and defendant.

Much of the evidence is conflicting. Upon an examination of it, we are satisfied as was the trial court. The plaintiff was engaged with a crew in operating a hay baling machine. The machine was run by an engine so connected that its power could be disengaged from the baling machine by the use of a clutch operated by a lever—a part of the machine. A pin in the machine broke and Carl Riggins, the operator in charge of the machine, threw it out of gear leaving the engine running, and went to the tool wagon nearby to make a wooden pin for repairs. He ordered the machine to be oiled while it was idle. There is a dispute as to whom the order was given; several, including the plaintiff, testified the order was given to the plaintiff who had usually performed that service since he had been working with the crew. While the plaintiff was thus engaged, the operator was driving the wooden pin, just made, into the machine, and in doing so, or while at that position, moved the lever which caused the clutch to engage the power which started the machine and caused the injuries complained of. Carl Riggins testified that the machine was thrown into gear accidentally. However, there is evidence which tends strongly to show that it was not accidentally but that he purposely threw it into gear; that almost immediately upon the happening of the accident he repeatedly said "why did I throw it into gear." He denied making the statement, but did admit that he paid no attention to any one else and did not notice that any one was oiling the machine.

(1) It is claimed the relation of master and servant between the parties did not exist at the time of the accident. There is convincing evidence to show substantially the following facts: That the defendant owned several farms in the vicinity and that on or about August 26 he employed the plaintiff, a stranger, to work at bailing hay on one of his farms. He took the plaintiff out to the farm and introduced him to the foreman, R. L. Riggins, who put plaintiff to work. The crew consisted of a number of men including Carl Riggins, a brother of the foreman. It appears that the baling machine was operated by the foreman most of the time but during his absence by his brother. The work was finished at this place on Saturday, Septem-

ber 6, when, at about eleven o'clock in the morning, the outfit and crew, including the foreman and his brother, were moved to the adjoining place belonging to one Usher. The foreman directed the work of moving the outfit. After moving, the crew went back to defendant's place for their noon day meal, after which they returned to work at the Usher place. The foreman, R. L. Riggins, operated the machine as usual that afternoon.

Thereafter, on the following Monday and Tuesday, the operation of the machine with essentially the same crew was under the immediate direction of Carl Riggins until plaintiff was hurt on the morning of the 9th. The foreman arrived at the scene a few moments before plaintiff was hurt. It is the theory of the defendant that he was in no way responsible for the use of the machine on the Usher place and that that work was being done by Carl Riggins wholly independent of any responsibility on the part of the defendant. In this he is corroborated by several witnesses including his foreman and Carl Riggins, and that the plaintiff was aware of the change of masters. That theory is flatly contradicted by the plaintiff. His evidence, strongly corroborated, shows that when first employed the defendant informed him he would need him at baling hay for six weeks and possibly longer if he could find hay to bale on the outside; that the foreman told him before finishing on defendant's place that when they moved over to the Usher place his brother "Carl will look after it", that he (the foreman) had a lot of work to do at home and would not be with the machine all the time.

The plaintiff further testified, "absolutely nothing was said to me by Mr. Anderson or Mr. Riggins or by anybody relative to their being any change in my employment at any time before I was hurt. If I had known

that there was any change, or if I had known that the
work was the individual work of Carl Riggins I would
not have continued in my employment." On finishing the work on defendant's place, nothing was said
about paying the crew and indeed the plaintiff and
his cousin, who were employed at the same time and
who worked together and quit at the same time, never
received any pay until after the plaintiff was hurt.
The machine belonged to two brothers named Mullen.
One of them testified, substantially, that the defendant
hired the machine saying he had two hundred tons of
hay and another fellow, named Usher, that much more.
That the next time he saw the machine it was on the
Usher place. He, his brother and defendant's foreman
were at the baler at the time the foreman said he would
like to finish that job for Usher and would bring the
baler back.

"He (the foreman) said that Usher had really gone
out of his way to do their threshing for them and they
would like to oblige him by doing his baling. After
that I did not have any conversation with R. L. Riggins
when Carl was present. Nothing was said about Carl
leasing the machine or anything of that kind, R. L.
Riggins was running it then, he was working it over
there and we imagined he was running it the same as
before. I did not know of any change in the contract."

The other brother testified to the same effect, and
further said that he didn't know there was any claim
that Carl was leasing the machine until after the plaintiff was hurt.

The plaintiff's proof is convincing, and the contention that he was not a servant of the defendant is un-
availing. Notwithstanding the conflict in the evidence,
we are satisfied that at the time the plaintiff was hurt
the responsibility was that of the defendant as the master and not that of Carl Riggins. Certainly he was
employed by the defendant. When did the relation ter-

minate? The owners of the machine never let it to
Carl Riggins, nor did they give the defendant any
authority to do so. Carl Riggins did not employ the
plaintiff, who says he would not have worked for him.
One has the right to know for whom he works and of
any attempt to enforce a change of masters. At the
time of the accident, there was nothing in the situation
inconsistent with the terms, scope and purpose of the
original employment, except as indicated by some of
the testimony of the foreman and his brother which is
flatly denied by the plaintiff and other witnesses and
the circumstances.

"The liability of a master to a servant does not cease
—the servant not having been informed of any change
—although, as between the master and a third person a
change is made by which thereafter the work is to be
done for such third person." 26 Cyc. 1087.

Being unable to agree with the defendant as to his
view of the facts it becomes unnecessary to discuss his
authorities upon this branch of the case.

(2) It is argued that Carl Riggins was not a vice-
principal of the defendant and that as he was
engaged in the immediate operation of the baler
at the time of the accident that therefore the
defendant is not liable. Having concluded the
plaintiff was in the defendant's employment at
the time of the injury, it follows that it was
the duty of the defendant to furnish the plaintiff
a reasonably safe place in which to work, that it be kept
in such condition, and that this duty could not be delegated to another in any manner to relieve the master
of the liability. While the work was being done on the
Anderson place, the foreman put his brother in charge
during his absence. The same rule was followed on the
Usher place. That was the station assigned to him
by the foreman within the knowledge of the plaintiff.

Such being the case, the duties discharged by Carl Riggins were delegated duties and passed to him from the general foreman, the master's primary representative. *Bailey v. Cascade Timber Co.*, 35 Wash. 295, 77 Pac. 377. The mere fact that Carl Riggins did not have authority to employ or discharge workmen as his brother did does not change the rule. The power of superintendence and control is the test. *Allend v. Spokane Falls & N. R. Co.*, 21 Wash. 324, 58 Pac. 244.

(3) It is contended against the right to recover that plaintiff, with full knowledge of danger, undertook to oil the machine in a dangerous and unsafe way when a safe method was open to him and that his own negligence caused the injury. The overwhelming weight of the evidence is to the contrary. His plan of carrying out the order of his superior was approved by nearly all the witnesses who testified. It was the same way he had theretofore performed the service during the whole time he worked with the crew. Certainly there was no danger until the machine was started, without any notice to him, by the person under whose order he was working and who negligently took no notice of him. *Dosset v. St. Paul & Tacoma Lum. Co.*, 40 Wash. 276, 82 Pac. 273.

(4) The contention that the work in which plaintiff was engaged at the time of the accident came within the purview of the industrial insurance act is answered, we think, by the cases of *Guerrieri v. Industrial Insurance Comm.*, 84 Wash. 266, 146 Pac. 608, and *Remsnider v. Union Sav. & Tr. Co.*, 89 Wash. 87, 154 Pac. 135, Ann. Cas. 1917D 40.

(5) Error is claimed upon the refusal of the court to admit in evidence a letter dated September 4, written by the defendant to his foreman concerning the delivery of the baler to Carl Riggins for the latter's own use. We think it was properly refused. It was

private correspondence between those parties and was in no way, directly or indirectly, called to the attention of the plaintiff either as to the fact that a letter had been written or as to the subject-matter discussed in it.

The judgment was for $4,331, consisting of $4,000 for personal injuries and $331 for expenses. It is claimed on the cross-appeal that the $4,000 award is inadequate. The evidence shows that the plaintiff was twenty-three years of age at the time he was hurt and that he suffered the loss of his right arm about six inches below the shoulder; that he was an experienced woodsman and had earned during six years from $4.40 to $9 per day; had lately engaged in the operation of a harvesting machine at $8 per day, and at the time of his injury was earning $5 per day; that he had earned practically nothing since the accident and, of course, is disabled from pursuing any of his former vocations. He is not prepared for any other kind of business. In consideration of the following authorities, viz.: *Shea v. Seattle Lumber Co.*, 47 Wash. 70, 91 Pac. 623, where a man twenty-seven years of age lost his left arm, and $8,000 was adjudged reasonable; *King v. Page Lumber Co.*, 66 Wash. 123, 119 Pac. 180, where a boy twenty years of age lost three fingers and a fourth one injured, and $4,500 was held reasonable; and *Baird v. Northern Pac. R. Co.*, 78 Wash. 67, 138 Pac. 325, where a laborer in a gravel pit was injured by the breaking of the large bone in his wrist causing a limitation of its motion of twenty-five to thirty per cent, and $4,000 was held reasonable; and other cases of a similar sort such as *Glucina v. Goss Brick Co.*, 63 Wash. 401, 115 Pac. 843, 42 L. R. A. (N. S.) 624, and *Woodard v. Cline Lumber Co.*, 81 Wash. 85, 142 Pac. 475, and also more or less independent of the results of those authorities, we are of the opinion, that while there can be no hard and fast rule in such cases because of the fluctuating purchasing power of money and circumstances more or less peculiar in each individual case, that in the present case the award made by the trial court is insufficient and that it should be and is increased to the sum of $7,500 in addition to the sum of $331 for the expenses incurred for hospital, doctors, nurses and drug bills.

Reversed on the cross-appeal and remanded with directions to the trial court to enter judgment accordingly.

PARKER, C. J., MAIN, and TOLMAN, JJ., concur.

[No. 16332. Department One. July 22, 1921.]

ADA McCARTHY, *Respondent*, v. HARRY OSCAR McCARTHY, *Appellant*.[1]

DIVORCE (36)—EVIDENCE—CRUEL TREATMENT. A husband's false accusations and charges against the chastity of his wife, made at various times and places and in the hearing of others, entitles her to a divorce on the ground of cruel treatment.

WITNESSES (55)—COMPETENCY—INFORMATION ACQUIRED BY PHYSICIAN—PERSONS ENTITLED TO OBJECT. Testimony by the family physician of parties to a divorce action that the husband had inquired of him what his physical examination of the wife had indicated with respect to her chastity was not a privileged communication so far as the husband was concerned, and was properly admissible in evidence against him.

Appeal from a judgment of the superior court for King county, Allen, J., entered October 13, 1920, upon findings in favor of the plaintiff, in an action for divorce, tried to the court. Affirmed.

James R. Chambers, for appellant.

Winter S. Martin and *Ralph H. Higgins*, for respondent.

[1]Reported in 199 Pac. 733.

Bridges, J.—The defendant has appealed from a decree granting the plaintiff a divorce, and awarding her certain property. The chief ground upon which the appellant seeks reversal is that the testimony was insufficient upon which to base the decree appealed from. It would not serve any useful purpose to recite in detail the facts as shown by the testimony; suffice it to say, that we have very carefully read all the testimony as it is contained in the statement of facts. The parties intermarried in the year 1914;.there is no issue of the marriage; the only property involved is that of the community and of relatively small value. It appears that during the earlier years of their marriage, the parties lived together with a reasonable degree of harmony, but in later years they have had constant bickerings, quarrels, and unfriendly relationship. At one time the appellant temporarily left the respondent; at another time the respondent left the appellant, and they lived apart for some time. A reconciliation did not last longer than a week or two, when they again separated.

The most serious testimony is the alleged expressions of the appellant concerning the good character of his wife. There is testimony tending to show that on various occasions and to various persons, appellant, either directly or by insinuations and indirectly, questioned her chastity. There is also testimony to show that at times he called her unbecoming names, and applied to her opprobrious epithets, and that on one or two occasions he struck her. It is true appellant stoutly denied all these accusations, and we are frank to concede that his denials have considerably impressed us. Yet we must remember that the trial court had the witnesses before him and was in very much better position than we to judge of their veracity. That court, apparently, did not consider the quarrels and bickerings between the parties as, in themselves, sufficient for a divorce, and in that regard we agree with him. He seems to have granted the divorce largely because of the testimony to the effect that the appellant had openly and covertly questioned the purity of respondent. We are not satisfied from the record that he was not guilty of these charges, and being in that frame of mind, we feel strongly disposed to follow the interpretation of the testimony made by the trial court. It found as a fact "that defendant made false accusations and charges against plaintiff's character at various times and places and in the hearing of others, and has falsely charged plaintiff with numerous acts of misconduct." If this finding is correct (and we are not disposed to interfere with it), it must follow that appellant has been guilty of such cruel treatment as to entitle respondent to a divorce.

The respondent introduced the testimony of the family physician to the effect that the appellant had inquired of him concerning respondent's chastity, and as to what the physical examination made by the witness of the respondent indicated in that respect. To this testimony the appellant objected on the ground that it was privileged and within the statute. Appellant does not cite any authorities in support of his argument, nor do we believe there are any. The wife might have claimed the privilege under the statute, but she alone could do it, and she having waived it, the respondent cannot claim it. In any event, this feature of the case is unimportant because the trial court more than once announced that he placed very little importance on that testimony.

The judgment is affirmed.

PARKER, C. J., MACKINTOSH, FULLERTON, and HOLCOMB, JJ., concur.

[No. 15585. *En Banc.* July 22, 1921.]

THE STATE OF WASHINGTON, *Respondent,* v. J. E. COLLINS, *Appellant.*[1]

CRIMINAL LAW (26, 45, 50)—JURISDICTION—OF JUSTICE OF PEACE—FORMER JEOPARDY. A justice of the peace is without jurisdiction to assess a fine and enter judgment based only on a plea of guilty of defendant that he had committed an assault, in view of the provisions of Rem. Code, §§ 1929-1931, to the effect that a defendant may plead guilty, but in all cases where the offense charged involves an injury to a particular person within the county, such person's attendance at the trial should be enforced, and the testimony of witnesses taken as to the circumstances of the transaction; hence such judgment of the justice would not constitute a bar, on the theory of former jeopardy, to a subsequent prosecution in the superior court for the same offense.

SAME (26, 45, 50). In a prosecution for assault, the refusal to admit in evidence the record of a justice of the peace to show a prior conviction for the same offense was proper, where the record was silent as to the steps necessary to sustain the jurisdiction of the justice to enter final judgment; there being no presumption attaching to the record that the justice proceeded properly under the statutes.

PARKER, C. J., MITCHELL, MACKINTOSH, and BRIDGES, JJ., dissent.

Appeal from a judgment of the superior court for Stevens county, Jackson, J., entered December 6, 1916, upon a trial and conviction of assault. Affirmed.

John Salisbury, for appellant.

L. B. Donley, for respondent.

ON REHEARING.

HOLCOMB, J.—A rehearing having been granted in this case, *En Banc,* a majority of the court have concluded that the Departmental opinion reported in 112 Wash. 201, 191 Pac. 831, should be rewritten. For the history of the case and the questions involved, see the Departmental opinion above cited.

[1] Reported in 199 Pac. 745.

The court is in hopeless division upon both of the principal questions involved herein, but in greater confusion over the first question upon which the Departmental opinion was based than upon the second, for the reason that some of the judges who are in accord upon the second ground disagree upon the first.

We believe that the result was correct but the first reason stated therefor was erroneous.

The statutes which provide that a defendant may plead guilty of any offense charged against him (Rem. Code, § 1929), provides also that in all cases where the offense charged involves an injury to a particular person who is within the county it shall be the duty of the justice of the peace to summon the injured person and enforce his attendance at the trial, if necessary; and further, that no justice shall assess a fine or enter a judgment until a witness or witnesses have been examined to state the circumstances of the transaction. (Rem. Code, §§ 1930-1931.)

These are positive mandates to a justice of the peace having a complaint made to him of an assault involving an injury to a particular person within his county. The evident purpose of these statutes was to prevent collusion and inadequate punishment in cases of assault. A justice of the peace has no more power or jurisdiction to assess a fine or enter a judgment until after he has summoned the injured party and enforced his attendance at the trial and heard the testimony of a witness or witnesses to state the circumstances of the assault, than he has to proceed in any criminal case without a complaint first being made to him. It is not a mere formality or directory matter that is required by the statute. It is a matter of substance and a matter of jurisdiction. It is unlike the case we had before us of *In re Casey,* 27 Wash. 686, 68 Pac. 185, where in a trial before a justice with a jury, the jury rendered a verdict of guilty but failed by its verdict to assess any punishment. Thereupon the justice assessed a fine, and the defendant refusing to pay it he was committed to jail. The statute involved in that case provided that, "such justice, or jury, if they find the prisoner guilty shall assess his punishment", etc. It was held that the procedure of the justice in assessing the penalty when the jury had failed to do so was simply irregular and voidable, but not void, for the reason that the justice court had jurisdiction of the person and of the subject-matter, and had power to render a judgment of the kind rendered, although it might have been avoided on appeal because of irregularities. Had there been no jury in that case, the justice alone would have assessed the punishment, but the jury having been called it was its duty to assess the punishment, and the duty of the justice to record the punishment fixed by the jury, if within the law. The proceedings were regular up to the time of judgment and the judgment was voidable because not fixed by the proper authority. That is not true of this case. Here the justice had no power to enter any judgment until he had summoned the injured party, enforced his attendance, and received the testimony of a witness or witnesses.

Nor can it be said that, because the record offered by the state was silent as to those steps, it must be presumed that the justice proceeded properly under the statute. It is elementary law that a court which is not a court of record must show its jurisdiction by showing that the steps specified by law necessary to sustain its jurisdiction, were taken. In this case the record is silent as to those steps necessary to sustain the jurisdiction of the justice to enter any final judgment, and therefore it cannot be presumed that he had power sufficient to proceed to judgment. The injured party was within his county and was not summoned, since the record is silent thereon, nor was any witness, so far as the record discloses, sworn and examined, much less any witness who stated the circumstances of the transaction. The justice's proceedings, therefore, fail to show a legal conviction of the defendant, and there was no error in rejecting as evidence the record showing such defective proceedings. For this reason the judgment is affirmed.

TOLMAN and MAIN, JJ., concur.

FULLERTON, J. (concurring)—As I read the record from the justice's court, it shows on its face two things, (1) that there was no valid complaint before the justice charging the defendant with crime, and (2) that the justice pronounced his judgment without complying with, and in disregard of, the plain mandate of the statute. This, in my opinion, resulted in a void, not a voidable, judgment, and, in consequence, it could be successfully attacked collaterally whenever claimed rights were sought to be maintained by it. I cannot agree with the opinion of Judge Holcomb, that a judgment of a court not a court of record may be attacked collaterally because it fails to show on its face that "the steps specified by law necessary to sustain its jurisdiction were taken." On the contrary, I think presumptions aid judgments of courts of this class, when the attack on the judgment is collateral as it was here, as well as they aid the judgments of courts of record and of general jurisdiction. But presumptions are indulged in only where the record is silent. The record is presumed to be regular because nothing appears to the contrary. Here, however, the record is not silent. The errors rendering it void appear upon its face. There is therefore no room for presumptions, and none can be called in aid of the judgment.

There should be an affirmance, and I concur in the opinion in so far as it announces that result.

MOUNT, J., concurs with FULLERTON, J.

MITCHELL, J. (dissenting)—There are two principal questions in this case, suggested by the state as follows: (1) the complaint on which the conviction was had before the justice of the peace did not state facts sufficient to constitute a crime; and (2) the proceedings before the justice of the peace were contrary to the provisions of the statutes governing proceedings in such cases.

Upon the first contention made, I am convinced the majority opinion in the Departmental hearing was erroneous and the dissenting opinion therein was correct.

As to the second contention, it is to be observed that, while the statutes provide that a defendant may plead guilty, they further provide that in all cases where the offense charged involves an injury to a particular person who is within the county, it shall be the duty of the justice of the peace to summon the injured person as a witness at the trial and to enforce his attendance by attachment if necessary; and further, that no justice shall assess a fine, or enter a judgment, until a witness or witnesses have been examined to state the circumstances of the transaction. The justice's docket which was offered in evidence and rejected shows a plea of guilty and a judgment imposing a fine and costs. It shows, "testimony having been offered", but is otherwise silent if a witness was sworn, nor does it affirmatively appear if the party injured was examined as a witness. Without doubt the statutes have an important purpose and should not be ignored or overlooked in proceedings before a justice of the peace. Nevertheless, the question remains was the judgment that was entered void or voidable only, and if the latter, was it sufficient, after having been performed by the defendant, to constitute a bar to another prosecution for the same offense.

There was no answer on the part of the prosecution to defendant's plea of former conviction, to the effect that the judgment of the justice of the peace was collusive on the part of the defendant, or at all. There was no presumption of collusion either by statute or other rule of law. Such an issue, if made, would be one of fact to be tried out as any other issue of fact. But the contention is that the judgment was void. The statute does not say so. The justice of the peace had jurisdiction over the crime charged and the person of the defendant. As it is with all public officers, so it is with courts of limited jurisdiction.

"The presumption that an official did his duty and acted within his authority is recognized in connection with criminal courts, where the record is silent, so that, if jurisdiction is obtained, the validity of a judgment will not be affected by mere irregularity and·want of form in the proceedings". 16 C. J. 183, 184.

In this case the defendant submitted to trial in the justice court, did nothing to influence the judgment and performed the judgment when it was imposed. True, the amount was small, possibly a matter of some importance if collusion were charged, but in no manner affecting its validity under the present issue.

On principle, a similar situation was involved in the case of *In re Casey*, 27 Wash. 686, 68 Pac. 185. A trial was had before a jury, resulting in a verdict of guilty, but the jury did not by its verdict assess any punishment. Thereupon the justice assessed a fine and upon the refusal of the defendant to pay it he was committed to jail. While so detained in custody, he applied to the superior court for a writ of habeas corpus which was denied and thence he appealed to this court. In the case reliance was had upon a statute (now § 1928, Rem. Code), which contains the following: "Such justice or jury, if they find the prisoner guilty, shall assess his punishment", etc. It was conceded by the state that the failure of the jury to fix the punishment, and the action of the court in fixing it in their stead would likely call for a reversal of the judgment if attacked by appeal, but that the proceedings were simply irregular and voidable, but not void, for the reason that jurisdiction of the person and of the subject-matter was in the justice court, and that the court had power under the pleadings and under the law to enter a judgment of the kind rendered, although it might have been voided on appeal because of irregularities committed by the court during the progress of the case. This latter view was adopted by the court, for, after reviewing cases relied on by the appellant, and finding them to be inapplicable, the court said:

"In this case a complaint was filed charging the offense. The accused was arrested and brought into court. The offense was within the jurisdiction of the justice. He thereby acquired jurisdiction of both the person and the subject-matter. The judgment entered was also within his jurisdiction under the pleadings in the case. The following general statement of the law, as found in 15 Am. & Eng. Enc. Law (2d ed.), p. 170, seems particularly applicable;

" 'But it is only when the court pronounces a judgment which is not authorized by law under any circumstances in the particular case made by the pleadings, whether the trial has proceeded regularly or otherwise, that such judgment can be said to be void', . . ."

The statute in question in that case was as mandatory upon the subject of procedure as is the one involved in the present case. In that case the judgment was within the pleadings and so it was in the present case.

Similarly, the case of *Everett v. Cowles*, 97 Wash. 396, 166 Pac. 786, discusses the conviction in a police court of one for the violation of a city ordinance. He appealed to the superior court wherein a new complaint was filed against him charging him with the same offense. In answer to the new complaint, he took the untenable position that the complaint filed in the police court did not state an offense and hence that the court was without jurisdiction over the offense, and that therefore the appeal could not vest jurisdiction in the superior court. This court said:

"But without noticing the contradiction involved in the argument, it is enough to say that the jurisdiction of the police court over the crime charged and the person of the defendant did not depend upon the sufficiency of the complaint. This the court had in virtue of the law. And having such jurisdiction, the judgment it rendered was voidable rather than void; enforceable against the defendant until reversed or set aside in some correctory proceeding. *In re Nolan*, 21 Wash. 395, 58 Pac. 222."

It follows from these cases and the reasons they furnish that, notwithstanding the alleged insufficiency of the complaint to state an offense, and notwithstanding the irregularity in the proceedings by which the justice of the peace arrived at the judgment entered, that the judgment though voidable on appeal was sufficient upon its having been performed by the defendant to make it proper evidence to be considered in support of appellant's plea of a former conviction of the same offense, and that the rejection of the complaint and justice's record was reversible error. There seems to be no question in the case of the identity of the person or of the act involved, as compared with those in the case before the justice of the peace. If there be any dispute in those respects, oral testimony may be re-

sorted to for the establishment of such identities if
necessary. 16 C. J., p. 425, § 769.

The judgment appealed from should be reversed.

PARKER, C. J., MACKINTOSH, and BRIDGES, JJ., concur
with MITCHELL, J.

[No. 16582. *En Banc.* July 22, 1921.]

A. D. WHITNEY, *Plaintiff*, v. PAGE & BOLSTER SHINGLE
COMPANY, INCORPORATED, *Defendant.*

MILL AND MINE SUPPLY COMPANY, *Plaintiff*, v. PAGE &
BOLSTER SHINGLE COMPANY, INCORPORATED, *et al.*,
Defendants.[1]

MASTER AND SERVANT (20-1)—WORKMEN'S COMPENSATION ACT—
PREMIUMS—LIENS FOR—PRIORITY. Under Rem. Code, § 6604-8 (as
amended by Laws 1917, ch. 120, § 5) providing that claims for industrial insurance premiums, in all cases of insolvency of the employer, shall have priority over all other claims except taxes, the
state's claim for such premiums has priority over labor liens given
to workmen by the provisions of Rem. Code, § 1152 *et seq.*

Appeal from an order of the superior court for King
county, Gilliam, J., entered February 15, 1921, decreeing distribution of proceeds of a receiver's sale in
favor of lien creditors, in preference to the state's
claim for industrial compensation. Reversed.

The Attorney General, John H. Dunbar, Assistant,
and *M. H. Wight,* for appellant.

A. D. Martin, W. G. Beard, and *Alexander, Bundy &
Swale,* for respondents.

HOLCOMB, J.—In 1920, the defendant, Page & Bolster
Shingle Company, was operating a small sawmill. On
October 6, 1920, it became insolvent and ceased operat-

[1]Reported in 199 Pac. 728.

ing. At that time it had on hand approximately 325,000 feet of lumber, and was indebted to plaintiff Whitney and other employees in excess of $3,000 for wages in the operation of the mill. On October 19, the plaintiff Whitney and other employees filed liens against the lumber under the provisions of Rem. Code, § 1152 *et seq*. These liens were assigned to plaintiff Whitney, who commenced the first of the above entitled consolidated cases for their foreclosure. Subsequently the plaintiff Mill & Mine Supply Company commenced the second of the consolidated cases for the appointment of a receiver, and respondent Gordon was appointed as such receiver. Later the two cases were consolidated, and the order of consolidation provided that plaintiff Whitney be permitted to foreclose his liens in the consolidated action, and that the respondent Gordon, as general receiver, act also as receiver in the lien foreclosure action.

Under an order of the court, the receiver sold the lumber for the sum of $2,000, which was less than the amount of the lien claims. The receiver applied to the court for an order for the distribution of the proceeds and upon hearing thereon, appellant, state of Washington, urged that its claim for compensation should be paid out of the proceeds in preference to the lien claims. The lower court held that the lien claims were entitled to the proceeds of the lumber, and an order was entered to that effect, from which the state has appealed.

The sole question in this appeal is as to the relative priority between the lien claims for labor and the claim for industrial insurance premiums filed in the insolvency proceedings in this action in the superior court. Appellant bases its claim of priority as against the labor claims upon the amendment of 1917 to § 6604-8, Rem. Code. (Laws of 1917, ch. 120, p. 487, § 5.) The amendment provides:

"In all cases of insolvency, assignment for the benefit of creditors, or bankruptcy, the claim of the state for payments due herein shall be a claim prior to all other claims except taxes. . . . ."

Respondent does not question but that the state has the power to provide that any claim of the state shall be entitled to priority, as against any other class of claims, but contends that the state is not entitled to such priority in the absence of an express enactment to that effect as against a specific lien.

It is contended by respondent that in the case of *Scandinavian American Bank v. King County,* 92 Wash. 650, 159 Pac. 786, we decided this question against appellant's contention, where we said:

"The state has an undoubted power to create a priority of lien in aid of its taxing power, but the general rule is that such priority will not be indulged unless sustained by some positive statute; it will not be sustained by resort to construction."

That case was one passing upon the question of whether a delinquent personal tax is a lien upon real property owned by the tax debtor at the time the tax was levied, but which was subject to a voluntary lien, or had been conveyed to another prior to the time the county treasurer selected real property to be charged with the delinquent tax, and noted the tax upon the tax roll. We, in effect, held that under the statutes governing that case it would be necessary to resort to construction to hold that real estate which had not been designated by the county treasurer upon which to impose the lien of unpaid delinquent personal property tax prior to the time the real estate had passed from the hands of the taxpayer to another, unaffected by any lien imposed thereon for delinquent personal taxes, and that we could not do so. We further said in that case:

"The very terms of the statute compel the conclusion that the tax is not a lien generally upon all property, but only upon such as may be thereafter specifically selected and charged. For the treasurer may not select and charge all real property arbitrarily, but shall 'select some particular tract or lots, etc.' (§ 9245)."

That case is not applicable here. Cases are cited and discussed from other states, but we must determine this upon our own statutes.

In addition to the portion of § 5, ch. 120, p. 487, Laws of 1917, heretofore quoted, that section also provides:

"In case of refusal or failure after written demand personally served to furnish such bond, the state in an action brought by the attorney general in its name shall be entitled to an injunction restraining such delinquent from prosecuting an extra hazardous occupation or work until such bond shall be furnished, and any sale, transfer or lease attempted to be made by such delinquent during the period of such default, of his works, plant or lease thereto shall be invalid until all past delinquencies are made good and such bond furnished. . . ."

The above provisions, in connection with the provisions first quoted, positively create a lien paramount and superior to any other lien *or claim* except for taxes. The exception alone excludes any other construction.

Respondent asserts that this is not a case of insolvency; that, so far as the fund in controversy is involved, it is a fund in the custody of the receiver, arising and to be distributed in the foreclosure action, and not in the general receivership action.

We are of the contrary opinion. This is a case of insolvency, the debtor having been declared insolvent and the receiver was appointed receiver of all the property.

The language of the statute (amendment of 1917) is clear and explicit in such cases, that the claim of the state shall be prior to all other claims except taxes, and there is no room for construction. To hold otherwise might seriously impair and deplete the industrial insurance funds which it was evidently the object of the legislature in enacting the amendment to avoid.

The judgment of the lower court is reversed.

PARKER, C. J., MITCHELL, TOLMAN, FULLERTON, MAIN, MACKINTOSH, and BRIDGES, JJ., concur.

[No. 16315. Department One. July 22, 1921.]

J. G. LUGER et al., *Respondents*, v. J. D. WINDELL et al., *Appellants*.[1]

APPEAL (218)—REQUISITES—GARNISHMENT PROCEEDINGS—NOTICE OF. APPEAL—SERVICE. On appeal by a garnishee defendant alone, notice of appeal to the original judgment defendant is not necessary.

INSURANCE (122)—INDEMNITY INSURANCE—CONTRACT—CONSTRUCTION—LIABILITY. A policy of casualty insurance issued to an automobile owner, which provided that the insurer would defend him against suits for damages, and also that no action would lie against the insurer under the policy unless brought by and in the name of the assured for loss actually sustained and paid in money by him in satisfaction of a judgment after actual trial of the issue, constitutes an indemnity and not a liability policy, against which there could be no recourse by a person injured by the assured (Overruling *Davies v. Maryland Cas. Co.*, 89 Wash. 571).

Appeal from a judgment of the superior court for Spokane county, Blake, J., entered June 26, 1920, upon findings in favor of the plaintiff, in an action in garnishment proceedings. Reversed.

Danson, Williams & Danson (*R. E. Lowe*, of counsel), for appellants.

Fred Miller and *E. Eugene Davis*, for respondents.

MACKINTOSH, J.—Luger recovered judgments against Windell on account of damages arising from an auto-

[1] Reported in 199 Pac. 760.

mobile accident. These judgments were affirmed by this court in *Luger v. Windell,* 110 Wash. 22, 187 Pac. 407. After the remittiturs had gone down, a writ of garnishment was served on the New Amsterdam Casualty Company, under the claim that it was indebted to, or had property of, Windell in its possession, which should be made to satisfy the judgments. The casualty company answered, denying any indebtedness; Luger controverted the answer by alleging that the casualty company had issued a policy of insurance upon the Windell automobile. Upon a trial of this issue, the lower court entered judgment against the casualty company, holding that the policy of insurance was a liability one, and that, consequently, the casualty company was liable to Luger. In so holding, the trial court felt compelled to follow the decision of this court in the case of *Davies v. Maryland Cas. Co., infra,* though that decision did not meet with his approval. The casualty company appealed from that judgment.

The respondent has moved to dismiss the appeal for the reason that the casualty company has not served Windell with notice of appeal, and that Windell, being an interested party, should have had such notice, and without it this court has not jurisdiction. In *Dittenhoefer v. Coeur d'Alene Clothing Co.,* 4 Wash. 519, 30 Pac. 660, and *Globe Electric Co. v. Montgomery,* 85 Wash. 452, 148 Pac. 596, this court has already held that where an appeal is taken by a garnishee defendant alone, that it is not necessary that notice of appeal should be given to the original judgment defendant. On the authority of those cases, the respondent's motion to dismiss the appeal is denied.

The policy written by the casualty company contained the following conditions:

"Condition C. If thereafter any suit is brought against the assured to enforce such a claim for damages, the assured shall immediately forward to such executive office of the company every summons or other process as soon as the same shall have been served on him, and the company will defend such suit, whether groundless or not, in the name and on behalf of the assured: the expenses incurred by the company in defending such suit; including costs, if any, taxed against the assured, will be borne by the company, whether the verdict is for or against the assured irrespective of the limits of liability expressed in the policy. In addition to the payment of expenses and costs as provided herein, the company will reimburse the assured for interest accrued on such part of the amount of the judgment after entry and payment thereof as shall not exceed the limits of liability expressed in the policy. The company shall have the right to settle any claim or suit at any time.

"Condition E. No action shall lie against the company to recover for any loss under or by reason of this policy unless it shall be brought by and in the name of the assured for loss actually sustained and paid in money by the assured in satisfaction of a judgment after actual trial of the issue; nor unless such action is brought within two years after such judgment against the assured has been so paid and satisfied. The company does not prejudice by this condition any defenses to such action as it may be entitled to make under this policy."

The question in this connection is whether a policy containing such provisions is a liability or an indemnity policy. The provisions quoted are identical in effect, and nearly so in language, with the provisions of the policy considered by this court in *Ford v. Aetna Life Ins. Co.,* 70 Wash. 29, 126 Pac. 69. The opinion in that case, written by Judge Gose, is a masterly review of the question, upon both reason and authority, and decides that a policy with those conditions is a policy of indemnity, and that a judgment creditor, when his judgment remains unpaid, cannot, by garnishment, compel its payment from the insurance company which had insured the judgment debtor. That decision leaves nothing to be added in support of the conclusion there reached. It establishes the rule by reason and shows that it is based upon the overwhelming weight of authority. Contrary to the rule there announced are the decisions of but two states; to wit, New Hampshire (*Sanders v. Frankfort Marine Ins. Co.*, 72 N. H. 485, 57 Atl. 655; *Lombard v. Maguire-Penniman Co.*, 78 N. H. 110, 97 Atl. 892), and Minnesota (*Patterson v. Adan*, 119 Minn. 308, 138 N. W. 281; *Standard Printing Co. v. Fidelity & Dep. Co.*, 138 Minn. 304, 164 N. W. 1022), and it is upon the decisions of those two courts, and the decision in the case of *Davies v. Maryland Cas. Co.*, 89 Wash. 571, 154 Pac. 1116, 155 Pac. 1035, L. R. A. 1916D 395, from this court (which we will hereafter refer to) that the respondent bases his argument in support of the lower court's judgment. The earlier New Hampshire decision was referred to and condemned in the *Ford* case, *supra*. The Minnesota cases must fall under the ban of the same argument, for they are based upon the reasoning of the New Hampshire court.

In addition to the cases cited in the *Ford* case in its support, may be added the following cases, which have been decided to the same effect but subsequently to the filing of the *Ford* opinion: *Schambs v. Fidelity & Casualty Co.*, 259 Fed. 55; *Maryland Casualty Co. v. Peppard*, 53 Okl. 515, 157 Pac. 106; *Curtis & Gartside Co. v. Aetna Life Ins. Co.*, 58 Okl. 470, 160 Pac. 465; *Riner v. Southwestern Surety Ins. Co.*, 85 Ore. 293, 165 Pac. 684; *Hebojoff v. Globe Indemnity Co.*, 35 Cal. App. 390, 169 Pac. 1048; *Emerson v. Western Automobile Ind. Ass'n*, 105 Kan. 242, 182 Pac. 647; *Kansas Free Air Ass'n v. Georgia Casualty Co.*, 107 Kan. 109, 190 Pac. 592; *Lorando v. Gethro*, 228 Mass. 181, 117 N. E.

185; *Eberlein v. Fidelity & Dep. Co.*, 164 Wis. 242, 159
N. W. 553; *Newton v. Seeley*, 177 N. C. 528, 99 S. E.
347; *McBride v. Aetna Life Ins. Co.*, 126 Ark. 528, 191
S. W. 5; *Hoagland Wagon Co. v. London Guaranty &
Accident Co.*, 201 Mo. App. 490, 212 S. W. 393; *Owens
v. Jackson-Hinton Gin Co.*, 217 S. W. (Tex. App.) 762.

It is the respondent's argument that the *Ford* case
has been overruled by the decision of this court in the
Davies case, *supra*. An examination of the latter case
will show that the original opinion was written upon
a theory not suggested by either party to the appeal,
and that the decision cites no authorities in support of
its conclusion upon the question before us, but trans-
forms an indemnity policy into one of liability on the
ground that the provision allowing the insurance company to conduct the defense waived the company's
right to exact prepayment by the assured of the judgment before it could be held on the policy. Upon a petition for rehearing, the *Ford* case having been called
to the attention of the court, it was sought to distinguish that case from the *Davies* case on the ground
that, in the *Davies* case, the judgment creditor was suing as an assignee of the policy. No such distinction
can be drawn between the conclusion in the *Ford* and
Davies cases. The court also used some language indicating an intention to modify the *Ford* case. When
all is said and done, the decision in the *Davies* case
was an overruling of the *Ford* case. There is no distinction that can be drawn between the two cases. In
the *Ford* case it was decided that the policy, with the
provisions which we have quoted, is a policy of indemnity, and in the *Davies* case it was held that such
a policy was one of liability. The *Davies* opinion is
contrary to reason and authority, and its entire refuta-
tion is contained in the exposition of the law made by
Judge Gose in the *Ford* case. Being satisfied that the

Ford decision is sound, we reaffirm it and overrule the *Davies* case upon this point.

Attention is called to our decision in *Fenton v. Poston*, 114 Wash. 217, 195 Pac. 31, where this court had before it a policy of insurance presenting the question whether it was one of liability or indemnity, and it was held to be a liability policy. That decision recognizes the rule in the *Ford* case, but decided the policy before the court to be one of liability for the reason "that the intention of the parties thereto was to protect the insured from liability for damages, or to protect persons damaged by injuries occasioned by the insured as specified in the contract, when such liability should accrue and be imposed by law (as by a judgment of a competent court)." Both the prevailing and the dissenting opinions in the *Fenton* case recognize the soundness of the doctrine of the *Ford* case, which we are reaffirming.

For the reasons stated, the judgment of the lower court is reversed.

PARKER, C. J., BRIDGES, FULLERTON, and HOLCOMB, JJ., concur.

[No. 16184. *En Banc.* July 25, 1921.]

Theodore Olson, *Respondent*, v. John Barton Payne et al., *Appellants*.[1]

Railroads (80)—Persons On or Near Tracks—Contributory Negligence of Person Injured. A boy twelve years of age and of average intelligence and experience was guilty of contributory negligence as a matter of law, where it appears that he had lived near railroad tracks and was conversant with the dangers through frequent warning by his parents, and was struck by the side of the engine or the first car of a train, while he was walking alongside of the track, the noise of the engine in laboring to draw a long train around a curve and to pick up speed being sufficient to apprise him of its approach.

Same (82)—Injury to Persons On or Near Tracks—Proximate Cause. The last clear chance doctrine is inapplicable in the case of a naked licensee on or near railroad tracks, where his presence was not known by persons on the engine causing his injuries, and his own negligence had not ceased but was continuing.

Appeal from a judgment of the superior court for Snohomish county, Alston, J., entered March 20, 1920, upon the verdict of a jury rendered in favor of the plaintiff, in an action for personal injuries. Reversed.

Thomas Balmer, for appellants.

Black & Black, for respondent.

Bridges, J.—This was a suit on account of personal injuries. There was a verdict and judgment for the plaintiff, and the defendant has appealed therefrom.

The jury having returned its verdict for the plaintiff, it will be our duty, in discussing most of the questions involved in this appeal, to look upon his testimony in the light most favorable to him. In so doing, we find testimony to support the following facts: In approaching the city of Everett from the north, the Northern Pacific and the Chicago, Milwaukee & St.

[1]Reported in 199 Pac. 757.

Paul Railroads' rights of way are in reasonably close
proximity, and where they go through that portion of
the city hereinafter mentioned the rights of way are
contiguous. Coming into the city from the north, one
first comes to the Northern Pacific depot, at the foot of
Pacific avenue. It is some 200 feet south of the depot
that the rights of way of the two railroads become contiguous. Some 600 feet south of the depot is what is
known as the "Fuel crossing" of the tracks for the
Eclipse mill. About 200 feet farther south from this
crossing is a switch stand, which was the point of the
accident. In this neighborhood, the distance between
the main line tracks of the two railroads is some ten
or twelve feet, and on each side of the main tracks are
certain side tracks. Both of these main tracks approach
from the north on a wide curve, which terminates at
about the mill crossing. Standing at that point and
looking north along the Northern Pacific tracks, a
train would come into view at about the depot, which
is some 600 feet away. For many years pedestrians
have been in the habit of traveling the right of way
from the depot to the south, past the point mentioned
and on toward the town of Lowell. The amount of
such travel on the right of way was such that those
operating the trains must have been aware of the custom. The Great Northern Railway also operates certain trains over these tracks. At the time of the injury, all the railroads were being operated by the appellant, as director-general of railroads.

About eight o'clock in the forenoon, on August 31,
1919, Theodore Olson, a boy practically twelve years
of age, was going fishing. He first came upon the railroad track at the Eclipse mill crossing. There he
stopped and looked both north and south along the
railroad tracks, and did not see any trains in either
direction. At that particular time, however, a Great

Northern freight train, operating on the Northern Pacific tracks, was approaching the Northern Pacific depot, but was then probably out of view of the boy, because of the curve in the railroad tracks. Not seeing any trains the boy turned southward, walking beside the Northern Pacific main line track, and close to the end of the ties. When he got to the switch stand, which is some 190 to 200 feet south of the mill crossing, where he had looked for the trains, the forepart of the engine of the approaching Great Northern freight train passed him, and he was hit by some part of the rear portion of the engine, or one of the cars immediately behind it. The blow caused him to be knocked under the train, and one of his legs was so nearly cut off that it was amputated as soon as he was taken to the hospital. There is nothing in the testimony to show that there was anything unusual projecting from the side of the engine or any of the cars, and if the boy was hit as he says he was, it must have been by the steps of the engine or some permanent portion of one of the cars immediately following it. The boy testified that the train in approaching him did not blow its whistle nor ring its bell, and that he did not hear its approach or know of it until the forepart of the engine passed him. As it came to the Northern Pacific depot, which is some 600 or 800 feet from the place of the injury, the train slowed down to about three or four miles an hour to receive certain orders, and then proceeded forward, gaining as much speed as it could by laboring hard. At the time it struck the boy, it was traveling about ten miles an hour. This engine was pulling between 55 and 60 freight cars and was making a great deal of noise. The boy had a long spell of dangerous sickness, hovering for weeks between life and death. The defendant's motion for nonsuit and for directed verdict and for judgment notwithstanding the verdict and for new trial were all denied.

The appellant contends that it was impossible for the injury to have happened in the way the boy testified it did, and it must be admitted that one studying the record is made to wonder whether the boy was mistaken. But, on the other hand, it is not impossible for the accident to have happened just as the boy testified. From the testimony, the jury had a right to believe that it happened in that way and by its verdict has bound us in that regard. We must, therefore, assume that the accident happened in the way the boy said it happened. But, so assuming, is he entitled to recover?

The chief question argued by both sides is as to whether the boy was guilty of such contributory negligence that, as a matter of law, and notwithstanding the verdict, we may say that he cannot recover. He is of average intelligence and experience. He has succeeded in making from year to year his various school grades. He was thoroughly acquainted with the immediate neighborhood where he was injured; he had been there and on those tracks a number of times, both alone and with his parents. He had some two or three years before lived within a block or two of a railroad. His parents had time and again warned him about the danger of being on the tracks. His age, his intelligence and his experience must have made him know as fully as any one could know, that he was in a place of danger; that he must keep away from the trains; that he would be killed or hurt if he got too close to them. That he knew and fully appreciated these things is shown by the fact that when he first came to the tracks he looked in both directions to see if any trains were coming.

Many, and probably a majority, of the courts of this country have held that a child five or six years of age or under, cannot, but that a boy of ten or twelve years of age may, under some circumstances, be guilty of such contributory negligence as will preclude recovery for his injury. The facts in any two personal injury cases are never the same. Each case must be decided upon its own peculiar facts. In determining whether this boy was guilty of such negligence as to preclude recovery, we must take into consideration his age, his intelligence, his experience and his knowledge of the surrounding circumstances. In so doing we must not hold the boy to that strict accountability to which we would hold one who had reached older years. But the matters for the respondent's consideration to assure his safety were of the most simple and elementary nature. There were no other noises or trains to confuse; the situation was not such as to require a sudden election what course to pursue. It is true he says the whistle was not blown and the bell was not rung, although nearly everybody else testified to the contrary, yet the purpose of giving those signals is to warn. In this case we have a freight train of some sixty cars approaching him, laboring heavily to make a curve and gain speed. It does not need testimony, although there is plenty in the record, to inform us that, under those circumstances, the train must have made a great noise. The boy says that he did not hear the noise of the oncoming train, but if he was exercising such reasonable care as a boy of his age, experience and intelligence must, as a matter of law, exercise under like circumstances, he must have heard it. There was nothing here, so far as the testimony shows, to distract his attention. It seems impossible to look upon this case otherwise than that the respondent wholly failed to give any heed to his surroundings. We must, of course, hold that he must have exercised at least a small amount of care, and yet it seems to us that he did not use any.

That the court is justified, notwithstanding the ver
dict of the jury, under proper circumstances, in holding, as a matter of law, that a child twelve years of age
has been guilty of such contributory negligence as precludes his recovery, is shown by the following citations,
selected from many of like character: *McGee v. Wa-
bash R. Co.*, 214 Mo. 530, 114 S. W. 33; *Studer v. South-
ern Pacific Co.*, 121 Cal. 400, 53 Pac. 942; *Texas & Pac.
R. Co. v. Phillips*, 91 Tex. 278, 42 S. W. 852; *Schoon-
over v. Baltimore & Ohio R. Co.*, 69 W. Va. 560, 73 S. E.
266; *Kyle v. Boston Elevated R. Co.*, 215 Mass. 260, 102
N. E. 310; *Adams v. Boston Elevated R. Co.*, 222 Mass.
350, 110 N. E. 965; *Derringer v. Tatley*, 34 N. D. 43,
157 N. W. 811. In this connection we call attention to
the notes commencing on page 10, L. R. A. 1917F;
notes commencing at page 123 of the same volume, and
notes commencing at page 172 of the same volume. The
authorities are elaborately collected and digested in
these notes. We have recognized the same doctrine in
the case of *Oregon R. & Nav. Co. v. Egley*, 2 Wash. 409,
26 Pac. 973, 26 Am. St. 860, where we held that a boy
nine and one-half years of age was, as a matter of law,
guilty of such contributory negligence as to bar his recovery. See, also, *Clark v. Northern Pacific R. Co.*, 29
Wash. 139, 69 Pac. 636, 59 L. R. A. 508.

A very conscientious study of the facts of this case
leads us to the necessary and inevitable conclusion that,
under all the circumstances, the respondent was, as a
matter of law, guilty of such contributory negligence
as bars his recovery.

It is argued by the respondent, however, that even
under these circumstances, the plaintiff is entitled to
recover on the doctrine of last clear chance, but we cannot accept this view. We do not think that doctrine is
involved in this case for at least two reasons: First,
because all the testimony shows that those in charge of

the train did not see the boy; there were three or four persons on the engine, and all of them testified that they did not see him; in fact, they contend the boy was not there as the engine approached or reached the place of the accident. Second, because the respondent's negligence had not ceased but was continuing. At most, it was a case of injury resulting from the continuing negligence of both parties. Again, the respondent was but a naked licensee on appellants' tracks and he could recover only for wantonness or wilfulness on the part of the appellant. In this as well as in other regards this case is controlled by *Scharf v. Spokane Inland Empire R. Co.*, 92 Wash. 561, 159 Pac. 797, and cases there cited. There is, therefore, nothing upon which to base the doctrine of last clear chance.

The judgment is reversed with instructions to dismiss the case.

PARKER, C. J., MACKINTOSH, FULLERTON, MAIN, HOLCOMB, TOLMAN, and MITCHELL, JJ., concur.

[No. 16506. Department One. July 27, 1921.]

THE STATE OF WASHINGTON, *Respondent*, v. FREDERICK S. WILES, *Appellant*.[1]

LICENSES (5)—MOTOR VEHICLES—UNITED STATES MAIL—CONTRACTOR'S LIABILITY. A person under contract with the United States for the transportation of mail to and from the post office and postal stations and depots, wharves and docks of a particular city, who uses his motor truck for the purpose, is subject to the motor vehicle license tax imposed by Laws 1915, p. 385 (as amended by Laws 1919, p. 90), such license tax in no way constituting a direct interference with the free and orderly performance of governmental functions nor with the conduct of government business.

Appeal from a judgment of the superior court for King county, Frater, J., entered January 6, 1921, after

[1]Reported in 199 Pac. 749.

a trial and conviction of operating a motor vehicle without a license. Affirmed.

Elias A. Wright and *Sam A. Wright*, for appellant.

Malcolm Douglas, *John D. Carmody*, and *Arthur Schramm, Jr.*, for respondent.

BRIDGES, J.—Appellant was charged by information with unlawfully using and operating a motor truck on the public highways of the county of King, state of Washington, without first obtaining a license therefor, as required by the state laws. He was found guilty, and has appealed from a judgment imposing a fine.

The facts are simple and stipulated, and are as follows: Prior to his arrest appellant had entered into a written contract with the United States government, whereby, for certain considerations, he agreed to carry the United States mail, in the city of Seattle, Washington, between the various depots, wharves, docks, post-office and substations therein. In carrying out his contract with the government, he used various motor trucks, including the one which he is accused of operating without first having obtained a license. These trucks were used by the appellant only in the business of carrying the mail under his contract. They had painted on them the usual insignia of vehicles used for these purposes, including the words "United States Mail". The terms of his contract required him to provide vehicles for the carriage of the mail, and to keep them properly equipped and in repair, and he was required also to furnish all necessary oil, gasoline, tires, upkeep and drivers. The contract further provided that such trucks should be used only in the business of carrying United States mail. At the time of his arrest, the appellant was in the exercise of the duties imposed upon him under his contract.

The 1915 session laws (Laws of 1915, p. 385), as amended by ch. 46, session laws of 1919 (Laws of 1919, p. 90), provide, among other things, that it shall be unlawful to operate automobiles and motor trucks on the public highways of the state without first having obtained a license therefor. The minimum license fee required of a motor truck is $10 per annum, and the fee increases as the weight and capacity of the truck increase. The 1919 act especially exempts "all motor vehicles owned by the United States government, and used exclusively in its service".

Appellant's argument is that the United States government has the constitutional right to carry its mails in any manner it may see fit, and without let or hindrance from any person or state; that in the use of his trucks he was in the performance of a governmental duty; that he was an instrumentality selected by the United States government for the purpose of carrying out and putting into effect its constitutional duty of carrying, delivering and caring for the mail; that such a tax or license fee could not be lawfully imposed on the government itself, if it had owned the trucks and operated them in the performance of the work which appellant was doing, and that since he is doing for the government what it might do for itself, to impose a tax on him would be in fact to impose it on the government, because any private person carrying the mail must require the government to pay him an additional amount equal to any such taxation as he may be required to pay. The principal cases cited by the appellant in support of his argument are the following: *Osborn v. Bank of United States*, 9 Wheat. (U. S.) 738, 6 L. Ed. 204; *McCullough v. State of Maryland*, 4 Wheat. (U. S.) 316; *Williams v. City of Talladaga*, 226 U. S. 404, 57 L. Ed. 275; *Western Union Telegraph Co. v. Texas*, 105 U. S. 460, 26 L.

Ed. 1067; and *Johnson v. State of Maryland,* 254 U. S. 51.

On the other hand, the respondent contends that the license fee is a tax imposed on the right to operate a motor truck on the public highways of the state, and is not a tax imposed on the right to carry the United States mail; that the state has sole control of its roads and highways, and that the agents of the United States are amenable to the reasonable rules and regulations governing the use of such highways; that the immunity of the Federal government from state taxation is not negotiable to the extent that it can transfer that immunity to every person who contracts with it to do any act for the furtherance of governmental business; that the mail contract between an individual and the Federal government does not render the former an essential governmental agent, and confer on him freedom from state control. In support of its argument, respondent cites and relies upon the following, among other cases: *Commonwealth v. Closson,* 229 Mass. 329, 118 N. E. 653, L. R. A. 1918C 939; *Ex parte Marshall,* 75 Fla. 97, 77 South. 869, L. R. A. 1918C 944; *Searight v. Stokes,* 3 How. (U. S.) 151, 11 L. Ed. 537, to which may be added: *Dickey v. Maysville etc. Turnpike Co.,* 7 Dana (Ky.) 113; *Western Union Tel. Co. v. Richmond,* 178 Fed. 310, 56 L. Ed. 710; *Fidelity & Deposit Co. v. Commonwealth of Pennsylvania,* 240 U. S. 319; *Lumberville Delaware Bridge Co. v. State Board of Assessors,* 55 N. J. L. 529, 26 Atl. 711, 25 L. R. A. 134.

The single legal question involved in this case is an interesting one. Although the same question, based upon identical facts, must exist in nearly every state of the Union, we have not been cited to a single case which is directly in point, nor has our independent search resulted in finding one.

We are of the opinion that the judgment appealed
from must stand. It is, doubtless, true that the states
may not directly tax the property of the Federal government, nor the instrumentalities which it uses to discharge any of its constitutional functions, nor may a
state, by taxation or otherwise, materially interfere
with the due, expeditious and orderly procedure of
that government while in the exercise of its constitutional powers. When it acts within its powers it is
supreme, and all the states are subordinate to it.
Being supreme, it must maintain its supremacy in
order that our form of government shall be and continue to be stable and lasting. It is on this broad
principle, as we understand it, that the Federal supreme court has always held that a state may not tax
the Federal government or its instrumentalities, or do
aught which would directly interfere with its lawful
operations, because had the various states such powers they might slowly but surely undermine and
weaken its foundations, independence and acknowledged supremacy. It was on these grounds and for
these reasons that the United States supreme court
held, in the epoch making cases of *McCullough v. Maryland, supra,* and *Osborn v. Bank of United States,
supra,* that a state did not have power to directly
tax the right of the United States bank to do business
in such states. But the law of those cases is not applicable to the facts of this case. In those cases the
bank was chartered by the United States, and controlled by Congressional acts as to the manner of doing
business. It was the direct issue and immediate instrumentality of the government. Its private property
within the state might be taxed like any other property, but for the state to require it to pay a tax for the
right to do business was equal to requiring the
government itself to pay a tax for the priv-

ilege of performing, within the borders of the
state, functions authorized or imposed on it by the
Federal constitution. But the case at bar cannot come
within the scope or spirit of those decisions. Here
there is no effort to tax the business of carrying the
mail. The appellant is not a direct instrumentality of
the government; he is a personal contractor, doing certain work for the government, at a fixed compensation.
In no sense is he the representative or agent of the
government nor an integral part of it. As was said
by the Federal supreme court in the case of *Fidelity
& Deposit Co. v. Commonwealth of Pennsylvania,
supra* (which case we will later notice in more detail):

"But mere contracts between private corporations
and the United States do not necessarily render the
former essential governmental agencies and confer
freedom from state control."

A person building a state road is nothing but a
contractor; he is no part of the state or its agencies,
and does not thereby inherit the various immunities
of the state. There is nothing in appellant's contract
which indicates that the government intended to pass
its immunities on to him. Under these circumstances it
should be presumed that it was the intention that he
should be subject to the general laws of the state.

Nor are those cases out of the supreme court of the
United States concerning taxation on interstate commerce in point. Such were the cases of *Western
Union Tel. Co. v. Texas, supra,* and *Williams v. City
of Talladaga, supra.* The state of Texas passed a law
imposing taxes on every chartered telegraph company
doing business in the state, and each such company was
thereby required to pay a tax of one per cent for each
full rate message sent and one-half cent for each message the toll for which was less than full rate. The
telegraph company was incorporated under the laws

of the state of New York. Many years ago the Congress of the United States passed an act authorizing telegraph companies to place their poles and other apparatus on all government property, reservations and post roads, in consideration of which government messages should have certain preferences in transmission. The Texas act was held unconstitutional in that it undertook to impose a direct tax on messages sent and received by and on behalf of the government, and on interstate messages. The *Williams* case, *supra,* was of like general character. We think it will at once be observed that these cases are not controlling of the case at bar. In discussing a somewhat similar question in the case of *Johnson v. State of Maryland, supra,* cited by the appellant, the court said:

"The cases upon the regulation of interstate commerce cannot be relied upon as furnishing an answer. They deal with the conduct of private persons in matters in which the states as well as the Federal government have an interest, and which would be wholly under the control of the states but for the supervening destination and the ultimate purpose of the acts. Here the question is whether the state can interrupt the acts of the general government itself."

That case is probably more nearly in point here than any of the cases cited by appellant or which we have found. Johnson was an employee of the post-office department of the United States, and while driving a government motor truck in the transportation of mail over certain highways in the state of Maryland, was arrested, convicted and fined for driving such truck without having a personal license as required by the laws of that state. The court stated the question involved to be: "whether the state has power to require such an employee to obtain a license by submitting to an examination concerning his competence, and paying $3, before performing his official duties in obedience to superior command." In determining the matter adversely to the state, the court said:

"It seems to us that the immunity of the instruments of the United States from state control in the performance of their duties extends to a requirement that they desist from performance until they satisfy a state officer, upon examination, that they are competent for a necessary part of them, and pay a fee for permission to go on. Such requirement does not merely touch the government servants remotely by a general rule of conduct; it lays hold of them in their specific attempt to obey orders, and requires qualifications in addition to those that the government has pronounced sufficient. It is the duty of the department to employ persons competent for their work, and that duty it must be presumed has been performed."

There is a wide and fundamental distinction between that case and the one at bar, for in that case the government owned the truck and the person required to pay the fee and obtain the license was its direct employee, engaged in the performance of his duties, while here the person required to pay the license fee was a simple contractor, a resident of the state, the owner and operator of the truck in question and engaged in a work which was to be performed entirely within the state. There the tax was, in effect, directly against the government, while here it is directly on the individual and affects the government only indirectly and incidentally.

In the recent case of *Fidelity & Deposit Co. v. Commonwealth of Pennsylvania, supra,* it was held by the Federal supreme court that a surety company does not by becoming, conformably to an act of Congress, surety on bonds required by the United States, a Federal instrumentality so as to be exempt from a state tax on the premiums received. Mr. Justice McReynolds, speaking for the court in that case said:

"That the challenged tax 'is an exaction for the privilege of doing business' seems plain; and undoubtedly a state may not directly and materially hinder exercise of constitutional powers of the United States by demanding in opposition to the will of Congress that a Federal instrumentality pay a tax for the privilege of performing its functions. But mere contracts between private corporations and the United States do not necessarily render the former essential governmental agencies and confer freedom from state control. Moreover, whatever may be their status, if the pertinent statute discloses the intention of Congress that such corporations, contracting under it with the Federal government, shall not be exempt from state regulation and taxation, they must submit thereto."

If the bonding company in that case was subject to the laws of that state, the appellant in this case ought to be subject to the laws of this state.

In the case of *Commonwealth v. Closson, supra,* it was held that one in charge of a vehicle transporting United States mail is not exempt from the operation of state statutes and municipal ordinances regulating traffic on the highways, although by Federal statutes the highways are post-roads. In that case Closson was arrested for violating a state statute concerning the conduct and operation of motor vehicles on the public highways. He defended on the ground that, being employed as a mail carrier, using a vehicle for the delivery of mail, he was immune from prosecution and punishment under the statute. The court said:

"The designated streets or ways are not, however, instrumentalities created by the general government, where 'exemption from state control is essential to the independent sovereign authority of the United States within the sphere of their delegated powers'. . . . . The facilities thereby afforded for transportation of the mails confer no extraordinary rights upon mail carriers to use the ways as they please, nor do they necessarily or impliedly do away with the power of supervision and control inherent in the state."

The case of *Ex parte Marshall, supra,* is an instructive and interesting one. During the world war, a military encampment of United States soldiers was located near Jacksonville, Florida. The officer in charge of that camp made a contract with Marshall, authorizing him to transport by motor bus the soldiers from the camp to the city of Jacksonville, upon certain terms and conditions particularly set out. He was arrested for not complying with a certain state law imposing a license tax somewhat similar to that involved in this case. He defended on the ground that he was engaged in the business of the United States government, and was its constituted agent for the purpose of transporting soldiers. He cited practically the same cases cited by the appellant in this case. Concerning them the court said:

"We are in accord with the holdings of all these cases, . . . but unfortunately for the petitioner, none of them fit the facts of the case in hand. In all of them a license tax was sought to be imposed by a state, county, or municipality, upon the right to do business either by a bank, a railroad company, or telegraph company that had been chartered, and had been granted its franchise and right to do business by the Congress of the United States, and in all of them it was held, in effect, that such a license tax was invalid because it was an unwarranted invasion of rights properly granted by the Federal government, and amounted virtually to an attempt to annul such Federal grant."

The judgment and sentence were affirmed.

But appellant further contends that to impose the license tax upon him would, in effect, be to impose it upon the Federal government in the transaction of its constitutional functions. This argument, however, proves entirely too much. The appellant admits, and

under like circumstances all the courts have held, that
the state has the right to levy a property tax on motor
trucks owned by him and used in the transportation of
the mail. In making his contract with the government
he, doubtless, took into consideration this tax, and it
would be in effect passed on to the government in
identically the same way that he contends the license
tax must be passed on to the government. We have in
this state a statute which requires every person driving or operating a motor vehicle to obtain a driver's
license before he will be permitted to operate such vehicle. If the state cannot compel appellant to pay the
motor license tax, for the same reason it cannot compel
him to license his drivers or himself as a driver. We
also have a law in this state imposing a small tax on
each gallon of gasoline sold. This tax is by the gasoline companies charged to the consumer, including the
appellant, and, he, doubtless, will, if he should renew
his contract with the government, pass that tax also on
to the government, and if he be exempt from the motor tax, he is, for the same reason, exempt from the
gasoline tax. Other like illustrations might be given.

While it is true, generally speaking, that a state may
not by its laws hamper and interfere with the free and
orderly performance of governmental functions, by
taxation or otherwise, yet that interference must be
substantial and direct. Every indirect and immaterial
interference with the conduct of government business
is not violative of the principles upon which the Federal government is founded and performs its duties. The
rule of reason must control in all such questions, otherwise the states will be greatly hampered in the conduct
of their affairs, without any correspondent benefit
flowing to the national government.

We are confident that the appellant is not, because
of the facts of this case, relieved from complying with

the state statute imposing upon him the motor truck license fee. The judgment is affirmed.

PARKER, C. J., MACKINTOSH, FULLERTON, and HOLCOMB, JJ., concur.

[No. 16509. Department Two. July 27, 1921.]

JOHN A. SWEITZER, *Respondent*, v. INDUSTRIAL INSURANCE COMMISSION, *Appellant*.[1]

MASTER AND SERVANT (121-2)—WORKMEN'S COMPENSATION—AWARD FOR INJURIES—REVIEW. The refusal of the industrial insurance commission to re-open a case and make an increased award cannot be said to be arbitrary and capricious action on its part, where it had taken the injured workman's application into consideration, heard his evidence and that of medical examiners, and reached an adverse conclusion; since "arbitrary and capricious" action within the purview of the statute means wilful and unreasonable action.

SAME (121-2)—CLASSIFICATION OF INJURIES—DEGREES—REVIEW. Where the industrial insurance commission properly classified a workman's injury as permanent partial disability, the amount of the award based upon a finding as to the degree of the injury is not subject to review by the courts in the absence of a showing that its action in that respect was arbitrary and capricious.

Appeal from a judgment of the superior court for Skagit county, Brawley, J., entered April 27, 1920, upon findings in favor of the plaintiff, on an appeal from an award of the industrial insurance commission. Reversed.

The Attorney General and *John H. Dunbar, Assistant,* for appellant.

John A. Hanson, for respondent.

FULLERTON, J.—On August 10, 1918, the respondent Sweitzer, while engaged in an extra hazardous occu-

[1]Reported in 199 Pac. 724.

pation within the meaning of the workmen's compensation act, fell from a scaffold and was injured. He applied to the industrial insurance commission for compensation, and that body found, after due investigation, that he had suffered from the accident a temporary total disability, and a permanent partial disability to his thumbs, and made him an award accordingly. On January 4, 1920, the respondent filed with the industrial insurance commission a written application for the re-opening of his case and a further award; setting forth therein the condition of his injuries and the effects therefrom in the following language:

"That at the time, as aforesaid, and while your said petitioner was so employed and engaged in his duties as a workman and was then and there discharging his duties, your said petitioner sustained an injury to his head, to the thumb on his right hand and the thumb on his left hand, and to his left eye; that the injury sustained by said petitioner to his head has caused a scar thereon about six inches long and has permanently disfigured and permanently disabled him; that said injury to his head is a constant worry to your said petitioner for the reason that said wound is not inclined to heal and foreign matters continue to run therefrom which causes boils and irritable sores; that the injury to your said petitioner's thumbs has caused them to become permanently stiff so as to handicap your said petitioner to a large extent from following his usual occupation and the injury to his left eye has to a partial degree destroyed his eyesight in that the eye-lid was cut and that said eye-lid now hangs down over the eye and partially covers same."

The board denied the application, and the respondent appealed from its order to the superior court. At the hearing on the appeal the superior court made the following finding of fact:

"That from the evidence of the said plaintiff on the hearing of said cause in said court and the evidence of Dr. Shorkley and Dr. Osterman, both qualified physicians, the court finds that the injury to said plaintiff's left hand had caused said hand to become useless to said plaintiff to such an extent that approximately seventy-five per cent of the use of said hand was lost to said plaintiff, and further that the medical examination made by the medical board of the industrial insurance commission upon the re-opening of said plaintiff's claim was made with reference to the permanent partial disability to plaintiff's left thumb and in making their findings the said medical board based their finding on the permanent partial disability of plaintiff's left thumb and not to the permanent partial disability to said plaintiff's entire left hand."

As conclusions of law, it held that the order of the board refusing to re-open the case was "arbitrary and capricious and not in accordance with the facts and the law and statutes in such case made and provided;" that the order was based on a permanent partial disability of the respondent's left thumb, which was a lesser disability than he had sustained; that the findings should have been based on a permanent partial disability to the respondent's entire left hand instead of restricting the findings of permanent partial disability to the left thumb. It was further concluded that the respondent was entitled to an award from the insurance fund "based on not less than seventy-five per cent of permanent partial disability to plaintiff's entire left hand." A judgment was entered directing the commission to re-open the case and to make the respondent an award based on an injury such as the court found to have been suffered. The commission appeals.

It is our conclusion that the judgment of the trial court must be reversed. There is no evidence in the record justifying its conclusion that the commissioners

in refusing to re-open the respondent's case acted
either arbitrarily or capriciously. On the contrary,
the evidence shows that they exercised the utmost good
faith in their consideration of the case. They not only
heard the respondent himself with respect to his ail-
ments, but they caused him to be examined by their
own medical examiners as well as by physicians not
connected with the department, who are acknowledged
experts on diseases and injuries of the character of
which he complained, and based their action upon the
results of these inquiries. The most that can be said
of their action, even from the respondent's point of
view, is that they erred in judgment. But this is not
arbitrary or capricious action. These terms, when
used in this connection, must mean wilful and unrea-
soning action, action without consideration and in disregard of the facts and circumstances of the case. Action is not arbitrary or capricious when exercised
honestly and upon due consideration where there is
room for two opinions, however much it may be believed
that an erroneous conclusion was reached.

We think the court erred also in finding that there
had been an insufficient award. While it must be con-
fessed that the statute defining the questions that may
be reviewed on an appeal from the conclusions of the
industrial insurance commission is somewhat indefinite, we have heretofore construed it to preclude a review of the amount of the award made by that body.

"The meaning of the act is that all questions going
to the classification of an injured workman and his
right to participate in the insurance fund are questions
of fact and subject to review, upon appeal, by court or
jury; but the amount of the award upon a proper classification is a matter resting in the broad discretion of
the department, and will not be interfered with:"
Parker v. Industrial Insurance Dept., 102 Wash. 54,
172 Pac. 830.

Here, there is no question that the department properly classified the injury. The law provides for but three classifications, namely, temporary total disability, permanent total disability, and permanent partial disability, and the respondent's injury, in so far as it is brought into question in the proceeding, is of the latter class. Within the latter classification there are of course degrees, some of which entitle the injured workman to a higher award than do others, but the degree of injury within the classification affects only the amount of the award and since it is the exclusive province of the department to determine the amount, it is likewise their exclusive province to determine the degree of the injury. A case can arise of course where the degree of the injury may be inquired into. If, for illustration, a workman's arm should be severed between the elbow and the wrist and the department should diagnose it as an injury to the thumb, unquestionably the court would say that an erroneous conclusion had been reached. But it would so say because the conclusion was without due consideration of the facts; in other words, that it was arbitrary and capricious. Where, however, as here, there is room for an honest difference of opinion, and the department, after due investigation, determines the injury to be of a certain degree within its proper classification, the courts have no warrant to interfere with their findings.

The judgment is reversed, with instructions to enter a judgment to the effect that the respondent take nothing by his appeal.

PARKER, C. J., MAIN, MITCHELL, and TOLMAN, JJ., concur.

[No. 16612. *En Banc.* July 27, 1921.]

CATHERINE S. SKIDMORE, *Appellant*, v. C. W. CLAUSEN, *as State Auditor, Respondent.*[1]

STATUTES (78)—TIME OF TAKING EFFECT—INITIATIVE AND REFERENDUM—SOLDIER'S BONUS. Under Const., art. 2, § 1d, providing that initiative and referendum measures shall be in operation thirty days after approval, the soldiers' compensation act, Laws 1920, ch. 1, approved by popular vote on November 2, 1920, did not go into effect until December 2, 1920; and the death of a soldier entitled to a bonus, four days prior to the date of taking effect of the measure, would not entitle his estate to take thereunder (BRIDGES, J., dissents).

Appeal from an order of the superior court for Thurston county, Wright, J., entered June 17, 1921, sustaining a demurrer to plaintiff's application for a writ of mandate, dismissing an action to recover under the soldiers' bonus. Affirmed.

Philip Tworoger, for appellant.

The Attorney General and *Nat U. Brown,* for respondent.

HOLCOMB, J.—This action was begun in the superior court of the state of Washington for Thurston county, by appellant in her own name, seeking a writ of mandate directed against C. W. Clausen, as state auditor, to compel the issuance to her of a warrant in her favor in the sum of $360. Appellant is the widow of Francis M. Skidmore, who died November 28, 1920. Mr. Skidmore, had he lived, would have been entitled to receive $360 from the state, under ch. 1, Laws of 1920, p. 7, known as the "Bonus Act", or "Soldiers Additional Compensation Act", for service performed in the army

[1] Reported in 199 Pac. 727.

of the United States during the late war. A demurrer
to the application was sustained by the lower court, and
appellant refusing to plead further, the action was dismissed. This appeal is from the order of dismissal.

In the lower court, appellant sought recovery as the
beneficiary under the terms of the act and set forth
in her affidavit that she was the dependent wife of the
deceased soldier, and therefore entitled to the compensation that would have gone to him. Section 1,
ch. 1, Laws of 1920, p. 7, provides compensation for dependent widows of soldiers who were killed or died in
the service. The deceased husband of appellant died
some five months after his discharge. In this court
appellant abandoned her claim as a dependent of the
deceased soldier, and seeks relief as administratrix of
the estate of her husband. This change was agreed to
by the attorney general.

As stated by appellant, the question is whether appellant is entitled to the relief demanded under an interpretation of the initiative and referendum amendment to the state constitution. The provision of the
initiative and referendum amendment affecting the
same, is:

"Any measure initiated by the people or referred to
the people as herein provided, shall take effect and become the law *if* it is approved by a majority of the
votes cast thereon: *Provided,* That the vote cast upon
such question or measure shall equal one-third of the
total votes cast at such election and not otherwise.
*Such measure shall be in operation on and after the
thirtieth day after the election at which it is approved.*"
(Italics ours). Const., art. 2, § 1d.

Appellant contends that the bonus law went into effect on November 2, 1920, the date on which the people
of the state by their referendum approved it; that its
operation was technically to commence on December 2,

1920, but that it actually went into effect on the date of its approval by the people.

The deceased husband died November 28, 1920, or four days before the act would become effective under the above quoted amendment.

Although this is a case appealing to us as a very meritorious one, we are forced to the conclusion that the contentions of appellant are untenable. In *Gottstein v. Lister*, 88 Wash. 462, 153 Pac. 595, Ann. Cas. 1917 D 1008, in construing the effect of the initiative and referendum amendment to the constitution, we held that an initiative measure became effective on the thirtieth day after the election at which it was approved. A referred measure is under the same terms as an initiative measure.

In *State ex rel. Atkinson v. Northern Pacific R. Co.*, 53 Wash. 673, 102 Pac. 876, 17 Ann. Cas. 1013, we held that:

"The general rule is that a statute speaks from the time it goes into effect, whether that time be the day of its enactment or some future day to which the power enacting the statute has postponed the time of its taking effect."

We quoted with approval 26 Am. & Eng. Ency. Law (2d ed.), p. 565, reading:

"A statute passed to take effect at a future day must be understood as speaking from the time it goes into operation and not from the time of passage. Thus the words 'heretofore', 'hereafter' and the like, have reference to the time the statute becomes effective as a law, and not to the time of passage. Before that time no rights may be acquired under it, and no one is bound to regulate his conduct according to its terms; . . ."

The *Atkinson case,* it is true, was reversed by the supreme court of the United States, *Northern Pacific R. Co. v. State ex rel. Atkinson,* 222 U. S. 370, but it was reversed on the ground that although it conceded the right of the state to apply its police power for the purpose of regulating interstate commerce, in a case like this it ''exists only from the silence of Congress on the subject, and ceases when Congress acts on the subject *or manifests its purpose to call* into play its exclusive power.'' This being the conceded premise upon which the state law could have been made applicable, it was held that the enactment of Congress of the law in question was an assertion of its power, and by the fact alone of such manifestation that subject was at once removed from the further operation of the authority of the state. The supreme court of the United States admitted the soundness of the rule declared by us, but held, as will be observed from the above statement, that its application did not apply to that case.

We are therefore obliged to affirm the order of the lower court.

Parker, C. J., Tolman, Fullerton, Main, and Mitchell, JJ., concur.

Bridges, J., dissents.

[No. 16501. Department Two. July 27, 1921.]

THE STATE OF WASHINGTON, *Respondent,* v. VERLE
BRUMMETT, *Appellant.*[1]

CRIMINAL LAW (21)—PARTIES TO OFFENSE—PRINCIPALS AND ACCESSORIES. Under Rem. Code, § 2007, abolishing the distinction between an accessory before the fact and a principal, the driver of an automobile who did not participate in the forcible act of robbing another, but who held the car in readiness for the active participants to escape, was equally guilty of the crime of robbery.

APPEAL (272)—RECORD—PROCEEDINGS NOT IN RECORD—AFFIDAVITS. An affidavit alleging the misconduct of a juror as ground for new trial in a criminal case, which appears in the clerk's transcript, but not in the statement of facts, will not be considered on appeal.

Appeal from a judgment of the superior court for Snohomish county, Alston, J., entered March 17, 1920, upon a trial and conviction of robbery. Affirmed.

E. C. Dailey and *A. E. Dailey,* for appellant.
Thos. A. Stiger, for respondent.

PARKER, C. J.—The defendant Brummett was, with Palmer R. Fosse and Arnold Fosse, by information, charged with the crime of robbery, committed at the ticket office of the Pacific Northwest Traction Company at Everett, in Snohomish county; in that they, with force and violence, took from the immediate possession and control of Nora Vaara the sum of $794, the property of that company, which was then and there in her possession and control as the ticket agent of the company. Trial in the superior court for Snohomish county resulted in a verdict, finding the defendant Brummett guilty as charged, upon which judgment was ren-

[1]Reported in 199 Pac. 726.

dered sentencing him to imprisonment in the penitentiary; from which he has appealed to this court.

There is no question before us calling for serious consideration, other than the contention here made in appellant's behalf that the evidence does not support the
verdict and judgment rendered against him. This contention seems to be mainly rested upon the fact that
he was not in the ticket office when the two other defendants committed the physical act of forcibly taking
the money from the possession of the ticket agent. But
the evidence plainly supports the verdict and judgment, in showing that appellant went with the other defendants to a place within a block of the ticket office, all
with the avowed purpose of taking the money by force
from the ticket agent, they all going there in an automobile, appellant driving and waiting for the other defendants to so procure the money, with a view of all
of them making a hasty escape; which they did, in the
automobile, immediately after the commission of the
crime. Plainly, under our statutes abolishing all distinction "between an accessory before the fact and a
principal," in crime, appellant was rendered as guilty
of this crime as if he had actually physically participated in taking the money from the ticket agent. Rem.
Code, § 2007.

Some contention is made that appellant is entitled to
a new trial because of the misconduct of a juror. This
contention seems to us so devoid of merit — even conceding that it is properly before us — as to not call for
discussion. We note that it is rested upon a showing
not appearing in the statement of facts. In support of
it, counsel for appellant refer to an affidavit which appears only in the clerk's transcript, and therefore does
not appear in the record in such manner that we can
know that the trial court ever saw it. Counsel for the
state, however, have not sought to avoid meeting this

contention upon the merits, being evidently willing that
we consider the affidavit as properly before us.

The judgment is affirmed.

MITCHELL, MAIN, HOLCOMB, and TOLMAN, JJ., concur.

[No. 16490.   Department Two.   July 27, 1921.]

W. H. SINCLAIR *et al.*, *Respondents*, v. WILES & FOY,
Defendants, C. YABE *et al.*, *Appellants*.[1]

MUNICIPAL CORPORATIONS (379, 380)—USE OF STREETS—COL-
LISIONS—ORDINANCES. The verdict of a jury finding the negligence
of the driver of a jitney bus as the proximate cause of injury to a
passenger in the bus, resulting from its collision with a mail truck,
was sustained by evidence showing that, under the city ordinances,
the mail truck had the right of way over other vehicles, and also
had the right of way over the jitney bus by first entering the intersection of cross-streets; that the jitney entered the intersection at
an excessive rate of speed; that the jitney driver did not heed the
proper signal given by the truck driver, nor give any signal which
would warn the driver of the truck; and that the jitney driver
turned his car to the right, while a turn to the left or a timely reduction of speed would have avoided the collision.

Appeal from a judgment of the superior court for
King county, Tallman, J., entered November 27, 1920,
upon the verdict of a jury rendered in favor of the
plaintiff, in an action for personal injuries. Affirmed.

Morris B. Sachs, for appellants.

William U. Park and *Paul S. Dubuar*, for respondents.

TOLMAN, J.—Respondents, as plaintiffs, brought this
action to recover for personal injuries sustained by
Bessie F. Sinclair while a passenger on a jitney bus
operated by appellant Yabe. From a verdict against

[1]Reported in 199 Pac. 725.

them in the sum of $2,000, and a judgment thereon, the appellants bring the case here for review on appeal.

The errors assigned all go to the sufficiency of the evidence to support the verdict, and may be considered together.

The jury having found the driver of the jitney bus guilty of negligence, which was the proximate cause of the accident, and occasioned the injuries, then, if there is any evidence in the case from which that conclusion can properly be drawn, the judgment must be affirmed.

An examination of the record reveals that there is evidence tending to show, and from which the jury may have found, that appellants' jitney bus, upon which the injured respondent was a passenger, collided with a mail truck operated by the defendant Wiles & Foy, a corporation, at the intersection of three streets, Olive, Westlake and Fifth avenues, in the city of Seattle; that a semaphore operated by a traffic officer is there maintained, which, when open for traffic on Olive street, closes all traffic on Westlake and Fifth avenues, and when open for Westlake is also open for Fifth avenue, and closed for Olive street. In other words, the semaphore has only the "go" and "stop" signs, which operate identically the same on Westlake and Fifth avenue traffic at all times. The jitney bus was traveling southerly on Westlake avenue, while the mail truck was crossing Westlake diagonally for the purpose of proceeding northwesterly up Fifth avenue. The semaphore showed the "go" sign for both. Under the city ordinance introduced in evidence mail trucks have the right of way over ordinary traffic. The mail truck first entered the intersection of the two streets which also would give it the right of way under the city ordinance. The driver gave the proper signal and there was nothing to obstruct the view of the driver of the approaching jitney. There was also evidence tending to

show that in view of the known density of the traffic at
that point, the driver of the jitney approached and entered the intersection at an excessive rate of speed under all the circumstances; gave no signal which would
warn the driver of the mail truck or call the attention
of his passengers to the situation, so that they could
brace themselves for the blow of the collision which
was impending, and turned his machine to the right
thus striking the rear of the mail truck, while a turn
to the left, or a timely reduction of speed would have
avoided the collision entirely. Under these conditions
which we must assume were the conditions actually
existing, the driver of the jitney bus was clearly bound
to exercise such a degree of care as was necessary to
protect his passengers from injury.

The trial court properly denied the motion for nonsuit, the motion for judgment *non obstante,* and the motion for a new trial, and did not err in entering judgment on the verdict.

The judgment is affirmed.

PARKER, C. J., FULLERTON, MAIN, and MITCHELL, JJ.,
concur.

[No. 16381. Department One. July 28, 1921.]

C. C. HARRIS, *Respondent*, v. NORTHWEST MOTOR COMPANY, *Appellant.*[1]

ELECTION OF REMEDIES (3)—ACTS CONSTITUTING ELECTION—MIS-
TAKE IN REMEDY. There was no election of remedies by a purchaser's action to recover from the seller the price of a car, wrongfully sold by the seller's agent, who was clothed with apparent
authority to sell, which would bar plaintiff's subsequent action of
replevin against defendant, who had seized the car as his own;
since the doctrine of election of remedies applies only in case of
the pursuit of inconsistent remedies against the same party and not
in case of a mistake in originally bringing action against the wrong
party.

EVIDENCE (104)—HEARSAY—STATEMENTS BY OTHER THAN PARTIES
OR WITNESSES—OWNERSHIP OF PROPERTY—COMPETENCY. In an action
of replevin for an automobile, the declaration of the seller of the
car, a former owner, that he was not the owner at the time he made
the sale to plaintiff, but would repurchase it and turn it over to him,
was inadmissible in evidence against plaintiff, though made in his
presence, where there was no showing that plaintiff acquiesced in
the statement and intended to be bound thereby.

PRINCIPAL AND AGENT (34-42)—AUTHORITY OF AGENT—EVIDENCE—
SUFFICIENCY. An automobile sales agent's real or apparent authority to sell second-hand cars, which was denied by defendant, was
properly a question for the jury, in an action of replevin, where the
evidence showed defendant conducted two departments, one for the
sale of new cars and the other for the sale of second-hand cars; that
the agent had received a second-hand car as part payment on the
sale of a new car and had placed the former in the proper department, from which he sold it without accounting to the defendant;
that the agent advertised a second-hand car for sale from his residence, and an inquiry at such place resulted in an authorized representative of defendant calling at the prospective purchaser's place
of business, and stating that the sales agent made a practice of ad-
vertising from his residence as a more likely means of making a
sale of second-hand cars than if they had been advertised from a
public garage or motor company.

SALES (96-99)—RIGHTS OF BUYER AS TO THIRD PERSONS—PROPERTY
OBTAINED BY LARCENY—STATUTES. Rem. Code, § 2129, providing that
"all property obtained by larceny, robbery or burglary shall be re-

[1]Reported in 199 Pac. 992.

turned to the owner, and no sale, whether in good faith on the part
of the purchaser or not shall divest the owner of his rights to such
property," is inapplicable in case of the embezzlement of the proceeds of sale of an automobile by an agent clothed with apparent
authority to make the sale, where the agent did not embezzle the
car itself.

Appeal from a judgment of the superior court for
King county, Jurey, J., entered August 23, 1920, upon
the verdict of a jury rendered in favor of the plaintiff,
in an action of replevin. Affirmed.

Kerr, McCord & Ivey, for appellant.
Ned Roney, for respondent.

Bridges, J.—Suit for possession of an Oakland automobile. The case was tried before a jury, which
rendered its verdict in favor of the plaintiff, and defendant has appealed from the judgment entered
thereon. The controlling facts are as follows: In
September, 1919, Mrs. Grottle, of Seattle, was the
owner of the Oakland car. During that period and
before and after, one C. A. Doty was in the employ
of the appellant as a sales agent of automobiles. As
such agent, he sold to Mrs. Grottle a Hudson car and,
on behalf of the appellant, received the Oakland car
as part payment. After this transaction, Doty sold
the used Oakland car to Compton & Martin, also of
Seattle, who were dealers in second-hand cars. Within
a few days thereafter, Compton & Martin sold the
same car to the respondent. The appellant had knowledge of the sale of the Hudson car to Mrs. Grottle and
the receipt of the Oakland car in part payment, but
it did not know that its agent Doty had sold the Oakland car, because Doty did not account to it for the
sales price. Learning that it did not have the car in
its used car department, the appellant commenced a
search for it and ultimately found it on the streets of

Seattle, where the respondent had left it. Appellant at once took the car into possession and refused to surrender it to the respondent, claiming that it was the owner of the car and that respondent did not have any title to it.

We will first dispose of certain preliminary questions: It appears that, as soon as the respondent learned that the appellant had possession of the Oakland car, he was by the latter put in touch with one of its attorneys, who was also its secretary. As a result of respondent's conference with the attorney, suit was started by him against Compton & Martin, as vendors, for the purchase price, alleging that they did not have title to the car when they sold it to him. Shortly thereafter the respondent, having obtained additional information, changed attorneys, dismissed the suit against Compton & Martin, and instituted this action. The appellant now claims that, by the bringing of the first suit, respondent had elected between remedies, and therefore cannot maintain this action. We cannot agree with this contention. Election of remedies cannot arise under these circumstances because there could not be two or more inconsistent remedies. If Compton & Martin were liable to respondent for the purchase price, the appellant would not be liable to him for the return of the car; and if the appellant were liable for the return of the car, Compton & Martin could not be liable for its purchase price. Here there was nothing more than respondent bringing his action against Compton & Martin for the purchase price, and being later convinced that he had sued the wrong parties, dismissed it and brought this action. There cannot be an election of remedies under such circumstances. 9 R. C. L. 962 lays down the principle as follows:

"The principles governing election of remedies are necessarily based upon the supposition that two or more remedies exist. If in fact or in law only one remedy exists, there can be no election by the pursuit of another and mistaken remedy. It is a well-established rule that the choice of a fancied remedy that never existed and the futile pursuit of it, either because the facts turn out to be different from what the plaintiff supposed them to be, or the law applicable to the facts is found to be other than supposed, though the first action proceeds to judgment, does not preclude the plaintiff from thereafter invoking the proper remedy. And likewise a mere mistake in selecting a wrong party does not preclude a party from asserting liability against the person liable when he is discovered. . . ."

The same rule has been laid down by this court in the case of *Roy v. Vaughan,* 100 Wash. 345, 170 Pac. 1019, where the late Justice Morris, in discussing the question of election of remedies, said:

"Before there can be an election of remedies, there must be two or more inconsistent remedies available to a party, any one of which he is at liberty to pursue. That respondents erroneously believed themselves entitled to the first remedy sought does not prevent them, upon learning that their provable facts were insufficient to maintain that remedy, from seeking another remedy their facts would sustain. A mistake in remedy can never be considered as an election of remedies."

See, also, extensive note to the case of *Clark v. Heath,* 101 Me. 530, 64 Atl. 913, 8 L. R. A. (N. S.) 144.

Appellant strongly relies upon the case of *Pickle v. Anderson,* 62 Wash. 552, 114 Pac. 177, and asserts that the doctrine of that case is contradictory to the doctrine in the case of *Roy v. Vaughan, supra.* We think there is a clear distinction between the two cases, and that the *Pickle* case is not at all controlling of the facts here.

During the progress of the trial the appellant sought to show that at one time Compton & Martin, in the

presence of the respondent, and during the period of
the suit against them, conceded that they were not
the owners of the car, and that appellant was such
owner, and offered to buy it from appellant and turn
it over to respondent in order to make good their obligation
to him. The court announced that he would
refuse to receive such testimony unless appellant
would also show that Compton & Martin had made such
statements with the consent of the respondent, and that
the latter concurred therein and agreed to be bound
thereby. The appellant did not offer any such testimony,
but limited its offer to the fact that Compton
& Martin had made the representations in the presence
of the respondent. We think the ruling of the court
was eminently correct. The respondent had bought
and paid for the car and the only thing he was interested
in was to get possession and good title. It
was, of course, immaterial to him whether Compton
& Martin repurchased the car from the appellant, and
his mere failure to object to such a proposition would
not be sufficient to show that he had concurred in the
representations and intended to be bound by them.
Appellant fails to bring itself within the rule contended
for by it, as contained in 22 C. J. 360, § 421, as
follows:

"Statements of a former owner of personal property,
made after he has parted with his title, are not
admissible in evidence either against the immediate
transferee of the declarant or against a subsequent
owner, unless the person against whom the statement
is sought to be used has acquiesced therein."

The appellant did not offer any testimony even tending
to show that the respondent acquiesced in the representations
or statements made by Compton & Martin.
While the offered testimony might have been compe-

tent in an action between appellant and Compton & Martin, it was not competent in this action.

The appellant further contends that the testimony was wholly insufficient to carry the case to the jury on the main question whether Doty had either the real or apparent authority to sell the used Oakland car to Compton & Martin. Appellant's testimony in this regard was that it had two distinct departments in its business; one being the sale of new automobiles, and the other the sale of second-hand cars obtained by it in the same manner the car in question was obtained, and that the only authority which Doty had was to sell new cars. It is admitted, however, that he had the right to take in second-hand cars in part payment of new cars sold by him. On the other hand, respondent's testimony tended to show that Doty had been employed by appellant for about two years, as its agent in selling cars, and that Compton & Martin knew him as such agent; that, when Doty undertook to sell to Compton & Martin the Oakland car, they supposed that in so doing he was acting as the agent of the appellant, and that nothing occurred at the time of the sale or prior thereto to indicate anything to the contrary. Not very long before the transaction involved here, Doty advertised in the daily papers a used car for sale; such advertisement coming from Doty's private residence. Compton & Martin, in answering this advertisement, telephoned to Doty's residence about the advertised car, and were informed by Mrs. Doty that, at that time, it was down town. Within the next day or two, one of the appellant's duly authorized representatives appeared at the place of business of Compton & Martin in response to their telephone inquiry at the Doty residence. At that time appellant's representative stated to Compton & Martin that Doty was a sales agent of

the appellant, and that he made it a practice to adver-
tise cars from his residence because prospective purchasers would more likely purchase such a car than one
advertised from a public garage or motor company.
There was also other testimony tending to show that
Doty had at least apparent authority to sell the car in
question. The law on this, question is tersely stated in
21 R. C. L. 856, as follows:

"Whenever a principal has placed an agent in such
a situation that a person of ordinary prudence, conversant with business usages, and the nature of the
particular business, is justified in assuming that such
agent is authorized to perform in behalf of his principal the particular act, and such particular act has
been performed, the principal is estopped from denying the agent's authority to perform it."

A similar principle is laid down in 2 C. J. 570, as
follows:

"While as between the principal and the agent the
scope of the latter's authority is that authority which
is actually conferred upon him by his principal, which
may be limited by secret instructions and restrictions,
such instructions and restrictions do not affect
third persons ignorant thereof; and as between
the principal and third persons the mutual rights and
liabilities are governed by the apparent scope of the
agent's authority, which is that authority which the
principal holds the agent out as possessing or which
he permits the agent to represent that he possesses,
and which the principal is estopped to deny, and the
principal will be bound by all acts of the agent performed in the usual and customary mode of doing the
particular business, although he may have acted in
violation of private instructions, unless there is something in the nature of the business or the circumstances
of the case to indicate that the agent is acting under
special instructions or limited powers."

Under these rules there cannot be any question but
that there was ample testimony to carry the case to

the jury on the question of the authority or apparent authority of the agent Doty to dispose of the Oakland car.

The appellant further contends that our recent case of *Linn v. Reid,* 114 Wash. 609, 196 Pac. 13, is controlling of this case in its favor. The facts in the *Linn* case were that he was the owner of a Maxwell car, and while driving it on the public road met two strangers driving a Hudson car. After certain negotiations, Linn traded his car for that which the strangers were driving, and at once surrendered it to them and took possession of their car. These strangers had stolen the Hudson car. Very shortly its owner found it in the possession of Linn and demanded and obtained possession of it. Thereupon Linn, after a search, located his Maxwell car in Reid's possession. The latter refused to surrender it to him and he instituted suit for its recovery. In that case Linn took the position that if it be conceded that the general doctrine is that, in the case of the sale and delivery by the owner of personal property, although he may have been induced to make such sale and delivery by fraudulent acts and representations amounting to a felony by statute, the vendee may convey a good title to a *bona fide* purchaser, yet that general rule had been changed by virtue of § 2129, Rem. Code, which is as follows:

"All property obtained by larceny, robbery or burglary shall be returned to the owner; and no sale, whether in good faith on the part of the purchaser or not, shall divest the owner of his rights to such property."

Linn contended that, inasmuch as the criminal statutes of the state provide that one obtaining property fraudulently and by misrepresentations was guilty of larceny, he was protected by § 2129. We held, however, that, when that section was enacted, the legisla-

ture had in mind the kind of larceny then defined by
the statutes, and that the fact that later statutes had
included other offenses under the head of larceny,
would not authorize the court to enlarge the meaning
of larceny as used in § 2129. But appellant here contends that Doty embezzled the Oakland car, and that,
at the time of the passage of § 2129, embezzlement was
a species of larceny, and consequently it is entitled to
protection under that section. It is our view that
neither the *Linn* case nor § 2129, Rem. Code, have any
bearing on this case. If it had been conceded in this
case, or the jury had found, that Doty had embezzled
the Oakland car, then the *Linn* case might be applicable. But the main question submitted to the jury
was whether Doty had actual or apparent authority, as
appellant's agent, to sell the Oakland car. If he had,
his sale was perfectly valid and there could not be
any question of embezzlement by him of the car. What
Doty embezzled was the money which he received from
the sale of the car and not the car itself.

We do not find any error; the judgment is affirmed.

Parker, C. J., Mackintosh, Fullerton, and Holcomb, JJ., concur.

[No. 16405. Department One. July 28, 1921.]

MRS. FRED ANDERSON, *Respondent*, v. INDUSTRIAL INSURANCE COMMISSION, *Appellant*.[1]

MASTER AND SERVANT (121-2)—WORKMEN'S COMPENSATION—PROXIMATE CAUSE OF DEATH—EVIDENCE—SUFFICIENCY. A widow is entitled to compensation under the workmen's compensation act, where a cut in the foot received by a workman in an extra-hazardous occupation bled profusely, leaving him in a weakened and fainting condition, and after removal to his home, twelve miles distant, in cold and inclement weather, pneumonia developed from which he died; the imprudence of the deceased in exposing himself to the weather in his weakened condition not barring her right, if the axe wound was the proximate cause which directly set in motion a train of events resulting in death (MACKINTOSH, J., dissents).

Appeal from a judgment of the superior court for Grays Harbor county, Sheeks, J., entered November 5, 1920, upon findings in favor of the plaintiff, reversing an order of the industrial insurance commission denying a claim for compensation. Affirmed.

The Attorney General and *John H. Dunbar, Assistant,* for appellant.

J. M. Phillips and *John C. Hogan,* for respondent.

FULLERTON, J.—On December 6, 1919, one Fred Anderson, while engaged in an extra-hazardous occupation, received a cut in the foot from an axe. Immediately after the injury, he was taken to a bunk house located near the place of the accident, where he received first aid. The wound bled somewhat profusely before the bleeding was finally checked, leaving him in a weakened and fainting condition. After the wound was dressed he was placed in bed, but, complaining

[1]Reported in 199 Pac. 747.

of the cold, he was taken to a stove in the bunk house, where a hot fire was burning. The accident happened at about ten o'clock in the morning, and later in the day, possibly about the middle of the afternoon, he desired to be taken to his home, some twelve miles distant. An automobile was called which could not approach the camp nearer than about one mile, and this distance he was compelled to walk. The weather was cold and otherwise inclement at the time, and Mr. Anderson was exposed to it until he arrived at his home at about seven o'clock in the evening. Shortly thereafter his wound was again dressed. At this time he again complained of being cold, and on the same evening had a chill. Two days later he developed a case of lobar pneumonia. His illness immediately became severe, and he died from its effect on December 28, 1919.

After the death of Mr. Anderson, his widow, the present respondent, made application to the industrial insurance commission for compensation. The commission rejected her application, basing its rejection upon the ground that the injury to the foot was not the proximate cause of Mr. Anderson's death. From the order of the board, the respondent appealed to the superior court of Grays Harbor county, and that court reversed the commission's order, directing that her claims be allowed. From the judgment of the superior court, the commission appeals to this court.

There is but little conflict in the evidence. The medical witnesses testify that the axe wound of itself would not cause pneumonia, yet all agree that the wound and the resultant weakened condition of Mr. Anderson rendered him much more susceptible to the disease than he otherwise would have been had he maintained his ordinary robust health. All of them testify moreover, that it was not beyond probability that he acquired pneumonia from his exposure to the weather because of his weakened condition, and some of them testify that it was highly probable that he did do so.

There is, of course, no question of contributory negligence or fault involved. The workmen's compensation act allows compensation regardless of questions of fault, and the fact that Mr. Anderson may have been imprudent in exposing himself to the weather in his weakened condition does not militate against the right of his widow to compensation for his death. Nor is it necessary that the axe wound should have been of itself the cause of the death. It is sufficient if it was the proximate cause—the cause which directly set in motion the train of events which brought about the death.

In our opinion, the evidence justifies this conclusion, and the judgment of the superior court will stand affirmed.

PARKER, C. J., HOLCOMB, and BRIDGES, JJ., concur.
MACKINTOSH, J., dissents.

[No. 16182. *En Banc.* July 28, 1921.]

In the Matter of the Estate of M. F. JONES.

ISABELLA JONES, *Respondent,* v. EVA A. BABCOCK *et al.,*
Appellants.[1]

JUDGMENT (106)—VACATION—ERROR OF LAW. Error of the court
in applying the law to the facts, in making a decree of final distribution of an estate under the provisions of Rem. Code, § 1341, would
constitute an "error of law"; and no distinction can be drawn between judgments in probate and other civil actions, nor from the
fact that an administratrix procured the decree exactly in the form
she asked it.

SAME (106). Under the settled practice of this state not to vacate judgments for error of law that could be corrected on appeal, a
petition for the vacation of a judgment for error of law, discovered
too late to be used on appeal, will not be entertained by the courts,
though apparently sanctioned by Rem. Code, §§ 303, 464, 465.

Appeal from a judgment of the superior court for
King county, Jurey, J., entered January 10, 1920, upon
findings in favor of the plaintiff, in an action to vacate
a judgment, tried to the court. Reversed.

James McCabe (*Hyman Zettler,* of counsel), for
appellants.

Karr & Gregory, H. G. Sutton, and *Burkheimer &
Burkheimer,* for respondent.

MACKINTOSH, J.—In October, 1917, M. F. Jones
died intestate, leaving surviving him a widow, the petitioner herein, who was appointed as administratrix
of his estate. He left surviving him no children, and
no direct descendants; no father, mother, brother, nor
sister, but twelve nieces and nephews, and children
of deceased nieces and nephews. Jones' estate consisted of community and separate property, and in
December, 1918, was in condition for the filing of the

[1]Reported in 199 Pac. 734.

final account and the securing of an order of distribution. In that month such an order was entered upon the petition of the administratrix, and by the order she received all the community property and all the personal property, while the separate real property was distributed one-half to her, as the widow, and one-half to the nieces and nephews and children of deceased nieces and nephews. The estate was administered and distributed upon the theory that these nieces and nephews were entitled, under § 1341, Rem. Code, to one-half of the separate realty of the deceased.

In July, 1919, after the filing of the final account and petition for distribution, the widow, having in the meantime consulted attorneys other than those that represented her in the settlement of her husband's estate, determined that, under § 1341, she was entitled to all of her deceased husband's separate realty, and that the distribution which had been made was erroneous. Therefore, in that month, she filed this her petition to vacate the decree of distribution and sought to have the entire property of the estate awarded her. In this effort she was successful in the lower court, and this appeal has been taken.

The filing of the petition by the respondent for vacation of the decree of distribution is claimed to be sanctioned by Rem. Code, § 303, and subds. 1 and 3 of § 464. To determine whether any such sanction exists is to determine this appeal. It is unnecessary to give to § 1341 of the probate code a determination as to whether the view of the law taken by the respondent during the administration of her husband's estate, or the view which she now contends for, be the correct one. An interesting and close question is presented by the language of that section, but we will assume that respondent's present view correctly interprets the language and meaning of the section, and that the

respondent and the court were in error at the time
the decree of distribution was made. It is incumbent
upon us to inquire into the nature of this mistake,
that is, whether it was a mistake of fact or a mistake
of law. To clear the ground for the question just
stated, it is necessary to first dispose of a few preliminary matters.

In the case of *Morgan v. Williams*, 77 Wash. 343,
137 Pac. 476, this court concisely defined an error of
law as being an "error in applying the law to the facts
as pleaded and established." That is the situation
here. The court had before it the names of nieces and
nephews and children of deceased nieces and nephews,
and referring to § 1341 of the probate code, under
which distribution is to be made, decided, as a matter
of law, that that section entitled these persons to a
share of the Jones' estate.

Argument is made that a distinction is to be drawn
between judgments or decrees entered in actually contested matters, and a decree in a probate proceeding where there has been no contest. The fact that
the administratrix had, as has been alluded to, secured the decree of distribution of which she now complains, exactly in the form in which she asked it, does
not affect the nature of the final decree. This court
has always held that a decree in probate and a judgment in other forms of action are not to be distinguished as to their effect, nor should there be any distinction between them in applying the general rules
as to new trials, vacations of judgment, etc. An error
of law, as we will hereafter show, does not furnish
ground for the vacation of judgment in an ordinary
civil proceeding, and there is no reason why it should
have a different effect in reference to probate decrees.
See *In re McKeever's Estate*, 48 Wash. 429, 93 Pac.
916; *In re Ostlund's Estate*, 57 Wash. 359, 106 Pac.

1116, 135 Am. St. 990; *Alaska Banking & Safe Deposit Co. v. Noyes,* 64 Wash. 672, 117 Pac. 492; *In re Hamilton's Estate,* 108 Wash. 326, 184 Pac. 337; *In re Nilson's Estate,* 109 Wash. 127, 186 Pac. 268.

We come now to the consideration of the question whether a petition for vacation of judgment may be entertained for error of law discovered too late to be used on appeal.

A literal reading òf Rem. Code, §§ 303 and 464, which are as follows:

"And the court may 'upon such terms as may be just, and upon payment of costs, relieve a party or his legal representatives, from a judgment, order or other proceeding taken against him through his mistake, inadvertence, surprise or excusable neglect'." Rem. Code, § 303.

"(1) By granting a new trial for the cause, within the time and in the manner and for any of the causes prescribed by sections relating to new trials.

"(3) For mistakes, neglect or omission of the clerk or irregularity in obtaining the judgment or order." Rem. Code, § 464, subds. 1 and 3.

together with the statutes relating to new trial (Rem. Code, §§ 465 and 399, sub. 7), as follows:

"When the grounds for a new trial could not with reasonable diligence have been discovered before, but are discovered after the term (time) when the verdict, report of referee or decision was rendered or made, the application may be made by petition filed as in other cases, not later than after the discovery, on which notice shall be served and returned, and the defendant held to appear as in the original action, . . . but no motion shall be filed more than one year after the final judgment was rendered." Rem. Code, § 465.

"The former verdict or other decision may be vacated and a new trial granted, on the motion of the party aggrieved, for any of the following causes materially affecting the substantial rights of such party,

"(7) Insufficiency of the evidence to justify the verdict or the decision, or that it is against the law." Rem. Code, § 399, sub. 7.

would seem to substantiate the right of the respondent to file her vacation petition, and respondent's attorneys have added to the mere reading of those sections an argument which is especially logical and persuasive, and did we consider the question an open one, it is probable that the interpretation which they advance would be adopted as the correct one. This court has, however, in so many cases decided that judgments will not be vacated for errors of law that it has become the fixed and settled rule of this state. Although it may not satisfy the strict letter of the law, it does satisfy the spirit thereof, and in the majority of cases it is more conducive to correct and satisfactory results than would be the contrary interpretation. Although never applied to exactly the same facts as are presented here, the rule has been consistently adhered to under the varying states of facts which have arisen in different cases, and it would only introduce confusion where there now exists a rule, established and understood, to make an exception in the present case. These decisions go back to a statement of the principle enunciated in 1 Black, Judgments (2d ed.), § 329:

"The power to vacate judgments, on motion, is confined to cases in which the ground alleged is something extraneous to the action of the court or goes only to the question of the regularity of its proceedings. It is not intended to be used as a means for the court to review or revise its own final judgments, or to correct any errors of law into which it may have fallen. That a judgment is erroneous as a matter of law is ground for an appeal, writ of error, or certiorari, according to the case, but it is no ground for setting aside the judgment on motion."

Some of the cases which have considered this question may be cited as follows: *Tacoma Lumber & Manufacturing Co. v. Wolff*, 7 Wash. 478, 35 Pac. 115, 755; *Bozzio v. Vaglio*, 10 Wash. 270, 38 Pac. 1042; *Dickson v. Matheson*, 12 Wash. 196, 40 Pac. 725; *Green v. Williams*, 13 Wash. 674, 33 Pac. 588; *Burnham v. Spokane Mercantile Co.*, 18 Wash. 207, 51 Pac. 363; *State ex rel. Grady v. Lockhart*, 18 Wash. 531, 52 Pac. 315; *Roberts v. Shelton Southwestern R. Co.*, 21 Wash. 427, 58 Pac. 576; *Kuhn v. Mason*, 24 Wash. 94, 64 Pac. 182; *State v. Boyce*, 25 Wash. 422, 65 Pac. 763; *State ex rel. Stratton v. Tallman*, 29 Wash. 317, 69 Pac. 1101; *Coyle v. Seattle Electric Co.*, 31 Wash. 181, 71 Pac. 733; *State ex rel. Hennessy v. Huston*, 32 Wash. 154, 72 Pac. 1015; *McInnes v. Sutton*, 35 Wash. 384, 77 Pac. 736; *Snohomish Land Co. v. Blood*, 40 Wash. 626, 82 Pac. 933; *Warren v. Hershberg*, 52 Wash. 38, 100 Pac. 149; *National Bank of Commerce v. Kilsheimer & Co.*, 59 Wash. 460, 110 Pac. 15; *Robertson Mtg. Co. v. Magnolia Heights Co.*, 65 Wash. 260, 117 Pac. 1121; *McElroy v. Hooper*, 70 Wash. 347, 126 Pac. 925; *Morgan v. Williams, supra; Faulkner v. Faulkner*, 90 Wash. 74, 155 Pac. 404; *In re Hamilton's Estate* and *In re Nilson's Estate, supra.*

For the reasons stated, the judgment of the lower court was erroneous in vacating the final decree of distribution and is reversed.

PARKER, C. J., BRIDGES, FULLERTON, MAIN, HOLCOMB, TOLMAN, and MITCHELL, JJ., concur.

[No. 16327. Department Two. July 28, 1921.]

ANNA BROWN, *Respondent*, v. J. H. HOFFMAN *et al.*,
Appellants.[1]

SALES (53)—RESCISSION BY BUYER—FRAUD—OPPORTUNITY FOR IN-
SPECTION. Where the sale of a rooming house was induced by false
representations of the seller as to the condition of the business and
its net income, the purchaser would be entitled to rescind the contract, notwithstanding an examination of the property had been
made before its purchase.

Appeal from a judgment of the superior court for
Spokane county, Blake, J., entered February 2, 1920,
in favor of plaintiff, in an action to rescind a contract
for fraud, tried to the court. Affirmed.

E. B. Quackenbush, for appellants.
Frank H. Kinsell, for respondent.

MAIN, J.—The purpose of this action was to rescind
a contract for the purchase of a rooming house in the
city of Spokane and to recover back the portion of the
purchase price which had been paid. The trial resulted
in a decree awarding to the plaintiff the relief sought.
From this judgment, the defendants appeal.

On the 24th day of June, 1918, the appellants were
the owners of a rooming house, and through negotiations conducted by the appellant J. H. Hoffman, the
same was sold to the respondent. The respondent remained in possession approximately one month, when
she notified the appellants of her intention to rescind
the contract, claiming that it had been induced by
fraudulent representations.

In the complaint, a number of false representations
are charged, but upon the trial the issue narrowed

[1] Reported in 199 Pac. 742.

practically as to whether there was a misrepresentation
as to the condition of the business and its net income.
Upon this issue the evidence is in direct conflict. The
trial court made no formal findings, but entered a decree which was equivalent to holding that the contract
had been induced by fraud. It would serve no useful
purpose to discuss the evidence in detail. It is sufficient
to say that, after a careful examination of all the evidence, we are of the opinion that the trial judge reached
the correct conclusion and that his judgment should be
sustained.

This case is very similar to that of *Sowles v. Fleetwood*, 97 Wash. 166, 165 Pac. 1056, where it was held
that the net income of a rooming house was a fact peculiarly within the knowledge of the seller and one upon
which the purchaser had a right to rely, and if misrepresentation as to this fact was made, it would
amount to fraud. So here, the respondent had a right
to rely upon the representation of the seller as to the
net income of the business. If the evidence offered on
behalf of the respondent is to be believed, there was a
serious misstatement of facts in this regard. The income was very materially less than it had been represented to be. The fact that the respondent examined
the property before its purchase does not relieve the
appellant from the charge of fraud, as held in the
Fleetwood case, if there was misrepresentation as to
the net income.

The judgment will be affirmed.

PARKER, C. J., FULLERTON, MITCHELL, and TOLMAN,
JJ., concur.

[No. 16596. Department Two. July 28, 1921.]

THE STATE OF WASHINGTON, *on the Relation of School District No. 102, Spokane County, Plaintiff,* v. C. W. CLAUSEN, *as State Auditor, Respondent.*[1]

SCHOOLS AND SCHOOL DISTRICTS (30)—LIMITATION OF INDEBTEDNESS—COMPUTATION—STATUTES—REPEAL. Laws 1917, p. 587, § 1, (ch. 143) limiting the indebtedness of all taxing districts on the basis of "1½ per centum of the last assessed valuation of the taxable property" in the district (thereby impliedly amending Laws 1909, ch. 97, Rem. Code, § 4607, which permitted school districts to incur indebtedness to 5 per cent of the taxable property in such districts) was not itself superseded by a later amendment of Rem. Code, § 4607, by Laws 1919, ch. 90, § 12, which, following the method of amending statutes prescribed by the constitution, set out the section as amended, and thus restated the portions which conflicted with the 1917 act.

STATUTES (47)—IMPLIED REPEAL—BY AMENDATORY ACT—AMENDMENT—EFFECT ON INTERVENING ACT. Where an act has been in part impliedly repealed and superseded by a conflicting act on the same subject, the subsequent amendment of the earlier act in the constitutional method of amending laws, without mention of the intervening act, does not amend or repeal by implication such intervening act so as to restore the conflicting portions of the first act.

Application filed in the supreme court June 8, 1921, for a writ of mandate to compel the state auditor to issue a warrant for bonds of a school district. Denied.

Wm. C. Meyer and *Clarence A. Orndorff,* for relator.

The Attorney General and *M. H. Wight,* for respondent.

MITCHELL, J.—The relator, School District No. 102 of Spokane county, seeks a writ of mandate to compel the respondent, C. W. Clausen, as state auditor, to issue a warrant in the sum of $45,000 for bonds of the school district it is alleged the state board of finance is

[1]Reported in 199 Pac. 752.

obligated to take. The controversy arises because of
diverse views as to the legality of the bonds with reference to the statutory limit of indebtedness. The contention of the relator is that the limit of indebtedness of
a school district is five per cent of the taxable property
in the district, while the respondent contends that it is
five per cent of the last assessed valuation of the taxable property in the district. If the relator's contention is correct, the writ must issue; otherwise, it must
be denied.

Section 1, p. 324, ch. 97, Laws of 1909 (Rem. & Bal.
Code, § 4607; Rem. Code, § 4607), empowered the board
of directors of any school district to borrow money and
issue negotiable coupon bonds therefor to any amount
not to exceed five per cent of the taxable property in
such district, as shown by the last assessment roll for
county and state purposes previous to the incurring of
such indebtedness, when authorized by a vote of the district so to do. Similar language was considered in the
case of *Hansen v. Hoquiam*, 95 Wash. 132, 163 Pac. 391,
wherein it was held that the constitutional limit of indebtedness of five per cent on the total value of the taxable property, to be ascertained by the last assessment
for state and county purposes previous to the incurring
of such indebtedness, does not mean five per cent of the
assessed valuation, where the assessing officers assess
property at fifty per cent of its value, but means five
per cent of its actual value, or that per cent of twice its
assessed value. Promptly, after that decision, the legislature enacted a law (Laws of 1917, p. 587, ch. 143),
which provides as follows:

"Section 1. No taxing district shall for any purpose
become indebted in any manner to an amount exceeding
one and one-half per centum of the last assessed valuation of the taxable property in such taxing district,

without the assent of three-fifths of the voters therein voting at an election to be held for that purpose, nor in cases requiring such assent shall the total indebtedness at any time exceed five per centum of the last assessed valuation of the taxable property in such taxing district: . . ."

Section 4 of the act (Laws of 1917, p. 589) defines the term "taxing district" to mean and embrace "all counties, cities, towns, townships, port districts, school districts, metropolitan park districts or other municipal corporations which now, or may hereafter exist."

Because of the well established rule, for which there is an abundance of authority, we think it must be held that the statute of 1917 superseded that portion of § 1, p. 324, ch. 97, Laws of 1909, with reference to the basis for computing the limit of indebtedness, because of the positive conflict between the two statutes; so that, after the effective date of the act of 1917, the limit of indebtedness of a school district was five per cent of the last assessed valuation of the taxable property in such district, rather than five per cent of the taxable property therein. We understand that counsel on both sides agree that such was the effect of the act of 1917. Thereafter, the legislature of 1919 (ch. 90), without directly or otherwise referring to the act of 1917, and following the form prescribed in the constitution, amended § 1, p. 324, ch. 97, Laws of 1909—Rem. & Bal. Code, § 4607. Chapter 90, p. 216, § 12, of the act of 1919, commences: "That § 4607 of Remington & Ballinger's Annotated Codes and Statutes of Washington be amended to read as follows:" Then follows therein, so far as it is material in the present case, a repetition of the words of the former statute to which the amendment is addressed concerning the power of the board of directors of any school district to borrow money and issue negotiable

coupon bonds therefor to any amount not to exceed five
per cent of the taxable property of such district, as
shown by the last assessment roll for county and state
purposes previous to the incurring of such indebtedness, when authorized by a vote of the district so to do,
and there is added in the amendment, *inter alia*, a proviso, "that from and after July 1, 1919, all bonds issued by any school district shall be issued in serial
form". And it is argued for the relator that the
amendment necessarily repeals and supersedes that
portion of the act of 1917 relating to school districts,
so that the limit of indebtedness of such districts is now
determined upon the basis of the taxable property in
the district rather than upon the assessed valuation
thereof—that the amendment in the fullness of its text
and terms is the law, so far as school districts are concerned, as if the statute of 1917 had never been enacted.

There is a conflict of authority as to whether a section which has been repealed can be amended. 25
R. C. L., p. 905, § 157; 36 Cyc. 1055; Lewis' Sutherland
Statutory Construction (2d. ed.), § 233. The authorities show, however, that "the question usually arises
where a section of an act is amended 'to read as follows', and is then again amended in the same manner
and by the same description, ignoring the first amendment". 25 R. C. L., p. 905, § 157.

We need not, nor do we, take sides in this conflict of
opinion, for, in the last analysis, the question here is
not if such an amendment can be made, but what is the
effect of such an amendment. In considering this precise question it will be noticed: (1) That the original
law, 1909, consisted of two important particulars,
among others, viz: the issuance of bonds not exceeding
five per cent of the taxable property in the district when
authorized by a vote of the district, and that the bonds

should bear interest at not to exceed six per cent per annum, payable annually or semi-annually, the bonds to mature as designated in the bonds not to exceed twenty years; (2) that the act of 1917, by necessary implication, repealed that part of the 1909 act by which the basis of valuation was changed from the value of the property to the assessed valuation of the property; and (3) that the amendatory act of 1919 repeated the provisions of the act of 1909 relating to the issuance of bonds not exceeding five per cent of the taxable property of the district when authorized by a vote of the district; it repeated the provision with reference to the rate and payment of interest, changed the wording of the old law as to the maturity of bonds, providing a greater length of time therefor, and in districts of the first class, where bonds were issued for certain specified purposes, the bonds should be made payable in semi-annual installments beginning the third year over any period not exceeding forty years; and added by further proviso that all bonds issued by any school district shall be issued in serial form. These were new and important changes and extensions in the amendatory act over the terms of the original act, upon particulars altogether foreign to the terms and purpose of the intervening act of 1917. The 1919 act was not a new and independent one, strictly speaking, but it took the form of an amendatory act.

Section 37, art. 2, of the constitution, provides: "No act shall ever be revised or amended by mere reference to its title, but the act revised or the section amended shall be set forth at full length". The reasons for this limitation upon the mode or form in which the legislative power to amend a law shall be exercised are elaborately expressed in the case of *Spokane Grain & Fuel Co. v. Lyttaker*, 59 Wash. 76, 109 Pac. 316, and authorities therein cited, and need not be repeated here. In construing the amendment of 1919, it is manifest that the use or repetition therein of language found in the original act, including that relating to the basis of the valuation of property of the district upon which the five per cent limit of indebtedness should be computed, which in no way interfered with the revisions and extensions the legislature desired and intended to accomplish by the amendment, was but a vehicle or means mandatorily required by the constitution. By repeating the language of the old law, it cannot be held that the legislature thereby repealed by implication the act of 1917 which necessarily repealed that portion of the old law fixing the basis of valuation of the property of a school district, and recreated the old law upon that particular feature (thus discriminating in favor of school districts over all other taxing districts of the state), since, as already observed, the legislature in 1919 was then engaged only in the process of amendment—that is, declaring for the first time certain things to be the law, impossible of achievement by amendment of a former law, under the inhibition of the constitution, except in the manner actually employed. To ascertain the effect of the amendment, it, in the light of the manner the constitution prescribes an amendment shall be effected, the old law amended, and the act of 1917 which changed the old law in one particular—the one particular here involved—must all be considered together.

McLaughlin v. Newark, 57 N. J. L. 298, presented a situation wherein the legislature of New Jersey amended an act concerning wards and district lines in the cities of the state. Intervening the original and amendatory acts, the legislature passed an independent act providing for the formation and establishment of wards in cities of the first class; and in presenting the

case to the court it was contended by counsel that the
original act and the intermediate one were inconsistent
and that the amendatory act evinced a purpose to repeal whatever laws were at that date inconsistent with
the original act. The court, after stating that, under
the constitution, an amended section must be recited at
length in the amended act, decided the case as follows:
"By observing the constitutional form of amending a
section of a statute the legislature does not express an
intention then to enact the whole section as amended,
but only an intention then to enact the change which is
indicated. Any other rule of construction would surely
introduce unexpected results and work great inconvenience." It was held the intermediate act was unim-
paired.

In the case of *Gordon v. People,* 44 Mich. 485, 7
N. W. 69, there was considered the effect of an amenda-
tory act upon an intervening act not referred to in the
amendatory act. In the opinion written by Judge
Campbell, concurred in by the other judges including
Judge Cooley, it was said:

"No one would claim for a moment that if § 7569 had
been amended as was formerly the custom—not by re-
publishing it as changed, but only by showing for what
part the new clause was substituted—any effect would
be produced on the remainder of the section. The
constitutional provision requiring amendments to be
made by setting out the whole section as amended was
not intended to make any different rule as to the effect of such amendments. So far as the section is
changed it must receive a new operation, but so far as
it is not changed it would be dangerous to hold that the
merely nominal re-enactment should have the effect of
disturbing the whole body of statutes *in pari materia*
which had been passed since its first enactment. There
must be something in the nature of the new legislation
to show such an intent with reasonable clearness before

an implied repeal can be recognized. Repeals by implication should not be established without satisfactory reason to believe such was the legislative will."

It appears in *Spokane Grain & Fuel Co. v. Lyttaker, supra,* by a quotation from *Warren v. Crosby,* 24 Ore. 558, 34 Pac. 661, that Oregon has a constitutional provision similar to ours. The case of *Small v. Lutz,* 41 Ore. 570, 67 Pac. 421, discusses a situation similar to those above referred to in the states of New Jersey and Michigan and reaches the same conclusion, citing therein other authorities.

The conclusion is that the amendatory act did not restore the provision of the old act, and that the law of 1917 declaring that the limit of indebtedness that may be authorized by a vote of a taxing district, including a school district, is five per cent of the last assessed valuation of the taxable property in such district remains controlling and unrepealed.

Writ denied.

PARKER, C. J., TOLMAN, and MAIN, JJ., concur.

[No. 16332. Department One. July 28, 1921.]

In the Matter of the PESHASTIN IRRIGATION DISTRICT.
BOARD OF DIRECTORS, PESHASTIN IRRIGATION DISTRICT,
Respondent, v. S. P. BEECHER *et al., Appellants.*[1]

WATERS (89)—IRRIGATION DISTRICTS—PROCEEDINGS TO ESTABLISH—
PUBLICATION OF NOTICES—SUFFICIENCY. The notices for the hearing
of a petition and for an election for the organization of an irrigation
district may properly be published in a newspaper of general circulation in the vicinity of the proposed district instead of in the designated official newspaper of the county, in view of Rem. Code, § 6417,
providing that it may be made in any newspaper of general circulation in the county, selected by the person or body charged with making the publication, which shall be the official newspaper for such
purpose.

SAME (89)—NOTICE—DESCRIPTION OF BOUNDARIES. A notice of
election for the creation of an irrigation district sufficiently describes courses and distances in establishing the district boundaries
by a designation of one point as "the most northerly point of lot 3,
Peshastin Orchard," and another point as "the northwest corner of
lot 6, Springdale Orchards," where the plats of such tracts were of
record in the county auditor's office, and the boundary of the district
was described in the notice as commencing at a specified point with
reference to a section corner of a specified township and range in
the county.

SAME (89)—PETITION—ORDER ESTABLISHING DISTRICT—FILING OR-
DER. Under Rem. Code, § 6490, as amended by Laws 1917, ch. 162,
p. 723, a petition for the confirmation by the superior court of proceedings organizing an irrigation district is only required to "state
generally that the irrigation district was duly organized," and need
not recite that a certified copy of the order of the county commissioners finally establishing the district was filed with the county
clerk pursuant to Id., § 6418, as amended by Laws 1917, ch. 162.

SAME (91)—BONDS—SUBMISSION TO VOTERS. Where the only
questions submitted to the voters of an irrigation district under a
notice calling an election to authorize a bond issue were the obtaining of additional water for irrigation and for the construction, reconstruction, betterment, extension and acquisition of the necessary
rights and property therefor, it was immaterial that a prior resolution of the board had also contemplated the submission of the question of raising funds for operating purposes.

[1] Reported in 200 Pac. 88.

SAME   (89) — PROCEEDINGS — CONFIRMATION — PETITION — SUFFI-
CIENCY. Where a petition for the confirmation of the organization
of an irrigation district fails to recite the publication of a notice for
a bond election, if conceded as necessary under Rem. Code, § 6490,
as amended by Laws 1917, ch. 162, the petition will be deemed
amended to correspond to the proof, where the fact of proper publication appears in the evidence.

SAME (89)—CONFIRMATION—ILLEGAL USE OF FUNDS. In a proceeding to confirm the organization of an irrigation district and its
proposed bond issue, any threatened illegal disposition of the proceeds of the bond issue is not a proper matter for consideration,
that being a matter for adjudication on the equity side of the court.

Appeal from a judgment of the superior court for
Chelan county, Allen, J., entered April 16, 1920, upon
findings in favor of the plaintiff, confirming proceedings for the organization of an irrigation district, and
for the issuance of bonds, tried to the court. Affirmed.

Ludington & Shiner and *Herman Howe,* for appellants.

Corbin & Easton and *Walter H. Hodge,* for respondent.

PARKER, C. J.—This is a special proceeding commenced in the superior court for Chelan county by the
board of directors of the Peshastin Irrigation District,
in that county, under §§ 6489-6493, Rem. Code, as
amended by chapter 162, Laws of 1917, p. 723, seeking
a decree confirming the proceedings for the organization of the district and the proceedings for the issuance
of bonds of the district in pursuance of an election held
for that purpose. S. P. Beecher and wife, owners of
land within the district, filed their answer resisting
confirmation of the proceeding as petitioned for by the
board of directors of the district. Thus, as provided by
§ 6492, Rem. Code, there arose this controversy, in
which the board of directors became the plaintiff and
Beecher and wife the defendants. A trial upon the

merits in the superior court, as between these parties, resulted in findings and a decree confirming the organization of the district and the proceedings therefor, and also confirming the proceedings for the issuance of the bonds of the district. From this disposition of the cause in the superior court, the defendants Beecher and wife have appealed to this court.

By the provisions of § 6417, Rem. Code, it is required, in the proceedings for the organization of an irrigation district, that two notices be published; a notice of the hearing before the county commissioners upon the petition of the owners of land within the proposed district, at which hearing the boundaries of the proposed district are finally determined and an election ordered by the county commissioners upon the question of whether or not the district shall be organized; and a notice of the election so ordered. These required notices were published in the Cashmere Valley Record, a weekly newspaper published at Cashmere, very near the proposed district and of general circulation in that neighborhood, and were not published in the newspaper which had been designated generally by the county commissioners as the official newspaper of the county; that newspaper being published at Wenatchee, several miles distant from the district. The publication of these notices in a newspaper other than the general official county newspaper, it is contended in appellants' behalf, constitutes a fatal defect in the proceedings, rendering the organization of the district void. We cannot agree with this contention. The concluding language of § 6417, Rem. Code, which section requires the publication of such notices, reads:

" . . . where in this act publication is required to be made in a newspaper of any county, the same may be made in any newspaper of general circu-

lation in any such county, selected by the person or
body charged with making the publication and such
newspaper shall be the official paper for such purpose.''

We do not find in the record before us any specific
order or direction made by the county commissioners
that these notices were to be published in any specified
newspaper. We think we may assume, therefore, that,
since they are to be given by the county auditor, they
were published in the Cashmere Valley Record by direction of that officer; and we note that recitals in the
subsequent proceedings by the county commissioners
plainly indicate that such publication was approved by
that body; indeed, there is a strong inference that that
body directed these notices to be published in the Cashmere Valley Record, though, as we have noticed, there
seems to have been no specific order made of record to
that effect. We are of the opinion that, in view of the
concluding language of § 6417, Rem. Code, above
quoted, the notices were lawfully published in the Cashmere Valley Record. It is not claimed that the notices were not fairly given, or failed to furnish ample
opportunity for all interested persons to be heard before the county commissioners and vote at the election.
Indeed, the location of the publication of the Cashmere
Valley Record in the immediate neighborhood of the
district strongly suggests that that paper was a more
appropriate paper for the publication of these notices
than the general official paper of the county would have
been.

It is further contended in behalf of appellants that
the description of the boundaries of the district in the
petition of the landowners, the notice of election and
the order of the county commissioners finally establishing its boundaries, is fatally defective. The boundary
description of the district found in these documents

commences at a specified point with reference to a section corner of a specified township and range in that
county, and proceeds therefrom by courses and distances to designated points and finally to the place of
beginning. One of these points is designated as "the
most northerly point of lot 3, Peshastin Orchard, Chelan county, Washington," and another as "the northwest corner of lot 6, Springdale Orchards, Chelan county, Washington." An engineer and surveyor of long
experience in surveying and tracing boundaries in Chelan county, testified in substance that the boundary description of the district as set forth in the petition and
order could be traced and located upon the ground, providing "that the points given as corners of lots of orchards are a matter of record." The county auditor
testified without objection that there were upon record
in his office official plats designated as "Peshastin Orchards" and "Springdale Orchards," but that he was
unable to say, not having the records before him at the
trial, in what section, township or range such orchard
plats were located. The argument of counsel for appellants is directed only to the supposed uncertainty
of location upon the ground of these two designated
points in Peshastin and Springdale orchards, and is in
substance that these points are rendered uncertain because of the fact that the county auditor was unable to
say in what township or range they are located, but
manifestly the other language of the description of the
boundary of the district renders it sufficiently fixed and
certain upon the ground to put them in a section, township and range that will make them fit the balance of
the boundary description. We are quite convinced that
the evidence at least makes a sufficient *prima facie*
showing to warrant the conclusion that these questioned points are capable of being located upon the

ground with sufficient certainty to satisfy the statute as to description of the boundary of the district. Our decision in *In re Wenatchee Reclamation District,* 91 Wash. 60, 157 Pac. 38, lends support to this conclusion.

It is further contended in behalf of appellants that the initial petition filed in the superior court in this proceeding by the directors of the district fails to show that a certified copy of the order of the county commissioners finally establishing the district was filed with the county clerk of Chelan county as required by § 6418, Rem. Code, as amended by ch. 162, Laws of 1917. The answer to this contention is found in the fact that § 6490, Rem. Code, as amended by ch. 162, Laws of 1917, p. 723, specifying what shall be alleged in the petition, does not require any such allegation, but only that the petition "shall state generally that the irrigation district was duly organized." It is plain from the record before us that a certified copy of the order of the county commissioners, finally establishing the district, was timely filed with the county clerk; though that fact does not appear in the petition.

It is further contended in appellants' behalf that the proceedings for the bond election are fatally defective in that there was submitted to the voters of the district the question of expending funds to be raised by the issuance of bonds, for the purpose of operating the irrigation system of the district; as well as the question of expending the funds to be raised by the issuance of the bonds for construction, betterment and extension of the irrigation system of the district. We may assume for present purposes that the statute (Rem. Code, § 6490, as amended by ch. 162, Laws of 1917, p. 723), does not authorize the raising of funds by the issuance of bonds of the district, to be expended in the operation of its irrigation system. In the resolution of the board of directors of the district providing for the holding of this bond election, it is true we find recited, among other things, that

"Whereas there are no funds of said Peshastin Irrigation District with which to so purchase, acquire, construct, reconstruct, better and extend and operate said irrigation system . . .; and

"Whereas the board of directors of the said Peshastin Irrigation District has caused to be made a careful estimate to determine the amount of funds necessary to be raised for the above purposes, and that such estimate is the sum of One Hundred Thousand Dollars ($100,000), . . .

"Be it further resolved that the said board of directors of said district do hereby call a special election for the purpose of voting on the question as to whether or not bonds of said Peshastin Irrigation District shall be issued in the amount above specified; . . ."

In the notice of election, however, following the adoption of this resolution, which notice of election was signed by all of the directors of the district, it is stated that the election is to be held

" . . . for the purpose of determining whether or not the bonds of said Peshastin Irrigation District in the amount of One Hundred Thousand Dollars ($100,000) shall be issued for the purpose of obtaining additional water with which to irrigate the lands in said district and for the construction, re-construction, betterment, extension and acquisition of the necessary property and rights therefor, . . ."

There is no mention whatever made in the notice of election that the proposition submitted to the voters included the raising or expenditure of funds for the operation of the district's irrigation system; so that when we critically examine the record of the proceedings of the board of directors, it appears that the question of raising or expending money for the operation of the irrigation system of the district was not submitted to the electors of the district; and that the board of directors abandoned all purpose of issuing the bonds to raise any funds for such purpose. Indeed, the notice of election, signed by all of the directors, seems to us to plainly evidence a rescission of any such purpose as may have been evidenced by its former resolution. A critical reading of the findings, conclusions and decree of the trial court we think renders it plain that the proceedings looking to the bond election and the issuance of the bonds were confirmed by the trial court upon the theory and assumption that there was no ultimate intention or purpose on the part of the directors of the district to submit to the voters of the district the question of so raising funds for the operation of its irrigation system, or to use any of the funds which might be so raised for any such purpose.

It is further contended in appellants' behalf that the petition filed by the board of directors of the district in this proceeding, asking confirmation of their proceedings, was defective in that it failed to affirmatively specifically allege the publication of a notice of the bond election. In view of the provisions of § 6490, Rem. Code, as amended by ch. 162, Laws of 1917, p. 723, we think that it was not necessary to specifically plead such fact in the petition. In any event, the proof shows a proper publication of such notice, and we must presume the petition to have been amended to fit such proof, in so far as such an amendment was necessary.

It is finally contended in appellants' behalf that the issuance of the bonds as proposed would be for a purpose which, because of legal obstacles, could not be carried out by the directors of the district. Whatever might be said of this contention were this a suit in equity seeking to restrain the commissioners from ex-

pending funds to be raised from this bond issue, in
some threatened manner, we think it has no place in
this case. Much argument is indulged in by counsel
for appellants, based upon evidence in the case, which
was admitted over the objection of counsel for the
board of directors, rested upon the theory that there is
disclosed by the evidence a threat on the part of the
board of directors to expend the proceeds of this bond
issue for purposes that would be illegal. We think we
are not concerned here, however, with the question of
any threat of the board of directors to make such illegal
expenditures of the funds to be raised by the bond issue. What we are here concerned with is, were the
proceedings leading up to the confirmation of the district and this bond election regular and valid? The
matters to be decided by the court in this special proceeding are set forth in § 6493, Rem. Code, as amended
by ch. 162, Laws of 1917, p. 723, as follows:

"Upon the hearing of such special proceedings, the
court shall have full power and jurisdiction to examine
and determine the legality and validity of and approve
and confirm each and all of the proceedings for the
organization of said district under the provisions of
this chapter, from and including the petition for the
organization of the district, and all other proceedings
which may affect the legality of the formation of said
district or the legality or validity of said bonds, and
the order for the sale, and the sale thereof, and all proceedings which may affect the authorization or validity
of contract with the United States."

Our attention is not directed to any provision of the
statute—and we think there is none—requiring the
board of directors of the district to submit for approval or disapproval to the electors of the district the plan
of construction, betterment and extension of the irrigation system, for which the money to be raised by
bond issue shall be expended; except such expenditure

involve the entering into a contract with the United
States, a matter with which we are not here concerned.
We think the court rightfully refrained from deciding
any question touching a supposed threat of the directors of the district to unlawfully use the funds which
might be raised from the issuance of the bonds. The
courts, on their equity side, are still open for the adjudication of any such question.

We are of the opinion that the decree of the superior
court must be affirmed. It is so ordered.

HOLCOMB, FULLERTON, MACKINTOSH, and BRIDGES,
JJ., concur.

[No. 16364. Department Two. July 28, 1921.]

DWYER & COMPANY, *Respondent*, v. THE CITY OF
SEATTLE *et al., Appellants.*[1]

GAMING (10)—DEVICES PROHIBITED—SLOT MACHINES. A machine
known as a "silent salesman," containing 3,000 tickets purchasable
for five cents each as they appear in the slots of the machine, the
large majority of which entitle the purchaser to nothing more than
a postal card of the value of one cent, some few of the tickets entitling the purchaser to articles of merchandise of considerably
more value, is a gaming device within the inhibition of the Seattle
ordinances and the statutes of the state against gaming devices.

Appeal from a judgment of the superior court for
King county, French, J., entered November 9, 1920, in
favor of the plaintiff, in an action for an injunction,
tried to the court. Reversed.

Walter F. Meier and *George A. Meagher,* for appellants.

Robinson, Murphy & Murphine, for respondent.

TOLMAN, J.—This action was instituted by respondent for the purpose of obtaining an injunction restrain-

[1]Reported in 199 Pac. 740.

ing the city of Seattle and its officers from interfering with the operation of a certain device known as the "Silent Salesman", of which Dwyer & Company is the lessee, and Joseph F. Dwyer, who intervened by permission of the court below, is the patentee and owner. From a decree as prayed for, the city and its officers, who were made defendants, appeal.

Briefly stated, the record reveals the following facts: Joseph F. Dwyer is the patentee, owner and proprietor of the device in question, and Dwyer & Company, a Washington corporation, is the lessee from Joseph F. Dwyer of all rights necessary to enable it to place the machines, with the tickets and merchandise used therewith, in the hands of those who operate places of business where men resort, and where it is likely to be used by the public. Each machine has five compartments or "slots", in each of which is placed a roll containing 600 tickets, numbered from 1 to 600, consecutively, but in inverse order, so that the first ticket drawn from each roll is numbered 600, and the last is numbered 1, and anyone can determine at a glance how many tickets remain upon each roll. Title to the machine remains at all times in Joseph F. Dwyer. Dwyer & Company place the machine with the local merchant, sell him three thousand tickets, and what purports to be $150 worth of merchandise, for $105, and the merchant's profit thereon is $45, or the difference between the $150 obtained from the sale of the three thousand tickets, at five cents each, and the $105 which he pays for the tickets and for the merchandise which is to be delivered to the players of the machine as the tickets are drawn. Each ticket has printed on its face:

"POST CARD 5c

"Purchaser agrees before sale that the complete transaction is for 5 cts. and that no option on, nor interest in the following offer is involved or implied. No agent has authority to change this agreement. Drawing sales tickets accepts the condition. Copyright 1920. Joseph F. Dwyer.''

As the machine stands ready for operation, the first ticket on each roll is in plain view of the one about to operate the device, but all subsequent tickets are concealed from view. As a ticket is drawn from either roll, the next succeeding ticket upon that roll is brought into view, and at irregular intervals, in addition to the printed matter quoted, there is printed with a rubber stamp upon a ticket the name of some article of merchandise worth much more than five cents, such as "electric heater," "camera", "briar pipe," "robe," and the like, and these articles or prizes are listed and displayed in proximity to the machine where they will attract the attention of the public and convey the idea that, by operating or playing the machine, one may obtain much more than the worth of his money. Needless to say that, as one approaches the machine, he sees exposed to view five tickets, each in a separate compartment, and each or either of which entitles him, by the payment of five cents, to a post card worth one cent (no prize ticket ever being left in view by the preceding player), but the suggestion is held out that by drawing one of these tickets, he may thereby bring into view, subject to immediate withdrawal upon the payment of another five cents, a ticket calling for a camera, or some article of considerable value; and the record reveals that, in actual operation, it is the custom of each player to buy not one, but three, five or more tickets before beginning to operate the device, in the hope that by buying one or more post cards, at five cents each, he may thereby gain an opportunity to obtain an expensive camera or a handsome pipe, or some other article of considerable value, for a like nominal sum.

The facts as stated supply their own argument, and demonstrate beyond question that, in its practical operation, this ingenious device is intended to, and does, appeal to the gambling instinct or habit, and were 'there none inclined to take chances in the hope of getting "something for nothing" there would be no tickets sold, and the machine would never be operated.

In no reported case from a court of last resort, so far as we are advised, has this particular device been passed upon, but it is so plainly a gaming device, and as such so clearly falls within the inhibition of our statute, and the ordinance of the city of Seattle, that no authorities are necessary to support the conclusion we here reach.

Remanded and reversed with directions to dismiss the action.

PARKER, C. J., MAIN, and MITCHELL, JJ., concur.

[No. 16435. Department One. July 28, 1921.]

ANGELA NORMILE, *Appellant*, v. ANNIE DENISON, *Individually and as Executrix of the Estate of S. Normile, Respondent.*[1]

DIVORCE (50-1)—JUDGMENT (227)—RES JUDICATA—MATTERS CONCLUDED—PROPERTY RIGHTS. Although the complaint of the wife in an action for divorce alleged that the parties "have made between themselves a complete adjustment and settlement of their property rights," a decree of divorce confirming their division of the community real estate, without attempting to dispose of their community personalty or mention of the agreement, which was not pleaded, and which was void for fraudulent concealment, is not *res adjudicata* as to personal property rights, and would not bar her from maintaining a subsequent action for the division of community personalty the existence of which had been fraudulently concealed from her at the time of the agreement between the spouses.

[1]Reported in 199 Pac. 995.

WITNESSES (44) — COMPETENCY — TRANSACTIONS WITH PERSON
SINCE DECEASED. In an action by a divorced wife to recover one-
half of community personal property fraudulently concealed from
her by her husband at the time of a property division agreement between them, her testimony that she relied upon the statements made
to her and obtained from other witnesses who testified as to representations made by her husband, since deceased, without attempting
to testify as to what was said by the latter, would not come within
the statutory prohibition against testifying as to transactions with a
deceased person.

Appeal from a judgment of the superior court for
King county, Wilmon Tucker, judge *pro tempore*, entered November 29, 1920, upon findings in favor of the
defendant, in an action to recover a community interest
in property. Reversed.

Preston, Thorgrimson & Turner, for appellant.

*Gill, Hoyt & Frye, Chadwick, McMicken, Ramsey &
Rupp,* and *John P. Garvin,* for respondent.

PER CURIAM.—The law of this case was practically
settled in nearly all respects in a former appeal, reported in 109 Wash. 205, 186 Pac. 305. Upon the going
down of the remittitur on the former appeal, issues
were settled by the filing of an answer containing denials and affirmative allegations, and an appropriate
reply thereto.

At the trial the evidence on behalf of the appellant
practically followed the allegations of the amended
and supplemental complaint, which we held in the former appeal stated a cause of action, and there was
very little contradiction of such evidence.

On behalf of respondent it was pleaded and shown
that, on the same day that the second contract was
entered into, referred to in the decision on the former
appeal, March 28, 1917, appellant began an action for
divorce against the deceased, S. Normile, in which she
alleged, among other things, that she and the defend-

ant "have made between themselves a complete adjustment and settlement of their property interests." This allegation in the divorce proceedings was admitted in the answer, and the decree in the divorce proceeding confirmed the division between the parties of the real property which had been divided between them, as made by them. There was no attempt made to dispose of the personal property in the divorce case, nor any notice taken thereof by the divorce court.

Upon this appeal three propositions are vigorously asserted by respondent, namely: (1) that appellant is estopped by the divorce proceedings from maintaining this action; (2) that the agreement of March 28, 1917, is binding upon the appellant; (3) that, even though the agreement of March 28, 1917, be cancelled and disregarded, appellant has received her full share of the property.

The second proposition was decided adversely to respondent in our former decision. The third proposition is not sustained by the evidence.

The first proposition deserves some discussion. Respondent contends that, in the divorce proceeding, it became an admitted and adjudicated issue between the parties by virtue of the allegations in the complaint, the admission in the answer, and the reference thereto in the decree, that there was a complete property division between the parties. It is admitted, however, that it is not necessary in a divorce proceeding that the property rights of the parties be adjudicated; but that, where the property question is brought before the divorce court by complaint, answer or cross-complaint, the court acquires jurisdiction of the property interests of the parties. *Ambrose v. Moore*, 46 Wash. 463, 90 Pac. 588, 11 L. R. A. (N. S.) 103. And it is contended, therefore, that, where the property question is before the court, the adjudication in the divorce court will be deemed final and conclusive upon the questions which were or could have been litigated (*Averbuch v. Averbuch,* 80 Wash. 257, 141 Pac. 701, Ann. Cas. 1916 B. 873), and that the parties are estopped from taking any inconsistent or contradictory position with reference thereto. *In re Clifford,* 37 Wash. 460, 79 Pac. 1001, 107 Am. St. 819.

It is further contended that this proceeding is, in effect, a collateral attack against the divorce proceeding.

Respondent is in error in assuming that there was a complete adjudication of the property rights in the divorce proceedings. The agreements entered into between the parties prior to the institution of the divorce suit were not brought into the proceedings in that case in any way except by the mere reference to the property settlement which had been made by the parties. The divorce court did not dispose of the personal property of the parties in any way, but did confirm the division of the real estate.

There is no dispute but that the settlement of the property rights between the parties referred to in the divorce complaint was the agreement of March 28, 1917. That agreement, we held on the former appeal, with the facts concerning the inducements and the concealment of property not included therein, was subject to being attacked and set aside for the fraudulent concealment. The divorce proceedings could not have confirmed that contract unless the contract had been alleged and one or the other of the parties asked that it be annulled or confirmed, and the divorce court had acted thereon. Such, as we have seen, was not the case.

We therefore conclude that the appellant is not estopped by the proceedings and the decree in the divorce case. For a further and more convincing argument to sustain the right of appellant to recovery, see the opinion on the former appeal, *supra*.

It is also contended that the testimony of the appellant, that in making the contract of March 28, 1917, she relied upon representations made to her, is incompetent and should be disregarded.

Appellant did not attempt to testify what was said to her by her deceased husband. Some of the statements as to his property were proven by other witnesses, and appellant testified that she also gained information from Mr. Hoyt, who was the attorney for Normile; and Mr. Preston, who was her attorney, testified as to information gained from Mr. Hoyt, who had a statement of the items of real and personal property and their respective values obtained from Normile. Appellant testified that she relied upon the statements and representations which were made to her and obtained from these other witnesses and attorneys. We have held that for a person to testify that he has relied upon statements of deceased is not within the prohibitions of the act against testifying to a personal transaction or communication between them. *O'Connor v. Slatter*, 46 Wash. 308, 89 Pac. 885.

The evidence showed the discovery by the respondent executrix of personal property of the deceased, as follows:

Bonds in Local Improvement District No.
    2718, City of Seattle, of the par value of $25,200.00
Bond in Local Improvement District No. 28,
    of the par value of....................   213.50
Bonds in Local Improvement District No.
    3262, amounting to..................   500.00

Making a total of personal property aggregating $25,913.50

which had been concealed from appellant by her husband when making the property settlement. Under our decision on the former appeal, she is entitled to one-half of this concealed property (being community property) as her absolute property.

We therefore feel compelled to reverse the judgment of the lower court, and adjudge the appellant to be entitled to the sum of $12,956.75, and costs.

[No. 16080. Department One. July 29, 1921.]

THE STATE OF WASHINGTON, *on the Relation of Arthur Seaborg et al., Plaintiff,* v. THE SUPERIOR COURT FOR WAHKIAKUM COUNTY, *Respondent.*[1]

EMINENT DOMAIN (42-1)—PROPERTY SUBJECT—CONSENT OF OWNER. Where a county instituted condemnation proceedings to establish a road along the top of a dike, and the diking district appeared and consented thereto, no question arises with respect to the right of a county to condemn the property of another municipal corporation.

Certiorari to review an order of the superior court for Wahkiakum county, Back, J., entered August 10, 1920, adjudging a public use and necessity in condemnation proceedings. Affirmed.

Wm. P. Lord, for relators.

J. C. McFadden, for respondent.

MACKINTOSH, J.—Certiorari to review an order of necessity, in a suit by Wahkiakum county for the condemnation of a right of way for a public road. The property sought to be condemned is the top of a dike in a diking district, organized by virtue of the laws of this state, and the only question to be determined is the right of the county to establish such a road.

[1] Reported in 199 Pac. 755.

The diking district and the various property owners through and upon whose property the dike is constructed were made parties to the condemnation proceeding, and the diking district appeared and consented to the establishment of the road. Several of the property owners are objecting to the condemnation for the reason, as they claim, that the county has no right to condemn property belonging to another municipal corporation, and rely upon our decision in the case of *State ex rel. Cle Elum v. Kittitas County*, 107 Wash. 326, 173 Pac. 698.

There is no question in this case but what there is a reasonable necessity for the construction of the road contemplated by this condemnation, and no question that the use for which it is being sought by the county is a different use from that to which it is now being devoted by the diking district, and that the use by the county would not be inconsistent nor in any way in conflict with the diking district's use, present or prospective. As we view it, the question of the county's right to condemn the property of another municipal corporation is not in this case, for the reason that the diking district has, through its proper officers, consented to the condemnation and has, in effect, licensed the use of its property for road purposes. This the diking district could do under the authority given its commissioners under § 4102, Rem. Code. The diking district does not own the fee of the dikes, it simply has an interest therein as provided in the diking acts, Rem. Code, § 4091 *et seq.* The case, therefore, does not fall within the rule announced in the *Cle Elum* case, *supra,* for there is not here presented the question of the power of the county to condemn in the absence of express grant of such power by statute. The consent of the diking commissioners, of course, does not absolve the

county from the necessity of condemning the land of
private property holders, and, as we view it, they have
no legal ground upon which to object to the proceeding.

The case falls within the principle announced in
State ex rel. Kent Lumber Co. v. Superior Court, 46
Wash. 516, 90 Pac. 663, where a right of way granted
to a city for a pole line was allowed to be condemned
for a railroad right of way, the city having consented
thereto, and it being determined that the two uses
could run together. It was there held the city could
dispose of its property, and that the interests of the
owner of the fee, after the grant of easement to the
city, were still subject to condemnation. In that case
we said:

"It is also contended that the respondent railway
company is not authorized to appropriate this land,
for the reason that it has already been appropriated
by the city for a pole line for the transmission of elec-
tricity to said city and for the further purpose of protecting its water supply. We may assume for the purposes of this case, without deciding, that relator can
raise these objections. It appears, that the city has
granted its permission for a right of way to respondent
company; that the city has the power to acquire property or to dispose of the same as the interests of the
same require. Pierce's Code, §§ 3728, 3732, 3735 . . .
§ 1 of the city charter. While the city does not own
the fee, it owns an interest in the land which may be
waived or granted to another public use (*Seattle v.
Columbia etc. R. Co.*, 6 Wash. 379, 33 Pac. 1048), subject to the rights of the owner of the fee. Whatever
rights the owner of the fee has left are subject to condemnation for a public use, especially where the two
uses can run together, as appears to be the case here."

The evidence disclosing that the construction of this
road is necessary, that the use to which it is to be devoted is not inconsistent with the interest and use of
the diking district, and that the diking district has

waived its right to object, we hold that the superior court was correct in entering its order of necessity, and the writ will be denied.

PARKER, C. J., BRIDGES, FULLERTON, and HOLCOMB, JJ., concur.

———————————

[No. 16465. Department Two. July 29, 1921.]

META MORRIS EVANS, *Appellant*, v. GEORGE WASHINGTON EVANS, *Respondent*.[1]

DIVORCE (105)—CUSTODY AND SUPPORT OF CHILDREN—DURATION AND TERMINATION. Under a decree of divorce providing that defendant pay the "sum of $60 per month from date hereof for the support, maintenance and education" of the children, and for the support and maintenance of the divorced wife, but without segregating the amount payable for maintenance and education of the children from the amount intended for support and maintenance of the wife, there could be no recovery against defendant after the first child became of age, in the absence of any modification of the decree thereafter.

Appeal from a judgment of the superior court for King county, Jurey, J., entered December 2, 1920, upon findings in favor of the defendant, in an action to recover alimony, tried to the court. Affirmed.

James B. Kinne, for appellant.

MAIN, J.—The purpose of this action was to recover alimony claimed to be due and unpaid, and the action is based upon a decree of the circuit court of the state of Illinois. The trial resulted in findings of fact, conclusions of law and a judgment denying recovery. The plaintiff appeals.

The parties were divorced on the 21st day of December, 1900, by decree of the circuit court for Cook

[1]Reported in 199 Pac. 764.

county, Illinois. At this time there were two minor
children, the custody of whom was awarded to the
mother, the appellant here. Covering the matter of
alimony and the maintenance and education of the
children, the decree contained the following provision:

"That the complainant have and recover from the
defendant, George Washington Evans, the sum of $60
per month from the date hereof, and that the defendant pay the said sum of $60 per month from date here-
of for the support, maintenance and education of said
children, Meta Morris Evans and George Chambliss
Evans, and for her own support and maintenance,
which monthly sum shall become due and payable on
or before the 15th day of the month for which the same
is due."

The oldest child attained the age of majority on
March 18, 1911. The present action was instituted on
April 12, 1911, and at that time it was claimed that
there was due and unpaid under the terms of the decree the sum of $2,160. The action did not come on for
trial until May 27, 1920. Between the time when the
complaint was filed and the date of the trial, a number
of supplemental complaints were filed covering the
amount which it was claimed was accruing from time
to time under the decree. There is some dispute in the
evidence as to whether anything was owing and unpaid at the time the action was instituted. The evidence, however, makes it reasonably clear that the respondent, at the time the action was begun, had paid
all the sums which had accrued under the divorce decree up to the time that the oldest child became of age.
The evidence upon this question is such that it leaves
little room for controversy.

The question in the case is whether the appellant
had the right to recover under the decree the amount
there specified after one of the children, or both, had

reached the age of majority. From the excerpt from the decree above quoted, it appears that the respondent was required to pay $60 per month to the appellant for the "maintenance and education of said children, Meta Morris Evans and George Chambliss Evans, and for her own support and maintenance." The decree does not segregate the amount which was intended for the maintenance and education of the children, or either of them, from the amount which was intended for the support and maintenance of the appellant. Under the language of the decree, if the respondent was delinquent as to any sum which accrued prior to the time when the first child became of age, there can be no question but what a recovery could be had. *Beers v. Beers*, 74 Wash. 458, 133 Pac. 605; *Britton v. Chamberlain*, 234 Ill. 246, 84 N. E. 895; *Rogers v. Rogers*, 46 Ind. App. 506, 89 N. E. 901; *Wells v. Wells*, 209 Mass. 282, 95 N. E. 845; *De Vall v. De Vall*, 57 Ore. 128, 109 Pac. 755, 110 Pac. 705. But the question is, can a recovery be had after one of the children becomes of age, when the decree does not make a segregation. After the first child became of age, the liability of the respondent under the decree for the maintenance and education of that child ceased. Likewise with reference to the second child. 19 C. J. 360.

At the time this action was instituted, there had been no proceedings in the Illinois court for the purpose of modifying the decree and fixing the amount which was intended for the maintenance and education of the children as distinct from the sum which was intended for the support and maintenance of the appellant. It seems plain that, before the appellant could prevail, it was necessary that she allege and prove the sum which she was legally entitled to. In other words, it was necessary that she establish, after the children became of age, the sum which was intended for her maintenance and support. It is admitted, of course, that this could only be done by the Illinois court. If the appellant were permitted to prevail in this action, a portion of the recovery would be for a sum which the respondent was under no legal obligation to pay because of the fact that the children had attained their majority. As already pointed out, at the time the first child became of age there was nothing due and unpaid under the decree.

The judgment will be affirmed.

PARKER, C. J., MITCHELL, and BRIDGES, JJ., concur.

[No. 16102. Department Two. July 29, 1921.]

THE STATE OF WASHINGTON, *Respondent*, v. HARRY GREENWALD *et al.*, *Appellants*.[1]

INTOXICATING LIQUORS (42)—OFFENSES—"JOINTIST"—INFORMATION —SUFFICIENCY. Under Laws 1917, ch. 19, § 17h, declaring that any person who opens up, conducts or maintains a place for the unlawful sale of intoxicating liquor is a "jointist," an information charging that defendants on a certain date "did then and there wilfully, unlawfully and feloniously conduct and maintain" a certain place, "the said place then and there being a place for the unlawful sale of intoxicating liquor," sufficiently charged the crime of being jointists.

SAME (50) — OFFENSES — "JOINTIST" — EVIDENCE — SUFFICIENCY. Though the main purpose of defendants' business is the operation of a restaurant or inn, evidence of occasional sales or gifts of liquor is sufficient to carry the question of guilt to the jury in a prosecution for the crime of being jointists.

SAME (51) — "JOINTIST" — INSTRUCTIONS AS TO OTHER OFFENSES. In a prosecution for the crime of being jointists, it was error to instruct the jury that, on the day of the offense charged, it "was unlawful for any one to give away, furnish, or exchange intoxicating liquor in any manner whatsoever, except for use in sacramental purposes," such instruction defining a crime not charged against the defendants.

[1] Reported in 199 Pac. 730.

Appeal from a judgment of the superior court for King county, Tallman, J., entered April 17, 1920, upon a trial and conviction of being a jointist. Reversed.

Wm. R. Bell (*J. Kalina,* of counsel), for appellants.
Malcolm Douglass and *John D. Carmody,* for respondent.

MAIN, J.—The defendants in this case were charged by information with the crime of being jointists. Motion for a new trial and in arrest of judgment being made and overruled, they appeal to this court.

The charging part of the information is as follows:

"They, said Harry Greenwald and Jennie Greenwald, and each of them, in the county of King, state of Washington, on the 9th day of November, 1919, did then and there wilfully, unlawfully and feloniously conduct and maintain a place known as Motor Inn, situate on the Pacific Highway near the town of Auburn, in said county and state, the said place then and there being a place for the unlawful sale of intoxicating liquor."

It is first claimed that the information is not sufficient, in that it does not contain a plain and concise statement of the facts constituting the offense charged. The information is very similar in language to that which was before the court in the case of *State v. Rousseau,* 111 Wash. 533, 191 Pac. 634, where the information was sustained. Under the statute (Laws of 1917, ch. 19, p. 60, § 17h), any person who opens up, conducts or maintains a place for the unlawful sale of intoxicating liquor "be and hereby is defined to be a 'jointist.'" It is the opening up and maintaining of the place and not the actual sale which constitutes the offense, but proof of an illegal sale or sales is admissible to show for what purpose the place was kept. In 2 Woollen and Thornton, The Law of Intoxicating Liquors, p. 1093, it is said:

"In all such instances it is the keeping of the place or public bar for an illegal purpose (or, in the last instance, for the sale of liquors) that constitutes the offense and not an actual illegal (or even other) sale. Therefore, to commit the offense a sale is not necessary and one need not be proven; but proof of an illegal sale or sales, is admissible to show for what purpose the place was kept."

Under the rule restated in *State v. Randall*, 107 Wash. 695, 182 Pac. 575, the information was sufficient.

It is further claimed that the evidence was not sufficient to establish the crime charged, and that the trial court erred in not sustaining either the motion for a directed verdict, made at the conclusion of the evidence, or the motion in arrest of judgment, presented after verdict. The tenor of the argument here is that, since the appellants were engaged in the business of operating a restaurant or inn for the convenience of motorists on the Pacific Highway near Auburn, in King county, and incidentally selling cigars, etc., that if, on a single occasion, or on several isolated occasions, they sold, or attempted to sell or give away, intoxicating liquor, they would not be guilty of the crime of being jointists. It is not necessary in order to establish the crime that the evidence should show that the principal purpose for which the place was opened up or conducted was the unlawful sale of intoxicating liquor. Even though the keeping of the place for the sale of intoxicating liquor was not its principal purpose, the offense may be as complete as if the entire building had been kept for that purpose. In 2 Woollen and Thornton, The Law of Intoxicating Liquors, p. 1094, it is said:

"Even though the keeping of the building for sales is not the main purpose of keeping it, yet the offense is as complete as if the entire building had been kept for that purpose."

The evidence was sufficient to carry the question of the guilt or innocence of the appellants to the jury.

The next question is whether there was error in the instructions by which the cause was submitted to the jury. Instructions 1, 2 and 3 are as follows:

"(1) Under the law of this state any person who opens up, conducts, or maintains, either as principal or agent, any place for the unlawful sale of intoxicating liquor, is defined to be a jointist.

"(2) You are further instructed that it is, and on the 9th day of November, 1919, was unlawful for anyone to give away, furnish, or exchange intoxicating liquor in any manner whatsoever, except for use in sacramental purposes.

"(3) To convict the defendants, or either of them of the offense herein charged, the state must prove to you beyond a reasonable doubt that the defendants, or either of them, in the county of King, state of Washington, on the 9th day of November, 1919, were conducting a place known as Motor Inn, situate on Pacific Highway near the town of Auburn in said county, and that at that time the said Motor Inn was a place for the unlawful sale of intoxicating liquor."

In instruction one is defined the crime of being a jointist. In instruction two the jury are told that it was unlawful on the 9th day of November, 1919, the date the crime charged is alleged to have been committed, for any one to give away, furnish or exchange intoxicating liquor in any manner whatsoever, except for use in sacramental purposes. This instruction defines a crime not charged and of which, under the evidence, the jury might have found the appellants guilty. In instruction three the jury were told that, before there could be a conviction, it was necessary for the state to prove that the appellants, on the 9th day of November, 1919, were conducting a place known as Motor Inn and that, at the time, this inn was a place for the unlawful sale of intoxicating liquor. This instruction tells the jury what it is necessary for them to find in order to convict the appellants, or either of them, of the crime charged. The jury are nowhere told that they may not convict the appellants, or either of them, of the crime defined in the second instruction.

In *State v. Hessel*, 112 Wash. 53, 191 Pac. 637, the defendant was charged with the crime of being a bootlegger. In submitting the case to the jury, there was an instruction to the effect that it was unlawful for any person other than a regularly ordained clergyman, priest or rabbi, to have in his possession any intoxicating liquor other than alcohol. Other matters were referred to in the instruction of which there was no evidence. After giving these instructions, the court went into other portions of § 17h, ch. 19, p. 60, Laws of 1917, in which is contained a prohibition against bootlegging, and told the jury that it was not necessary for the state to prove matters and things contained in the balance of that section which the court had just quoted. It was there held that the giving of the instruction with reference to a crime with which the defendant was not charged and calling the jury's attention to matters of which there was no evidence was erroneous and prejudicial, as it tended to confuse the issue before the jury.

In principle, the holding in that case cannot be distinguished from the present one. In § 17h, the crime covered by instruction number two in this case, and by one of the instructions given in the *Hessel* case, and the crimes of being a jointist and bootlegger, are all defined. In this case the jury might have concluded, under the evidence, that the appellants were not guilty of the crime of being jointists, but they were guilty of the crime of having intoxicating liquor unlawfully in their possession. Here, as in the *Hessel* case, the giving of instruction number two tended to confuse the issue before the jury and was prejudicial.

The other question presented upon this appeal is such as is not likely to arise upon a second trial, and therefore it is not necessary at this time to consider it.

The judgment will be reversed, and the cause remanded for a new trial.

PARKER, C. J., MITCHELL, TOLMAN, and BRIDGES, JJ., concur.

[No. 16395. Department Two. July 29, 1921.]

ELLA NORDSTROM *et al.*, *Appellants*, v. M. P. ZINDORF, *Respondent*.[1]

HIGHWAYS (62)—DEFECTIVE SIDEWALK—ACTION FOR INJURY—COMPLAINT—SUFFICIENCY. In an action to recover damages for injuries caused by a fall upon a defective sidewalk, a complaint against the abutting property owner was good as against a general demurrer, where it alleged that some four or five years before the accident it had been negligently and defectively constructed by defendants; that nails of proper size and sufficient in number to hold the boards for any length of time had not been used, thus making the sidewalk an unsafe place to walk upon; that, though unsafe, it presented a sound appearance, inviting its use by the public; that plaintiff was tripped and received the injuries complained of when a companion with whom she was walking stepped upon one end of a board which had become loose from the stringer to which it had been defectively nailed; that this board had been in such condition for a long time, and the defective condition of the walk was known, or by the exercise of reasonable care should have been known by defendant; and that the defective condition of the sidewalk was due to the carelessness and negligence of defendant.

[1] Reported in 199 Pac. 741.

Appeal from a judgment of the superior court for King county, Smith, J., entered January 24, 1920, upon sustaining a demurrer to the complaint, dismissing an action in tort. Reversed.

Robert G. Cauthorn, for appellants.

McClure & McClure and *Walter S. Osborn,* for respondent.

MITCHELL, J.—The only assignment of error is the action of the court below in sustaining a demurrer to the amended complaint on the ground that it failed to state a cause of action. The appellants sued to recover for personal injuries suffered by Mrs. Nordstrom due to a fall she sustained while walking on a board sidewalk the respondent had constructed on Lakeview Boulevard, in King county. The respondent owned the abutting property. Altogether the amended complaint is somewhat voluminous and contains some repetition, but in substance it is alleged, that the sidewalk had been negligently and defectively constructed so as to be unsafe, in that sufficient nails had not been used to hold the boards for any length of time; that the nails used were not of the proper size, making the sidewalk an unsafe place to walk upon; that the sidewalk, while in fact unsafe and dangerous to one who might walk upon it, presented a sound appearance so as to invite anyone to go upon it, and was so defectively constructed that it would become more dangerous; that it had been built some four or five years before the accident complained of. It is alleged that one of the boards had become loose at one end from the stringer to which it had been defectively nailed, and that another person walking with Mrs. Nordstrom stepped on one end of the board and caused it to fly up and trip Mrs. Nordstrom, thereby causing the injuries

complained of. It is further alleged "that this board
had been in this condition for a long time prior thereto,
and defendant knew, or by the exercise of reasonable
care should have known, of said defective condition of
said sidewalk. And such condition was the result of
the defective manner in which said walk had been constructed, and was due to the carelessness and negligence of defendant in his maintenance or lack of
maintenance of said sidewalk."

In support of the demurrer, it is, in effect, argued
by the respondent that the amended complaint is susceptible of no other construction than that of charging
him with the negligence of not maintaining a sidewalk
in a reasonably safe condition for public use, and that,
under the law which imposes that burden upon the
county, the allegation that the accident occurred so
long a time after the abutting property owner built
the sidewalk does not state a cause of action. If such
were the only effect of the allegations of the amended
complaint it would appear as if the conclusion drawn
is correct, under the statute and the rule announced in
the case of *Bullock v. Yakima Valley Transp. Co.*, 108
Wash. 413, 184 Pac. 641, 187 Pac. 410, and cases therein cited. But the complaint is capable of, and must receive, a more liberal construction. It was not moved
against in any manner, but tested solely by general
demurrer. In such case all reasonable intendments in
favor of the complaint must be indulged in, because of
the statute compelling liberal construction of pleadings.

While it is true the amended complaint alleges that
the accident occurred some four of five years after the
sidewalk was built, it nevertheless is also alleged that
the fault was in the negligent and defective construction; and referring to the particular board that caused

the fall, it is averred, in addition to its defective original fastening, that it would fly up and again "fly back in place so that no one could notice that said board was loose; and that this board had been in this condition for a long time prior thereto (the accident), and defendant knew, or by the exercise of reasonable care should have known, of said defective condition of said sidewalk." For what length of time prior to the accident that condition existed the amended complaint gives no information; and thus respondent has rested upon a general demurrer against allegations which altogether are ample to admit proof sufficient to establish actionable negligence on the part of the respondent—negligence not of a passive kind in failing to maintain the walkway in a safe condition, but of an active sort consisting of defective original construction not readily or reasonably observable to others.

Reversed and remanded with directions to overrule the demurrer.

PARKER, C. J., MAIN, MACKINTOSH, and TOLMAN, JJ., concur.

[No. 16374. Department Two. July 29, 1921.]

WORTHY CREEK SHINGLE COMPANY, *Appellant*, v.
CHARLES A. ANDERSON *et al.*,
Respondents.[1]

ESTOPPEL (46, 54)—PUBLIC WAY—ACQUIESCENCE IN USE—EVI-
DENCE—SUFFICIENCY. In an action to prevent defendants' interference with plaintiff's use of a roadway over the land of defendants on
the ground they were estopped by conduct to deny the use of the
road to plaintiff, held that the evidence was insufficient to support
plaintiff's cause of action.

TRESPASS (15, 16)—DAMAGES TO REAL PROPERTY—EVIDENCE—SUF-
FICIENCY. A judgment for damages for trespass was unwarranted,
where it appeared that defendant, in making use of a private roadway over plaintiff's land for which it paid a rental, was compelled
to make a slight detour because the roadway had been partially destroyed in blasting stumps and rocks.

Appeal from a judgment of the superior court for
Snohomish county, Brawley, J., entered July 30, 1920,
in favor of the defendant, in an action for equitable
relief, tried to the court. Modified.

Thos. A. Stiger and *Wm. Sheller,* for appellant.

MITCHELL, J.—This action was brought to prevent
the respondent from interfering with appellant's use
of a roadway on the east side of Worthy Creek across
respondent's lands, upon the ground that the roadway
is public by adverse user; and further, that in the
event it is not such a public way, that the respondent is
estopped by his conduct to deny the use of the road to
the appellant. The respondent denied that the road
was public by prescription or otherwise, denied the
allegations charging him with estoppel, and filed a
cross-complaint claiming damages by reason of trespass on the part of the appellant. The court, without

[1]Reported in 199 Pac. 756.

making findings, entered judgment denying the appellant any relief and allowed respondent damages in the sum of $100, from which the appeal has been taken.

Upon the subject of the character of the road, while there is a conflict in the evidence, we are satisfied it preponderates in favor of the conclusion reached by the trial court.

As to the charge of estoppel against the respondent, it appears that the premises occupied by the appellant, upon which it established a shingle mill in the early part of the year 1920, is separated from a public road by the premises of the respondent, across which runs the roadway in question that was used as an outlet by the appellant until prevented by the respondent about May 1, 1920. In establishing the mill, and thereafter until prevented, the appellant used the private road ·of the respondent as a means of going and coming. There is a sharp conflict in the evidence as to the representations made by the respondent concerning the right of the appellant to use the roadway upon which it claims it depended in locating its mill. There can be no question, however, that a number of years ago partial steps were taken to establish a public road through respondent's lands on the west side of the creek, and that such way had been opened sufficiently to permit public travel thereon for several years, but thereafter, and for the last eight or ten years, that way had fallen into disuse and was unfit for travel.

The appellant corporation was organized about January, 1920, the officers and stockholders of which are the same persons who in October or November, 1919, purchased by contract, with the right of removal, the timber upon the land whereon the mill was later placed. About the time of the purchase of the timber, they interviewed the respondent with reference to a way of

ingress and egress, and at the trial testified that he
gave them to understand the roadway east of the creek
was a public way and could be used by them, and that
had they not been so informed they would not have
purchased the timber nor established the mill. On the
contrary, the respondent's proof shows that, while
he orally consented to the temporary use of his private
way, the public way he mentioned to them was on the
other or west side of the creek. This conflict in the
evidence is positive. Appellant, to some extent, is
corroborated, but such corroborating evidence and circumstances are not inconsistent with respondent's ver-
sion that appellant or its predecessors in interest were
to have only the temporary use of the private roadway.
The burden of proof was upon the appellant, and we
are satisfied, as was the trial court, that it was not met,
in view of circumstances and other proof corroborating the respondent, among which are the following:
About the time of the purchase of the timber those
who are now officers and stockholders of the appellant
corporation, together with the respondent, on more
than one occasion interviewed the board of county commissioners to have the old road reopened; and it appears also that later the appellant sought the assistance of the owner of the land upon which the mill was
located to get the commissioners to open up the way;
and still further, some time about April 1, 1920, while
appellant was still using the private road, the respondent asked and received of the appellant, by its
manager (a stockholder and director), $20 for the use
of the private road until May 1, 1920. We conclude
there was no estoppel against the respondent.

As to respondent's damages, we do not agree with
the trial court. Such alleged damages, as defined
by the evidence, consisted of so-called trespass upon

the meadow land in making a slight change from the road used by the appellant. It occurred a few days prior to the expiration of the period for which appellant had paid for the use of the road. But the record shows that the slight detour was made necessary because the respondent had destroyed the roadway at places by blasting stumps and rocks. In making and using the detour it appears that as little damage was caused as possible.

The cause is remanded with directions to the trial court to modify the judgment by eliminating therefrom damages awarded to the respondent. Appellant will recover its costs on the appeal.

PARKER, C. J., MAIN, HOLCOMB, and TOLMAN, JJ., concur.

[No. 16382. Department Two. July 29, 1921.]

In the Matter of the Estate of AUGUSTA P. TUCKER. PRENTISS TUCKER, *as Administrator etc., Appellant,* v. JAMES E. SEARGEANT, *as Trustee in Bankruptcy etc., Respondent.*[1]

APPEAL (88)—RIGHT TO APPEAL—PERSONS INJURED OR AGGRIEVED—ADMINISTRATORS. A personal representative of a decedent's estate of which he was also a beneficiary, who filed his petition for final distribution, praying that the estate be awarded to the other beneficiaries on the ground that his indebtedness to the estate exceeded his share, had no right of appeal from an order distributing his share to his trustee in bankruptcy, since he was not a "party aggrieved" within Rem. Code, § 1716, limiting the right of appeal to such parties only.

Appeal from an order of the superior court for King county, Gilliam, J., entered April 29, 1920, distribut-

[1]Reported in 199 Pac. 765.

ing the estate of a decedent, after hearing objections
to the petition for distribution. Appeal dismissed.

Russell & Blinn, for appellant.

Greene & Henry, for respondent.

TOLMAN, J.—Augusta P. Tucker died in King county, Washington, in September, 1915, leaving a last will
and testament executed on March 17, 1911, by which
she bequeathed to her three sons, Edward C. Tucker,
Louis Tucker, and Prentiss Tucker, all of her estate in
equal shares, one-third to each, and named Edward C.
Tucker as executor. The executor named in the will
duly qualified and proceeded to administer the estate, but before the estate was closed he died, and
thereafter, in September, 1916, Prentiss Tucker was,
by the superior court, duly appointed administrator
with the will annexed. While so acting as administrator, Prentiss Tucker filed a petition in voluntary
bankruptcy, and on April 6, 1918, was duly adjudged
a bankrupt. Thereafter respondent, James E. Seargeant, was duly appointed trustee in bankruptcy for
the estate of Prentiss Tucker, and has since been the
duly qualified and acting trustee for said bankrupt
estate.

In his petition to be adjudged a bankrupt, Prentiss
Tucker listed certain indebtedness amounting to $2,500
and interest as due from him to his mother's estate.
No note or memorandum in writing signed by him was
ever made evidencing these loans, nor was any interest
paid within such time as would toll the statute of limitations, and the only written evidences of such indebtedness are the schedules in bankruptcy, made and signed
by Prentiss Tucker long after the statute of limitations
would have run, and the inventory listing such claims
as assets of his mother's estate, filed by Prentiss

Tucker as administrator, after having filed his petition in bankruptcy. Thereafter and in due course, Prentiss Tucker, as administrator with the will annexed of the estate of Augusta P. Tucker, filed his final account and petition for distribution, praying that the estate be distributed wholly to Louis Tucker and the estate of Edward C. Tucker, deceased, upon the ground that, by reason of the unpaid indebtedness above referred to, which exceeded in amount what would pass to him under the terms of the will, Prentiss Tucker was not entitled to have any part of his mother's estate distributed to him. Respondent, as trustee in bankruptcy, filed objections to this manner of distribution, and prayed that one-third of the estate be distributed to him as trustee in bankruptcy of the estate of Prentiss Tucker, a bankrupt. The trial court thereupon entered an order distributing the estate of Augusta P. Tucker, one-third to Louis Tucker, one-third to the estate of Edward C. Tucker, deceased, and one-third to respondent as trustee in bankruptcy of the estate of Prentiss Tucker, and from this order of distribution Prentiss Tucker, as administrator with the will annexed, has appealed.

No question was raised in the court below, nor is any raised here, as to the accuracy and correctness of the accounts of Prentiss Tucker as administrator. His final accounts were approved as filed, without contest or objection by any one.

Respondent has interposed a motion to dismiss the appeal upon the ground that Prentiss Tucker, as administrator, is not aggrieved by the judgment from which the appeal is prosecuted, and has no right or legal capacity to prosecute such an appeal. Our statute on appeals, Rem. Code, § 1716, provides that, "Any party aggrieved may appeal to the supreme court," and it follows that no one has a right to prosecute an appeal unless he has been aggrieved within the meaning of the statute. This question has been passed upon by this court in *In re Cannon's Estate*, 18 Wash. 101, 50 Pac. 1021; and *Cairns v. Donahey*, 59 Wash. 130, 109 Pac. 334; where, following what seems to be the general rule, the doctrine was laid down that an administrator or executor, as such, may not take sides as between claimants on final distribution, and has no interest in the subject-matter in dispute between such claimants. See, also, *In re Ayers' Estate*, 175 Cal. 187, 165 Pac. 528; *In re Craig's Estate*, 101 Neb. 439, 163 N. W. 765; *In re Vincent's Estate*, 84 Ver. 89, 78 Atl. 714. Appellant, however, contends that a different rule is established in *In re Sullivan's Estate*, 48 Wash. 631, 94 Pac. 483, but in this we think he is mistaken. In denying the motion to dismiss the appeal by the administrator, it was there said:

"As administrator he has an appealable interest, to the end that it is his duty to guard against the error of a distribution without some ample provision for all known obligations of the estate."

So that the appeal was there entertained, not because of any supposed interest of the administrator in who should take under the decree of distribution, but solely upon the ground that he should preserve the estate until provision was made for the payment of all known obligations, and therefore no different rule was there announced from that laid down in the authorities heretofore referred to. The motion is well taken and must be granted.

Appeal dismissed.

PARKER, C. J., FULLERTON, MAIN, and MITCHELL, JJ., concur.

[No. 16507. Department Two. July 29, 1921.]

CONTINENTAL TRADING COMPANY, *Appellant*, v. SEATTLE
NATIONAL BANK *et al., Respondents.*[1]

SALES (77, 82)—EVIDENCE (104)—HEARSAY—EXCUSE FOR FAILURE
TO DELIVER. In an action by a trading company for the return of a
deposit of money made by it to secure a contract of sale and delivery of one hundred tons of Chinese peanuts to be shipped from
Japan within specified dates, which it alleged it was excused from
performing under the boycott and strike provisions of the contract,
it is incompetent, upon an issue as to the existence of a boycott in
Chinese ports against loading vessels carrying the Japanese flag, to
offer the testimony of one who had not been within four hundred
miles of the Chinese port from which the shipment was to be made,
or letters and telegrams from correspondents in Japan referring to
the boycott and its effect on the proposed shipment, based upon reports and hearsay, and not under oath; none of the evidence going
to the fact that the particular shipment from China to Japan was
prevented by the boycott or strike.

Appeal from a judgment of the superior court for
King county, Jurey, J., entered October 18, 1920, in
favor of the defendants, notwithstanding the verdict
of a jury rendered in favor of the plaintiff, in an action
on contract. Affirmed.

Flick & Paul, for appellant.

Bausman, Oldham, Bullitt & Eggerman, for respondents.

TOLMAN, J.—On June 17, 1919, appellant's assignors,
Brown & Mahoney, Ltd., a copartnership, entered into
a written agreement with respondent, National Importing & Trading Company, Incorporated, for the
sale and delivery of one hundred tons of Chinese
shelled peanuts, of certain specified quality, to be
shipped from Japan during June, July and August,
1919. Among the conditions set forth in the contract
was the following:

[1]Reported in 199 Pac. 743.

"The sellers and suppliers, their agents and principals shall not be under any obligations under this contract if the performance thereof is prevented or impeded either wholly or in part by strikes or the effects thereof; lockouts of workmen, fire, riots or disturbances local or otherwise; stoppage or obstruction of navigation or railways or interruption or shortage of transportation of any kind whatsoever; act of God, force mejeure, restraints of Princes, Rulers, or peoples; requisitioning, loss of or delay to steamers relied on by the sellers as likely to be available for service under this contract; licensing rules or other regulations or directions of embargoes or restrictions of any government or any department of any government or any person acting or purporting to act with authority of any government. If the cargo described in this contract is detained or delayed at the point of original shipment, the contract is not to be invalidated and the sellers not to be held responsible."

At the time of the execution of the contract, the sellers therein named deposited with the respondent Seattle National Bank $4,625 as security for the faithful performance of the contract and the delivery of the peanuts within the time limited. The time for delivery was afterwards extended to October 30, 1919, and no delivery having then been made, on November 3, 1919, upon demand of the National Importing & Trading Company, the bank paid to it the amount so deposited. Brown & Mahoney, Ltd., having assigned to appellant all their rights therein, appellant, as plaintiff, brought this action against the bank and the importing company to recover the amount so deposited with the bank and paid over to the importing company, alleging in its complaint:

" . . . that said peanuts could not be shipped out of China, by reason of the existence of a well established and effective boycott which was designed and intended to obstruct and stop all trade relations between the peoples of China and those of Japan, and that said boycott was originated by the peoples of China on or about July 1, 1919, and was put in immediate effect and has been ever since of such character that it was entirely impossible to ship out of China any goods that had for their transhipment place any point in Japan, or which goods were in anywise to be delivered to a Japanese agent, broker, shipper or carrier, or through such race to others.

"That the cargo herein referred to was duly at hand at Tsingtau in ample time for shipment as contemplated by said contract, excepting as hereinafter qualified, but that it was during all times from July on, and is now being detained and delayed at said point of original shipment by reason of said boycott, and obstructed as herein just recited."

The case was tried to a jury, which found a verdict in favor of appellant for the full amount sued for. A motion on behalf of both respondents for judgment notwithstanding the verdict was interposed and granted, from which judgment appellant prosecutes this appeal.

It was contended and sought to be shown that, though the contract calls for shipment from Japan, it was well known to the trade generally and to the importing company that the peanuts must first be shipped from China to Japan, and that shipment could not be made from China because of the boycott pleaded. It may be a debatable question whether, under the terms of the contract calling for shipment from Japan, the boycott in China would be an excuse for the non-shipment; but however that may be, we think the judgment of the trial court was right, because of the absence of any competent evidence in the record that such boycott in fact existed at the Chinese port of shipment, or, if so, that it was of sufficient force or effectiveness to prevent this particular shipment. The evidence introduced by appellant, and upon which it relies upon this point, consists of the testimony of a Mr. Priestley, who was in China during the early summer of 1919, but who left there early in July, and was not at any time in that year within four hundred miles of Tsingtau, the port from which it was claimed the peanuts were to be shipped; had no personal knowledge of conditions there at any time during the year, and, of course, no personal knowledge of conditions anywhere in China after his departure. He testified that the boycott existed in Shanghai which applied only to Japanese goods and Japanese vessels and was of varying degrees of severity, according to the class of commodities affected, but did not attempt to say in what class peanuts fell, or whether they were affected in any degree by the boycott. He further testified that the Chinese coolies were largely unable to read, knew nothing of manifests or shipping bills, and judged only by the flag, refusing to load or unload vessels carrying the Japanese flag, and that an American firm would have no difficulty on account of the boycott in loading a shipment, unless it was known that it was acting in the interest of the Japanese. Since the time for shipment specified in the contract was June, July and August, and was afterwards further extended, this testimony falls far short of showing such a prevention or impeding of the shipment as is contemplated by the excusatory clause of the contract.

Appellant also introduced, over respondents' objections, certain letters and cablegrams from its Japanese correspondents, referring to the boycott and its effect on the proposed shipment, which, since the writers were not under oath or subject to cross-examination, and since the statements made in these communications were based on reports or hearsay and not upon personal knowledge of the writers, cannot be deemed any evidence upon the point now under consideration; nor can the testimony of the witnesses Ogurra and Fujimori, based entirely upon these communications and like information, be considered any evidence of conditions existing at the Chinese port of shipment. We quite agree with the views expressed by the trial court in granting the motion for judgment *non obstante*. He said:

"Then the burden was upon the plaintiff to prove by competent evidence that the boycott or strike did in fact prevent this particular shipment from Tsingtau to Japan. This burden the plaintiff has not sustained.

"It is not a case of sufficiency of the evidence but a case of no competent evidence to sustain it. Plaintiff's sole showing on this question consisted of letters and cablegrams mostly from its own people to the effect that it was impossible to make the shipment on account of the boycott or strike. These were admitted in evidence under the strenuous objection of counsel for defendants and were admitted and I think properly for some special purpose and never to establish the fact of a boycott or its effect upon this particular shipment. It is true some of the documents may appear from the record to have gone in without objection, but unquestionably the objections of counsel for defendants to that character of evidence were broad enough to cover all the documents in question. There were many questions involved in the case where such evidence was competent, such as notice, customs or knowledge of the trade and the like, but a positive fact such as that a boycott or strike not absolute in its effect did in fact prevent a particular shipment cannot be established by such evidence. This alone regardless of any other feature of the case is controlling and conclusive against the right of the plaintiff to recover."

The judgment appealed from is affirmed.

PARKER, C. J., MAIN, MACKINTOSH, and MITCHELL, JJ., concur.

[No. 16320. Department Two. July 30, 1921.]

In the Matter of the Estate of ANTON ADLER.
MOLLIE ADLER, *as Administratrix etc., Respondent,* v.
SCANDINAVIAN-AMERICAN BANK, *Appellant.*[1]

EXECUTORS AND ADMINISTRATORS (146)—SET-OFF AND COUNTER-CLAIM—PRESENTATION OF CLAIM. The right of a bank under Rem. Code, § 268, to set off the debt of a decedent to it against the deposit of the decedent in the bank would not in any way be affected or altered by the fact that the bank deposit of the decedent had been shifted to the name of his personal representative prior to the assertion of the set-off.

SAME (146)—BANKS AND BANKING (22)—DEPOSITS—SET-OFF—APPLICATION OF DEPOSITS TO DEBTS DUE BANK. Under Rem. Code, §§ 266, 268, a right of set-off against an executor who brings action upon a claim due the deceased exists without the presentation of any claim under the statute of non-claim; and the statute of non-claim requiring an action on a rejected claim within thirty days does not apply, although a claim was presented and rejected on the set-off demand before suit by the executor.

SAME (146)—BANKS AND BANKING (22)—DEPOSITS—SET-OFF. Where a personal representative continued the bank account of her decedent, had it changed to her own name, and deposited in the account funds coming to her as administratrix, the right of the bank to set off against the deposit a debt of the decedent to it would not extend beyond the amount of the deposit at the time of the debtor's death.

Appeal from a judgment of the superior court for King county, Frater, J., entered November 23, 1920, upon findings in favor of the plaintiff, in an action to recover a deposit in a bank, tried to the court. Reversed.

Ballinger, Battle, Hulbert & Shorts, for appellant.
Rummens & Griffin, for respondent.

MITCHELL, J.—Mollie Adler, as administratrix of the estate of Anton Adler, deceased, and the Scandinavian-

[1] Reported in 199 Pac. 762.

American Bank of Seattle, Washington, are the parties to this controversy. Upon stipulation of the parties, the trial court made findings of fact which are substantially as follows: Anton Adler died intestate on December 1, 1919, possessed of an account, subject to check, of $4,331.11 in the Scandinavian-American Bank; the bank being the owner and holder of a promissory note in the sum of $5,000 made by Anton Adler to the bank on October 1, 1919, due December 30, 1919. On December 9, 1919, Mollie Adler, the surviving spouse, was appointed and qualified as administratrix of the estate of Anton Adler. After his death and prior to her being appointed administratrix, she caused to be deposited in the bank in the checking account of Anton Adler the further sum of $917, making a total of $5,248.11 in that account at the date she qualified as administratrix, whereupon, on her application, the account was transferred on the books of the bank from the name of Anton Adler to the name of Mollie Adler, administratrix of the estate of said deceased. Thereafter she made daily deposits and withdrawals for the use and benefit of the estate until June 3, 1920, at which time there was $4,975.60 in the account, all of which belonged to the estate.

Subsequent to prompt notice to creditors, the bank presented to the administratrix its duly verified creditor's claim in the sum of $5,000, based on the promissory note then due. Some months later, not having received any notice of what action the administratrix had taken upon its claim, and having learned that the Adler estate was insolvent, the bank gave notice, on June 3, 1920, to the administratrix that it applied the $4,975.60 in the checking account as a credit on the $5,000 note due the bank. On June 2, 1920, the administratrix endorsed her approval on the creditor's claim of the bank without giving the bank any notice thereof, and upon receiving notice on June 3, 1920, from the bank that it had applied the checking account of the administratrix as a credit on the note, the administratrix promptly cancelled her former approval of the creditor's claim and so notified the bank on June 4, 1920. On June 11, 1920, the administratrix served on the bank her written rejection of the bank's creditor's claim based on the note. On June 15, 1920, the administratrix made and presented to the bank for payment her check in the sum of $4,975.60, which was refused by the bank upon the claim that it had already been appropriated by the bank according to its former notice. Claims allowed and approved against the estate aggregate $50,000, while the assets of the estate do not exceed $27,500. The bank has not instituted any action upon its rejected claim.

On August 16, 1920, the administratrix commenced this action against the bank to recover the sum of $4,975.60, claimed to have been wrongfully appropriated by the bank. The trial court concluded the bank was without right in applying the deposit on the note, and that since it had not commenced any action against the estate within thirty days after notice of the rejection of its claim on the promissory note, that the claim was barred. Upon the findings and conclusions, a judgment was entered against the bank in the sum of $4,975.60, from which it has appealed.

It has been seen that the bank gave notice of its application of the deposit as a credit on the note prior to notice of any action by the administratrix on the bank's creditor's claim, prior to the rejection of the claim by the administratrix, after the bank had learned of the insolvency of the estate, and after the maturity of the note due to the bank. It did not sue the estate or its representative, but only set off the note when it was sued by the administratrix.

Section 268, Rem. Code, provides:

"In actions brought by executors and administrators, demands against their testators and intestates, and belonging to defendant at the time of their death, may be set off by the defendant in the same manner as if the action had been brought by and in the name of the deceased."

Section 266, Rem. Code, so far as it is material here, provides:

"The defendant in a civil action upon a contract expressed or implied, may set off any demand of a like nature against the plaintiff in interest, which existed and belonged to him at the time of the commencement of the suit. . . ."

In the case of *Fishburne v. Merchants Bank of Port Townsend*, 42 Wash. 473, 85 Pac. 38, in construing these statutes, it was held that, in an action by an administrator to recover the amount of the check account of the decedent at the time of his death, the bank was entitled to set off a note belonging to it at the time of the death of the deceased, which matured after such death but before the commencement of the action, without the bank's having presented any claim therefor against the estate, being limited to the extinguishment of the debt sued on if no claim had been presented against the estate, and that the special statute of limitation within which an action must be commenced upon a claim rejected by an executor or administrator does not apply as to such set-off.

That the presenting of a claim to an executor or administrator is not a prerequisite to asserting it as a set-off, provided the obligation had matured and was existing and belonged to the defendant at the time the action was commenced against him, was later declared in *Mendenhall v. Davis*, 52 Wash. 169, 100 Pac. 336, and *Hanson v. Northern Bank & Trust Co.*, 98 Wash.

124, 167 Pac. 97. The statute provides for a set-off
in such cases, that is, where the action is brought by
the legal representative of the deceased person—in
the same manner as if the action had been brought by
and in the name of the deceased, that is, in the same
manner as if the person deceased were yet alive and
brought the action in his own name, for an amount
personally due to him.

It is contended by the respondent, however, that the
rule is applicable in those cases only where the deposit
remains upon the bank's books in the name of the
decedent until the time the suit against the bank is
commenced, and that it does not apply in the present
case because the deposit was changed or transferred
from the name of Anton Adler, thus extinguishing the
relation of debtor and creditor between them, to the
name of Mollie Adler as administratrix, thus creating
the relation of debtor to her as its creditor. Concerning the change of the name of the creditor, caused by
the transfer of the account to the administratrix, as
affecting the right of the bank to use its set-off, it was,
we think, unimportant and immaterial. Strictly or
legally speaking, upon the death of Anton Adler the
bank was no longer his debtor, for he was non-existent.
The bank continued the debtor, but it was, after his
death, the debtor of his estate to be represented legally
by an appointment suggested by the law and to be
made by the court. After the appointment was made,
the individual name of the creditor then became known,
but the process or change in name upon the books of
the bank in no way disturbed the bank's right to assert
or interpose a set-off in an action brought by the only
one entitled to sue, the legal representative of the
bank's original creditor.

The other argument of the respondent upon this
feature of the controversy is that, upon transferring

the account to the name of the administratrix, she, as such creditor, became the owner of the amount due by the bank as a trustee for the benefit of all parties interested in the estate, and that to allow the set-off, the estate being insolvent, would prevent the enforcement of other statutes with reference to priorities and the pro rata distribution of the estate. But the answer is that the deposit of $4,331.11, on hand at the date of Anton Adler's death, later placed to the credit of the administratrix in his stead, was not a trust fund at the time it was received by the bank. The set-off was the matured note of Anton Adler due the bank, and interposed in an action by the legal representative to collect from the bank a deposit that had, in part, been made by Anton Adler in his individual right. This distinction marks the difference in the relation of the original deposit to the right of a set-off as compared with the remainder of the total deposits of $4,975.60 involved in this suit. That is, the bank may apply the debtor's deposits on his debts as they become due. 7 C. J., Banks and Banking, p. 653, § 351. Continuing, the same authority says: ''While the universal recognition of this rule has led the courts, on a few occasions, to make a general statement to the effect that a bank has a lien on deposits, the more accurate view appears to be that this right of a bank is not really in the nature of a lien but is rather a right of set-off or application of payments.'' See, also, *Furber v. Dane*, 203 Mass. 108, 89 N. E. 227. This theory is tersely put and illustrated in the case of *Wynn v. Tallapoosa County Bank*, 168 Ala. 469, 53 South. 228, to the effect, that the word ''lien'' is inaptly applied to a general deposit which is the property of the bank itself, but can properly be applied to special deposits of chattels, choses in actions, valuables, etc.

Finding that this right of the bank is not in the nature of a lien, but rather a right of set-off or application of payments, and that it relates to deposits made by the debtor, it follows that the rule of application of payments or set-off does not apply where the money received by the bank is of a fiduciary character and deposited by one other than the party whose individual indebtedness the bank seeks to set off.

In the present case, the original amount of $4,331.11 was deposited by Anton Adler as his individual funds and is applicable to the satisfaction of his individual debt, while the difference between that amount and the $4,975.60 embraced within the judgment, to wit, $644.49, was, within the knowledge of the bank, deposited and held by the administratrix in a fiduciary capacity and is not thus applicable, nor does it constitute a liability of the bank of that character against which it may set off the individual liability of Anton Adler. We must and do conclude from the findings made by the trial court that, at all times after the transfer of the original account to the administratrix, she had not less than $4,331.11 to her credit in the bank, and that to that extent the bank had the right to set off the note, but as to the remainder, viz, $644.49, no such right existed.

Reversed, with directions to enter judgment accordingly.

Parker, C. J., Fullerton, Main, and Tolman, JJ., concur.

[No. 16495.   Department Two.   August 4, 1921.]

DEM. SPIROPLOS, *Appellant*, v. SCANDINAVIAN-AMERICAN
BANK OF TACOMA *et al.*, *Respondents*.

KONSTANTINOS N. DIMOS, *Appellant*, v. SCANDINAVIAN-
AMERICAN BANK OF TACOMA *et al.*, *Respondents*.[1]

BANKS AND BANKING (26)—GENERAL OR SPECIAL DEPOSITS—PRE-
FERRED CLAIMS. The purchase of a draft from a bank would not
constitute the money or its equivalent paid therefor a special deposit, since the transaction merely creates the relation of debtor
and creditor, unless it be shown that in some way the net cash
assets of the bank are increased thereby; and such assets were not
increased by the deposit, since it created a corresponding liability.

SAME (6)—INSOLVENCY—DEPOSITS AFTER INSOLVENCY—FRAUD.
Where a draft by plaintiff from defendant bank on a Greek bank
was handled by the drawing of two drafts by the local bank, one on
the New York correspondent of the Greek bank, and one on its own
New York correspondent, to meet the draft on the Greek bank,
which its New York correspondent refused to accept and pay because of notice of the subsequent insolvency of the defendant bank,
the transaction between plaintiff and defendant bank would not
amount to a special deposit so as to constitute plaintiff's claim a
preferred one; and it cannot be said that a fraud was worked on the
depositor from the fact that the bank was insolvent on the day the
deposit was received.

Appeal from judgments of the superior court for
Pierce county, Card, J., entered April 16, 1920, in favor
of the defendants, dismissing consolidated actions to
establish claims against an insolvent bank, tried to the
court. Affirmed.

Govnor Teats, Leo Teats, and *Ralph Teats*, for appellants.

Guy E. Kelly, Thomas MacMahon, and *F. D. Oakley*,
for respondents.

MAIN, J.—These two cases in the superior court were
consolidated for the purpose of trial and are presented

[1]Reported in 199 Pac. 997.

here upon the record there made. The plaintiffs, by
their actions, sought to establish and recover as preferred claims the sums which they had respectively
paid for drafts issued by a bank which a few days
later was closed by the bank commissioner and placed
in the hands of a receiver. At the conclusion of the
trial, the court dismissed the actions and the plaintiffs
appealed.

The case of Dem. Spiroplos will be considered first,
and the facts of that case essentially to be stated are
these: On the eleventh day of January, 1921, Spiroplos, a Greek resident of Tacoma, went to various
banks in that city for the purpose of ascertaining
where he could get the best rate of exchange for the
purchase of a ten thousand dollar draft on the National
Bank of Greece. On the following day he purchased
the draft from the Scandinavian-American bank of
that city, and in payment thereof indorsed to the bank
a cashier's check drawn by another bank in the same
city. The Scandinavian-American bank, in the customary form, drew a draft on the National Bank of Greece,
at Athens, for 132,460 drachmas (Greek money). At
the same time the Scandinavian-American bank drew
a draft in favor of the Guaranty Trust Company of
New York upon the National Park Bank of the same
city, to meet the draft which it had drawn upon the
Greek bank. The National Park Bank was the Scandinavian bank's New York correspondent, but that bank
was not a correspondent of the bank of Greece. The
Guaranty Trust Company was such a correspondent.
The money represented by the cashier's check which
the Scandinavian bank received for the draft on
Greece went into its general funds. On January 15,
1921, the bank commissioner, finding that the Scandinavian-American Bank was insolvent, took charge of

its affairs for the purpose of liquidation. The National Park Bank of New York was notified of this fact and it declined to pay the draft drawn upon it. Had the bank examiner not taken over the affairs of the Scandinavian bank, Spiroplos would have received credit in the Greek bank for the number of drachmas represented by the draft, because the draft drawn in favor of the Guaranty Trust Company upon the National Park Bank would have been paid in due course, there being funds in that bank sufficient to meet it.

On January 17, 1921, the National Park Bank charged off the deposit which the Scandinavian bank had with it against certain liabilities. Between the time when the draft was purchased and the time when the bank examiner took over the affairs of the Scandinavian bank, there was in the vaults of that bank more than sufficient money to cover it. Spiroplos presented a claim to the receiver of the Scandinavian bank, seeking to have a preferred claim in the money that he had paid for the draft. The receiver disallowed the claim as a preferred claim and allowed it as a general claim. The present action was brought to establish and recover the money paid over to the bank as a preferred claim.

The principal question in the case is whether, when Spiroplos purchased the draft and paid for it with a cashier's check, which we will treat as equivalent to cash, the transaction was one whereby the money going into the Scandinavian bank became a special deposit. If it were a special deposit, the right to recover would exist. Where it is sought to establish that the deposit was special, the theory of the action necessarily is the same as though the action were to recover property, and the fact that it is sought to recover property in a changed or substituted form does not change the ground of recovery. In order to establish a special deposit, upon which the action is predicated, it was necessary for Spiroplos to show that the money which he paid into the bank at least came into the hands of a receiver in a substituted form and that it swelled the net assets thereof. *Rugger v. Hammond*, 95 Wash. 85, 163 Pac. 408; *Zimmerli v. Northern Bank & Tr. Co.*, 111 Wash. 624, 191 Pac. 788. It may be assumed that Spiroplos' money passed into the hands of a receiver in a substituted form, but the more serious question is whether it increased the net assets of the bank. The receiving of money on deposit by a bank does not ordinarily swell its assets because it creates a debt of the bank to the depositor equal to the amount of the money so received. In the *Rugger* case it was said, speaking of the money there involved:

"True this money in a sense went into the assets of the trust company, but so does all money which is deposited in a bank, since title thereto passes to the bank. It is not enough, however, for our present purpose that the money physically became a part of the trust company's assets, it must have actually swelled the net assets of the trust company and passed in some form to the hands of the receiver. Manifestly the receiving of money on deposit by a bank does not ordinarily swell its assets, for it creates a debt of the bank equal to the amount so received."

The question then arises whether, when the bank received Spiroplos' money and issued the draft, it created an obligation on the bank equal to the amount of money so received. If it did, the rule of the cases just cited would control. The bank, by drawing and delivering the draft, thereby agreed that, if it be duly presented, it would be accepted and paid by the drawee, and in case of default, if notified of the dishonor, would pay it. The drawee entered into no contract relations until the draft had been accepted by it. Up to that time the payee looked exclusively to the drawer for his protection. In *Grammel v. Carmer,* 55 Mich. 201, 21 N. W. 418, in the opinion written by the late Judge Cooley, it was said:

"The drawer, by drawing and delivering the paper to the payee, agrees that if duly presented it shall be accepted and paid by the drawee, and that in default thereof he will, if duly notified of the dishonor, pay it himself. The drawee enters into no contract relations with the payee in respect to it until it is presented to him, nor then unless he does so by acceptance. If he accepts, he undertakes to pay according to the terms of the bill or of the acceptance; but up to the time of that act the payee looks exclusively to the drawer for his protection. . . ."

In *Clark v. Toronto Bank,* 72 Kan. 1, 82 Pac. 582, a resident of the state of Iowa sold some cattle in Woodson county, Kansas, through an agent there, who accepted in payment a check drawn on the bank of Toronto in that county. The agent presented the check at the bank, and upon his request was given in payment a draft payable to the order of his principal, drawn by the Toronto Bank upon a Kansas City bank against a fund on deposit there to its credit. Shortly afterwards the Toronto Bank was closed by the bank commissioner, and in due course of time a receiver was appointed. A draft was presented for payment to the Kansas City bank, which having notice of the failure of the issuing bank, refused, for that reason, to pay it. The holder of the draft brought an action against the receiver and sought to recover from him the full amount of the draft, upon the theory that he was entitled to a preference. It was said:

"In the petition an attempt was made to give the transaction described the color of a special deposit, or a contract for the transferring of a fund in specie

from Toronto to the plaintiff's home in Iowa. As
clearly appears from the statement made, however, the
facts will not bear that construction. The transaction
was the ordinary one of the purchase of a draft for
convenience in the remitting of money, and the giving
to it of a different name cannot alter its essential
character.''

In *Jewett v. Yardley,* 81 Fed. 920, it was held that
the relation between the bank and the holder of drafts
issued by it was that of debtor and creditor, and that
the holder of the draft upon the bank that had
become insolvent was not entitled to a preference. It
follows, therefore, that the relation between Spiroplos
and the Scandinavian bank, after the transaction of
the purchase of the drafts, was that of debtor and
creditor, and therefore the deposit was not special,
because the net assets of the bank were not augmented
by the transaction. The case of *Carlson v. Kies,* 75
Wash. 171, 134 Pac. 808, is distinguishable. There
the money was placed in the bank to be held until the
return of proper vouchers from heirs of an estate who
lived in Sweden, and a receipt issued for the money.
It was held that it was the obvious intent of both
parties to the transaction to make a special and not a
general deposit.

In the present case, the facts will not bear the inference that it was the intention of the parties to make
the deposit special. In the briefs and in the argument,
the transaction was referred to as a purchase of Greek
money, but it was an ordinary transaction by which
Spiroplos desired to have money placed to his credit
in Greece, and the fact that the appellant may have
thought he was purchasing Greek money does not
change its essential nature. Upon the trial, the appellant offered to prove that the bank was insolvent on

the day the deposit was received, and for this reason
a fraud was worked upon him.   Error is assigned
upon this ruling, but it does not seem to be specially
relied upon, though argued to some extent both orally
and in the briefs.   There was no error in this ruling.
Of the cases cited by the appellant, the one most nearly
in point is that of *Widman v. Kellogg*, 22 N. D. 396, 133
N. W. 1020, 39 L. R. A. (N. S.) 563, but that case is
different in its facts.   There, the bank had, at the time
it drew the draft, no money on deposit with· the
drawee, and it was there said that, under the facts of
that case, the cash assets of the insolvent bank were
enhanced by the receipt of the money.   As above
pointed out, under the doctrine of this court as stated
in the case of *Rugger v. Hammond, supra,* the net cash
assets of the Scandinavian bank were not enhanced.

The case of Dimos is in all essential particulars the
same as that of Spiroplos, and it is not necessary to
discuss this case in detail, as the result in both cases
must be the same.

The judgment in each case will be affirmed.

PARKER, C. J., MACKINTOSH, MITCHELL, and TOLMAN,
JJ., concur.

[No. 16331.   Department One.   August 4, 1921.]

KETTLE RIVER INDUSTRIAL AND DEVELOPMENT COMPANY,
Appellant, v. FERRY COUNTY, *Respondent.*[1]

TAXATION (202, 210)—REDUCTION OF ASSESSMENT—EXCESSIVE VAL-
UATION—EVIDENCE—SUFFICIENCY. An assessed valuation of property
for tax purposes will not be set aside as constructively fraudulent,
in that it was arbitrary and excessive, where the evidence fails to
show such excessive valuation with that degree of conclusiveness
which would justify the interference of the courts.

Appeal from a judgment of the superior court for
Ferry county, Neal, J., entered September 18, 1920,
upon findings in favor of the defendant, in an action to
set aside the assessed valuation on certain lands, tried
to the court. Affirmed.

Zent & Jesseph and *W. Lon Johnson,* for appellant.
Charles P. Bennett, for respondent.

PER CURIAM.—Appellant is the owner of approximately 556 acres of land in Ferry county, and complains of the assessed valuation placed thereon, for
the years 1916, 1917 and 1918, for the purposes of taxation. The valuation of which complaint is made is
$8,082 for 1916, $8,086 for 1917, and $7,348 for 1918.
Its contention is that the assessed value of the property
should have been $1,500 for each of those years. It
has tendered, as the amount which it thinks due
for taxes for the three years combined, the sum of
$118.54, whereas the county, the respondent, claims
taxes in about five times that amount. The appellant
makes no assertion that the respondent's assessing
officers were guilty of any actual fraud, but founds its
action on the doctrine of constructive fraud, in that the

[1]Reported in 199 Pac. 722.

assessed valuation placed upon the land was arbitrary and excessive.

A statement of facts of 533 pages was produced in the trial of this action, which consumed fourteen days. The abstract, consisting of 186 pages, has been carefully read. The result of such reading leads us to adopt the following portion of this court's opinion in the case of *Trimble v. Kitsap County,* 113 Wash. 527, 194 Pac. 799, where we said:

"The only evidence tending to show that the assessed valuation put upon the lands by the taxing officers of the county was fraudulently excessively made, is the testimony of witnesses tending to show that the lands were assessed in excess of fifty per cent of their actual value, and in excess, proportionately, of the assessment of other similar lands in the county. A painstaking review of the evidence, practically all of which was opinion evidence, and by no means free from conflict, convinces us that it does not warrant the conclusion that the lands in question were valued by the assessing officers in excess of fifty per cent of their real value, as limited by § 9112, Rem. Code, nor that the lands were assessed at a value materially in excess of that at which other similar lands in the county were assessed;—that is, that the evidence does not show such excessive valuation with that degree of conclusiveness calling for interference by the courts in such cases. We think it would be unprofitable to review the evidence in detail in this opinion. The judgment is affirmed."

And so, also, is the judgment of this case affirmed.

[No. 16148.   *En Banc*.   August 8, 1921.]

NORTH BEND LUMBER COMPANY, *Respondent*, v. THE
CITY OF SEATTLE, *Appellant*.[1]

NEGLIGENCE (16, 18)—CONTRIBUTORY NEGLIGENCE—NATURE AND
ELEMENTS—CARE REQUIRED AS TO USE OF PROPERTY. The fact that a
property owner knew or suspected that the negligence of another
might cause damage to his property and made no effort to counteract it, would not constitute contributory negligence on his part,
since the rule of personal conduct which requires one to make a
reasonable effort to protect his person from the known negligence
of another does not extend to the use of property.

WATERS AND WATER COURSES (79, 87)—PUBLIC SUPPLY—DAMAGES
FROM NEGLIGENCE. In an action for damages against a city for the
destruction of plaintiff's mill property by the flooding of a creek on
which the mill was located, a question for the jury was presented
where there was evidence showing that the flood had been swelled
by the bursting out of water through one wall of defendant's reservoir, which wall was a glacial moraine of pervious character util-
ized for the purpose, through which there had always been seepage
within the knowledge of defendant.

Appeal from a judgment of the superior court for
King county, Smith, J., entered May 4, 1920, granting a new trial, after the verdict of a jury rendered in
favor of the defendant, in an action in tort. Affirmed.

Walter F. Meier and *Frank S. Griffith*, for appellant.

Peters & Powell, for respondent.

BRIDGES, J.—Boxley creek is a small mountain
stream in King county, having its source near Rattle-
snake lake, and running thence in a southerly direction for some three miles, empties into the south fork
of the Snoqualmie river. The plaintiff, North Bend
Lumber Company, had its sawmill located on both sides
of this creek, at a point about one mile above its mouth.
The Druid Lumber Company's sawmill was located on

[1]Reported in 199 Pac. 988.

the same creek, but very near its mouth. These mills were built during the years 1905 and 1906, and from time to time since have been enlarged. The plaintiff built a dam across the creek a short distance above its mill for the purpose of creating a pond of water in which to store its saw logs. A platform crossed the creek from one part to another of the sawmill. This platform rests upon piling driven in the banks and bed of the stream.

Cedar river flows through Cedar lake, which is located near the foot of Mount Washington. The river, after flowing out of the lake, takes, for a number of miles, a general westerly course. In 1914, the city of Seattle constructed a large dam in this river at a point about two miles west of the lake. The purpose of the dam was to impound waters in the canyon of the river between the lake and the dam, to be used by the city in generating electric power. The northerly bank of this reservoir is for the most part a glacial moraine. Whether this moraine formation would permit much of the water of the reservoir to leak out has been a question from the beginning, and has, to a considerable extent, disturbed the minds of the city authorities. This glacial moraine covers several hundred acres and a part of it is within the watershed of Boxley creek, and a part within the Cedar river watershed. The divide between the two watersheds is less than one mile in width.

Immediately prior to December 23, 1918, there had been heavy rains which caused the waters of Boxley creek to become very considerably swollen. On that date the sawmills of the North Bend Lumber Company and of the Druid Lumber Company were either wholly or partially destroyed by high water. The plaintiff sued the city of Seattle for its damage, and also for damage to the property of the Druid Lumber Company, the latter having assigned to the former its claim of damages. The plaintiff contends that its damage was caused by the waters from defendant's reservoir seeping through the coarse ground forming the moraine and tending in a westerly direction, suddenly breaking out in great quantities near the westerly edge of the moraine, thence being conveyed into the watershed of Boxley creek, and ultimately into that creek above plaintiff's works.

The plaintiff charged the city with negligence in the construction and maintenance of its reservoir, and particularly the north bank thereof, and in permitting the waters of Cedar river to be diverted in part into the channels of Boxley creek. The city denied negligence upon its part, and denied that any of the waters had found their way into Boxley creek, to the damage of the plaintiff, and alleged that the damage done to its property was caused by the waters coming from the natural watershed of Boxley creek. It further alleged contributory negligence on the part of the plaintiff in building and maintaining its log pond in the creek, and in partially closing up the creek by means of piling, logs and debris.

Upon these issues the case went to trial before a jury, which returned its verdict in favor of the defendant. The plaintiff's motion for a new trial was granted by the trial court, and the defendant has appealed therefrom.

The trial court gave three instructions on contributory negligence wherein, among other things, it told the jury that it was to determine whether the plaintiff used such degree of care and prudence as an ordinarily prudent person, under the same or similar circumstances, would have used, and that in determining

whether it did use such degree of care and caution, the
jury had the right to, and should, take into consideration any knowledge which the plaintiff had of the danger, and should consider all the circumstances and
conditions surrounding the situation.

At the hearing of the motion for a new trial, the
court concluded that it had erred in giving these instructions on contributory negligence, and for that
reason granted a new trial. The respondent argues
that there is not, and cannot be, in this case any question of contributory negligence; that the only question
involved is whether, because of the negligence of the
appellant, any of the waters belonging to the Cedar
river watershed were suddenly diverted into the
watershed of Boxley creek, to the respondent's damage; and that, if this question be answered in the
negative, then, under no circumstances, could the appellant be held liable; and that, if it be answered in
the affirmative, then, even if respondent's works in
the bed of the creek did block the stream more or less,
and did cause or aggravate the injury to its property,
still, there would be no question of contributory negligence, because respondent would not be required, under
any circumstances, to so use its property as to protect
itself against the wrongful act of the appellant in di-
verting large quantities of the waters of Cedar river
into their unnatural watershed and into Boxley creek.

If the destruction of respondent's property was
caused by the waters naturally coming from the watershed of Boxley creek, or if appellant was not guilty of
the negligence charged against it, then that would be
an end of the case, for it is plain that, under those
circumstances, contributory negligence could not be involved, because contributory negligence of the plaintiff
grows out of, and is necessarily associated with, the
negligence of the defendant.

But appellant argues that the question of its negligence was for the jury, and that, if the finding was against it in that regard, then it would be proper for the jury to consider whether respondent contributed to its damage by putting its dam across the creek and by driving piling in the bed of the stream, thus restricting its natural capacity. In this connection it asserts that there was testimony to show that some of respondent's officers had lived many years in the immediate vicinity of Cedar lake; knew that the appellant was creating the great reservoir; knew that its north bank was a moraine, and knew as much as the city officers concerning whether it was pervious to water, and because of this information had reason to anticipate that the very thing which happened might happen; that, notwithstanding all this knowledge, it afterwards caused the channel of the creek to be blocked in such a way as to impede the flow of the waters therein. To these facts (and it may be conceded that there was testimony tending to show such to be the facts) it applies the doctrine that one must protect himself and his property against such acts of negligence of others as a reasonably prudent person would have reason to anticipate.

Appellant's reasoning is plausible but not sound. We need not here decide whether one may use and improve his property in total disregard of a danger, resulting from the negligence of someone else, which he knows exists and which he is morally certain will damage him. There is no evidence showing or tending to show this condition. We hold, however, that one is not bound to use his property in anticipation of a situation arising which, because of the negligence of someone else, known to or suspected by him, may or may not cause him damage. The use one may make of

his property is not to be measured or limited by any
such unstable rule as that contended for by appellant.
At least, up to the point where one has become morally
certain that the negligence of another will injure him,
he may make any proper and customary use of his
property in total disregard of any negligence of that
other, whether such negligence be known to him or not.
One owns real estate for the use he may make of it.
Being the owner, he may make such use of it as he sees
fit, so long as he does not injure his neighbor or violate
some principle of the doctrine of police regulation.
His neighbor may not say to him, "you must not improve your land nor plant it to crop, because I have
been guilty of such negligence as may cause your improvements or your crop to be damaged or destroyed."
Any other rule would permit one guilty of wrongdoing
to deprive another of the right of making any lawful
use of his property. If appellant's theory of the law
is to prevail, then every man who owns real estate
below a reservoir of water must use it at his peril, if
he have reason to suspect the dam, through the negligence of the owner, has become weakened; and a farmer takes his chances in planting his land to crop,
simply because he knows a culvert has been so negligently built by another that it will not carry away flood
waters, but may cause them to wash over his land to
his damage. The rule which requires one to make a
reasonable effort to protect his person from the known
negligence of another is a rule of personal conduct and,
in the nature of things, cannot be extended to the use
of property. Respondent knew something about the
moraine and it knew that it formed the northerly bank
of appellant's reservoir. It did not know that it was
or was not impervious to water. From its standpoint,
there was no certainty that what it claims happened

would happen. Must it then, at its peril, make use of the land because of the knowledge it had. If it was guilty of contributory negligence in putting a dam in Boxley creek, it was guilty of contributory negligence in constructing its mills on the bank of the stream.

An extensive examination of the authorities on this question convinces us that they are not in entire accord, and that the subject has not always been treated with the thoroughness its difficulties and importance deserve.

We will first examine the cases out of this court which affect the question. Appellant calls our attention to the case of *Box v. Kelso,* 5 Wash. 360, 31 Pac. 973, which it claims is contrary to our conclusion here. In that case the facts were that the plaintiff had cut some shingle bolts and left them in the woods, under such surroundings as that he knew they were in danger of being destroyed by fire. They were so destroyed, and he charged defendant with negligently causing the destruction. The defendant pleaded contributory negligence. Judge Anders, speaking for the court, among other things, said:

"While it may be true that this property might not have been destroyed if it had been in some other place, or differently situated, still we are of the opinion that ordinary prudence did not require the respondents to provide against the negligent acts of others *which they had no reason to anticipate."* (Italics ours).

But that the court did not use those words in the sense appellant construes them is shown by the facts in the case and by what the court later said in the opinion, as follows:

"They had a perfect right to cut their timber into shingle bolts and to leave them upon their own premises as they did, and as was said by this court in *Tacoma Lumber & Mfg. Co. v. Tacoma,* 1 Wash. 12, 'were entitled at any and all times to have them protected from the wrongful and negligent acts of any and all persons'. From what we have said it follows that the court committed no error in failing to instruct the jury upon the question of contributory negligence.''

Counsel for appellant also call our attention to a quotation from Cyc. found in the recent case of *Rainier Heat & Power Co. v. Seattle,* 113 Wash. 95, 193 Pac. 233, as follows:

"The general rule is that every person has a right to presume that every other person will perform his duty and obey the law, and *in the absence of reasonable ground to think otherwise* (Italics ours) it is not negligence to assume that he is not exposed to danger which can come to him only from violation of law or duty to such other person. Hence failure to anticipate defendant's negligence does not amount to contributory negligence, even though he places his property in an exposed or hazardous position.'' 29 Cyc. 516.

The italicized portion of this quotation may be correct as applied to individual conduct, such as is involved in a personal injury suit. Indeed, the text shows that subject was under consideration, because, in connection with the discussion, it is said:

"This rule (to use reasonable effort to avoid danger) is subject to the exception that as a person is entitled to use his own premises for any lawful purpose, his failure to protect it from the negligence of another will not be contributory negligence.'' 29 Cyc. 516.

Our holding in that case supports our conclusion here. There the facts were that the heat and power company had its plant located in a basement, thirty feet below the level of the street grade. One of the city's water mains, laid in an adjoining street, burst and flooded the cellar and injured and damaged the heating plant therein. Speaking of the question of contributory negligence, we said:

"We are of the opinion that the maintaining of appellant's plant at the level of approximately thirty feet below the street grade was not contributory negligence, and that it must be here so decided as a matter of law. . . . It may have been obliged to anticipate damage from the natural flow of water and the accumulation of surface water, but manifestly, it was not obliged to anticipate danger from any such source as the bursting of this water main."

The appellant contends that the case of *Woolworth Co. v. Seattle*, 104 Wash. 629, 177 Pac. 664, is contrary to our conclusion. But that case, in our judgment, is easily distinguishable from this one. It was there held that no recovery could be had for damages because of the flooding and injury to goods located in a basement, where such flooding was caused by a city sewer of insufficient capacity, and the failure of the plaintiff to maintain and keep in proper repair a back water valve, required by ordinance to be installed. It will be observed that plaintiff was denied recovery because he had violated an express provision of a city ordinance.

In *Fraler v. Sears Union Water Co.*, 12 Cal. 556, 73 Am. Dec. 562, discussing this question, the court said:

"The defendants were bound to see to their own property, and to so govern and control it that injury would not result to their neighbor's. If, in consequence of gross neglect on the part of the plaintiffs, the injury happened, a different rule might be applied; but a mere want of reasonable care to prevent the injury does not impair the right to recover."

In the case of *Clark v. Dyer*, 81 Tex. 339, 16 S. W. 1061, the plaintiff was a farmer and his crops had previously been drowned out because of an insufficient road culvert. Notwithstanding such knowledge, the farmer again planted his ground to grain and again it was destroyed, and upon a suit for damages the defense of contributory negligence was made. The court, discussing this question, said:

"The owner in lawful possession of his land is entitled to use in it any lawful manner he may desire, for any purpose for which it may be adapted. The owner in the exercise of this right is not guilty of negligence if he does not anticipate the results and consequences of acts that are remote, and may never happen, and of which he is not the promoting cause. The negligence that would defeat his recovery must be such as would proximately contribute to the injury. It cannot be said that the owner is guilty of negligence if he plants a crop on land that may be overflowed, when there are no present indications of that fact. . . . The law does not require that the owner should preserve and guard his premises from the effects of injuries caused by the wrongful acts of another before he is justified in the use thereof. A different rule would virtually deprive the owner of the beneficial rights that flow with and are incident to the enjoyment of his estate."

In the case of *Kendrick v. Towle*, 60 Mich. 363, 27 N. W. 567, the court said:

"The obligation of care to prevent the fire from the defendant's engine burning the plaintiff's mill rested upon the defendant, and the fact that old, combustible matter accumulated about the mill, and in near proximity to the railroad, cannot be urged as contributory negligence on the part of the plaintiff. He had a right to use the offal of his mill to fill up the waste and low places about it, just as he was accustomed to do before the railroad was built. He was not obliged to guard his premises to relieve the defendant from liability for his negligent acts."

In support of this general rule see the following cases: *Mississippi Home Ins. Co. v. Louisville, New Orleans & T. R. Co.*, 70 Miss. 119, 12 South. 156; *Helpand v. Independent Tel. Co.*, 88 Neb. 542, 130 N. W. 111; *McLennan v. Brownsville Land & Irrigation Co.*, 46 Tex. Civ. App. 249, 103 S. W. 206; *Emison v. Owy-*

hee Ditch Co., 37 Ore. 577, 62 Pac. 13; *Philadelphia etc.
R. Co. v. Smith*, 64 Fed. 679; *Hollenback v. Dingwell*,
16 Mont. 335, 50 Am. St. 502; *Gulf C. & San Francisco
R. Co. v. Clay*, 28 Tex. Civ. App. 176, 66 S. W. 1115;
Underwood v. Waldron, 33 Mich. 232; *Fritz v. First
Division, St. Paul & Pacific R. Co.*, 22 Minn. 404; *Kellogg
v. Chicago & Northwestern R. Co.*, 26 Wis. 223;
Cook v. Champlain Transportation Co., 1 Denio
(N. Y.) 91; *Yik Hon v. Spring Valley Water Works*, 65
Cal. 619, 4 Pac. 666.

There are many cases touching the question of
whether a railroad company may defend on the ground
of contributory negligence, where private property adjoining the right of way has been destroyed by fire
which was the result of negligence in operating trains.
While such cases are not controlling of this case, they
involve the same general question. A large number of
such cases have been collected and digested in the note
to *Walker v. Chicago, R. I. & P. R. Co.*, 76 Kan. 32,
90 Pac. 772, 12 L. R. A. (N. S.) 624.

We have said that the cases on this question are not
harmonious. One which may be contrary to our conclusion is *Emry v. Raleigh & Gaston R. Co.*, 109 N. C.
589, 14 S. E. 352. Plaintiffs owned land a short distance from a culvert by means of which the defendant's
road crossed a certain creek. It was claimed that this
culvert was too small to allow the waters of the creek
in times of freshet to pass through or under it, and
that as a result a pond was created which overflowed
plaintiff's land and damaged it, and also a brick yard
located on the land. The plaintiffs testified that this
overflow and damage occurred on an average of every
four out of five years. The court said:

"It seems to us clear, and we cannot hesitate to
decide, that no prudent business man would place and
keep his brick-yard and brick-kilns at a place like that

in question, when he would hazard the loss or serious
injury described by the plaintiff four years out of
five. . . . A prudent business man would establish
his business elsewhere and seek his remedy for injury
to his land. . . . The defendant's insufficient culvert caused the flooding of the plaintiff's land. The
latter well knew of this for years; still, they put their
brick-kilns where they had strong reason to believe
they too would be flooded and injured or destroyed.
Thus they contributed to their own injury."

While this case may be distinguished on the facts
from the case at bar because in the one the landowner
had "strong reasons" to believe defendant's negligence would injure his land, because during previous
years it had so done, while in the other case the landowner did not have "strong reasons" to believe it
would be injured, because at no previous time had it
been injured, yet we cannot follow the reasoning of the
cited case. The idea that one by his wrongful act may
drive an owner from his land and force him to "establish his business elsewhere" does not appeal to us.
The plaintiff there owned the land and had a right to
make any lawful use of it. If he could not establish
his brick-kilns there, then he could not plant his crops,
and thus is entirely deprived of any use of his lands.
The foregoing is the strongest case cited by appellant,
and we do not consider it necessary to review any
others. Most of them are personal injury cases or
cases involving flooding of cellars because of defective
sewers, in all of which different principles of law are
involved.

We therefore conclude that the question of contributory negligence is in no wise involved in this case,
and that the court was right in granting a new trial
because he had erred in instructing the jury on that
question.

But appellant contends that, aside from the question of contributory negligence, the court erred in granting a new trial because there was not sufficient evidence of its negligence to carry the case to the jury. We cannot sustain this position. At the trial the appellant's contention was that the waters which damaged respondent's property were those belonging to the natural watershed of Boxley creek, and that none of them came from appellant's reservoir. On the other hand, respondent contended that the waters which injured it seeped from the reservoir through the moraine and were there stored in great quantities till they suddenly broke out and found their way into Boxley creek, and that appellant knew, or should have known, of the pervious character of the moraine. There was testimony to support each of these theories or contentions. It was, therefore, the duty of the court to submit to the jury the question of appellant's negligence.

The judgment is affirmed.

Parker, C. J., Mackintosh, Fullerton, Main, Holcomb, Tolman, and Mitchell, JJ., concur.

[No. 16365.   Department One.   August 8, 1921.]

A. D. ANDREWS, *Appellant*, v. ALETHA W. C. ANDREWS, *Respondent*.[1]

FRAUDS, STATUTE OF (18)—CONTRACT TO DEVISE—PERFORMANCE. An oral promise to make a will in favor of another is enforcible, if founded upon a valuable consideration and deliberately entered into by the deceased, where there has been a full or partial performance of the contract on the part of the promisee; but it must be supported by the strongest evidence of a valuable consideration.

APPEAL (348, 373½)—ASSIGNMENT OF ERROR—REVIEW—TRIAL DE NOVO. Where an equity case is tried *de novo* on appeal, the court has power to reject incompetent evidence in the record which had been admitted in favor of the appellant, and upon which there is no assignment of error.

WITNESSES (41-1)—COMPETENCY—TRANSACTIONS WITH PERSONS SINCE DECEASED—PARTY IN INTEREST. An agreement by a father to will his property to his son in return for the care and support of his parents could not be proved by the testimony of the son's wife, inasmuch as the property to be acquired would constitute community property, being dependent on the rendition of services by the community composed of the son and his wife; and her testimony would be barred under Rem. Code, § 1211, prohibiting a party in interest from testifying in his own behalf as to any transaction with or statement made by a deceased person.

HUSBAND AND WIFE (57)—COMMUNITY PROPERTY—EARNINGS OF HUSBAND AND WIFE. Property to be acquired by a husband under a contract for its devise in return for services rendered would be community property and not be in the nature of a gift, within the meaning of Rem. Code, § 5915, declaring that property and pecuniary rights acquired by a husband "by gift, bequest, devise, or descent" shall constitute his separate property.

Appeal from a judgment of the superior court for King county, Jurey, J., entered October 9, 1920, in favor of the defendant, in an action on contract, tried to the court. Affirmed.

'Reported in 199 Pac. 981.

Jas. A. Dougan and *William A. Gilmore,* for appellant.

Thomas H. Bain, for respondent.

BRIDGES, J.—A. D. Andrews brought this suit for the purpose of establishing and enforcing an alleged oral contract with his father, Joshua Andrews, to the effect that the latter would, by will or otherwise, at the time of his death, give to the plaintiff all property then owned by him. Upon a trial on the merits, the lower court dismissed the action, and the plaintiff has appealed.

The direct and surrounding facts are as follows: Joshua and Harriet Andrews were, respectively, the father and mother of the appellant, and lived in the city of Seattle, while the appellant with his family lived in West Seattle. This was in 1903. At that time, Joshua and his wife owned certain lots in the city of Seattle, on which they lived. Mrs. Andrews, senior, was afflicted with cancer, and for many months the wife of the son, A. D. Andrews, daily at times, and at other times less frequently, went to the home of Mrs. Andrews, senior, and nursed her and took care of her wants. After some months of this manner of care, it was agreed between the two families that Joshua and his wife should move to West Seattle and live in the home of their son and his family. This contemplated move was made sometime in 1903. The mother continued to reside in the home of her son until her death, and the father lived there much longer.

In the early part of January, 1904, it became apparent that Mrs. Andrews, senior, was approaching death, and she desired to make disposition of her property. She seems to have felt herself much indebted to her son and his family for their services to her in

her long and serious sickness, and it was her desire
that they should be compensated. During January,
1904, she made a will giving all of her property to her
husband, but in the will expressed the desire that, at
the death of her husband, the property should go to
their son, the appellant. For some reason which is
not made clear from the testimony, at the same time
Mrs. Andrews, senior, made her will, she and her husband made a deed to appellant covering the property
then owned by them, and immediately thereafter appellant executed a quitclaim deed of the same property
to the father, Joshua Andrews; apparently the deeds
were made with the view of vesting in Joshua the full
title to the property. Mrs. Andrews, senior, died
within a month or two after making her will. The
appellant alleges that, at the time Mrs. Andrews,
senior, made her will, and at the time of the execution
of the deeds above mentioned, it was orally agreed
between Joshua Andrews and the appellant that the
former should continue to live with the latter and receive his care and attention for such length of time as
Joshua should desire to live with him, in consideration
of which Joshua orally agreed that, at the time of his
death, he would will all of his property to his son.
This alleged oral agreement was made, if at all, on
the 2d of January, 1904.

After the death of his wife, Mr. Andrews, senior,
continued to abide with the son and his family until
about the middle of the year 1905, when the son, for
business reasons, went to Nome, Alaska, with a view
to remaining there for at least several years. Mrs.
Andrews, junior, however, continued to reside in the
West Seattle home until July, 1906, when she and her
family moved to Nome. During all of the time previous to the departure of Mrs. Andrews, junior,

Joshua lived with her in her home and she took care of him and furnished him board. When the son's family went to Nome they solicited the father to go with them and agreed to give him a home there. In fact, the testimony shows that arrangements at Nome had already·been made by the son for the proper care of his father. The latter, however, deemed himself too old to make the trip or to live in the rigorous climate of the far north, and refused to accompany the family thence. He continued, however, to live at the son's home in West Seattle, but took care of himself and paid his own living expenses, until 1908, when he was married to the respondent. Shortly thereafter he and his wife took up their residence in the city of Seattle, where they continued to reside until his death several years after. Long after the appellant and his family moved to Nome, and on November 20, 1907, Joshua undertook to make his will. That instrument, however, was void as a will because it had but one witness instead of two, as required by statute. This purported will gave certain small sums to the children of appellant, and all remaining of the estate to the appellant. Still later, and long after he was remarried, and on August 20, 1918, Joshua attached a codicil to the previous will, modifying it to the extent of giving his wife $500 in cash, the household furniture, and the use of the homestead for a period of five years. Except as indicated in the codicil, the will was left as originally written. This codicil was also illegal because it had but one witness.

All the briefs in the case refer to a memorandum opinion of the trial court and quote extensively therefrom, referring to it as part of the record. It is not, however, a part of the record, but from the assertions in the briefs, we take it that the trial court found as a fact that the oral contract was made substantially as contended for by the appellant, but that the latter breached it by moving to Nome.

This court has more than once held that an oral contract of the character here mentioned is enforcible notwithstanding the statute of frauds, if there has been full or partial performance. In fact, that question seems to be so well settled in this court that we deem it unnecessary to do more than cite some of the cases: *Velikanje v. Dickman*, 98 Wash. 584, 168 Pac. 465; *Alexander v. Lewes*, 104 Wash. 32, 175 Pac. 572; *Worden v. Worden*, 96 Wash. 592, 165 Pac. 501; *Swash v. Sharpstein*, 14 Wash. 426, 44 Pac. 862, 32 L. R. A. 796. In the *Lewes* case we said:

"Cases of this kind are not favored, and when the promise rests in parol are even regarded with suspicion, and will not be enforced except upon the strongest evidence that it was founded upon a valuable consideration, and deliberately entered into by the deceased. But while not favored and rarely enforced upon oral proofs, the power to make a valid agreement to dispose of property by will in a particular way has long been recognized."

The first question we must discuss is whether the original contract was made. It is a well settled principle of law that contracts of this character must be established by clear and convincing evidence. The appellant undertook to establish the existence of this contract by the testimony of his wife. At the trial the respondent objected to her testifying concerning any conversations on this subject had between Joshua Andrews and the appellant, for the reason that the appellant's wife was a party in interest. The respondent's objections were overruled. The appellant neither in his brief nor in his oral argument touched the question as to the competency of his wife to testify

concerning the contract, and the respondent makes no
further argument on the subject than that his "objections to all of her testimony should have been sustained. She was the wife of the plaintiff and therefore
vitally interested. She will surely be benefited if he
prevails in this action." The question, however, is
foremost in the case and must be decided. While the
judgment of the lower court ran in favor of the respondent, against whom this witness testified, and
respondent has not appealed, yet this is an equity case
and we must hear it *de novo;* consequently, we must
consider only such testimony as is competent. Section
1211, Rem. Code, is as follows:

"No person offered as a witness shall be excluded
from giving evidence by reason of his interest in the
event of an action, as a party thereto or otherwise;
but such interest may be shown to affect his credibility: *Provided, however,* That in an action or proceeding where the adverse party sues or defends as executor, administrator, or legal representative of any deceased person, or as deriving right or title by, through,
or from any deceased person, or as the guardian or
conservator of the estate of any insane person or of
any minor under the age of fourteen years, then a
party in interest or to the record shall not be admitted
to testify in his own behalf as to any transaction had
by him with or statement made to him by any such
deceased or insane person, or by such minor under the
age of fourteen years. . . . ."

This court has expressly held that, if a like oral contract with the husband was concerning community
property, or if the property sought to be acquired by
the suit would be community property when acquired,
then the wife is an interested party and is forbidden
by the statute to testify concerning the contract. In
the case of *Whitney v. Priest,* 26 Wash. 48, 66 Pac. 108,
the facts were as follows: Whitney was a physician

and surgeon and claimed to have entered into a verbal contract with Harriet S. Priest, agreeing to perform certain professional services for her, for which she agreed to pay him an agreed amount. She subsequently died, and Whitney instituted suit against her estate to recover the amount of the alleged agreed compensation. He undertook to prove by his wife the conversations between himself and Mrs. Priest concerning the amount of compensation agreed to be paid. After quoting the statute, we said:

"The plaintiff and the witness Josephine Whitney were husband and wife. The professional services which were the subject of contract between plaintiff and the deceased involved the community interest. The compensation for such services belonged to the community. Mrs. Whitney was interested equally with her husband. She must necessarily be said, therefore, to be a party in interest, and the transaction and the statements made to plaintiff must equally involve his wife. The witness then falls within the disability of the proviso of the statute, and it was error to admit her testimony as to the transaction and statements made by the deceased to the plaintiff."

The whole question here, then, resolves itself into the proposition whether the property which the appellant sought to recover would have been, had he succeeded in recovering it, community property or his separate property. If it would have been community property, then the wife was a party in interest and could not testify, and the objection of the respondent should have been sustained.

We are convinced that the property sought to be acquired by this action would have been community property had it been acquired. Section 5915, Rem. Code, defines the separate property of the husband as follows:

"Property and pecuniary rights owned by the husband before marriage and that acquired by him afterwards by gift, bequest, devise or descent, with the rents, issues and profits thereof, shall not be subject to the debts and contracts of his wife, and he may manage, lease, sell, convey, encumber or devise by will, such property without the wife joining in such management, alienation or encumbrance, as freely and to the same extent as though he were unmarried."

Section 5916, Rem. Code, defines in substantially the same words the separate property of the wife. Section 5917, Rem. Code, defines community property as follows:

"Property, not acquired or owned as prescribed in the next two preceding sections, acquired after marriage by either husband or wife, or both, is community property."

The main question is, was the property sought to be obtained by this suit acquired by "gift, bequest, devise or descent," within the spirit of the statute?

We are satisfied that it would not have been so acquired. It would have been acquired by contract. There is no element of gift, bequest or devise involved in this case. Joshua Andrews, according to the alleged agreement, was to will his property to his son for a consideration, and that consideration was that the latter was to maintain and support him during the remainder of his life, or such portion thereof as he might elect to accept such maintenance and support. The testimony was that the services to be performed in payment of the property to be acquired were performed by the appellant and his wife. It was their community property which housed and sheltered Joshua Andrews; it was the community money of the appellant and his wife which furnished, and was to furnish, the table from which Mr. Andrews, senior, was to eat. The testimony shows that the appellant's wife did the housework and cooked the food, and did the other usual duties in the maintenance of the home, and in the care and attention given to Mr. Andrews, senior. Everything that went into his maintenance was the joint effort of the appellant and his wife. In no true sense was the appellant to acquire this property by gift. He was to acquire it by virtue of a contract which was to be performed on the one side by himself and his wife. Bouvier's Law Dictionary defines "Gift" as a "voluntary conveyance or transfer of property; that is, one not founded on the consideration of money or love. A voluntary, immediate, absolute transfer of property without consideration." The "gift, bequest, devise or descent" contemplated by the statute as constituting separate property is not based upon contract or consideration, and property willed by one to another in compliance with a contract between the parties is not a gift or bequest in contemplation of the statute. If the appellant had alleged and shown that the contract was a personal one between his father and himself and was to be performed, and was performed, by means of his separate property and his individual endeavors, then the property to have been acquired might have been his separate property, and his wife might have testified as to the terms of the contract. But this situation is not before us and we do not decide it. But, even in that instance, it would be his separate property by purchase, and it would not have been his by gift, devise or descent within the spirit of the statute. If the alleged contract had been made by the appellant with a stranger and not with his blood relation, then it would seem to us that everyone must say that the property to be acquired under it would be community property, because we have always held that property acquired by the joint efforts of the husband and wife is presumed to be community property. The mere fact that it is alleged that the contract here was made with the appellant's father could not change the legal situation, and the legal effect must be the same as if the contract had been made with entire strangers.

Without the testimony of the appellant's wife, there is not sufficient evidence upon which to base any contract. While the self-sacrifice made by the appellant, and particularly by his wife, is to be highly commended, the rules of law forbid them any compensation.

The judgment must be affirmed.

PARKER, C. J., MACKINTOSH, FULLERTON, and HOLCOMB, JJ., concur.

[No. 16313.   Department One.   August 8, 1921.]

J. I. FARRIER et al., Respondents, v. RITZVILLE WAREHOUSE COMPANY, Appellant.[1]

CORPORATIONS (26, 27)—BY-LAWS—AMENDMENT. A by-law of a corporation, discriminating, within reasonable limits, respecting dividends payable to stockholders who deal with the corporation and thereby increase its profits, and those who do not deal with it, is a valid exercise of corporate power.

SAME (69, 70)—DIVIDENDS—VESTED RIGHTS OF STOCKHOLDERS. Where a corporate by-law gave stockholders a ten per cent dividend on the par value of their stock and distributed the balance of the net profits to the stockholders hauling and selling wheat to the company, an amendment of the by-law reducing the dividend of the common stockholders to seven per cent against their protest was invalid as an interference with vested rights.

SAME (69, 70). Stockholders having a vested right in dividends, are not estopped to object to an amendment of the by-laws affecting their rights, where they acted promptly, although they failed to act and are estopped as to a prior amendment.

[1]Reported in 199 Pac. 984.

Appeal from a judgment of the superior court for Adams county, Truax, J., entered January 19, 1920, in favor of the plaintiffs, in an action for equitable relief, tried to the court. Modified.

C. W. Rathbun, for appellant.

Adams & Miller, for respondents.

MACKINTOSH, J.—In 1907, the appellant was incorporated for the purpose of conducting a farmers' grain and warehouse business, and adopted, as one of its by-laws, a provision that the dividends of the corporation should be distributed among the stockholders by an equal distribution to them of fifty per cent thereof, and that the remaining fifty per cent should be divided among the stockholders hauling and selling wheat to the company, in proportion to the amount of wheat so sold and hauled. Another by-law provided that the by-laws might be amended, repealed or altered by a majority vote of the stockholders.

The respondents were subscribers to, and original stockholders in, the appellant company. Over the objection, or, at least, without the consent of the respondents, the by-law in regard to dividends was amended in 1912, so that the stockholders should receive ten per cent dividend on the par value of their stock, and the balance of the net profits should be distributed among the stockholders hauling and selling wheat to the company, in proportion to the amount so hauled and sold. In June, 1919, over the protest of the respondents, this by-law was again amended so that the dividends should be paid to each stockholder at the rate of seven per cent on his stock, and the balance of the net profits should be divided among the stockholders hauling and selling wheat to the company, in proportion to the number of bushels so hauled and sold. The respondents thereupon instituted this action to enjoin the corporation from distributing profits in accordance with this latest by-law.

As stated by Thompson, Corporations, § 971:

"A corporation authorized by its charter to make such by-laws as may be necessary to attain the objects for which it is created and to carry on and transact its business affairs, on the plainest principles of right, as well as by its inherent power, has the power to alter, amend or repeal such by-laws from time to time, when necessary to carry out the objects of the corporation or for the better conduct of its business. 'The power to enact by-laws' said the Supreme court of Indiana, 'is inherent in every corporation as an incident of its existence. This power is a continuous one. No one has the right to presume that by-laws will remain unchanged. Associations and corporations have a right to change their by-laws when the welfare of the corporation or association requires it, and it is not forbidden by the organic law. The power which enacts may alter or amend'. This power to amend or repeal by-laws, even when expressly conferred by the charter, it must be remembered, cannot be exercised by the corporation itself in such manner as to impair any rights that have been given and vested by virtue of such by-laws."

The question then arises in this case whether these amendments to the by-laws are invalid by reason of their affecting or destroying vested rights. In other words, whether the respondents, at the time that they became subscribers to the capital stock of the appellant, had a vested right given them by the then existing by-laws in the distribution of dividends, fifty per cent to the stockholders, the remaining fifty per cent to such stockholders as might have done business with the company.

There is no question that the original by-law is a valid exercise of the powers of the company; the rule being, that a by-law may discriminate within reasonable limits between stockholders who deal with the corporation and who thereby increase its profits, and those who do not deal with it. *Mooney v. Farmers' Mercantile & Elevator Co. etc.*, 138 Minn. 199, 164 N. W. 804. This right has been tacitly recognized by this court in the case of *Johnson v. Goodenough*, 103 Wash. 625, 175 Pac. 306. The briefs of neither party refer to any case which bears directly upon the point before us, and so far as our independent search has led us, the case most nearly in point upon the question here is that of *Kent v. Quicksilver Mining Co.*, 78 N. Y. 159, which is a thoroughly considered authority, and the reasoning of which seems conclusive. The facts in that case were that the shares of the capital stock in the company involved in that litigation were divided equally in amount, and were entitled to an equal distribution of dividends, but thereafter, by a majority vote of the stockholders, the stock was divided so that a portion of it was given preference over the other in sharing in the earnings. The New York court, in passing upon these questions, said:

"Then there arises the query, whether there was at that time power in the corporation to distinguish between the stockholders in it, to form them into two classes, and to give to one class rights in the corporate property, business and earnings from which the other was shut out.

"We are not prepared to say that, at the first, the corporation might not have lawfully divided the interest in its capital stock into shares arranged in classes, preferring one class to another in the right it should have in the profits of the business. The charter gave power to make such by-laws as it might deem proper, consistent with constitution and law; and to issue certificates of stock representing the value of the property. We know nothing in the constitution or the law that inhibits a corporation from beginning its cor-

porate action by classifying the shares in its capital
stock, with peculiar privileges to one share over another, and thus offering its stock to the public for subscriptions thereto. No rights are got until a subscription is made. Each subscriber would know for what
class of stock he put down his name, and what right he
got when he thus became a stockholder. There need
be no deception or mistake; there would be no trench-
ing upon rights previously acquired; no contract, express or implied, would be broken or impaired.

"This corporation did otherwise. A by-law was
duly made, which declared the whole value of its property and the whole amount of its capital stock, and
divided the whole of it into shares equal in amount,
and directed the issuing of certificates of stock therefor. It is not to be said that this by-law authorized
anything but shares equal in value and in right; or that
the taker of one did not own as large an interest in the
corporation, its capital, affairs, and profits to come, as
any other holder of a share. Certificates of stock were
issued under this by-law, that gave no expression of
anything different from that. When that by-law was
adopted, it was as much the law of the corporation as
if its provisions had been a part of the charter. . . .
Thereby, and by the certificate, as between it and every
stockholder, the capital stock of the company was fixed
in amount, in the number of shares into which it was
divisible, and in the peculiar and relative value of each
share. The by-law entered into the compact between
the corporation and every taker of a share; it was in
the nature of a contract between them. The holding
and owning of a share gave a right which could not be
divested without the assent of the holder and owner; or
unless the power so to do had been reserved in some
way. . . . Shares of stock are in the nature of
choses in action, and give the holder a fixed right in the
division of the profits or earnings of a company so long
as it exists, and of its effects when it is dissolved. That
right is as inviolable as is any right in property and
can no more be taken away or lessened, against the will
of the owner than can any other right, unless power is

reserved in the first instance, when it enters into the
constitution of the right; or is properly derived afterwards from a superior law giver. The certificate of
stock is the muniment of the shareholder's title, and
evidence of his right. It expresses the contract between the corporation and his co-stockholders and himself; and that contract cannot, he being unwilling, be
taken away from him or changed as to him without his
prior dereliction, or under the conditions above stated.
Now it is manifest that any action of a corporation
which takes hold of the shares of its capital stock
already sold and in the hands of lawful owners, and
divides them into two classes—one of which is thereby
given prior right to a receipt of a fixed sum from the
earnings before the other may have any receipt therefrom, and is given an equal share afterwards with the
other in what earnings may remain—destroys the
equality of the shares, takes away a right which
originally existed in it, and materially varies the effect
of the certificate of stock.

"There is a power in this charter to alter, amend,
add to or repeal, at pleasure, by-laws before made. It
is argued from this that it was in the power of the corporate body, in due form and manner, to alter the by-
law which had fixed the amount of the capital stock
and the number and relative value of the shares thereof.
The power to make by-laws is to make such as are not
inconsistent with the constitution and the law; and the
power to alter has the same limit, so that no alteration
could be made which would infringe a right already
given and secured by the contract of the corporation.
Nor was the power to alter, to the extent of affecting
the contracted relative value of a share, reserved when
the share was sold to the stockholder, so as to enter
into and form a part of the contract. An alteration is
a *pro tanto* repeal; but no private corporation can repeal a by-law so as to impair rights which have been
given and become vested by virtue of the by-law afterwards repealed. All by-laws must be reasonable and
consistent with the general principles of the laws of
the land, which are to be determined by the courts,
when a case is properly before them. . . . A by-

law may regulate or modify the constitution of a corporation, but cannot alter it. . . . The alteration
of a by-law is but the making of another upon the same
matter. If the first must be reasonable and in accord
with principles of law, so must that which alters it.
If then the power is reserved to alter, amend or repeal, and that reservation enters into a contract, the
power reserved is to pass reasonable by-laws, agree-
able to law. But a by-law that will disturb a vested
right is not such. . . . And it differs not when the
power to make and alter by-laws is expressly given to
a majority of the stockholders, and that the obnoxious
ordinance is passed in due form.

"But there remains a serious question; whether,
though there was at the outstart a minority of the
stockholders who gave no assent to the corporate act,
there has not been such tacit acquiescence and delay in
action by that minority as to amount to indefensible
laches and estoppel upon those who constituted it and
their assigns. In our judgment there has; and we find
here a safe place on which to rest our decisions in these
cases. The findings show that the by-laws empowering
the creation and issue of the preferred stock were
authorized at a stockholders' meeting regularly called
and held and conducted; that the stock was at once offered for subscription to all of the stockholders; that
a circular informing thereof was issued by authority
and distributed to the stockholders; that though all of
them did not avail themselves of the chance to take it,
it was not because the chance was not known; a large
number of them did subscribe, and paid money for the
privilege to the corporation, and that money went into
the assets and business of the company; certificates for
the preferred stock were thereupon issued, and it, as
well as the common stock, was dealt in by the public,
sales were made of the two kinds openly at the Stock
Exchange, at prices for the one larger than for the
other, and quoted in the daily public prints; and from
year to year for four years the annual reports of the
directors to the stockholders spoke of the two kinds of
stock. There was ample knowledge, or means of knowledge, on the part of all stockholders, of the action of

the corporation in the creation of the two kinds of stock, of the issue of certificates for the preferred stock, of the entry of that stock into the channels of trade, of the public dealings in it at the especial marts for the sale of such property, and of the continued recognition of its existence and validity by the company and the public. It is not to be conceived that the owners of the common stock of this corporation did not have actual knowledge that there had been created a stock having ostensibly greater right and value than their own, and that it had gone into the market and was dealt in by the public interested in the validity of it. For the lapse of four years, however, there was no action of the company, or of an individual stockholder, to have a judicial declaration that the company had exceeded its powers in the creation of the stock, and that it was invalid. We think that these facts, most of which are set forth in the findings in two of the cases, warrant the conclusion of law therein, that the stockholders, by acquiescing in the action of the corporation in making the preferred stock, have ratified and assented thereto, and that the same is binding on them by reason of such assent and ratification.''

This court in two cases seems to have expressed the same idea. In *Seattle Trust Co. v. Pitner,* 18 Wash. 401, 51 Pac. 1048, it was said:

''We view the by-law relative to dividends as in effect appropriating the net proceeds arising from the company's business. Eight per cent was payable to the preferred stockholders, and a dividend was payable at the date fixed by the company. After such date was fixed and the 8 per cent, due annually, paid to the preferred stockholders, the net profits remaining were devoted to the common stockholders. This by-law had the force and effect of a contract, and we see no good reason why it should not be given its full effect.''

In *State ex rel. Gwinn v. Bucklin,* 83 Wash. 23, 145 Pac. 58, L. R. A. 1915D 285, the court observed:

'' 'Each stockholder shall have the right to inspect the books and records of the company at any time dur-

ing regular business hours of said company'. This by-
law, we think, has all the force and effect of a statute
containing such a provision.''

Under the original by-law, the then stockholders had
stock which was to receive one-half of the dividends declared by the company, and the remaining one-half of
the dividends was to be divided among such of them as
did business with the company. Under the last by-law,
of which complaint is now made, the present stockholders have stock which is limited to dividends in the
amount of seven per cent, with the provision that out of
the net proceeds a bonus shall be paid to such stockholders as do business with the company.

A very decided and marked difference is made by
these two by-laws as to the participation of the stock
in the profits of the corporation. Under the original
by-law, the stockholders had a vested right to have
dividends applied as there provided; under the last by-
law, the stock is confined to a seven per cent profit, unless held by one of those stockholders who have transacted some business with the company. Whether or
not, in the conduct of the business of the company, the
latter provision might be more advantageous to the
stockholder than was the original one, is entirely beside
the question; even if more advantageous, the majority
of the stockholders cannot compel the minority owners
to submit to such a change. The matter is entirely for
the minority stockholder's determination as to whether
he is willing to allow the vested right which he has acquired under the original by-law to be taken from him,
and to have substituted therefor a fixed rate of interest
upon his stock investment.

The question then arises whether the respondents,
having in 1912 acquiesced in the modification of the
original by-law as to dividends, should not now be de-

nied the right to question the authority of the majority of the stockholders to again alter the by-laws on that subject. Although the respondents are estopped by reason of their failure to take any action to have set aside the amendment of the by-law passed in 1912, and by accepting dividends under the terms of that by-law they will not now be allowed to question its validity, it cannot be said that they are estopped from complaining of this last amendment, which materially reduced the amount of dividends provided for the common stock. Having acted promptly after the passage of this amendment, which was carried without their consent, they are now privileged to maintain this action.

The decree of the trial court will be modified so as to annul the by-law of 1919, leaving in effect and operation the one of 1912, which the respondents have estopped themselves from complaining of.

PARKER, C. J., BRIDGES, FULLERTON, and HOLCOMB, JJ., concur.

[No. 16565.   *En Banc.*   August 8, 1921.]

H. H. CLARK, *Appellant,* v. DORA KILIAN *et al., Respondents.*[1]

CHATTEL MORTGAGES (23, 43-2)—VALIDITY—FAILURE TO RECORD—RIGHTS OF SUBSEQUENT PURCHASERS. A chattel mortgage not filed for record within ten days after its execution is void, as against a subsequent purchaser in good faith, notwithstanding the mortgage may have been recorded prior to the acquisition of title by such purchaser, under Rem. Code, § 3660, providing that a chattel mortgage not so recorded shall be void as to all creditors of the mortgagor, existing or subsequent, whether they have a lien or not, and as against all subsequent purchasers in good faith.

SAME (43)—NOTICE OF MORTGAGE—BURDEN OF PROOF. In a contest between a chattel mortgagee whose mortgage was not recorded and a subsequent purchaser of the mortgaged property, the burden of proof is upon the mortgagee to show that the purchaser had actual notice of the existence of the mortgage.

Appeal from a judgment of the superior court for King county, Frater, J., entered December 6, 1920, in favor of the defendants, in an action to restrain a mortgage foreclosure sale, tried to the court. Reversed.

Walter G. Kienstra, for appellant.

Robert D. Hamlin, for respondents.

MACKINTOSH, J.—Does a mortgagee, who has failed to file his chattel mortgage within ten days from the time of its execution, have any rights against a purchaser of the chattel whose bill of sale was given him two months subsequently to the actual filing of the chattel mortgage? An answer to this question will dispose of this appeal.

The facts are: On May 24, 1919, respondent Kilian sold a boat to C. E. King, who gave a chattel mortgage

[1]Reported in 199 Pac. 721.

thereon, which was not filed with the county auditor until July 15, 1919. Kilian, on September 22, 1919, conveyed the boat by bill of sale to the appellant, free of all incumbrances. The notes to secure which the chattel mortgage was given not being paid, Kilian attempted to foreclose his mortgage by notice and sale. Thereupon the appellant brought this action, alleging that he was the owner of the property, and asking to have the sale restrained.

Prior to the legislative session of 1915, the requisites necessary to the giving of a chattel mortgage were contained in § 3660, Rem. & Bal. Code, and under that section, in as far as it relates to the question of the necessity of filing the chattel mortgage within ten days from its execution, this court has held that a chattel mortgage was valid, as to creditors other than those who had acquired some form of lien upon the mortgaged property, whether the mortgage was properly recorded or not. *Heal v. Evans Creek Coal & Coke Co.*, 71 Wash. 225, 128 Pac. 211. It has also been held that an unrecorded mortgage might, after the ten-day period provided by the statute, be recorded and become effective after the date of such recording as to all creditors, both prior and subsequent, except such creditors as may have had a lien prior to the filing. *Pacific Coast Biscuit Co. v. Perry*, 77 Wash. 352, 137 Pac. 483; *Watson v. First Nat. Bank*, 82 Wash. 65, 143 Pac. 451; *Keyes v. Sabin*, 101 Wash. 618, 172 Pac. 835, and other cases cited in these opinions.

In view of these decisions, and with the obvious purpose of changing the rule they announced, the legislature, in 1915, passed the act (Rem. Code, § 3660), which provides that a chattel mortgage not filed within ten days from the time of its execution is void "as against all creditors of the mortgagor, both existing and subse-

quent, whether or not they have or claim a lien upon
such property, and against all subsequent purchasers,
pledgees, and mortgagees and incumbrancers for value
in good faith. . . ." Under this statute, a chattel
mortgage not recorded within the time is void as to all
the persons mentioned, and as to them is of no effect,
even though it may be filed subsequently to the ten-day
period. The belated filing may carry actual notice to
subsequent purchasers, pledgees, mortgagees and incumbrancers for value so as to take them out of the protection of the "good faith" clause of the statute. As we
have held in *Othello State Bank v. Case Threshing Machine Co.*, 113 Wash. 680, 194 Pac. 563, citing several
decisions of this court, "good faith" includes "without
notice."

In the case of *Robertson, Thieme & Morris v. Whit-
tier*, 112 Wash. 6, 191 Pac. 763, the rule which we announce is suggested, although the decision went off on
another point.

Although the record is silent upon this question
whether the appellant took his bill of sale without notice of the prior chattel mortgage, this is not sufficient
to defeat his claim. The burden of alleging and proving notice is upon one claiming the personal property
under the alleged chattel mortgage. In *Manhattan
Trust Co. v. Seattle Coal & Iron Co.*, 16 Wash. 499,
48 Pac. 333, 737, we said:

"There is no evidence whatever that the petitioners
had any notice of the existence of any chattel mortgage
in favor of the plaintiff. Counsel for plaintiff and receiver argued that as petitioners, as creditors, have not
negatived notice or knowledge on their part, it should
be inferred against them; but this would be a novel
rule and one which we have never seen applied. Such
allegation and proof of notice should come from the one
claiming the personal property under the alleged mortgage."

Under the plain language of the statute, the chattel mortgage in this case was void as to the appellant if he was a subsequent purchaser in good faith.

There being no proof to contradict his good faith, the lower court should have enjoined respondent's sale, and for failure to do so, the judgment is reversed.

PARKER, C. J., BRIDGES, FULLERTON, MAIN, HOLCOMB, TOLMAN, and MITCHELL, JJ., concur.

[No. 16634.   Department Two.   August 9, 1921.]

THE STATE OF WASHINGTON, *on the Relation of John Z. Bayless, Plaintiff,* v. THE SUPERIOR COURT FOR KING COUNTY, *Boyd J. Tallman, Judge, et al., Respondents.*[1]

CERTIORARI (6, 13)—WHEN LIES—ADEQUACY OF REMEDY BY APPEAL—ORDER DENYING INJUNCTION. The action of the superior court in denying a temporary injunction to restrain the sheriff from selling mortgaged personalty on a foreclosure of a mortgage by notice and sale, pending proceedings by the mortgagor contesting the amount due, is subject to review by writ of certiorari, since the remedy by appeal from final judgment would be inadequate if the sheriff should be allowed to proceed with the sale.

Certiorari to review an order of the superior court for King county, Tallman, J., entered July 12, 1921, refusing to enjoin proceedings to foreclose a chattel mortgage. Reversed.

Piles & Halverstadt, for relator.

MITCHELL, J.—John Z. Bayless mortgaged certain personal property to Frank O. Gordon to secure the payment of two promissory notes. After maturity of

[1]Reported in 199 Pac. 977.

the notes, the mortgagee proceeded to foreclose his
mortgage by notice and sale under § 1104 *et seq.*, Rem.
Code, relating to the foreclosure of chattel mortgages.
Promptly, the mortgagor, contesting the amount
claimed to be due in the notice and proposed sale by
the sheriff, commenced an action therefor in the superior court against the mortgagee and against the
sheriff to enjoin that process of foreclosure. On the
hearing of the show cause order and notice why injunction should not issue, the sheriff having been temporarily restrained in the meantime, the superior
court dissolved the emergency restraining order and
refused injunction. The mortgagor has, by writ of
review proceedings, called in question the action of the
superior court, claiming he has no plain, speedy and
adequate remedy at law, and that the superior court
in making its determination violated to the prejudice
of the relator a rule of law affecting his rights.

Section 1110, Rem. Code, provides that the right of
the mortgagee to foreclose by notice and sale by the
sheriff, as well as the amount claimed to be due, "may
be contested by any person interested in so doing, and
the proceedings may be transferred to the superior
court, for which purpose an injunction may issue if
necessary." Certainly the mortgagor is a "person interested", and there can be no question that injunction is necessary where, as here, the mortgagee resists
the application for it and insists that the sheriff shall
not be disturbed in the summary proceedings and sale.
That is, injunction is necessary if there shall be an effective transfer of the cause to the superior court as
contemplated by the statute.

Citing *State ex rel. Lilly Co. v. Brawley*, 104 Wash.
374, 176 Pac. 337, respondent herein relies upon the
rule:

"This court has uniformly held that an extraordinary writ will not issue to review or supersede an order denying a temporary injunction, which by statute is not appealable, unless there is a finding of insolvency, because the legislative intent is that such orders shall be reviewed only on appeal from the final judgment."

But the reason of that rule and the authorities which announce it rest on cases where the trial court had and exercised jurisdiction over all matters pertaining to the controversy between the parties, and it was apparent that no substantial right was denied. That rule is not applicable here. It was decided in *Mack v. Doak*, 50 Wash. 119, 96 Pac. 825, that the statutory form of foreclosure by notice and sale by the sheriff constituted process sufficient to protect the sheriff against the claim of conversion; so that in the present case, without an injunctive order against the sheriff, the court will not have jurisdiction of all matters pertaining to the controversy. While the court is engaged in settling the account between the parties, the sheriff will be permitted to proceed with the foreclosure for the full amount of the face of the obligations, in defiance of the mortgagor's protest as he seeks to avail himself of a specific statute to transfer the whole matter to the superior court. Respondent's argument is accepted that there is no appeal from the order of the superior court except as it may be brought up by an appeal from a final judgment. Manifestly an appeal at that time would not be adequate, for the reason that the statute provides for transferring the proceedings, not simply a part of them, to the superior court. It does not propose that the court shall control a part of the controversy while the sheriff shall carry on the foreclosure. Where the remedy by appeal is inadequate, we have always recognized the right to an extraordinary writ. *State ex rel. Silver Basin Mining Co. v. Superior Court*, 110 Wash. 559, 188 Pac. 384.

One of the questions involving the merits to be determined by the court upon the hearing in writ of review proceedings is, "Whether in making the determination, any rule of law affecting the rights of the parties thereto has been violated to the prejudice of the relator." Rem. Code, § 1010. The right to transfer the foreclosure proceedings from the sheriff to the superior court is unqualified in the statute, and the refusal of the court to enjoin the sheriff where necessary, as we find the case to be here, amounts to the denial of a rule of law, prejudicially affecting the rights of the relator.

Reversed, with directions to the superior court to issue the injunction prayed for by the plaintiff in that case, the relator here, upon his furnishing a proper bond.

PARKER, C. J., MAIN, BRIDGES, and TOLMAN, JJ., concur.

[No. 16286.   Department Two.   August 9, 1921.]

THE STATE OF WASHINGTON, *on the Relation of
Joseph B. Lindsley, Prosecuting Attorney
for Spokane County, Respondent,* v. JOHN
GRADY *et al., Defendants,* BERNARD
PARENT, *Appellant.*

THE STATE OF WASHINGTON, *on the Relation of
Joseph B. Lindsley, Prosecuting Attorney
for Spokane County, Respondent,* v.
JOHN GRADY *et al., Defendants,*
JOHN GRADY, *Appellant.*

THE STATE OF WASHINGTON, *on the Relation of
Joseph B. Lindsley, Prosecuting Attorney
for Spokane County, Respondent,* v.
JOHN GRADY *et al., Defendants,*
CHARLES CRAIG, *Appellant.*[1]

VENUE (18)—CHANGE—PREJUDICE OF JUDGE—CONTEMPT—STATUTES—CONSTRUCTION. One cited for contempt, charged with the violation of an injunction order by acts not committed in the presence of the court, is entitled to a change of judges on affidavits setting up the prejudice of the presiding judge.

Appeal from judgments of the superior court for Spokane county, Webster, J., entered July 12, 14, 17, 1920, upon trials and convictions of contempt. Reversed.

W. C. Donovan, for appellants.

W. C. Meyer, for respondent.

TOLMAN, J.—On January 5, 1920, the superior court for Spokane county issued an injunction in this cause, restraining and forbidding the defendants, and all others who were associated and acting in concert with them, from doing certain things not necessary to be

[1]Reported in 199 Pac. 980.

here detailed. Appellant John Grady was a defendant
in the original action, while the appellants Craig and
Parent were not parties thereto.

In July, 1920, separate affidavits were filed in the
cause, charging each of the appellants separately with
violating the injunction order by acts not committed in
the presence of the court. Bench warrants were issued and each was brought into court to answer to the
charge of contempt. Upon his first appearance on
said charge, each of the appellants moved for a change
of judges, and each motion was duly supported by the
usual affidavit, charging that the presiding judge before whom the case was then pending was prejudiced.
This motion was denied in each proceeding, as also
were motions to quash, and demands for jury trials.
Thereafter each appellant was tried, found guilty of
contempt, and sentenced to serve a term in the county
jail. Each appeals, and by stipulation the cases are
here consolidated, because each presents the same
question.

Although the question is here raised by appeal instead of by applying for a writ of mandate, an examination of the record convinces us that the point involved is identical with that decided in *State ex rel.
Cody v. Superior Court,* 112 Wash. 571, 192 Pac. 935,
and *State ex rel. Russell v. Superior Court,* 77 Wash.
631, 138 Pac. 291, and since our views have been fully
expressed in those cases, a rediscussion of the matter
seems unnecessary.

Upon the authority of those cases, we hold that it
was error to deny the motions for a change of judges,
and the judgments appealed from must be, and they
are, reversed.

PARKER, C. J., MAIN, MITCHELL, and BRIDGES, J.J.,
concur.

[No. 16328.   Department Two.   August 9, 1921.]

THE STATE OF WASHINGTON, *on the Relation of Sarah B. Foley et al., Respondents,* v. CLAUDE C. RAMSEY *et al., as County Commissioners of King County, Appellants.*[1]

MANDAMUS (31, 35)—ACTS OF PUBLIC OFFICERS—COUNTY BOARD—MATTERS OF DISCRETION. Mandamus will not lie to compel the board of county commissioners to act upon a petition for a rehearing of their order establishing a drainage district, upon an allegation that the order was based upon a mistake of fact as to the existence of a protest against the establishment of the district, where it does not clearly appear that the order had been entered by mistake under such circumstances as would make it the duty of the board to correct the mistake, and that they, arbitrarily and without the exercise of any discretion, have refused to take the steps necessary to make the correction.

Appeal from an order of the superior court for King county, Tallman, J., entered December 7, 1920, directing the board of county commissioners to proceed to a rehearing upon a petition for the establishment of a drainage district. Reversed.

Fred C. Brown and *Howard A. Hanson,* for appellants.

Elias A. Wright, Sam A. Wright, Jay C. Allen, and *S. H. Steele,* for respondents.

TOLMAN, J.—On or about February 18, 1918, certain owners of property in the Snoqualmie Valley, in King county, filed a petition with the county commissioners of that county, seeking to have a drainage district established under the provisions of Rem. Code, § 4226. Thereafter the preliminary work was done apparently as required by the statute, and on January 6, 1920, the county engineer filed with the clerk of the board of

[1]Reported in 199 Pac. 978.

county commissioners his report covering the matters
which the statute requires, and recommending the establishment of a drainage district as prayed for in the
petition theretofore filed, whereupon the board of
county commissioners fixed a time and place for a hearing upon such petition and report, and gave notice
thereof by publication in the official newspaper of King
county for the time and in the manner which the statute
directs. Pursuant to such notice, a hearing was had at
the office of the board on February 9, 1920; no one in
any manner appearing in opposition, or then protesting, the board entered its order establishing the drainage district.

Thereafter, on March 25, 1920, respondents, as relators, filed their petition in the superior court, in
which they alleged, among other things, that, shortly
after the petition for the establishment of the drainage district was filed with the board of county commissioners, they employed an attorney to represent them
as protestants; that a protest was prepared, signed by
more than thirty-five of the property owners of the
district, which protest was turned over to the attorney,
and afterwards by him duly filed with the clerk of the
board of county commissioners; that such attorney
continued in charge of their interests, and they relied
upon him to notify them of any hearing ordered, so
that they might appear in support of their protest;
that, during a period of practically two years which
intervened between the filing of the petition for the
drainage district and the filing of the report of the
county engineer, their attorney so employed kept constantly in touch with the board of county commissioners, examined the files from time to time, kept himself
acquainted with the situation, so that if a hearing were
ordered a proper showing might be made; visited the

office of the county commissioners more than fifty
times during such period, and that such attorney was
informed by the clerk of the board and by the board
that he would receive notice from them of the time of
the hearing, if one were ordered, so that his clients
might be heard; that, in January, 1920, the attorney
representing petitioners became ill with pneumonia,
was confined to his bed and was unconscious for a considerable length of time, and from the time of so becoming ill until after the hearing on February 9, was
wholly unable to give any attention to business; that
the notice published by order of the county commissioners fixing the date of the hearing was published in
remote country newspapers of limited circulation and
many miles from the residences of petitioners; were
not seen by petitioners, who had no knowledge or notice of said hearing, and no notice thereof was given to
their attorney, and neither petitioners nor their attorney had any knowledge of such hearing until after the
same had taken place, when they learned of the results of such hearing through the news columns of the
daily newspapers.

It is further alleged that the written protest which
had been filed with the clerk of the board was never
placed in the records and files of the proposed drainage district; was lost, or had disappeared before the
day of the hearing, and that such protest was not in
any manner considered by the board at such hearing,
and the fact that such written protest had not been
properly filed and was lost was unknown to petitioners
and their attorney; that, upon learning that the hearing had been had and the order entered establishing
the drainage district, petitioners immediately went to
the city of Seattle, and there discovered that their attorney was ill, confined to his home under a doctor's
care, and not in condition to attend to business or to

see them; that petitioners immediately employed other
counsel and went before the board of county commissioners, advised them fully of the situation, and that
the board gave them until the next day in which to file
a petition for a rehearing; that, accordingly, relators,
on the next day, duly filed with the board of county
commissioners their written petition setting forth all
the facts and in great detail the grounds of their objections to the establishment of the district, and the
reason for their non-appearance at the time of the
hearing, and prayed that a rehearing be granted, and
offered to pay in cash the expense incident to such rehearing, or furnish a bond conditioned for the payment by them of all such expenses. Many other allegations are made which, if true, tend to show that a grave
injustice was done to the relators by the entry of the
order establishing the drainage district; but, as all such
allegations are denied, and as, if true, they form no
basis for a decision in the present state of the record,
we find it unnecessary and useless to set them forth in
detail.

Relators further allege that their petition for rehearing was brought on for hearing before the board
in open session, at which time the members of the
board individually admitted the facts and circumstances alleged, and the justice and merit of the relators' demands, but decided that the board had no
legal right or authority to open up the matter and
grant a rehearing, and upon advice of counsel, the
board refused to either grant such petition or to deny
the same, but ordered it placed on file. Relators further alleged that they have no other remedy, and that
they will be able to establish all of the facts set forth
in their petition for a rehearing if one be granted, and
prayed for a peremptory writ of mandate directing

the board of county commissioners to hear their petition and grant or deny the same.

A show cause order was duly issued to the county commissioners as defendants, and after their demurrer had been overruled they answered, denying all of the material allegations of the petition, and pleading affirmatively, first, that the relators had appealed from the order of the board of county commissioners entered on February 9, 1920, establishing a drainage district, to the superior court for King county, and that the appeal was then pending; and for a second affirmative defense, set up all of the steps taken by them under the petition for the establishment of the drainage district, showing that the board had proceeded duly and regularly in the matter; that no protests, either oral or written, had ever been made or filed, and, while admitting that a petition for rehearing had been filed after the entry of the order establishing the district, alleged that such petition is not authorized by law, and had no legal effect. Relators duly replied, placing in issue many of the facts pleaded in the second affirmative answer, and thereafter the cause coming on for hearing, the defendants moved for judgment on the pleadings, which motion was denied, and thereupon, without taking any testimony, an order was entered directing the board of county commissioners to fix a time and place for the hearing of relators' petition for a rehearing, and to proceed to a hearing of such petition and to either grant or deny the same; from which order this appeal is prosecuted.

Relators seem to rely chiefly upon the case of *State ex rel. Ross v. Headlee,* 22 Wash. 126, 66 Pac. 126, where it was said:

"The general powers of the county commissioners are extensive, under the statute. They are the financial agents of the county, and it would be a harsh rule to lay down that a mistake which they had made in the transaction of their business could not be rectified. It is a matter of common knowledge that the members of boards of county commissioners are not, as a rule, technical lawyers, and of necessity their acts are more or less informal, and cannot be expected to meet the requirements of technical exactness which characterizes the actions of superior courts; and the proper administration of the law intrusted to their care demands a liberal construction of their acts, to the end that substantial justice shall be attained. We think the commissioners in this case had authority to revoke their former action and to make a levy in accordance with the business necessities of the county, as it was made to appear to them.''

It will be observed that the court was there dealing with the general powers of the county commissioners as the financial agents of their county, and not with special powers as here granted by a particular statute for a particular purpose, and further, there a writ was sought not to compel the commissioners to make an order rectifying an alleged or even an admitted mistake, but the writ was directed to the auditor requiring him to carry into effect an order already made by the commissioners—a very different situation, controlled by very different principles of law.

But, assuming that the *Ross* case holds that the county commissioners may, in all cases where they have made a mistake, rectify it by a subsequent order, still it does not meet the present situation. Respondents assert that, notwithstanding the denials in their answer, appellants admitted upon the trial below all of the allegations of their petition. This contention is strenuously denied by appellants, and as we can find no support for it in the record, we must assume that no admissions were made except as shown by the pleadings. This being the situation, it does not now appear from the record that the county commissioners made any mistake. Upon a trial of the issues it might appear that the respondents never made or filed any written protest, and that their present situation is due wholly to their own neglect and carelessness; or, if it should appear otherwise, it might also appear that the county commissioners never had any knowledge or notice of such protest, proceeded regularly in all respects, made no mistake, either of fact or law, or if so, have, in the exercise of a proper discretion, determined that the final results must be the same in any event, and hence have not abused their discretion (if they be entitled to exercise discretion) in refusing to grant a rehearing.

Treating a mistake as one of fact as distinguished from an error of judgment, and assuming, without deciding, that the commissioners may, and in a proper case should, correct an order made by mistake, still, before a mandate may issue directing the appellants to hear the petition for a rehearing, it must clearly appear that the original order was entered by mistake under such circumstances as to make it the duty of the commissioners to correct that mistake, and that they have, arbitrarily and without the exercise of any discretion, refused to take the steps necessary to make the correction. *State ex rel. Godfrey v. Turner*, 113 Wash. 214, 193 Pac. 715, and cases there cited.

For the reasons given, the order appealed from is reversed.

PARKER, C. J., MAIN, MITCHELL, and BRIDGES, JJ., concur.

[No. 16429. Department Two. August 9, 1921.]

THE STATE OF WASHINGTON, *Respondent*, v. G. L. GLEASON (*informed against as Gertie Gleason*), *Appellant*.[1]

INTOXICATING LIQUORS (30, 33)—STATUTES (47)—UNLAWFUL POSSESSION—IMPLIED REPEAL—AMENDATORY ACT. Laws 1917, ch. 19, making possession of intoxicating liquor unlawful is not in conflict with Rem. Code, § 6262-4, which forbids the manufacture, sale, barter, exchange or giving away of intoxicating liquor, except insofar as the proviso to such section allows one in lawful possession of intoxicating liquor to give it to a guest in his dwelling, to be drunk on the premises; hence the later law impliedly repeals only the proviso, without working a repeal of the body of the section to which the proviso is attached.

WITNESSES (120, 124) — IMPEACHMENT — INCONSISTENT STATEMENTS—REBUTTAL. Where a witness on cross-examination denied making certain prior statements inconsistent with his testimony, after the time, place and circumstances were called to his attention, the testimony of other witnesses as to his having made such statements was properly admissible to impeach him.

Appeal from a judgment of the superior court for Whitman county, McCroskey, J., entered January 15, 1921, upon a trial and conviction of giving away intoxicating liquor. Affirmed.

Hanna, Miller & Hanna, for appellant.

G. A. Weldon and *W. L. Lafollette*, for respondent.

TOLMAN, J.—Appellant was tried and convicted under Laws of 1915, p. 3, § 4 (Rem. Code, § 6262-4), of the offense of giving away intoxicating liquor to one not a guest in his private dwelling or apartment. He here seeks reversal upon the theory that the section of the 1915 law referred to was repealed by ch. 19, p. 46, Laws of 1917.

[1]Reported in 199 Pac. 739.

It is manifest that the original act recognizes that one may be in lawful possession of intoxicating liquor, and that being so in possession, he may give it to a guest in his private dwelling, to be drunk on the premises; but the later act of 1917 abolishes the permit system which was authorized by the prior act, and therefore § 17h, p. 60, Laws of 1917, is inconsistent with the proviso contained in § 4 of the prior act. In *State v. Giaudrone*, 109 Wash. 397, 186 Pac. 870, Mr. Justice Fullerton, speaking for this court upon this identical question, said:

"But as to the first of these sections, it will be noticed that it is a part of the original initiative measure, and that the section cited as containing the prohibition is amendatory of the original measure and a later expression of the legislative will. In so far as there is a conflict between them, the earlier provision is superseded by the later, and in so far as the language of the later section is direct and mandatory and free from ambiguity, it is to be construed without reference to the language of the earlier provisions. That there is a conflict must be conceded. A man cannot lawfully give his neighbor drink of that which he may not himself lawfully possess. But it is also true that the later act is in its language direct and mandatory and without ambiguity. We cannot, therefore, but conclude that the earlier provision was superseded by the later one."

The only question left to be determined then, is, How far and to what extent do the two provisions conflict? It is beyond question that the 1917 act makes possession of intoxicating liquor unlawful, with the exceptions which are therein clearly stated, and since possession is unlawful, the proviso in § 4 of the earlier act, being in conflict, is directly affected thereby, and is the earlier provision referred to by Judge Fullerton as superseded by the later one. There is nothing in the later act which is in any wise in conflict with the body of § 4 of the earlier act, which, in set terms, forbids the manufacture, sale, barter, exchange or giving away of intoxicating liquor; and as the legislature, by this later act, did not in terms amend or repeal this section, and did not undertake to again legislate upon the subject covered by the body of the section, we can only conclude that it was the legislative intent that the section should stand as originally written, except only the proviso, which, being in direct conflict with the later legislation, must yield thereto. And since the body of the section in no wise conflicts with the later legislation, there is no room for holding that the whole section falls.

Error is also assigned upon the ruling of the trial court in permitting certain impeaching questions to be put to the witness Ganley, and after he had denied making the statements attributed to him, in permitting the state on rebuttal to introduce the evidence of two witnesses to the effect that Ganley had made the statements to them or in their presence. The matters inquired about were material, and since the attention of the witness was directed to these statements and the time, place and circumstances called to his attention, while he was on the stand, and he denied having made such statements, which were in conflict with his testimony given on the stand, it was proper to offer proof by other witnesses to the effect that such conflicting statements had been made by the witness at the time, place and under the circumstances indicated in the questions propounded to him.

The judgment is affirmed.

PARKER, C. J., MAIN, MITCHELL, and BRIDGES, JJ., concur.

[No. 16446.   Department Two.   August 11, 1921.]

FRANK MASTERSON, *by his Guardian ad Litem, D. L. Masterson, Appellant,* v. MRS. JAMES LEONARD *et al., Respondents.*

D. L. MASTERSON, *Appellant,* v. MRS. JAMES LEONARD *et al., Respondents.*[1]

NEGLIGENCE (23) — IMPUTED NEGLIGENCE — RIDER OF BICYCLE. Where two boys engaged in the joint enterprise of covering a newspaper route which belonged to one of them, but in which he was sometimes assisted by the other, were both riding the same bicycle, the owner on the cross-bar and his friend in the seat and controlling its guidance, the negligence of the latter in colliding with an automobile while coasting down a street is attributable to the other.

TRIAL (99)—INSTRUCTIONS—REQUESTS FOR SPECIFIC INSTRUCTIONS. An instruction that the plaintiff must prove that "the defendant was negligent as charged in this complaint," should not be deemed erroneous, in view of the fact that all acts of negligence were pleaded in one paragraph, and there were no requested instructions asking specific charges upon the different acts of negligence, viewed separately.

Appeal from judgments of the superior court for Spokane county, Frater, J., entered August 10, 1920, upon verdicts rendered in favor of the defendants, in actions for personal injuries sustained in a collision with an automobile. Affirmed.

E. A. Cornelius, for appellants.

Lee & Kimball, for respondents.

PARKER, C. J.—These two actions, though separately commenced and finally disposed of in the superior court by separate verdicts and judgments, were, by agreement of all parties, tried together. The plaintiff Frank Masterson, by his guardian *ad litem,* seeks re-

[1] Reported in 200 Pac. 320.

covery of damages claimed as the result of personal
injuries suffered by him from the alleged negligent
operation of an automobile by the defendants. The
plaintiff D. L. Masterson, father of the plaintiff Frank
Masterson, seeks recovery of damages claimed as the
result of the same alleged negligence on the part of the
defendants; which claimed damages are for medical
and hospital expenses incurred by him for his son's
care, rendered necessary by the injuries received by
the son. The trial resulted in verdicts and judgments
in favor of the defendants, denying recovery to both
of the plaintiffs, from which they have appealed to
this court.

The plaintiff Frank Masterson and his companion,
Edward Buck, who was with him at the time of the
accident, were at the time each twelve years old. They
were ordinarily bright and intelligent boys of that age,
and were possessed of such experience in the city life
of Spokane — wherein the accident happened — as
newspaper boys ordinarily possess, and were well
acquainted with the conditions of the streets at and
in the immediate neighborhood of the accident. Frank
was injured in being thrown from a bicycle, on the
frame of which he was riding just behind the handle
bars, Edward sitting on the seat of the bicycle, having
hold of the handles and controlling it in the usual
manner, save for the fact that he had to reach his arms
past Frank, on each side, to the handles. Riding in
this manner, the boys coasted west for a distance of
two blocks down 5th avenue, on a descending grade
averaging about nine per cent, and, when arriving at
the foot of the grade at the intersection of Walnut
street, were thrown from the bicycle, either by coming
into collision with the defendants' automobile, which
was at that moment crossing 5th avenue going south

on Walnut street, or by being thrown from the bicycle
in an effort on the part of Edward to avoid the collision with the automobile. Frank was quite severely,
though apparently not permanently, injured; Edward
escaped with but slight injury. The bicycle belonged
to Frank's father, but Frank had been riding it for
about a year, and he then had it in his possession with
the privilege of using it. All of these facts are undisputed.

In view of the question of the negligence of Edward
being imputed to Frank and thus making such negligence Frank's contributory negligence, presently to be
considered, it is necessary that we have a correct view
of the evidence touching the relationship of the boys
to each other in their undertaking of this hazardous
journey in the manner above noticed. Edward testified
for the plaintiffs as follows:

"Q. You were with the Masterson boy the day of
the collision? A. Yes. Q. Where did you come
from on that day? A. From our house. Q. Where
is your home? A. On Fifth avenue, between Jefferson and Adams. Q. And what direction from the
place of the collision? A. East. Q. How far away?
A. Two blocks and a half. Q. What direction were
you going to reach this avenue and Walnut? A. West.
Q. Just state when—what you did from the time you
left until the collision? A. We went up the hill together and there is a little hill in front of our house
that goes up to Fifth and Adams—we started at our
house and went to Fifth and Adams, it is about a half
a block uphill, we walked up there and we decided to
ride Frank down the hill and he got on the cross bar
and I got on the saddle and we started down the hill,
there are two hills, we came to the bottom of the first
hill, and there was an old lady crossing the road and
we slowed up for her, and then coasted on down to
where we bumped into the automobile. . . . Q.
Where were you going from there? A. For the

papers. . . . Q. Whose paper route is that? A.
It is mine. Q. Why was Frank going along? A. He
was going to substitute on my route if I was sick.
Q. He had been over the route with you before that?
A. Yes. Q. How many times? A. He used to go
off and on. Q. And you always got the papers at the
same place? A. Yes. Q. You always went over
then in the same way on bicycle? A. Yes. Q. Did
you have a bicycle? A. Yes. Q. Did Frank have a
bicycle? A. Yes. Q. Whose were you using this
night? A. It was Frank's. . . . Q. Now you
went up to the top of the hill of Adams and Fifth avenue, and you said something to him about whether he
could ride you or you ride him? A. Yes. Q. And
it finally run to your lot to run the bicycle? A. Yes,
sir. Q. Now you got on the saddle and he got on the
cross-bars, which way did his feet point, which way
did he face? A. To the left. . . . Q. Now you
say you went on down here to Walnut, coasting all the
way down, were you? A. Yes. Q. Frank was sitting in front of you and your arms on either side of
him, and you had hold of both handlebars . . .
A. Yes, sir.''

This testimony is all of the evidence having any substantial bearing upon the relationship of the boys to
each other in their then enterprise or adventure.
While Frank testified in the case, his testimony was
not in the least in conflict with the facts disclosed by
the above quoted testimony of Edward, and there is
no other testimony or circumstance in the case which
in the slightest degree points to the relation of the
boys to each other, or their purpose in coasting down
5th avenue upon the bicycle.

It is contended that the trial court erred in giving
its instructions to the jury, in assuming, as claimed by
counsel for appellants, that whatever negligence
Edward was guilty of in the control of the bicycle was

imputable to and became the negligence of Frank, and thus became Frank's contributory negligence. We assume, for argument's sake, that the instructions given by the trial judge in effect so decided this question as one of law; that is, that Edward's negligence in the management of the bicycle became by imputation, as a matter of law, Frank's contributory negligence; clearly leaving to the jury, however, the question of whether or not Edward was negligent. In support of this contention, counsel cite and particularly rely upon our decisions in *Wilson v. Puget Sound Elec. R. Co.*, 52 Wash. 522, 101 Pac. 50, 132 Am. St. 1044, and *Allen v. Walla Walla Valley R. Co.*, 96 Wash. 397, 165 Pac. 99. The *Wilson* case involved injury resulting in the death of a passenger who was being carried in an automobile for hire. The *Allen* case involved an injury to a guest or companion riding in a buggy, who apparently had no control whatever over the driving of the buggy; nor did it appear that the driver and the injured person were engaged in any common enterprise. Judge Webster, speaking for the court, said in part:

"The basic thought upon which the doctrine or principle of imputed negligence rests is that the relationship of master and servant or principal and agent must exist between the driver and the occupant at the time of the injury. In the absence of such a relationship, the negligence of the one will not be attributed to the other."

Counsel for appellants also cite in support of their contention, but without comment thereon, the following decisions of this court: *Brabon v. Seattle*, 29 Wash. 6, 69 Pac. 365; *Shearer v. Buckley*, 31 Wash. 370, 72 Pac. 76; *Cathey v. Seattle Elec. Co.*, 58 Wash. 176, 108 Pac. 443; *Field v. Spokane, Portland etc. R. Co.*, 64 Wash. 445, 117 Pac. 228; *McCanna v. Silke*, 75

Wash. 383, 134 Pac. 1063; *Beach v. Seattle*, 85 Wash. 379, 148 Pac. 39.

A critical reading of these decisions we think will readily disclose that they all involve injuries either to mere guests, employees, or passengers being carried for hire, none of whom had any control over the operation of the respective vehicles on which they were riding when injured. We are of the opinion, in view of the ownership of the bicycle, the general possession of and control over it by Frank, the acquiescing by him in the temporary control over it by Edward for the purpose of conveying them both on this hazardous journey, which we think was their common enterprise or adventure, that the trial court did not err in telling the jury, in effect, that whatever negligence Edward was guilty of, in carrying out this their joint enterprise or adventure, was attributable to Frank and became, in law, his negligence. In other words, the trial judge did not err in so deciding as a matter of law, in view of the undisputed facts on that subject. Observations made in the text of Huddy, Automobiles (5th ed.), at § 682, and the decisions there cited, lend strong support to this conclusion. The decisions of the Virginia and Utah courts in *Washington & O. D. R. Co. v. Zell's Adm'r*, 118 Va. 755, 88 S. E. 309, and *Derrick v. Salt Lake & O. R. Co.*, 50 Utah 573, 168 Pac. 335, seem to us, in principle, to be directly in point.

Contention is made that the trial court erred in giving to the jury the following instruction:

"In order for the plaintiff to recover in this case he must satisfy you by a fair preponderance of the evidence that the defendant was negligent as charged in his complaint, and as to the truth of all the material allegations contained in his complaint."

The argument is that this was erroneous, since the complaint alleged several acts of negligence and that

proof of one or more might sustain recovery without
proof of all. The acts of negligence are not plead
separately in the complaint. The summary made of
them in appellants' brief is as follows:

"(1) That the automobile was being driven south
at a high, dangerous and negligent rate in the excess
of thirty-five miles per hour. (2) That Margaret
Leonard negligently and carelessly failed to keep a
proper lookout. (3) That Margaret Leonard negligently and carelessly failed to sound a horn or give any
other warning of her approach and negligently and
carelessly failed to so operate said automobile as to
avoid collision.

"The paragraph in the complaint is not divided into
sections, in the manner in which we have written it,
but the several distinct charges of negligence are there,
and if the jury believed any one of them, it would be
sufficient to be the foundation of a judgment against
respondent."

This challenged instruction does not stand out by
itself, but is embodied in a general instruction given by
the court touching the question of burden of proof.
No instructions were requested in behalf of the plaintiffs. Other instructions were given which seem to
leave the jury free to find in favor of the plaintiffs and
award them recovery on some one or more of these
acts of negligence without finding the defendants
guilty of all of them. However that may be, it seems
to us, in view of the fact that these acts of negligence
are all plead together in one paragraph of the complaint, separated only by commas, and in view of there
being no requested instructions in behalf of the plaintiffs, asking the court to specifically instruct the jury
as to what it might find touching these acts of negligence, viewed separately, that the plaintiffs are not
in a position to now complain of the particular instruction which they question.

One or two other claims of error are made, but we think they are so wholly without merit as to not call for discussion.

The judgments are affirmed.

MITCHELL, FULLERTON, MAIN, and TOLMAN, JJ., concur.

[No. 16283. Department Two. August 12, 1921.]

THE STATE OF WASHINGTON, *Respondent*, v.
R. D. STEPHENS, *Appellant*.[1]

INTOXICATING LIQUORS (6) — PROHIBITION — BOOTLEGGING — 18TH AMENDMENT. Prosecution under state laws for bootlegging and conducting illegal liquor joints is lawful as in aid of the enforcement of the 18th amendment to the constitution of the United States and the Volstead act passed pursuant thereto.

APPEAL (277)—OBJECTIONS OR EXCEPTIONS—ARGUMENT OF COUNSEL. Misconduct of the prosecuting attorney in his argument to the jury will not be considered on appeal, where there is no showing that any objection or exception was taken at the time, or request made to have the jury instructed to disregard the alleged improper statement, and the only showing of misconduct in the record appears in the affidavit of defendant in support of his motion for new trial.

Appeal from a judgment of the superior court for Snohomish county, Alston, J., entered May 20, 1920, upon a trial and conviction of being a bootlegger. Affirmed.

O. T. Webb and *Coleman & Fogarty,* for appellant.
Thos. A. Stiger and *Q. A. Kaune,* for respondent.

TOLMAN, J.—Appellant appeals from a conviction upon a charge of being a bootlegger, and assigns as error the overruling of his motion for a new trial, (a) because of certain statements alleged to have been

[1]Reported in 200 Pac. 310.

made by the deputy prosecuting attorney in his closing argument to the jury; and (b) because, it is contended, the state prohibition law is superseded or suspended by the eighteenth amendment to the constitution of the United States, and the Volstead act passed pursuant thereto.

Upon the ground last stated, this court has already passed, holding adversely to appellant's contention. *State v. Turner,* 115 Wash. 170, 196 Pac. 638.

Upon the first contention, it is sufficient to say that the matters complained of are shown in the record only by affidavit of the appellant in support of his motion for a new trial, made a part of the statement of facts, and it does not appear that any objection was made or exception taken at the time, or that any request was then made to have the jury instructed to disregard what are now said to be improper statements by the prosecutor. Furthermore, it does appear by the same affidavit that the jury was instructed to disregard any statements of counsel not borne out by the testimony, and the prosecutor, by counter affidavit, denies having made the prejudicial remarks attributed to him, and sets forth what he claims was said, amounting to no more than that which frequently occurs in the heat of trial and under provocation from opposing counsel.

The trial judge who presided was of the opinion that the prosecutor made no statements which were prejudicial to the appellant, and, in view of the state of the record, we are not disposed to inquire into the matter. But if we were, we could not find that the trial court erred in so holding.

Judgment affirmed.

Parker, C. J., Holcomb, Main, and Mitchell, JJ., concur.

[No. 16505. *En Banc.* August 18, 1921.]

In the Matter of the Application of LETTIE WILLIAMSON *for a Writ of Habeas Corpus.*[1]

STATES (26)—APPROPRIATION—NECESSITY—EFFECT OF FAILURE TO MAKE. Where, through the failure to make an appropriation, the operation of the Women's Industrial Home and Clinic, to which certain classes of female offenders were to be sentenced, was suspended, the requirement of the act that convicted offenders be sentenced to such institution was likewise suspended, thereby subjecting such class of offenders to the operation of the general laws which provide for the imprisonment of persons convicted of crimes.

STATUTES (51)—REPEAL—REVIVAL OF ACT REPEALED—EXCEPTIONS. Where an original statute is left in force on the passage of a subsequent act, which modifies it only to the extent of excepting certain cases from its operation, the taking away of the exception by suspension or repeal revives the original statute, which continues in force to be applied without the exception; since the rule against revival of a statute by the repeal of a repealing statute relates to absolute repeals only.

STATES (3, 25, 26)—LIABILITY—POWER TO INCUR DEFICIENCY—APPROPRIATIONS. An administrative officer charged with the management and control of a reformatory institution, for which the legislature has failed to make an appropriation for maintenance, is under no obligation to incur a deficiency to continue its operation; in view of Rem. Code, §§ 5025-5027, which prohibit expenditures in excess of appropriations and provide that the officer making such expenditures is guilty of misdemeanor and liable personally and on his official bond for the amounts so expended.

HABEAS CORPUS (21, 24, 25)—PROCEEDINGS—JUDGMENT—DISPOSITION OF PERSON—DISCHARGE. On an original application in the supreme court for a writ of habeas corpus directed to the officer who has a petitioner in custody, that court, being without authority to direct by mandate the proper sentence to be rendered, should order the officer having the petitioner in charge to take her before the court in which she was convicted for a proper sentence, and that she should be discharged if no further action be taken by the lower court (TOLMAN, HOLCOMB, and MITCHELL, JJ., dissenting).

Application filed in the supreme court April 27, 1921, for a writ of habeas corpus to release the petitioner

[1]Reported in 200 Pac. 329.

from the county jail of Spokane county, after conviction and sentence to the women's industrial home and clinic. Denied.

Richard S. Munter and *Munter & Munter*, for petitioner.

T. T. Grant, for respondent.

The Attorney General (Nat U. Brown, of counsel), *amicus curiae*.

FULLERTON, J.—The legislature, at its biennial session of 1919, provided for the creation of a penal institution to be known as the "Women's Industrial Home and Clinic." (Laws of 1919, p. 570, ch. 186.) The act, as expressed in its title, was designed to provide a place for the "custody, training and treatment of delinquent and diseased women." The body of the act was somewhat broader than its title indicated. Aside from a few excepted instances, it provided for the confinement therein of all women convicted of crime in any of the courts of the state exercising criminal jurisdiction,. whether felonies, gross misdemeanors, or misdemeanors, and whether the convicted woman was diseased or otherwise. The remainder of the act related to the erection, management and control of the institution. It provided for the appointment of a board of directors, and imposed upon such board the duty of selecting a site for the institution, erecting suitable buildings thereon, and selecting its officers and employees, who should have immediate charge of the inmates committed to the institution. The act also provided that, when the institution should be ready for the reception of inmates, the board should so certify to the governor, and made it the duty of that officer to issue a public proclamation to that effect. The act also provided somewhat minutely for the care and treatment of the women sentenced to it, and the conditions upon which its inmates could be paroled or discharged therefrom. The act created no new offenses, nor any new methods or modes of trial, nor did it on its face repeal, or purport to repeal, any of the existing general statutes relating to crimes and their punishment. The specific provision relating to the persons who should be sentenced thereto reads as follows:

"From and after the proclamation of the governor, provided for in section 4 of this act, all women over sixteen years of age belonging to any of the following classes sentenced to imprisonment by any court of criminal jurisdiction may be committed to and confined in, and all women over eighteen years of age belonging to any of the following classes sentenced to imprisonment by any court of criminal jurisdiction must be committed to and confined in said institution:

"First: Women convicted of or who plead guilty to the commission of felonies, except murder in the first and second degree, arson in the first degree, and robbery, who have not been twice before convicted in this state or elsewhere of crimes which under the laws of this state would amount to felonies.

"Second: Women convicted of or who plead guilty to the commission of gross misdemeanors or misdemeanors as defined by law.

"The court imposing sentence on offenders of either of the above classes shall not fix the time of such commitment. Commitment to such institution shall be executed, within one week after sentence is imposed, by a woman guard appointed by the court for that purpose or sent from said institution on notice of the issuance of the commitment. The expenses of such commitment shall be paid in the same way as commitment to other penal institutions of the state. The trial court shall cause a record of the case to be sent with commitment papers on blanks furnished by the institution.

"Any girl between the ages of sixteen and eighteen years who shall be found to be delinquent or dependent under the provisions of chapter 160 of the laws of 1913, may be committed to said institution, and if committed, the commitment shall be executed by a juvenile officer, or a woman guard from said institution.

"The duration of such commitment for Class 1, including the time spent on parole, shall not exceed the maximum term specified by law for the crime for which the offender was sentenced, and in such cases it shall be the duty of the trial court to specify the maximum term for which the offender may be held under commitment.

"The duration of such commitment for all other classes shall not exceed three years unless, in the opinion of a board of experts composed of one jurist and two physicians one of whom shall be a recognized neurologist, a longer detention shall be recommended.

"If, through oversight or otherwise, any person be sentenced to confinement in said institution for a definite period of time, such sentence shall not for that reason be void but the persons so sentenced shall be entitled to the benefits and subject to the liabilities of this act in the same manner and to the same extent as if sentence had been given in the terms required by this section; and in such cases said board of directors shall deliver to such offender a copy of this act and written information of her relation to said board.

"Immediately upon the arrival of any person committed to said institution a careful physical and mental examination of such person shall be made by a competent physician."

In the act authorizing the institution, the legislature appropriated sufficient funds for its maintenance during the ensuing biennium. At its biennial session in 1921, however, it failed to make an appropriation for the coming biennium, and as a result thereof the institution was closed on April 1, 1921, for want of funds for its support.

On April 8, 1921, after the institution had been
closed, one Lettie Williamson was convicted in the
superior court of Spokane county of the crime of adul-
tery, and was by that court committed to the institution for a term not exceeding two years. There being
no way of carrying the commitment into effect, the
convicted woman is now held in the county jail of Spokane county by the sheriff of that county. The proceeding now before us is an original application made
in her behalf to this court for a writ of habeas corpus,
seeking her discharge from custody.

Basing his argument upon the contention that the
provisions of the act relating to the classes of women
who are required by the act to be sentenced to the institution have existence independent of the existence
of the institution itself, the petitioner's counsel argues
that it is the mandatory duty of the courts to sentence
all women offenders convicted of crime to the institution; and, since the institution is closed for the reception of inmates, there is no other remedy to pursue
than to discharge the convicted person from custody.
Doubtless, if we were to accept as sound the contention made, we would be compelled to accept the conclusion drawn therefrom. We cannot, however, think
the contention tenable. Appropriation bills of a legislature are laws, as all other constitutional enactments
of a legislature, are laws. While they are limited in
duration by reason of constitutional provisions, yet,
during the period of their existence, they have the same
force and effect as do laws of unlimited duration.
When, therefore, the legislature fails to make an appropriation for an institution of its own creation, that
is to say, an institution the existence of which depends
solely upon its own will, its failure operates to suspend the operation of the institution as effectually as

it would were an express declaration made to that
effect. Again, an act of the legislature, which de-
nounces as a crime the doing of some particular thing
by an individual but prescribes no penalty for the
crime, or if it prescribes a penalty and provides no
means of carrying the penalty into execution, is, in
effect, in so far as the criminal courts are concerned,
no law. Courts are not required to do useless or sense-
less things. They need not so waste their time, or the
state's substance, as to enter upon the trial of an offender when the result of the trial, whether a conviction
or an acquittal, must end in an absolute discharge. It
it apparent, also, that the particular act here in question is a special, rather than a general law. As we have
said, it creates no new offenses. All that it does is to
select from the general class of offenders a particular
class and provide that this particular class shall be
punished by commitment to the institution. It must
follow necessarily, we conclude, that the provision of
the act requiring a commitment to the institution is
so far dependent upon the maintenance of the institution that the one cannot exist as law without the other,
and that the suspension of the operation of the institution suspends the requirement that convicted offenders be sentenced to it; this for the manifest reason that
a law which as a whole is without sanction can have
no sanction in its separate and individual parts.

It is argued, however, that this conclusion leaves
the matter where it was before; that the act operated
to suspend the general statutes in so far as it conflicted
with them, and that these statutes are not revived by
the suspension of the suspensatory act. But the rule
is otherwise. The rule against the revival of a statute
by the repeal of a repealing statute relates to absolute
repeals only, and not to instances where the statute is

left in force and all that is done in the way of repeal is to except certain cases from its operation. In such instances, the original statute does not need to be revived, for it remains in force, and the exception being taken away, the statute is to be applied without the exception. 25 R. C. L. 934. See, also, *Manchester Township Supervisors v. Wayne County Commissioners,* 257 Pa. St. 442, 101 Atl. 736, Ann. Cas. 1918 B 278, and the note thereto, where the cases will be found collected.

Another matter is proper to be noticed. In a proceeding presenting somewhat similar features to the one here presented, it was argued that the officer in whom the law now vests the management and control of the state institutions is obligated to maintain this institution, notwithstanding the legislature has failed to appropriate the necessary funds for that purpose and notwithstanding he must incur a deficiency in so doing, and from this the conclusion is drawn that the institution is a going concern, and that the requirement that certain persons be committed thereto is still operative. But it is a sufficient answer to say that the maintenance of any state institution, not required by the higher authority to be maintained, rests in the will of the legislature, not in the will of the executive officers whose duty it is to execute the legislative will. Further than this, the argument overlooks the provisions of the law relating to the expenditure of money for the maintenance of a public institution in excess of the amount appropriated by the legislature therefor. Rem. Code, §§ 5025, 5026 and 5027. By these provisions not only are such expenditures positively prohibited, but the officer causing the expenditure is made guilty of misdemeanor, and is made liable personally and liable upon his official bond for the amounts so expended. In view of these positive prohibitions of the statute, it is at least doubtful whether an officer can create a liability against the state by expending money in excess of an appropriation; but be this as it may, surely it ought not to be held that it is his duty so to do contrary to the provisions of a positive law. It is true that the legislature (Laws of 1921, p. 16, ch. 7, § 15, subd. 7), sought to empower the administrative board to authorize the incurring of a deficiency when a necessity exists therefor, but it is a sufficient answer to. any argument based upon this clause of the statute to say that the board has suffered this institution to be closed without action looking to its continued maintenance.

From these considerations, it follows that the trial court before whom the petitioner was convicted was without authority to sentence her to this institution, and that it should have sentenced her to that punishment provided by the general statutes for the offense of which she was convicted. Since, however, this proceeding is an original application made to this court directed to the officer who has the petitioner in custody, this court has no authority to direct by mandate the proper sentence to be made. The order will be, therefore, that the officer having the petitioner in charge take the petitioner before the court in which she was convicted for a proper sentence, and if no further action be taken by the court, that she be discharged.

Parker, C. J., Mackintosh, Bridges, and Main, JJ., concur.

Tolman, J. (dissenting)—I cannot agree with the views expressed by the majority. The act referred to, in positive terms requires:

"From and after the proclamation of the governor, provided for in section 4 of this act, all women over six-

teen years of age belonging to any of the following
classes sentenced to imprisonment by any court of
criminal jurisdiction may be committed to and confined
in, and all women over eighteen years of age belonging
to any of the following classes sentenced to imprisonment by any court of criminal jurisdiction must be committed to and confined in said institution:

"First: Women convicted of or who plead guilty
to the commission of felonies, except murder in the
first and second degree, arson in the first degree, and
robbery, who have not been twice before convicted in
this state or elsewhere of crimes which under the laws
of this state would amount to felonies.

"Second: Women convicted of or who plead guilty
to the commission of gross misdemeanors or misdemeanors as defined by law." Laws 1919, p. 574, ch.
186, § 9.

Consequently this act, complete in itself, superseded
all prior law upon this subject. The legislature did
make an appropriation for the maintenance of this institution, and after its final adjournment the governor
vetoed such appropriation, except as to the sum of
$5,000, for the maintenance of the buildings, thus caus-
ing the institution to close. While admitting the governor's power to veto an appropriation, I cannot consent
to the idea that by such veto the governor can, in effect,
repeal prior properly enacted, positive statutory provisions for the punishment of crime. In my judgment,
the petitioner is entitled to her discharge, and I therefore dissent.

MITCHELL, J., concurs with TOLMAN, J.

HOLCOMB, J. (dissenting)—I concur with the views
of Judge Tolman, and would add that the law is universal that a sentence by a court that does not comply
with the statute providing for sentence is void. The
majority will now have courts sentencing women to

places forbidden by statute for certain classes of women to be committed.

This decision is judicial legislation, reviving laws that the legislature superseded and never intended to be revived.

[No. 16522. *En Banc.* August 18, 1921.]

In the Matter of the Petition of AUTTIE CANARY *for a Writ of Habeas Corpus.*[1]

REFORMATORIES (2)—COMMITMENT—TRANSFER OF PRISONERS. A woman sentenced to commitment in the Women's Industrial Home and Clinic, on conviction of grand larceny, was transferable to the state prison by order of the board of directors of the industrial home, under the authority conferred by Laws 1919, p. 570, § 13; the determination by the board of the necessity for the transfer not being the exercise of a judicial function.

HABEAS CORPUS (8-1)—GROUNDS—CORRECTION OF ERROR. Mere error on the part of the board of directors of the Women's Industrial Home and Clinic, committed in the exercise of acknowledged power to make transfers of inmates to the state prison, is not subject to review in habeas corpus proceedings.

Application filed in the supreme court April 30, 1921, for a writ of habeas corpus to release a person held in custody in the state penitentiary, upon transfer from the women's industrial home and clinic. Denied.

Beeler & Sullivan, for petitioner.

The Attorney General, for respondent.

FULLERTON, J.—This is an original application made to this court for a writ of habeas corpus. The petitioner alleges in her petition that she entered a plea of guilty to an information filed against her in the superior court of Spokane county charging her with the

[1]Reported in 200 Pac. 307.

crime of grand larceny; that, upon her plea of guilty, she was adjudged guilty by the court, and was thereupon committed to the institution known as the women's industrial home and clinic; and that, on March 28, 1921, she was transferred by the officers of that institution to the state penitentiary, where she is now confined. As causes for granting the writ, she makes the general allegation that the transfer was without authority of law and against her will. In the argument at bar, the more specific objections were made, (1) that the directors of the institution were without power to make the transfer; and (2) that, conceding that the directors had such power, they wrongfully exercised the power.

With reference to the first objection, it is provided in the act authorizing the creation of the institution known as the women's industrial home and clinic (Laws of 1919, p. 577, ch. 186, § 13):

"The board of directors may transfer to the state prison any inmate of said institution who shall appear to said board to be incorrigible, or whose presence in said institution may be seriously detrimental to its well being."

Obviously the legislature, by this provision of the statute, attempted to confer power on the board of directors to make the transfer, and unless it is to be held that the legislature was in itself without power so to do, there is warrant for the act of the board of directors. But we see no valid objection that can be based upon this ground. The crime of which the petitioner was adjudged guilty is a felony. It is a crime long recognized as punishable in a penal institution, and it is solely for the legislature to prescribe the character of that institution. They could have provided directly for her punishment by confinement in the state prison, and no logical or sound reason can exist why that body may not provide that a convicted person be first confined in some other institution and thereafter for stated causes be transferred thereto. The objection that to transfer is to exercise a judicial function was met and answered in the negative by us in *Pellissier v. Reed,* 75 Wash. 201, 134 Pac. 813.

As a basis for the second contention, it is claimed that the petitioner was not incorrigible and that her presence in the institution named was not detrimental to its well being. But these are questions not cognizable in this proceeding. The writ of habeas corpus is not in this state a writ of review, and mere errors on the part of a court, board or person, committed in the exercise of acknowledged powers, will not be reviewed in such a proceeding. *In re Newcomb,* 56 Wash. 395, 105 Pac. 1042. The question was also before us in *Pellissier v. Reed, supra,* where the same conclusion was reached. As we said in that case, we again say here, that we do not wish to be understood as holding that a prisoner is denied the right of showing, in an appropriate proceeding, an abuse of discretion on the part of the board in making the transfer. All we hold is that such a question must be brought before the courts by some form of proceedings authorized to be brought for the correction of errors, and that habeas corpus is not such a proceeding.

The petition is denied.

PARKER, C. J., BRIDGES, MAIN, and MACKINTOSH, JJ., concur.

[No. 16592. *En Banc.* August 18, 1921.]

THE STATE OF WASHINGTON, *on the Relation of Thomas E. Skaggs, as Director of Business Control, Plaintiff,* v. EVERETT SMITH, *Judge of the Superior Court for King County, Respondent.*[1]

PROHIBITION (33)—JURISDICTION AND PROCEEDINGS—OBJECTIONS IN LOWER COURT. The writ of prohibition may properly issue from a supervisory to an inferior court, without a previous application to the inferior court for relief, where something is done by the inferior court from which the inference may fairly be drawn that, unless prohibited, such court will act beyond and in excess of its jurisdiction; or where the question involved relates to public affairs and interests, and a prolonged trial may prove detrimental to such affairs and interests.

SAME (20, 22)—GROUNDS—EXCESS OF JURISDICTION—CONTEMPT PROCEEDINGS. A citation of an administrative officer for contempt, for failing to deliver a prisoner to an institution that was closed, is subject to a writ of prohibition as in excess of the jurisdiction of the court and interfering with the duties of the officer, where, in habeas corpus proceedings for the discharge of a woman detained in custody under sentence to confinement in the Women's Industrial Home, to which she had been refused admission on the ground that it was closed, it appears that the administrative officer, charged with the control of the institution, was not a party to the record, nor responsible for its closing, and without power to cause it to be reopened.

Application filed in the supreme court June 3, 1921, for a writ of prohibition to prevent the superior court for King county, Smith, J., from proceeding with a cause. Granted.

The Attorney General, for relator.

Beeler & Sullivan, for respondent.

FULLERTON, J.—On April 25, 1921, one Lucile Brown was convicted of the crime of vagrancy, in a justice's court for King county, and committed by that court

[1]Reported in 200 Pac. 92.

to the institution known as the women's industrial
home and clinic. After her commitment, she was
placed in the custody of the sheriff of the county, and
was by him detained in the county jail to await the
coming of a guard to transfer her to the institution
named. No guard appeared within the seven days fixed
by the statute, whereupon she applied to the superior
court of King county for a writ of habeas corpus, alleging in her petition that she was detained by the sheriff
against her consent and without authority of law. The
writ applied for was granted, and the application came
on for hearing before the court on May 6, 1921, Honorable Everett Smith presiding. At the conclusion of
the hearing, the court made and entered the following
order:

"This cause having come on regularly for hearing
before the undersigned, one of the judges of said court,
on the 5th day of May, 1921, the petitioner being present in person and represented by Beeler & Sullivan,
her attorneys, and the respondent being represented by Chester A. Batchelor, deputy prosecuting attorney, and the matters connected with
said petition having been duly advised therein and finding that the petitioner Lucile Brown,
was on the 25th day of April, 1921, duly and
regularly committed to the women's industrial home
and clinic at Medical Lake, by Honorable C. C. Dalton,
justice of the peace, in and for Seattle precinct, King
county, state of Washington, and that the respondent,
Matt Starwich, sheriff of King county, Washington,
has since said 25th day of April, 1921, been holding
said petitioner, Lucile Brown, in the county jail of
King county, Washington, awaiting a guard from the
said women's industrial home and clinic, and it further
appearing that no guard has arrived from said
women's industrial home and clinic, and that more than
seven days since the date of her commitment has expired, and it further appearing to the court that said

petitioner should be forthwith removed from the King county jail to the women's industrial home and clinic at Medical lake, and the court being fully advised in all the facts and premises;

"It is now by the court adjudged and ordered that the petition of said Lucile Brown for a writ of habeas corpus herein be and the same is hereby denied to which petitioner excepts and exception is hereby allowed.

"It is further ordered by the court that Mrs. Jackson Silbaugh, a satisfactory and suitable woman be and she is hereby appointed guard of the said Lucile Brown, and said Mrs. Jackson Silbaugh shall be and she is hereby directed and ordered to forthwith take the said Lucile Brown from said King county jail to said women's industrial home and clinic at Medical lake, Spokane county, Washington, and to deliver her to the superintendent and officials thereof, to which the petitioner excepts and exception is hereby allowed."

Pursuant to the order, the guard caused the applicant to be transported to the institution named. She found no one in charge of the institution who would receive the prisoner, whereupon she returned her to the sheriff of King county, making and filing with the court an affidavit as follows:

"Mrs. Jackson Silbaugh, being first duly sworn, upon oath, deposes and says: That she is the duly appointed, qualified and acting traveling guard, appointed by the superior court of King county, state of Washington, for the purpose of accompanying Lucile Brown, sentenced to the women's industrial home and clinic at Medical lake in Spokane county, state of Washington; that she did, on the 9th day of May, 1921, take said Lucile Brown to said women's industrial home and clinic at Medical Lake, presented said Lucile Brown to the superintendent of said women's industrial home and clinic, and requested the superintendent in charge to take charge of said Lucile Brown and care for her in accordance with order directing that said Lucile Brown

be sent to women's industrial home and clinic at Medical lake, in case No. 150869 in the superior court of
the state of Washington, for King county; that the
superintendent, Margaret Gillam, notified this affiant
that said home had been closed and that she would not
receive said Lucile Brown as an inmate thereof, and
thereupon refused to take over the custody of said
Lucile Brown or to permit her to enter said women's
industrial home and clinic.''

Thereafter, the applicant for the writ, through her
attorneys, applied to the court for an order directed
to the relator in the proceeding now before us, as the
director of business control, commanding him upon a
day certain to show cause why he should not be punished as for a contempt of court. The application was
accompanied by the affidavit of Lucile Brown, in which
she recited in substance the matters hereinbefore
stated. The application was heard on May 31, 1921,
whereupon the court entered the following order:

"This matter having come on for hearing on the
written motion of Beeler & Sullivan, as attorneys for
Lucile Brown, and on the sworn affidavit of the said
Lucile Brown, for an order directing the Honorable
Thomas E. Skaggs as director of business control, one
of the state administrative departments of the state of
Washington, to show cause why he should not be adjudged as in contempt of court; and it appearing to
the court from the affidavit of the said Lucile Brown,
which is on file herein, that on or about the 25th day
of April, 1921, she was duly and regularly committed
to the women's industrial home and clinic at Medical
lake, Spokane county, Washington, as is more clearly
shown by Exhibit 'A' attached to the affidavit of the
said Lucile Brown; and it further appearing to the
court that the said Lucile Brown was thereafter, to-
wit: on the 6th day of May, 1921, directed by this court
to be taken to the said women's industrial home and
clinic, and that thereafter, to-wit, on or about the 9th
day of May, 1921, the said Lucile Brown, in custody of

a guard appointed by this court to take her to said
institution, was thereupon taken by said guard to said
women's industrial home and clinic, and offered to the
superintendent in charge thereof, but that said superintendent then and there neglected, failed and refused
and still refuses to take said Lucile Brown and confine her in said institution; and the court being fully
advised in the contents of said affidavit, and the records
and files in this cause, and having examined the exhibits, and being fully advised in the premises:

"It is now by the court adjudged and ordered that
the said Thomas E. Skaggs, as director of business control, be and he is hereby ordered and directed to be
and appear before the Honorable Everett Smith, one
of the judges of the superior court of King county,
state of Washington, in Department No. 8 thereof, on
Saturday the 4th day of June, 1921, at the hour of
10:30 o'clock a. m., then and there to show cause, if
any he has, why he should not be punished as for contempt of court, for having failed to accept, receive,
take and commit the said Lucile Brown to the said
women's industrial home and clinic at the time she was
presented by the guard appointed by the court to take
and deliver her to said women's industrial home and
clinic.

"It is further ordered that a certified copy of this
order may be served upon Thomas E. Skaggs, as director of business control, by any officer of Thurston
county competent to make service of process."

Upon the service of this last mentioned order on the
relator, he applied to this court for a writ prohibiting
the court from further proceeding with the cause, basing the application upon the ground that the court was
acting without and in excess of its jurisdiction. In his
petition for the writ, after reciting the proceedings had
in the court below, he sets forth—what the court perhaps knows judicially, in any event—that there was no
appropriation by the legislative department of the state
for the maintenance, during the present biennium, of

the institution known as the women's industrial home
and clinic, and that, in consequence, the institution was
closed to the reception of inmates on April 1, 1921, and
has been so closed since that time; that he, as director
of business control, has no power or authority to direct
it to be opened for the reception of persons committed
thereto, nor power or authority to incur obligations
for its maintenance obligatory upon the state, should
it be so opened; since to do so would be to expend a
greater sum of money than was appropriated by the
legislature for the use of the institution, an act positively prohibited by law, rendering him liable to punishment as for a misdemeanor, and rendering him liable
personally and upon his official bond for the liabilities
incurred. He further set forth that he was not a party
to any of the proceedings had in the superior court;
that no notice of any of the hearings had in that court
was served upon him; and that the first notice thereof
so served was the order of May 31, 1921, by which he
was directed to appear before the court and show cause
why he should not be punished as for a contempt. The
return of the judge of the superior court, filed in answer
to the alternative writ issued out of this court, does not
contravert the allegations of the petition, further than
it is alleged therein:

"That it was the opinion and conclusion of respondent upon the facts alleged in the affidavit upon which
the said order to show cause directed to relator Skaggs
herein, dated May 31, 1921, was based, and from all
the files and records in said habeas corpus proceedings,
that said women's industrial home and clinic was, at
the time of making such order and at the time when
said Lucile Brown was taken thereto as aforesaid,
actually and lawfully open for the reception of inmates."

In this court, counsel for the respondent makes the preliminary objection that the application for a writ of prohibition is premature, invoking the general rule that the supervising court will not issue a peremptory writ of prohibition against an inferior court until application is made to that court for relief and the court has in some way indicated that its decision will be adverse to the objector, and then only when there is no remedy by appeal. But to this general rule there are exceptions as well established as the rule itself. If something is done by the court from which the inference may fairly be drawn that the court, unless prohibited, will act beyond and in excess of its jurisdiction, so that it is reasonably certain that any application to it will prove futile; or where the question involved relates to public officers, or public affairs and interests, and a prolonged trial may prove detrimental to such affairs and interests, application for relief to the supervisory court on the ground of want of jurisdiction may be made without first suggesting the question to the court of trial. The exceptions are applicable in the present instance. The trial court has already prejudged the main issue. This not only appears from the fact that it caused the party before it to be conveyed to the site of the institution to which she was committed and tendered to some person found in charge thereof, and from the fact that the order served upon the relator is to answer as for a contempt in refusing to receive the committed person, but also from the fact that the court recited in its return that it was its "opinion and conclusion . . . upon the facts . . . and from all the files and records . . . that the women's home and clinic . . . was actually and lawfully open for the reception of inmates." Necessarily, before the relator can be punished for contempt for refusing to confine a person committed to the institution, it must be established that the institution is open for the reception of the committed person. This question the relator has had no opportunity to meet; it has been so adjudged without notice to him, and he can have no defense in the court to which he is cited to the charge made against him. Obviously it would seem that he should be permitted to inquire into the jurisdiction of the court to compel him to answer, before he is subjected to punishment.

The other ground suggested is likewise pertinent. The relator is a state officer. His duties are arduous and cover a wide field in state affairs. The charge against him here is in its effect malfeasance of official duty, and a defense to the charge will necessarily take him from the discharge of his official duties for a considerable period of time. Plainly, before the state should be thus deprived of his services, it ought to be clear that the court proceeding against him has jurisdiction to so proceed. We think, therefore, that the case is one where the relator may rightfully invoke the writ, and we hold that the proceedings are not improvidently taken.

On the principal question involved there is need of but little discussion. Plainly the court is proceeding in excess of its jurisdiction. The proceeding before it was one in habeas corpus by a woman convicted of a crime in a justice court and held under the sentence of that court, who charges that she is detained without authority of law. Doubtless the court, in virtue of the proceedings, had power and authority to inquire into the jurisdiction of the court in which the conviction was had, and into the regularity of the commitment under the judgment of conviction. It had jurisdiction, also, to inquire whether the convicted person is being confined in the institution to which she was committed, and it could, if it is found that the person is not so confined, direct that she be transferred to the proper institution or be discharged. But the court has gone much farther than this. It has determined that the institution known as the women's industrial home and clinic, although actually closed by the executive department of state against the reception of inmates, is not lawfully so closed, and is seeking to punish as for contempt a state officer not a party to the record, who is in no wise responsible for its closing and who is without power to cause it to be re-opened, for refusal to receive a person committed thereto for confinement therein. The statement of the proposition exposes its fallacy. There may be a proper proceeding by which the courts can inquire into the question whether the institution named is or is not lawfully closed. But it must be a proceeding instituted for that purpose, in which the parties responsible are made parties and given an opportunity to defend. Habeas corpus is manifestly not such a proceeding.

Let the alternative writ heretofore issued be made peremptory.

PARKER, C. J., BRIDGES, MAIN, HOLCOMB, TOLMAN, and MACKINTOSH, JJ., concur.

MITCHELL, J., concurs in the result.

[No. 15662. Department One. August 22, 1921.]

THE STATE OF WASHINGTON, *Respondent*, v. A. F. SIGLER, *Appellant*.[1]

CRIMINAL LAW (107)—EVIDENCE—OTHER OFFENSES. In a prosecution for unlawfully having sexual intercourse with a female child under the age of eighteen years, evidence that defendant had given the prosecuting witness capsules to prevent pregnancy, and that he had arranged with a physician to operate upon her to bring about a miscarriage, was properly admissible as directly tending to establish his guilt of the crime charged, though such proof tended to show guilt of other offenses.

RAPE (1, 5)—STATUTES—"PREVIOUS CHASTE CHARACTER"—DEFENSES. Under Rem. Code, § 2436, making it a crime to carnally know a female child "fifteen and under eighteen years of age, and of previously chaste character," a requested instruction "that the phrase 'previously chaste character' is not limited alone to sexual intercourse, but includes purity in conduct and principle up to the time of the commission of the alleged offense," was properly refused, since the term "previously chaste character" means an actual physical condition as distinct from a chaste state of mind.

RAPE (19)—EVIDENCE—"PREVIOUS CHASTE CHARACTER"—PRESUMPTIONS. In a prosecution for having carnal knowledge of a female child between fifteen and eighteen years of age, a requested instruction that "previously chaste character . . . . is not presumed but must be proven by the state as a fact," was properly refused, the rule in this state being that the chastity of the woman will be presumed in cases of this character.

TRIAL (101)—INSTRUCTIONS—REQUESTS ALREADY GIVEN. The refusal of a proper requested instruction is not error where the court, in its own language, substantially charges the jury to the same effect.

CRIMINAL LAW (358, 362)—NEW TRIAL—CUMULATIVE EVIDENCE. The refusal of the court to grant a new trial because of newly discovered evidence did not show an abuse of discretion, where it appeared that the new evidence was largely cumulative, and would not be likely to change the result at another trial.

Appeal from a judgment of the superior court for Yakima county, Holden, J., entered February 24, 1919, upon a trial and conviction of rape. Affirmed.

[1]Reported in 200 Pac. 323.

H. J. Snively, for appellant.

O. R. Schumann and *J. Lenox Ward,* for respondent.

BRIDGES, J.—The defendant was convicted of the crime of having unlawful sexual intercourse with a certain female child, not his wife, of previous chaste character, who, at the time of such offense, was more than fifteen and less than eighteen years of age. He appeals to this court for redress.

His first complaint is that the court permitted the state to introduce evidence showing, or tending to show, the commission by him of other and independent crimes. The testimony particularly objected to is that of the prosecuting witness to the effect that the defendant would take her to the big cities and make money with her, and that he kept certain capsules which he gave her for the purpose of preventing pregnancy, and also certain other testimony tending to show the appellant's connection with an abortion operation performed, or planned to be performed, upon the person of the prosecuting witness. The rule in this jurisdiction, with reference to these matters, is that:

"Proof of the commission of a separate and distinct crime will not be admitted for the purpose of aiding the conviction of defendant for the crime charged. There are exceptions, however, to this general rule, as where the testimony shows a connection between the transaction under investigation and some other transaction, and where they are so interwoven that the omission of the testimony in relation to the other crime would detract something from the testimony which the state would have a right to introduce as tending to show the commission of the crime charged by the defendant. . . . ." *State v. Gottfreedson,* 24 Wash. 398, 64 Pac. 523; *State v. Kaukos,* 109 Wash. 20, 186 Pac. 269.

The rule is well stated in *State v. Geddes,* 22 Mont. 68, 55 Pac. 919, as follows:

"While it is thoroughly well established that the commission of one crime cannot be proved on the trial of a defendant for another, merely for the purpose of inducing a belief in the minds of the jury that the accused is guilty of the crime for which he is being tried, on the other hand it is a part of the criminal law that whatever testimony directly tends to establish the guilt of a person on trial of the crime charged is proper, even though it tends to show guilt of another distinct offense."

The testimony objected to here was not in violation of the principles so announced. One of the questions to be proved by the state and determined by the jury was whether the appellant had carnal knowledge of the prosecuting witness. Any testimony tending to show that such relationship had existed was competent, and so testimony to the effect that the appellant obtained and gave to the prosecuting witness capsules to prevent her from becoming pregnant had a strong tendency to prove the charge that he had had sexual relations with her. Also, the testimony to the effect that the appellant had made arrangements with a certain physician to perform an operation upon the prosecuting witness for the purpose of bringing about a miscarriage was proof tending to show that the appellant was responsible for the condition of the witness. The state would not have had any right to go into the details concerning these matters. This the trial court recognized, and constantly kept such details out of the case. In fact, time and again during the trial, it warned the jury that they were to try the defendant on the charge specified in the information, and that they should consider testimony concerning other offenses only in so far as it bore upon the guilt or innocence of the defendant of the crime with which he was charged. There was no error in receiving this testimony. What we have said will be sufficient to answer the objections of appellant concerning certain statements made by the prosecuting attorney in his opening statement.

The statute under which the information was drawn is § 2436, Rem. Code, and reads as follows:

"Every person who shall carnally know and abuse any female child under the age of 18 years, not his wife, shall be punished as follows: .   .   .

"(3)   When such child is fifteen and under eighteen years of age, and of previously chaste character, by imprisonment in the state penitentiary for not more than ten years, or by imprisonment in the county jail for not more than one year".

The trial court instructed the jury that if, before the time alleged in the information, the prosecuting witness had been carnally known she would not be of previous chaste character, and that, "No act of indiscretion or indecorum on her part, no matter how serious, could constitute her unchaste within the meaning of these instructions, if she had not been carnally known." The appellant requested, and the court refused to give, the following instruction:

"You are instructed that the phrase 'previously chaste character' is not limited alone to acts of sexual intercourse, but includes purity in conduct and principle up to the time of the commission of the alleged offense."

The appellant's argument is that:

"The common understanding of the word 'character'   .   .   .   does not include a physical condition, but instead, it is understood, as applied to a human being, to define and describe a condition arising largely from the action of the mind".

The substance of appellant's argument on this question is tersely stated in the case of *Andre v. State,* 5

Iowa 389, 68 Am. Dec. 708, cited by him, where that
court said:

"We cannot think that a female who delights in
lewdness—who is guilty of every indecency, and lost
to all sense of shame, and who may be even the mistress
of a brothel—is equally the object of this statute (if she
has only escaped actual intercourse) with an innocent
and pure woman. . . . The statute is for the protection of the pure in mind, or the innocent in heart,
who may have been led astray, seduced from the path
of rectitude . . .

"Finally, it seems to us, that if the legislature intended, as argued by the prosecution, it would have
used the phrase 'a woman previously chaste' or 'of previous chastity' or the like, which are directly natural
words to express the idea of actual chastity or chastity
in fact. . . ."

The appellant's contention is novel and interesting,
but, in our judgment, unsound. Indeed, the question
is not an open one in this jurisdiction.

The case of *State v. Dacke*, 59 Wash. 238, 109 Pac.
1050, was one under the statute here being considered.
We there said:

"The term 'of previously chaste character' means
the same in law as in morals. It describes a condition
of sexual purity. It means a female who has never
submitted herself to the sexual embraces of man, and
who still retains her virginal chastity."

The case of *State v. Workman*, 66 Wash. 292, 119
Pac. 751, was also a case of the same character as that
now before us. We there said:

"The obvious purpose of the statute is to protect
females of fifteen and under eighteen years of age,
even in case of actual consent. The words 'previously
chaste character' as used in the statute must, therefore, be construed to mean an actual physical condition,
as distinct from a chaste state of mind as shown by
general conduct."

The courts generally are in accord with this court in the construction of similar statutes. Some of such cases are the following: *Marshall v. Territory,* 2 Okl. Cr. App. 136, 101 Pac. 139; *Kenyon v. People,* 26 N. Y. 203, 84 Am. Dec. 177; *Carpenter v. People,* 8 Barb. (N. Y.) 603, 35 N. Y. Cr. 341; *People v. Clark,* 33 Mich. 112.

While the appellant cites several cases in support of his contention, in addition to *Andre v. State, supra,* none of them, other than the *Andre* case, supports him. We have no doubt that the previous decisions of this court on this question are correct, and we have no disposition to depart from them.

Appellant also complains that the court did not give his requested instruction as follows:

"You are instructed that an element of this alleged offense is the previously chaste character of Elsie Stump. This is not presumed but must be proven by the state as a fact, like any other fact, and beyond a reasonable doubt, and if you have any reasonable doubt as to whether or not Elsie Stump was of previously chaste character, prior to the commission of the alleged offense, then the defendant should be acquitted."

Appellant argues that the chastity of the prosecuting witness will not be presumed, but must be proved by the state. While the courts are not in harmony on this question, this court has long since held that, in cases of this character, the chastity of the woman will be presumed and that it is not necessary that the state prove it. *State v. Jones,* 80 Wash. 588, 142 Pac. 35; *State v. Storrs,* 112 Wash. 675, 192 Pac. 984, 197 Pac. 17.

The appellant also claims error because the court refused to give the following instruction requested by him:

"You are further instructed that, in considering whether or not Elsie Stump, at the time of the commis-

sion of the alleged offense, was of previously chaste
character, you may give full weight to all circumstantial evidence bearing upon the said issue, and if
you find that there be any circumstantial evidence from
which you can infer any fact bearing upon such issue,
you should consider the same and give it full force and
effect in connection with all of the other evidence in
the case.''

The trial court permitted the appellant to put in
much testimony showing the character and conduct of
the prosecuting witness, from which the jury might
have concluded that she was not chaste prior to the
time of the alleged offense. While the court refused to
give the instruction requested by the appellant, it did
give one substantially to the same effect, for it informed the jury that:

''Before the defendant can be convicted you must be
convinced, beyond a reasonable doubt, that, at the time
of the act of intercourse with the defendant, if there
was one, Elsie Stump was of previously chaste character, and in passing on this question you should consider all facts and circumstances disclosed by the evidence which relate to this question, and give them such
weight or credence as you deem them fairly entitled
to.''

The instruction thus given was amply sufficient for
the purpose.

It is further contended that the court erred in refusing to grant a new trial, first, because the evidence
was insufficient to support the verdict; and second, because of newly discovered evidence.

That there was amply sufficient evidence to support
the verdict, there cannot be any reasonable question.
The chief defense was that the prosecuting witness was
not of previous chaste character. On this question
there was a direct conflict of the testimony. The prosecuting witness herself testified that her first act of

intercourse was with the appellant at the time alleged
in the information.

Nor do we think the court was in error in failing to
grant a new trial because of newly discovered evidence.
The record discloses that such newly discovered evidence was that of one Lola Fern Allen and a girl
named "Sunshine" Johnson. Both of these persons
made affidavits to the effect that, some months previously to the time of the alleged offense, Elsie Stump
had told them that she had theretofore had sexual relations with certain young men. It is also shown by the
affidavits that, at the time of the trial, neither the defendant nor his attorneys knew, nor by the exercise of
reasonable care could they have known, that these two
young ladies would testify as shown by their affidavits.
In addition to this newly discovered evidence being of
a cumulative nature, its strength was greatly weakened
by counter-affidavits presented by the state. One of
those affidavits was made by "Sunshine" Johnson, in
which she states that her previous affidavit erroneously
stated the facts, and that the prosecuting witness had
not told her, as therein stated, that she had previously
had sexual relations with young men, but that what
she had said was that she had permitted certain young
men to do with her as they liked. The state also produced affidavits which tended strongly to show that,
prior to the time of the alleged offense, both Miss Johnson and Miss Allen had stated that they knew nothing
derogatory of the character of the prosecuting witness,
or concerning her chastity, and the prosecuting witness
also made an affidavit denying that she had had any
such conversations with those two young ladies. The
trial court manifestly believed that such newly discovered evidence would not, at another trial, be likely
to change the result. Under such circumstances, we

feel impelled to hold that the showing with reference to the newly discovered evidence was insufficient to require us to hold that the court abused its discretion in failing to grant a new trial on that account.

We do not find any prejudicial error, and the judgment is affirmed.

PARKER, C. J., FULLERTON, and HOLCOMB, JJ., concur.

[No. 16324. Department One. August 22, 1921.]

THE STATE OF WASHINGTON, *Respondent*, v. ALFRED PETTILLA *et al., Appellants.*[1]

CRIMINAL LAW (137) — EVIDENCE — HEARSAY — DECLARATIONS BY THIRD PERSONS. In a prosecution for criminal syndicalism, it is prejudicial error to admit hearsay testimony by witnesses who had talked with various persons, at different times and places, who, the witnesses believed, were members of the I. W. W., or assumed by the witnesses to be members, and that in those conversations such persons had revealed the purposes and objects of the I. W. W. organization.

INSURRECTION—CRIMINAL SYNDICALISM—EVIDENCE—ADMISSIBILITY. In a prosecution for criminal syndicalism, witnesses may testify as to statements, speeches, and declarations made by members of the I. W. W. organization, or in their presence, at recognized meetings or assemblages of the organization in their various headquarters, or in such places and on such occasion as are proven to have received the sanction of the organization; and may also testify as to conversations, in which are revealed the principles, teachings, objects and purposes of the organization, with members whose membership is shown by competent testimony and proven to be of such a character as to show it carried the authority of the organization to make the declarations as to its purposes, objects, principles, and teachings.

JURY (59-1)—PEREMPTORY CHALLENGES—JOINDER—CODEFENDANTS. Under the statute granting defendants six peremptory challenges in criminal cases, where there are several defendants, all must join in the challenges, the statute not contemplating that each defendant shall have a right to the full number of peremptory challenges.

[1] Reported in 200 Pac. 332.

Appeal from a judgment of the superior court for
Pierce county, Fletcher, J., entered March 3, 1920,
upon a trial and conviction of criminal syndicalism.
Reversed.

George F. Vanderveer, Ralph S. Pierce, and
Leslie B. Sulgrove, for appellants.

William D. Askren and *Earl V. Clifford,* for respondent.

MACKINTOSH, J.—The defendants were convicted of
the crime of criminal syndicalism and have made many
assignments of error, a renewed discussion of a majority of which is unnecessary, as they have been disposed of adversely to defendants' position in many
recent cases involving the same section of the criminal
law.

Among these assignments, however, are several
which refer to the admission of testimony of several
witnesses who were allowed to say upon the stand that
they had talked with various persons, at different
times and places, who, the witnesses believed, were
members of the I. W. W., by reason of the possession
by some of them of membership cards, by statements
made by others that they were members, and by the
assumption of the witnesses that they were such members, and that, in those conversations, those persons
had revealed the purposes and objects of the I. W. W.
organization.   These witnesses also testified as to
speeches and remarks made at meetings of I. W. W.'s
and various I. W. W. assemblages.   Under the decision
of this court, in *State v. Gibson,* 115 Wash. 512,
197 Pac. 611, the testimony of these witnesses as to
statements made to them by persons who they had
reason to believe were I. W. W.'s as to the objects and
purposes of the organization, was inadmissible and

constituted prejudicial error which entitles the appellants to a new trial.

The rule is: That the ban of hearsay testimony must be placed upon the use of witnesses whose testimony is a recital of what they have been told by persons who they have reason to believe are I. W. W's, either by the discovery upon them of membership cards, or by their declarations of membership, or other facts which lead the witnesses to the belief of the membership in the organization of the persons with whom they have held the conversations touching the purposes and objects, the principles and teachings of the organization; but that witnesses may testify as to statements and speeches and declarations made by members of the organization, or in their presence, at recognized meetings of the organization or assemblages of the organization in their various headquarters or halls, or in such places and on such occasions as are proven to have received the sanction and countenance of the organization, and that the witnesses may also testify as to conversations in which are revealed the principles and teachings, the purposes and objects of the organization, with members of the organization whose membership is shown by competent testimony, and whose membership is proven to be of such a character as to show it carried with it the authority of the organization to make such declarations as to its purposes, objects, principles and teachings.

A point is made of the court's denial to each of the defendants of the right to six peremptory challenges. The courts of a few of the states of the Union have held that, where several defendants are tried at once, each of them has a right to the full number of peremptory challenges. The overwhelming weight of authority, however, under statutes which are similar to ours, requires codefendants to join in the peremptory challenges, and we are satisfied that this is the correct and better rule.

It is also alleged that several of the defendants were not properly identified. From an examination of the record and the briefs of appellants upon this point, we cannot say, as to any special defendant, that there was not some evidence entitling the jury to pass upon his guilt. In view of the disposition we are making of the case, we have not felt it necessary to take up each individual appellant and refer to the testimony which tended to establish his membership in the organization.

For error in the admission of hearsay testimony, as previously indicated in this opinion, the conviction is set aside and appellants are granted a new trial.

PARKER, C. J., BRIDGES, FULLERTON, and HOLCOMB, JJ., concur.

[No. 16587. Department One. August 23, 1921.]

THE STATE OF WASHINGTON, *Respondent*, v.
O. KOWALCHUK *et al.*, *Appellants*.[1]

CRIMINAL LAW (137)—EVIDENCE—HEARSAY—DECLARATIONS BY THIRD PERSONS. In a prosecution for sabotage under Laws 1919, ch. 173, a witness, who had been at one time a member of the I. W. W. organization and acquainted with its leaders and organizers, could testify without violating the hearsay rule, as to what the organizers, leaders, and officers taught him were the doctrines and teachings of the organization respecting injury and destruction of the working appliances of the employers for whom the members of the organization might work.

SAME (140)—EVIDENCE—ACTS OF CODEFENDANTS—UNLAWFUL ACTS OF MEMBERS—ADMISSIBILITY. Specific acts of lawlessness committed by members of an unlawful organization, under the direction or with the sanction of its recognized officers or representatives, are admissible in evidence as proofs of its teachings, purposes, and objects.

[1]Reported in 200 Pac. 333.

SAME (225)—TRIAL—RECEPTION OF EVIDENCE—COMPULSORY PROCESS FOR ATTENDANCE OF WITNESSES. In a prosecution for sabotage, the denial of an application by defendants for the issuance of subpoenas for witnesses residing in the state, but outside of the county of trial, was not a violation of the constitutional right of accused persons to have compulsory process to compel the attendance of witnesses in their behalf, where the only showing of the materiality of such evidence was that the witnesses were librarians having among their books kept for general circulation certain of the literature of the I. W. W.

WITNESSES (81)—CROSS-EXAMINATION—IMMATERIAL MATTERS. In a prosecution for sabotage, committed by defendants as members of the I. W. W. organization, the refusal to permit defendants to cross-examine witnesses who testified respecting specific cases of sabotage by other members of the organization as to whether prosecution had been instituted against such offenders, did not constitute error, since it was not material to the inquiry before the court.

Appeal from a judgment of the superior court for Walla Walla county, Mills, J., entered May 8, 1920, upon a trial and conviction of sabotage. Affirmed.

Leslie B. Sulgrove and *Ralph S. Pierce,* for appellants.

Earl W. Benson and *A. J. Gillis,* for respondent.

FULLERTON, J.—The appellants were convicted of the crime of sabotage, as defined and denounced in ch. 173, p. 517, Laws of 1919, and appeal from the judgment and sentence pronounced upon them. In the brief of counsel, filed in support of the appeal, a large number of assignments of error are made and discussed, but on the oral argument many of these were not dwelt upon, counsel conceding that they had been met and determined by decisions of this court handed down prior to the oral hearing, although subsequent to the preparation of the brief. There were certain of the assignments which it was contended fell within the rule of the case of *State v. Gibson,* 115 Wash. 512, 197

Pac. 611. These were urged orally as constituting reversible error, and these only will be noticed.

The first section of the sabotage act makes it a
felony to commit wilfully any act which shall injure,
interfere with, or obstruct any agricultural, stockrais-
ing, lumbering, mining, quarrying, fishing, manufacturing, transportation, mercantile, or building enterprise,
wherein persons are employed for wage, or wilfully to
destroy or attempt to destroy, or wilfully to derange or
attempt or threaten to derange any mechanism or appliance whatsoever used in the pursuit of the enterprises mentioned. The second section makes it a felony
unlawfully to take or retain, or attempt or threaten
unlawfully to take or retain, any property or instrumentality used in the enterprises enumerated in the
first section, with intent to supplant, nullify or impair
the owner's management and control thereof. By subd.
1, § 3 (p. 517), of the act it is made a felony to advocate,
advise or teach the necessity, duty, propriety or expediency of doing or practicing any of the acts denounced
in the two preceding sections; and by subd. 4 (p. 518)
of the same section it is made a felony to organize,
help to organize, give aid to, be a member of, or voluntarily to assemble with, any group of persons
formed to advocate, advise or teach such necessity,
duty, propriety or expediency. The appellants were
charged with being members of a group of persons
known as the Industrial Workers of the World, an organization charged to have been formed to advocate,
advise and teach the necessity, duty, propriety, and
expediency of doing and practicing the acts made unlawful by the first sections of the act.

To show that the organization named was organized
for the unlawful purposes mentioned, the state called
as a witness one William Josh. This witness, after

testifying that he was at one time a member of the
organization, and acquainted with its leaders and organizers, was permitted to testify, over the objection
of the appellants, to the statements and declarations
made by these persons to members of the organization
as to their duties as such members. Specifically, he
testified that members of the organization were instructed by them to do, in all instances, no more work
than they were compelled to do to continue on a job,
and to do such work as they did, so far as they could,
in such a manner as to cause it to be done over again;
that, if they were railway employees, it was their duty
to lose all the freight possible, and their duty to send
such of it as they could to stations to which it was not
consigned; that, if they were working in the mills, in
other industries, or in the woods, it was their duty to
let the steam in the engines operating the power-driven
machinery die down, and thereby cause stoppages and
delays in the work; to misplace, lose and destroy as
many of the working tools as possible, and generally to
do anything they could to injure property and "make
a hole in the boss' pocket;" the object and purpose being to make the operation of industries unprofitable to
their owners, and cause their abandonment, when they
could be seized and operated by the workers themselves.

It is objected to this testimony that it is in its nature
hearsay, and inadmissible under the general rule excluding testimony of that nature, and specifically so
under our decision in the case of *State v. Gibson,
supra.* Treating the question as an open one, we cannot think the evidence here admitted falls within the
ban of the rule invoked. Hearsay evidence is defined
in Corpus Juris (22 C. J. 199) as evidence the pro-
bative force of which depends, in whole or in part, on

the competency and credibility of some person other
than the witness by whom it is sought to produce it.
In other words, it is to permit a witness, who has himself no knowledge of a fact, to testify what he heard
some other person say, or what some other person told
him was the fact. The inquiry here was as to the doctrines and teachings of the organization known as the
Industrial Workers of the World, of which organization the defendants were members. The witness testifying was formerly a member of the organization.
Manifestly, he could testify as to these doctrines and
teachings in so far as they were within his own knowledge, and could testify without violating the hearsay
rule, what the organizers, leaders and officers taught
him were the doctrines and teachings of the organization. This is to testify to the fact directly, not what
some third person stated to him was the fact.

Nor does the case of *State v. Gibson* lay down a different rule. There the question at issue was, in substance, the question at issue here. In making proof
of the objects and purposes of the organization known
as the Industrial Workers of the World, the state
called as witnesses persons not members of the organization, who were permitted to testify what certain
other persons, who claimed to be members of the organization, in private conversations, told them concerning its objects and purposes. But it is at once apparent that the witnesses testifying to the facts related
were not testifying as of their own knowledge. In this
sense their testimony was hearsay, and was held to be
within the ban of the hearsay rule. It is plain, however, that the question now before us is not the question there presented. Here the witness did not testify
to facts told him by others concerning the doctrines and
teachings of the organization, but to facts within his

own knowledge—to matters actually taught by the
representatives and officers of the association at authorized meetings of the association held for the purpose
of promulgating its doctrines. The case falls within
the rule announced in *State v. Pettilla, ante* p. 589, 200
Pac. 332, where it was held that statements and·decla-
rations concerning the teachings, purposes and objects
of the organization could be shown when made at
authorized meetings of the organization, whether private or public, by persons purporting to represent the
organization; "and that the witnesses may also testify
as to conversations in which are revealed the principles
and teachings, the purposes and objects of the organization, with members of the organization, whose membership is shown by competent testimony, and whose
membership is proven to be of such a character as to
show that it carried with it the authority of the organization to make such declarations as to its purposes,
objects, principles and teachings."

Another witness for the state, who was also at one
time a member of the organization, was permitted to
testify to specific acts of lawlessness while working for
a ship-building concern; such as loosening bearing
shafts, putting grit into bearings, drilling out rivets
inserted in the sheetings forming the sides of a vessel
on which they were working, and the like. It is objected
to this that it is testimony highly prejudicial in its effects upon a jury, and testimony that is vicious and
dangerous if not properly guarded, since any workman,
whether a member of the organization or not, may
commit such acts, and since a member of the organization may commit the acts, although they be not authorized by the organization, and that here the court did
not sufficiently guard the testimony. But we think the
trial court exercised all due caution in this respect. It

admitted the testimony only after it was shown that
the general literature of the organization taught the
duty of committing acts of this kind, after it was shown
that such were the teachings at the public and private
meetings of the organization, and after it had been
specially shown that these specific acts had been agreed
upon at a "job meeting" of members of the organization held shortly prior to their commission to devise
ways and means for "slowing up the job." It is perhaps unnecessary to add that, where the teachings, objects and purposes of a society, or other organized
body of persons, is a question at issue, specific acts
committed by the members of the particular organization in question, committed under the direction or with
the sanction of its recognized officers or representatives, are admissible in evidence as proofs of its teachings, purposes and objects.

Prior to the trial of the cause, the defendants,
through their attorney, sought an order from the trial
court directing subpoenas to issue for certain named
witnesses residing within the state but outside of the
county in which the trial was had. The court denied
the application, and it is urged that the appellants were
thereby deprived of material evidence necessary for
their defense. With respect to one of the witnesses,
no showing whatever was made as to what the defendants expected to prove by him. As to the others, it
was shown that they were librarians having charge of
libraries in which books were kept for general circulation, and that among such books were certain of the
literature of the Industrial Workers of the World,
which the state would introduce as a part of its evidence to show that that organization taught by its literature the duty of its members to commit acts denounced
by the act under which the defendants were informed

against. In the early cases of *State ex rel. Thurston County v. Grimes*, 7 Wash. 445, 35 Pac. 361, and *State ex rel. Carraher v. Graves*, 13 Wash. 485, 43 Pac. 376, it was held that, while it was the constitutional right of a defendant to have compulsory process to compel the attendance of witnesses in his behalf without advancing fees therefor, he was not entitled to subpoena at the state's expense whomsoever he pleased, but that he must, before he is entitled to such a subpoena, "make a showing in general terms of the materiality of the testimony he expects from the witnesses" for whom the subpoenas are sought. Following this rule, the trial court denied the application, holding that there was no sufficient showing of the materiality of this testimony. We find no error in this conclusion. The fact sought to be shown could have no possible bearing upon the issue the jury were required to determine.

On cross-examination of the witnesses testifying to acts of sabotage, the defendants sought to show that the persons charged with the acts had not been prosecuted therefor. The court sustained objections to the questions, and complaint is made that, by so doing, the defendants were unduly limited in the cross-examinations of these witnesses. But plainly there is no error in the ruling of the court. It might have been material, as bearing upon the credibility of the witnesses testifying to the acts, to inquire whether they had made complaint to the proper authorities of the commission of the act, but to show merely that no prosecution had been instituted against the offenders would prove nothing material to the inquiry before the court.

We find no error in the record, and the judgment appealed from will stand affirmed.

PARKER, C. J., HOLCOMB, BRIDGES, and MACKINTOSH, JJ., concur.

[No. 16272. Department One. August 23, 1921.]

THE STATE OF WASHINGTON, *Respondent*, v. FLORENCE PICKEL, *Appellant*.[1]

CRIMINAL LAW (17, 19)—RAPE (27)—PRINCIPALS AND ACCESSORIES—EVIDENCE—SUFFICIENCY. Under Rem. Code, § 2260, declaring one who abets, encourages, or induces a crime to be a principal therein, a woman was properly convicted as principal in the crime of rape upon a girl under the statutory age of consent, where the evidence showed she introduced the man to the girl and invited him to call on her, absenting herself from home at the time of the visit until late in the evening, retiring shortly after her return, leaving the couple alone, and in the morning asking the girl if she got any money out of him; that on the night of the offense charged, at the invitation of the defendant, the man came to the house bringing another man with him about 10 p. m., the four of them remaining in a darkened room until 2 a. m. during which time the man and girl had sexual intercourse in the presence of defendant.

SAME (19)—RAPE (35)—AIDING AND ABETTING OFFENSE—INSTRUCTIONS. In a prosecution of a woman as principal in the rape of a girl under the age of consent, a requested instruction that the defendant was under no legal obligation to prevent, either by word or action, the having carnal knowledge of the girl by the man was properly refused, it being for the jury, under the evidence, to decide whether the defendant aided, assisted and abetted the perpetration of the offense.

SAME (451)—APPEAL—HARMLESS ERROR—CONDUCT OF COUNSEL. In a prosecution charging defendant with abetting and encouraging carnal intercourse with a girl under the age of consent, the misconduct of the prosecuting attorney on cross-examination in asking defendant whether she had not stayed certain nights in certain hotels with certain men was not prejudicial error, where the court sustained objections to that line of examination.

SAME (217)—TRIAL—CONDUCT OF JUDGE—COMMENTS ON EVIDENCE. The remark of the court in sustaining objections to improper questions by the prosecuting attorney that they called for repetition was not a comment on the facts to be determined by the jury.

WITNESSES (101)—IMPEACHMENT OF ACCUSED. Where a female defendant in a criminal prosecution charging a sexual offense becomes a witness in her own behalf she is subject to impeachment

[1]Reported in 200 Pac. 316; 204 Pac. 184.

by evidence showing that her reputation for morality and chastity in the community in which she lives is bad.

ON REHEARING.

CRIMINAL LAW (116)—EVIDENCE—CHARACTER OF ACCUSED—PARTICULAR ACTS. In a criminal case in which the accused had not put her character in issue, it is reversible error to allow witnesses to testify that her reputation for morality and chastity in the community in which she lived was bad.

Appeal from a judgment of the superior court for Spokane county, Oswald, J., entered August 12, 1920, upon a trial and conviction as an accessory to the crime of rape. Affirmed.

John M. Gleeson and *A. G. Gray,* for appellant.

Joseph B. Lindsley and *James Emmet Royce,* for respondent.

HOLCOMB, J.— Appellant appeals from a judgment of conviction and sentence thereon, upon an information charging that, "on or about March 1, 1920, in Spokane, Washington, she did then and there wilfully, feloniously and unlawfully aid, abet, encourage, and permit one Charles Jennings to commit the crime of carnal knowledge and abusing a female child under the age of eighteen years, to wit: one Tillie Schmidtz, the said Tillie Schmidtz being of the age of fourteen years and not then and there being the wife of the said Charles Jennings."

The evidence for the prosecution tended to show these facts: Tillie Schmidtz lived in the town of Davenport, where appellant and her husband also resided for a number of years. In the summer of 1919, Charles Jennings met appellant in Davenport. Early in the year 1920, appellant and her husband and children left Davenport and moved to Spokane. The husband returned to Lincoln county within two days after moving to Spokane, and secured steady employment, and was absent from home all week, seeing his family only on Sundays. When appellant and her family moved to Spokane, the Schmidtz girl went with them, with the permission of the mother of the girl, and upon the understanding that the girl was to make her home with appellant. On the night of February 21, 1920, appellant and the Schmidtz girl were returning from a dance hall on the "Owl" car. Jennings was on the car, and appellant addressed him and reminded him of their having met in the street at Davenport the previous year. She introduced him to the Schmidtz girl, and invited him to visit them. He went out the next night, Sunday, February 22. He arrived there about six p. m. and appellant was not at home, and did not return until 10 p. m. She remained down stairs for a time, and then retired. She asked the Schmidtz girl the next morning if she got any money from Jennings. Appellant again invited Jennings to the house, requesting that he bring another man with him, and arranged to meet him the following Tuesday night, February 24. Jennings went to the house Tuesday night, the 24th, and took another young man with him, arriving there about 10 p. m. Jennings and the Schmidtz girl, and appellant and the other young man, entertained each other in the front room until about 2 a. m. Jennings and the girl occupied the sofa, and both testified that they had sexual intercourse there, both appellant and the other young man being present. Sometime during the evening the light in the room was extinguished, either by burning out or by being turned off, and was not renewed. The light burned in the adjoining room and shone through the open door into the front room.

Jennings was a young man of about twenty-one years. Appellant was of the age of twenty-eight, a married woman, mother of four living children, the eldest being a daughter about thirteen years of age, and the Schmidtz girl was between fourteen and fifteen years of age.

The crime charged is that of carnally knowing and abusing a female child under the age of consent, as an accessory before the fact.

The distinction between an accessory before the fact and a principal, or a principal in the second degree, is abolished by § 2007, Rem. Code, which provides that all persons concerned in the commission of an offense, whether they directly counsel the act constituting the offense, or counsel, aid and abet in its commission, though not present, shall hereafter be indicted, tried and punished as principals. Section 2260, Rem. Code, also defines a principal as every person concerned in the commission of a felony, gross misdemeanor, or misdemeanor, whether he directly commits the act constituting the offense, or aids or abets in its commission, and whether present or absent; and every person who directly or indirectly counsels, encourages, hires, commands, induces, or otherwise procures another to commit a felony, gross misdemeanor or misdemeanor, is a principal and shall be proceeded against and punished as such.

The state was required to, and did, elect to rely upon the alleged intercourse occurring Tuesday night, February 24, as the crime charged. The jury were instructed to disregard all evidence concerning any subsequent alleged intercourse, and to consider prior alleged intercourse, if any, for the purpose of corroboration of the offense alleged on February 24.

It is elementary that every person who counsels a crime or contributes to it, directly or indirectly, has a guilty participation in that crime. Under our statute, encouragement is made an element of the offense of aiding and abetting in the commission of a crime, and encouragement may be by either words or deeds. To encourage is defined as: "To help, forward, incite, stimulate, countenance, advise." Webster's International Dictionary. The encouragement by appellant of Jennings to commit the crime upon the girl consisted, if at all, in these facts and circumstances: Appellant took a girl of very immature age, night after night, to public dance halls; she kept the girl out late at night; she permitted the girl to make promiscuous acquaintances among men; she herself remained out late at night, knowing the girl was at home and expecting the young man; she frequently remained out all night, to the girl's knowledge; she invited a man of whom she knew nothing to visit the girl in her home, and then absented herself on the night of his coming. She suggested to the girl, by questioning, that she should get money out of the young man; she, according to the state's evidence, was in the immediate presence of Jennings and the girl when the act of February 24th was said to have been committed. These facts and circumstances certainly constitute encouragement and incitement towards the commission of the offense, and it would be no defense to show that the offense would have been committed although the incitement had never taken place. 2 Starkie, Evidence (3d ed.), p. 9. Nor is it necessary to show that the criminal act was specifically commanded or advised. 12 Cyc. 191.

Appellant complains that the court erred in its refusal to give requested instruction No. 2 of appellant, as follows:

"The jury are instructed that the said defendant, Florence Pickel, was under no legal obligation to prevent either by word or action the said Charles Jennings from having carnal knowledge of the said Tillie Schmidtz.''

We cannot give our assent to the requested instruction as a statement of the law, under the circumstances here shown. The girl was a very young girl, the man was a young man, and the appellant very much older than either of them and a mature woman. The girl was an inmate of her household, and appellant stood somewhat in the relation of a parent towards her for the time being. Under such circumstances, it was her duty to, at least by word of warning, have prevented Jennings from having carnal knowledge of the girl, if appellant knew, or had reason to believe, that it was about to occur. It was held in *State v. Jackson*, 65 N. J. L. 105, 46 Atl. 764, that a woman who furnishes a room where a man and girl under the age of consent may indulge in sexual intercourse may be convicted as a principal in the second degree, or accessory before the fact. If that decision be sound in principle, as we consider it is, the instruction requested by appellant is very unsound. It has also been held that the presence of a defendant at the commission of a crime would be a circumstance tending to show complicity. It was for the jury to decide, upon all of the evidence and circumstances proven, whether the person who was present aided, assisted and abetted the perpetration of the offense. *People v. Woodward*, 45 Cal. 293, 13 Am. Rep. 176; *State v. St. Clair*, 17 Iowa 149, 22 L. R. A. (N. S.) 835; *Brown v. State*, 28 Ga. 199; *Strawhern v. State*, 37 Miss. 422.

Although appellant complains, the court correctly instructed the jury as to the elements of the offense, and the manner in which it should be proven, and it will serve no good purpose to further elaborate upon the instructions given or refused. Nor is it necessary to discuss appellant's claim that the court erred in not dismissing the jury at the close of the plaintiff's case, or in refusing to direct a verdict in her favor, because the crime had not been proven against appellant. The evidence was sufficient, if believed by the jury, to prove the perpetration of the offense charged.

Other claimed errors, however, deserve discussion.

It is claimed that the court erred in allowing testimony to be introduced to the effect that appellant had stayed down town on several occasions away from the family, because the same was irrelevant and tended to prejudice the jury. The Schmidtz girl had testified that the appellant on other occasions, and on the nights when Jennings visited the house, absented herself and stayed down town somewhere. In her direct examination appellant attempted to justify herself and show the innocence of her staying down town at nights. She said she stayed down town one or two nights only and in company with lady friends. Having so testified in chief, cross-examination by the prosecution made her admit to a number of nights she stayed out all night, and attempted to show that she stayed down town, not with lady friends, but with men other than her husband, naming the men. She denied any such occurrences. When the questions were put to her as to staying certain nights in certain hotels with certain men, objections were interposed, and the court sustained the objections on the ground that the questions would call for repetition, and with this ruling we think appellant must be content. Whatever the ground of rejection was, it was rejected; nor can it be assigned as misconduct on the part of the prosecution that the questions were propounded to appellant upon cross-examination, when the evidence was rejected. Neither did the reason assigned by the court for the rejection constitute unconstitutional comment upon facts to be determined by the jury.

Appellant also complains of the admission of testimony on the part of the state to the effect that appellant was a person of immoral character, when she had not put her character in issue. These witnesses were allowed to testify to the effect that the *reputation* of appellant for *morality and chastity* in the community in which she lived was bad. Such evidence tending to impeach the character of a female witness was approved in *State v. Coella*, 3 Wash. 99, 28 Pac. 28, as being founded upon the text of Underhill, Criminal Evidence (2d ed.) § 237, and also in *State v. Jackson*, 83 Wash. 514, 145 Pac. 470, and *State v. Gaul*, 88 Wash. 295, 152 Pac. 1029, none of which cases have ever been overruled, and stand as the law of this state at this time. It is also the accepted rule in this state that, when a defendant becomes a witness, he or she is subject to impeachment according to the same rules as govern other witnesses.

Many other errors are claimed by appellant, but we find none which we consider prejudicial in anywise to a fair trial of appellant.

Finding no errors warranting a reversal, the judgment is affirmed.

PARKER, C. J., and BRIDGES, J., concur.

ON REHEARING.

[*En Banc*. February 14, 1922.]

PER CURIAM.—On rehearing *En Banc* in this case, the majority of the court are of the opinion that the opinion heretofore rendered in this case, while correct in all other respects, is in error in affirming the action of the lower court in admitting testimony on the part of the state to the effect that appellant was a person of immoral character, when she had not put her character in issue.

Witnesses were allowed to testify to the effect that the reputation of appellant for morality and chastity in the community in which she lived was bad. The cases cited in the opinion relate to female witnesses who were not the accused in the case, and the rule should not be extended to cases like this. The question presented is governed by our decision in *State v. Shaw*, 75 Wash. 326, 135 Pac. 20.

For this error the judgment is reversed and a new trial granted, and the former opinion to that extent is overruled.

[No. 16299. Department Two. August 24, 1921.]

THE STATE OF WASHINGTON, *Respondent*, v. GEORGE STEINLE, *alias* GEORGE BENSON, *et al.*, *Appellants*.[1]

CRIMINAL LAW (460)—INTOXICATING LIQUORS (30, 51)—UNLAWFUL POSSESSION—FORMER CONVICTIONS—INSTRUCTIONS. In a prosecution for the aggravated offense of bootlegging after having been previously convicted of violation of the liquor laws, under Laws 1917, ch. 19, which provides (§ 15) that a certified record of a former conviction "shall be sufficient evidence and proof of such previous conviction or convictions," it is error to instruct that the jury had no right to take into consideration the prior conviction of defendant of the offense of violating the liquor laws of the state, except so far as it might affect his credibility as a witness; since under Art. 1, § 22, of the constitution, guaranteeing the right of trial by jury in criminal cases, the legislature could not empower the courts to declare as a matter of law that the "proof" produced was sufficient.

SAME (460)—INTOXICATING LIQUORS—FORMER CONVICTIONS—STATUTES—AMENDMENT—PROOF AND SUFFICIENCY OF EVIDENCE. An instruction in a prosecution for bootlegging that, if the jury failed to find the defendant guilty of that charge, they might find him guilty of the lesser charge of unlawful possession of intoxicating liquor, was erroneous, where the evidence on which the instruction was based was that, at another time and place, a small quantity of in-

[1]Reported in 200 Pac. 313.

toxicating liquor of similar appearance was found at his home, which was considerably distant from the place where he was charged with bootlegging.

Appeal from a judgment of the superior court for San Juan county, Pemberton, J., entered October 30, 1920, upon a trial and conviction of bootlegging. Reversed.

Clarence L. Reames, for appellants.

The Attorney General, O. R. Schumann, Assistant, and *Samuel R. Buck (Nat U. Brown*, of counsel), for respondent.

TOLMAN, J.—Appellants were separately informed against, charged with the crime of bootlegging. The information against George Steinle charged that he had theretofore been twice convicted of an offense in violation of the prohibition statutes, and the information against Ernest Steinle charged one such prior conviction. The causes were consolidated and tried together. The jury returned a verdict against each of the appellants, "guilty of unlawful possession of intoxicating liquor," and from a judgment on the verdict, the defendants appeal.

The trial court, over the objections and exceptions of appellants, instructed the jury:

"I charge you that you have no right to and must not take into consideration the fact that the defendant or defendants have heretofore been convicted of an offense of violating the liquor laws of this state, except so far as it may affect their credibility as a witness in this case."

Substantially the same instruction was passed upon by this court in *State v. Dale*, 110 Wash. 181, 188 Pac. 473, and there held to be erroneous, and since the subject was there fully discussed and the reasons for the ruling stated, we need not again review the subject.

But it is pointed out by the state that the statute with reference to previous convictions which was considered in the *Dale* case was Rem. Code, § 6262-32, which reads:

" . . . and a certified transcript from the docket of any justice of the peace or a certified copy of the record under seal of the clerk of any court of record shall be sufficient evidence of any previous conviction or convictions of violations of this act;"

while the present prosecution is based upon the amendment of 1917 (ch. 19, Laws of 1917, p. 61, § 15), which inserts, after the word "evidence", the words "and proof," so that the statute now reads:

" . . . and a certified transcript from the docket of any justice of the peace, or a copy of the record of any court of record, certified by the clerk thereof under the seal of the court, shall be sufficient evidence and proof of such previous conviction or convictions."

We cannot hold that the change in the statute alters the situation. Under the constitution, art. 1, § 22, the right of trial by jury is unqualifiedly accorded to one charged with a crime, and in the face of that provision the legislature may not (if the amendment was so intended), empower the courts, as a matter of law, to declare the proof sufficient, and the defendant therefore guilty.

Since our conclusion upon the point just discussed calls for a new trial, we find it necessary to refer to only one other of the many errors assigned. The court instructed the jury, in effect, that if the jury failed to find the defendants guilty of bootlegging, as charged, then it might find them guilty of the lesser charge of unlawful possession of intoxicating liquor, and defined such possession, apparently following the instructions approved in the case of *State v. Spillman*, 110 Wash. 662, 188 Pac. 915; but the evidence in the *Spillman* case justified such a charge, while here it did not. The evidence of the person said to have purchased the liquor from the appellants was of such a character that, if believed by the jury, must have been followed by a verdict of "guilty as charged"; but in rebuttal, under a so-called "gentleman's agreement", the state was permitted to offer evidence to the effect that, after the arrest of appellants, and while they were confined in jail, their home, which was considerably distant from the place where the offense charged in the informations was said to have been committed, was searched and a small amount of liquor, similar in appearance to that which they were alleged to have sold, was there found. While the similarity in appearance of the liquor found with that alleged to have been sold might make this evidence proper on rebuttal, the jury should have been advised that the evidence was admitted only for the purpose of corroborating the prosecuting witness. The failure to so limit the effect of this evidence, and the giving of the instruction now under consideration, erroneously permitted the jury to find that the appellants had no liquor and sold none at the time and place charged, but were guilty of having unlawful possession of intoxicating liquor at a wholly different time and place; or, in other words, while not guilty of the offense charged, were guilty of a wholly different and separate offense committed at a wholly different time and place, with which they were not charged. We do not understand that there is any authority for a criminal prosecution except the nature and cause of the accusation be set forth as required by the constitutional provision hereinbefore referred to.

. The judgment of conviction is reversed, and the cause remanded with instruction to grant the motion for a new trial.

PARKER, C. J., FULLERTON, MAIN, and MITCHELL, JJ., concur.

[No. 16350. Department Two. August 24, 1921.]

THE STATE OF WASHINGTON, *Respondent*, v. KENNETH McLENNEN, *Appellant.*[1]

EVIDENCE (2)—JUDICIAL NOTICE—WORDS OF COMMON MEANING— "SABOTAGE." A court may take judicial notice of the meaning of the word "sabotage," though a statute relating to the offense does not expressly define it.

CRIMINAL LAW (299) — TRIAL — INSTRUCTIONS — DEFINITION OF TERMS—"SABOTAGE." In a prosecution for criminal syndicalism, it was prejudicial error for the court to charge the jury that sabotage is a crime under the laws of the state and that any person practicing it is guilty of a felony, after declaring that it is defined as follows: . . . . . (giving the statutory definition of criminal syndicalism, which does not mention sabotage.)

Appeal from a judgment of the superior court for King county, Ronald, J., entered April 24, 1920, upon a trial and conviction of criminal syndicalism. Reversed.

George F. Vanderveer and *Ralph S. Pierce,* for appellant.

Fred C. Brown and *Chas. Ethelbert Claypool,* for respondent.

BRIDGES, J.—The appellant was charged by information as follows:

"He, said Kenneth McLennen, in the county of King, state of Washington, on the 28th day of January, 1920, did, then and there being, wilfully, unlawfully

[1]Reported in 200 Pac. 319.

and feloniously, be and is a member and organizer and did give aid to and did voluntarily assemble with, a group of persons formed to advocate, advise and teach crime, sedition, violence, intimidation and injury as a means and way of effecting or resisting an industrial, economic, social and political change, to-wit: By being a member and organizer of the Industrial Workers of the World, known as the I. W. W. The said Industrial Workers of the World being and is a group of persons or an organization advocating, advising, teaching crime, and justify crime, sedition, violence, intimidation or injury as a means or way of effecting or resisting an industrial, economic, social or political change."

He was convicted and has appealed. Most of the reasons given by him for reversal of the case have heretofore been by this court determined against him in the case of *State v. Hennessy*, 114 Wash. 351, 195 Pac. 211, and subsequent cases. It will not be necessary for us to consider more than one or two of the points argued by him.

During the trial, the state introduced in evidence, and sufficiently identified, a pamphlet by Vincent St. John, entitled: "The I. W. W.; Its History, Structure and Methods", published by the I. W. W. publishing bureau. It was by this pamphlet that the state undertook to prove the objects and purposes of the organization, and that it came within the state syndicalism act, Laws of 1919, chs. 173, 174, pp. 517, 518. Among other things in the pamphlet is the following: "Failing to force concessions from the employers by the strike, work is resumed and 'sabotage' is used to force the employers to concede the demands of the workers."

The state did not offer any explicit testimony to show the meaning of the word 'sabotage', but the court instructed the jury concerning its meaning as follows:

"You are instructed that sabotage is a crime under the laws of the state of Washington, and is defined as follows:

"Whoever with intent that his act shall, or with reason to believe that it may, injure, interfere with, or obstruct any agricultural, stock raising, lumbering, mining, quarrying, fishing, manufacturing, transportation, mercantile or building enterprise wherein persons are employed for wage, shall wilfully injure or destroy, or attempt or threaten to injure or destroy any property whatsoever, or shall wilfully derange, or attempt or threaten to derange, any mechanism or appliance, shall be guilty of a felony.

"'Whoever, with intent to supplant, nullify or impair the owner's management or control of any enterprise described in the preceding section, shall unlawfully take or retain, or attempt or threaten unlawfully to take or retain, possession or control of any property or instrumentality used in such enterprise, shall be guilty of a felony.'" Laws of 1919, p. 517, §§ 1, 2.

The appellant objected to the giving of this instruction, and here vigorously attacks it. If the word "sabotage" has a common and well-understood meaning, then the court, without any testimony as to its meaning, had a right to define to the jury its meaning as commonly understood. But if the word does not have a commonly understood meaning, then the court would not be authorized to define its meaning, at least without testimony in the case showing what its meaning was. We have no doubt that the word "sabotage" has a common and well understood meaning, and that the court in this case had a right to tell the jury what that meaning was. Though the word is of somewhat recent coinage, its use has become so general and common that the court may take judicial knowledge of its meaning. A very recent edition of the Americana defines the word as follows:

"Sabotage, a method used by labor revolutionists to force employers to accede to demands made on them. It consists in a wilful obstruction and interference with the normal processes of industry. It aims at inconveniencing and tying up all production, but stops short of actual destruction or of endangering human life directly. The practices are varied. The original act of sabotage is said to have been the slipping of a wooden shoe, or 'sabot', of a workman into a loom, in the early days of the introduction of machinery, to impede production. Some of the more common forms are waste of materials; telling the exact truth to customers; obeying orders punctiliously, especially on railroads; using of bad materials so as to impair the standing of the employers; placing sand or emery in wheel bearings; loosening screws and nuts; cutting belts; sitting idle at machines; mislaying tools, and any number of petty devices for hindering and delaying production. . . ."

The court could, of course, define the word in its own language, or adopt for that purpose words from any other person or any statute. But there may be a question whether the statute quoted by the court gives, or was intended to give, a definition of the word "sabotage." It does not on its face purport so to do, nor is the word to be found anywhere in the act or its title. We do not, however, decide that the act does or does not properly define the common meaning of the word. But if it should be conceded that it is there properly defined, yet we are convinced the court committed prejudicial error in informing the jury "that sabotage is a crime under the laws of the state of Washington", and that any person practicing it "shall be guilty of a felony." The fact that, under the statute, sabotage is a crime can have no possible bearing on the definition of the word. It is not at all improbable that, by this instruction, the jury was misled into the belief that the defendant was charged with the statutory crime of

sabotáge and not with a violation of the syndicalism
law of the state, or the jury may have been otherwise
prejudiced against the appellant because of the instruction to the effect that sabotage was a crime and punishable by imprisonment in the penitentiary. The court
should simply have given the commonly accepted definition of the word sabotage, without instructing the jury
that one guilty of practicing it had committed a crime
under the law of the state.

The appellant raises certain other questions which
we have not heretofore decided, but we find them to be
without substantial merit.

For the error pointed out, the judgment must be reversed and the cause remanded for a new trial. It is
so ordered.

PARKER, C. J., MAIN, MITCHELL, and TOLMAN, JJ.,
concur.

———————

[No. 16333. Department Two. August 24, 1921.]

CON HAMBURG, *as Guardian ad Litem of Catherine
Hamburg, a Minor, Appellant,* v. GENEVA EAGLESON,
Respondent.

CON HAMBURG, *as Guardian ad Litem of Pauline Hill, a
Minor, Appellant,* v. GENEVA EAGLESON, *Respondent.*[1]

MALICIOUS PROSECUTION (4, 15)—MALICE—EVIDENCE—SUFFICIENCY.
In an action for malicious prosecution in swearing out a search
warrant against a domestic servant and procuring a search of the
home of her parents, a directed verdict for defendant was proper,
where the evidence showed that defendant, upon missing a fur,
made inquiries at places where she might have left it, without result, but after the search, the defendant recovered the fur from a
place she had theretofore visited, and expressing regrets to the
servant for having suspected her, their relations were amicably
maintained until the father of the servant took the latter away
and began an action for damages.

[1] Reported in 200 Pac. 306.

SAME (4)—MALICE—MISTAKE OF OFFICER. Where one acted in good faith and upon probable cause in signing a blank complaint for a search warrant for a lost fur, which the justice of the peace later filled out so as to charge an essentially different offense, the carelessness and mistake of the officer would not establish malice on the part of the complainant.

Appeal from judgments of the superior court for Walla Walla county, Mills, J., entered January 15, 1920, upon verdicts of a jury rendered in favor of the defendants by direction of the court, in consolidated actions for malicious prosecution. Affirmed.

J. W. Brooks, for appellants.

J. L. Sharpstein and *T. A. Paul,* for respondent.

MITCHELL, J.—These two cases were tried together and are thus presented on appeal. They are malicious prosecution actions. In each case there was a directed verdict for the defendant, and plaintiffs have appealed.

The arguments are predicated on the case of Catherine Hamburg, and we follow that course. She was, and for some months had been, a domestic servant of the respondent's mother, at whose home respondent resided. She and her employer's family, including the respondent, were on the best of terms—all were pleased, except that there were evidences of a secretive disposition on the part of the appellant and minor irregularities, including prowling about portions of the house, not required or expected in the performance of her duties. Catherine's friend Pauline Hill often called in the evenings and stayed until both would leave about eight o'clock, and Pauline also took more or less liberties about the place. The respondent missed a fur that until lately she had in her possession at the residence. It possessed a peculiar value to her. All members of

the household engaged in a fruitless search for it and
Catherine was told of the loss. Careful consideration
and discussions were had by members of the family as
to the different places visited and apparel worn by the
respondent since the last time they had seen it, which
failed to account for it. It was known that, in the
meantime, no one at all outside the members of the
family and Catherine and her friend Pauline had been
in the house. Inquiries at places there was a possibility of its having been left were unrewarded.

In these circumstances, the respondent interviewed a
deputy sheriff, under whose advice both of them went
to a justice of the peace (who, under § 2237, Rem. Code,
if the complainant believes the property is concealed in
any particular house or place, shall issue a search warrant for such property if "he be satisfied that there is
a reasonable cause for such belief") and advised him
of the situation. He had her sign an instrument in
blank form intended for the issuance of a search warrant against the appellant. The instrument, signed by
the respondent, was later filled out by the justice of the
peace in her absence, and thereafter a search warrant
was placed in the hands of a deputy sheriff, who
searched the house of the appellant without finding the
fur. After the search, the respondent recovered the
fur from a place she had lately visited. Immediately
respondent and her mother expressed to appellant their
regrets for having suspected her. The appellant, who
was seventeen years of age, was scarcely perturbed,
and without cessation at any time, continued her services until the father, the nominal appellant here, went
to the home of respondent's mother in an angry mood
and against the daughter's wishes took her away. His
demeanor at the house at that time was such that at

one time his daughter "pushed him away", and later, before leaving, she told the family they had been so kind and good to her she did not want to leave, but that her father would not let her stay; and on leaving was advised that the family would at any time give her recommendations as a house servant. There are some other facts in the case of minor importance we do not set out that negative the charge of malice and strengthen the defense of probable cause. We are of the opinion this case, without question, is as strong or stronger in support of the judgment than were the facts, similar in many respects, in the malicious prosecution case of *Ton v. Stetson*, 43 Wash. 471, 86 Pac. 668, in support of the judgment therein, in which case we said:

"Appellate courts have frequently sustained or directed nonsuits upon clearer evidence tending to show malice than that in the case at bar. See, *Hatjie v. Hare*, 68 Vt. 247, 35 Atl. 54; *Perry v. Sulier*, 92 Mich. 72, 52 N. W. 801; *Richter v. Koster*, 45 Ind. 440; *Willis v. Knox*, 5 Rich. (S. C.) 474."

Also, the judgment appealed from is sustained by reference to the principles stated in *Saunders v. First National Bank of Kelso*, 85 Wash. 125, 147 Pac. 894.

The conclusion here reached is not overcome by the fact that the justice of the peace carelessly and erroneously filled in the complaint, after the respondent had signed it in blank, so as to charge an essentially different offense. It was known to the officers it was the fur that was wanted, and it was that the sheriff did search for. She obeyed the instructions of the justice of the peace in signing the instrument, and his carelessness in later erroneously filling out the complaint, of which mistake she, of course, was wholly unaware, cannot prevail against her, in the face of her having acted in good faith and upon probable cause in seeking a warrant for the search of the fur. *O'Brien v. Frasier,* 47 N. J. L. 349.

The judgment in each case is affirmed.

PARKER, C. J., MAIN, MACKINTOSH, and TOLMAN, JJ. concur.

[No. 16581. *En Banc.* August 25, 1921.]

THE STATE OF WASHINGTON, *on the Relation of the City of Yakima, Plaintiff,* v. C. W. CLAUSEN, *as State Auditor, Respondent.*[1]

MUNICIPAL CORPORATIONS (9)—CLASSIFICATION OF CITIES—ADOPTION OF COMMISSION FORM OF GOVERNMENT—STATUTES—CONSTRUCTION. Under Rem. Code, §§ 7670-1 to 7670-24, providing that cities having a population from 2,500 to 20,000, on adopting a commission form of government, should have the powers of, and be governed by the laws applicable to, second-class cities, a third-class city adopting the commission government did not thereby become a city of the second class, though entitled to such rank by reason of population; since a city can advance from one classification to another only by taking the steps provided in Rem. Code, § 7482 *et seq.*

Application filed in the supreme court May 26, 1921, for a writ of mandamus to compel the state auditor to issue warrants to a city in a certain amount against the primary highway maintenance fund. Denied.

Thos. E. Grady (*Grady, Shumate & Velikanje,* of counsel), for relator.

The Attorney General and *Nat U. Brown,* for respondent.

MACKINTOSH, J.—In July, 1911, Yakima was a city of the third class, although it possessed sufficient population to have entitled it to classification as a city of the second class, had it complied with the law in rela-

[1]Reported in 200 Pac. 311.

tion to the raising of the classification of cities. In
that month it organized itself under the commission
form of government, in pursuance of the provisions
of the Laws of 1911, ch. 116, p. 521 (§§ 7670-1 to
7670-24, Rem. Code), and ever since that time has been
operating under that form of government.

The act just referred to provides that any city in
the state having a population of 2,500 and less than
20,000 may organize under the provisions of the act,
and that cities so organized shall have applicable to
them all the laws governing cities of the second class
not inconsistent with the provisions of the act. The
act also provided that cities organized under the act
shall have the powers of cities of the second class, and
the act further provided, in the event a city decided to
abandon the commission form of government, that,
upon such abandonment, the city shall take classification according to its then population. Laws of 1921,
ch. 96, p. 251, creating a "Primary Highway Maintenance Fund," provides that the state shall pay to cities
of the first and second class in which there are streets
forming a part of a primary state highway a sum
equal to $500 per mile for each mile of such highway,
and that cities of the third and fourth class shall receive $300 per mile. The state auditor, claiming that
Yakima is a city of the third class, has remitted $300
per mile; Yakima claims to be a city of the second
class, and that it should receive $500 per mile. This
action is one in mandamus to compel the payment of
the larger amount. The question, therefore, is whether
Yakima is a city of the second or third class.

Sections 7482 to 7488, Rem. Code, had not been followed at the time that Yakima adopted the commission
form of government, and although, as has been said,
it had a population sufficient to allow it to avail itself

of the statutory procedure to. raise its classification to that of the second class, it had done nothing in that regard. It is relator's contention that, although it had not availed itself of the statutory rights conferred by these sections, by the adoption of the commission form of government, it automatically advanced from the third class to the second class. Section 10, art. 11, of the constitution provides that the legislature, by general law, can prescribe the classification of cities and towns in proportion to their populations, and in pursuance of that constitutional decree, the legislature, in § 7479, Rem. Code, made the classification so that cities having a population of more than 10,000 and less than 20,000 shall be known as those of the second class, and cities of more than 1,500 and less than 10,000 shall be cities of the third class. To advance from one class to another, the method provided in § 7482 *et seq.* must be followed. As we said in *State ex rel. Sylvester v. Superior Court*, 64 Wash. 594, 117 Pac. 487, cities must comply with these statutory requirements in order to attain the advanced classification.

The law of 1911, which allows cities of the second class and a certain portion of those of the third class to adopt a commission form of government, did not create a separate and distinct classification of cities, but merely directs that third class cities having a population of 2,500 and more, and second-class cities, could adopt that form of government, and when they so adopted it they should have the powers, and be governed by, the general laws applicable to second-class cities. The effect of the act is merely to create a class within a class, otherwise the act would be in conflict with the constitution, which classifies cities according to population. The prescription by the act of powers and limitations referred only to the method of administering the form of government provided for in the act, and did not re-classify all cities that accept that form of government, but left them in the classification in which they were at the time they took advantage of the 1911 law. In other words, Yakima is still a city of the third class, operating under a commission form of government, and, by act of the legislature, that form of government is administered as is the government of cities of the second class, but as to all other matters which do not relate to its form of government, it retains the classification it had at the time it became a commission governed city. If it desires to advance itself from the third to the second class, the statutory procedure is open to it to do so, having the requisite population to make the advance. That statutory procedure is available no matter what form of government it may be operating under. To hold otherwise would be to say that cities whose population is less than that specified as necessary under the general laws to make them cities of the second class become cities of that class by adopting the commission government. This would result in the possibility of cities lying side by side, one of them with a population of 2,500, being classified as a second-class city, and its neighbor, with a population of 9,999, remaining a third-class city, because of different forms of government, thus violating the intent of the constitution that cities should be classified according to population.

In the absence of an express declaration by the legislature of its intention to make commission governed cities, cities of the second class, even though the constitution did not inhibit such classification, we are powerless to so interpret the act of 1911. This question has been once before presented to this court in the case of *State ex rel. Hunt v. Tausick*, 64 Wash. 69, 116 Pac. 651, where we said:

"That uniformity was not the object is evidenced by the fact that special charters in existence when the constitution was adopted were, by a further provision of § 10, art. 11, *supra*, permitted to continue in operation, and cities of more than 20,000 population were, by the same section, authorized to frame their own charters. Moreover, there is nothing in the constitution or in any statute of this state providing that, when a municipality organized as a city of the third class may attain a population of 10,000 or more, it shall *ipso facto* become a city of the second class. On the contrary, it will remain a city of the third class until by proper procedure and vote it decides to advance itself to, and become organized as, a city of higher grade. Thus, it may be seen that cities of the third class may progress to more than 10,000 population, without changing their organization or classification. It is evident that all laws pertaining to municipalities in this state must be general in their terms. By the enactment of this statute which is a general law, the legislature has created another class of cities in proportion to population, for the purpose of authorizing their incorporation and organizing under a commission form of government, to be adopted by them at their option. We find no constitutional inhibition against its enactment or against the creation of such a class of cities. Notwithstanding appellant's contention to the contrary, we conclude the act in no way seeks to amend or repeal any statute creating cities of the second and third classes. It only creates a new classification of all cities having the population of cities of the second class and a portion of cities of the third class, without repealing or destroying their original classification."

When the act of 1921 referred to payments to cities of the different classes, it applied to the classification of the cities of the state according to their classification as regards population, and not as to the form of government under which they might be operating. The state auditor was therefore correct in apportioning to Yakima on the basis of its being a city of the third class. It will be entitled to the larger amount when it makes use of the statutory machinery to advance to the classification to which its population entitles it. The writ is denied.

PARKER, C. J., BRIDGES, FULLERTON, MAIN, HOLCOMB, MITCHELL, and TOLMAN, JJ., concur.

[No. 16488. Department Two. August 25, 1921.]

In the Matter of the Estate of SCOTT McDONALD.
FRANK D. ALLEN, *Appellant,* v. RUTH McDONALD *et al., Respondents.*[1]

EXECUTORS AND ADMINISTRATORS (160, 167)—FINAL ACCOUNT—ADDITIONAL COMPENSATION—ATTORNEY'S FEES—TIME FOR APPLICATION. The failure of an executor, upon the hearing in the trial court of exceptions to his final account, to present testimony as to the reasonable additional compensation due him on account of the employment of an attorney to resist the exceptions, which were sustained by the court, would not foreclose proof upon such issue upon a rehearing by the trial court after reversal of its order sustaining the exceptions.

APPEAL (494)—DECISION—POWERS AND DUTIES OF LOWER COURT—INCIDENTAL RELIEF. Where a judgment sustaining exceptions to an executor's final account was reversed and remanded without directions to enter a specific judgment, upon which the trial court entered judgment overruling the exceptions, it was entitled to consider as incidental to such judgment the amount of compensation to be awarded the executor for attorney's services in resisting the exceptions.

SAME (375)—REVIEW—MATTERS NOT BEFORE LOWER COURT. On appeal from a judgment of the trial court upon an executor's final account to which exceptions had been sustained; appellant was not required to present the question of allowance of attorney's fees in resisting the exceptions, since such question had not been litigated in the lower court and there was no evidence in the record upon which the appellate court could base a directed judgment.

[1] Reported in 200 Pac. 308.

Appeal from a judgment of the superior court for Spokane county, Oswald, J., entered March 3, 1921, upon findings in favor of the defendants, denying additional compensation for attorney's services in resisting exceptions to the final account of executors, after a hearing before the court. Reversed.

Alex M. Winston, for appellant.

Henry L. Kennan, for respondents.

MAIN, J.—Frank D. Allen, for many years one of the executors of the last will and testament of Scott McDonald, deceased, filed a petition in this case asking that he be allowed additional compensation in order that he might pay an attorney whom he had employed to resist exceptions to his final account. The trial resulted in a judgment sustaining certain of the exceptions, and from this judgment the petitioner appealed. In 1900, Scott McDonald died testate, and two years later Allen was appointed to fill a vacancy in the number of executors, and acted in this capacity until his resignation was accepted August 19, 1919, and his final account as such executor approved and settled on the fourth day of November, 1919. In March, 1918, the then executors filed their annual reports for the years 1916 and 1917. To these reports exceptions were filed. A trial was had upon the exceptions on February 3, 1919, and judgment was rendered by the trial court sustaining the exceptions. From this judgment, Frank D. Allen, one of the executors, appealed. While the appeal was pending, Allen filed in the superior court a petition and report praying for an order approving the final accounts fixing the amount of compensation to be paid to him on account of services rendered as executor and attorney for the estate and asking that he be discharged as such executor. As above

stated, on November 4, 1919, an order was made discharging him as executor and fixing and allowing compensation as such executor and trustee for all services
rendered by him to the estate of Scott McDonald, deceased.

When the exceptions were filed to the appellant's
report, he employed Alex M. Winston, an attorney-at-
law, to defend against them. When the order of November 4, 1919, was entered, Mr. Winston had rendered
all the services which he was required to render, with
the exception of preparing and filing the reply brief
and arguing the case orally in this court. The executor
prosecuted an appeal from the order sustaining the
exceptions, and in *In re McDonald's Estate*, 110 Wash.
366, 188 Pac. 523, the judgment of the trial court in
sustaining the exceptions was reversed and the cause
remanded with direction to overrule the exceptions.
After the remittitur in that case was filed in the superior court, the appellant presented an application
requesting that he be allowed compensation in order
that he might pay Mr. Winston for the services which
he had rendered in resisting the exceptions. The matter of allowing additional compensation came on for
hearing and testimony was taken. The court made
findings of fact in which it was stated that $1,500 was
a reasonable fee. To this finding no exception has been
taken, and the parties seem to be in accord that the fee
is reasonable if additional compensation is to be
allowed.

The first question is whether the appellant was required in the hearing in the trial court at the time the
exceptions were sustained, to offer testimony as to
what would be a reasonable additional compensation
to him on account of the necessity of employing an
attorney to resist the exceptions. The respondent's

position is that, not having asked for the compensation
at that time, the present application comes too late. It
is suggested that, since the matter of fixing the compensation of executors and administrators is a subject
for determination upon the settlement of the final account and that such judgment is a final judgment, as
held in *In re Doane's Estate*, 64 Wash. 303, 116 Pac.
847, and other cases, that the present application was
not timely. But that rule is not controlling here. The
trial court held and entered a judgment sustaining the
exceptions, and if this judgment had been sustained
the appellant would not have been entitled to any compensation on account of expense incurred in resisting
such exceptions. Both parties to this appeal recognize
the rule that, where exceptions are filed to the accounts
of an executor and are sustained, the executor is entitled to no compensation from the estate for resisting
such exceptions, but that, where exceptions are overruled, he is entitled to compensation. The trial court
being of the view, and entering a judgment accordingly, that the exception should be sustained under the
rule, any evidence offered by the appellant looking to
compensation for services in resisting the exceptions
would have been entirely immaterial and irrelevant.
Had such testimony been offered, the trial court might
well have held that, under its view of the law, such
evidence had no bearing upon the case. The appellant
was not required to anticipate that the judgment might
be reversed and proceed upon such hypothesis, because,
under the judgment of the trial court, he was entitled
to nothing if sustained; and, in addition to this, it could
not be known at that time how much future litigation
there might be with reference to the matter.

The next point is that the judgment, when the remittitur went down, was one directed by this court and

that all that the trial court could do would be to enter
the judgment overruling the exceptions. In support of
this position, reliance is placed upon the holding in
German-American State Bank v. Sullivan, 50 Wash.
42, 96 Pac. 522, and other like cases, where it is held
that, where a cause is remanded from this court with
directions to enter a specific judgment, the trial court
is without power to do other than enter the judgment
directed; but that rule is not controlling here. The
judgment sustaining the exceptions was reversed.
When the cause was remanded, the trial court entered
another judgment overruling the exceptions. For the
first time there was a judgment entered in the trial
court under which the appellant was entitled to additional compensation in resisting the exceptions. When
this judgment was entered, as incidental to it would
arise the matter of compensation. There is nothing
in the directions given, when the judgment was reversed upon the former appeal, which would indicate
that the trial court might not consider as incidental
to the judgment to be entered that compensation might
be awarded.

There is another contention that the appellant should
not be allowed compensation because he did not ask
for it while the cause was pending in this court and
before the remittitur was returned to the trial court.
The question presented here was whether the trial
court erred in sustaining the exceptions to the final
account. Upon the appeal a new element could not be
brought into the case. Had the request been made
while that case was pending here it would have been
an attempt to introduce into the case an element which
was not in it in the trial court, and, as above pointed
out, which was not required to be litigated in that court
at the time the matter of the exceptions to the account

was being heard. There was no evidence in the record upon which this court could base a directed judgment.

The judgment will be reversed, and the cause remanded with directions to the superior court to enter a judgment for the sum stated in the findings as reasonable additional compensation.

PARKER, C. J., HOLCOMB, and MITCHELL, JJ., concur.

[No. 16422. Department One. August 26, 1921.]

MITSUBISHI GOSHI KAISHA, *Respondent*, v. CARSTENS PACKING COMPANY, *Appellant*.[1]

ARBITRATION AND AWARD (9)—NOTICE OF AWARD—SERVICE—SUFFICIENCY. Where an award had been made pursuant to the provisions of Rem. Code, §§ 420-430, under an agreement for arbitration, service of notice of the award by registered mail was sufficient, under Id., §§ 244-247, where the person making the service and the person on whom it was made resided at different places between which there was regular communication by mail; such notice not coming within the exception against the service of "summons or other process" by such method.

PROCESS (1)—NOTICE—REQUISITES—STATUTORY PROVISIONS. Where one part of the code defines what constitutes service of notice, the use of the term "service" in another part of the code applying to notice must be construed as coming under such definition.

Appeal from an order of the superior court for King county, Frater, J., entered February 19, 1920, denying a motion to vacate a judgment entered upon an award of arbitrators, after a hearing before the court. Affirmed.

Kerr, McCord & Ivey, for appellant.

Bausman, Oldham, Bullitt & Eggerman, for respondent.

[1] Reported in 200 Pac. 327.

FULLERTON, J.—On July 25, 1919, the respondent, Mitsubishi Goshi Kaisha, contracted to sell to the appellant, Carstens Packing Company, some three hundred barrels of China refined edible cottonseed oil, the oil to be shipped from the Orient in August or September following the date of the contract. The contract contained the following provision:

"Any dispute arising under this contract shall be settled by arbitration of M. J. Falkenburg & Company, upon the immediate demand on the part of either the seller or the buyer; the decision of the arbitrator shall be final for both parties."

The oil was delivered pursuant to the terms of the contract and paid for by the appellant. Subsequent thereto a dispute arose between the parties as to the quality of the oil delivered, the appellant contending that it was not edible as required by the contract. No agreement having been reached by the parties themselves, the respondent submitted the contract to the arbitrators named therein, with a request that the dispute be arbitrated. Pursuant thereto, the arbitrators caused notice to be given to each of the parties that the matter would be heard on February 16, 1920, at 10 o'clock a. m., at the office of the arbitrators. At the time appointed, the appellant did not appear. The respondent, however, appeared and submitted his evidence, and the arbitrators thereafter made a formal decision in writing, deciding the dispute in favor of the respondent. The written award was sealed and delivered to the prevailing party, who delivered it without breaking the seal to the clerk of the superior court of the county wherein the arbitration was held, who caused it to be entered of record. A copy of the award, signed by the arbitrators, was also delivered to the respondent, who caused service thereof to be made on the appellant by registered mail. No exceptions thereto were taken by the appellant within twenty days after the service, and the respondent thereupon applied to the superior court for a judgment upon the award, and a judgment was entered thereon by the court on February 24, 1920.

On January 18, 1921, the appellant appeared specially in the superior court and moved to set aside the judgment, basing the motion on the ground that the service of the award was insufficient to give the court jurisdiction of the person of the appellant, and that in consequence the court was without jurisdiction to enter a judgment upon the award. The motion was heard in due course and denied by the court, and from its order, the present appeal is prosecuted.

The single question presented by the appeal is whether the service of the award by registered mail was a sufficient service.

The statute relating to the arbitration of disputes and for judgment thereon is found at §§ 420 to 430 of the Code (Rem.). It provides that all persons desirous to end by arbitration any controversy, suit, or quarrel may submit their differences to the award or umpirage of any person or persons mutually agreed upon. The agreement to so submit must be in writing, signed by the parties. The procedure in making the award is prescribed with some minuteness, and was substantially followed by the procedure taken in the instant case as we have outlined it. The manner of serving the required notices is not prescribed by the particular statute, but is covered elsewhere in the statutes. Rem. Code, §§ 244-247. These provide for service by mail where the person making the service and the person on whom it is made reside at different places between which there is regular communication by mail. It is provided, however, that the particular provision shall not apply "to the service of a summons or other process or of any paper to bring a party into contempt."

It follows that, if the notice of this award was not a "summons or other process," the service by mail was sufficient. It is our opinion that it is neither of these. It was not the proceeding by which the appellant was brought into court, or the means through which the court acquired jurisdiction over its person; it is what the statute denominates a notice to distinguish it from a summons or process; in this instance its purpose is to give the party an opportunity to appear and object to the award if he so desires, and perhaps, also, to fix a time at which his right to so object shall be cut off. Jurisdiction of the subject-matter of the award and of the persons of the parties was acquired by consent; it arose from the agreement to arbitrate. As we said in *Tacoma Railway & Motor Co. v. Cummings*, 5 Wash. 206, 31 Pac. 747, 33 Pac. 507, every agreement to arbitrate

"is entered into in view of the law upon the subject, and every party to such arbitration consents to such jurisdiction on the part of the court in regard to the controversy as has been by law provided. And the law having provided that the filing of such award with the written agreement to submit the same to arbitration should give the court jurisdiction of the persons of the parties to the arbitration and of the subject-matter of the controversy, every one entering into such an arbitration must be held to have consented thereto."

So, also, to the same purport is *Dickie Mfg. Co. v. Sound Const. & Eng. Co.*, 92 Wash. 316, 159 Pac. 129, where we said:

"Those who enter into arbitration accept in advance the jurisdiction of the superior court . . . Common law arbitration has ceased to exist. If there is no proper agreement under the statute, then there is no arbitration at all. But once the parties do properly agree on arbitration, there can be no revocation."

The appellant argues that, where a statute requires a notice to be served but does not prescribe the manner of service, a personal service is required. But the rule could be operative in this instance only on the theory that the general statutes relating to service are without application to this particular proceeding. This theory we think untenable. The chapter of the code relating to arbitration and award is in no sense a special statute. It was enacted with the code of civil procedure and forms an integral part thereof. So, likewise, were the sections of the statute relating to service of notice, process, and summons; although these latter have been amended since the enactment of the original code. But the amendment does not change the governing principle. The statute is a whole and must be read and construed as a whole. Wherever, therefore, it speaks of service it means service as that term is elsewhere defined therein.

We find no error in the ruling of the court, and its order will stand affirmed.

PARKER, C. J., HOLCOMB, MACKINTOSH, and BRIDGES, JJ., concur.

[No. 16346. Department Two. August 26, 1921.]

IONIA FITZSIMMONS, *Respondent,* v. ROBERT C.
FITZSIMMONS, *Appellant.*[1]

DIVORCE (109)—RIGHTS OF DIVORCED PARTIES—PROPERTY DISPOSED
OF BY STIPULATION — CONTRACTS — ENFORCEMENT — FRAUD. Where,
pending a divorce proceeding, a man and wife entered into a written contract purporting to settle their property rights, by the terms
of which the husband agreed to convey certain property to the wife,
an action by the wife, after divorce, for the specific performance of
the contract would not be defeated by evidence showing that, at the
time the property settlement was entered into, letters were written
to the wife by another man, couched in endearing terms and of a
nature to indicate the writer had reason to believe his attentions
were welcomed by the wife; since such misconduct on her part did
not constitute fraud inhering in the contract between them.

SAME. A property settlement pending divorce whereby the husband agreed to convey certain property to her was enforcible by
her, where the evidence showed her separate property had been consumed by the community, and there was no showing of gross misconduct or of fraud on her part which produced for her an advantage which would be unfair and unjust.

Appeal from an order of the superior court for Spokane county, Blake, J., entered October 9, 1920, granting a new trial, after a judgment entered in favor of
the defendant, in an action for specific performance.
Affirmed.

Ferris & Ferris, for appellant.
Davis & Heil, for respondent.

TOLMAN, J.—Respondent brought this action to enforce the specific performance of a contract to convey
to her certain real estate situated in Spokane county.
It appears that the parties hereto were formerly husband and wife, and while an action for divorce was
pending, they entered into a written contract purport-

[1] Reported in 200 Pac. 305.

ing to settle their property rights, by the terms of
which, among other things, the husband agreed to convey, or cause to be conveyed to the wife, the property
in question.

Appellant defended upon the ground that he had
expressly stated, at the time the contract was entered
into, that, if there was no other man in the case, he
would make the settlement the wife wished, but if she
was involved with another man, he would make no
property settlement whatever with her, and upon her
assurance that she never had anything to do with any
other man, he executed the agreement. No stipulation
with reference to this subject was embodied in the
contract. Appellant produced, and offered in evidence
at the trial, letters written to the wife at about the
time the property settlement was made, by another
man, couched in most endearing terms, and of a nature
to indicate that the writer had reason to believe that
his attentions were welcomed by the recipient. At the
close of the testimony, the trial court indicated that
if it were conceded that the conversation relating to
another man in the case never took place, or was such
as not to constitute any actual misrepresentation, yet
the letters indicated enough to defeat the rights of the
respondent, and therefore entered a judgment denying
her any relief. Upon the argument of a motion for a
new trial, the court's attention was called to the case.
of *Krug v. Krug*, 81 Wash. 461, 142 Pac. 1136, whereupon the judgment previously entered was set aside
and a new trial granted, from which order the defendant appeals.

The testimony of appellant regarding the conversation at the time of the making of the contract, as to
there being no other man in the case, is denied *in toto*
by the wife, and also by the attorney who drew up the

contract, and in the absence of any finding upon that
subject by the trial court we might well hold that appellant has failed to sustain the burden of proof in
that respect; but however that may be, we cannot hold
that the representations, if made, related to a material
fact and constituted a fraud inherent in the contract.

We recognize that specific performance is not a matter of right, but of equity, and a prayer therefor is
addressed to the sound legal discretion of the court,
and before a court of equity will decree specific performance it must appear that the contract had been
fairly entered into.

Here the contract, as in the *Krug* case, recognized
the pendency of the divorce action, and was not made
upon the assumption that the marriage relation was to
be continued, and as was there said:

"Giving the evidence of the facts which occurred
prior to the execution of the agreement their severest
interpretation against the appellant, they would yet
fall short of showing positive immoral conduct. That
the appellant associated with a man not her husband,
and that this was not known to respondent at the time
the contract was executed is plain; but the contract
being executed with a view to a separation, which occurred, and ultimately a divorce, it would seem that
the conduct of the wife was not a fault sufficient to
constitute a fraud which inhered in the contract."

True, in the *Krug* case it was sought to set aside a
contract, and not to have it specifically performed, but
there the court denied the equitable relief sought because the fraud did not inhere in the contract, and here
the equitable relief sought should be granted for the
same reason. Moreover, in view of our community
property law, and the evidence in the case to the effect
that the wife's separate property had been consumed
by the community, and this property was given her in

lieu thereof, it would be highly inequitable to deny relief to the wife except for her gross misconduct, or a fraud which produced for her an advantage which would be unfair and unjust. There being no attempt made here to show that the property settlement in question was in any respect unfair or unjust, the agreement should be enforced.

The judgment is affirmed.

PARKER, C. J., FULLERTON, MAIN, and MITCHELL, JJ., concur.

[No. 16414. Department One. August 29, 1921.]

HATTIE MARIA GLASS, *Appellant*, v. WILLIAM HENRY GLASS, *Respondent*.[1]

DIVORCE (80)—DIVISION OF PROPERTY—AWARD—EVIDENCE—SUFFICIENCY. In an action for divorce by a wife, in which she was awarded from the husband's separate property $15,000 in cash and real property valued at $5,000, she cannot complain of the inadequacy of the award, where the evidence shows that, at the time of marriage, the husband was seventy-seven years of age, that she had no property of her own, that she married him on account of his wealth, and instituted her action for separation in something over two and one-half years after marriage.

Appeal by plaintiff from a judgment of the superior court for King county, Smith, J., entered January 15, 1921, upon findings in favor of the plaintiff, in an action for divorce, tried to the court. Affirmed.

Trefethen & Findley, for appellant.

E. H. Guie, for respondent.

PER CURIAM.—The appellant, Hattie Maria Glass, and the respondent, William Henry Glass, intermarried in May, 1917. At that time the respondent had passed in age his seventy-seventh year. In January, 1920, the appellant instituted this action for a divorce and for a share of the respondent's property holdings. At the hearing, the court granted the appellant a divorce, and awarded her from the respondent's separate property the sum of fifteen thousand dollars in cash and certain real property valued at five thousand dollars. This appeal questions only the property award.

It is our opinion that the appellant obtained all the property to which she can justly lay claim. The evidence makes it clear that the respondent's wealth constituted the sole attraction which induced the appellant to enter into the marriage. She admits that she had no love or affection for the respondent at the time of the marriage, and while she says that she then had regard for him, even that the evidence leaves in doubt. At the time of the marriage, she had nothing in the way of property. The marriage has put upon her no infirmity or increase of burden, and it is clear that the unhappy condition of the marriage relation was largely due to her own fault.

The statute (Rem. Code, § 989) provides that the court, in granting a divorce, shall make such disposition of the property of the parties as shall appear just and equitable, having regard to the respective merits of the parties, the condition in which they will be left by the divorce, and to the party through whom the property was acquired. The trial court's award was made in consonance with this statute and we think it should not be disturbed.

Affirmed.

[No. 16321. Department One. August 29, 1921.]

THE STATE OF WASHINGTON, *Respondent*, v.
C. E. PAYNE, *Appellant*.[1]

EVIDENCE (79) — SECONDARY EVIDENCE — PHOTOGRAPHIC COPIES.
Photographic copies of books and documents are admissible in evidence, where it is shown that the originals are in possession of some third person out of the state and beyond the jurisdiction of the court, who refused to surrender them.

CRIMINAL LAW (138) — EVIDENCE — DECLARATIONS BY THIRD PERSONS — LETTERS WRITTEN TO ACCUSED. A letter addressed to defendant and found in his possession at the time of his arrest is admissible in evidence in a prosecution for criminal syndicalism, where the evidence shows that it was upon the usual letter-head of the I. W. W. organization and was written by the secretary-treasurer of a branch thereof in answer to a letter by defendant.

INSURRECTION — EVIDENCE — SUFFICIENCY TO SUPPORT CONVICTION — I. W. W. MEMBERSHIP. In a prosecution for criminal syndicalism under Laws 1919, p. 518, membership of defendant in the I. W. W. organization was sufficiently established by evidence showing that from August 7, to December 31, 1918, he was a delegate and organizer of Industrial Union 573 of the order; that, from November 1918 to November 22, 1919, he was editor of an official weekly publication of the I. W. W. while at the same time a member of Industrial Union 573; that, on severing his connection as editor of such official organ, he came to this state; and that, when arrested, there was found in his possession much I. W. W. literature, including copies of the preamble and constitution of the order, a supply of membership cards, blanks for application for membership, and other matter tending to show he was still a member on the date mentioned in the information.

Appeal from a judgment of the superior court for Pend Oreille county, Neal, J., entered August 10, 1920, upon a trial and conviction of criminal syndicalism. Affirmed.

George F. Vanderveer and *Ralph S. Pierce*, for appellant.

The Attorney General, O. R. Schumann, Assistant, J. A. Rochford, and *Sidney W. Rogers*, for respondent.

[1] Reported in 200 Pac. 314.

Bridges, J.—The information in this case charged the appellant with the crime of criminal syndicalism, as shown by the laws of the state of Washington. Laws of 1919, p. 518. It charges the commission of the crime on the 23d day of December, 1919, in the county of Pend Oreille, state of Washington. He was convicted and has appealed to this court.

In his brief here he admits that most of the assignments of error have heretofore been disposed of adversely to him in the case of *State v. Hennessy*, 114 Wash. 351, 195 Pac. 211, and subsequent cases out of this court. His argument here only questions the admissibility of certain testimony presented by the state, and whether the testimony was sufficient to authorize the case to be sent to the jury on the question of his membership in the order commonly known as the I. W. W.

The state put in evidence certain photographic copies of a book and certain other papers which had previously been taken by the authorities in the city of Chicago during a raid. These copies were presented through the witness McDonough. It is shown that that witness was a part of the police department of Chicago and, as such, made a raid on the offices of one James Crowley on December 23, 1919, at which time he took from the possession of Crowley the originals of which the photographs in question are supposed to be copies. The testimony shows that, at the time of the raid, Crowley was the secretary of Workers' Union, No 573, of the I. W. W.

The appellant first contends that these photographs were secondary evidence, and that the testimony failed to show that the originals could not have been produced in court. We think this position is untenable. The witness McDonough testified that the original books and papers were in the possession and under the control of the assistant state's attorney in Cook county, Illinois, and that before starting west to attend this trial, he had tried to obtain the originals to bring with him, but that the assistant state's attorney in Chicago would not surrender them to him because he wanted to use them in a trial soon to be had in that city. This was a sufficient showing of the inability of the state to present the originals.

There appear to be two lines of decisions, one holding that a photographic copy may be introduced if the original is in the possession of some third person, who is out of the state, and that, under such circumstances, it is not necessary to show that an effort was made to obtain the original. The other line of cases is to the effect that it is not sufficient to show alone that the original is in the possession of someone out of the state and beyond the jurisdiction of the court, but that it must also be shown that a reasonable effort has been made to obtain and have at the trial such original. *Federal Chemical Co. v. Jennings,* 112 Miss. 513, 73 South. 567, L. R. A. 1917D 529, and notes; *Burton v. Driggs,* 87 U. S. 125, 22 L. Ed. 299; *Fuller v. Robinson,* 230 Mo. 22, 130 S. W. 343; 17 Cyc. 529. It is unnecessary for us to here determine which line of authorities on this question we will follow, because the testimony in this case was amply sufficient to accord with the views of either or both of those lines of cases.

But appellant claims that the photographs were not admissible because they were not sufficiently identified. Suffice it to say that the witness McDonough amply identified the photographs as being correct copies of the originals.

The state introduced in evidence a letter, dated at Butte, Montana, December 20, 1919, written by the

secretary-treasurer of a branch of the·I. W. W. organization, addressed to the appellant and found in his
possession at the time of his arrest. He contends that
the letter was wrongfully received in evidence against
him, on the theory that a defendant cannot be held
responsible for the assertions contained in letters
which may be written to him. In support of his argument, he quotes from the case of *State v. Roberts*, 95
Wash. 308, 163 Pac. 778, to the effect that:

"It is well established, not only in reason but by
authority as well, that letters written by a third party
to one who is charged with a crime are not to be taken
as an admission against him, but are to be rejected as
hearsay."

While the general rule is as stated by us in that case,
there are exceptions, one of which was noticed by us
in the opinion in that case, for we there said:

"But this rule has a well-defined exception: 'Letters written to a party and received by him may under
some circumstances be read in evidence against him,
but before they can be received as admissions against
him, there must be some evidence besides the mere
possession showing acquiescence in their contents, as
proof of some act or reply or statement.' Jones, Evidence (2d ed.), § 269."

In the case of *Spies v. People*, 122 Ill. 1, 12 N. E.
865, 17 N. E. 898, 3 Am. St. 320, the rule is laid down
as follows:

"In the celebrated trial known as the Anarchist
case, it was held that an unanswered letter found in
the possession of a defendant may be received in evidence as in the nature of an admission, if, from its
terms, it may be gathered that he invited it, or if evidence is adduced that he acted on it."

The letter in question here comes within the recognized exception to the general rule, for it is written on
the usual letterhead of the I. W. W. and is an answer

to a letter written by the appellant. It reads in part
as follows:

"Received yours of the 18th. I am glad you got
safely back among the stumps once more, and I am
sure a few weeks work there will do you a great deal
of good. Have not heard from any of the fellow-
workers in Seattle since you left here, and if I do get
any news will keep you posted. . . . With best
wishes, and hoping to hear from you again soon, I
remain, Yours for One Big Union . . ."

Lastly, it is contended that the evidence concerning
the appellant's membership in the I. W. W. was insufficient to support the verdict. A reading of the
testimony convinces us that there was ample evidence
for this purpose. The state's testimony tended to
show that, from August 7 to December 31, 1918, appellant was a delegate and organizer of Industrial Union,
573, I. W. W.; that, from November, 1918, to November 22, 1919, he was the editor of "The New Solidar-
ity," an official weekly publication of the I. W. W.,
and that, during such period, he was also a member
of Union No. 573. The testimony also tended to show
that, during the latter part of November, 1919, the
appellant ceased to be the editor of "The New Solid-
arity" and came at once from Chicago to this state,
where he was arrested, and that, when he was arrested, there was found in his possession much I. W. W.
literature, a supply of membership cards, blanks for
application for membership, many copies of the preamble and constitution of the I. W. W., and much other
matter tending to show that, at the time of his arrest,
and on the date mentioned in the information, he was
still a member of the I. W. W.

We do not find any error, and consequently affirm
the judgment.

PARKER, C. J., MACKINTOSH, HOLCOMB, and FULLER-
TON, JJ., concur.

[No. 16380. Department One. August 29, 1921.]

H. J. WALLER, *Appellant*, v. KAY SMITH, *Respondent.*[1]

NEGLIGENCE (6)—INJURY TO PROPERTY—DUTY TO LICENSEE. Where plaintiff, on a hunting trip, parked his automobile for a period of ten days on government land, in the vicinity of logging operations conducted by defendant under contract with the government, plaintiff was a mere licensee, and not entitled to recover for injuries to his car from being struck by a falling tree which had swerved from the course intended by the faller, there being no evidence of wanton or wilful acts on the latter's part causing the injury.

Appeal from a judgment of the superior court for Pierce county, Clifford, J., entered September 30, 1920, upon findings in favor of the defendant, in an action in tort, tried to the court. Affirmed.

Lyle, Henderson & Carnahan, for appellant.

Wm. H. Pratt, for respondent.

FULLERTON, J.—In this action the appellant, Waller, sought to recover in damages from the respondent, Smith, for injuries to his automobile. From an adverse judgment, entered by the trial court on a trial of the action without a jury, Waller appeals.

On conflicting evidence, the court found the facts as follows:

"(1) That the plaintiff herein is the owner of a certain Buick automobile.

"(2) That, during the months of September and October, 1919, the defendant was engaged in logging operations in the vicinity of Brinnon, Washington, and removing the timber upon certain land belonging to the United States government, under contract held with the government for removing the same; that adjacent to the place where said defendant was conducting his logging operations was an abandoned road, which had been blocked up and unused at that point for a period

[1]Reported in 200 Pac. 95.

of some four years and the used road transferred some
distance therefrom, both of said roads and said logging
operations being located on United States government
property.

"(3) That, on or about the 23d day of September,
1919, the plaintiff parked his Buick automobile on the
unused part of said road adjacent to where the defendant was conducting said logging operations, and
the defendant, at the time the plaintiff parked his said
automobile at said place, was then engaged in the cutting of trees in said logging operations but a little distance from said place, and said plaintiff, after so park-
ing his automobile, left and went on a hunting trip in
the mountains and was gone for a period of ten days,
and during said time left his said automobile there for
said period, unwatched and unattended; and that, at
the time the plaintiff so left his automobile in said position, he knew of said logging operations and that the
same were being carried on adjacent to said place, and
knew of the danger of falling trees in the position
where he had left his said automobile, and that during
the time said automobile was left standing in said
place, one of the employees of the defendant was cutting down a tree in the conduct of said logging operations, and the said tree accidentally and unavoidably
fell so that it struck the plaintiff's automobile and
injured the same, but that said employees were reasonably careful, and the striking of said automobile by
said tree was the result of unavoidable accident and
was not the wanton or wilful act of the said defendant's employee."

On the question of the weight of the evidence, it preponderates, in our opinion, with the findings of the
trial court. Clearly, there is no evidence showing that
the act causing the injury was wanton or wilful, and
it supports the conclusion that the employee of the
respondent exercised reasonable care in falling the
tree which caused the injury. The accident was not,
of course, unavoidable in an absolute sense, as it could
have been avoided had the respondent ceased entirely

the work of falling timber during the time of the presence of the automobile on the premises, and it could perhaps have been avoided had the respondent refrained from falling the particular tree which caused the injury, but it was unavoidable in the sense that the faller of the tree could not foresee the conditions which caused the tree to swerve in falling from its intended course to a course in the direction of the automobile. The question then is whether, under the facts as found, the appellant is entitled to recover. We are of the opinion that he is not. Contrary to his contention, he did not have the same rights on the premises as the respondent had. The land was the property of the government, and the government had granted its temporary use to the respondent. It had granted no rights therein to the appellant. As between himself and the respondent he was at most a mere licensee, and the respondent's utmost duty towards him and his property was not to inflict upon him or upon his property a wilful or wanton injury. *Smith v. Seattle School District No. 1*, 112 Wash. 64, 191 Pac. 858.

There being no evidence of a wanton or wilful injury, it follows that the judgment must stand affirmed. It is so ordered.

PARKER, C. J., BRIDGES, MACKINTOSH, and HOLCOMB, JJ., concur.

[No. 16383. Department Two. August 29, 1921.]

PIERRE P. FERRY *et al.*, *Respondents*, v. THE CITY OF SEATTLE, *Appellant*.[1]

INJUNCTION (30)—PROCEEDINGS OF CITY COUNCIL—VALIDITY OF ORDINANCE—REVIEW. Where a city council acts in good faith upon a matter within the scope of its authority, its exercise of discretion will not be controlled by injunction by a court of equity, in the absence of fraud.

MUNICIPAL CORPORATIONS (398) — INJUNCTION (30) — PARKS— USES—DIVERSION—CONSTRUCTION OF RESERVOIR. Where a city acquired land in fee simple by purchase, without any restriction on its use, which it devoted to park and reservoir purposes, its threatened use of a portion of the park land for increased reservoir purposes is not subject to restraint by a court of equity.

SAME (398)—PARKS—CHARTER PROVISIONS—AUTHORITY OF COUNCIL—LEGISLATIVE POWERS. The city charter of Seattle, which creates a board of park commissioners, does not confer on such board power to control the disposition to be made of such property, but confers merely administrative powers, the legislative power over city property being vested in the city council.

NUISANCE (2, 18)—WHAT CONSTITUTES—ACTIONS FOR ABATEMENT— EVIDENCE. An objection to the construction of a city reservoir to store water for domestic use on the theory that the drainage from a neighboring cemetery would contaminate the water was not sustained where the evidence showed that, by reason of the contour of the land, the drainage would be away from the reservoir, and further that the pressure of water would cause the reservoir water itself to leak out, and naturally, even if there were drainage from the cemetery, it could not leak in.

SAME (2, 5)—ACTIONS FOR ABATEMENT. In an action to enjoin the construction of a city reservoir on the ground that it would obstruct the free use of the residential property of plaintiffs and interfere with their comfortable enjoyment of life and property, thus constituting a nuisance within the terms of Rem. Code, §§ 943, 944, *held*, that the evidence was insufficient to support the complaint (Overruled on rehearing).

INJUNCTION (11)—GROUNDS FOR RELIEF—DEFENSES—INCONVENIENCE TO PUBLIC. An injunction will not issue to restrain the construction and maintenance of a reservoir for the storage of water

[1]Reported in 200 Pac. 336; 203 Pac. 40.

for domestic use, though based upon evidence of the fears of apprehended injuries to the persons or property of adjoining owners,
where the weight of the evidence shows that such apprehended injuries are not the necessary or probable results of the maintenance
of the reservoir (Overruled on rehearing).

MACKINTOSH, J., dissents.

ON REHEARING.

NUISANCE (2, 5, 18)—WHAT CONSTITUTES—ACTIONS FOR ABATE-
MENT. A city reservoir, impounding water by a fifty-six foot embankment of soil subject to slides and inevitable leakage, will be enjoined as a nuisance, interfering with the comfortable enjoyment of
life and property, where a large section of the city, composed of men
and women not ready dupes of conjectural and imaginary fears,
have a real and present reasonable apprehension that their lives
and properties will be jeopardized by the maintenance of the reservoir (MITCHELL, MAIN, and TOLMAN, JJ., dissenting).

Appeal from an order and judgment of the superior
court for King county, Tallman and Allen, JJ., entered
September 30, 1920, and December 14, 1920, in favor
of the plaintiffs, in an action to enjoin the construction of a reservoir in a city park, after a hearing
before the court. Reversed.

Walter F. Meier and *Edwin C. Ewing*, for appellant.

*C. H. Hanford, Kerr, McCord & Ivey, John F.
Murphy*, and *Samuel Hill*, for respondents.

MITCHELL, J.—This is an appeal from a final decree
of the superior court of King county, by the terms of
which the city of Seattle was enjoined from constructing, at a selected site in Volunteer Park, a reservoir
for the storage of water for the uses of the city and its
inhabitants. The appeal also involves an allowance
imposed as terms upon granting a trial amendment of
the city's answer that necessitated a continuance.

The city owns and operates its waterworks system,
and the growing need for an additional reservoir has
been apparent to the city authorities for several years.
A number of sites were carefully considered and inves-

tigated, with the result of the selection of the site proposed. The drift of the judgment of the city council has been towards this site, during which time, and for the last four or five years, the subject has been discussed in the press, in open sessions of the city council, and in the sessions of its appropriate committee. There appears to be no question of the wisdom in the selection of the site from the standpoint of economy and the practical distribution of the water. By appropriate ordinances, the city adopted plans and specifications and proposed the sale of utility bonds, payable out of the revenues of the waterworks system, for the construction of the reservoir and the relining of a reservoir already in the park, among other expenditures, as betterments to and extensions of its present system. Upon calling for bids for making the necessary excavation and earthen embankments, this action was commenced by a number of persons in their own behalf and for all others similarly situated, taxpayers and owners of property in the vicinity of the park, to prevent the construction of the reservoir. The suit resulted, as already stated, in favor of the plaintiffs. During the suit, a temporary injunction was entered against the city, whose appeal therefrom is now presented with its appeal from the final decree. The disposition of the final appeal will dispose of the merits of the appeal from the interlocutory order.

It may be observed, that, assuming the city council acts in good faith and within the scope of its lawful authority, courts of equity are generally without power to interfere, or as stated in *State ex rel. News Publishing Co. v. Milligan,* 3 Wash. 144, 28 Pac. 369, viz.:

"No principle of equity jurisprudence is better established than that courts of equity will not sit in review of proceedings of subordinate political or municipal tribunals, and that where matters are left to the discretion of such bodies the exercise of that discretion in good faith will not, in the absence of fraud, be disturbed. High on Injunctions (3d ed.), § 1240.''

See, also, *Ewing v. Seattle*, 55 Wash. 229, 104 Pac. 259; *Twitchell v. Seattle*, 106 Wash. 32, 179 Pac. 127; Pomeroy's Equity Jurisprudence (4th ed.), vol. 4, § 1765.

Volunteer Park consists of about fifty acres, acquired as follows: Forty acres from James M. Colman and wife by warranty deed to the city June 12, 1876, and the east half of blocks E and F, Phinney's Addition to Seattle, located immediately west of the forty-acre tract and separated from it by an avenue afterwards vacated, by warranty deeds to the city in the year 1902. All of the conveyances were by straight warranty deeds, none of which contained any reservation, restriction or limitation upon the title or use of the property thereby conveyed.

In 1887, by ordinance, the city converted the forty-acre tract into a park. Later it made provision for a water tank which was constructed in the park, then called the City Park. In 1901, by ordinance, the park was given the name of Volunteer Park. In 1900 and 1901, the city constructed a reservoir, still in use, in the park. The city has spent about $139,000 in improving the park.

The first theory of the complaint and argument of respondents is that the ordinance of the city declaring the property to be a public park, the subsequent use of it as such, and the expenditure of public money for its adornment, amount to an irrevocable dedication of it for park purposes. Indeed, it is argued that the course of the city with reference to the park operates as a conveyance of the land to the public for that specific use, so that it may not be thereafter devoted to a different use otherwise than by the exercise of the power of eminent domain; and for the support of such claim, reliance is had on the cases of *Cincinnati v. Louisville & N. R. R.*, 223 U. S. 390, 56 L. Ed. 481; *Cincinnati v. White*, 6 Pet. (U. S.) 431, 8 L. Ed. 452; and *Hoadley's Adm'rs v. San Francisco*, 124 U. S. 639.

The argument is without merit, we think, and the cases cited are not applicable here. *Cincinnati v. Louisville & N. R. R.* was a case involving the right of a railroad company to condemn a right of way for an elevated track across a public landing at Cincinnati that had been dedicated by the former owner for public use. It was decided that condemnation might be had, and, among other things, it was said, in effect, that a dedication by a private owner of land as a common, for the use and benefit of the town forever, as shown on a plan, and the acceptance by the town and sale of lots under the plan, constitutes a contract. The case of *Cincinnati v. White* involved the dedication of privately owned land to a city for public use, accepted and used as such by the city. It was held that a person who thereafter acquired a paper title from the former owner to the same property could not disturb the city in its right to the title and use of the common. The case of *Hoadley's Adm'rs v. San Francisco* related to land that was granted by Congress to the city for the purpose of public use as squares, and it was held "lands so dedicated could not lawfully be conveyed by the city to private parties." The doctrine of such cases is well established and recognized, but they are outside of the inquiry here. The city of Seattle acquired this property in fee simple, by purchase. During its ownership it has used it to its own fancy for the purposes of a park and a reservoir. The situation falls within the rule laid down in the case of *Caldwell*

v. Seattle, 75 Wash. 565, 135 Pac. 470, wherein owners
of property abutting upon a public park were denied
injunction against the location of a main trunk sewer
through the park, located so that a part of the sewer
was above the ground. In that case it was said:

"The particular tract upon which appellants' property abuts was deeded without reservation and the full
fee simple title was conveyed. Under such conditions,
the city holds clothed with every incident of ownership. Parks are relatively necessary in modern cities,
but sewers are absolutely necessary, and courts will
not control the discretion of the governing bodies of
cities when they have ordained that a sewer shall be
placed in a park, nor will the necessity of laying the
sewer on top of the ground be reviewed.

"The judgment of the court is sustained by reference to the principles announced in *Seattle Land &
Imp. Co. v. Seattle,* 37 Wash. 274, 79 Pac. 780. The
building of the sewer upon the city's property is not
necessarily a diversion of the uses of the park, and
is as to appellants *damnum absque injuria.*"

And here, as in that case, there is no destruction of
the park, but only an appropriation of a part of the
total area for a necessity different from strictly park
purposes.

Further, it is contended by the respondents that the
city charter, which was adopted after Volunteer Park
had been established, forbids interference by the city
council with the use of the public park as such. It
contains no specific provision to that effect. The charter distributes the corporate powers of the city under
fourteen different departments, including the "department of parks" in charge of a board of park commissioners. Numerous provisions of the charter are referred to which it is claimed show that the park board
and not the city council has ultimate control in deciding if a portion of the park shall be used for a reservoir. A repetition and analysis of all such provisions

is unnecessary here.   An examination of them convinces us, as it did the trial court, against this contention of the respondents.   There is not to be found in the charter or in the statutes any attempt to make of the department of parks or the board of park commissioners a separate entity such as a municipal corporation.   Many of the cases relied on by the respondents, such as *McCormick v. South Park Commissioners,* 150 Ill. 516, 37 N. E. 1075; *City of Chicago v. Pittsburg, C. C. & St. L. R. Co.,* 242 Ill. 30, 89 N. E. 648, and *City of Fargo v. Gearey,* 33 N. D. 64, 156 N. W. 552, are cases wherein the parks involved were under the control of boards of commissioners which by statute were made municipal corporations with the power to acquire, hold, own and possess real property and to levy and collect taxes and assessments.   No such authority is given to the board of park commissioners of Seattle.   However, ample authority is given to the legislative department of the city.   In paragraph 3, § 18 of art. 4, it is provided that the city council shall have power by ordinance "to control the finances and property of the city; *Provided,* That the city council shall have no administrative as distinguished from the legislative power."   Paragraph 4 of the same section provides that the city council shall have power by ordinance .

"to acquire by purchase, or by exercise of the right of eminent domain or otherwise, and for the use and in the name of the city, such lands and other property as may be deemed necessary, proper or convenient for any of the corporate uses provided for by this charter, and to acquire for the use of the city any property by gift, bequest or devise, and to dispose of all such property as it shall have, as the interests of the city may from time to time require."

. The relative powers of the department of parks and of the city council are that those of the one are administrative, while those of the other are legislative. Having acquired the full fee simple title to the property, the city holds it clothed with every element of ownership, to be controlled under and by the final and superior authority of its legislative department. This view is in accord with the conclusion and reason of the rule of *Caldwell v. Seattle, supra.*

Another theory of the complaint (supported by some lay evidence) that has not been sustained, in our opinion, is that the selected site, by reason of its proximity to a cemetery, is an improper place to store water to be supplied for domestic use. The proof clearly shows two satisfactory answers: (a) The contour of the ground is such that the drainage from the cemetery is away from the site of the reservoir; and (b) the common sense view of the city health officer (an experienced sanitary expert), who, after listening to the construction and engineering experts testify that it was impossible to prevent all leakage from a reservoir constructed as this would be with a lining of concrete, upon being asked as to the danger of the water becoming contaminated and polluted because of the nearness of the cemetery, replied by saying: "It is impossible, the lining of concrete cannot leak both ways."

By far the greater part of the large record in this case is devoted to the subject of nuisance. Respondents rely on §§ 943 and 944, Rem. Code, §§ 8231 and 8232, Pierce's 1919 Code, which provide, among other things, that "an obstruction to the free use of property, so as to essentially interfere with the comfortable enjoyment of the life and property, is a nuisance, and the subject of an action for damages and other and further relief," and that "such action may be brought by any person whose property is injuriously affected or whose personal enjoyment is lessened by the nuisance." The present reservoir in the park

holds twenty-three million gallons of water. It is
charged in the complaint that the placing of the additional reservoir therein, if permitted, would constitute
a nuisance and menace to the property and lives of
the respondents and others. More specifically, it is
alleged that a reservoir in the situation chosen would
create a condition conducive to a landslide and flooding of the hillside below the reservoir that would destroy some of the residential property owned by the
respondents, and be an immediate danger by depreciat-
ing the market value of the property and its value for
living in security and comfort therein. The proposed
basin is to be constructed on a slope near the crest of
the hill on which the park is located, about four hundred feet above the sea level. The structure will consist of an earthen embankment on the lower side about
fifty-six feet high at one point. The inside incline of
the embankment will be one to one and a half, and the
outside one to two. The whole of the earthen basin is
to be treated and prepared for a lining of concrete
slabs seven inches thick, the joints of which are to be
sealed with copper according to an improved method.
The top of the reservoir on the side of the embankment
will be forty feet in width and level with the top of
the existing reservoir.

None of the witnesses would expect to find artesian
water in the hill. The evidence shows that there has
been no perceptible subsidence or disintegration of
the embankment of the existing reservoir since it was
built twenty years ago and that, as the trial court
found, it is entirely safe at the present time. The evidence shows with convincing force that the geological
formation of the site and hill is highly suitable for the
safe construction and maintenance of the additional
reservoir; it shows, in the same manner, that the con-

sensus of engineering opinion is that earthen dams or embankments are the stablest kind, and that it is perfectly safe and suitable for impounding water to construct a reservoir on the side of a hill by excavating a portion of the earth and using the material to form an embankment on the lower side—a very general practice in American cities. The evidence shows also, in the same manner, that the building of a reservoir according to the completed plans and specifications, under the supervision and directions of the city's engineer, and the maintenance of it thereafter under the customary and required inspections of the public authorities, can and will cause no damage or menace to the respondents or their property or others in the vicinity, or at all. The record abounds with endorsements of the plans and specifications by a large number of persons skilled and experienced as hydraulic and construction engineers, many of whom have a knowledge of the geological formation of the hill and of the surrounding country generally, while many of them have been engaged in connection with public works and the study of the different kinds of soils in and about the city for years.

On the contrary, there were expert witnesses for the respondents who testified in reason to the incompleteness of the plans and specifications with reference to the total project, including the matter of drainage. That testimony was given, however, at a time when the city, by its answer, was apparently committed to a defense of its plans and specifications for the construction of the earthen dam only as affording a safe and proper structure. Thereafter, upon application and order, the city's answer was amended to show that the completed work was to be accomplished by units, and that, after the earthen work was done, still another

contract was to be let and carried out for the concrete
lining and proper provision made for drainage. It
was after the amendment of the answer that the city's
proof was introduced; but after the amendment, only
two of appellant's witnesses then testified in criticism
of the total plans and specifications, or that the reservoir would be unsafe or a menace to persons or property. Of these two witnesses, one frankly admitted he
had made no examination of, and was unacquainted
with, the ground where the reservoir is to be located;
and withal, while admitting the general sufficiency of
the plans and specifications, the principal objection of
both witnesses was that no detail of plan had been
made to take care of drainage during the construction,
nor for inevitable leakage, to some extent, during the
maintenance of the reservoir—that is, the plans and
specifications were not precise in those particulars.
However, the objection is fully answered by general
provisions, such as are customarily and usually found
in such contracts and instruments. The evidence
shows the impossibility of providing by specific details in advance for all possible contingencies that may
arise. The necessary and intelligent provisions for
such contingencies can be estimated and determined
only as the excavation and construction proceed, and
are to be then taken care of under clauses in the contract, such as are found here, authorizing the engineer
or board of public works to make such provisions as
may then appear to be necessary, either by payment at
a price then agreed on or by force account.

The relief here sought is an appeal to equity. Under
the facts, we are compelled to find against the respondents. The reservoir is a necessity. The construction
and maintenance of it in a proper manner and place
would not constitute a nuisance in a legal sense; nor

would it, as a matter of fact, under the evidence in this case. In this class of cases the courts are not called upon to determine only if plaintiffs, or any one of them, entertain fears for the safety of themselves or their property, but to ascertain if, by evidence that is clear and satisfactory, it is shown that such injuries are or will be the necessary or probable results of the action sought to be restrained. The test is not what may possibly occur, but what may be reasonably expected to happen. This rule is well stated in *People v. Canal Board of New York*, 55 N. Y. Ct. App. 390, as follows:

"To entitle a plaintiff to prohibition by injunction from a court of equity, either provisional or perpetual, he must not only show a clear legal and equitable right to the relief demanded or to some part of it, and to which the injunction is essential, but also that some act is being done by the defendant, or is threatened and imminent, which will be destructive of such right, or cause material injury to him. A state of things from which the plaintiff apprehends injurious consequences to himself, but which neither actually exists nor is threatened by the defendants, nor is inevitable, is not a sufficient ground for an injunction.

"Injury, material and actual, not fanciful or theoretical, or merely possible, must be shown as the necessary or probable results of the action sought to be restrained."

In the case of *City of Rochester v. Erickson*, 46 Barb. (N. Y.) 92, it was said:

"It is not enough to make out a doubtful or possible case of danger; but the danger apprehended must appear to be imminent, and in the natural course of events clearly impending, and the mischief in its nature and character irreparable."

In *Missouri v. Illinois*, 180 U. S. 208, 40 L. Ed. 497, it was said:

"We fully agree with the contention of defendants'
counsel that it is settled that an injunction to restrain
a nuisance will issue only in cases where the fact of
nuisance is made out upon determinate and satisfactory evidence; that if the evidence be conflicting and
the injury be doubtful, that conflict and doubt will be
a ground for withholding an injunction; and that,
where interposition by injunction is sought, to restrain
that which is apprehended will create a nuisance of
which its complainant may complain, the proofs must
show such a state of facts as will manifest the danger
to be real and immediate."

In *Lake Erie & W. R. Co. v. City of Fremont,* 92 Fed.
721, it was said:

"But it is well settled that an injunction does not
issue in such cases unless the probability of danger is
clearly shown, and the existence of the nuisance clearly
made out upon determinate and satisfactory evidence,
and that in no case will the chancellor interfere by injunction where the nuisance sought to be abated. or
restrained is eventual or contingent, or where the evidence is conflicting, and the injury to the public, or to
the individual complaining, doubtful."

Again, the rule is stated and supported by a long
list of cases in 14 R. C. L., p. 354, § 57, as follows:

"A mere apprehension of future injury is not
enough to warrant the issuance of a permanent injunction; it must appear, to the satisfaction of the
court, that such apprehension is well grounded, that
there is a reasonable probability that a real injury, for
which there is no adequate remedy at law, will occur
if the injunction be not granted. If it is doubtful or
contingent equity will not interfere by injunction."

Some of the cases in this court to the same effect are
Hughes v. McVay, 113 Wash. 333, 194 Pac. 565;
Rea v. Tacoma Mausoleum Ass'n, 103 Wash. 429, 175
Pac. 961; *Winsor v. Hanson,* 40 Wash. 423, 82 Pac.
710; *Rockford Watch Co. v. Rumpf,* 12 Wash. 647,

42 Pac. 213; *Morse v. O'Connell,* 7 Wash. 117, 34 Pac. 426.

The conclusion reached on the merits of the case makes it unnecessary to discuss or otherwise dispose of the second branch of the appeal relating to the terms imposed by the court on granting the city leave to amend its answer.

The judgment is reversed, with directions to set aside the injunction and dismiss the action.

PARKER, C. J., MAIN, and TOLMAN, JJ., concur.

MACKINTOSH, J., dissents.

ON REHEARING.
[*En Banc.* January 3, 1922.]

MACKINTOSH, J.—Upon a reargument of this case, the court has decided that the opinion of the Department on the prior hearing is incorrect, and that the judgment of the trial court should have been affirmed.

A reference to the prior opinion is sufficient to give an understanding of the facts of the case. Without determining whether Volunteer Park has been dedicated by declaration, use and the expenditure of public money thereon to exclusive park purposes, so that it cannot now be used for any other purpose, and without determining whether exclusive jurisdiction has been placed in the park department rather than in the city council, and leaving undetermined the question of whether the respondents are entitled to an injunction against the appellant based on the impairment of the beauties of the park, leaving also undetermined the question whether the proposed reservoir might be contaminated by its proximity to a large burial ground, we will pass to the question which determines the respondents' rights to an injunction.

The respondent property owners complain against the construction of this reservoir in Volunteer Park, on a side hill which extends westerly a considerable distance, with its fifty-six foot embankment as the only protection between their homes and the mass of water impounded behind it, for the reason that they claim its existence will constantly menace their lives and property. It is true that expert witnesses called on behalf of the city testified that a reservoir constructed in this place and manner would present no such peril as the respondents picture, and the city points to another reservoir in this park, which has existed some twenty years and never has occasioned damage to adjacent property. The old reservoir, it must be remembered, is small compared with the proposed one, and its westerly side is protected by an embankment only about one-third as high as would be that of the new reservoir. But at that, the fact that the old reservoir has occasioned no damage is far from conclusive proof that a new one, constructed under different conditions, would be equally as harmless. On the other hand, experts on behalf of the respondents testified that the proposed reservoir would continually threaten danger. With such a record before us, it is difficult to say that the respondents have not a reasonably grounded apprehension.

The test as to whether a structure of the proposed character is to be declared a nuisance turns on whether the complaining property owners are under a reasonable apprehension of danger, and the question of the reasonableness of the apprehension turns again, not only on the probable breaking of the reservoir, but the realization of the extent of the injury which would certainly ensue. That is to say, the court will look to consequences in determining whether the fear existing is reasonable. For instance, if the reservoir were being built in some place where, should it break, the resultant damage would be merely to property which could ade-

quately be recompensed, the court would be more apt to
hesitate in declaring it a nuisance than where, should
a break occur, not only property of immense value
would be destroyed, but many lives would be lost
as well.

It cannot be said that the property owners dwelling
in the shadow of the fifty-six foot embankment would
not live under a reasonable apprehension, based upon
the testimony in this case, that sooner or later they and
their property would be destroyed by this contemplated
reservoir. Reservoirs built upon the expert advice of
city engineers, and sealed with the approval of other
experts called in to substantiate that advice, have been
known to not hold water. All the experts agree that
there will be an inevitable leakage, to some extent, in
the proposed reservoir. With this advice of these
experts, and with a general knowledge of the contour of
the ground, the nature of the soil, the prevalence of
slides in similar situations in Seattle, and the disasters
that have happened from the bursting of impounded
waters, the respondents have, as a result of all these
things, a fear which interferes with their comfortable
enjoyment of life and property, and allege that the construction of the reservoir annoys, injures and endangers their comfort, repose and safety, and renders them
insecure in life and the use of their property. If they
have reason for this attitude they must succeed in this
action. If this situation supports a reasonable expectation that disaster may happen, and such expectation
leads to a depreciation in the value of adjoining properties, the structure will be considered a nuisance.

This court has already held in *Everett v. Paschall*, 61
Wash. 47, 111 Pac. 879, Ann. Cas. 1912B 1128, 31 L. R.
A. (N. S.) 827, that the building of a tuberculosis sani-
tarium in the residential section of a city will be en-

joined as a nuisance where its construction creates fear
and dread of disease, which will result in a depreciation of the value of adjacent property, and where it
will affect the mind, health and nerves of the occupants
thereof. Sections 943 and 8309, Rem. Code (P. C.
§§ 8231, 9131-68), describe as a nuisance anything
which is injurious to the health, or which is an obstruction to the free use of property, so as essentially to interfere with the comfortable enjoyment
of life and property. The court said, in the sanitarium case, *supra,* that, although the danger of
communication of disease might be reduced to a
negligible quantity, and that such a sanitarium
might be constructed with due regard to the safety
of patients and the public, and that there might be no
danger to persons living in the immediate vicinity, and
that the sanitarium would be a great benefit to the general community, yet that it constituted a nuisance for
the reason that there had grown into the law of nuisances an element not recognized at common law; that
is, that making uncomfortable the enjoyment of another's property is a nuisance. It was there held that,
though the fear of disease might be unfounded, imaginary and fanciful, yet where there is a positive dread
which science has not yet been able to eliminate, such
dread, robbing as it did the home owner of the pleasure
in and comfortable enjoyment of his home, would make
the thing dreaded an actionable nuisance, and the depreciation of the property consequent thereon would
warrant a decree against its continuance. Further,
that dread of disease and fear induced by the proximity
of the sanitarium, if that in fact destroys the comfortable enjoyment of the property owners, is not unfounded and unreasonable when it is shared by the
whole of the interested public, and property values become endangered, and that:

"The question is, not whether the fear is founded
in science, but whether it exists; not whether it is imaginary, but whether it is real, in that it affects the
movements and conduct of men. Such fears are actual,
and must be recognized by the courts as other emotions
of the human mind. . . . Comfortable enjoyment
means mental quiet as well as physical comfort. . . .
Nuisance is a question of degree, depending upon varying circumstances. There must be more than a tendency to injury; there must be something appreciable.
The cases generally say tangible, actual, measureable,
or subsisting. But in all cases, in determining whether
the injury charged comes within these general terms,
resort should be had to sound common sense. . . .
The theories and dogmas of scientific men, though
provable by scientific reference, cannot be held to be
controlling unless shared by the people generally. . .
The only case we find holding that fear alone will not
support a decree in this class of cases is Anonymous, 3
Atk. 750. . . . Our statute modifies, if indeed it was
not designed to change this rule. Under the facts, we
cannot say that the dread which is the disquieting element upon which plaintiffs' complaint is made to rest,
is unreal, imaginary or fanciful."

It was held in *Goodrich v. Starrett*, 108 Wash. 437,
184 Pac. 220, that under §§ 943 and 8309 of Rem. Code
(P. C. §§ 8231 and 9131-68), which define nuisance, and
which add to the common law definition the new element
of "comfortable enjoyment of one's property", that
an undertaking establishment in the residential section
of a city, so constructed as to affect property values in
the neighborhood, is a nuisance and will be enjoined.
In that case the case of *Rea v. Tacoma Mausoleum
Ass'n*, 103 Wash. 429, 174 Pac. 961, 1 A. L. R. 541, referred to in the department opinion, was discussed and
held not to be in conflict with the case of *Everett v. Paschall, supra.* The reference to cases from other juris-
dictions which follow the common law rules on nuisance,

or statutory rules not so broad as those obtaining with us, are of very little help in solving this question.

In the case of *Hughes v. McVay*, 113 Wash. 333, 194 Pac. 565, it was held that the facts showed that the property of the persons complaining was so far away from the situation of the detention home that the fears of the complainants were based only on imagination, conjecture and uncertainty, and were the product of a fastidiousness which the law would not sanction. These cases and the cases upon which they are founded present facts which the writers of the opinions in *Goodrich v. Starrett* and *Hughes v. McVay, supra,* hold distinguish them from the situation here. In the present case, we find a very large section of the city of Seattle, composed of men and women who, in the ordinary business of life, are not to be charged as victims of hysteria, nor ready dupes of conjectural and imaginary fears, having a very real and present apprehension that their lives and properties will be jeopardized by the hanging of this modern sword of Damocles above their heads, and that fear is bolstered by the testimony of expert witnesses, and confirmed by the common sense of any one to whom the facts come. It does not take the testimony of experts, although that was produced, to advise one that the proposed structure would cause a most serious depreciation of property values within the affected area. It is an obstruction to the free use of property, as it interferes essentially with the comfortable enjoyment of life and property. It is a nuisance, for it annoys, injures and endangers the comfort, repose, health and safety of these respondents and renders them insecure in life and the use of their property. The Department opinion refers to the reservoir as a necessity, and it may be so, but there is no contention made that the necessity exists to the point where it must be erected at this particular spot and no other.

From our review of the testimony, it is clear and satisfactory to us that the injury to these respondents will be the probable effect of the action which they seek to restrain. The judgment of the lower court is affirmed.

Hovey, Bridges, Fullerton, and Holcomb, JJ., concur.

Parker, C. J. (concurring)—While I concurred with the majority of Department Two upon the former hearing, further reflection has convinced me of the error of that conclusion. I am moved to concur in the result reached in the opinion of Judge Mackintosh, more because of what seems to me would be the appalling nature of the catastrophe which would result from the breaking of the proposed reservoir, than because of the probability of such break occurring. If the breaking of the proposed reservoir would probably result in comparatively small damage and no loss of life, I would not demand proof of its safety with a high degree of certainty; but in view of what now seems to me would be the appalling result of such breaking, I would want the necessity of its location there, and its safety, to be proven beyond all doubt, before withholding the injunctive relief prayed for. I think the evidence falls short of satisfying this view of judicial duty in this case. I therefore now concur in the conclusion reached by the majority opinion of the court sitting *En Banc*.

Mitchell, J. (dissenting)—I adhere to the views expressed in the former opinion, for the reasons therein given, and therefore dissent.

Main and Tolman, JJ., concur with Mitchell, J.

[No. 16267. Department Two. August 30, 1921.]

THE STATE OF WASHINGTON, *Respondent*, v.
FAY McDONALD, *Appellant*.[1]

FORGERY (7)—EVIDENCE—ADMISSIBILITY. In a prosecution for
forgery, written instruments signed by defendant, which were in
no way connected with the crime charged, were properly introducible in evidence for the purpose of comparing her signatures
with the alleged forgery.

CRIMINAL LAW (448)—APPEAL—HARMLESS ERROR—ADMISSION OF
EVIDENCE. Evidence that a check, the indorsement upon which was
alleged to be forged, was presented by defendant's sister in payment
for goods at a store, conceding its inadmissibility as failing to connect defendant with the crime, would not constitute prejudicial
error.

SAME (107)—EVIDENCE—OTHER OFFENSES. Testimony connecting
a defendant with another and distinct crime is admissible, if it is
closely associated with the crime charged and furnishes evidence
material to that crime.

SAME (107). In a prosecution for forgery by the indorsement
of payee's name on a check, it was admissible to show in evidence
that the check had been given to a certain man for delivery to the
payee: that the check was in his possession when he visited defendant in her apartment; that this man was killed while in defendant's
rooms and his body buried some distance from the city; and that,
upon disinterment of his body, the check was not upon his person
although other personal articles were found there; such evidence
being relevant for the purpose of showing how defendant might
have become possessed of the check, though having a tendency to
indirectly connect her with another crime.

Appeal from a judgment of the superior court for
Spokane county, Hill, J., entered April 26, 1920, upon
a trial and conviction of forgery. Affirmed.

C. T. McDonald, F. W. Girand, and *C. W. Green-
ough,* for appellant.

J. B. Lindsley, W. C. Meyer, and *Clarence A. Orndorff,* for respondent.

[1]Reported in 200 Pac. 326.

BRIDGES, J.—The information in this case charged the defendant with forging the name of the payee named in a certain check. The state's testimony tended to show that one Mabel J. Musser drew her check to the order of Mrs. Wonderlick for $93.33, and that the defendant wrongfully obtained possession of this check and committed the forgery by indorsing the name of the payee on the back thereof. She was convicted and has appealed to this court.

The appellant first complains that the court permitted the state to introduce in evidence a certain bill of sale given by the defendant, and also a certain check signed or indorsed by her. It seems to be contended that these instruments were not admissible because they did not in any way tend to establish the crime with which appellant was charged. Those instruments showed the signature of the appellant and were introduced for the purpose of comparing the signatures on those instruments with that which was claimed to be a forgery. For this purpose the court properly admitted these papers in evidence.

It is next contended that it was error to permit the state to introduce testimony to the effect that the forged check was presented at a certain store in Spokane for payment, such presentation not having been made by the appellant. There was testimony, however, tending to show that the check was presented by appellant's sister, Marie McDonald. But if this testimony should be considered inadmissible because it failed to connect the appellant with the alleged crime, it certainly was not prejudicial, and under no circumstances could it be said that the error, if it was such, would be cause for reversal.

The state's testimony tended to show that the check given by Mabel J. Musser to the order of Mrs. Wonder-

lick had, at the request of the maker, been delivered
into the possession of one McNutt for the purpose,
doubtless, of the same being delivered by him to the
payee; that McNutt had this check in his possession
when he visited the appellant and her sister at their
rooms in the Wolverine Apartments, and that, while in
those rooms, McNutt was killed and his body thereafter buried some distance from Spokane, and that
the body of the dead man had been disinterred and the
check was not then upon his person, although other
personal articles were found. The appellant particularly objects to that portion of the testimony concerning the killing of McNutt while he was in the Wolverine Apartments, because it is claimed it had a tendency
to connect her with a crime other than that for which
she was being tried. Since the state accused the appellant of the forgery of the check in question, it became proper, and probably essential, that it should
also prove, if it could, how the appellant came into possession of the check to enable her to commit the
forgery. It is true, the testimony to which objection
is made may have had a tendency to indirectly connect
the appellant with another crime, yet that fact alone
would not deprive the state of the right to show how
the appellant might have become possessed of the
check. Testimony connecting a defendant with another and distinct crime is admissible if it is closely
associated with the crime charged and furnishes evidence material to that crime. *State v. Kaukos,* 109
Wash. 20, 186 Pac. 269; *State v. Sigler, ante* p. 581, 200
Pac. 323. All the state attempted to show in this
connection was that McNutt, who had the possession of the check in question, was killed while in the
apartments occupied by the appellant, and we think it
was proper that that testimony should be introduced.

It would have been improper for the state to show the details of the killing of McNutt, and it did not undertake to prove such details. It may be that, in answer to proper questions propounded by the prosecuting attorney, the witness gave more of the details of the killing than were necessary, but the questions did not call for such details and the appellant did not undertake to stop the witness, nor did she move to strike any testimony concerning the details. At the trial, the position of the appellant seems to have been that no testimony concerning the killing should be admitted in evidence. We are unable to find any reversible error in the introduction of this class of testimony.

It is also claimed that the cross-examination of Marie McDonald by the prosecuting attorney was improper and prejudicial. Since the appellant has made no further argument on this matter than to claim that it was prejudicial and improper, we do not deem it necessary to say more than that, while the court may have allowed the cross-examiner a wide latitude, we are unable to say that the appellant was in any wise prejudiced thereby.

The judgment is affirmed.

PARKER, C. J., MAIN, MITCHELL, and TOLMAN, JJ., concur.

[No. 16448. Department One. September 1, 1921.]

W. P. Kaufman, *Respondent*, v. August Sickman *et al., Appellants.*[1]

Highways (58)—Use for Travel—Driver of Automobile—Contributory Negligence. One lawfully using a public highway is not required by any rule of law to be constantly looking and listening to ascertain if an automobile is approaching, in order that he may avoid any imputation of contributory negligence for injuries received.

Same (52, 57)—Use for Travel—Driver of Automobile—Negligence—Evidence—Sufficiency. In an action for damages resulting from a collision between automobiles, the negligence of defendant was established by evidence showing that the chauffeur was driving at the rate of thirty to forty-five miles an hour through a village, that he had an unobstructed view of the road for over 300 yards, that he glanced aside to wave to a friend and did not see the signal of the driver of the other car indicating that he was going to turn across the road.

Same (58)—Use for Travel—Contributory Negligence—Evidence—Sufficiency. Whether a person injured in the collision of two automobiles as the result of the negligence of the other driver was himself guilty of contributory negligence was for the jury, where the evidence showed he stopped at the side of the highway, and, intending to turn to the left, glanced behind some fifteen seconds before getting in his car, saw no approaching car, then released the brake, started his car, and threw out his hand as a signal that he was going to turn to the left, and his car was struck by the other car on the left-hand side behind the front wheel and carried a distance of about seventy-five feet.

Damages (80)—Personal Injuries—Excessive Verdict. In an action for personal injuries, a verdict for $1,185 for pain, suffering and shock, $958.33 for permanent injuries; $534 for loss of time, and $122 for medical and hospital expenses, was not excessive, where it appeared plaintiff was seriously injured, the skin and flesh from his forehead were lacerated to the bone and hung down over his eyes, he was delirious for some time, remained in the hospital ten days, suffered severe mental shock and his neck was probably permanently injured.

Mackintosh, J., dissents.

[1] Reported in 200 Pac. 481.

Appeal from a judgment of the superior court for Adams county, Truax, J., entered November 17, 1920, upon the verdict of a jury rendered in favor of the plaintiff, in an action for personal injuries sustained in an automobile collision. Affirmed.

G. E. Lovell and *E. A. Davis,* for appellants.

Adams & Miller and *S. B. Kaufman,* for respondent.

Holcomb, J.—The collision involved in this action occurred upon a broad, straight, dry, improved highway, in broad daylight. The facts which could be found in favor of respondent were as follows: At about 11 o'clock a. m., on May 6, 1920, respondent, driving a Ford touring car, stopped on the right side of the road, in front of a store, to inquire his way. Upon being informed, he returned to his car, cranked the engine, closed the door to the back seat, looked back of him towards the north, from which direction he had come, to see if any cars were approaching behind him, saw none, got in the car, released the brake, threw out his left hand as a signal that he was going to turn to the left, and started, within a quarter of a minute after his look backward, slowly to turn around and go in the opposite direction. The Ford car had been headed south, and when starting to turn around proceeded very slowly from where it was standing, and when almost to the middle of the road, and almost cross-wise of the road, was struck by a Buick limousine belonging to appellants Rieker and wife, and driven by appellant Sickman, their agent, and at a rate of speed estimated by witnesses at from thirty to forty-five miles per hour. The Ford was struck by the other car on the left-hand side behind the front wheel, and was carried south a distance of about seventy-five feet, and, according to witnesses, was carried forty feet or more before striking the ground.

The store where respondent stopped was at the side of the highway in the village of Ralston. The road was a permanent, improved highway, and straight to the north, until it crossed a railroad track at grade, for about three hundred yards, and for about fifty yards beyond the railroad track, to where it makes a turn. It was therefore possible to see from the store up the road over three hundred yards. There were no travelers, either vehicles or pedestrians, to distract the attention, and the whole road for the time being was for the use of each of the vehicles in question, subject only to the rights of the other; and yet the collision occurred. There is testimony also that, just before striking respondent's car, Sickman, the driver of the limousine, glanced to the right side of the road, recognized an acquaintance, and waved his hand at him. Sickman admitted seeing the Ford car about fifty feet in front of him before he struck it. He said he attempted to avoid striking it by first turning to the right, and then turning to the left; that he was obliged to release the brakes on his car because it was skidding. He gave no signal by horn or otherwise. There was testimony that the Buick could have been stopped in twenty or twenty-five feet had it been going at the rate of twenty or twenty-five miles per hour, as claimed by Sickman, on a smooth dry road.

Appellants rely on three contentions for reversal: (1) plaintiff's evidence is insufficient as to defendants' negligence; (2) plaintiff's evidence shows contributory negligence on behalf of the plaintiff, and (3) the damages were excessive.

Appellants contend that the law of the case, if the case should be submitted to the jury, was as requested in their requested instruction No. 3, as follows:

"You are instructed that when the driver of an automobile is about to cross a highway it is his duty to look behind him and ascertain whether an automobile is approaching from that direction; and if he does not look he is guilty of negligence in the operation of his car."

There is no imperative rule of law requiring one, when lawfully using public highways, to be constantly looking and listening to ascertain if an automobile is approaching, under the penalty that, upon failure so to do, if he is injured, his own negligence must be conclusively presumed. *Hennessey v. Taylor*, 189 Mass. 583, 76 N. E. 224; *Gerhard v. Ford Motor Co.*, 155 Mich. 618, 119 N. W. 904; *Rogers v. Phillips*, 206 Mass. 308, 92 N. E. 327, 28 L. R. A. (N. S.) 944, the same case on second appeal, 217 Mass. 52, 104 N. E. 466; *Johnson v. Johnson*, 85 Wash. 18, 147 Pac. 649. Some of the cases above cited are cases of pedestrians crossing streets, but we know of no stricter rule as to the duty of a person in an automobile crossing a street or a country road than applies to pedestrians. In the *Johnson* case, above cited, we said:

"While it is also true that there was nothing to prevent the respondent's glancing in the direction of the automobile and governing her progress by its actual rather than its presumed movements, it is also true that there was nothing to prevent the driver from glancing in the direction of the crossing and seeing that the respondent was taking a straight course thereon unconscious of the dangerously rapid approach of the automobile, and governing his movements accordingly."

and further:

"The inquiry is thus narrowed to this: was the respondent, as a matter of law, guilty of contributory negligence in not continuously observing the automobile, which she saw a block distant when she entered upon the crossing, in order to avoid being run down by it?"

The same reasoning applies here. Respondent was in a place with his car where he had a right to be. Fifteen seconds before starting to turn, he looked and saw no car coming from the rear. He had the right to assume that any other person upon the highway in an automobile would exercise due care for his safety. Under the evidence in support of his case, he showed that he observed the rule of the road, or custom, by putting out his hand to the left as a signal that he was going to turn to the left. Had the driver of appellants' car been exercising due care for respondent's safety, instead of at the moment observing a person at the side of the road and waving to him, he might have seen the signal given by respondent and averted the collision.

At any rate, it seems clear that the negligence of appellants is established by the evidence, and that the question of whether or not respondent used due care for his own safety, under the circumstances, was a question for the jury. We are not willing to lay down the rule that a person in an automobile, driving across the road under such circumstances as appear to have existed in this case, would necessarily be negligent, as a matter of law, if he did not instantly look behind him before starting across the road. *Rogers v. Phillips, supra.*

We conclude, therefore, that the instruction requested was properly refused, and also that the case was one for the jury.

It is also contended that the verdict was excessive.

Respondent was very seriously injured. The skin and flesh from his forehead were lacerated to the bone and hung down over his eyes. He was delirious for some time and it was twenty-four hours before he could be removed to a hospital, where he remained ten days. A doctor testified that, besides the cuts and bruises above mentioned, his nose was deeply cut; that his left knee cap was scraped; that he vomited blood; that he suffered severe mental shock and continued nervousness; and that his neck was severely injured so that it still left an impairment to the movement of the neck, and some discomfort, which will probably be permanent.

The jury allowed $1,185 for pain, suffering and shock; $958.33 for permanent injuries; $534 for loss of time, and $122 for medical and hospital expenses. We are unable to say that these damages were in any way excessive under the evidence which supported the various items.

Judgment affirmed.

PARKER, C. J., BRIDGES, and FULLERTON, JJ., concur.

MACKINTOSH, J., dissents.

[No. 16375. Department Two. September 1, 1921.]

N. PAOLELLA, *Respondent*, v. EUGENE BRUNNER *et al.*, *Appellants*.[1]

BILLS AND NOTES (78-1, 93)—PLACE OF PAYMENT—ACTIONS—CONDITIONS PRECEDENT—DEPOSIT OF NOTE. The placing of a promissory note in a bank where it was made payable was not a prerequisite to the maintaining of action on it, where the evidence showed that there was no agreement requiring it to be left at such bank and that the failure to so place it was not the cause of its nonpayment when due.

Appeal from a judgment of the superior court for King county, Jurey, J., entered September 27, 1920, upon findings in favor of the plaintiff, in an action on promissory notes, tried to the court. Affirmed.

[1]Reported in 200 Pac. 481

John F. Murphy, for appellants.

H. Albert George and *W. A. Keene (James H. Buchanan*, of counsel), for respondent.

MAIN, J.—This action was brought to recover a judgment on promissory notes and for the foreclosure upon certain corporate stock which had been given as collateral security for the payment of the notes. The case came on for trial before the court and a jury. At the conclusion of the evidence, a motion being made, the court withdrew the case from the jury, made findings of fact, conclusions of law, and entered a judgment as prayed for in the complaint. The defendants appeal.

The facts out of which the action arose may be summarized as follows: On December 1, 1919, the appellant, Eugene Brunner, executed and delivered to one Joe Filiberto thirteen promissory notes, each for the principal sum of $750, except the note numbered thirteen, which was for one thousand dollars. Note one was payable on or before January 1, 1920. The remaining notes matured monthly thereafter. Contemporaneously with the delivery of the notes and as part of the same transaction, and for the purpose of securing the same, Brunner pledged 249 shares of the capital stock of the Jefferson Hotel Company, a corporation, and deposited the stock in the Scandinavian-American Bank of Seattle. At the time of the execution of the notes, an agreement collateral thereto was made covering the matter of the pledge of the stock and the depositing of the same in escrow in the bank. By this agreement the stock was to be placed in the bank, but no mention is made as to the notes. The notes on their face provide that they are payable at the same bank, and were in fact placed there, together with the notes and the collateral agreement. After the execution and delivery of the notes and agreement, and before maturity of any of them, the respondent purchased the notes from Filiberto, paying therefor the sum of $9,558. After respondent purchased the notes, they were withdrawn from the bank, indorsed and delivered to him and placed in the Guardian Trust & Savings Bank, with the exception of note number one, which was due on January 1, 1920, and which was paid some days after the due date. Note number two which was due on February 1, 1920, was not paid.

The present action was begun on March 1 thereafter, by filing the complaint in the clerk's office. The principal contention of the appellants seems to be that, since the notes provided that they should be paid at a certain place, to wit, the Scandinavian-American Bank, and that note number two was not there on the due date, one prerequisite to the right to maintain the action was lacking. The collateral agreement did not require the notes to be placed in that bank, and the evidence shows without substantial controversy that the failure of note number two to be in the Scandinavian-American Bank was not the cause of its nonpayment when it became due. The appellants knew the bank in which the note was deposited and did not make any tender of payment at the bank where the note specified it was payable. Under these facts, the respondent had a right to maintain the action, even though note number two was not in the Scandinavian-American Bank at the time it became due and payable.

The judgment will be affirmed.

PARKER, C. J., HOLCOMB, TOLMAN, and MITCHELL, JJ., concur.

[No. 16322. Department Two. September 1, 1921.]

M. McINNIS et al., Appellants, v. B. A. WATSON,
Respondent.[1]

FRAUDS, STATUTE OF (44)—OPERATION OF STATUTE—MODIFICATION
OF LEASE. Under the rule that a contract required by law to be in
writing cannot be modified by parol, excepting that an oral modification which has been performed may be set up as a defense, in an
action on a farming lease requiring a portion of the crop to be paid
as rental, the lessee cannot prove a verbal modification of the lease
tending to reduce the rental, where there was no showing of anything done in performance of such alleged oral modification.

Appeal from a judgment of the superior court for
Walla Walla county, Mills, J., entered June 9, 1920,
upon the verdict of a jury rendered in favor of the
defendant upon his counterclaim, in an action on contract. Reversed.

J. W. Brooks, for appellants.

Reynolds & Bond, for respondent.

MACKINTOSH, J.—By written lease, the appellants
rented farming land to the respondent for a term of
years, the rent to be paid by a portion of the crop.
This action was begun to recover damages for failure
to deliver certain portions of the rent and for failure
to harvest portions of the crop. To the complaint the
respondent filed an answer which contained, among
other things, the allegations that there had been a
verbal modification of the lease whereby the rental
had been reduced, in that it is alleged the appellants
agreed to pay for the sacks in which the portion of the
crop coming to them for rent was to be delivered, this
agreement having been made to induce the respondent to continue the lease. The respondent also plead
a counterclaim for the value of the sacks. The case was

[1]Reported in 200 Pac. 578.

tried to a jury, and resulted in a verdict for the respondent on the counterclaim.

The evidence shows that, after the rent had been paid by the respondent for a time, he discovered that, on account of the rolling character of the land (his counsel justifies this description of the land by the fact that, in attempting to harvest the crop, the whole crew, header and horses rolled over into the canyons below the property), it was impossible, under the lease, to make any profit, and being discouraged, the modification above referred to was made by the appellants and the respondent, and under this modification he continued to farm the land for another year.

Many errors are assigned by the appellants which relate to the ruling out of opinion testimony, and the admission of testimony as to the meaning of terms in the lease, and to instructions given; it is unnecessary to review these various assignments, as a careful examination of the record relating to them, in our opinion, shows no error. The important question in the case is as to whether the testimony concerning the verbal modification of the written lease was admissible.

The general rule is that a contract which, under the law, is required to be in writing may not be modified by parol. It should be borne in mind that we have not here under consideration the right to modify by parol an original contract that was in fact reduced to writing but was not required to be so by law. Some states have departed from the general rule and their decisions are in direct variance with it, as, for example, *Nonomaker v. Amos*, 73 Ohio St. 163, 76 N. E. 949, 112 Am. St. 708, 4 L. R. A. (N. S.) 980; *Wilson v. Peoples' Gas Co.*, 75 Kan. 499, 89 Pac. 897. In other states the general rule has been modified by special statutory provisions, as, for example, California,

§ 1698 of whose civil code provides that "a contract in writing may be altered by a contract in writing or by an executed oral agreement and not otherwise." A similar provision occurs in the statutes of North Dakota, South Dakota, Oklahoma and Montana. In this state the rule was early adopted and has been followed since, that a contract modifying or abrogating a prior contract, required by statute to be in writing, must itself be in writing to be obligatory. *Spinning v. Drake,* 4 Wash. 285, 30 Pac. 82, 31 Pac. 319; *Thill v. Johnston,* 60 Wash. 393, 111 Pac. 225. In *Gerard-Fillio Co. v. McNair,* 68 Wash. 321, 123 Pac. 462, this rule was followed, with the modification that "an executed oral contract to modify or abrogate a written contract, required by statute to be in writing, can be successfully pleaded as a defense to an action on the original contract." In *Oregon & Wash. R. Co. v. Elliott Bay Mill & Lum. Co.,* 70 Wash. 148, 126 Pac. 406, it was held that, in a case where the contract was required to be in writing, an oral modification which had been performed and was recognized by the subsequent forbearance of the appellant might be proven. See, also, *Farley v. Letterman,* 87 Wash. 641, 152 Pac. 515; *Stoner v. Fryett,* 91 Wash. 89 157 Pac. 213; *Woolen v. Sloan,* 94 Wash. 551, 162 Pac. 985; *Clements v. Cook,* 112 Wash. 217, 191 Pac. 874.

As we view it, there is no question presented in this record as to whether there was such performance or part performance of the modification, or such acts as amounted to an estoppel against the appellants, as to bring this case within the rule which allows oral modifications of written contracts, required by law to be in writing, to be testified to. There was nothing done in this case in regard to the modification of the rental requirements which would amount to a performance or part performance, for that must consist in the doing or the suffering of something not required to be done or suffered by the terms of the original writing.

Attention is called to the case of *Bono v. Warner,* 108 Wash. 180, 182 Pac. 946, where a question was submitted to the jury as to whether there had been a verbal modification of a lease such as we have before us in this case. An examination of the opinion in that case and the record discloses no question there raised as to the admissibility of the evidence of modification, the claim being that no modification had in fact been made. That case, therefore, is not authority upon the point under discussion.

By reason of the fact that the court allowed the evidence of the verbal modification of the lease to be introduced, the judgment is reversed.

PARKER, C. J., MAIN, MITCHELL, and TOLMAN, JJ., concur.

[No. 16291. Department Two. September 1, 1921.]

NORTHERN PACIFIC RAILWAY COMPANY, *Appellant*, v.
WALLA WALLA COUNTY *et al., Respondents.*[1]

WATERS (92)—IRRIGATION DISTRICTS—ASSESSMENTS—BENEFITS TO
PROPERTY—STATUTES. The inclusion of land within the boundaries
of an irrigation district does not necessarily mean that it is capable
of receiving benefit from the district's irrigating system, and thus
liable to contribute to the maintenance of the system.

SAME (92). Land included in an irrigation district which is in-
capable of irrigation and cultivation would not be subject to maintenance charges, in view of Rem. Code, § 6433, providing that assessments therefor "shall be made in proportion with the benefits accruing to the lands assessed," and Id., § 6452, providing that such
charges may be collected "from all persons using said canal for
irrigation and other purposes."

SAME (92)—RECOVERY OF ASSESSMENT—FRAUD—COMPLAINT—SUF-
FICIENCY. In an action to recover money paid on an assessment for
maintenance of an irrigation system which was illegally exacted
from plaintiff, the complaint would not be demurrable for failure
to allege fraud or wilful misconduct on the part of the directors of
the district, since the allegations of the complaint sufficiently show
legal fraud when they set up that the plaintiff's land had been
charged with an assessment when it was not in fact benefited by the
maintenance of the irrigation system.

Appeal from a judgment of the superior court for
Walla Walla county, Mills, J., entered November 4,
1920, upon sustaining demurrers to the complaint, dismissing an action to recover a tax paid under protest.
Reversed.

*Geo. T. Reid, J. W. Quick, L. B. da Ponte, C. A.
Murray,* and *John H. Pedigo,* for appellant.

A. J. Gillis and *Moulton & Jeffrey,* for respondents.

PARKER, C. J.—The plaintiff railway company commenced this action in the superior court for Walla
Walla county, seeking recovery of the sum of $230.87,

[1]Reported in 200 Pac. 585.

claimed to have been unlawfully exacted from it by
the officers of the defendants county and irrigation district as an assessment upon certain lands owned by
it, for the expense of operating and maintaining the
irrigation system of the defendant district; which sum
was paid by the railway company under protest for
the purpose of preventing the casting of a cloud upon
its title to the land in the form of a sale thereof in
satisfaction of the claimed lien of the assessment
thereon. The county and irrigation district demurred
to the complaint of the railway company upon the
ground of insufficiency of facts to constitute a cause of
action. The demurrers were by the court sustained,
and the railway company electing to stand upon its
complaint and not plead further, judgment of dismissal
with prejudice was rendered against it, from which it
has appealed to this court.

Following the allegations of the corporate existence
of the railway company, the county and the irrigation
district, and the ownership of the land by the railway
company, the complaint alleges:

"   . .   . which property was acquired and
owned for the purpose of constructing sand guards or
fences in order to protect plaintiff's railway track
from being buried and obstructed by drifting sand.
Said lands are within the bounds of defendant irrigation district, but the same are not susceptible of any
use for agriculture and could not be devoted to such
use because of their nature and topography, being
nothing but drifting sands in which it would be impossible to grow any crops, trees or shrubs of any kind
whatever.

"On or about the 13th day of September, 1918, defendant irrigation district, acting through its duly
authorized officers and agents, passed a resolution as
follows:

" 'Be it resolved, that there shall be and is hereby
levied against all lands in said irrigation district in-

cluded in the assessment roll as benefited lands, an assessment in the aggregate of $18,200 to cover the following items which are hereby declared to be the necessary amounts for interest, maintenance and operation, and emergency, deficit:

Interest on bonds issued..............$ 1,040
Expense of operation and mainte-
   nance for the ensuing year........ 14,560
Fund to cover deficit............... 2,600
                                     _____
        Total $18,200

and be it further resolved that the Sec. be and is hereby directed to extend the assessment roll as against such tract of land appearing thereon, in accordance with the ratio of benefits as heretofore fixed and established; and upon said extension being made the Sec. is directed to file the assessment roll with the county treasurer as by law provided.

" 'Passed by the board of directors this 13th day of September, 1918.

" 'J. H. Sharry, Sec.
" 'A. H. Hawkins, Pres.'

"Pursuant to said resolution, there was levied an assessment against plaintiff's land in the sum of $14.06, interest on bonds, the sum of $195.94 for maintenance of the irrigation system used for furnishing water to lands within the district, and the sum of $34.93 for a deficit on account of previous years' maintenance of said irrigation works, or a total of $244.93, . . . Said assessment was duly certified to the county treasurer and was by that officer spread on the tax rolls for the year 1918. . . .

"Said assessment is illegal and void to the extent that the same was levied against plaintiff's lands for the maintenance of said irrigation system for the year 1918 and for said deficit for previous years' maintenance, in that there is no provision or authority of law for levying an assessment for maintenance on any lands within the district which are not being irrigated or are not susceptible of irrigation and cultivation on account of their character and topography, . . .

". . . the only portion of said assessment which could be lawfully levied upon plaintiff's lands was that for interest on bonds in the sum of $14.06, as aforesaid.

"On the 31st day of December, 1918, plaintiff duly tendered to the county treasurer of defendant county said sum of $14.06 in payment of said assessment, said tender being made unconditionally and without prejudice to the right of said county or said irrigation district to claim and recover the full amount appearing to be due. . . . The defendant county refused to accept said tender for no other reason than that it did not include the amount levied for the maintenance of said irrigation works, . . . Thereupon, and on the 31st day of December, 1918, plaintiff paid to defendant county the full amount appearing to be due in the sum of $244.93, protesting that the same was illegal in the sum of $230.87, as aforesaid, . . . Said payment was made for the purpose of relieving plaintiff's property from the lien and cloud cast thereon bv reason of said pretended assessment appearing on the general tax rolls of defendant county, and to protect its property from being sold in payment thereof."

No contention is here made that this is not an appropriate form of action, or that it was not timely commenced for the purpose of testing the legality of the assessment in question. The only question presented in the briefs of counsel is whether or not the assessment was lawfully made against the land of the railway company, assuming, as we must for the present, that the allegations of its complaint are true. We think the allegations of the complaint must be viewed as meaning that the maintenance of the irrigation district could not, under any circumstances, result in any benefit to the land in question. The argument of counsel for respondents seems to be that the question of the land being benefited by the maintenance of the irrigation system is foreclosed by the fact that it was,

we shall assume, lawfully included within the boundaries of the district. We cannot give assent to this
view. We do not think that the mere fact that the
land happens to be within the boundaries of the district necessarily means that it is capable of receiving
benefit from the maintenance of the irrigation system
of the district, in the sense of becoming liable to contribute toward the maintenance of the irrigation system of the district. The provisions of the irrigation
statutes which seem to call for notice in our present inquiry, referring to the sections of Rem. Code, are the
following:

"§ 6432. Said bonds . . . [bonds for construction, and acquisition of property] shall be paid by revenue derived from an annual assessment upon the real
property of the district, and all the real property in
the district shall be and remain liable to be assessed
for such payments as hereinafter provided. . ."

"§ 6433. Assessments made in order to carry out
the purposes of this act shall be made in proportion
with the benefits accruing to the lands assessed. . ."

"§ 6452. The cost and expense of purchasing and
acquiring property, and construction, reconstruction,
extension, and betterment of the works and improvements herein provided for, and the expenses incidental
thereto, and indebtedness to the United States for district lands assumed by the district, and for the carrying out of the purposes of this chapter, may be paid
by the board of directors out of the funds received
from bond sales. For the purpose of defraying expenses of the organization of the district, and of the
care, operation, management, repair and improvement
of such portions of said canal and works as are completed and in use, the board may either fix rates or
tolls and charges, and collect the same from all persons using said canal for irrigation and other purposes,
or they may provide for the payment of said expense
by a levy of assessment therefor, or by both said tolls
and assessment; if by the latter method, such levy
shall be made on the completion and equalization of

the assessment-roll each year, and the board shall have
the same powers and functions for the purpose of said
levy as possessed by it in case of levy to pay bonds
of the district.''

There may be some room for arguing that this land,
by the mere fact of being within the boundaries of the
district, is subject to assessment, viewed as a general
tax, to aid in paying for the construction of, and acquiring property rights for, the irrigation system.
Counsel for appellant seem to concede this much for
the purposes of this case; but if such be a correct view
of the provisions of § 6432, Rem. Code, in view of the
statement in that section that ''all the real property
in the district shall be and remain liable to be assessed
for such payments,'' we think it does not follow that
the property in question became liable for maintenance
charges if it is in fact not capable of being benefited
by the maintenance of the district's irrigation system,
as alleged in the complaint. It will be observed that,
by the express provisions of § 6433, Rem. Code, the
assessments ''shall be made in proportion with the
benefits accruing to the lands assessed.'' If this does
not apply to the assessment or tax to pay for construction and property acquisition bonds, we think it in
any event applies to maintenance cost, in view of the
provisions of § 6452, Rem. Code.

Some contention is made in respondents' behalf that
the allegations of the complaint fail to show ''fraud
or wilful misconduct on the part of the board of directors of the irrigation district.'' The argument seems
to be that they must be presumed to have acted honestly, in the absence of some specific allegation to the
contrary. This is not so much a question of the hon-
esty of purpose of the board of directors in a moral
sense, as whether or not they have charged the railway company's land with this assessment, when in fact

it is not and cannot be benefited by the maintenance of
the irrigation system. If this occurred, a legal fraud
was worked upon the railway company; and the allegations of the complaint show such a fraud.

We conclude that the order of the trial court sustaining the demurrers to appellant's complaint, and
the judgment rendered thereon dismissing the action,
must be reversed and the cause remanded to the trial
court with directions to overrule the demurrers, and
for further proceedings. It is so ordered.

MAIN, MITCHELL, and MACKINTOSH, JJ., concur.

[No. 16511. Department One. September 2, 1921.]

WILLIAM LUCKKART et al., Appellants, v. DIRECTOR
GENERAL OF RAILROADS et al., Respondents.[1]

MUNICIPAL CORPORATIONS (383, 391)—STREETS—AUTOMOBILES—
CONTRIBUTORY NEGLIGENCE—EVIDENCE—SUFFICIENCY. In an action for
damages for personal injuries, plaintiffs were properly nonsuited,
where the evidence showed their injuries resulted from driving
their automobile in the nighttime into a light pole, set in the middle of a space devoted to traffic and which at the time was unlighted,
and it appears plaintiffs were familiar with the surroundings, that,
in making a turn and driving slowly in low gear which would enable
them to stop within a couple of feet, the car was driven into the
pole, the presence of which should have been noted by a careful
driver as his front lights swept across it in making the turn (FUL-
LERTON, J., dissenting).

Appeal from a judgment of the superior court for
Yakima county, Taylor, J., entered May 26, 1920, upon
granting a nonsuit, dismissing an action for personal
injuries. Affirmed.

O. B. Root and Harold B. Gilbert, for appellants.

Geo. T. Reid, J. W. Quick, L. B. da Ponte, and Rigg
& Venables, for respondents.

[1]Reported in 200 Pac. 564.

BRIDGES, J.—The plaintiffs appeal from a judgment of nonsuit in their action to recover damages on account of personal injuries. Construing the testimony in the light most favorable to them, it is shown that their accident occurred in the following manner: The depot of the Northern Pacific Railway Company, in the city of Toppenish, is reached from the city by means of a driveway located on the railway company's private right of way, which driveway was laid out and is maintained by the railway company. Within the right of way and in front of the depot, is located a small park on one side of the driveway, and the freight depot on the other side. Where the driveway goes between the freight depot and the park it is more than one hundred feet in width. The space between the depot and the park and freight depot is open and used exclusively for a roadway. In about the center of that portion of the driveway located between the freight depot and the park was a large electric light pole, placed there long ago by the defendant Pacific Power & Light Company, upon which wires were strung which conveyed all the electric light used at the depot. The pole was about 55 feet from the park, 75 feet from the freight house, and about 90 feet from the depot. The plaintiffs are farmers and reside within two or three miles of Toppenish.

In August, 1919, very early in the morning, plaintiffs brought their daughter with them in their automobile to the depot that she might take a train leaving there about three o'clock a. m. At that time it was dark, and there were no lights of any character on the electric light pole, or in its immediate vicinity, nor was the private driveway in any manner lighted. Having put their daughter aboard the train, they again entered their automobile, which was immediately in front of the depot, for the purpose of returning to their home. Mr. Luckkart was driving, and his wife was in the front seat with him. His front lights were burning brightly and his brakes were in good order. In order to get out to the city street they desired to take, it was necessary for them to make a turn to the left on the driveway within the private grounds of the railroad company. In so doing, the automobile came into collision with the electric light pole and both plaintiffs were injured. From the time the automobile left the door of the depot to the time of its collision with the pole, it was being driven in low gear, at the rate of about five miles per hour, and could have been stopped within a foot or two. The right front spring of the car struck the pole.

Mr. Luckkart testified that he did not see the pole before striking it, and that he could not have seen it because his car was approaching it on a curve to the left, and that his lights would not be thrown upon it. It seems clear to us, however, that the physical facts conclusively show that the driver of the automobile could have seen the pole in time to have avoided the collision. One important fact stands out, and that is that it was the right front spring of the automobile which hit the pole. Since the car was turning to the left, it must follow that, at some time before the collision, the lights must have shone fully on the pole, and during that period it was directly in front of the car. Such being the facts, we must conclusively presume that the driver of the car could have seen the pole in time to have avoided the accident. But the fact that he could have seen it was not sufficient to nonsuit him. To justify that action we must be able to say that, not only could he have seen the pole, but that had he used reasonable care, under all the circumstances, he would have seen it in time to have avoided hitting it. The only question, therefore, is whe-

ther, under all of the circumstances, we can say that, if
the driver of the car had used ordinary care, he would
have seen the pole and avoided the collision. We think
the ruling of the trial court was right. Both Mr. and
Mrs. Luckkart were fairly familiar with the whole
situation, although they did not know, or at least
remember, that there was a pole located in the driveway. They had been on these grounds before, and
for some years had lived within two or three miles of
them. When the driver was some distance from the
pole, he must have been driving directly at it, with
the front lights shining squarely on it. There was no
other traffic on the roadway or in the immediate vicinity, and there was nothing to confuse the driver of
the automobile or distract his attention. Under these
circumstances, it would seem quite impossible for him
not to see the pole, if he was paying any attention to
where he was going. But the rules of law impose that
duty on the driver—to keep his senses about him; to
look where he is going; to pay reasonable heed to his
surroundings. Had he done so, it is manifest that he
must have seen the pole in plenty of time to have
avoided striking it. We cannot escape the conclusion
that the collision was the result of the negligence of
the driver of the automobile.

The judgment is affirmed.

PARKER, C. J., MACKINTOSH, and HOLCOMB, JJ., concur.

FULLERTON, J. (dissenting)—The driveway mentioned in the majority opinion was opened by the railway company as a means of approach to its depot, and
any member of the general public was invited to use
it when upon lawful business with the railway company. The electric light pole mentioned stood in the
middle of this highway, and was at all times a menace

to its use, and particularly so in the nighttime, since
it was left without a light or any form of guard to
mark its position. The appellants, at the time they
were injured, were in lawful use of the highway, and
had a right to suppose that nothing would be left in it
in the form of an obstruction which might result in
their injury. They did not know of the presence of
the pole, and therefore were not obligated to give it
the same attention as they would have been obligated
had they known of its existence. It seems to me,
therefore, too much to say that they are conclusively
presumed to be negligent because they failed to discover its presence and avoid it. It is true, undoubtedly, that in making the turn in the passage from the
depot to the pole, the lights of the automobile flashed
over the pole; and it is possible, also, that the appellants, had they been at that instant looking in that direction, would have discovered the pole. But I cannot think this the question at issue. The question, to
my mind, is, were they legally obligated to look for it.
I cannot conclude that they were, and without so concluding I cannot conceive that they were guilty of contributory negligence, as matter of law, in failing to see
it. I am constrained therefore to dissent from the
conclusion reached by the majority.

[No. 16438.   Department Two.   September 2, 1921.]

OLYMPIA NATIONAL BANK, *Respondent*, v. MURPHY
MOTOR CAR COMPANY, *Appellant*.[1]

CORPORATIONS (151, 160)—POWERS AND LIABILITIES—PROMISSORY
NOTES—ASSUMPTION OF LIABILITY—EVIDENCE—SUFFICIENCY. Where
an individual organized his business into a corporation, which assumed the assets and liabilities of his business, a note executed by
him as officer of the corporation in renewal of a personal note given
by him while conducting the business as an individual is binding on
the corporation.

APPEAL (429, 437)—REVIEW—HARMLESS ERROR—PLEADING—DECI-
SION CORRECT ON MERITS. Error in permitting plaintiff to file a reply
setting up estoppel and ratification, in an action by it on a promissory note of a corporation, was harmless, where the judgment was
sustainable upon the theory that the obligations of a concern were
assumed by defendant at the time of taking over its assets.

Appeal from a judgment of the superior court for
Thurston county, Wright, J., entered March 4, 1921,
in favor of the plaintiff, in an action on promissory
notes, and to foreclose collateral security, tried to the
court. Affirmed.

Thos. L. O'Leary, for appellant.

Geo. F. Yantis and *Troy & Sturdevant*, for respondent.

MAIN, J.—This action was brought for the appointment of a receiver, for judgment on four promissory
notes, and for the foreclosure of two chattel mortgages
and certain collateral security. The receiver was appointed, and the trial resulted in a judgment upon the
notes and a foreclosure of the securities and chattel
mortgages. From this judgment, the defendant appeals.

The facts essential to be stated are as follows: Prior
to the month of May, 1920, one A. R. Murphy owned

[1]Reported in 200 Pac. 577.

and conducted an automobile and garage business on
west Fourth street, in the city of Olympia, under the
name of the West Fourth Street Garage. On or about
the first of the month named, the Murphy Motor Car
Company was incorporated, the capital stock of which
was $5,000, divided into fifty shares of the par value
of $100. Murphy subscribed for twenty-four shares
of this capital stock; one C. M. Poncin, for twenty-
four shares, and M. O'Bannon for two shares. The
Murphy Motor Car Company began doing business
on Columbia street, in the city of Olympia, on or about
May 3, 1920. Between the first and the third of May
the physical property which had been situated at the
West Fourth Street Garage was transferred to the
place of business of the appellant company. At about
this time, Poncin left Olympia on an extended trip and
did not return until the latter part of October, 1920.
Some time prior to his return, and on October 5, 1920,
the appellant corporation was in financial difficulty.
At the time the business was taken over by the appellant, the respondent held four promissory notes signed
by Murphy individually. After the business had been
taken over, these were renewed and the renewal notes
were signed by the appellant corporation by Murphy
as manager. It is these notes that are involved in
this action.

The defense is that they were the notes of Murphy
individually, and that therefore the corporation was
not liable. Upon the question as to whether, when the
assets of the West Fourth Street Garage were taken
over by the appellant, that corporation assumed the
liabilities of Murphy, the evidence is in direct conflict,
Murphy testifying that the corporation took over the
assets and assumed the liabilities; Poncin testified
directly to the contrary. Upon this conflicting evi-

dence the trial court, in a memorandum opinion, expressed the view that:

"The statement made by Mr. A. R. Murphy is a true and correct delineation of the circumstances surrounding the creation of the Murphy Motor Car Co. When this corporation was perfected it assumed the indebtedness of the West Fourth Street Garage, which was conducted by, and was the business of, A. R. Murphy. When the notes were renewed and signed by the Murphy Motor Car Company, the company was simply giving these notes in place of the notes it assumed and agreed to pay and did not change its obligation."

After reading the record, we are in accord with the view of the trial court upon the facts. If this view is correct, then the judgment of the trial court was right. The corporation, when it took over the assets, had a right to assume the liabilities.

The appellant relies principally upon two cases from this court. If its view of the facts were adopted, the cases would be in point and controlling. The first case is that of *Mooney v. Mooney Co.*, 71 Wash. 258, 128 Pac. 225, where it was held that, when one of the officers of a corporation gave a note of the corporation in renewal of his personal note, such transaction was presumptively *ultra vires,* and one dealing with such officer was presumed to know that he could not bind the company by the renewal note for which it received no consideration. The other case is that of *Hoffman v. Gottstein Inv. Co.*, 101 Wash. 428, 172 Pac. 573, and the facts are similar. There the renewal note was given by a corporation for the individual note of one of its officers, and it was held that the corporation could not be held to pay the personal debt of the officer by the execution and delivery of the renewal note, there being no consideration moving to the corporation for such note. Those cases are distinguishable from the present, in that here the evidence shows that, when the business was taken over by the appellant, it was the agreement that it should receive not only the assets but assume the liabilities. In executing the renewal notes the appellant was only giving its own notes in place of the obligation which it had already assumed.

It is also claimed that the trial court erred in permitting a reply which is construed by the parties as pleading estoppel and ratification. Assuming, without deciding, that this was a departure from the complaint, the appellant was in no way harmed thereby. The case was fully tried upon the facts and, as already pointed out, the judgment of the trial court should be sustained upon the theory that the obligations, at the time the assets were taken over, were assumed.

The judgment will be affirmed.

PARKER, C. J., MITCHELL, TOLMAN, and FULLERTON, JJ., concur.

[No. 16373.   Department One.   June 9, 1921.]

SACAJAWEA LUMBER & SHINGLE COMPANY, *Appellant*, v. SKOOKUM
LUMBER COMPANY *et al.*, *Respondents*.[1]

Appeal from an order of the superior court for Thurston county,
Wilson, J., entered October 18, 1920, overruling plaintiff's motion
to set aside an order of dismissal.   Reversed.

F. Campbell and *H. H. Johnston*, for appellant.

PER CURIAM.—This case is controlled by our decision in the case
of *Sacajawea Lumber & Shingle Co. v. Skookum Lumber Co.*,
ante p. 75, 198 Pac. 1112, where the same facts and questions are
disposed of, and is therefore reversed and remanded with the same
instructions to the lower court.

[No. 16518.   Department Two.   June 14, 1921.]

EMMA AROLA, *Respondent*, v. W. F. HAYS, *Appellant*.[2]

Appeal from a judgment of the superior court for King county,
Frater, J., entered November 16, 1920, upon findings in favor of the
plaintiff, in an action for money received, tried to the court.   Affirmed.

Kelleran & Hannan, for appellant.
J. Grattan O'Bryan, for respondent.

PER CURIAM.—In this action, which was begun by a client against
her attorney for the return of money received by him, he has set
up a counterclaim seeking to recover for legal services performed
for her and at her request.   The only question presented on the
appeal is as to the proper amount to be allowed on this counterclaim.   An examination of the record does not disclose any reason
why we should interfere with the amount awarded by the trial
court, and the judgment is therefore affirmed.

[1]Reported in 198 Pac. 1114.
[2]Reported in 198 Pac. 1119.

[No. 16420. Department One. June 28, 1921.]

H. A. RISPIN, *Appellant*, v. GEORGE F. VANDERVEER *et al.*, *Respondents.*[1]

Appeal from a judgment of the superior court for King county, Hall, J., entered December 27, 1920, upon findings in favor of the defendants, in an action on a promissory note, tried to the court. Affirmed.

Dwight N. Stevens and *Jones, Riddell & Brackett*, for appellant.
Ralph S. Pierce, for respondents.

PER CURIAM.—This is an action upon a promissory note which was given in payment for an oil-drilling rig. One of the defenses was, that upon an examination of the rig, it developed that certain essential parts were missing, and that the respondents therefore refused to accept the property and rescinded the sale.

While there are other questions presented by the appellant, the main and determinative one involves the authority of one Williams to act as appellant's agent in making the sale. This presented purely a question of fact, with the superior court's determination of which we find no reason to interfere.

The judgment is therefore affirmed.

[No. 16440.   Department Two.   July 7, 1921.]

JOHN J. SNYDER *et al.*, *Respondents*, v. E. O. MARKEN *et al.*, *Appellants.*[2]

Appeal from a judgment of the superior court for King county, Tallman, J., entered November 13, 1920, upon the verdict of a jury rendered in favor of the plaintiffs, upon sustaining a demurrer to defendants' affirmative defense, in an action for personal injuries sustained in an automobile collision. Affirmed.

Hartman & Hartman, for appellants.
Flick & Paul, for respondents.

PER CURIAM—This suit is to recover damages for injuries to Mrs. Snyder and to an automobile belonging to the respondents. It presents substantially the state of facts presented in the case of *Snyder v. Marken, ante* page 270, 199 Pac. 302. For the reasons given in that case, the judgment here appealed from is affirmed.

[1]Reported in 199 Pac. 235.
[2]Reported in 199 Pac. 303.

[No. 16407. Department One. July 8, 1921.]

Rose A. Moore, *Respondent*, v. James B. Moore, *Appellant.*[1]

Appeal from an order of the superior court for Okanogan county, Neal, J., entered November 8, 1920, denying defendant's motion to vacate a decree, in a divorce action. Reversed.

Ferris & Ferris, for appellant.
P. D. *Smith* and W. *C. Brown*, for respondent.

Per Curiam.—Respondent, on March 19, 1920, was granted a decree of divorce from the appellant, which decree awarded her the custody of their six minor children, there being no appearance by the appellant. On April 16, 1920, the appellant served and filed a motion to have the decree vacated and his default set aside on the ground that the order of default and decree had been taken against him through his inadvertence and excusable neglect. The trial court entered an order refusing to vacate the decree, from which order the appellant has brought this appeal.

It is not necessary to detail the facts alleged by the respondent as showing a reason entitling him to have his default set aside and the decree opened. It is only necessary to say, upon the authority of *Jarrard v. Jarrard, ante* p. 70, 198 Pac. 741, that the relief asked for by the appellant should have been granted.

The order of the trial court, refusing to set aside the default and vacate the decree, is reversed, and that court is directed to allow appellant to file his answer, and to proceed to hear the case upon its merits.

[1]Reported in 198 Pac. 99.

INDEX

Affidavits—Continued.

For publication of summons in tax foreclosure proceedings, see
TAXATION, 1.

Agency:

See PRINCIPAL AND AGENT.

Agreement:

See CONTRACTS.

Agriculture:

Irrigation, see WATERS AND WATER COURSES, 5-13.

Alimony:

For support and maintenance, duration of, see DIVORCE, 7.

Allowance:

Of compensation to administrator *de bonis non*, see EXECUTORS AND
ADMINISTRATORS, 6.

Alteration:

Of dangerous structures, under building code, see MUNICIPAL COR-
PORATIONS, 2-5.

Alteration of Instruments:

Forgery, see FORGERY.

Amendment:

Of by-laws reducing dividends, see CORPORATIONS, 1, 6, 7.
Of articles of incorporation, see CORPORATIONS, 3, 4.
Of pleading, see PLEADING, 2, 3.
Of statute limiting indebtedness of taxing districts, see SCHOOLS AND
SCHOOL DISTRICTS.
Of statute, see STATUTES, 1.

Amount in Controversy:

Jurisdictional amount, see APPEAL AND ERROR, 1, 2.

Appeal and Error:

In disbarment proceedings, see ATTORNEY AND CLIENT, 3.
Existence of remedy by appeal, where inadequate, see CERTIORARI.
Criminal appeals, see CRIMINAL LAW, 22, 24.
Stipulations between parties to appeal, see STIPULATIONS.

III. DECISIONS REVIEWABLE.

1. APPEAL (23)—DECISIONS REVIEWABLE—SUITS IN EQUITY. The
provision of the constitution, Art. 4, § 4, denying appellate jurisdiction to the supreme court where the original amount in controversy
is less than $200, does not preclude appeal from an injunctive order

Appeal and Error—Continued.

Appeal and Error—Continued.

VII. REQUISITES FOR TRANSFER OF CAUSE.

IX. SUPERSEDEAS.

X. RECORD.

XI. BRIEFS.

Appeal and Error—Continued.

will not interfere on the ground of its inability to determine which items were found in favor of one party and which in favor of the other. *Pettijohn v. Ray*..................................... **136**

20.   APPEAL (429, 437) — REVIEW—HARMLESS ERROR—PLEADING—DECISION CORRECT ON MERITS.   Error in permitting plaintiff to file a reply setting up estoppel and ratification, in an action by it on a promissory note of a corporation, was harmless, where the judgment was sustainable upon the theory that the obligations of a concern were assumed by defendant at the time of taking over its assets. *Olympia National Bank v. Murphy Motor Car Co*.............. **695**

XVII.   DETERMINATION AND DISPOSITION OF CAUSE.

21.   APPEAL (494)—DECISION—POWERS AND DUTIES OF LOWER COURT—INCIDENTAL RELIEF.   Where a judgment sustaining exceptions to an executor's final account was reversed and remanded without directions to enter a specific judgment, upon which the trial court entered judgment overruling the exceptions, it was entitled to consider as incidental to such judgment the amount of compensation to be awarded the executor for attorney's services in resisting the exceptions. *In re McDonald's Estate*................................ **625**

Appearance:

Of parties of record to confer right to appeal, see APPEAL AND ERROR, 4.

Application:

For additional compensation for attorney in resisting exceptions to final account of executors, see EXECUTORS AND ADMINISTRATORS, 5.
Of payments, see PAYMENT.

Appointment:

Of executor or administrator, see EXECUTORS AND ADMINISTRATORS, 1.

Appropriation:

Of state funds, see STATES.
Of water rights in general, see WATERS AND WATER COURSES, 3.

Arbitration and Award:

Reference of issues under order of court, see REFERENCE.

1.   ARBITRATION AND AWARD (9)—NOTICE OF AWARD—SERVICE—SUFFICIENCY.   Where an award had been made pursuant to the provisions of Rem. Code, §§ 420-430, under an agreement for arbitration, service of notice of the award by registered mail was sufficient, under Id., §§ 244-247, where the person making the service and the person on whom it was made resided at different places between which there was regular communication by mail; such notice not comi within the exception against the service of "summons or othe

Banks and Banking—Continued.

would not amount to a special deposit so as to constitute plaintiff's claim a preferred one; and it cannot be said that a fraud was worked on the depositor from the fact that the bank was insolvent on the day the deposit was received. *Spiroplos v. Scandinavian-American Bank of Tacoma*.................................... 491

2. BANKS AND BANKING (26)—GENERAL OR SPECIAL DEPOSITS—PRE-FERRED CLAIMS. The purchase of a draft from a bank would not constitute the money or its equivalent paid therefor a special deposit, since the transaction merely creates the relation of debtor and creditor, unless it be shown that in some way the net cash assets of the bank are increased thereby; and such assets were not increased' by the deposit, since it created a corresponding liability. *Spiroplos v. Scandinavian-American Bank of Tacoma*.......... 491

Bar:

Of prosecution by former conviction, see CRIMINAL LAW, 5-7.
Of action by former adjudication, see DIVORCE, 4; JUDGMENT, 3.
By election of remedy, see ELECTION OF REMEDIES.

Benefits:

To property from irrigation district, see WATERS AND WATER COURSES, 11, 12.

Bequests:

In general, see WILLS.

Best and Secondary Evidence:

In civil actions, see EVIDENCE, 4.

Bias:

Of judge as ground for change of venue, see VENUE, 2.

Bicycles:

Imputed negligence of rider guiding machine, see NEGLIGENCE, 3.

Bills and Notes:

Authority of officers to execute notes on behalf of corporation, see CORPORATIONS, 10.
Forgery of check, see FORGERY.

1. BILLS AND NOTES (78-1, 93)—PLACE OF PAYMENT—ACTIONS—CONDITIONS PRECEDENT—DEPOSIT OF NOTE. The placing of a promissory note in a bank where it was made payable was not a prerequisite to the maintaining of action on it, where the evidence showed that there was no agreement requiring it to be left at such bank and that the failure to so place it was not the cause of its nonpayment when due. *Paolella v. Brunner*.............................. 677

Certainty:

As to amount or extent of damages, see DAMAGES, 1.

Certiorari:

Cessation of Controversy:

On appeal, see APPEAL AND ERROR, 6.

Challenge:

To juror, see JURY.

Change:

Of name of paper, see NEWSPAPERS, 2.

Change of Venue:

Of civil actions, see VENUE.

Character:

Of accused as evidence, see CRIMINAL LAW, 11.
Previous chaste character of female, see RAPE.
Of witness, see WITNESSES, 7.

Charge:

To jury in criminal prosecutions, see CRIMINAL LAW, 2, 20, 25, 26.
To jury in civil actions, see TRIAL, 1, 2.

Charter:

Powers conferred on park commissioners by, see MUNICIPAL COR-
PORATIONS, 15.

Chattel Liens:

See LIENS.

Chattel Mortgages:

Review of order denying temporary injunction to restrain sale on
foreclosure, see CERTIORARI.

Collusion:

Between parties to divorce, see DIVORCE, 2.

Comment:

On evidence by judge, see CRIMINAL LAW, 17.

Commitment:

Errors and irregularities as to giving right to discharge, see HABEAS CORPUS, 1.

Transfer of prisoners, see REFORMATORIES.

Community Property:

See HUSBAND AND WIFE.

Compensation:

Pecuniary compensation for injuries caused by unlawful acts of another, see DAMAGES.

For property taken for public use, see EMINENT DOMAIN, 2.

Attorney's fees on settlement of estate, see EXECUTORS AND ADMINISTRATORS, 5.

Of executor or administrator, see EXECUTORS AND ADMINISTRATORS, 6.

For use of money, see INTEREST.

Review of award by industrial insurance commission to injured workman, see MASTER AND SERVANT, 7-9.

Of civil service employee on reinstatement, see MUNICIPAL CORPORATIONS, 6.

Time of taking effect of Soldiers' Compensation Act, see STATUTES, 3.

Competency:

Of evidence in civil actions, see EVIDENCE, 2, 3, 5.

Of witnesses in general, see WITNESSES, 1-4.

Complaint:

In civil action, see PLEADING.

Compromise and Settlement:

Property settlement by parties to divorce, see DIVORCE, 8, 9,

Conclusion:

Of witness, see EVIDENCE, 6.

Condemnation:

Taking of property for public use, see EMINENT DOMAIN.

Condition:

Precedent to action on note, see BILLS AND NOTES.

Precedent to action by seller for damages, see SALES, 5.

Conditional Sales:

See SALES, 10.

Conditions:

In lease, construction, see LANDLORD AND TENANT, 1.

Conduct of Counsel:

Review of rulings as dependent on presentation of objections in record, see APPEAL AND ERROR, 12.

Confirmation:

Of organization of irrigation district, see WATERS AND WATER COURSES, 7-9.

Consent:

Of owner to condemnation, see EMINENT DOMAIN, 1.
Of owner as affecting right to lien, see LIENS.

Consideration:

Of contract in general, see CONTRACTS, 2.

Constitutional Law:

Jurisdiction of particular courts, see COURTS.
Compulsory process to compel attendance of witnesses, see CRIMINAL LAW, 18.

1. CONSTITUTIONAL LAW (39)—STATUTES (2-3)—LEGISLATIVE POWERS —ACTS — TIME OF TAKING EFFECT — DETERMINATION OF EMERGENCY. The Administrative Code (Laws 1921, p. 9, ch. 7) is not subject to referendum under Art. 2, § 1, of the state constitution as amended; in view of the emergency clause which recites that the revenues of the state are insufficient to support the state government and its existing public institutions and that it is necessary that the existing administrative agencies of the state government be consolidated and coordinated in order to bring the cost of supporting the state government and its existing institutions within the possible revenue of the state; which is a statement of fact, which the court cannot, from its judicial knowledge, say does not exist. *State ex rel. Short v. Hinkle* 1

2. SAME. In a mandamus proceeding to compel the secretary of state to submit to referendum a legislative act reciting an emergency for its taking effect immediately, the court is without power to grant the writ, in view of the presumption of verity attaching to the legislative declaration of emergency, unless it can say from judicial knowledge that a patent contradiction exists upon the face of the enactment sufficient in law or in reason to justify the court's denial of the declaration of emergency. *State ex rel. Short v. Hinkle* 1

3. SAME. A legislative act is properly one for the support of the government, if its purpose is to give the government and its existing public institutions the greatest benefit from the revenues which are

Construction:

Of contracts, see CONTRACTS, 2.
Of highway contract, see HIGHWAYS, 1.
Of insurance contract, see INSURANCE.
Of conditions in lease, see LANDLORD AND TENANT, 1.
Of building ordinance, see MUNICIPAL CORPORATIONS, 2-5.
Of contract of sale, see SALES, 2.

Contempt:

Restraining contempt proceedings, see PROHIBITION, 2.
Bias of judge as authorizing change of venue, see VENUE, 2.

Continuance:

Presumptions in absence of showing made by defendant in record, see APPEAL AND ERROR, 7.
In criminal prosecutions, see CRIMINAL LAW, 16.
Demand for on allowance of amendment, see PLEADING, 2.

Continuance—Continued.

1. CONTINUANCE (4)—PENDENCY OF OTHER ACTION—ISSUE NOT DEPENDENT ON OUTCOME. In an action for damages for failure to prosecute and pay the costs of an appeal from the Federal district court to the circuit court of appeals, it is proper to deny a continuance pending the outcome of litigation in the Federal court to quiet title to certain lands. *Hays v. Sumpter Lumber Co* 90

Contractors:

On public work, see HIGHWAYS, 1.

Liability of United States mail carrier for motor vehicle tax, see LICENSES.

Contracts:

Agreement to arbitrate, see ARBITRATION AND AWARD.

For purchase of corporate stock, see CORPORATIONS, 5.

Damage for breach, see DAMAGES, 1.

Property settlement by parties to divorce, see DIVORCE, 8, 9.

Agreements within statute of frauds, see FRAUDS, STATUTE OF.

For construction or repair of roads, see HIGHWAYS, 1.

Of insurance in general, see INSURANCE.

Employment, see MASTER AND SERVANT, 1.

Sales of personalty, see SALES.

Shipping articles, see SEAMEN.

Stipulation in actions, see STIPULATIONS.

1. CONTRACTS (40)—VALIDITY—STATUTES—LEVER ACT. The Lever Food Control Act fixing a minimum price for wheat is not a prohibition against sales at a price in excess thereof. *Jones-Scott Co. v. Ellensburg Milling Co* 266

2. CONTRACTS (66)—LANDLORD AND TENANT (15)—LEASE—CONSTRUING INSTRUMENTS TOGETHER. An agreement for renewal of a lease, bearing same date as the lease and making reference to that instrument, must be considered as a part of the leasing agreement and supported by the same consideration; the fact that the renewal agreement was not acknowledged until five days after the date of the lease being immaterial. *Spotts v. Westlake Garage Co* 255

Contribution:

1. CONTRIBUTION (4)—PERSONS ENTITLED. Where a joint purchase of harvesting machinery on deferred payments was made by two farmers, and thereafter, under an alleged agreement between them, one was released from liability by the seller, the payment by the other of the balance due to the seller would not entitle the payor to contribution against his copurchaser. *Pettijohn v. Ray* 136

Contributory Negligence:

Of driver of automobile, see HIGHWAYS, 3, 4.

In adopting method of work, see MASTER AND SERVANT, 6.

Contributory Negligence—Continued.

Of person struck by automobile, see MUNICIPAL CORPORATIONS, 12.

Of driver of auto in colliding with light pole, see MUNICIPAL CORPORATIONS, 13.

In failure to protect property from damage, see NEGLIGENCE, 2.

Of person on or near track, see RAILROADS, 1.

Conveyances:

Of personalty as security for debt, see CHATTEL MORTGAGES.

By corporations, see CORPORATIONS, 11.

In fraud of creditors, see FRAUDULENT CONVEYANCES.

Convicts:

Transfer of prisoners, see REFORMATORIES.

Corporations:

See MUNICIPAL CORPORATIONS.

Competency of evidence of value of stock, see EVIDENCE, 2.

1. CORPORATIONS (26, 27)—BY-LAWS—AMENDMENT. A by-law of a corporation, discriminating, within reasonable limits, respecting dividends payable to stockholders who deal with the corporation and thereby increase its profits, and those who do not deal with it, is a valid exercise of corporate power. *Farrier v. Ritzville Warehouse Co.* 522

2. SAME (28)—CAPITAL STOCK—REDUCTION. Under a contract providing for the sale of mining claims to a corporation, all of the stock of which except a certain number of shares given the claim owners was to be sold and the proceeds turned over to them, the stock, pending sales, being deposited in bank as a pledge for the purchase price, there was no diminution of the capital stock or assets, within the prohibition of Rem. Code, § 3697, where no stock had been issued which was not paid for, and nothing was taken out of the assets to pay for the stock. *Turner v. Tjosevig-Kennecott Copper Co.* 223

3. CORPORATIONS (46)—STOCK SUBSCRIPTIONS—ACTIONS ON—AMENDMENTS. A subscriber to the capital stock of a banking corporation would not be released by the amendment of its articles of incorporation so as to change its name and increase its capital stock for the purpose of absorbing the assets and assuming the liabilities of another bank, since such amendment did not end the corporate existence of the original bank. *German-American Mercantile Bank v. Foster* 313

4. SAME (46). An error in judgment on the part of the bank examiner in permitting one bank to absorb another, resulting in loss to the former, would not constitute a defense against the liability of a nonassenting stockholder in an action to recover on his subscrip-

Corporations—Continued.

sumed the assets and liabilities of his business, a note executed by him as officer of the corporation in renewal of a personal note given by him while conducting the business as an individual is binding on the corporation. *Olympia National Bank v. Murphy Motor Car Co.* 695

11. CORPORATIONS (172) — PROPERTY AND CONVEYANCES — DISPOSAL OF CORPORATE ASSETS. A transfer of all the property of a corporation by its officers and some of its stockholders to a trustee to be by him transferred to a new corporation on its organization would not defeat the right of dissenting or omitted stockholders to sue the purchasing company for the value of the stock. *Wunsch v. Consolidated Laundry Co.* 44

12. CORPORATIONS (195)—ACTIONS—VENUE—TRANSACTION OF BUSINESS. Where a trust company in the course of its business acquired by foreclosure fruit land in another county which it was compelled to cultivate until able to dispose of it, such cultivation would not constitute the transaction of its ordinary or customary business in such county, and hence it would not be liable to suit therein under Rem. Code, § 206, providing that "an action against a corporation may be brought in any county where the corporation transacts business." *State ex rel. American Savings Bank & Trust Co. v. Superior Court* 122

Costs:

1. COSTS (24)—SECURITY—CHARACTER OF PARTIES—ANCILLARY PROCEEDINGS. A petition for the modification of a divorce decree being an ancillary proceeding and not an original action, would not subject petitioner to the operation of Rem. Code, §§ 495, requiring non-resident litigants to furnish security for costs. *Smith v. Frates* 108

2. COSTS (48)—REFEREE'S FEES. An allowance of a referee's fees as costs under a statute therefor does not deprive a litigant of any constitutional right, inasmuch as costs are a part of the burden of litigation. *Daniel v. Daniel* 82

3. SAME (88)—REMEDIES FOR COLLECTION—STAY OF SUBSEQUENT PROCEEDINGS. A motion for a stay of proceedings upon a petition for the modification of a divorce decree until petitioner should satisfy the costs in the divorce action was properly denied where it was shown that she was wholly unable to satisfy them. *Smith v. Frates* 108

Counties:

Establishment of drains, see DRAINS.
Condemnation of property for road, see EMINENT DOMAIN, 1.
Mandamus to control acts of county board, see MANDAMUS.
Injuries to riparian rights, see NAVIGABLE WATERS.

Counties—Continued.

County Board:

Courts:

1. COURTS (2)—JURISDICTION—NATURE AND SOURCE. Const., art. 4,
§ 6, defining the jurisdiction of the superior courts, does not purport
to control the manner in which such courts shall exercise jurisdiction, but this is left as a prerogative of the courts and of the law-
making power, which can be lawfully exercised in any manner
which the constitution does not directly prohibit. *Daniel v. Daniel*
.... 82

Credibility:

Criminal Law:

Criminal Law—Continued.

Criminal Law—Continued.

Criminal Law—Continued.

Criminal Law—Continued.

Daily Papers:

What constitutes, see Newspapers.

Damages:

1. Damages (3, 106)—Certainty as to Amount—Evidence—Admissibility. Upon an issue as to damages through an architect's breach of contract in the preparation of plans and specifications for a hospital building, which could not be constructed within the estimate, an item of damages in the sum of $1,000 for costs of excavating the basement for the building, prior to discovery of inability to bring the expense of construction within the estimate, was properly withdrawn from the jury, where the excavation also included a cesspool and a long drain leading thereto, which were not included in the plans, and the defendants were unable to segregate the cost of the cesspool and drain items from the excavation. *Nevins v. Scace* 215

2. Damages (80)—Personal Injuries—Excessive Verdict. In an action for personal injuries, a verdict for $1,185 for pain, suffering and shock, $958.33 for permanent injuries; $534 for loss of time, and $122 for medical and hospital expenses, was not excessive, where it appeared plaintiff was seriously injured, the skin and flesh from his forehead were lacerated to the bone and hung down over his eyes, he was delirious for some time, remained in the hospital ten days, suffered severe mental shock and his neck was probably permanently injured. *Kaufman v. Sickman* 672

3. Damages (86)—Inadequate Damages—Injury to Arm. Damages to plaintiff in the sum of $4,000 for the loss of his right arm about six inches below the shoulder should be increased to $7,500, where the evidence showed he was twenty-three years of age, an experienced woodsman who during six years had earned from $4.40 to $9.00 per day, and in recent farm work had earned from $5.00 to $8.00 per day. *Barney v. Anderson* 352

4. Damages (88)—Excessive—Injury to Leg. A verdict for $10,000, for injuries to plaintiff's leg, about five inches above the ankle, for which he was in the hospital sixty-eight days and the leg was rendered about one-half inch short, with a slight backward bow, was excessive, and should be reduced to $5,000. *O'Brien v. Griffiths & Sprague Stevedoring Co.* 302

Dentists:

Malpractice, see PHYSICIANS AND SURGEONS.

Deposits:

In bank, see BANKS AND BANKING.

Of note in bank as condition precedent to action, see BILLS AND NOTES.

Set-off of debt of decedent against deposit in bank, see EXECUTORS AND ADMINISTRATORS, 2-4.

Desertion:

Of ship by seamen, see SEAMEN.

Devise:

See WILLS.

Disbarment:

Of attorney, see ATTORNEY AND CLIENT, 1-4.

Discharge:

On habeas corpus, see HABEAS CORPUS, 2.

Discretion:

Review of discretion of city council, see INJUNCTION, 3.

Mandamus to control acts involving discretion of officers, see MANDAMUS.

Discretion of Court:

Presumptions as to proper exercise of in refusing to grant continuance, see APPEAL AND ERROR, 7.

Continuance, see CRIMINAL LAW, 16.

Vacation of default decree, see DIVORCE, 3.

Discrimination:

Special privileges or immunities and class legislation, see CONSTITUTIONAL LAW, 6, 7.

Dismissal and Nonsuit:

Dismissal of appeal for failure of parties of record to appear below, see APPEAL AND ERROR, 4.

Right of parties to dismiss action without consulting attorneys, see ATTORNEY AND CLIENT, 5.

Districts:

Drainage districts, see DRAINS.

Irrigation districts, see WATERS AND WATER COURSES, 5-13.

Diversion:

Of use of city park, see MUNICIPAL CORPORATIONS, 14.

Of water course, see WATERS AND WATER COURSES, 1, 2.

Dividends:

On corporate stock, see CORPORATIONS, 1, 6, 7.

Division:

Of property on divorce, see DIVORCE, 4, 5.

Divorce:

Appealability of order modifying order awarding custody of child, see APPEAL AND ERROR, 3, 6.

Costs on petition for modification of decree, security for, see COSTS, 1.

Divorce—Continued.

Domicile:

As affecting community nature of property, see HUSBAND AND WIFE, 1.

Of parties as affecting venue, see VENUE, 1.

Draft:

Purchase of as creating special deposit, see BANKS AND BANKING.

Drains:

1. DRAINS (4-1)—ESTABLISHMENT BY CITIES—AREA LYING WITHIN CORPORATE LIMITS. The power to establish diking and drainage districts within the corporate limits of cities and towns being conferred by Rem. Code, §§ 4120 and 4162, the county commissioners have no authority, under the powers granted by Id., § 4226-1 *et seq.* as amended and supplemented by Ch. 130, Laws 1917, p. 517, to create such a district where the territory to be included lies wholly within the corporate limits of a city. *Weatherwax v. Grays Harbor County* 212

Earnings:

Dividends on corporate stock, see CORPORATIONS, 1, 6, 7.

Of husband and wife, see HUSBAND AND WIFE, 2, 3.

Election:

To take under will or statute, see WILLS, 3.

Election of Remedies:

1. ELECTION OF REMEDIES (3)—ACTS CONSTITUTING ELECTION—MISTAKE IN REMEDY. There was no election of remedies by a purchaser's action to recover from the seller the price of a car, wrongfully sold by the seller's agent, who was clothed with apparent authority to sell, which would bar plaintiff's subsequent action of replevin against defendant, who had seized the car as his own; since the doctrine of election of remedies applies only in case of the pursuit of inconsistent remedies against the same party and not in case of a mistake in originally bringing action against the wrong party. *Harris v. Northwest Motor Co* 412

Elections:

For bond issue for irrigation district, see WATERS AND WATER COURSES, 5-10.

Emergency:

Legislative acts, time of taking effect, see CONSTITUTIONAL LAW, 1-4.

Eminent Domain:

Taking of property within police power, see CONSTITUTIONAL LAW, 5.

1. EMINENT DOMAIN (42-1)—PROPERTY SUBJECT—CONSENT OF OWNER. Where a county instituted condemnation proceedings to establish a

Eminent Domain—Continued.

Employees:

See MASTER AND SERVANT.

Civil service employees, compensation of, see MUNICIPAL CORPORATIONS, 6.

Encroachment:

On adjoining land, see ADJOINING LANDOWNERS.

Entry:

Townsite entries of public lands, see PUBLIC LANDS.

Equal Protection of Laws:

See CONSTITUTIONAL LAW, 6, 7.

Equitable Estoppel:

See ESTOPPEL.

Equity:

See INJUNCTION.

Equitable action of account, see ACCOUNT.

Reviewability of suits in equity, see APPEAL AND ERROR, 1.

Scope and extent of review in equitable actions, see APPEAL AND ERROR, 14.

Erosion:

Injury to riparian rights, see NAVIGABLE WATERS.

Damages to lands by improvements in channel of stream, see WATERS AND WATER COURSES, 1, 2.

Error of Law:

Ground for vacation of judgment, see JUDGMENT, 1, 2.

Establishment:

Of drains, see DRAINS.

Of irrigation district, see WATERS AND WATER COURSES, 5-10.

Evidence—Continued.

To sustain conviction of lesser offense, see CRIMINAL LAW, 26.

Certainty as to amount of damages, see DAMAGES, 1.

Of cruelty, for divorce, see DIVORCE, 1.

Collusion of parties to divorce, see DIVORCE, 2.

Adequacy of property award on divorce, see DIVORCE, 5.

Condemnation proceedings, see EMINENT DOMAIN, 2.

Estoppel to deny use of roadway, see ESTOPPEL, 1.

Comparison of signatures with alleged forgery, see FORGERY.

For injuries in highway, see HIGHWAYS, 2, 4.

Community or separate character of property, see HUSBAND AND
WIFE, 3.

In prosecution for criminal syndicalism, see INSURRECTION.

In prosecution for being jointist, see INTOXICATING LIQUORS, 6.

In action for malicious prosecution, see MALICIOUS PROSECUTION.

Employment and relation, see MASTER AND SERVANT, 1, 11.

Proximate cause of death of employee, see MASTER AND SERVANT, 10.

For injuries to servant, see MASTER AND SERVANT, 11.

Of negligent driving of automobile, see MUNICIPAL CORPORATIONS,
11, 12.

In action for death of child in swimming pool, see NEGLIGENCE, 4, 5.

Verdict or findings contrary to evidence, see NEW TRIAL.

In action to enjoin construction of reservoir as nuisance, see
NUISANCE, 1-3.

Existence of partnership, see PARTNERSHIP.

To prove fact of agency, see PRINCIPAL AND AGENT, 1-3.

Authority of agent, see PRINCIPAL AND AGENT, 4-6.

Previous chaste character of female, see RAPE, 2.

To sustain excuse for failure to deliver goods, see SALES, 6.

Of excessive tax, see TAXATION, 2.

Damage to real property, see TRESPASS.

Mistake, undue influence, or fraud in making or procuring will, see
WILLS, 2.

Competency, attendance, credibility and examination of witnesses,
see WITNESSES.

1. EVIDENCE (2)—JUDICIAL NOTICE—WORDS OF COMMON MEANING—
"SABOTAGE." A court may take judicial notice of the meaning of
the word "sabotage," though a statute relating to the offense does
not expressly define it. *State v. McLennen* 612

2. EVIDENCE (48)—COMPETENCY—VALUE OF CORPORATE STOCK. In an
action to recover the value of stock in an old corporation all the
property of which had been transferred to a new corporation, under
an agreement for an issue of new stock "dollar for dollar," evidence
of the value of the stock in the new corporation was admissible
as tending to show the value of the stock of the old corporation.
Wunsch v. Consolidated Laundry Co 44

Evidence—Continued.

Executors and Administrators:

1. EXECUTORS AND ADMINISTRATORS (1, 29½)—NECESSITY OF ADMINIS-
TRATION—ADMINISTRATORS DE BONIS NON. Where an executor for an
estate died after eighteen years of incumbency without having
closed and procured distribution of the estate, nor given the notice
to creditors ordered by the court at the time of his appointment, the
court had jurisdiction to appoint an administrator *de bonis non* with
the will annexed; since creditors of the estate had not been conclusively barred; and Rem. Code, § 1368, providing nonliability of an
estate for debts unless letters of administration be granted within
six years after death of the decedent is inapplicable in view of the
actual appointment of an executor. *In re Curtis' Estate*...... 237

2. EXECUTORS AND ADMINISTRATORS (146) — SET-OFF AND COUNTER-
CLAIM—PRESENTATION OF CLAIM. The right of a bank under Rem.
Code, § 268, to set off the debt of a decedent to it against the deposit of the decedent in the bank would not in any way be affected
or altered by the fact that the bank deposit of the decedent had
been shifted to the name of his personal representative prior to the
assertion of the set-off. *In re Adler's Estate*.................... 484

3. SAME (146) — BANKS AND BANKING (22)—DEPOSITS—SET-OFF—
APPLICATION OF DEPOSITS TO DEBTS DUE BANK. Under Rem. Code,
§§ 266, 268, a right of set-off against an executor who brings action
upon a claim due the deceased exists without the presentation of
any claim under the statute of non-claim; and the statute of non-
claim requiring an action on a rejected claim within thirty days
does not apply, although a claim was presented and rejected on the
set-off demanded before suit by the executor. *In re Adler's Estate*
.... 484

4. SAME (146) — BANKS AND BANKING (22) — DEPOSITS — SET-OFF.
Where a personal representative continued the bank account of her
decedent, had it changed to her own name, and deposited in the account funds coming to her as administratrix, the right of the bank
to set off against the deposit a debt of the decedent to it would not
extend beyond the amount of the deposit at the time of the debtor's
death. *In re Adler's Estate*................................. 484

5. EXECUTORS AND ADMINISTRATORS (160, 167) — FINAL ACCOUNT —
ADDITIONAL COMPENSATION—ATTORNEY'S FEES—TIME FOR APPLICATION.
The failure of an executor, upon the hearing in the trial court of
exceptions to his final account, to present testimony as to the reasonable additional compensation due him on account of the employment of an attorney to resist the exceptions, which were sustained

Executors and Administrators—Continued.

Exemptions:

False Representations:

Fees:

Filing:

Fires:

Floods:

Food:

Forfeiture:

Forgery:

Forgery—Continued.

1. FORGERY (7) — EVIDENCE — ADMISSIBILITY. In a prosecution for forgery, written instruments signed by defendant, which were in no way connected with the crime charged, were properly introducible in evidence for the purpose of comparing her signatures with the alleged forgery. *State v. McDonald*.................. 668

Former Adjudication:

As bar to action, see JUDGMENT, 3.

Former Jeopardy:

Bar to prosecution, see CRIMINAL LAW, 5-7.

Fraud:

Receiving deposits after insolvency, see BANKS AND BANKING, 1.

In property settlement by parties to divorce, see DIVORCE, 8.

In sale of personalty, see SALES, 3.

In levy of assessment for irrigation district, see WATERS AND WATER COURSES, 13.

Frauds, Statute of:

1. FRAUDS, STATUTE OF (18) — CONTRACT TO DEVISE — PERFORMANCE. An oral promise to make a will in favor of another is enforcible, if founded upon a valuable consideration and deliberately entered into by the deceased, where there has been a full or partial performance of the contract on the part of the promisee; but it must be supported by the strongest evidence of a valuable consideration. *Andrews v. Andrews*.. 513

2. FRAUDS, STATUTE OF (44)—OPERATION OF STATUTE—MODIFICATION OF LEASE. Under the rule that a contract required by law to be in writing cannot be modified by parol, excepting that an oral modification which has been performed may be set up as a defense, in an action on a farming lease requiring a portion of the crop to be paid as rental, the lessee cannot prove a verbal modification of the lease tending to reduce the rental, where there was no showing of anything done in performance of such alleged oral modification. *McInnis v. Watson* 680

Fraudulent Conveyances:

1. FRAUDULENT CONVEYANCES (16)—PROPERTY TRANSFERRED—EXEMPT PROPERTY. Grain needed for stock and seed by a farmer and householder, being exempt from attachment or levy and sale on execution under Rem. Code, § 563, could be transferred to a creditor to apply on indebtedness to him, free from the lien of attachment or execution levy. *Cummings v. Erickson*...................... 347

Funds:

Of irrigation district, see WATERS AND WATER COURSES, 9.

Gambling:

Devices prohibited, see GAMING.

Gaming:

1. GAMING (10)—DEVICES PROHIBITED—SLOT MACHINES. A machine known as a "silent salesman," containing 3,000 tickets purchasable for five cents each as they appear in the slots of the machine, the large majority of which entitle the purchaser to nothing more than a postal card of the value of one cent, some few of the tickets entitling the purchaser to articles of merchandise of considerably more value, is a gaming device within the inhibition of the Seattle ordinances and the statutes of the state against gaming devices. *Dwyer & Co. v. Seattle* 449

Garnishment:

Notice of appeal by garnishee alone, see APPEAL AND ERROR, 9.

Habeas Corpus:

1. HABEAS CORPUS (8-1) — GROUNDS — CORRECTION OF ERROR. Mere error on the part of the board of directors of the Women's Industrial Home and Clinic, committed in the exercise of acknowledged power to make transfers of inmates to the state prison, is not subject to review in habeas corpus proceedings. *In re Canary* 569

2. HABEAS CORPUS (21, 24, 25) — PROCEEDINGS—JUDGMENT—DISPOSITION OF PERSON — DISCHARGE. On an original application in the supreme court for a writ of habeas corpus directed to the officer who has a petitioner in custody, that court, being without authority to direct by mandate the proper sentence to be rendered, should order the officer having the petitioner in charge to take her before the court in which she was convicted for a proper sentence, and that she should be discharged if no further action be taken by the lower court. *In re Williamson* 560

Harmless Error:

In civil actions, see APPEAL AND ERROR, 20.
In criminal prosecutions, see CRIMINAL LAW, 23, 24.

Hearsay:

In criminal prosecutions, see CRIMINAL LAW, 12-14.
In civil actions, see EVIDENCE, 5; SALES, 6.

Highways:

1. HIGHWAYS (33) — CONSTRUCTION — CONTRACTS — RESERVE FUND. Under a contract between the state and a contractor for the construction of a highway pursuant to Rem. Code, §§ 5867-5878, which does not authorize the retention of a percentage of the contract price for the protection of those supplying labor and material, no trust fund is created in favor of the latter by the provisions of the

Highways—Continued.

tripped and received the injuries complained of when a companion with whom she was walking stepped upon one end of a board which had become loose from the stringer to which it had been defectively nailed; that this board had been in such condition for a long time, and the defective condition of the walk was known, or by the exercise of reasonable care should have been known by defendant; and that the defective condition of the sidewalk was due to the carelessness and negligence of defendant. *Nordstrom v. Zindorf*.... 468

Husband and Wife:

Divorce and judicial separation, see DIVORCE.

1. HUSBAND AND WIFE (45)—COMMUNITY PROPERTY—WHAT LAW GOVERNS — PROPERTY ACQUIRED IN ANOTHER STATE. Personal property acquired in another state by one of the spouses of a community composed of husband and wife domiciled in this state is presumptively community property, and hence not liable for the separate debt of one of the spouses; the fact that the law where the property was acquired would make it separate property not affecting its status in this jurisdiction. *Snyder v. Stringer*....................... 131

2. HUSBAND AND WIFE (57) — COMMUNITY PROPERTY — EARNINGS OF HUSBAND AND WIFE. Property to be acquired by a husband under a contract for its devise in return for services rendered would be community property and not be in the nature of a gift, within the meaning of Rem. Code, § 5915, declaring that property and pecuniary rights acquired by a husband "by gift, bequest, devise, or descent" shall constitute his separate property. *Andrews v. Andrews* 513

3. HUSBAND AND WIFE (58, 60)—COMMUNITY PROPERTY—PRESUMPTION —EVIDENCE—SUFFICIENCY. The presumption of the community character of property acquired during coverture is not overcome by a showing that the separate property and community earnings of the spouses were commingled in the acquisition of what is claimed as community property. *In re Curtis' Estate*..................... 237

Identity:

Of offense under plea of former jeopardy, see CRIMINAL LAW, 7.

Impeachment:

Of witnesses, see WITNESSES, 5, 7, 8.

Implied Repeal:

Of statute, see INTOXICATING LIQUORS, 4; STATUTES, 1.

Imprisonment:

Of convicts on failure to make appropriation for maintenance of penal institution, see STATES.

Injunction—Continued.

2. INJUNCTION (11) — GROUNDS FOR RELIEF — DEFENSES — INCONVEN-
IENCE TO PUBLIC. An injunction will not issue to restrain the construction and maintenance of a reservoir for the storage of water
for domestic use, though based upon evidence of the fears of apprehended injuries to the persons or property of adjoining owners,
where the weight of the evidence shows that such apprehended injuries are not the necessary or probable results of the maintenance
of the reservoir (Overruled on rehearing). *Ferry v. Seattle.*. 648

3. INJUNCTION (30) — PROCEEDINGS OF CITY COUNCIL — VALIDITY OF
ORDINANCE—REVIEW. Where a city council acts in good faith upon
a matter within the scope of its authority, its exercise of discretion
will not be controlled by injunction by a court of equity, in the absence of fraud. *Ferry v. Seattle*............................. 648

Insolvency:

Receiving deposits after insolvency, see BANKS AND BANKING, 1.

Inspection:

Of property before purchase, see SALES, 3.

Instructions:

Review of rulings as dependent on specification of error in brief,
see APPEAL AND ERROR, 13.
In criminal prosecutions, see CRIMINAL LAW, 2, 20, 25, 26; INTOXI-
CATING LIQUORS, 7; RAPE.
In civil actions, see TRIAL, 1, 2.

Insurance:

1. INSURANCE (122) — INDEMNITY INSURANCE—CONTRACT—CONSTRUC-
TION—LIABILITY. A policy of casualty insurance issued to an automobile owner, which provided that the insurer would defend him
against suits for damages, and also that no action would lie against
the insurer under the policy unless brought by and in the name of
the insured for loss actually sustained and paid in money by him
in satisfaction of a judgment after actual trial of the issue, constitutes an indemnity and not a liability policy, against which there
could be no recourse by a person injured by the assured (Overruling
Davies v. Maryland Cas. Co., 89 Wash. 571). *Luger v. Windell.*. 375

Insurrection:

1. INSURRECTION—CRIMINAL SYNDICALISM—EVIDENCE—ADMISSIBILITY.
In a prosecution for criminal syndicalism, witnesses may testify as
to statements, speeches, and declarations made by members of the
I. W. W. organization, or in their presence, at recognized meetings
or assemblages of the organization in their various headquarters,
or in such places and on such occasions as are proven to have received the sanction of the organization; and may also testify as

Jeopardy:

Former jeopardy bar to prosecution, see CRIMINAL LAW, 5-7.

Jitneys:

Regulation of by city as denial of equal protection of laws, see CONSTITUTIONAL LAW, 6, 7.

Regulation of by city, see MUNICIPAL CORPORATIONS, 8-10.

Joinder:

Of codefendants in peremptory challenges, see JURY.

Joint Adventures:

See PARTNERSHIP.

Jointist:

Sufficiency of information, see INTOXICATING LIQUORS, 5.

Sufficiency of evidence, see INTOXICATING LIQUORS, 6.

Judges:

Conduct of judge in criminal trial, see CRIMINAL LAW, 17.

Conduct of judge in civil trial, see TRIAL, 3.

Change of, see VENUE, 2.

Judgment:

Review in general, see APPEAL AND ERROR.

Effect of motion to vacate judgment on time to appeal, see APPEAL AND ERROR, 8.

Supersedeas or stay pending appeal, see APPEAL AND ERROR, 10.

On appeal, see APPEAL AND ERROR, 17.

Powers of lower court on remand of cause on appeal, see APPEAL AND ERROR, 21.

Vacation of divorce decree, see DIVORCE, 2, 3.

Conclusiveness of divorce decree as to property rights, see DIVORCE, 4.

1. JUDGMENT (106)—VACATION—ERROR OF LAW. Error of the court in applying the law to the facts, in making a decree of final distribution of an estate under the provisions of Rem. Code, § 1341, would constitute an "error of law"; and no distinction can be drawn between judgments in probate and other civil actions, nor from the fact that an administratrix procured the decree exactly in the form she asked it. *In re Jones' Estate*............................ 424

2. SAME (106). Under the settled practice of this state not to vacate judgments for error of law that could be corrected on appeal, petition for the vacation of a judgment for error of law, discovered too late to be used on appeal, will not be entertained by the court, though apparently sanctioned by Rem. Code, §§ 303, 464, 465. *In Jones' Estate* 42

Judgment—Continued.

Judicial Notice:

See EVIDENCE, 1.

Judicial Power:

Encroachment on legislature, see CONSTITUTIONAL LAW, 1-4.

Jurisdiction:

Jury:

Justices of the Peace:

Knowledge:

Of agent's authority, see PRINCIPAL AND AGENT, 4.

Laches:

As ground for estoppel, see ESTOPPEL, 2.
As affecting right to injunction, see INJUNCTION, 1.

Landlord and Tenant:

Construction of lease, see CONTRACTS, 2.
Requirements of statute of frauds as to leases, see FRAUDS, STATUTE
OF, 2.

1.   LANDLORD AND TENANT (15)—LEASE—CONSTRUCTION AND OPERA-
TION—CONDITIONS. A condition in a lease requiring the lessees to
deliver a bond in the sum of $5,000 as security for the performance
of its terms was waived by the acceptance of $1,000 in lieu thereof,
which sum was to be returned on the substitution of $2,400 in stock
of the corporation to be formed by the lessees, and on tender of the
stock the lessor said he did not care for it, that he had used the
$1,000, and asked that the sum be applied on the rent, and at no
time thereafter during the term of the lease ever demanded the delivery of the $5,000 bond. *Spotts v. Westlake Garage Co.*........ 255

2.   SAME (15). The failure of a lessee to pay the rent due for certain months under a lease must be deemed waived by a subsequent
agreement modifying rentals for the future, which made no reference to the prior delinquent rent, and hence such failure would not
defeat the lessee's right to renewal of the lease under the agreement
between the parties. *Spotts v. Westlake Garage Co.*............ 255

3.   SAME (15). Slight damages resulting from alterations or failure
to repair would not defeat the right of a lessee to a renewal of his
lease under an agreement providing therefor at the expiration of
the original term. *Spotts v. Westlake Garage Co.*.............. 255

4.   LANDLORD AND TENANT (30)—EXTENSIONS AND RENEWALS—COVE-
NANT FOR RENEWAL. Under a lease providing for renewal at the expiration of the term at the same rentals paid during the last year of
the term, the lessee is entitled to a renewal at the reduced rental
paid during the last year of his tenancy, under a modification of the
rental terms of the original lease. *Spotts v. Westlake Garage
Co.* 255

Lands:

See PUBLIC LANDS.

Lapse of Time:

As affecting right to appeal, see APPEAL AND ERROR, 6.

Larceny:

Sales of property obtained by larceny, see SALES, 7.

Master and Servant—Continued.

to delegate the duty of operating it to his brother, constituted the latter a vice-principal of defendant, charged with the duty of furnishing plaintiff a reasonably safe place in which to work. *Barney v. Anderson* 352

5. SAME (77). In determining whether an employee occupies the position of vice-principal, the power of superintendence and control is the test, and not the question whether he had authority to employ or discharge workmen. *Barney v. Anderson*.................... 352

6. SAME (113)—CONTRIBUTORY NEGLIGENCE—METHODS OF WORK. The fact that a safer method of oiling a baling machine existed does not establish contributory negligence on the part of plaintiff, where it appears there was no danger in the method pursued until the machine was started without any notice to him by the person under whose order he was working and who negligently took no notice of the situation of plaintiff. *Barney v. Anderson*.............. 352

7. MASTER AND SERVANT (121-2)—WORKMEN'S COMPENSATION—REMEDIES—APPEAL—REVIEW. Under Rem. Code, §§ 6604-5, 6604-20, an award by the industrial insurance commission for an injury, properly classified as "permanent partial disability" not being subject to review by the courts, except for arbitrary or capricious action on its part, an award of $400 will not be disturbed where it appears the commission acted upon the testimony of competent physicians, some of them considering plaintiff's injury to be very severe and probably lasting, while others concluded that his injury was not so severe. *Whipple v. Industrial Insurance Commission*.................... 341

8. MASTER AND SERVANT (121-2)—WORKMEN'S COMPENSATION—AWARD FOR INJURIES—REVIEW. The refusal of the industrial insurance commission to re-open a case and make an increased award cannot be said to be arbitrary and capricious action on its part, where it had taken the injured workman's application into consideration, heard his evidence and that of medical examiners, and reached an adverse conclusion; since "arbitrary and capricious" action within the purview of the statute means wilful and unreasonable action. *Sweitzer v. Industrial Insurance Commission*.................. 398

9. SAME (121-2)—CLASSIFICATION OF INJURIES—DEGREES—REVIEW. Where the industrial insurance commission properly classified a workman's injury as permanent partial disability, the amount of the award based upon a finding as to the degree of the injury is not subject to review by the courts in the absence of a showing that its action in that respect was arbitrary and capricious. *Sweitzer v. Industrial Insurance Commission*............................. 398

10. MASTER AND SERVANT (121-2)—WORKMEN'S COMPENSATION—PROXIMATE CAUSE OF DEATH—EVIDENCE—SUFFICIENCY. A widow is en-

Master and Servant—Continued.

titled to compensation under the workmen's compensation act, where a cut in the foot received by a workman in an extra-hazardous occupation bled profusely, leaving him in a weakened and fainting condition, and after removal to his home, twelve miles distant, in cold and inclement weather, pneumonia developed from which he died; the imprudence of the deceased in exposing himself to the weather in his weakened condition not barring her right, if the axe wound was the proximate cause which directly set in motion a train of events resulting in death. *Anderson v. Industrial Insurance Commission* 421

11. SAME (130-1)—ACTIONS—ADMISSIBILITY OF EVIDENCE—EXISTENCE OF RELATION. A letter written by defendant to the foreman in charge of a hay-baler concerning the delivery of the machine to the foreman's brother for the latter's own use was properly excluded in an action by a servant against defendant for personal injuries due to negligence in the operation of the baler, where the writing of the letter or its subject-matter was in no way, either directly or indirectly, called to the attention of plaintiff. *Barney v. Anderson* 352

Measure of Damages:

For breach of contract of sale, see SALES, 8, 9.

Mechanics' Liens:

See LIENS.

Method of Work:

Contributory negligence in adopting unsafe method of oiling machine, see MASTER AND SERVANT, 6.

Mines and Minerals:

Transfer of mining claims to corporation, see CORPORATIONS, 2, 5, 8.

Misconduct:

Of counsel, necessity of objections or exceptions in record for purpose of review, see APPEAL AND ERROR, 12.
Of trial judge, see CRIMINAL LAW, 17; TRIAL, 3.
Of counsel ground for reversal in criminal prosecutions, see CRIMINAL LAW, 24.

Misrepresentation:

Affecting validity of sale, see SALES, 3.

Mistake:

Affecting validity of election of remedy, see ELECTION OF REMEDIES.
Of officer as inference of malice, see MALICIOUS PROSECUTION, 2.

Modification:

Oral modification of lease, see FRAUDS, STATUTE OF, 2.

Mortgages:

Of personal property, see CHATTEL MORTGAGES.

Motions:

For new trial in civil action, see TRIAL, 4.

Motor Vehicles:

Regulation of jitneys by city as denial of equal protection of laws, see CONSTITUTIONAL LAW, 6, 7.

License tax for, see LICENSES.

Regulation of jitneys in city streets, see MUNICIPAL CORPORATIONS, 8-10.

Municipal Corporations:

Regulation of jitney busses as denial of equal protection of laws, see CONSTITUTIONAL LAW, 6, 7.

Drainage districts, within limits of city, see DRAINS.

Exercise of power of eminent domain, see EMINENT DOMAIN.

Enjoining proceedings of city council, see INJUNCTION, 3.

Enjoining construction of city reservoir, see NUISANCE, 1-3.

Negligence in flooding lands by seepage from reservoir, see WATERS AND WATER COURSES, 4.

1.   MUNICIPAL CORPORATIONS (9)—CLASSIFICATION OF CITIES—ADOPTION OF COMMISSION FORM OF GOVERNMENT—STATUTES—CONSTRUCTION. Under Rem. Code, §§ 7670-1 to 7670-24, providing that cities having a population from 2,500 to 20,000, on adopting a commission form of government, should have the powers of, and be governed by the laws applicable to, second-class cities, a third-class city adopting the commission government did not thereby become a city of the second class, though entitled to such rank by reason of population; since a city can advance from one classification to another only by taking the steps provided in Rem. Code, § 7482 *et seq. State ex rel. Yakima v. Clausen*.. 620

2.   SAME (50)—ORDINANCES—CONSTRUCTION AND OPERATION. The building code of Seattle, providing, in § 1035 of the part relating wholly to "alterations and repairs" of existing buildings, that "nothing in this part shall be construed to prevent the superintendent of buildings from requiring unsafe or dangerous structures to be made safe under the powers granted elsewhere in this code," has a special and limited effect to the control only of alterations and repairs. *Coffin v. Blackwell* 281

3.   SAME (50). The building code of Seattle, § 103, providing that "nothing in the building code shall be construed as requiring that

Municipal Corporations—Continued.

buildings heretofore constructed and equipped must be reconstructed, rearranged or otherwise equipped unless it be by ordinance specially provided," took from the administrative officers of the city all power to require reconstruction or equipment, unless specifically provided by ordinance to that effect. *Coffin v. Blackwell* 281

Municipal Corporations—Continued.

Municipal Corporations—Continued.

unlighted, and it appears plaintiffs were familiar with the surroundings, that, in making a turn and driving slowly in low gear which would enable them to stop within a couple of feet, the car was driven into the pole, the presence of which should have been noted by a careful driver as his front lights swept across it in making the turn. *Luckkart v. Director General of Railroads*........... 690

Names:

Change in name of paper, see NEWSPAPERS, 2.

Navigable Waters:

Bodies and streams of water not capable of navigation, see WATERS AND WATER COURSES.

Necessity:

Of administration of estate, see EXECUTORS AND ADMINISTRATORS, 1.

Negligence:

Inadequate and excessive damages, see DAMAGES, 2-4.
In use of highway, see HIGHWAYS, 2-4.
In maintenance of defective sidewalk, see HIGHWAYS, 5.
Of employers, see MASTER AND SERVANT.
Malpractice by dentist, see PHYSICIANS AND SURGEONS.
In operation of trains, see RAILROADS.
Injuries by flooding land, see WATERS AND WATER COURSES, 4.

Negligence—Continued.

1. NEGLIGENCE (6)—INJURY TO PROPERTY—DUTY TO LICENSEE. Where plaintiff, on a hunting trip, parked his automobile for a period of ten days on government land, in the vicinity of logging operations conducted by defendant under contract with the government, plaintiff was a mere licensee, and not entitled to recover for injuries to his car from being struck by a falling tree which had swerved from the course intended by the faller, there being no evidence of wanton or wilful acts on the latter's part causing the injury. *Waller v. Smith* 645

2. NEGLIGENCE (16, 18) — CONTRIBUTORY NEGLIGENCE — NATURE AND ELEMENTS—CARE REQUIRED AS TO USE OF PROPERTY. The fact that a property owner knew or suspected that the negligence of another might cause damage to his property and made no effort to counteract it, would not constitute contributory negligence on his part, since the rule of personal conduct which requires one to make a reasonable effort to protect his person from the known negligence of another does not extend to the use of property. *North Bend Lumber Co. v. Seattle* 500

3. NEGLIGENCE (23) — IMPUTED NEGLIGENCE — RIDER OF BICYCLE. Where two boys engaged in the joint enterprise of covering a newspaper route which belonged to one of them, but in which he was sometimes assisted by the other, were both riding the same bicycle, the owner on the cross-bar and his friend in the seat and controlling its guidance, the negligence of the latter in colliding with an automobile while coasting down a street is attributable to the other. *Masterson v. Leonard* 551

4. NEGLIGENCE (35)—ACTIONS—EVIDENCE—PREVIOUS ACCIDENTS—ADMISSIBILITY. In an action for damages for the death of a young child in a swimming pool, alleged as due to the negligence of the attendant to reasonably observe the movements of those using the pool, evidence of previous accidents therein is inadmissible. *Corum v. Blomquist* 196

5. NEGLIGENCE (38)—ACTIONS—EVIDENCE—SUFFICIENCY. In an action for damages for the death by drowning of a minor son in a swimming pool, operated by defendants, a motion for nonsuit was properly denied, where, upon an issue as to whether defendant furnished a reasonably attentive and competent attendant, the evidence showed that the boy while using the pool was missing from ten to fifteen minutes without his absence being noted, and when brought out of the water breathed a few times under manual manipulation. *Corum v. Blomquist* 196

Negotiable Instruments:
See BILLS AND NOTES.

Newly Discovered Evidence:
Ground for new trial, see CRIMINAL LAW, 21.

Newspapers:

New Trial:

Notes:

Notice:

Nuisance:

Nuisance—Continued.

Objections:

Occupation:

Officers:

Opinion Evidence:

Oral Contracts:

Physicians and Surgeons—Continued.

testimony that the tooth was loose, and that the bridge could not be removed without extracting the tooth to which it was attached. *Pedersen v. Norris*.. 338

2. SAME (12)—INSTRUCTIONS. In an action for damages for negligently extracting a tooth where there was conflicting evidence as to its soundness, a requested instruction, that "if said tooth was diseased, then I charge you . . . the extraction was a benefit to the plaintiff and not a damage," was properly refused, since it would not follow as a matter of fact or of law that a tooth which was diseased or not sound should be extracted. *Pedersen v. Norris* 338

Place:

Of payment of note, see BILLS AND NOTES.

Residence of parties to action as affecting venue, see VENUE, 1.

Pleading:

Review of rulings as dependent on prejudicial nature of error, see APPEAL AND ERROR, 20.

Complaint for injury from fall on defective sidewalk, see HIGHWAYS, 5.

In action to recover assessment paid to irrigation district, see WATERS AND WATER COURSES, 13.

1. PLEADING (14)—ALLEGATIONS INCONSISTENT WITH WRITTEN INSTRUMENTS. Where a cause of action is pleaded as being founded upon certain contracts which are set out, the pleadings must give way to the contrary provisions of the contract. *Turner v. Tjosevig-Kennecott Copper Co*.. 223

2. SAME (109) — CONDITION OF CAUSE — ASKING CONTINUANCE. The amendment of a complaint in the course of a trial cannot be claimed as prejudicial on appeal, where defendant did not demand time to prepare to meet the new allegations. *Wunsch v. Consolidated Laundry Co.* 44

3. PLEADING (112) — AMENDMENT OF COMPLAINT — NEW OR DIFFERENT CAUSE OF ACTION. A trial amendment of a complaint, even if it changes the cause of action from one sounding in tort to one sounding in contract, is permissible under the code. *Wunsch v. Consolidated Laundry Co*.. 44

Pledges:

Of corporate stock, see CORPORATIONS, 2, 5, 8.

Police Power:

Of state, see CONSTITUTIONAL LAW, 5.

Of municipality, see MUNICIPAL CORPORATIONS, 7.

Policy:

Of insurance, see INSURANCE.

Population:

As determining classification of city, see MUNICIPAL CORPORATIONS, 1.

Possession:

Illegal possession of liquor, see INTOXICATING LIQUORS, 2-4.

Powers:

Of lower court on remand of cause on appeal, see APPEAL AND ERROR, 21.

Of board of law examiners in disbarment proceedings, see ATTORNEY AND CLIENT, 1, 2.

Of corporation, see CORPORATIONS, 1.

Of corporate officers, see CORPORATIONS, 9, 10.

Of county board, see DRAINS.

Of officers to require alterations in buildings, see MUNICIPAL CORPORATIONS, 2-5.

Of city to regulate jitneys, see MUNICIPAL CORPORATIONS, 8-10.

Legislative powers of city council, see MUNICIPAL CORPORATIONS, 15.

Practice:

See APPEAL AND ERROR; COSTS; DIVORCE; INJUNCTION; PLEADING; PROHIBITION.

Grounds for continuance of action, see CONTINUANCE.

Exercise of jurisdiction, see COURTS.

Vacation of judgment, see JUDGMENT, 1, 2.

Prejudice:

Ground for reversal in civil actions, see APPEAL AND ERROR, 20.

Ground for reversal in criminal prosecution, see CRIMINAL LAW, 23, 24.

Change of judges for, see VENUE, 2.

Premiums:

Priority of claim for industrial insurance premiums, see MASTER AND SERVANT, 3.

Prescription:

See WATERS AND WATER COURSES, 3.

Presentment:

Of claim against estate of decedent, see EXECUTORS AND ADMINISTRATORS, 2, 3.

Presumptions:

On appeal, see APPEAL AND ERROR, 7.

As to community nature of property, see HUSBAND AND WIFE, 1, 3.

As to previous chaste character of female, see RAPE, 2.

Price:

Contracts in violation of statute fixing minimum price for commodity, see CONTRACTS, 1.

Principal and Accessory:

See CRIMINAL LAW, 1-3.

Principal and Agent:

Representation of corporation by agent, see CORPORATIONS, 10.

Principal and Agent—Continued.

Priorities:

Prisons:

Privileged Communications:

Process:

Publication:

Legal publications in daily papers, see NEWSPAPERS.

Service of process in tax foreclosure proceedings, see TAXATION, 1.

Of notice of proceedings to establish irrigation district, see WATERS AND WATER COURSES, 5, 6, 8.

Public Debt:

See SCHOOLS AND SCHOOL DISTRICTS.

Public Lands:

Public Use:

Taking property for public use, see EMINENT DOMAIN.

Punishment:

Of second and subsequent offenses, see CRIMINAL LAW, 25, 26.

Question for Jury:

Contributory negligence of driver injured in collision, see HIGHWAYS, 4.

Negligence of dentist in extracting tooth, see PHYSICIANS AND SURGEONS, 1.

Railroads:

Records:

Review of rulings as dependent on presentation of same in record, see APPEAL AND ERROR, 7.

Transcript on appeal or writ of error, see APPEAL AND ERROR, 7, 11, 12; CRIMINAL LAW, 22.

Chattel mortgage, see CHATTEL MORTGAGES.

Of justice court as evidence of former conviction of same offense, see CRIMINAL LAW, 6.

Reduction:

Of capital stock of corporation, see CORPORATIONS, 2.

Reference:

See ARBITRATION AND AWARD.

Fees of referee as item of costs, see COSTS, 2.

1. REFERENCE (2) — COMPULSORY REFERENCE — STATUTES — VALIDITY. Rem. Code, § 369 et seq., expressly providing that a compulsory reference may be ordered by the trial court where the issues involve a long account on either side, does not contravene Const., Art. 4, §§ 1, 6, 23, creating courts, defining their jurisdiction, and providing for the appointment of court commissioners. *Daniel v. Daniel* 82

Referendum:

Emergency acts defeating right to, see CONSTITUTIONAL LAW, 1-4.

Reformatories:

Effect of failure to make appropriation for, see STATES.

1. REFORMATORIES (2) — COMMITMENT — TRANSFER OF PRISONERS. A woman sentenced to commitment in the Women's Industrial Home and Clinic, on conviction of grand larceny, was transferable to the state prison by order of the board of directors of the industrial home, under the authority conferred by Laws 1919, p. 570, § 13; the determination by the board of the necessity for the transfer not being the exercise of a judicial function. *In re Canary* 569

Regulation:

Of jitneys in city streets, see MUNICIPAL CORPORATIONS, 8-10.

Rehearing:

See NEW TRIAL.

Remand:

Of cause on appeal or writ of error, see APPEAL AND ERROR, 21.

Removal of Causes:

Change of venue or place of trial, see VENUE.

Renewal:

Of lease, see LANDLORD AND TENANT, 2-4.

Rent:

See LANDLORD AND TENANT, 2, 4.

Repeal:

Of proviso relating to possession of liquor, see INTOXICATING LIQUORS, 4.

Of statute limiting district indebtedness, see SCHOOLS AND SCHOOL DISTRICTS.

Of statute, see STATUTES, 1, 2.

Reputation:

Of accused as evidence, see CRIMINAL LAW, 11.

Of witness, see WITNESSES, 7.

Requests:

For instructions in civil actions, see TRIAL, 1, 2.

Rescission:

Of contract for sale of goods, see SALES, 3, 4.

Reserve Fund:

In highway contract for protection of laborers and materialmen, see HIGHWAYS, 1.

Reservoir:

Enjoining construction of in city park, see INJUNCTION, 2; MUNICIPAL CORPORATIONS, 14.

Right to abate as nuisance, see NUISANCE, 1-3.

Res Gestae:

In civil actions, see EVIDENCE, 3.

Residence:

Of parties to action as affecting venue, see VENUE, 1.

Res Judicata:

See JUDGMENT, 3.

Divorce decree as bar to action for division of personal property, see DIVORCE, 4.

Bar by election of one of two inconsistent remedies, see ELECTION OF REMEDIES.

Revenue:

See TAXATION.

Review:

See HABEAS CORPUS.
In civil action, see APPEAL AND ERROR.
Scope and extent, see CERTIORARI.
In criminal prosecution, see CRIMINAL LAW, 22, 24.
Enjoining exercise of discretion by city council, see INJUNCTION, 3.

Revival:

Of repealed statute, see STATUTES, 2.

Riparian Rights:

See NAVIGABLE WATERS.

Roads:

Condemnation of property for county road, see EMINENT DOMAIN, 1.
Streets in cities, see MUNICIPAL CORPORATIONS, 8-13.

Robbery:

Accessory to offense, see CRIMINAL LAW, 3.

Sabotage:

Evidence in prosecution for, see CRIMINAL LAW, 13, 15.
Instructions defining crime, see CRIMINAL LAW, 20.
Judicial notice of meaning, see EVIDENCE, 1.

Safe Place to Work:

See MASTER AND SERVANT, 4.

Sales:

Rights of subsequent purchasers of mortgaged property, see
   CHATTEL MORTGAGES.
In violation of statute fixing minimum price, see CONTRACTS, 1.
Contribution between joint purchasers, see CONTRIBUTION.
Of corporate stock, see CORPORATIONS, 2, 5, 11.
Authority of agent to sell, see PRINCIPAL AND AGENT, 4, 5.

Sales—Continued.

Seamen—Continued.

shipping articles are signed by men employed as seamen, fishermen, beachmen and trapmen, under a contract to sail a vessel from Seattle to a port in Alaska, work during the fishing season as fishermen, beachmen or trapmen, and at the close of such season sail the vessel back to Seattle, the contract as a whole is of a maritime character, notwithstanding the extra provisions covering fishery services. *Heino v. Libby, McNeill & Libby*............................ 148

3. SAME—WAGES—FORFEITURE. Seamen employed under shipping articles to sail a vessel on the return voyage from an Alaskan port to Seattle, have no justification for abandoning their contract on the ground of the unseaworthiness of the vessel, where a survey of the vessel was made by three disinterested master mariners, and also by a board of survey consisting of the commander of a U. S. coast guard cutter and three other officers of his ship, the surveyors in both instances finding the vessel seaworthy and fit to make the voyage from Alaska to Seattle; and their refusal to serve as seamen, without making any demand for a survey, constituted them deserters under the statutes of the United States. *Heino v. Libby, McNeill & Libby* 148

4. SAME—WAGES—FORFEITURE—DESERTION. A deserting seaman not only forfeits his wages or emoluments which he has earned, but also forfeits the right to recover upon a quantum meruit for services rendered in part performance of his contract. *Heino v. Libby, McNeill & Libby*... 148

5. SAME—WAGES—ISSUANCE OF CERTIFICATES—EFFECT. Labor certificates issued to a crew of seamen and fishermen, stating the amounts that would become due them on fulfillment of their contract would not estop the employer to deny the right of recovery, where the certificates were secured by coercion after the crew had become deserters under their shipping contract. *Heino v. Libby, McNeill & Libby* 148

Secondary Evidence:

In civil actions, see ACCOUNT, 2; EVIDENCE, 4.

Security:

For costs, see COSTS, 1.

Servants:

See MASTER AND SERVANT.

Service:

Of notice of award, see ARBITRATION AND AWARD.
Of process, see PROCESS.

Set-off and Counterclaim:

Right of bank to set off debt of decedent against deposit, see EXECU-TORS AND ADMINISTRATORS, 2-4.

Settlement:

By executor or administrator, see EXECUTORS AND ADMINISTRATORS, 5, 6.

Shares:

Of corporate stock, see CORPORATIONS, 2-8, 11.

Shipping:

See SEAMEN.

Sidewalks:

Injuries from defects, see HIGHWAYS, 5.

Slot Machines:

As gambling device, see GAMING.

Soldiers' Bonus:

Time of taking effect of act, see STATUTES, 3.

Special Deposits:

See BANKS AND BANKING.

Specifications of Errors:

In briefs, see APPEAL AND ERROR, 13.

Specific Performance:

Of contract for property settlement, see DIVORCE, 8, 9.

States:

Highway construction contracts, see HIGHWAYS, 1.

1. STATES (3, 25, 26)—LIABILITY—POWER TO INCUR DEFICIENCY—AP-PROPRIATIONS. An administrative officer charged with the management and control of a reformatory institution, for which the legislature has failed to make an appropriation for maintenance, is under no obligation to incur a deficiency to continue its operation; in view of Rem. Code, §§ 5025-5027, which prohibit expenditures in excess of appropriations and provide that the officer making such expenditures is guilty of misdemeanor and liable personally and on his official bond for the amounts so expended. *In re Williamson* 560

2. STATES (26)—APPROPRIATION—NECESSITY—EFFECT OF FAILURE TO MAKE. Where, through the failure to make an appropriation, the operation of the Women's Industrial Home and Clinic, to which certain classes of female offenders were to be sentenced, was suspended, the requirement of the act that convicted offenders be sen-

States—Continued.

tenced to such institution was likewise suspended, thereby subjecting such class of offenders to the operation of the general laws which provide for the imprisonment of persons convicted of crimes. *In re Williamson*.. 560

Statutes:

See DRAINS; FRAUDS, STATUTE OF; INTOXICATING LIQUORS, 4.

Time of taking effect, emergency clause, see CONSTITUTIONAL LAW, 1-4.

Granting special privileges or immunities, see CONSTITUTIONAL LAW, 6, 7.

Contracts in violation of statute, see CONTRACTS, 1.

Recovery of value of improvements placed on lands, see IMPROVEMENTS.

Classification of cities, see MUNICIPAL CORPORATIONS, 1.

City ordinances, see MUNICIPAL CORPORATIONS, 2-5, 7-10.

Service of notice, see PROCESS.

Townsites, see PUBLIC LANDS.

Compulsory reference by trial court, see REFERENCE.

Sales of property obtained by larceny, see SALES, 7.

School district indebtedness, see SCHOOLS AND SCHOOL DISTRICTS.

1. STATUTES (47)—IMPLIED REPEAL—BY AMENDATORY ACT—AMENDMENT—EFFECT ON INTERVENING ACT. Where an act has been in part impliedly repealed and superseded by a conflicting act on the same subject, the subsequent amendment of the earlier act in the constitutional method of amending laws, without mention of the intervening act, does not amend or repeal by implication such intervening act so as to restore the conflicting portions of the first act. *State ex rel. School District No. 102 v. Clausen*........................ 432

2. STATUTES (51)—REPEAL—REVIVAL OF ACT REPEALED—EXCEPTIONS. Where an original statute is left in force on the passage of a subsequent act, which modifies it only to the extent of excepting certain cases from its operation, the taking away of the exception by suspension or repeal revives the original statute, which continues in force to be applied without the exception; since the rule against revival of a statute by the repeal of a repealing statute relates to absolute repeals only. *In re Williamson*..................... 560

3. STATUTES (78)—TIME OF TAKING EFFECT—INITIATIVE AND REFERENDUM—SOLDIER'S BONUS. Under Const., art. 2, § 1d, providing that initiative and referendum measures shall be in operation thirty days after approval, the soldiers' compensation act, Laws 1920, ch. 1, approved by popular vote on November 2, 1920, did not go into effect until December 2, 1920; and the death of a soldier entitled to a bonus, four days prior to the date of taking effect of the measure, would not entitle his estate to take thereunder. *Skidmore v. Clausen* 403

Stay:

Pending appeal, see APPEAL AND ERROR, 10.

Of subsequent action until costs of prior suit are paid, see COSTS, 3.

Stipulations:

1. STIPULATIONS (3)—CONCLUSIVENESS AND EFFECT—PERSONS CON-
    CLUDED. Under a stipulation between parties to an appeal in an ac-
    tion to recover the value of corporate stock that, in case the su-
    preme court should hold plaintiff entitled to a money judgment,
    then no question shall be raised as to the amount of the money
    judgment rendered by the trial court, the appellant is concluded
    from urging on appeal that the stock had no value. *Wunsch v. Con-
    solidated Laundry Co*   44

Stock:

Corporate stock, see CORPORATIONS, 2-8, 11.

Stockholders:

Of corporations, see CORPORATIONS.

Streets:

See MUNICIPAL CORPORATIONS, 8-13.

Condemnation of lands for, see EMINENT DOMAIN, 2.

Negligent use of highway, see HIGHWAYS, 2-4.

Submission of Controversy:

To arbitrators by agreement of parties, see ARBITRATION AND AWARD.

Subscriptions:

To corporate stock, see CORPORATIONS, 3.

Summons:

Affidavit for publication of, see TAXATION, 1.

Supersedeas:

On appeal or writ of error, see APPEAL AND ERROR, 10.

Supreme Court:

Jurisdiction to issue writ, see PROHIBITION, 2.

Surveys:

To determine seaworthiness of vessel, see SEAMEN.

Taxation:

Motor vehicle tax, see LICENSES.

Limitation of indebtedness of school district, see SCHOOLS AND
    SCHOOL DISTRICTS.

Assessment for irrigation district, see WATERS AND WATER COURSES,
    11-13.

Torts—Continued.

Agents, see Principal and Agent, 1, 6.

Diversion of natural water courses, see Waters and Water Courses, 1, 2.

Towns:

Townsite entries of public lands, see Public Lands.

Townsites:

See Public Lands.

Transfer:

Of corporate shares, see Corporations, 2, 5, 11.

Of prisoners, see Reformatories.

Trees:

As nuisance on adjoining land, see Adjoining Landowners; Nuisance, 4.

Trespass:

1. Trespass (15, 16)—Damages to Real Property—Evidence—Sufficiency. A judgment for damages for trespass was unwarranted, where it appeared that defendant, in making use of a private roadway over plaintiff's land for which it paid a rental, was compelled to make a slight detour because the roadway had been partially destroyed in blasting stumps and rocks. *Worthy Creek Shingle Co. v. Anderson* 472

Trial:

Review of rulings as dependent on presentation of same by record, see Appeal and Error, 7, 11, 12, 16.

Review as dependent on specifications in assignment of error, see Appeal and Error, 13.

Scope and extent of review as dependent on theory of case, see Appeal and Error, 15, 16.

Review of rulings as dependent on prejudicial nature of error, see Appeal and Error, 20.

Submission of controversy to arbitration, see Arbitration and Award.

Continuance in civil actions, see Continuance.

In criminal prosecutions, see Criminal Law.

Instructions in criminal action, see Criminal Law, 2.

Motions and grounds for new trial, see New Trial.

Instructions in action for malpractice by dentist, see Physicians and Surgeons, 2.

Amendment of pleadings at trial, see Pleading, 2, 3.

Place of trial, see Venue.

Competency and examination of witnesses, see Witnesses.

Trial—Continued.

Trover and Conversion:

Undue Influence:

United States:

Vacation:

Voters:

Submission of bond issue for irrigation district, see WATERS AND WATER COURSES, 10.

Wages:

Forfeiture of by deserting seamen, see SEAMEN.

Waiver:

Of error on appeal, see APPEAL AND ERROR, 18.
Of conditions of lease, see LANDLORD AND TENANT, 1, 2.

Waters and Water Courses:

Works for protection or improvement of lands, see DRAINS.
Enjoining use of splash dams in driving logs, see INJUNCTION, 1.
Enjoining construction of reservoir, see INJUNCTION, 2.
Waters capable of navigation, see NAVIGABLE WATERS.

1. WATERS AND WATER COURSES (35, 72)—DIVERSION—FLOWAGE—ACTION FOR INJURIES. Where adjoining counties, under express legislative authority, improve a navigable stream for the purpose of preventing it from overflowing its banks and doing damage to public property, they are liable to a landowner, under Const., art. 1, § 16, prohibiting the damaging of private property for public use without compensation, if, because of such improvements and the manner in which they are made, his property is eroded and washed away. *Conger v. Pierce County*............................... 27

2. WATERS AND WATER COURSES (44)—DAMAGES (9)—DIRECT OR CONSEQUENTIAL—IN GENERAL. The erosion and washing away of a property owner's land on the banks of a stream, due to deflecting the current of the stream by improvements in the channel made by defendants, cannot be said to be an indirect or consequential damage, where it appears that defendants through their engineer had knowledge that such an injury would probably result from the improvement. *Conger v. Pierce County*............................... 27

3. WATERS AND WATER COURSES (58)—PRESCRIPTION—ADVERSE CHARACTER OF APPROPRIATION. The filing by a public service corporation with the secretary of state of the plat and notice required by law showing that it was organized for the purpose of driving logs in a certain river was not sufficient to initiate an adverse claim or assertion of a legal right necessary to the support of prescriptive title. *Price v. Humptulips Driving Co*........................ 56

4. WATERS AND WATER COURSES (79, 87)—PUBLIC SUPPLY—DAMAGES FROM NEGLIGENCE. In an action for damages against a city for the destruction of plaintiff's mill property by the flooding of a creek on which the mill was located, a question for the jury was presented where there was evidence showing that the flood had been swelled by the bursting out of water through one wall of defendant's reser-

Waters and Water Courses—Continued.

voir, which wall was a glacial moraine of pervious character util-
ized for the purpose, through which there had always been seepage
within the knowledge of defendant. *North Bend Lumber Co. v.
Seattle* 500

5.   WATERS (89)—IRRIGATION DISTRICTS—PROCEEDINGS TO ESTABLISH—
PUBLICATION OF NOTICES—SUFFICIENCY. The notices for the hearing
of a petition and for an election for the organization of an irrigation
district may properly be published in a newspaper of general circulation in the vicinity of the proposed district instead of in the designated official newspaper of the county, in view of Rem. Code, § 6417,
providing that it may be made in any newspaper of general circulation in the county, selected by the person or body charged with making the publication, which shall be the official newspaper for such
purpose. *In re Peshastin Irrigation District*.................. 440

6.   SAME (89)—NOTICE—DESCRIPTION OF BOUNDARIES. A notice of
election for the creation of an irrigation district sufficiently describes courses and distances in establishing the district boundaries
by a designation of one point as "the most northerly point of lot 3,
Peshastin Orchard," and another point as "the northwest corner of
lot 6, Springdale Orchards," where the plats of such tracts were of
record in the county auditor's office, and the boundary of the district
was described in the notice as commencing at a specified point with
reference to a section corner of a specified township and range in
the county. *In re Peshastin Irrigation District*............... 440

7.   SAME (89)—PETITION—ORDER ESTABLISHING DISTRICT—FILING OR-
DER. Under Rem. Code, § 6490, as amended by Laws 1917, ch. 162,
p. 723, a petition for the confirmation by the superior court of proceedings organizing an irrigation district is only required to "state
generally that the irrigation district was duly organized," and need
not recite that a certified copy of the order of the county commissioners finally establishing the district was filed with the county
clerk pursuant to Id., § 6418, as amended by Laws 1917, ch. 162. *In
re Peshastin Irrigation District*............................. 440

8.   SAME   (89) — PROCEEDINGS — CONFIRMATION — PETITION — SUFFI-
CIENCY. Where a petition for the confirmation of the organization
of an irrigation district fails to recite the publication of a notice for
a bond election, if conceded as necessary under Rem. Code, § 6490,
as amended by Laws 1917, ch. 162, the petition will be deemed
amended to correspond to the proof, where the fact of proper publication appears in the evidence. *In re Peshastin Irrigation District* 440

9.   SAME (89) — CONFIRMATION — ILLEGAL USE OF FUNDS. In a proceeding to confirm the organization of an irrigation district and its
proposed bond issue, any threatened illegal disposition of the pro-

Wills—Continued.

Witnesses:

Witnesses—Continued.

Words and Phrases:

Work and Labor:

Contracts of employment, see MASTER AND SERVANT, 1.
Seamen on vessels, see SEAMEN.

Workmen's Compensation Act:

Employees within scope of, see MASTER AND SERVANT, 2.
Priority of state's claim for premiums, see MASTER AND SERVANT, 3.
Award of compensation to injured workman, review, see MASTER AND SERVANT, 7-9.

Writings:

Comparison of signatures with alleged forgery, see FORGERY.
Requirements of statute of frauds, see FRAUDS, STATUTE OF.
Pleading written instruments, see PLEADING, 1.

Writs:

See CERTIORARI; HABEAS CORPUS; INJUNCTION; MANDAMUS; PROHIBITION.